Insurance Industry
Mergers & Acquisitions

Insurance Industry
Mergers & Acquisitions

EDITED BY

Jim Toole
Tom Herget

WITH AUTHORS

John Butler
Tom Corcoran
Mike Gabon
Alan Hines
Ken LaSorella
Hugh McCormick
Owen Ryan
Erika Schmidt
Dale Yamamoto
Laird Zacheis

PUBLISHED BY

Society of Actuaries

475 N. Martingale Road, Suite 600
Schaumburg, IL 60173
www.soa.org

ISBN 0-9759337-0-1

First Edition
First Printing

Printed in the United States of America
09 08 07 06 05 5 4 3 2 1

Edited by Bob Barnett
Proofread by Megan Potter
Society of Actuaries Liaisons:
Clay Baznik, Director of Publications
Jacque Kirkwood, Communications Associate
Cover and interior design by Susie Ayala
Printed by Edwards Brothers Incorporated, Ann Arbor, Mich.

Table of Contents

Chapter Four
Valuation Techniques 104

Chapter Five
Due Diligence 184

Chapter Six
Corporate Benefits & Insurance Programs 236

Chapter Seven
Taxation 276

Detailed Table of Contents

LIST OF TABLES AND FIGURES

TABLES

Figures

FOREWORD

External and internal factors drive demand for M&A in the insurance industry, whether or not senior management is focusing on survival or growth. Externally, companies are looking to M&A to respond to changing demographics and to satisfy customer demands. In addition, many companies turn to cross-border acquisitions to successfully compete in the globalizing financial services industry. Finally, pressure from rating agencies and stock analysts to boost earnings and improve capital positions drives a number of companies to enter the M&A arena.

Internally, companies look to gain access to needed capital, new customer segments, and new geographic markets. They also look to build critical mass in key businesses, achieve economies of scale, divest non-core businesses, and improve margins. The bottom line is that insurance executives believe M&A is important to their businesses.

But despite their initial promise, many mergers and acquisitions never fully achieve their potential benefits. Companies that have undergone a merger or acquisition give them mixed marks. Fifty years of research suggests that most mergers have either a neutral or negative impact on profitability. In addition, research indicates that 70% of acquisitions fail to meet the expectations of their architects and between one-third and one-half of all acquisitions are subsequently divested.

There are many possible reasons, ranging from soft items, like incompatible cultures and clash of management styles, to concrete things, like overpaying for the target company. Most of these reasons can be linked to failures or omissions at key stages in the M&A process, such as rationale, due diligence, and implementation.

This book provides an in-depth look at the entire M&A process, from financing to due diligence to tax and accounting issues to post-acquisition integration. It contains a wealth of information on insurance M&A transactions and should prove to be a valuable resource to any participant in the M&A process. I believe it is one of the most comprehensive and up-to-date resources available.

It will be especially valuable to the actuary, who has a crucial role to play in most insurance M&A transactions. In many cases, the actuarial appraisal is the underpinning of the price at which companies change hands. Unfortunately, for such an important activity, there has been very little in actuarial literature to assist the practicing actuary. Since the first groundbreaking papers written in the 1970s and early 1980s, not much has been published. This book offers a unique look at the role of the actuary in insurance M&A transactions. During my nearly 30 years as a consultant to the insurance industry, there were many times when I wished I had such a tool.

Whether you read this book cover to cover, or simply use it as a resource for specific aspects of the M&A process, I'm sure you will find it enlightening. I especially enjoyed the commentary and case examples included throughout the book that offer interesting perspectives and insights from company executives and outside advisors who have participated in the M&A process. I would like to extend my compliments to Jim Toole, Tom Herget, and the entire team of authors who made this book possible.

Patricia L. Guinn, FSA, MAAA
Managing Director
Towers Perrin

Preface

Welcome

This book is a unique collection of knowledge, insights, and opinions, bringing together for the first time in a single publication the various points of view necessary to execute an insurance company acquisition and merger. While numerous professionals are involved in executing transactions, our text will focus on the involvement of accountants, actuaries, investment bankers, and lawyers.

An insurance transaction deserves its own treatment for numerous reasons, from unique regulatory and financial reporting requirements to the intractable problem of valuing insurance liabilities. Accounting, actuarial, tax, and regulatory standards are painfully arcane, driven by the need to both honor the complex web of interlocking promises and balance the sometimes conflicting interests of various stakeholders. Sources of information are disparate in scope and quality, and the opinions of experts can, and do, differ greatly.

M&A practices vary across the industry in ways that frustrate observers and practitioners alike. Expectations between prudent buyers and enthusiastic sellers can deviate wildly. Assumptions, methodologies, and results exhibit broad variations between firms and even offices within firms, particularly when anything is out of the ordinary (which, in M&A, is typically all of the time).

Little can be said to generalize across the industry as a whole. Even those whose entire careers have been spent in the field can find the industry daunting. Most of what is taken as "common knowledge" is absorbed in the trenches by apprenticing with practitioners. Beyond the introductory level, little information on the nuts and bolts of insurance M&A is codified, and different professionals will use different approaches. While we acknowledge that the methodologies presented here are not the only correct approaches, it is certainly our intention to set a minimum bar.

Scope

This is intended to be a practical text; few simplifying assumptions have been made. Our focus will be primarily on acquisitions, although every acquisition has an element of merger and vice versa. More specifically, we will not be analyzing deal structures surrounding joint ventures, bancassurance deals, start-up operations, or strategic partnerships.

The text is designed to assist the reader in understanding the sale process; it does not purport to shed light on how to make the decision to "go shopping," determine an optimal time to buy, or select the "right" property. While the academic community is locked in seemingly eternal discussion as to the efficacy of acquisitions in adding to shareholder value, it does appear that in certain instances and for certain companies an acquisition strategy is effective. We do not presume to weigh in on this debate; our goal is to help those who do, do.

We will use the terms merger, acquisition, and M&A interchangeably to indicate the process of buying and selling a stock company. Mutual companies exist in a separate world, which, for various reasons, limits the degree to which they can participate in M&A activities. The considerations of buying and selling a block of business will be identified separately and discussed where appropriate. Target (seller) and acquirer (buyer) are understood to be potential until the ink is signed.

"Insurance company" means life, health, or property and casualty unless otherwise specified. Property and casualty will also be referred to as P&C. Accounting, tax, and regulatory issues will be presented from a U.S. perspective; however, the majority of what is presented in this text is applicable globally. And while the differences between insurance M&A and other industries are important, we will be quick to highlight similarities between insurance and non-insurance transactions as well as areas that actuarial analysis can add value such as valuation, due diligence, and enterprise risk management to transactions in other industries.

Finally, our intention is to clarify the prudent steps of a "normal" acquisition process (if such a thing exists). We then proceed to shatter this reverie with pearls of wisdom (tales from the "crypt") shared by actual practitioners, scattered throughout the text to reflect the depravity and manic eccentricity of real life deals, when money and egos collide.

Approach

The first step in bringing this book to fruition was our collaboration on *Actuarial Considerations in Insurance Mergers and Acquisitions: An International Perspective*. While preparing what was to be a definitive treatment of actuarial involvement in insurance M&A, because of the importance of teams in the M&A process the solo actuarial treatment ended up feeling hollow. Based on the success of *US GAAP for Life Insurers*, a full text treatment seemed achievable, and we were able to get the support from the Society of Actuaries (SOA) to sponsor the project.

The structure and collaborative nature of the book were inspired by broad-ranging discussions in the SOA Strategic Planning Committee, a response to the need to better communicate the value of actuarial analysis outside the silo of our profession. M&A is perhaps the greatest challenge that any professional faces, both technically and from a communications standpoint. Appraisals are of necessity dense, stylized documents that represent huge investments of time and money, further complicated by the fact that report users have widely varying levels of experience (and interest in reading them). A professional may be required to present the salient aspects of his or her report representing 500 hours of work in 15 minutes or less, while all the audience wants to know is "total appraisal value." By presenting the full M&A process as well as the construction, content, and caveats of an actuarial appraisal in one place, we hope that readers will gain a greater appreciation of the role of the various participants while improving communications and, hopefully, overall results.

Our goal was to create an integrated text representing best practices within the industry. Every effort was made to include members of leading companies, accounting firms, and consulting firms to make sure consensus views were presented. Our author team met three times (in generally sunny climes) to develop the outline, write, and finally review the book as a team. Chapters were co-authored by qualified professionals and reviewed by the editors. Each of the chapters was sent to industry experts for external peer review, with a final editorial review by professional publishing staff.

For the student, we hope this text clearly addresses the topic in a timeless fashion. For the practitioner, we hope you can use this book as a resource to assist you with the challenges you face. For actuaries, we hope the perspectives of other professions facilitate communication and your participation in the process. For non-actuaries, we hope the veil is lifted: there is value behind the actuarial curtain.

We appreciate your feedback for the next edition.

Jim Toole
Tom Herget

AUTHOR BIOGRAPHIES

JIM TOOLE, FSA, MAAA

Jim is the managing director of the life and health practice of MBA Actuaries, Inc., a full service, independent consulting firm offering a wide range of actuarial, management, and strategic consulting services.

Jim has served on the Society of Actuaries' Strategic Planning Committee, the International Policy Committee, and various section councils. Jim is a frequent speaker at industry meetings, seminars, and universities in the United States and Latin America. His most recent paper, *"Actuarial Considerations in Insurance M&A: An International Perspective,"* was published as part of the Society of Actuaries Monograph series and is included on the SOA's Course 8 Finance exam syllabus.

Jim is an experienced M&A practitioner working from both the buy and sell side in life, health, and P&C lines of business. Before joining MBA Actuaries, Jim worked for Tillinghast in their Mexico City office and Milliman USA. Jim graduated *cum laude* from Wake Forest University with a degree in Mathematics.

R. THOMAS HERGET, FSA, MAAA

Tom is executive vice president at PolySystems, Inc., a software and services provider to the life insurance industry. Tom manages the installation, advisory services, and customer services components of his business.

Tom has served as a board member of the Society of Actuaries and as chair of its Financial Reporting Section. Tom was a leader in the American Academy of Actuaries' Unified Valuation System task force whose work serves as the basis for capital and reserve adequacy studies performed by the Academy. Tom is also the chief editor of the Society's *US GAAP for Life Insurers* textbook.

Tom has served many acquisitions in implementing forecasting and valuation software, affirming value anticipated in due diligence for both new and existing business.

Tom has worked for The Hartford and CNA as well as the public accounting firm Peat Marwick & Mitchell prior to his current position. Tom holds a BS in Actuarial Sciences from the University of Illinois.

JOHN M. BUTLER

John is a senior vice president in the Financial Institutions Group of Houlihan Lokey Howard & Zukin, an international investment banking firm, which provides a wide range of services including mergers and acquisitions, financing, financial opinions, advisory services, financial restructurings, and merchant banking.

He specializes in advising financial services companies, including insurance companies and insurance brokers, on mergers, acquisitions, divestitures, and raising private capital. John has advised on numerous corporate transactions on behalf of insurance carriers and insurance services companies.

John is a frequent contributor to insurance and finance publications and regularly speaks at insurance industry conferences.

He holds a Series 7 certification from the NASD and a Series 63 certification from the NASAA.

Prior to joining Houlihan Lokey, he worked in the corporate finance department of Fox-Pitt, Kelton and in the M&A group at Prudential Securities. Previously, John practiced corporate and securities law, representing insurance companies and banks. He earned his BA in government, *cum laude*, from Georgetown University and earned his JD from Fordham University School of Law.

Thomas R. Corcoran, FSA, MAAA

Tom is a principal with the Tillinghast business of Towers Perrin located in the firm's Hartford office. He provides consulting services to the insurance industry, specializing in group long-term disability, group short-term disability, special risk, accident, and individual health product lines.

Tom's professional activities include the Board of Governors of the Society of Actuaries and chair of the Society of Actuaries' Health Practice Area, Health Section, and Disability Special Interest Group.

His areas of expertise include appraisals, valuations, financial modeling and projections, and product development and pricing. He is regularly involved in his firm's activities relating to all aspects of mergers and acquisitions and is a frequent industry speaker on the topic.

Prior to joining Tillinghast, Tom was chief financial officer for GroupAmerica Insurance Company.

Tom holds a BS in applied mathematics from Brown University.

Michael E. Gabon, FCIA, FSA

Mike is president of AIRCO Ltd., an AIG subsidiary and global reinsurer located in Bermuda. He oversees the operations and is actively involved in structuring reinsurance solutions to achieve financial, risk, and strategic objectives.

Mike has structured and underwritten several reinsurance blocks and entities for acquisition, primarily through use of reinsurance tools and techniques. Earlier in his career, he authored several actuarial study manuals. Mike is a frequent speaker at industry and professional meetings and is an active volunteer within the profession over a broad range of project groups, councils, and committees.

Prior to his current position, Mike has held retail, institutional, brokerage, and consultant roles in the insurance industry, working at Desjardins Financial Group, Scottish Re Group, Aon Re Worldwide, and KPMG. Mike holds a BSc in actuarial science and major in commerce earned with high distinction from the University of Toronto.

Alan M. Hines, FCAS, MAAA

Alan is a consulting actuary for PricewaterhouseCoopers, specializing in property casualty risk and exposure. Alan provides audit support and actuarial consulting services to insurance companies, self-insured corporations, risk retention pools, and captive insurers, with an emphasis on reserve adequacy, strategic underwriting, and pricing.

Alan has served in a leadership role on a number of continuing education committees within the Casualty Actuarial Society. He has served as secretary to the board of directors and is a frequent speaker at continuing education seminars sponsored by the Casualty Actuarial Society.

Alan has participated in numerous mergers and acquisitions providing sell-side and buy-side valuations, due-diligence, and transition support for property casualty insurance companies. Alan also specializes in evaluating and restructuring property casualty insurance programs for corporate acquisitions, including those that use captive insurance companies to finance their property and casualty exposure.

Prior to joining PricewaterhouseCoopers, Alan was vice president of underwriting and marketing for Plymouth Rock Assurance and served on the board of directors for Adirondack Insurance Company. He has also worked as a licensed insurance agent and held various management level positions at Aetna Life and Casualty. Alan earned a BS and an MS in mathematics from the University of Connecticut.

Kenneth A. LaSorella, FLMI, FSA, MAAA

Ken is vice president, US GAAP, at Sun Life Financial, a Canadian financial services company with multinational operations.

Ken is responsible for all actuarial aspects of US GAAP for the company worldwide as well as being a significant contributor to embedded value reporting.

Ken is a frequent writer and speaker at industry and professional meetings. He chaired a committee to develop the actuarial textbook for the LOMA exam syllabus. Ken is vice chair of the American Academy of Actuaries' Life Financial Reporting Committee, focusing on US GAAP and international GAAP. He serves as co-chair of an Academy committee to develop a monograph on purchase GAAP.

Ken has been heavily involved with GAAP conversions and with acquisitions and their accounting.

Ken has worked for Sun Life and KPMG Peat Marwick where he dealt with GAAP conversions, mergers and acquisitions, and purchase GAAP. Ken attended Roosevelt University and UCLA.

Hugh T. McCormick

Hugh is executive vice president, corporate development, at Scottish Re Group Limited, where he is involved in M&A transactions, development of new reinsurance markets, reinsurance-based securitization transactions, and similar projects. Prior to joining Scottish Re, he was a senior partner in the New York office of LeBoeuf, Lamb, Greene & MacRac L.L.P., a large international law firm with significant presence in the insurance industry, where he advised domestic and foreign insurance and reinsurance companies on tax, regulatory, and corporate matters arising in connection with mergers and acquisitions, demutualizations, reinsurance transactions, and insurance products.

From 2002 to 2004, he served as president and chairman of the board of directors of the Insurance Tax Conference, Inc. Hugh is a member of the board of advisors and contributors of the *Journal of Taxation of Investments*. He is also a correspondent member of the Regulation and Tax Committee of the Reinsurance Section of the Society of Actuaries.

Hugh regularly speaks and writes on insurance tax issues and contributed the chapter on "US Regulatory Issues" for *International Life Insurance* (Chancellor Publications Ltd. (UK), 2002).

From 1977 to 1981 Hugh was an attorney-advisor with the Interpretative Division of the Office of Chief Counsel of the Internal Revenue Service. Hugh received a BA from the University of Michigan, a JD from Rutgers University School of Law, and an LLM (Taxation) from Georgetown University.

Owen M. Ryan Jr., CPA

Owen is the U.S. and Global Insurance Practice managing partner of Deloitte & Touche, LLP.

Owen's responsibilities include creating, implementing, and managing Deloitte's insurance business strategy and resources. He is also the vice chairman of Deloitte's Global Financial Services Practice as well as the U.S. managing partner, financial services, for Deloitte's M&A practice, which provides advice in all aspects of M&A activities including acquisitions, mergers, roll-ups, joint ventures, strategic alliances, divestitures, M&A strategy, target selection, transaction execution, and post-merger integration.

His 20 years of professional services experience include 200 merger and acquisition transactions in over 25 countries throughout the Americas, Europe, and Asia. He is a frequent lecturer at seminars on M&A topics, particularly focusing on how to capture the value in a transaction.

Owen obtained his BS from New Jersey City University and his MBA from Columbia University. He is a member of the AICPA and is a certified public accountant in Connecticut, New Jersey, and New York.

Erika A. Schmidt, CPA

Erika is a senior manager in the New York Mergers and Acquisitions Group of Deloitte & Touche LLP. She has over eight years of experience in the financial services industry and specializes in insurance industry transactions.

Erika provides consulting and advisory services to a variety of clients on life and annuity, property and casualty, reinsurance, and insurance brokerage transactions.

She has experience in conducting intensive and accounting due diligence services for financial and strategic buyers. She has worked on major transactions with many of Deloitte's leading insurance clients and has had significant experience with cross-border insurance transactions, primarily in South America and Asia.

Prior to her current position, Erika worked in the accounting and auditing practice of PricewaterhouseCoopers, serving public and private clients in the insurance sector. She earned her BA in accounting, *magna cum laude*, from the University of Houston.

Dale H. Yamamoto, FCA, FSA, MAAA, EA

Dale leads the healthcare actuarial practice for Hewitt Associates, a global human resources consulting firm providing services to more than half of the Fortune 500 companies.

He consults to a broad variety of employers on healthcare issues including managed care, consumer-driven alternatives, and retiree healthcare.

Dale is a frequent speaker at industry and professional meetings and has written extensively on the topic of healthcare and financial security.

He has been a key contributor to the firm's general guidelines in merger and acquisition consulting and has been involved with several M&A projects in the last 10 years.

Prior to his current position, Dale held a similar role at Towers Perrin and, before that, he worked at The Boeing Company and SAFECO Life Insurance Company. He earned a BS in mathematics from the University of Nebraska.

Laird Zacheis, FSA, MAAA

Laird is a principal of the life insurance practice of Milliman, Inc. He specializes in consulting on mergers and acquisitions and the development of actuarial appraisals. Laird also consults in the areas of financial planning and capital management, US GAAP issues including purchase GAAP, asset-liability management, and strategic planning.

Laird has consulted for buyers or sellers in approximately half of the largest life insurance transactions in the United States since 1990, consisting of over 40 transactions with a total value in excess of $75 billion. In addition, Laird has consulted on a number of the largest life insurance transactions in Japan and Korea.

Laird received a BS, *summa cum laude*, from Yale University and an MBA with high honors from the University of Chicago.

ACKNOWLEDGMENTS

So many people contributed to this effort that it is difficult to know where to begin or how to properly express our thanks. As with any M&A transaction, the importance of teamwork in bringing this project to successful fruition cannot be understated. Likewise, the amount of effort required turned out to be singularly understated. Everyone gave 110%. Some gave so much more—for that we are truly grateful. The book reflects the passion and commitment of these many individuals.

First and foremost, we would like to thank the authors. They did not know what they were in for; they certainly rose to the challenge. As if the challenges of researching, writing, editing, and rewriting were not enough, our authors were faced with the tasks of coordinating with fellow authors while reconciling terminology and methodologies across professions and actuarial disciplines. We have much to show for our efforts and much to be proud of.

Behind the author team were the families that supported us through the late nights and endless shifting deadlines (again, much like the average M&A deal). The editors would like to thank uber-frau Christine Toole and Allyson Herget for allowing us to yet again get in over our heads, trusting that we would manage to strike a balance while achieving our goal. The authors wish to acknowledge the support of their families including Amanda, Kelly, and Karen Hines; Barbara LaSorella; Anna, Elizabeth, and Jennifer Ryan; Jimmy, Robert and Dean Toole; Suzanna Weingarten; Louise Yamamoto; and Sunhee Lee and Julian and Claire Lee-Zacheis.

We benefited greatly from the advice, contributions, and assistance of numerous additional participants. The book is richer and more robust for their advice and criticism. Each person was selected for his or her specific expertise in one or more areas to ensure that the text was authoritative. Their experience and insight has made this book infinitely more valuable to the practitioner. We appreciate them sharing their hard earned wisdom with us.

We would like to thank the individuals who gave their time to review one or more portions of the text: Paul Bell, Sue Collins, Charles Cox, Rob Daly, Doug Doll, Dale Filsinger, Charles Friedstat, Phoebe Glass, Patricia Guinn, Jim Hawke, Norm Hill, Jay Jaffe, Dan Kunesh, Neil Lund, James Marple, Randy Maultsby, Hubert Mueller, James Murray, John Nigh, Jay Novik, Glenn Orr, Julie Perks, Dave Rogers, Joy Schwartzman, Shirley Shao, Robert Shapiro, Ken Smith, Michael Smith, Harry Soo, Howard Stecker, Wayne Stuenkel, Al Weller, Jennifer Wong, and Bart Zanelli.

In addition to the chapter review team, we wish to thank the many individuals who contributed and/or reviewed additional portions of the text: Mike Bell, Bob Beuerlein, Craig Buck, Garry Eckard, Morris Fishman, Debi Gero, Albert Gonzalez, Al Greenberg, Patricia Guinn, George Hammond, Jim Hawke, Art Hazlitt, Paul Hekman, Norm Hill, Jay Jaffe, Tom Koltis, Dan Kunesh, Jack LaGue, Anil Manji, Don Maves, Peter Mavrogenes, Tonya Maxwell, Mike

McLaughlin, Brett Morris, Theresa Resnick, Dave Rogers, Steve Rooney, Gail Ross, Bill Sakel, John Schaefer, Jeff Schlinsog, Val Schnell, Bob Shapiro, Bob Sharkey, Rob Sheridan, Henry Siegel, Brent Steele, Wayne Stuenkel, Vince Tsang, Christopher Walker, Rod Warren, Chris Wright, and Mel Young.

We would like to thank the various members of our respective staffs who put up with our absences and countless requests, including, but certainly not limited to Debbie Christensen, Erin Clougherty, Tom Cook, Sam Das, Philip Marak, Jim McDermott, Patty Pape, Jill Rierson, Veronica Saldana, Lucille Tate, and Mary Tucker.

Last but certainly not least, we would like to thank the Society of Actuaries and their expert staff who truly gave shape to this idea. In particular, we would like to thank SOA Publishing Director Clay Baznik who bought into the vision early on and provided the resources and husbanding to make this the successful project it was. SOA Board Member Shirley Shao went the extra mile, participating in two of our writing meetings to make sure we were on track. We would like to thank Jacque Kirkwood for her steady hand in guiding us through the publication process and keeping us, if not on track, at least pointed in the right direction. We are grateful to Susie Ayala who took a concept and designed and flawlessly executed the beautiful layout of this book, and Bob Barnett for his painstakingly reviewing each sentence, making our fractured prose into a more integrated whole.

We apologize to those we may have inadvertently left out. We are very grateful for the support and participation we received from the community on the project.

Chapter One

Introduction

1.1 INTRODUCTION

The U.S. insurance industry is fragmented compared with other financial services industries. There are over 2,000 life and health companies and 3,100 property and casualty (P&C) companies licensed to operate in the United States. Notwithstanding a wave of consolidation that hit the United States in the late 1990s, the total number of insurance companies operating since 1995 has increased. Despite the occasional high-profile mega-merger, the U.S. insurance sector has plenty of room for consolidation.

For example, the percentage of the market controlled by the top 10 life insurers dropped from 35% in 1997 to 31% in 2003. By comparison, since 1995 the 10 largest U.S. banking organizations have increased their share of domestic banking assets from 29% to 46% at year-end 2003, while the number of commercial banks has shrunk 23%, from 10,000 to 7,700. While subject to anti-trust scrutiny, even the largest insurance mergers in the United States pass untouched by justice authorities due to the level of fragmentation of the insurance market.

The buzzwords driving mergers in the twenty-first century are globalization and financial services convergence. Given the commoditized nature of the product and barriers to entry (capital requirements, distribution challenges, and the need to establish credibility), industry consolidation would seem to be inevitable. However, despite regular predictions that the U.S. insurance industry would follow the lead of the banking industry and begin the process of consolidating into a limited number of national mega-insurers and super-regionals, broad-based consolidation has yet to happen in the United States.

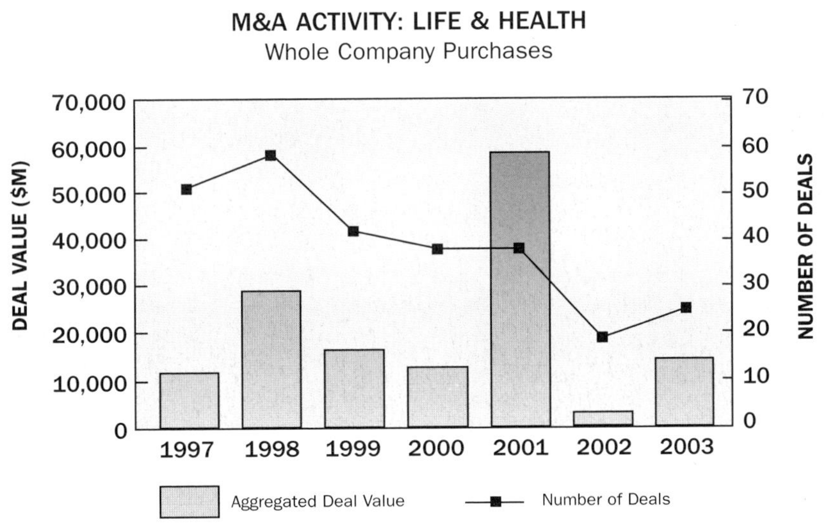

FIGURE 1.1 **Source:** SNL Financial

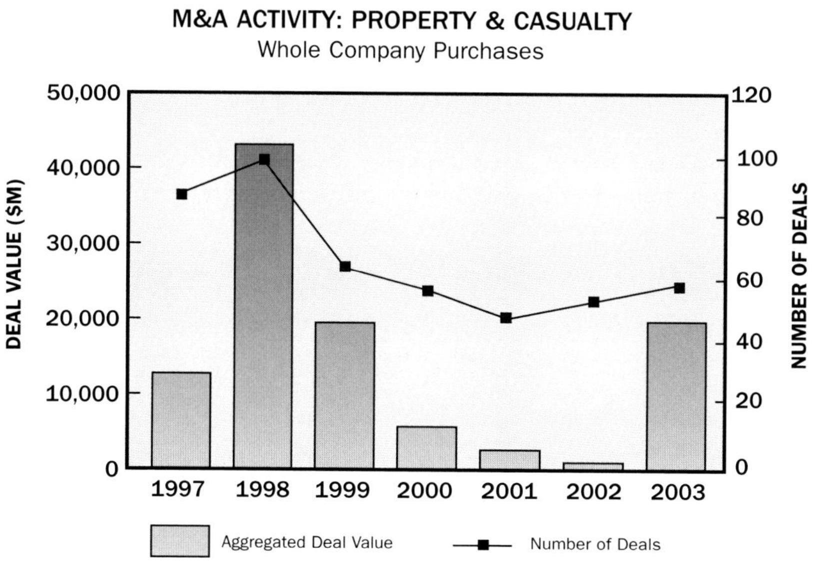

FIGURE 1.2 **Source:** SNL Financial

There are a number of reasons why the insurance industry in the United States has resisted consolidation, despite the various efficiencies that consolidation would likely create. The reluctance to merge is, in part, a consequence of the unique history of the development of the insurance market in the United States. The insurance industry, while highly regulated, has been regulated in a decentralized, state-by-state, fashion.

Another impediment to consolidation is the perceived status and importance of insurance companies within the communities they serve. Because of the unique nature of the product they manufacture, insurance companies are very often viewed as serving a public trust. Historically, insurance companies encouraged this perception by participating actively in their communities, building large monument buildings, and actively engaging in philanthropic causes. As a result, for personal, emotional, and political reasons, boards of directors of local insurance companies, and the politicians in those communities (and there is often some overlap between the two), can be reluctant to sell to a foreign institution even if it makes economic sense.

1.2 WHAT IS INSURANCE?

Simply put, insurance is the promise to pay for a loss (indemnify) in exchange for a premium based on the occurrence of an insurable event. Within this broad definition, there are literally thousands of different permutations for insurance products. The indemnity can be a fixed amount, a series of payments, or contingent based on damages incurred. The premium can be single, periodic, or limited; level, increasing, or decreasing; fixed or flexible.

At the heart of the concept is the definition of insurable event. The insurable event needs to be at some level predictable to the insurer but random and undesirable for the insured. In some instances, such as death, the event is clear. In other instances, such as a fire, the event may be clear, but the amount of the indemnity may be uncertain for some time. In other instances, such as professional liability, the existence of an insured event must be defined in the courts and may take years to establish.

An insurance organization, be it a company, a captive, pool, or self-insured group, is basically a mechanism for transferring risks and re-distributing losses, with an element inuring to the risk-bearing entity for expenses, uncertainty, investment, and profit. In assembling a group of risks, there is always a tension between risk sharing and charging equitable premiums. The more accurately a risk can be underwritten, the more accurately a premium can be assigned. But the more homogenous the risk pool, the less true risk sharing there is. Taken to its extreme, the pool can be allocated so that each individual is charged his or her expected value, with no actual sharing of risk at all, just the timing of losses.

SIDE NOTE

MORAL HAZARD

There are several requirements for a risk pool to function efficiently and to prevent excess losses from occurring due to the existence of the insurance coverage (the moral hazard).

First, there must be an insurable interest on the behalf of the policy owner. It is unwise, and potentially dangerous, to allow someone to insure property that is not theirs or that involves lives in which they have no legitimate interest.

Second, the offer of insurance may attract individuals or institutions that may already be aware of losses or be at greater risk for the condition or event. This is known as anti-selection and can significantly drive up the costs of some insurance. In order to prevent this, insurers typically utilize risk underwriting or have some combination of premium and product designs that compensate for the effect of anti-selection.

Finally, the amount payable should not be so high as to tempt the owner to incur the event. The indemnification should be for less than the amount of the potential loss. Hence, there is typically the need for loss controls and/or financial underwriting as well as risk underwriting.

1.3 INDUSTRY CHARACTERISTICS

Within the U.S. industry, there are four main lines of business: accident and health, life and annuity, P&C, and retirement/pension. Within each line of business there are numerous subdivisions and distinct product categories. The basic coverages are typically highly regulated and perceived by consumers as commodities, with the distinguishing aspects being price and image of the insurer. Insurers do their best to develop value-added features that respond to the needs of the marketplace and give the company a marketing edge. However, product innovation is not patentable, so product design is not typically a barrier to entry.

1.3.1 ACCIDENT AND HEALTH

Health insurance companies issue a broad spectrum of products including major medical, critical illness, accident, short-term disability, and long-term disability. The offerings are broken into two main categories: medical expense and disability income. Medical expense is typically in the form of indemnity or expense reimbursement. It can be limited in focus (e.g., cancer, vision, or dental) or cover virtually all the expenses associated with medical care and hospital usage.

The valuation of many health companies is straightforward because the products are annually renewable and do not have asset valuation concerns. On the other hand, companies with large blocks of disability or long-term care risks pose significant challenges to buyer and seller alike.

1.3.2 LIFE AND ANNUITY

Life insurance companies provide several types of services to their policyholders. They cover the risk of premature death through life insurance, they provide investment services for savings, and they cover longevity risk by providing annuities. Life and annuity reserves are established by law statutorily. Due to the long-term nature of these liabilities, life insurance companies are some of the most important investors in mid- and long-term capital markets. Life insurers must be constantly aware of the credit risks and asset liability matching risks associated with their portfolio. Because of these challenges, valuing life and annuity companies is more involved than with other lines of business.

1.3.3 PROPERTY AND CASUALTY

Property and casualty (P&C) is broken into personal lines (coverages purchased by individuals) and commercial lines (coverages purchased by businesses). Numerous product types exist within each group. Most P&C products are contracts with one year of exposure. However, long delays in both the reporting and ultimate settling of claims may require reserves to continue to be held for decades after premiums have been collected. This period after the exposure has expired but while the liabilities are still being run off is known as the tail.

The second broad generalization that can be made within P&C is to distinguish between long tail lines and short tail lines. Environmental exposures can take a generation to emerge and even longer to settle issues in the courts. Personal lines coverages such as auto and homeowners are largely completed in a few short years.

Rather than calculating formula reserves defined statutorily, claim reserves and reserves for loss adjustment expenses (LAE)[1] are estimated by actuaries using a variety of statistical and

[1] Loss adjustment expenses are expenses that the company incurs that directly relate to the management and adjudication of claims. Theoretically, the LAE reserve is the projected cost to administer claim payments associated with existing exposures if the company were to stop writing new business.

stochastic methods. Typically there are two primary reserves established: (1) case reserve for claims already reported and (2) incurred but not reported (IBNR) for claims that have likely been incurred but not yet reported to the insurer. Each type of P&C exposure has a different claim reporting and loss payment pattern. The resulting cash flows for two insurance companies writing the same exposure may differ significantly due to different underwriting and claim handling procedures.

1.3.4 RETIREMENT/PENSION

Retirement security is typically provided within a three-tiered framework: government systems (Social Security in the United States), employer-provided benefits, and private savings. Employer retirement benefits are highly regulated at the federal, state, and even local level. As a result, statutory liabilities can become distorted when regulations do not keep pace with academic or market innovations. As such, a plan may be significantly over- or underfunded depending on the economic environment, health of the company, and management practices. The existing and relative degree of funding for defined benefit plans, particularly for older, smokestack industries, may have a significant impact on the marketability of a company. Mergers can significantly impact defined benefit plan service accruals and resulting liabilities. In a merger and acquisition situation, defined benefit liabilities are typically considered as part of an overall package with other employee benefits such as other qualified plans, non-qualified plans, and group benefit programs.

1.3.5 REINSURANCE

Reinsurance refers to the purchase of insurance by insurance companies to cover their exposures. There are many reasons why a direct writer might purchase reinsurance. In addition to providing capacity to smaller companies (enabling them to write larger risks), reinsurers provide expertise to write difficult or unfamiliar risks, help to manage large claims, and offer access to scarce capital. Reinsurers offer various services to facilitate transactions between direct writers.

1.3.6 STOCK VS. MUTUAL

More so than in other industries, the mutual concept has thrived in insurance. The mutual concept was in vogue in the early 1900s when a number of stock companies mutualized. The trend reversed at the end of the century when a wave of large demutualizations occurred.

In the mutual legal structure, participating policyholders rather than stockholders are the owners of the company and vote for its board of directors. Participating policyholders also receive dividends, which are a reflection of the performance of their class. The issues of participation, ownership, and equity suddenly became problematic when non-participating products such as universal and variable life burst onto the scene and were embraced by stock and mutual companies alike. Esoteric discussions about class equity and capital management became popular insurance circles in the 1990s in conjunction with a great wave of demutualizations, including Prudential, MetLife, and MONY.

However, the mutual concept does thrive and contributes to the large numbers of smaller insurance companies. It is still a viable form; as of 2003 there were over 150 fraternal and mutual life and health companies and over 750 mutual P&C companies in the United States. Many mutual and reciprocal insurance companies were formed by social or professional organizations that were underserved. Owned by their policyholders, these companies have no shareholders seeking to maximize an investment. Mutual insurance companies are generally prohibited from merging or being acquired by stock companies. While this limits their access to capital, it does provide a degree of stability of coverage and employment.

1.4 REGULATORY BODIES

Insurance is a promise to pay—in some cases, a promise that lasts for a very long time. Because the costs of failure are so high and because past experience has shown that relying on markets to police themselves is both perilous and inefficient, the government takes an interest in seeing that those promises are kept. One of the many additional hurdles insurance M&As face is that transactions are not just regulated by the Securities and Exchange Commission (SEC); regulators at the states of domicile for the companies involved have input into the transaction, particularly as to whether it is in the interests of policyholders. In certain situations, such as transactions involving bankruptcy or assumption reinsurance, regulators and/or guarantee funds from every state in which the company has policyholders may become involved.

1.4.1 STATE REGULATION

In the United States, the insurance industry is highly, if unevenly, regulated at the state level. State insurance law and regulations adopted by the state insurance regulatory authority are the primary legal basis for the regulation of insurance in the United States. The state insurance regulatory authorities may also issue opinions, bulletins, and other documents of lesser authority than statute and regulation. Every state has an insurance regulatory authority, although the position of the department of insurance within the regulatory structure differs from state to state.

Massachusetts and New York pioneered the development of state insurance regulation from the mid-nineteenth century onward. Massachusetts Commissioner Elizur Wright (1858-66) pioneered the minimum net premium-based statutory reserves and minimum nonforfeiture benefits for the protection of insurers and policyholders. New York's Armstrong Investigation in 1905 resulted in strong statutory requirements for insurer governance that have protected the industry for over a century.

The insurance regulatory authority of an insurer's state of domicile is the primary regulator of that insurer. However, an insurer must comply with the applicable laws and regulations of the other states in which it operates. The insurer must be able to demonstrate that its reserves in the aggregate comply with the minimum requirements of every state in its territory. Under statutory codification, insurers must also compare financial statements as filed with the individual state insurance regulatory authorities with the basis prescribed by the Accounting Practices and Procedures Manual maintained by the National Association of Insurance Commissioners.

1.4.2 NATIONAL ASSOCIATION OF INSURANCE COMMISSIONERS

Founded in 1871, the National Association of Insurance Commissioners (NAIC) is a not-for-profit corporation serving the 50 separate insurance commissioners. In addition to providing centralized data-gathering support to the individual state insurance regulatory authorities, the NAIC:

(1) develops and adopts model laws, regulations, and guidelines for the consideration of the individual state insurance regulatory authorities and legislatures

(2) co-ordinates periodic financial and market conduct examinations of insurers for the individual state insurance regulatory authorities

(3) maintains the Accounting Practices and Procedures Manual (APPM), which is the highest authority for codified statutory accounting

(4) maintains the reporting blanks for the different types of insurers regulated and the instructions for completing these blanks

(5) determines through its Securities Valuation Office (SVO) statement values for reporting of assets in the reporting blanks

(6) maintains accreditation standards for state insurance regulatory authorities.

The adoption of the standard valuation and standard nonforfeiture laws (SVL and SNFL, respectively) by the various states was a major twentieth century NAIC accomplishment, which was complete by January 1, 1948.

In response to the needs of insurers with national operations, in 2002 the NAIC proposed for state adoption an Interstate Insurance Product Regulation Compact under which the individual states would delegate certain aspects of their regulatory authority (e.g., policy form approval for designated lines of insurance) to a centralized authority governed by the compacting states. The compact proposal was a response to advocacy for an alternative federal track regulation for insurers.

1.4.3 NATIONAL ORGANIZATION OF LIFE AND HEALTH GUARANTY ASSOCIATIONS

Unlike the banking industry, insurance companies are not federally insured. Each state maintains its own guarantee fund for the benefit of policyholders living in the state according to its own statutory rules. Funds are maintained by levying assessments on companies doing business in the state.

The system faces a number of challenges. From a risk standpoint, states with strong regulatory structures shoulder a disproportionate share of the burden from weaker states if one accepts the premise that weak regulation increases the risk of failure. A failure in a state with weak oversight impacts the cost of doing business in states with good management. For example, the state with the most effective oversight is responsible for indemnifying residents insured with any and all out-of-state companies whose oversight is worse, whereas companies domiciled in the better-regulating state pose less of a risk to the guarantee structure in other states. This treatment is in sharp contrast to regulatory oversight, where the state of domicile of the company, rather than the residence of the policyholder, is the overriding factor. This discrepancy and how to manage the costs of failure are recurring sources of tension between states.

Because of the structure of the guarantee funds, failures of companies writing in multiple states lead to a great deal of legal confusion and expense, to the detriment of all involved. The National Organization of Life and Health Guaranty Associations (NOLHGA) promotes coordination of action when insurers are placed under conservation or receivership by state insurance regulatory authorities.

When an insurer is declared insolvent, NOLHGA, on behalf of state guaranty associations, assembles a task force of guaranty association officials. This task force, with the support of NOLHGA staff, legal experts, actuaries, and financial experts, develops a plan for resolving the insolvency. Typically, the task force develops an accounting of the company's assets and liabilities, ensures that covered claims are paid, and prepares the block of business for sale to a healthy insurer.

The task force also supports the efforts of the receiver to dispose of the company's assets in a way that maximizes the value of those assets. If, after assets are disposed of, there is a shortfall of estate assets to fulfill all of the covered policyholder obligations of the insolvent insurer, guaranty associations assess the licensed insurers in their states a proportional share of the funds needed to make up the shortfall.

There are several key benefits that NOLHGA provides the guaranty system in its efforts to resolve insolvencies. Chief among these is that NOLHGA involvement decreases costs to state guaranty associations. Instead of having each state association hire legal and financial experts, NOLHGA uses one team of experts, greatly reducing costs to guaranty associations and ultimately the insurance companies that fund them. This coordination of effort also reduces the length of time it takes to develop a plan of rehabilitation or to otherwise resolve a multi-state insolvency.

1.4.4 U.S. FEDERAL GOVERNMENT

Nineteenth-century court decisions in the United States generally rejected federal government involvement in the regulation of the insurance business. However, federal court decisions in the twentieth century increased the role of the federal government in insurance regulation. With the adoption of Social Security in 1935 and Medicare in 1965, the federal government and its contractors became the largest single insurer in the nation.

There is an active segment of the insurance industry that advocates an alternative federal-track regulation of the insurance business to escape the inefficiencies of dealing with 50 state insurance departments. It is a barrier to entry, particularly to international insurers, and is responsible for the market in "shell" companies that have no actual insurance in force but consist solely of active licenses to do business in particular states.

1.4.4.1 Employee Retirement Income Security Act

Federal government involvement in the insurance business is strongest in employer-sponsored benefit plans. The Employee Retirement Income Security Act (ERISA) of 1974 pre-empted much state authority for insured plans in this domain. Specifically, states may not regulate the business of insurance when it applies to an employee benefit plan. However, state insurance law may still apply to the extent that a plan provides "insured" benefits because insurance companies and not the plan are still subject to state law. Federal legislation and various court decisions since that time have focused on insurer ownership structures and distribution mechanisms. State governments have had to adopt legislation relating to agent licensing to avoid pre-emptive exercise of authority by the federal government.

As the name of the act implies, ERISA's primary focus is retirement plans. However, its reach applies to all employee benefit plans such as health care, disability, vacation benefits, death benefits, and prepaid legal services.

ERISA imposes broad reporting and disclosure requirements on employee benefit plans. The disclosure rules are administered by the Department of Labor and the financial reporting is sent to the Internal Revenue Service. The law also provides rules for persons responsible for administering various aspects of the plans (plan fiduciaries) and provides for remedies and sanctions for noncompliance.

An employee benefit plan may be insured or self-funded and is required to have a written plan document describing the plan. The plan document also needs to describe the claims procedures under the plan, including how they are submitted and the process for appeals and denials.

Although one of ERISA's goals was to make its requirements applicable to all employee benefit plans, one situation still distinguishes insured and self-funded plans. Insured plans are still subject to any state-mandated benefits while self-funded plans are not. This exemption is the primary reason why self-funded medical plans are popular among employer-sponsored plans, especially for companies with multi-state operations.

1.4.4.2 Gramm-Leach-Bliley Act

The 1933 Glass-Steagall Act, which separated the financial services industries, set the stage for most of the regulatory challenges facing the insurance industry in the twentieth century. The loosening of these restraints in the form of the Gramm-Leach-Bliley Act in 1999 was expected to revolutionize the insurance industry. Citicorp struck first with its purchase of Travelers in 1998 for $38.6 billion, one of the country's largest mutli-line insurance companies. While analysts and consultants believed this to be a harbinger of a wave of bank-insurance acquisitions, the silence that followed this transaction was deafening.

A scant three years after the deal was consummated, Citicorp spun off the larger P&C portion of Travelers into a stand-alone operation. Less than two years after that, Travelers P&C was again in the news when the merger with St. Paul was announced with a purchase price of $16 billion. Yet more post-merger reserve strengthening at Travelers calls into question the appropriateness of this price, as well as the adequacy of the due diligence of this transaction.

The U.S. banking industry has, to date, rejected the notion of European-style bancassurance, with the bank as manufacturer and distributor, and is instead focusing on distribution only. Insurance agencies have been snapped up by banks at a remarkable pace in some regions, while other bank players are content to serve as distributors for product manufacturers in their own brick and mortar.

1.4.4.3 ***Sarbanes-Oxley***

During the early 2000s, several once well-regarded corporations in the United States collapsed due to accounting irregularities. In order to curb corporate scandals and restore investor confidence in U.S. financial markets, Congress enacted a corporate governance and accounting oversight act known as the Sarbanes-Oxley Act of 2002.

The act has broad implications and effects on many corporations' executives, boards of directors, accountants, lawyers, and external auditors. This act:

(1) created a Public Company Accounting Oversight Board for supervising public accounting firms and accounting professionals

(2) limited the scope of non-audit and consulting services to be provided by accounting firms to their audit clients

(3) required certifications from principal executives and principal financial officers regarding the quality of submitted quarterly and annual financial reports

(4) enhanced the required financial disclosures of the Securities Exchange Act of 1934

(5) enhanced Chapters 63 and 73 of title 18, United States Code, regarding corporate fraud and criminal fraud offenses.

The act affects mergers and acquisitions in many areas including, but not limited to, due diligence and quality of consolidated financial statements after the purchase. The act requires the purchasing company's signing officers (chief executive officer and chief financial officer) to certify the appropriateness of the combined company's internal control disclosure.

Because many corporations have restated their financial statements, the purchasing company should also evaluate this possibility in the target company. The purchasing company should only issue certification on the target company's internal controls after it has completed a well-designed due diligence. The prior practice of performing a limited scope due diligence in a relatively short time frame is not just inappropriate; it may also lead to adverse legal consequences. The act also focuses on the accuracy of the financial report and whether it is prepared in accordance with or reconciles to U.S. generally accepted accounting principles. This focus may affect the financial reporting of the target company after the purchase.

1.4.5 SECURITIES AND EXCHANGE COMMISSION

In 1933, the U.S. Congress enacted the Securities Act of 1933 to regulate the securities markets. The Act required registration of securities prior to their public sale and also required disclosure of certain financial and other data in order to assist investors in making informed decisions. The SEC's role is not to disallow an issue but to ensure that enough information is provided to investors. The Act also included provisions prohibiting false representations and disclosures. The enforcement of these laws became the responsibility of the Securities and Exchange Commission with the Securities Exchange Act of 1934.

While the Financial Accounting Standards Board (FASB) is the primary standard setter, the SEC can also be considered an accounting standard setter for those companies that fall within its regulatory reach. The SEC, through its rules and regulations, prescribes the form and content of financial statements that are filed with it. In some cases the requirements are the same as those set forth by FASB. In other cases the requirements may not be the same and may go beyond those of existing literature. The SEC's financial statement rules for insurance companies are set forth in "Regulation SX" Section 210.7. The SEC also periodically issues Staff Accounting Bulletins (SABs), which are intended to address specific accounting issues as they arise.

There are multiple situations in which companies are required to produce financial statements or other financial reporting information for the SEC. These include:

- 10-K: submitted annually; includes comprehensive information such as earnings, cash flow, balance sheet, executive pay, litigation, and management discussion and analysis
- 10-Q: submitted quarterly; a shorter version of the 10-K
- 8-K: submitted whenever any development that is material to shareholders and the company; examples include a merger, acquisition, accounting problems, or hiring and firing of key executives
- 13D: submitted whenever an individual or corporation acquires a 5% stake
- 14A: a proxy statement that includes details of issues to be voted on and background on management and the board of directors.

This list is not intended to be exhaustive because the accounting literature changes over time. The requirements of such statements are subject to interpretation by companies, their auditors, and the rule-making bodies.

1.5 INSURANCE RATING AGENCIES

Consumers pay a premium to insurance companies for the promise of indemnification in the event of a claim. In weighing offers between providers, the astute purchaser may contemplate the possibility that the insurer may or may not be around to pay the claim. Despite the multi-pronged regulatory approach, there is little information geared towards assisting consumers with these sorts of decisions. While most industries have debt ratings and stock analysts to provide insight and opinions on the soundness of a company and its ability to meet its obligations, because of the specialization in the industry, a separate group of analysts and ratings organizations has evolved offering their opinions, typically in terms of a letter grade, as to the company's ability to meet ongoing obligations to policyholders.

In some instances, the rating agencies' opinion will carry more weight than regulators' opinions. The rating is an independent opinion based on an evaluation of a company's balance sheet, operating performance, and business profile. This is different from, but not unrelated to, a company's ability to service debt. Policyholders are typically the most senior creditors of an insurer and have the most senior claim on assets in the case of default. As such, any insurance company debt will be of necessity rated lower than the overall creditworthiness of the operating insurer.

Changes in ratings can be tumultuous. Whereas upgrades in ratings are a cause for celebration, they rarely translate into immediate market momentum. On the other hand, a downgrade is a significant cause for concern and can translate into an immediate erosion in market share and the existing book of business. In extreme cases, it can cause a liquidity crisis. A ratings downgrade in 1999 eventually sent General American into the arms of a rescuer, Metropolitan.

The ability of a company to pay policyholder claims versus its ability to service its (or its parent's) debt are two different capabilities. In 1999, A.M. Best expanded its product line to include the rating of debt and structured finance separately from its analysis and rating of an insurer's ability to meet ongoing obligations to policyholders. The credit rating of each issue is an opinion as to the issuer's ability to meet its financial obligations to the security holders when due. These ratings are assigned to individual debt and preferred stock issues.

1.6 INSURANCE ACCOUNTING

An accounting system is a mechanism for determining a balance sheet and its consequent emergence of earnings. Unlike other industries, insurance is characterized by a surfeit of accounting bases, each with a different approach and purpose: statutory, generally accepted accounting principles (GAAP), tax, mutual company GAAP, innumerable management reporting bases, embedded value, fair value, etc. Because of this, it can be difficult for company insiders, much less outside observers, to agree exactly where an insurance company stands financially at any given point in time.

Why do accounting systems matter? After all the premiums have been collected and all claims and expenses paid, the accounting basis used will not have any impact on the total amount of profits made. The accounting basis does establish the reporting value of liabilities and assets, which shapes the emergence of earnings from period to period. If the discount rate is equal to the earned rate, then the present value of profits will be the same in any accounting scenario, and the accounting system will not matter because investment income on retained earnings will offset the effect of discounting. However, if the discount rate is higher than the earned rate (typically the case for any capital investment or shareholder yield objective), the earlier earnings emerge, the more valuable the book of business is to the investor or shareholder.

Some approaches, such as embedded value, tend to reflect profits earlier, more towards policy issue. Other approaches, like U.S. statutory, establish more conservative reserves, which delays the emergence of earnings in the interest of policyholder security. Application of U.S. GAAP generally results in a level emergence of earnings over the life of the contract. The conservatism inherent in statutory accounting is more of an issue in long-term contracts, such as life insurance and annuities, than in short-term contracts.

Optimizing an insurance accounting system involves reconciling the tensions inherent in the conflicting objectives of policyholder security, shareholder value, and the alignment of earnings with services performed. In the United States, statutory accounting generally requires conservative mortality tables and interest rates. As a result of these assumptions, higher reserves are established in early years, conserving profits for release in later years as liabilities expire. As reserves are released, profits emerge due to the conservatism implicit in statutory assumptions. US GAAP is used for financial reporting to shareholders and creditors in the United States, utilizing a separate set of assumptions and at times wholly different methodologies.

Internationally, various jurisdictions are contemplating using fair value accounting to present insurance company financial statements to regulators and markets. In the United States,

FASB has stated its interest in developing fair value reporting for financial institutions: fair value as a concept has intellectual appeal; fair value as an accounting basis may introduce rules and guidance that create unwarranted volatility. While determining the fair value of an asset may not be controversial, the lack of observable market values for liabilities creates many paths that fair value of liability determination could take.

1.7 TAXATION

Taxation is the longest-standing involvement of the federal government in the insurance industry. Insurance companies have been subject to the federal income tax since its inception in 1913. Major changes relating to the taxation of insurers were adopted in 1959 (multiple-phase tax for life insurers) and 1984 with the introduction of specific federal income tax basis reserves (yet another accounting basis for insurers).

The Internal Revenue Code (IRC) and its implementing regulations define the tax basis for insurers. The rules generally follow the statutory accounting paradigm as adopted by the individual states described previously. However, tax reserves are modified for certain accounting practices and use generally less conservative assumptions for reserve computations, which has the effect of accelerating earnings (and hence collecting taxes earlier).

The IRC also defines taxation of insurance products at the policy owner level. Most importantly, life insurance death benefit proceeds are exempt from tax, as is indemnification of loss as a general rule. The deferral of taxation on the "inside build-up" of life insurance and annuity products (excess of cash value above premium basis) has been almost as important to the promotion of the insurance industry in the United States in the twentieth century as the mortgage interest deduction has been in promoting home ownership.

State taxes on insurance consist primarily of a tax on premiums originating in the state rather than a tax on corporate profits.

1.8 DISTRIBUTION

There are many types of insurance distribution channels, each with its own cost structure. The history of the industry can be read through the evolving layers of its distribution channels: home service, debit, career agent, agency, broker, direct marketing, bancassurance, Internet, non-traditional, etc.

Distribution is as critical to insurance as it is expensive. By comparison with manufactured and other financial products, insurance is expensive to distribute. This cost is increasingly coming under pressure from alternatives such as mutual funds and bank certificates of deposit, which compete for savings dollars at significantly lower cost than traditional insurance distribution channels.

Such costs are the principal expenses incurred by a life insurance company in marketing its products. Those costs include commissions, overriding commissions, expense allowances, bonuses and other incentive plans, fringe benefits, fees, salaries, reimbursements, and direct paid expenses such as rent, clerical expenses, and other costs of doing business. Special plans frequently exist for agency heads, supervisory personnel, specialists, newly hired agents, top producers, and brokers. Methods may differ by distribution system, by product, or by market.

Special attention must be paid to the expense limitation laws and regulations of New York State. These statutes have a significant impact on the practices of life insurance companies licensed to do business in that state. The New York limits apply wherever a company does business, not just in New York alone.

An insurer (risk bearer) may be viewed as a manufacturer with the need to find distribution for the product. Many insurers are experimenting with multiple distribution channels, sometimes within the same company or sometimes through different brands, acquired or built. Other companies are seeking to enforce fiscal discipline by establishing distribution centers as independently managed profit centers rather than as unaccountable cost centers. Buyers may seek to acquire strategic partners for their complementary distribution channels. Channel conflict is an issue for companies with multiple distribution channels. The decision to acquire an insurance company versus a block of business often comes down to the choice of buying versus building the distribution channel.

Depending on the era, the value of new business can either be a significant element of the purchase price or a small component of the purchase price. The value of new business in any other industry is the goodwill ascribed to a trademark or brand name. In an actuarial appraisal, the value of new business might be considered a proxy for brand value.

1.9 A FEW WORDS ABOUT ACTUARIES

Chances are that the reader who is not associated with the insurance industry knows little about actuaries. Actuaries are specialists in analyzing, quantifying, and leveraging the economic consequences of risk. The profession has its roots in the insurance industry and is a proponent of a scientific principle, substituting facts for impressions. As will be seen in later chapters, the speed at which M&A transpires causes its players to have little time to convert impressions to facts.

The actuary plays a key role in insurance M&A transactions. Actuaries are experts in the valuation of insurance industry tangibles (existing business) and intangibles (new business, goodwill, brand value). But the actuarial approach to valuation (discounted cash flow) and due diligence (value optimization through risk management) are just as applicable to other industries, complementing the work of other professionals and their methodologies.

Like most professionals, actuaries are specialized. Although the profession is relatively small (17,500 members in the Society of Actuaries and 3,900 members of the Casualty Actuarial Society), actuaries practicing in different lines of business may have little in common with one another other than the analysis of risk. However, those risks vary greatly between lines, along with the language and methodology for analyzing that risk, making for broad gulfs between actuaries practicing in different fields.

Since World War II, four main actuarial disciplines have been prevalent, more or less corresponding to the types of risks under review: health, life, P&C, and retirement/pension. Since the 1990s, in response to industry needs, two new actuarial disciplines have emerged. One is expertise in financial analysis (the modeling of assets, options, and economic risks); the other is in the field of enterprise risk management. The later chapters present the perspectives of each of these actuarial disciplines.

There are a number of different professional bodies addressing the educational and professional needs of these different professionals.

1.9.1 THE AMERICAN ACADEMY OF ACTUARIES

The American Academy of Actuaries (AAA) is the organization representing the entire U.S. actuarial profession, both nationally and internationally, by establishing, maintaining, and enforcing professional standards of qualification, practice, and conduct.

To assist in this role, the academy has established the Actuarial Standards Board (ASB) as an independent entity. The ASB has the authority to approve exposure of proposed standards, to hold public hearings on them, and to adopt recommended standards of practice. The ASB also provides continuous review of the existing Actuarial Standards of Practice (ASOPs) to determine whether they are in need of amendment, alteration, expansion, or elimination.

1.9.2 SOCIETY OF ACTUARIES

The Society of Actuaries (SOA) has members all over the world, but the majority of them live in the United States and Canada. It is dedicated to education, research, and professionalism for its members, who are involved with the modeling and management of financial risk and contingent events.

Members achieve the designation of Fellow (FSA) or Associate (ASA) through completion of SOA-sponsored examinations. The SOA also sponsors continuing education through meetings, seminars, and publications. The SOA as a whole, its practice areas, and its special interest sections have a coordinated mechanism for performing and delivering research that supports the needs of its members.

1.9.3 CASUALTY ACTUARIAL SOCIETY

The Casualty Actuarial Society (CAS) serves casualty actuaries in the United States and Canada and also has members in Europe and Asia. It is dedicated to the advancement of the body of knowledge of actuarial science for its members, who evaluate the financial effects of economic, legal, and social trends on future events in property, casualty, and similar types of insurance.

Members achieve the designation of Fellow (FCAS) or Associate (ACAS) through completion of CAS-sponsored examinations. Members work for insurance companies, ratemaking organizations, regulatory entities, independent consultants, and educational institutions.

The CAS sponsors continuing education through meetings, seminars, publications, and two special interest sections devoted to regulation and reinsurance. The CAS is also dedicated to providing its members with research in such areas as ratemaking, reserving, dynamic financial analysis, and enterprise risk management.

1.9.4 AMERICAN SOCIETY OF PENSION PROFESSIONALS AND ACTUARIES

The American Society of Pension Professionals and Actuaries (ASPPA) is an organization whose primary purpose is to educate pension actuaries, consultants, and other benefits professionals about the private pension systems in the United States. Although founded with a strong emphasis on serving pension actuaries, the organization has evolved to serve a variety of benefits professionals, including administrators, consultants, financial planners, attorneys, accountants, and others.

For actuaries, ASPPA provides a series of examinations leading to professional designations as Fellow (FSPA) and Member (MSPA). It also provides review courses for the enrolled actuary (EA) examinations. The EA designation is required by the federal government for much of the actuarial work related to private pensions.

ASPPA has a mission to enhance the private pension system in the United States. To fulfill that mission, ASPPA frequently makes extensive comments about proposed laws and regulations to the IRS, the Department of Labor, the Pension Benefit Guaranty Corporation (PBGC), and others.

1.9.5 CONFERENCE OF CONSULTING ACTUARIES

The Conference of Consulting Actuaries (CCA) represents consulting actuaries in the United States and Canada. It focuses on strengthening the practice of actuarial consulting and the ability of its members to serve their clients and the public. Members practice in the health, life, P&C, and retirement/pension fields.

CCA has three levels of membership, the highest being Fellow, then Associate, and finally Member. Prospective members must meet an experience requirement consisting of a certain number of years of responsible actuarial work and must have obtained membership in one of the other North American actuarial organizations. CCA members must meet an annual continuing education requirement consisting of basic actuarial practice and professionalism. CCA provides meetings and seminars to assist its members in fulfilling those requirements.

1.10 OVERVIEW

The remainder of the book is devoted to the M&A process, particularly as it applies to insurance companies. Chapter 2 provides an overview of the entire M&A process. Even if the reader has been involved in a number of transactions, there are likely a number of elements that an active professional may never have had an opportunity in which to become involved. The chapter provides a discussion of the various types of M&A processes, the roles of the professionals involved on the M&A team, and the marketing of a property to the prospective buyer.

Chapter 3 examines the intricacies of financing an M&A transaction. The characteristics of different financing instruments, from debt to equity to everything in between, are presented. The many considerations that go into determining the amount and type of financing to use, both in general and those particular to the insurance industry, are discussed.

Chapter 4 details the valuation of insurance products and companies. Common Wall Street valuation methods are explained, as is the actuarial appraisal. The basic methodology employed is a discounted cash flow (DCF) model using best estimate assumptions to attempt to value the distributable earnings of the target. Considerations unique to particular lines of business and product types are also discussed.

Chapter 5 discusses the complex dance known as due diligence. It is a massive undertaking in normal circumstances, further complicated by the nature of insurance liabilities. All of the members of the buyer's team have an important role to play and each of their roles is laid out in this chapter. In addition, the special concerns and considerations of each of the actuarial disciplines and the reasons why they are critically important to address before the negotiation process is complete are examined.

Chapter 6 examines the role of the actuary in due diligence for non-insurance companies, particularly the risk management and human resource (HR) programs. HR programs of particular importance include employee benefits (group benefits, pensions, etc.), which can significantly impact large and many medium size transactions. The role of risk management is examined because it is an issue where non-insurance companies manage elements of their risk portfolio by means of self-insurance and wholly owned captives. Actuaries are needed to analyze the structure of these retained liabilities to determine their materiality to the deal. Just as an environmental review for a real estate transaction is common today but unheard of 25 years ago, a deal review by a risk management professional will eventually become the industry standard. While review of HR and risk management programs may not often be the primary cause for transactions breaking down, they do shape deals and often serve as a leading indicator of success.

Chapter 7 provides an overview of federal income tax issues that arise in connection with M&A transactions involving insurance companies. This chapter provides an introduction to some of the unique aspects of the taxation of insurance before discussing tax issues involved in structuring insurance company acquisitions, as well as valuation-related tax issues.

Chapter 8 deals with purchase accounting (PGAAP) for insurance transactions in the United States. This is a very technical subject with ample room for disagreement among experts because the authoritative literature that does exist is not comprehensive. The chapter discusses the wide range of practices within the industry.

Chapter 9 illuminates a subject few M&A specialists are familiar with: post-acquisition integration. The financial goals of a transaction may hinge on achieving post-merger efficiencies or cross-selling synergies. How can this possibly be accomplished in the crush of post-merger activity, all the while maintaining share value, customer loyalty, and employee morale? More than in other phases, the role of project management is important, and measurable indicators of success and failure are available.

Chapter Two

M&A Process Overview

2.1 INTRODUCTION

The process of buying, selling, merging, or divesting companies is a difficult, time consuming, and expensive proposition in any industry. Nevertheless, merger and acquisition (M&A) has played, and will continue to play, an important role in the continuing development of virtually every industry and sector. Given the financial and regulatory dynamics of the insurance industry, the risks and rewards of engaging in M&A activity are particularly significant for insurance companies.

The process of buying or selling companies varies from transaction to transaction. The facts, circumstances, and players involved in the transaction will dictate a unique path for each deal. While the process of acquiring a family-owned insurance brokerage seems to bear little in common with a hostile takeover of a multi-billion public life insurance company,[1] there are nonetheless certain fundamental transaction tasks and issues common to all insurance mergers and acquisitions. The purpose of this chapter is to provide an overview of a "typical" M&A transaction as it relates to insurance companies.

2.1.1 SCOPE

This scope of this chapter is limited to M&A transactions within the insurance industry in the United States. Although the M&A process is roughly analogous in Europe and most westernized countries, the process described in this chapter is focused solely on the method of buying or selling insurance companies within the United States and does not address the complexities associated with cross-border insurance transactions.

In addition, except where specifically mentioned, the process described in this chapter generally applies to all M&A activity involving insurance companies irrespective of their ownership structure or status (i.e., regardless of whether the companies involved are public companies or are privately owned).

In order to provide the reader with a comprehensive overview of the insurance M&A process, this chapter focuses on the fully marketed[2] sale of an insurance company notwithstanding the fact that many companies are sold in a truncated sale process.[3] In addition, this chapter generally assumes that the seller initiates the sale process. While that is generally the case, buyers frequently approach sellers and make offers directly. Regardless of how the process is initiated and who initiates it, the relevant steps in the process are virtually identical.

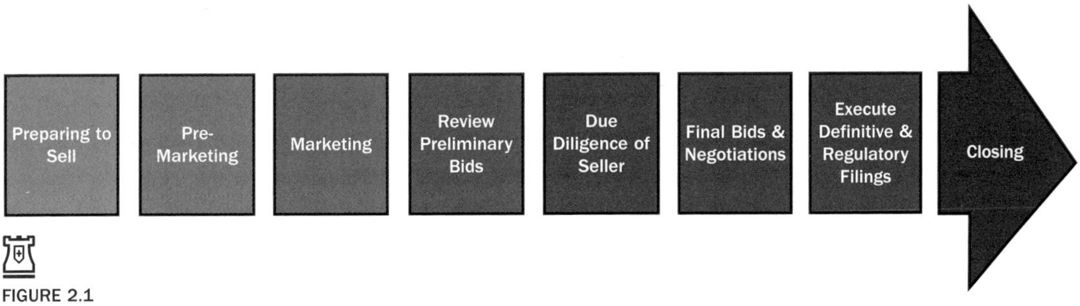

FIGURE 2.1

[1] AIG's hostile bid for American General in 2000 is a classic example of a successful hostile takeover in the insurance context (outmaneuvering Prudential PLC). For a gripping account of one of the most storied corporate takeovers in U.S. history not in the insurance arena, see *Barbarians at the Gate: The Fall of RJR Nabisco*, Bryan Burrough and John Helyear (1990).

[2] A fully marketed sale generally entails the seller's hiring of a transaction team, preparation of detailed marketing materials, and the distribution of such materials to a reasonably wide range of prospective acquirers.

[3] For example, the seller may know the buyer and simply call up the CEO or chairman and begin a non-competitive, one-on-one sale process.

2.1.2 ROADMAP

This chapter sets forth the tasks and milestones of the M&A process generally and, to the extent they diverge from one another, from the perspectives of each of the sell side and the buy side of the transaction. The chapter begins with an introduction to the strategic and financial considerations that drive M&A activity and then provides an overview of the key players in the transaction process and details their respective roles in the process.

The chapter next covers the progression of a "typical" transaction including:

- types of sale processes
- selection of potential buyers
- preparation of marketing materials and the actuarial appraisal
- marketing of the seller
- sell side and buy side due diligence
- negotiations and transaction structuring
- execution of a definitive agreement and announcement to various stakeholders.

The chapter ends with a discussion of the post-announcement transaction process culminating in the closing of the transaction.

2.2 M&A DRIVERS: AN OVERVIEW

There are ample risks and rewards throughout and at the end of the M&A process. The M&A market itself fluctuates based on many factors. Both financial and strategic objectives influence the final value of an acquisition. This section addresses these drivers.

2.2.1 THE BENEFITS AND RISKS OF M&A

The benefits of successfully executed and integrated corporate transactions can be enormous. First and foremost, a merger or acquisition can provide short-term and long-term financial benefits to the acquirer's shareholders by increasing corporate earnings and cash flow, thereby driving up the value of shareholders' equity. As importantly, mergers and acquisitions can provide immediate and long-term strategic benefits, which would be impossible, impractical, or simply more expensive to generate organically. Strategic benefits could include a meaningful gain in market share; geographic or product diversification; and access to new technology, distribution channels, and key personnel.

As with any major corporate decision, the potential benefits of acquisitions need to be weighed against the risks inherent in executing such transactions. There are, of course, major financial risks, including overpaying due to overly optimistic cost saving or revenue synergy assumptions or insufficient due diligence of the seller's liabilities. There are also strategic risks, such as creating "channel conflict" (i.e., alienating a distribution source by acquiring competing distribution). Finally, there is simple execution risk. This means that even if the transaction is priced properly and fits strategically, failure to integrate the transaction properly can cause disruption to the orderly business of the combined firm. This disruption can manifest itself in any number of ways, including the loss of, or damage to, key employee and customer relationships.

In addition to the aforementioned risks that relate only to buyers, information asymmetry presents a risk for both buyer and seller. The sell side typically has several months of lead-time and full access to the seller's resources and data to prepare a compelling sell side story. The buy side, on the other hand, generally has limited access to information and a limited time frame within which to submit its bid.[4] This information asymmetry increases the risk for potential buyers.

[4] On the other hand, the buyer may have a better sense of the seller's true value in the open market. Active buyers generally have excellent intelligence on valuation trends and the degree of competition for similar companies. This information asymmetry obviously benefits the buyer.

2.2.2 THE ACQUISITION MARKET

M&A activity among insurance companies is driven by the overall M&A market as well as strategic and financial considerations. The M&A market fluctuates based on a number of factors, including the (a) availability of financing from both the bank acquisition loan market and the debt and equity capital markets, (b) rising stock prices and rising P/E multiples, which provide acquirers with strong acquisition currencies, (c) ongoing restructuring as businesses shed underperforming or ancillary businesses to focus on core competencies, (d) tax implications (i.e., lower capital gains tax rates), (e) wealth transfer between generations, and (f) market psychology.

2.2.3 FINANCIAL OBJECTIVES

The primary objective in any M&A transaction is to promote corporate growth. "Growth" is generally short-hand for revenue growth and/or earnings growth. Revenue growth is important because the markets assign a premium valuation (all else being equal) to companies that are growing the "top line" (revenue) more rapidly than their peers—organically or via acquisition.[5] The reason for this phenomenon is the perception that rapid revenue growth presages future earnings growth, and most public companies are valued, at least theoretically, on estimated future earning power. Earnings growth is important because most companies are valued, more or less directly, on the basis of anticipated future corporate earnings.

A publicly traded buyer is generally expected to quantify (for its shareholders and for Wall Street) the financial impact of any anticipated improvement in competitive position arising from an acquisition. This topic is generally discussed in terms of the impact the transaction will have on pro forma[6] financial and operational statistics and ratios, including asset, equity, operating, and financial leverage ratios, and, most importantly, earnings.

Publicly traded companies are loath to make acquisitions that are not accretive to earnings per share within a reasonable time frame.[7] However, as a practical matter, many transactions are not accretive to earnings unless there are legitimate and identified expense savings or revenue synergies. An example of an expense reduction strategy is acquiring "orphan" blocks of life insurance business and administering them in run-off as a low-cost service provider. Revenue synergies are derived from increased sales of different product lines (cross-selling opportunities). For example, a bank purchasing an insurance company with the intention of cross-selling fixed annuities to the bank's customer base is a synergistic revenue-enhancing acquisition.

---

[5] The market generally values organic growth more highly than growth via acquisition, except in highly fragmented industries and for companies where acquisitions are fundamental to the business plan (i.e., roll ups).

[6] Pro forma (in the context of finance) describes a presentation of data, typically financial statements, where the data reflect the world on an "as if" basis. In other words, current financial data of an acquirer are often presented "as if" the merger or acquisition contemplated has already occurred. In addition to utilizing pro forma financial statements on a "forward looking" basis, pro formas are also useful retrospectively. For example, after a sizeable acquisition has been consummated, the acquirer's pre-transaction financial statements may bear only passing resemblance to the post-transaction financial statements, thereby impeding comparability over time and skewing analyses of "core" performance trends. In that case, it may be helpful to prepare pro forma financial statements that present data "as if" the acquisition occurred several years earlier. It should be noted that "pro forma" financial statements generally do not comply with generally accepted accounting principles. It also important to note that companies frequently utilize pro forma earnings outside of the transactional context, typically to emphasize financial results that would have been achieved but for a "one time" or "extraordinary" event.

[7] There is a widespread perception among executives and bankers that dilutive transactions will depress the buyer's stock prices notwithstanding the fact that EPS accretion (or dilution) is frequently a function of the accounting conventions and regulations rather than cash flows. *Do Appearances Matter?: The Impact of EPS Accretion and Dilution on Stock Price*, Gregor Andrade, Assistant Professor, Harvard Business School (1999). Moreover, short-term earnings accretion or dilution should be less important to executives and investors than ascertaining whether the returns generated by an acquisition clear the acquirer's "cost of capital" or "hurdle rate."

The anticipated value generated by revenue-enhancing synergies or operational leverage (expense saves) is often the edge that drives a winning bid. Unfortunately, realizing projected synergies and savings after the transaction closes is challenging and often elusive. The gap is generally caused by either (a) overly optimistic assumptions ahead of time or (b) difficulties optimally integrating the seller into the buyer's organization. An analysis of the challenges, lessons, and best practices in post-merger integration is presented in Chapter 9.

It is worth noting that even without synergies or expense savings, certain transactions are inherently accretive to the buyer's earnings. This phenomenon occurs when the market values the buyer's earnings more highly than the seller's earnings. In a stock-for-stock acquisition, the transaction is generally accretive to the acquirer's earnings if the acquirer's stock trades at a higher multiple of earnings (P/E ratio) than the multiple at which the seller's stock trades.

For example, in Table 2.1 below, Acquirer's stock is trading at 10 times Acquirer's annual earnings whereas Target is trading at five times Target's earnings. In this case, the market values $1 of Acquirer's earnings twice as highly as $1 of Target's earnings. As a result, Acquirer is in a position to buy that $1 earnings using its stock and thereby effectively double the market value of those earnings by adding them to Acquirer's own income statement. In other words, thanks to the P/E arbitrage, Acquirer can double its earnings from $1 million to $2 million as in the illustration in Table 2.1 while only issuing 50% more shares. To put it another way, the dilution suffered by Acquirer's shareholders as the result of Acquirer issuing more stock to buy Target is more than offset by the impact that the additional earnings will have in Acquirer's stock price. The result is that the additional earnings per share propels the stock price ever higher as long as the P/E ratio remains the same.

GROWTH IN EARNINGS PER SHARE BY ACQUISITION – STOCK SWAP

	ACQUIRER	TARGET	MERGED FIRM
P/E	10 X	5 X	10 X
Earnings	$1,000,000	$1,000,000	$2,000,000
Shares Outstanding	1,000,000	1,000,000	1,500,000
EPS	$1.00	$1.00	$1.33
Market Valuation Per Share	$10.00	$5.00	$13.33
Total Market Valuation	$10,000,000	$5,000,000	$20,000,000

TABLE 2.1

Of course, all of this favorable algebra evaporates once the Acquirer's P/E ratio declines, which typically happens when the Acquirer reaches critical mass and growth slows down. At that point, without the favorable high P/E multiple, Acquirer's ability to use its stock to make accretive acquisitions is curtailed, which compounds the already slowing corporate growth.[8]

[8] The merger booms of the 1960s and the late 1990s were driven, in part, by "pain free" stock-for-stock acquisitions in which companies with high P/E ratios acquired companies with lower P/E ratios. Because the stock market deemed the acquirer's earnings per share "more valuable" than the acquired companies' earnings, the transaction was generally accretive. From the acquirer's perspective, such transactions are almost always compelling because any additional earnings will result in a higher stock price (assuming the P/E ratio holds steady). *Mergers, Acquisitions & Corporate Restructurings*, Third Edition, by Patrick Gaughan. For a highly publicized example of the downside of the "earnings game," see AOL's acquisition of Time Warner.

2.2.4 STRATEGIC OBJECTIVES

While the transaction's financial impact often captures the newspaper headlines, the transaction's strategic impact is often more significant over the long term. Most M&A transactions are consummated, in part, to achieve strategic objectives above and beyond the transaction's financial impact. The strategic rationale may be to improve the buyer's long-term competitive position by eliminating a competitor, gaining access to more markets, creating economies of scale, leveraging technology, gaining market share/pricing power, or improving distribution, among other reasons.

2.2.4.1 Horizontal vs. Vertical Integration

Horizontal integration is essentially acquisition of market share in a company's existing competency, typically at the expense of rivals. Increased market share may lead to advantages in pricing, expenses, and attracting and retaining talent. Also, larger companies have advantages in terms of access to capital markets and investor/market visibility. Reaching certain market capitalization thresholds will "qualify" the stock to new groups of institutional investors, which can drive trading volume and stock prices upward.

A sub-segment of horizontal integration is geographic integration. A company may have a market position within a certain region and wish to expand into another region, creating expense or distribution advantages. Insurance companies frequently expand through acquisitions in new geographic markets.

Diversifying into new geographic markets in the insurance industry is fraught with peril, regardless of whether the expansion is organic or via acquisition. There is, however, a school of thought that organic growth, when effectuated through broker channels, is particularly risky given the likelihood of adverse selection because the brokers do not have longstanding relationships with the insurer and are frequently placing only small amounts of business in the new markets (i.e., "testing the waters").

Vertical integration is the process of gaining control over additional "links" in the value chain. In this manner the buyer gains greater access to a product source (backward integration) or the "end" consumer (forward integration). There are many reasons to vertically integrate, including stabilization of supply, price, and availability; access to captive distribution capacity; or potentially lower overall transaction costs. Buyers may seek to acquire strategic partners for complementary distribution channels. The classic example is a life insurance company purchasing a life insurance agency to gain consistent access to the agency's insured customer base.

2.2.4.2 Diversification

Theoretically, a diversified revenue stream should result in less volatile earnings as compared to a less diversified peer. The diversification of risk, particularly using a holistic or enterprise risk management[9] approach, makes sense when the company's core business is the acquisition, management, and transfer of risk. The insurance industry is both a seller of diversification opportunities (in the form of catastrophe bonds, uncorrelated with any economic risk) and a net acquirer of risk in terms of assets, liabilities, and its management. Insurance diversification plays include a life insurance company with mortality risk acquiring an offsetting position through the purchase of an annuity or group pension provider. Another example is a variable annuity writer acquiring a fixed annuity writer because variable annuity sales and fixed annuity sales are inversely correlated.[10]

[9] "Enterprise risk management" is generally defined as a coordinated approach to assessing and responding to all risks that affect the achievement of strategic and financial objectives, including both upside and downside risks.

[10] While equity market performance is not the sole determinant of demand (e.g., interest rates play a major role), when equity markets perform well, variable annuity sales tend to increase and fixed annuity sales tend to decrease. Conversely, when equity markets perform poorly, variable annuity sales suffer and fixed annuity sales increase.

U.S. regulations require P&C and life companies to have separate legal entities, but are able to operate within the same corporate structure. An example of a successful diversified insurance company is AIG. AIG is diversified across casualty, property, life, and health insurance, as well as retirement savings; provides reinsurance as well as direct writing; and operates in over 130 countries. In 2004, AIG's market capitalization was the largest of any insurer, while its shareholder returns have consistently outperformed the market.[11]

2.2.4.3 *Regulation*

Obtaining permission to sell insurance products in a particular state can be a difficult and time-consuming process. In the insurance industry there is a bustling practice in the sale of insurance state licenses in "shell" companies (companies with operating licenses but little or no business in force). At one time, the average price of a state license served as a barometer for the fortunes of the industry. Such transactions are rarer as a result of changes in the assumption reinsurance market that made creating clean shell companies more of a challenge. Nevertheless, market entry may be easier through acquisition of operating companies rather than "greenfield" development.

2.2.4.4 *Accounting and Tax*

Companies that possess undervalued assets due to tax and accounting anomalies become attractive targets to acquirers that believe they can unlock the deferred or hidden value. Accounting and tax "plays" have been significant drivers of past M&A transaction activity across all industries. Insurance company assets could be undervalued or overvalued by the market at a given point in time, and "creative" transaction structuring could mean the difference between winning and losing the bid. In addition, as in other industries, acquiring insurance companies or brokers with significant net operating losses may be an appealing way to shelter, in whole or in part, future operating earnings from federal taxation.

2.2.4.5 *Research and Development*

In other industries, the value of patents and intellectual property can be a significant M&A driver. While patents are rare in the insurance industry, acquiring research and development or specific marketing expertise can be an acquisition motive. For example, it may be cheaper and faster to enter a particular market by buying specific product expertise when innovations surge and time is of the essence, which was true during the heyday of universal life in the 1980s and variable annuity products in the 1990s.

2.3 PREPARING TO SELL

This section covers the major preparatory steps, from reviewing strategic alternatives to assembling the "deal team" to deciding on the correct type of sale process and the fundamental sale structure.

2.3.1 REVIEWING STRATEGIC ALTERNATIVES

Before committing to pursuing a material corporate transaction, including a change of control transaction, the board of directors generally undertakes a comprehensive review of all of the available strategic alternatives. Management may conduct this process independently or with the assistance of outside advisors.

[11] For an interesting discussion of the history of AIG and its iconic architect, Hank Greenberg, see *Schiff's Insurance Observer*, David Schiff, Vol. 16 (2004).

CRYPT 2.1

Buy Only What You Really Want

When buying a life insurance company, there may be a segment of the business in which the buyer has minimal interest. This may be because of negative feelings or lack of expertise regarding the segment.

My advice is "Don't give up hope." We were evaluating a company for purchase and were in a situation in which we could place a high value on a large portion of the business of a company. However, we viewed a certain block of the business very negatively.

We submitted a bid for the business that we wanted and specifically excluded the block of business that we did not want from the bid. Another bidder had used a similar strategy, but excluded a different block of business. There were no bids that met the seller's expectations for the entire company.

As a result of this, the seller changed its approach and sold selected lines of business while keeping ones that were not attractive to the bidders. This enabled the seller to recognize maximum value for certain lines of business while holding other lines of business to be "tidied up" for a sale in the future.

A financial advisor, typically an investment bank, is often retained to formally review the seller's strategic alternatives. Hiring a financial advisor to assist in the process has a number of advantages over a purely internal review. First, an investment bank is, in theory, impartial as to which option is selected. Different constituencies within a company may have different agendas. For example, an older management team may favor a sale to provide liquidity whereas a younger management team may wish to defer a sale to stay entrenched or create additional value. Second, because investment banks work consistently with companies evaluating strategic alternatives, the financial advisors may present options management had not considered.

As a corollary, financial advisors generally may have insight into not only what is the most desirable alternative, but also what are the most feasible (i.e., realistic and viable) alternatives. Moreover, a financial advisor is essential to provide advice as to the risks, opportunities, and timing associated with each alternative. Finally, the presentation the financial advisors make to the board is an important confirmation that the directors have fulfilled their fiduciary duties, including the duty of care,[12] by thoroughly considering all of the options available prior to choosing a course of action.

Once the alternatives have been presented to the board, it must undertake its own independent evaluation and reach its own conclusions as to the best approach to maximizing shareholder value. This may entail maintaining the status quo; pursuing a host of internal changes (i.e., non-transactional), which can run the gamut from minor operational tinkering to a wholesale change of business plan; or pursuing any of a wide variety of transactions, including buying other companies, selling assets or business lines or all or a portion of the company's common equity, or raising capital externally or internally.

2.3.2 ASSEMBLING THE DEAL TEAM

Assuming the board opts to pursue a sale of the company (meaning a sale of substantially all of the assets or a sufficient amount of the voting rights or financial interests in the common equity to constitute a change of control), the next step is to begin assembling the key players to assist in the execution of the sale transaction.

---

[12] The duties imposed on directors in these situations are generally referred to as "Revlon duties," named for the case, *Revlon Inc. v. MacAndrews & Forbes Holdings*, 506 A.2d 173 (Del. 1986). Once Revlon duties are triggered, consideration of nonshareholder interests potentially constitutes a breach of a board of directors' fiduciary duties, regardless of whether the transaction is a friendly or a hostile takeover. On a side note, Felix G. Rohatyn, the investment banker formerly at Lazard Freres & Co., likened Perelman to "the Huns and the Visigoths" for his hostile raid on Revlon.

Given the number and variety of tasks that need to be completed to accomplish a successful sale, buyers and sellers must assemble experienced transaction teams to plan and execute the transaction. For a sale to be successful, both transaction teams must be able to communicate the selling company's "story" and explain in a consistent, focused manner the rationale for the transaction, including the strategic and financial benefits of the contemplated transaction, to a variety of audiences.

A transaction team typically consists of a core group of employees and a group of external professionals, each with a specific expertise and transactional function. Internally, the sell side team would initially consist of the chief executive officer, the chief financial officer, the chief actuary, and the general counsel. External team members for transactions in any industry would typically include representatives from an investment bank or other financial advisory firm, a transactional law firm, and the seller's accounting firm. In addition to these members, external team members for transactions in the insurance industry would typically also engage a regulatory law firm and an independent actuary to perform an actuarial appraisal (standard for life companies, less common for P&C). On the buy side, the team will typically include the chief risk officer (if the acquiring firm has designated the position) in addition to the aforementioned professionals.

Because senior management time is scarce and valuable, efficiency is important. It is important to identify a core group of professionals who are exclusively focused on the sale process. In addition to a full-time project coordinator, significant commitments are needed from senior members of the actuarial, accounting, marketing, treasury, legal, compliance, and information technology areas. Coordination of efforts with the financial and other advisors is needed to minimize the duplication of efforts within the company. Early circulation of a detailed participant list including home and business addresses, phone numbers, cell phone numbers, and e-mail addresses is essential. Such lists not only help identify who the players are, but facilitate quick document circulation. However, the participant list should be limited to the core deal team, and information should be distributed only on a "need to know" basis.

The first major step for the seller is to begin interviewing and retaining a "transaction team" to plan and execute the transaction. The first and most important selection for the acquisition team is choosing a financial advisor who may, or may not, have advised the company previously with a formal review of strategic alternatives. Once selected and engaged, the financial advisor should help in assembling the rest of the team.

2.3.2.1 *Financial Advisors*

An investment bank is a financial advisor with expertise in assessing strategic alternatives for corporations, analyzing the value of a corporation's securities, providing fairness opinions[13] as appropriate, and facilitating the execution of major transactions. There are other types of financial advisors (such as consultants or business brokers) who perform some, but usually not all, of the functions typically carried out by investment bankers. For the purposes of this chapter, the broader term "financial advisor" is used except when the function is unique to an investment bank.

A financial advisor is retained to facilitate a smooth, efficient, and successful M&A process. A financial advisor's experience in the larger marketplace is useful to validate price expectations, identify the appropriate merger partners or targets, facilitate acquisition financing (if necessary), and assist with financial modeling. The financial advisor may also be engaged to render a fairness opinion to the seller's board of directors. In the event of a lawsuit against the seller and/or its board, a fairness opinion is evidence that the seller's board of directors[14] did not breach its

[13] An opinion rendered by an investment bank that the consideration to be received by the sellers' shareholders in a transaction is "fair" from a financial point of view.

[14] Although generally not required, buyers will obtain fairness opinions from investment banks under certain circumstances.

duty of care and is therefore subject to the protection of the business judgment rule.[15]

2.3.2.1.1 Selecting a Financial Advisor—The "Beauty Contest"

Whether or not the company has undertaken a formal review of strategic alternatives, the first major issue companies confront after deciding to sell is retaining an appropriate advisor to assist the company in accomplishing a sale. If the company retained a financial advisor to assist in the review of strategic alternatives, or if the company has worked successfully with an advisor in the past, the choice of advisor is typically predetermined.

If not, the best approach to hiring an advisor is to cast a wide net, reaching out to most of the logical banks (e.g., banks with reputations in the industry or sector or banks that have advised on transactions involving competitors), requesting preliminary credentials and information, narrowing the list based on the information provided, and interviewing the remaining banks. Sellers typically interview several investment banks before selecting one and negotiating an engagement. This process, informally referred to as a "beauty contest," is an opportunity for selected investment banking firms to "pitch" seller's management team on the investment banking firm's services, domain knowledge, credentials, relevant experience, and industry connections.

The seller is well advised to choose financial advisors who have worked on a large number

CRYPT 2.2

Whom Can You Trust?

As outside investment manager for the Orange Life, the company being acquired, I was asked to assist with the due diligence as part of the sale of the company by its parent, Paper Products, to GXX, a multi-national holding company.

The Wall Street firm of Bennington Dove was the investment bank representing, oddly enough, both the selling and the acquiring companies. As part of the negotiation, Bennington Dove offered to do a "free" asset liability analysis once the price was agreed to but before the deal was final. This way, both parties could be assured that interest rate movements during this narrow period of time would not impact the transaction price. In the event that there was any mismatch, Bennington Dove would execute transactions to match the duration and convexity of assets and liabilities.

Not surprisingly, Bennington Dove's rather cursory work suggested that there was an unexpectedly large duration difference in the portfolio. Their proposed transactions to bring the portfolio into line resulted in a sale and repurchase of $750 million of bonds, about 25% of the entire portfolio. While this hedging could have been done in the exchange traded futures and options markets for little cost, the investment banker recommended the sale and repurchase of actual bonds. Bennington Dove assured all that, with their time-honored tradition of putting the interests of their clients first, they could rest assured that the transactions would be executed as efficiently as possible.

This is where I stepped in. I was asked at the 11th hour by the seller to review the transaction prices so that Paper Products could verify that they received "best execution."

It wasn't hard to notice that the proposed transaction prices were well off the market. My team reviewed the bonds with the trading desk and adjusted the prices to actual levels. Needless to say, Paper Products was furious with Bennington Dove. I estimated that the price adjustments saved our client over five million dollars.

What did I learn from this? Do not hire outside advisors that have incentives that are not aligned with their clients.

---

[15] The business judgment rule requires that a board's decisions be reasonably informed and rational, in the sense that some prudent person would agree with the choice made, even though reasonable persons might differ on the wisdom of the decision. In other words, directors are not deemed guarantors of their business judgment and U.S. courts will generally not hold a board liable for good faith decisions even if those decisions are unwise in retrospect.

of acquisitions. As a general matter, whether the individual financial advisor is associated with a large or well-known firm is less important than that individual's credibility, integrity, industry knowledge, transactional experience, and skill set. However, there are situations when it is important for the financial advisor to be associated with a larger firm with a broad set of products or with special relationships.[16]

Ultimately, the seller should concentrate on hiring financial advisors who understand the business, have deep experience as M&A advisors, and ideally have successfully advised similar companies. The financial advisor selected should have demonstrated expertise at valuing companies in the relevant industry. For insurance transactions in particular, hiring bankers with demonstrated expertise in the industry and sector is essential. The complexity and peculiarity of insurance sector financial statements, accounting treatment, and regulatory environment pose unique challenges for the financial advisor. It is also important to select advisors who have represented both the buy and sell side in transactions so they understand all aspects of the deal.

The following is a list of the areas in which the financial advisor should have experience:

- familiarity with the relevant industry, sector, and sub-sector
- valuation expertise, including familiarity with the relevant financial metrics
- relevant M&A experience
- knowledge of, and contacts at, likely buyers
- sophisticated financial structuring experience
- strategic vision
- process prowess
- negotiating skills.

The buy side process of retaining a financial advisor and the considerations in selecting a financial advisor are analogous to the sell side process and considerations. The majority of buyers engage a financial advisor as soon as they have identified an attractive target to pursue. The financial advisor may assist in the bidding and negotiating process and is thus up to speed as the transaction proceeds.

Some buyers prefer not to retain a financial advisor until they have proceeded to the "finals" of a bidding process or until they have actually executed a non-binding letter of intent and are preparing for due diligence. At this point, most buyers prefer to have a financial advisor retained if only as a counterbalance to the sellers' financial advisors. Buyers may engage a financial advisor for a limited purpose engagement, such as assisting with due diligence or rendering a buy side fairness opinion. Buyers with extensive M&A experience sometimes opt not to engage investment bankers unless the deal is relatively large, complex, involves a publicly traded entity, or requires specific industry or other expertise.

The beauty contest is typically the last opportunity to elicit certain critical information from the prospective financial advisors. Because many larger investment banks have multiple "teams" covering each industry, the client is well advised to conduct behind-the-scenes due diligence to ascertain whether the team pitching the business is the "A" insurance team and not the weaker "B" team. In addition, it is important for clients to make the investment banks commit ahead of time that the "deal team" will be the same as the "pitch team." While most banks will not link the engagement to the identity of specific bankers (because the firm is retained, not individual bankers), the client should ask the bankers that are pitching the business who will run the process, conduct negotiations, etc.

[16] For example, if financing is required to consummate the transaction, both seller and buyer would be well served by hiring investment banks with demonstrated expertise in raising debt and equity.

2.3.2.1.2 The Process of Retaining a Financial Advisor

Once a seller has selected a financial advisor, the next step is to enter into a binding contract with the financial advisor. This contract is called an engagement letter. An engagement letter sets forth the rights and duties of each party, including the banker's role in the transaction process, the fees to be paid to the bankers, and the indemnification.

The following are the elements of a typical engagement letter between a seller and a financial advisor:

- a definition of the "transaction" or "assignment"
- the role of the advisor, including specific tasks to be performed
- a fee schedule, which covers retainer, fairness opinion fee, a success fee, a termination fee (if applicable), and reimbursement for reasonable out-of-pocket expenses
- a description of the engagement period, including a detailed description of each party's rights and duties in the event of termination of the contract by either party
- an indemnification provision in which the company retaining the investment bank agrees to indemnify and hold harmless the investment bank for any losses it incurs or expenses it has to pay for any legal proceedings that arise out of the assignment unless the losses or expenses result from the investment bank's own gross negligence or bad faith (or some similar high standard).

The cost of engaging a financial advisor is negotiable. In most cases, the bulk of the financial advisor's fee is contingent upon execution of a definitive agreement or closing of the transaction, although the client normally would be required to pay the banker's out-of-pocket costs. Most reputable advisors also request an up-front payment or a retainer. A retainer may be requested to cover the advisor's initial expenses and the financial advisor's opportunity cost (i.e., he or she could be working for other clients). An upfront retainer is also important to assess the level of the seller's institutional commitment to the sale process (i.e., to ensure that the seller is not simply undertaking a free valuation exercise).

2.3.2.2 Legal Counsel

It is important that the attorney selected be affiliated with a law firm that has the right set of capabilities. The attorney should be a specialist in corporate transaction work as well as have experience working in the insurance field.

The lead lawyer and the client in large transactions need to clarify roles early. Sometimes a client prefers to establish goals but otherwise remain in the background, deferring to the financial advisor and lawyer to control the dynamics of the transaction. Frequently, deals, whether large or small, will hinge on the client's skills and personality. At some point, the client must break the ice on intractable deal points. In public deals, lawyers often assume a large and continuing role once the financial advisor and buyer and seller have struck an economic deal.

The following is a list of the areas in which the seller's attorney and law firm may need to have experience:

- preparing bids in the form of letters of intent for the purchase of private companies
- negotiating the terms of purchase agreements on behalf of buyers of private companies
- negotiating supply agreements between the sellers and buyers in change of control transactions
- negotiating the terms of financing with sources of senior debt, subordinated debt, and equity
- negotiating intercreditor agreements
- negotiating shareholder agreements among the equity investors in a change of control transaction
- preparing incorporation documents for the company
- negotiating employment agreements for senior management.

Legal counsel performs a variety of critical functions on the buy side, from providing advice on the structuring of the acquisition through the process of documenting the transaction and obtaining necessary regulatory approvals to the post-transaction implementation phase. Lawyers are also involved in orchestrating the close of buyouts on behalf of buyers.

2.3.2.3 Accountants

The role of the accountants on the sell side is typically limited. Final audited financial statements need to be produced. The accountants may be queried for their opinion on tax implications and accounting impact of certain deal structures.

It is important to select a reputable accounting firm that provides a wide array of services. This is because several individuals will be performing the financial due diligence. The more reputable the firm, the more weight their opinion will carry in the event of accounting disputes with the seller. It is also important to choose an accounting firm with experience performing financial due diligence for acquisitions. The following is a list of the areas in which the seller's accounting firm may need to have experience:

- reviewing the target's audited financial statements and providing a "quality of earnings" report
- issuing reports focused on key deal issues
- advising on indemnities required in the letter of intent and adjustments to the purchase agreement
- creating partial-year audits upon close of the transaction
- advising on a tax efficient deal structure
- analyzing employee benefit packages
- analyzing risk management (insurance)
- assessing the target's information technology systems (generally only larger accounting firms do this work).

Accountants always play a large role on the buy side, especially in due diligence and in advising on tax and complex technical accounting matters. Depending on the history of the relationship between the client and accountant, especially in smaller deals, the accountant may actually lead the deal.

2.3.2.4 Actuaries

The scope of an actuary's role in an M&A process depends upon several factors. Chief among these factors is the character of the seller's liabilities. Specifically, companies with long duration liabilities (e.g., life and certain P&C lines) and that are heavily dependent on contingent factors (such as interest rates, mortality, and morbidity) should have an actuarial appraisal performed in support of an M&A transaction. Accordingly, seller life insurance companies almost always retain an independent actuarial firm to perform an appraisal, whereas seller P&C insurance companies have historically been less inclined to retain an actuarial firm to perform an appraisal. More commonly, a P&C company will hire an external actuary to review and provide an independent opinion on IBNR and other statement liabilities.

After a draft of the appraisal report is developed, it is usually distributed to the people who were closely involved in its development in order to ensure consistency with the management view and obtain buy-in from the parties involved.

The following is a list of the areas in which the seller's actuarial firm may need to have experience:

- liability modeling and valuation
- asset modeling and valuation
- valuation of alternative distribution channels
- review of reserves and statement liabilities
- experience analysis
- expense analysis
- brand valuation
- due diligence
- modeling on statutory and US GAAP basis
- tax modeling.

> **MOBIUS DEADLINE**
>
> One week we worked day and night to value a life insurer and its affiliates. We were trying to meet a deadline that had passed before we were even hired.

2.3.3 COORDINATION AND COMMUNICATION

As evidenced in the above description, there are numerous players involved in a transaction. Transaction teams can become large and unwieldy. It is critically important to designate the leader of the acquisition team who will orchestrate the efforts of the financial institutions, investing partners, valuation firms, accountants, legal counsel, and other professional advisors who may be required for the transaction. This role typically falls to the financial advisor because the financial advisor is well positioned to serve a dual role as both gatekeeper to the opposing side and coordinator of information and scheduling within his or her team. Management's focus should not be diverted from running its business and the strategic considerations of the acquisition effort.

It is important to maintain open lines of communication with all key players. The financial advisors should provide regular status updates on the process to management and, if appropriate, the board. The seller should dictate the amount and mode of communication. Regular and open communication with the rest of the acquisition team is critical to the quality of the end product for each stage. Coordinating the parties for the duration of the process is a daunting challenge but critically important given the stakes in an M&A transaction.

2.3.4 TYPES OF SALE PROCESSES

There are a wide variety of sale processes. They range from public auctions (in which the intention to sell is publicly announced) to privately negotiated transactions (in which buyer and seller enter into deal discussions without the seller marketing itself to the universe of potential buyers) to modified public auctions (which blend elements of both). The choice of sale process is a significant strategic decision. The seller's financial advisor should be able to outline the pros and cons of different marketing processes. Ultimately, the decision on which approach to take will depend upon the facts and circumstances of the seller and the goals of the seller's shareholders.

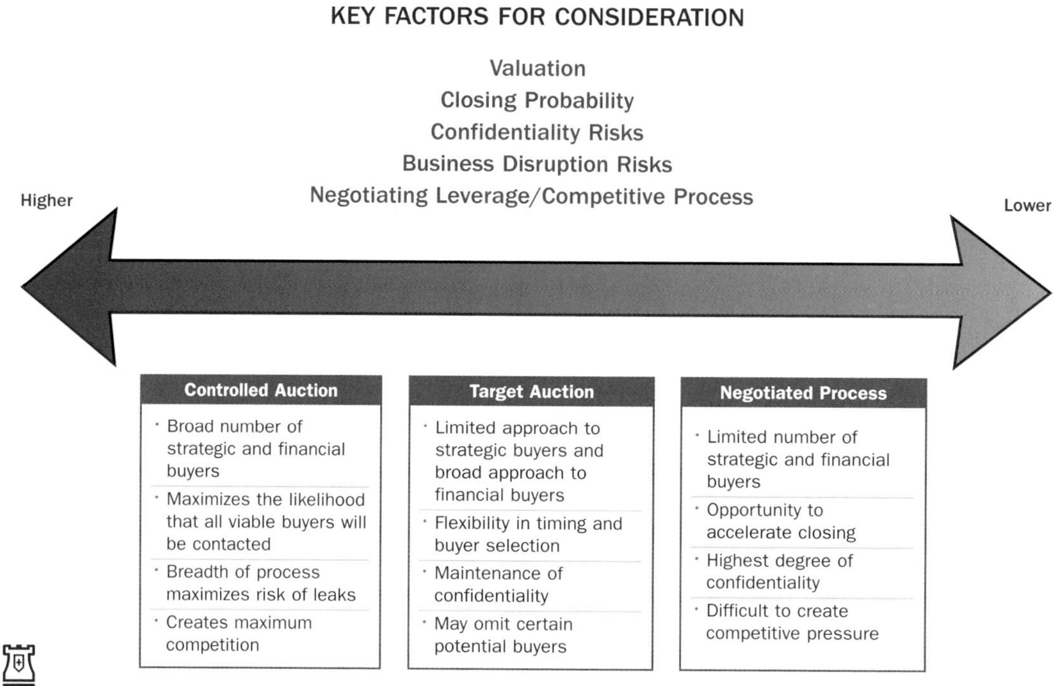

FIGURE 2.2

2.3.4.1 *The Public Auction*

A public auction generally entails the seller (or the seller's parent) issuing a press release announcing that the board of directors is considering "strategic alternatives" for the company and that the board has retained a certain investment bank to assist with the process. This is a thinly veiled message that the company is open to a transaction of some sort and effectively puts the company "in play."

By naming a financial advisor, the company effectively directs all inquiries to the bankers. The bankers then are given the task of vetting all proposals, inquiries, and offers and steering the parties towards a transaction that would satisfy the company's board of directors and shareholders. Many of the parties that initially make contact are disqualified by any of several factors, including the type of transaction they would like to pursue, lack of financing, unsuitability from a regulatory perspective, or lack of relevant experience. The remaining parties are informed by the bankers of the timetable, including the relevant deadlines for performing due diligence, submitting bids, etc.

The efficacy of the classic public auction is a matter of some debate in the academic as well as the investment banking community. It is typically a high risk, high reward approach. The key advantage is that the announcement puts all prospective buyers on notice and theoretically maximizes the number of potential bidders.[17] In addition to the sheer number of bidders, the public auction can create a public, super-heated bidding environment that enhances the consideration ultimately paid to shareholders. However, it is important to note that it is probably only appropriate for companies that have a reasonably high profile and are likely to generate ardent interest from a broad spectrum of potential buyers. If it is not highly likely to close, it is generally wise to opt for another type of sale process.

[17] Auctions may be more suitable when M&A transactions are in vogue and there is pressure to acquire. For example, when organic growth slows in the P&C market during a "soft cycle," there is a frenzy to buy quality P&C insurance companies. Channeling that frenzy through the use of an auction process is typically the best way to maximize shareholder value for the seller.

There are several disadvantages to this process. One key risk is that the announcement of a potential sale may damage the business by unnerving suppliers, distribution, rating agencies, and customers, as well as energizing key competitors to use the distraction to lure away customers. If the auction fails to generate sufficient interest, or at least sufficient interest at a valuation that appeals to shareholders, the company is generally perceived as "damaged goods" by its constituencies, including Wall Street, ratings agencies, and customers.

2.3.4.2 *Privately Negotiated Transactions*

A privately negotiated transaction is at the other end of the spectrum from the public auction. By definition, a privately negotiated transaction involves discussions with one potential buyer in a non-competitive environment. This type of transaction typically arises organically when companies are business partners, either through a commercial relationship or a formal joint venture. In addition, private transactions are frequently driven by personal relationships between chief executives and/or board members. The advantage to the seller is that if the transaction is not consummated, the core business has typically been protected from serious damage by maintaining confidentiality.

The key disadvantage is that a seller's board is subject to "second guessing" when a sale is consummated through a non-competitive process. The board can address this issue by undertaking a post-agreement market check and/or procuring a fairness opinion. A provision permitting a post-agreement market check may be structured into a merger agreement when a board opts to undertake single-bidder negotiations. This enables the seller's board to demonstrate that it has exercised its fiduciary duties by remaining "open" to a "topping bid" by another potential acquirer.[18] In addition to a market check, a seller's board will typically seek to procure a fairness opinion from a reputable investment banking firm. A fairness opinion acts as additional evidence that the seller's board exercised reasonable business judgment in agreeing to the transaction.

Given the enhanced scrutiny of public companies and their boards pursuant to the Sarbanes-Oxley Act of 2002, it is generally assumed that boards will be less inclined to undertake privately negotiated M&A transactions. However, it is interesting to note that the St. Paul-Travelers mega-merger in 2004 was a classic privately negotiated transaction arising out of the relationship between the two chief executive officers.[19]

2.3.4.3 *Modified Public Auction*

In many cases, a modified public auction is favored. This process is generally characterized by a targeted marketing campaign aimed at only the most likely candidates to acquire the seller and generally uses a more flexible bidding and due diligence schedule with no "drop dead" dates.

To maintain secrecy, the first step may be to contact the potential buyers on a "no names" basis to ascertain interest. The advantage is that the advisors are able to eliminate potential bidders and, therefore, further winnow the number of companies that learn the seller's identity. The disadvantage is that many potential bidders remain noncommittal in the absence of certain key information, such as the identity of management, which effectively discloses the identity of the potential seller. This process does not eliminate the problem of "window-shopping" from potential buyers that are not sincerely interested in acquiring the company but are instead interested in gathering competitive information.

---

[18] Acquirers, on the other hand, typically negotiate for provisions that enhance the likelihood of consummation of the transaction, including large "break up" fees, "no shop" clauses and, more controversially, "no talk" clauses.

[19] However, the torrent of bad press and litigation arising out of the 2004 AXA-MONY transaction underscores the risks of non-auction M&A processes. On the other hand, in the end the Delaware courts ruled in favor of MONY's board and, perhaps most importantly for insurance companies, were receptive to the argument that auction processes are inherently risky for companies that are reliant on third-party distribution such as life and annuity companies with independent agency forces.

The remainder of this chapter presumes that the seller has selected a modified auction process.

2.3.5 PRELIMINARY STRUCTURING CONSIDERATIONS

Although the seller generally need not make definitive decisions with respect to the preferred form of consideration and related issues, its financial advisor is well advised to engage the seller in a discussion on the topic early in the process.

The first issue is whether the seller's shareholders would accept cash, stock, or some combination of both, in exchange for their interests in the seller. The stock-versus-cash decision is generally a risk/reward decision. The decision is whether to accept cash and incur an immediate taxable event in exchange for the certainty of "cash in hand" or take stock and the risks associated with holding the buyer's stock in exchange for the ability to defer taxation in a so-called tax-free reorganization.

Of course, a transaction that uses a mix of consideration is frequently an appealing compromise for both seller and buyer. As a general matter, if a substantial portion (between 40% and 80%, depending on the form of the transaction) of the consideration is in the buyer's stock, the transaction may be treated as a tax-free reorganization, and the seller only incurs an immediate tax bill for the cash portion of the transaction. The selling shareholders are taxed only upon sale of the buyer's stock consideration received in the transaction.

Accepting the buyer's stock may be an opportunity as well as a risk. If the buyer's stock would represent an attractive investment opportunity irrespective of the M&A transaction (either because of the stock's dividend stream or the likelihood of share price appreciation), the seller's shareholders may want to hold onto the stock even after any restrictions on re-sale elapse. In addition, if the buyer represents an attractive acquisition target, the stock may have "double-dip" potential if the buyer is subsequently acquired. In the interim, the buyer's stock may be attractive based on its dividends, as well as its likelihood of stock price appreciation irrespective of M&A. Finally, when a fairly illiquid public company acquires another public company in a stock swap, the acquirer's stock may benefit from the additional liquidity associated with the issuance to additional shareholders.[20]

When publicly traded companies are involved in a merger or acquisition, the stock prices of both buyer and seller are generally impacted. All other things being equal, the stock price of a publicly traded buyer generally declines while the stock price of the seller usually increases upon announcement of a proposed merger or acquisition. Even if the acquisition appears to be compelling financially and strategically, the buyer's stock price usually declines, at least temporarily, due to the risks associated with consummating and integrating a transaction.

If serious skepticism exists among research analysts, investors, or commentators regarding the acquisition, the decline in stock price may be severe and prolonged. The seller's stock price generally increases, regardless of the efficacy of the transaction, to a stock price slightly lower than the announced acquisition price. This discount reflects the risk that the deal will not be consummated for any number of reasons, including anti-trust or other regulatory concerns. Of course, if the market believes that another bidder will emerge and trump the prospective buyer's offer, the seller's stock price would increase to a premium over the announced stock price to reflect this possibility.

2.3.5.1 Asset vs. Entity Sale

One of the fundamental questions in any M&A process is what exactly is being merged or acquired. The two most common types of transactions are asset deals and stock deals. For

[20] The additional liquidity should lead to a higher volume of buy and sell transactions. All other things being equal, substantial additional liquidity should mitigate the implicit discount in the buyer's stock, and the combined company's stock price should improve as a result.

example, the seller may want to dispose of one or more assets but remain a going concern. If the seller wants to sell substantially all of its assets, the seller is seeking to sell its business or, effectively, itself. If a seller is seeking to sell itself, the question becomes whether to structure the transaction as a sale of assets or as a sale of equity.

A buyer must decide whether it wants to acquire a going concern, consisting of the target's employees, marketing force, and insurance licenses for future business purposes, or if it's interested only in acquiring a book of business. Further complicating matters, a target may have significant legal exposures resulting from market conduct, employment, or other issues, or a buyer may have regulatory impediments to acquiring the legal entity.

Ownership of a legal entity generally brings with it all of the target's contractual benefits and liabilities. For example, if the seller has been the target of class action lawsuits or has taken past aggressive tax or employment positions, it might have potentially significant liabilities. The buyer, working with its financial and legal advisor, must evaluate the relative advantages and disadvantages of acquiring the entity. If the disadvantages outweigh the advantages, or if the buyer simply has no use for the corporate structure of the target, an asset acquisition is the alternative.

In the insurance industry, an asset acquisition (typically a block of policies or line of business) is accomplished through one or more reinsurance transactions. When feasible, an assumption reinsurance transaction is generally desired by both buyers and sellers. In an assumption reinsurance transaction, the selling insurer is relieved of liability to policy owners (or ceding insurers if the transaction involves the sale of a book of reinsurance) and is completely removed from the business. The assuming insurer or reinsurer is substituted for the seller and becomes directly obligated to policy owners *as if the buyer had written the assumed business directly*. In many cases, however, the seller will retain exposure to various pre-sale liabilities.

In assumption reinsurance transactions, the selling insurer will be relieved of all liability only if the original party to the contract agrees (by actual or deemed consent, referred to as a "novation") to the substitution of the assuming insurer as the party to the insurance contract. Because this is difficult to accomplish in practice for any number of reasons, the accepted approach is to structure an asset sale instead as a 100% coinsurance with an agreement that novations will be obtained when practical by the assuming insurer. The assuming insurer typically takes over administration of the business as part of the transaction. If novations are not obtained, the selling insurer will generally retain at least residual liability under the original contract.[21] This is particularly important if the assuming insurer should experience financial difficulties.

2.3.5.2 Tax Issues

As a general matter, there are several major taxation issues that arise in most M&A transactions:

- Will the buyer be able to "step up" the tax basis of the seller's assets to reflect the purchase price?
- Will the seller be able to defer its gain (if any) upon sale?
- If the seller recognizes a gain at sale, how is that gain calculated? (e.g., is a Section 338(h)(10) election available?)
- Is there anything "unique" or "unusual" about the target's business that will impact tax liability going forward?
- Is there any other tax-efficient way to sell the business?

Chapter 7 provides a full treatment of the M&A tax implications.

[21] See National Association of Insurance Commissioners Assumption Reinsurance Model Act, which describes a procedure for obtaining novations, but also specifies that policyholders have the right to reject the substitution of a new insurer.

2.4 PRE-MARKETING

Once the preparatory steps have been completed, the deal team begins to focus on preparing to formally "market" the seller. This involves analyzing who the likely buyers are and preparing marketing material and related documentation to present a comprehensive and accurate description of the seller in a favorable light.

2.4.1 PREPARING THE BUYER LIST

One of the financial advisor's key functions is to work with the seller to prepare a list of qualified potential buyers. In order to perform this responsibility effectively, the financial advisor must solicit input from the seller, consider a broad universe of potential buyers, cull the list in a reasonable manner, and pre-qualify buyers.

One of the threshold considerations is whether a potential acquirer can "afford" to buy the seller. For financial buyers, the analysis is fairly simple. Financial buyers need only have access to the capital necessary to make the purchase, the willingness to look at acquisitions of this size

CRYPT 2.3

Amateur Hour

We are a mid-sized property and casualty firm. We thought we could tame the annuity market. But after several years of unending capital contributions, we rethought our position. The life company had to go.

After screening several suitors, we honed in on an appealing presentation made by someone new to the insurance industry. Their firm was largely backed by inherited money. Soon after visiting our offices, they submitted an offer that was almost too good to be true. As it turns out, it was.

Moving forward under the belief that they were serious buyers, we told other suitors that we had a serious buyer lined up and would be limiting our negotiations to it. While we didn't end conversations with other potential acquirers, we left the door open slightly. Weeks turned into months and it finally became apparent that Amateur was simply a buyer with a gleam in its eye and little in the way of capital. Along the way they continued to maintain their interest and certainly did a fair amount of research that reinforced that position, but in the end it became apparent that they had marginal skills and financial capacity.

So what did we learn?

- *Execute a due diligence on the potential buyer that is as complete as the one they do on you. In this case, had we spent more time early in the process finding out about their capital plan, we would have realized much sooner that even if they had the money to buy our company, they really did not have the capacity to maintain the growth needed to make our company profitable. We should have discovered much sooner their true financial weaknesses.*
- *Evaluate the potential acquirers' due diligence staff. Our preliminary impression of their due diligence team was not favorable. It was apparent that they had a serious lack of experience in the annuity market. They asked the same basic questions repeatedly. Worse yet, as they brought in additional "experts," it became even more obvious that they were unable to tap into a pool of talented, experienced annuity professionals.*
- *Ask detailed questions about the proposed transition plan. As we asked more and more detailed questions, we quickly confirmed that they really had no plan. For example, their clerks were going to do the data conversion.*
- *If secondary sources of capital are central to the deal, find out everything you can about those sources. In this situation, there were a number of assertions that reinsurers would play a key role in providing the funding required to acquire and support growth. Since regulators would most likely confirm the existence of such financial guarantees from the reinsurer, as the seller we should have done the same.*

in the insurance industry, and possess a reasonable likelihood of passing regulatory scrutiny.[22] If the financial buyer has sufficient uninvested funds on hand (or subject to call) and the investment would not create concentration risk (too much invested in any one company or sector), the financial buyer may be assumed to be capable of purchasing the seller. Although it may not be strictly speaking necessary, it is also helpful if the financial sponsor has invested in, or at least seriously studied, the sellers' sector (insurance) and line of business (life, health, P&C, etc.).

In terms of qualifications for strategic buyers, the threshold considerations are affordability and regulatory qualifications, including anti-trust issues. The issues are reasonable access to capital and the impact that the transaction would have on the buyer post-transaction. The seller's financial advisor generally performs a preliminary affordability analysis, which examines possible or likely financing scenarios and the impact the transaction would have on various financial metrics. The seller's financial advisor should consider whether consummating a transaction would create too great a financial strain on the buyer, either by relying on excess financial leverage, by impairing the buyer's earnings too severely (i.e., causing earnings dilution) or otherwise by impairing the buyer going forward.[23] The operating premise of such an analysis is that a rational buyer either would not or could not successfully consummate a transaction that would certainly harm it and, therefore, contacting such a buyer would be a fruitless and potentially distracting exercise.

When evaluating potential buyers, insurance companies should also be cognizant of insurance-specific considerations such as the impact of the transaction on the buyer's liquidity, operating leverage, financial leverage, and any other metrics the relevant state insurance departments may consider. For example, if the acquisition could potentially result in the buyer suffering a ratings downgrade, the advisor would caution the seller to consider carefully the risks associated with pursuing such a transaction. In addition to affordability, the financial advisor should consider whether the buyer would be a logical buyer from a strategic point of view and is in a "buying mode."

The advisor must bear in mind that in most states, when an insurance company sells a material amount of its equity, the seller and potential buyer must jointly make a filing with the insurance department in the seller's state of domicile. The state department of insurance must approve this filing, generally referred to as a Form A filing, prior to consummation of the transaction. Therefore, the seller and its advisors would do well to consider issues such as the reputation of the buyer (e.g., whether the buyer has any legal or financial troubles in its past), the impact the transaction will have on employment in the seller's home state (e.g., whether there will be large-scale layoffs), and a host of other issues that could derail the closing. It is always best to vet those issues up front so that all parties are aware of the execution risks associated with certain potential buyers.

[22] For example, the financial advisor should consider whether a transaction would potentially trigger antitrust concerns. The Herfindahl-Hirschmann Index is a handy and widely used measure of market concentration, which is calculated by summing the squares of the percentages of a market as represented by each competitor.

[23] Of course, short-term earnings accretion or dilution should be less important to executives and investors than ascertaining whether the returns generated by an acquisition clear the acquirer's "cost of capital" or "hurdle rate." During the 1990s Conseco's stock performed remarkably well as it acquired dozens of companies in accretive transactions. Unfortunately, many of the transactions actually destroyed shareholder value.

CRYPT 2.4

An Offer That Couldn't Be Refused

One condition a state insurance department imposed on the merger of mutual companies A and B was that there wouldn't be undue layoffs in the home state of the acquired insurer. While the venture did expect to save money by reducing staff, this imposition would not be a problem.

One component of the plan to reduce expenses was to offer a liberal early retirement/severance package to the employees of both organizations. This offer was temporary; any employees subsequently laid off would not be eligible for the same package.

Company A was the larger of the two organizations and was anticipated to be the senior partner. When it made the early retirement/severance offer to its staff, about 15% accepted, which was approximately what had been expected.

When Company B extended its offer, it emphasized that no jobs were guaranteed. Apparently its employees took this warning to heart. Just one year earlier, Company B had completely restructured the company by "firing" every single employee and making everyone apply and interview for the new "open" jobs. This extreme strategy was designed to allow Company B to restructure in hopes of avoiding possible exposure to age and other discrimination lawsuits because the "best" candidate would always be hired. While this was apparently successful legally, it did engender considerable resentment on the part of Company B's employees. After this year-long process, Company B's employees had been assured that the turmoil was over. The merger announcement was a disillusioning surprise.

Their resentment was evidenced when, instead of the expected 15%, about 70% of Company B's employees accepted the early retirement/severance package. This created a crisis!

The deal was now in violation of the state-imposed condition of employee retention. The high level of terminations would put Company B staff far below the negotiated fixed level of employee count. The merger was now in jeopardy!

Company B management opened up a "reconsideration" window and indicated that the job security situation would likely be more reliable than its original communication might have implied. This encouraged many employees to rescind their initial decision. However, Company B was still several hundred employees short of the agreed-upon minimum.

To remedy that situation, Company B instituted a crash-hiring program. It retained dozens of temporary human resources personnel to set up and process interviews and hired several hundred employees in a matter of a few weeks, thereby meeting the conditions of the state agreement and allowing the merger to go through.

Advisors should qualify prospective buyers to determine each company's capability of completing a transaction of the size contemplated. At the same time, the advisor should have a discussion at the outset with the seller as to the company's willingness and ability to help finance the deal by accepting notes, non-competes, and employment contracts as part of the purchase price. The seller should be aware that it can be difficult to secure bank financing for certain transactions and in certain industries, including highly regulated industries such as insurance.

It is important for the advisor to review with the seller any prior transactional conversations or inquiries the seller has received in order to understand what the market may know about the seller's plans and the extent of any substantive transaction conversations. Parties that have expressed an interest in the seller in the past are obvious starting points in the search for potential buyers.

At this point the financial advisor then begins preparing a preliminary list of potential strategic and financial buyers based upon the advisor's knowledge of the sector, the major companies in the business, and the intentions or desires with respect to those companies expressed by management.

In addition, the banker must consider whether "out of market" companies should be contacted. Out of market companies are companies that are not currently in the seller's line of business and/or focus on a different region, yet may wish to explore diversification opportunities. For example, there was a trend in the 1980s and 1990s for health insurance companies to acquire P&C companies concentrating on the worker's compensation line of business. Because there is a significant medical component to worker's compensation, it was thought that the two lines of business would be complementary. Although in practice the hoped-for synergies of the combination were not realized, a savvy financial advisor during this period would have suggested including health insurance companies in the potential buyer universe for P&C companies specializing in worker's compensation.

Once the financial advisors have compiled a preliminary list, the seller reviews the list and provides feedback. One of the most common issues for the seller is whether the most likely buyers are, or are perceived to be, competitors. The seller's legitimate concern for confidentiality may deter an approach to the most likely buyers. The advisor must endeavor to convince the client that a controlled approach to the most synergistic prospects can be structured to protect the integrity of the business while realizing the highest price. This approach would consist of the following:

- careful preparation and use of confidentiality agreements and blind inquiries
- release of proprietary and financial information in stages so that the client has the opportunity to gain confidence in the integrity and legitimate interest of the prospect as negotiations proceed
- qualification of the prospect's strategic objectives and financial capacity
- research of previous acquisitions completed by the prospect and its reputation in its industry
- encouragement of contact with competitors, suppliers, and customers as the assignment progresses and as the seller becomes more relaxed about confidentiality; the client must be made to realize that such parties will place the highest value on his business.

2.4.2 PREPARING MARKETING MATERIALS

In the marketing process, the seller commonly sends out preliminary offering documents and solicits expressions of interest based on the pool of information provided to all potential buyers. The advisors and lawyers typically collaborate on drafting the key marketing materials. The bulk of the information necessary to draft the documents is obtained in the course of sell side due diligence. The seller, of course, has final sign off on any and all documents to be circulated.

The seller's advisors will also perform a due diligence review of its client for two reasons. The first is to ensure that the seller brings to light, and the advisors fully understand, any issues that may arise in the selling process. The second is to ensure that any statements made in offering documents are accurate.[24] One of the issues that frequently arises at this stage of the process is to determine how "seller-friendly" the relevant agreements will be. There are significant tactical advantages in approaching the market with offering documents that are carefully based on a realistic evaluation of the seller's position.

The key marketing documents are the "teaser," the confidentiality agreements (CA), the confidential information memorandum (CIM), and the "bid process letter." It is important to note that these documents must be drafted carefully and be reviewed thoroughly by seller's attorneys. While the teaser and CIM are marketing documents, they are essentially offering documents and may be construed as a prospectus under Section 5 of the Securities Act of 1933. Even if they are not so construed, the seller (and by extension bankers and attorneys involved in the preparation of these documents) is undoubtedly subject to the anti-fraud provisions of the Securities Exchange Act of 1934.

2.4.2.1 The Teaser

A teaser is a brief (one-to-three page) document that is prepared and distributed by the financial advisors to attract potential investors. The teaser briefly describes the selling company,

[24] In addition to general concerns about accurate disclosure, the U.S. Supreme Court has held that if the transaction involves the sale of stock, the anti-fraud provisions of §10(b) of the Securities Exchange Act of 1934 will be applicable. *Landreth Timber Company v. Landreth*, 471 U.S. 681 (1985).

highlights the attractive attributes for the selling company, and provides summary financial information that gives potential buyers a sense of the size and relative financial performance of the seller. The teaser may contain summary financial projections, although many bankers and companies are not comfortable with disclosing such information (and it would be inappropriate for a public company). If the potential buyer remains interested after reviewing the "teaser," the bidder communicates this interest to the seller's financial advisors. The bankers then send out a confidentiality agreement.

2.4.2.2 The Confidentiality Agreement

The CA is a contract between the seller and the potential buyer. The contract is, simply stated, intended to protect the seller from the potential buyer's unauthorized use or sharing of confidential information provided as part of the transaction process. A draft CA is prepared early in the process by the seller's attorneys and reviewed and commented upon by the seller and the financial advisors. No additional information about the seller should be provided to potential buyers until executed CAs are received.

CAs are particularly important if the seller is a publicly traded company. Without the CA's protection, the seller could release material non-public information that leads to insider trading activity and would subject the company itself to liability. In addition, if the seller discloses certain information to prospective buyers, it may trigger an obligation under Regulation FD to disclose the same information to the investing public.

2.4.2.3 The Confidential Information Memorandum

The CIM is the primary document used to market to the seller. It is typically a relatively lengthy, fairly dry document that describes the seller and the seller's industry in great detail. A well-prepared CIM reads like a formal, factual, and comprehensive recitation of the facts, while emphasizing the seller's strong points. While it is important to candidly acknowledge the seller's shortcomings and risks associated with the transaction, the CIM is an opportunity to explain and contextualize the risks.

While the CIM is prepared in advance of the formal marketing process, it is only shared with potential buyers who have met certain conditions. Specifically, the CIM is shared with potential buyers who have reviewed the teaser and indicated a continuing interest in exploring a transaction with the seller and have signed a CA with the seller. Once a mutually agreeable CA has been executed, the financial advisors send the CIM to the potential buyer.

The typical CIM includes the following:

- an executive summary
- key investment characteristics
- overview of the organization, including corporate and functional organizations charts
- a description of the business
- a description of the industry
- detailed historical financial and operating performance
- detailed financial projections
- management and board biographies
- other information, such as material litigation or real estate owned.

Prospective bidders may also request additional detail around the financial projections or more detailed product information in advance of due diligence. Typically the more information that is provided, the more reliable and accurate the pricing of the non-binding bids received. The most common requests are for recent audited GAAP financial statements and recent statutory statements for each insurance entity. This information is generally gathered ahead of time by the financial advisors in anticipation of such requests.

2.4.2.4 The Bid Process Letter

The financial advisors will prepare a letter to accompany the CIM when it is sent to a prospective bidder. Depending on the sale process, it may be nothing more than a brief cover letter or, in an auction format, the cover letter may constitute a bid process letter. A bid process letter can be delivered to potential bidders later in the process if the process is more open ended than a typical auction.

A bid process letter will usually include a description of the general process to be followed (auction, modified auction, etc.) and establish the deadlines, if any, for submitting an indication of interest (bid). In addition, the letter will typically instruct the prospective buyer to address the following topics in their indications of interest:

- identity of the acquiring entity
- proposed form of consideration (stock or asset)
- source of financing
- range of values for the seller
- treatment of liabilities in an asset purchase
- accounting treatment
- proposed tax treatment
- employee matters
- anticipated time to closing.

2.4.3 ACTUARIAL APPRAISAL AND RESERVE REVIEW

For long tail lines, an independent actuary is usually brought in to perform an appraisal soon after the decision to sell has been formally made. Although companies may have performed similar exercises internally, it is usually a penny-wise strategy to rely on internally produced valuations because the impartiality of the results is questionable at best. Relying on an internally produced appraisal (or worse, failing to provide one) usually causes far more problems during the negotiation process than the trouble and cost that it saves.

It is typically necessary for the independent actuary to visit the company to gather data, interview management personnel, and establish working relationships. Depending on the preparedness of the company, it may be important to spend significant time on-site to develop experience assumptions, become comfortable with management, and review operations.

In the normal course of preparing the appraisal report, the actuary may come across inconsistencies in data or processes across departments that are not always obvious to the seller's management team. One of the important roles of the independent actuary, along with the rest of the seller's team, is to detect and correct such problems in preparation for due diligence. Nothing can damage a sale process more than to have significant issues arise during the due diligence process for which the seller is unprepared. The actuary should proactively seek to understand any significant tax, regulatory, or economic issues that could materially affect the industry or, more specifically, the value of the seller's business. To the extent that likely prospective material changes are not reflected in the base case, specific scenarios may be prepared to reflect other possible outcomes. The technical aspects of preparing an actuarial appraisal are treated in greater detail in Chapter 4.

Ideally, the actuarial appraisal is completed before formal marketing of seller begins, which enables the seller and its financial advisors to send out the appraisal with the CIM if that is deemed the best course of action. It is, however, more common to send the appraisal report as an interim step after delivery of the CIM and prior to a formal visit to the data room. Occasionally, the appraisal is not provided until a buyer visits the data room. There are, however, active buyers that as a matter of policy will not send a deal team to perform due diligence until the appraisal has first been provided and reviewed.

For short tail lines, prospective bidders will typically request the opportunity to review the most recent loss reserve study prepared by the seller's external actuary. The actuarial firm typically requires that the seller obtain a consent from each party that reviews the report. The decision as to whether to send this information out ahead of time or hold it back for review on site is discretionary.

2.4.4 COMPILING THE DATA ROOM

The sell side team (typically the financial advisor with the assistance of a company point person) begins at this point to build a "data room," which consists of detailed, often highly sensitive, information on the seller. The sell side organizes the data room to highlight data that supports the CIM and actuarial appraisal and to present other material information in the interests of full disclosure. A poorly organized data room calls into question the accuracy of its contents and shoots up red flags for the buyer's due diligence team.

At a minimum, the data room should contain the information used to create the offering memorandum and the actuarial appraisal and any other material information omitted therefrom. In addition, each potential buyer typically provides a data request prior to its arrival at the target company. This enables the sell side to provide the information efficiently and timely. If the seller is not responsive in providing requested information, it is incumbent on the financial advisor to explain why the information is important and to help to loosen the impediments to timely production of the information.

2.5 MARKETING

Once all of the aforementioned preparation is completed, the marketing of the seller begins in earnest. With marketing materials drafted and a contact list assembled, the financial advisor is in a position to begin contacting prospective buyers.

2.5.1 INITIAL CONTACT WITH PROSPECTIVE BUYERS

The process of contacting prospective buyers is fairly straightforward. The financial advisors contact all of the potential buyers on the list. The financial advisors typically have a "sell script" that entails a brief introduction (if necessary), explains the reason for the call, and provides a quick overview of the company's most compelling characteristics. When contacting strategic buyers, the financial advisor should also be prepared to explain why it would make a good strategic fit for the company contacted. If the potential buyer has even a mild level of interest, the buyer will typically agree to review the teaser.

Regardless of the expressed level of interest, it is important for the financial advisor to gather detailed feedback from each party contacted. If the potential buyer is reluctant to provide a specific reason for rebuffing the inquiry, the advisor should force the issue a bit. At the end of the day, the potential buyers' reaction (or lack of reaction) is important feedback for the seller. The potential buyers' feedback, taken together as a whole, should provide the financial advisor with valuable information on general buyer sentiment, buyer views on seller's sector, product line or geography, and a preliminary sense as to which aspects of seller's story resonate and which are problematic. The financial advisor should provide seller with regular summaries of the feedback received.

2.5.2 FOLLOW-UP WITH INTERESTED PARTIES

The next step for the financial advisors is to send the teaser to parties that expressed an interest in learning more about the opportunity. As a practical matter, the teasers are sent out on a rolling basis as the potential buyers express an interest in evaluating the opportunity. The financial advisor should follow up a day or two after the teaser has been received to ascertain whether the potential buyer wants to move forward in the process. This is another important opportunity for the financial advisor to gauge the level of preliminary interest in the seller and to determine potential sticking points. If the potential buyer remains interested after reviewing the teaser, the banker sends out the standard, pre-prepared CA drafted by counsel.

Although most CAs used in this context are reasonably similar, obtaining an executed CA is typically somewhat of a drawn-out process. There is usually a fair amount of haggling over a number of issues, including the scope of what constitutes confidential information, exceptions to the prohibition against potential buyer disclosing confidential information, and the duration of the term of the agreement. The financial advisor must balance the important goals of maintaining the seller's confidentiality and remedies against the equally important goal of moving the sale process along in an orderly fashion.

Once both parties have executed a CA, the financial advisor sends out the CIM, typically accompanied by a cover letter. In the case of a flexible process without a specific deadline, the cover may be perfunctory and contain limited information or, in the case of a modified auction, the letter may describe the bidding process, due diligence, overall timing, and anticipated content of the bid letter or purchase agreement. As mentioned previously, the CIM is a comprehensive offering document that is intended to provide the prospective bidder with sufficient information for it to prepare a preliminary, non-binding bid. In practice, prospective bidders usually request additional information such as statutory statements or an actuarial appraisal.

As discussed previously, a packet of additional information may be prepared and provided to potential bidders. However, it is important that the financial advisor refrain from providing additional information to a sub-set of potential buyers if that information will provide those parties with an advantage in the buying process. The financial advisor may also spend a fair amount of time fielding follow-up questions and providing answers and clarification. To ensure a consistent message and level playing field, the other advisors are typically not in direct contact with the buyer teams at this time.

2.5.3 PRELIMINARY BIDS

After fielding follow-up questions and providing additional information where appropriate, the financial advisor generally asks for a formal, written expression of interest in advance of due diligence. A buyer's expression of interest frequently takes the form of a non-binding bid letter (also known as a non-binding letter of intent) setting out a preliminary purchase price and material terms that the potential buyer would be willing to offer, based on the information provided by the seller. The seller will review such letters in order to determine the potential buyers that seem most likely to meet the seller's terms.

Because most reputable potential buyers are unwilling to prepare such a letter in the absence of sincere (if preliminary) interest, and because most buyers need to obtain internal approval prior to submitting such a letter, this request will usually narrow the field of interested parties dramatically. This approach has the advantage of limiting the number of parties that are provided access to the data room and are treated to management presentations, safeguarding seller's confidential information, and reducing the amount of management time devoted to the sale process. However, this approach may be inappropriate in a variety of circumstances, particularly if there is some aspect of the business that is difficult to capture or quantify in a CIM. For example, if management is one of the principal selling points of the company, prospective buyers may balk at providing a preliminary bid without first meeting with management.

On the other hand, in a distressed sale where time is of the essence and interested and qualified buyers are scarce, it may be advisable to get right to the point, which might entail inviting any interested party that has executed a CA and reviewed the CIM to the seller's offices to meet with management. The financial advisors and seller should consider these issues ahead of time and carefully weigh the pros and cons of permitting management meetings or data room visits prior to preliminary bid submissions.

2.5.4 REVIEWING PRELIMINARY BIDS

Once the non-binding bid letters have been received, the seller and its financial advisor should carefully review the results. If there are only a limited number of parties that have expressed interest, or if the proposed valuation ranges diverge significantly from seller's expectations, the seller should consider all of its available options. Having invested substantial time in the process, the seller may instruct the bankers to explore alternative transactions structures, approach additional parties not originally contacted, re-approach other parties that chose not to participate for "non-fatal" reasons, or inform each bidder that its proposed valuation will need to be re-evaluated to guarantee continued participation in the process. The latter approach is obviously the most muscular, high-risk approach, and bidders may refuse to "bid against themselves."

CRYPT 2.5

Closing Costs

After their spring planning retreat, a major life insurance company decided to sell a significant division. The company established an objective to close the transaction by the end of the current calendar year.

The information on the division and related block of business was packaged in the normal way, and the package of material was provided to the potential buyers in June of that year. By the end of July, six serious candidates emerged, and each was provided two days of on-site due diligence. The seller planned to manage a process wherein two candidates would be selected to go through a more extensive due diligence and submit a binding offer to the company by early September, leaving plenty of time for the transaction to be closed by year-end.

One of the six candidates was a relatively new buyer. It was a large company that clearly had the means as well as a strategic interest to make the acquisition. This company became aggressive and took a pre-emptive approach to the transaction. They proposed a high price and promised to complete their due diligence within three weeks. This buyer convinced the seller to give them an exclusive relationship under these terms.

Once the exclusivity was in effect, the buyer proceeded to drill down their value and the terms of the transaction. Ultimately the seller had to break the exclusivity agreement because it became clear that the buyer's chief financial officer was not experienced in mergers and acquisitions and operated under the approach of "get a foot in the door and then drive the terms you want."

The end result was that the seller had to sheepishly go back to one of the other candidates, explain the "broken" transaction, and request that a new process be initiated to attempt to get the transaction done by the end of the year. In this case they were fortunate. They were able to negotiate an acceptable (but more reasonable) price and related terms with this second organization. However, the lesson here is clear. The seller needs to do due diligence on the buyers and the buyers' representatives early in the game because the buyers' capacity and professionalism to do a deal is an important element of closeability.

A key role for the financial advisor is managing the seller's expectations. Unrealistic expectations can lead to failed transactions and months of fruitless labor. A financial advisor should explain to the seller that preliminary bids rarely match a seller's expectations. It is even more important for the seller to understand that buyers have an incentive to inflate the preliminary valuation range to ensure continued participation in the bidding process. In other words, final bids are typically below, not above, the initial valuation range. On the other hand, if there is serious interest from multiple parties, bidders have been known to increase their final bids.

In any event, once the seller and its advisors determine which of the potential buyers have proffered the most attractive non-binding offers, the financial advisor notifies both the parties that have been selected and the parties that have not been selected. The parties that are judged to have submitted the most promising bid packages move into a second round of consideration. At this point, these potential buyers are invited to review more detailed information on the target in the data room and may be presented with the seller's version of a stock or asset purchase agreement.

CRYPT 2.6

Chin Up

Once there was a small company that had all sorts of problems. Everybody had told the board how terrible the place was. In a mood of discouragement, the directors decided to sell the company. The first two bidders agreed with the gloomy view and prognosis. But then some people arrived on the scene who seemed to think there was not only existing value but great potential. So did the next two visitors.

The company sold for far more than the board ever thought it was worth.

We should always listen to the people who disagree, as well as agree, with us.

2.5.5 PRELIMINARY DUE DILIGENCE OF THE SELLER: SELL SIDE PERSPECTIVE

Assuming that one or more of the preliminary bids is acceptable from the seller's perspective, the approved bidders are invited to spend time (generally one or two days) in the data room, reviewing information and interviewing senior management. A prudent seller will invite in every party that submitted a "serious bid" even if the valuation range does not match the seller's ultimate expectations on value. This is a conservative approach that provides a hedge if other parties drop out during due diligence. If nothing else, it encourages continued participation by "stalking horse" bidders. Maintaining a competitive process potentially provides seller with leverage to negotiate a better offer from the preferred buyer.

CRYPT 2.7

Never Quit

Many years ago I was involved in the transfer of a significant size book of business. While technically not an acquisition, it had all the financial and emotional characteristics of one.

This transfer of a book of business involved a plan sponsor, the current carrier, and several prospective carriers. The current carrier understood the reasons for the change and was cooperative in the process. It identified several new carriers and eventually settled on one company. There were two other carriers that finished a close second in the selection process.

As the transition was underway, the president of one of the second place carriers kept in touch with the plan sponsor. These communications were kept low-key, but the president always offered to help in any way.

Quite unexpectedly, the winning bidder suffered a severe financial setback in an area of the company that was not involved with the transaction. There were provisions in the agreement with the new carrier that the plan sponsor could move the block if its financial position changed. As a result, the block became in play again.

The plan sponsor then contacted the president who had been calling. Everyone knew the circumstances and the need for making a fast deal. Because of the continuing contact with the president of the second place company, it was possible to move forward with great speed and complete the transition in an unusually short time.

The moral of this story is that sometimes finishing second works out in the end. When done properly, a second place finisher should keep in touch with the other parties to a deal. Occasionally things happen and being in the right place at the right time is sometimes the most important factor to complete a deal.

2.5.5.1 *Due Diligence Strategy for the Seller*

Due diligence is a critical phase of the transaction process. Most sellers, unfortunately, dread the invasive and time consuming due diligence process. Potential acquirers spend hours scrutinizing every aspect of the seller's business, asking uncomfortable questions and requesting reams of follow-up information. Even in the most smoothly run sale processes, due diligence is by its very nature a disruptive process for management and employees. Depending on the number of bidders, the process of due diligence can take a month or more, which is an enormous time commitment on the part of management.

Anxiety during due diligence is only heightened by concerns about confidentiality.[25] It is imperative that the process be safeguarded from competitors, suppliers, customers, agents and brokers, the press, and the general public. The process is even more fraught with peril when bidders are the seller's competitors or potential competitors. In addition to the safeguards afforded by a well-drafted CA, sensitive information can be disclosed in a staged fashion, so long as it does not appear that the seller is "burying" damaging information.

Internally, management must decide which employees need to know about the prospective transaction and can be trusted to maintain confidentiality, subject to the constraints that the seller team should be large and experienced enough to promptly deliver correct and complete information and respond to follow-up questions. However, even with an off-site due diligence, it can be difficult to assemble the personnel and documents without arousing suspicion from the rank-and-file employees.

Nevertheless, the seller must understand that the due diligence process needs to be embraced, not simply endured. It is, after all, an opportunity to demonstrate the best features of the seller to a third party. Ideally, management should embrace the opportunity to (modestly) boast about the company's achievements, as a parent would his or her child.

2.5.5.2 *Data Room Strategy*

The seller's financial advisor must ensure that the data room has all of the information and technology necessary to run a smooth process. The financial advisor should organize and index the documentation, ensure that the information is fully secured at all times, and establish a process for copying documentation (on site or off site) and for reviewing documentation that is too sensitive to be copied. The seller's representative or the financial advisor must be present in the data room at all times.

It is not uncommon for financial advisors to establish a "check out" process, whereby the buy side team reviews the index and requests the document in writing to gain access to it. While cumbersome, this process enables the sell side to track the buy side's areas of focus. This is useful information in terms of defusing potential issues.

As a general rule, it is courteous to provide another room (that does not contain sensitive data) for the buy side team members to make personal phone calls and otherwise meet. However, it is extremely important for the financial advisor to organize the on-site diligence process so that the buy side team is prevented from roaming about seller's offices.

2.5.5.3 *Management Presentation*

Due diligence is far more than merely inviting bidders in to scrutinize documents. For the seller, it is first and foremost an opportunity to "tell the story" in person so as to present the company in a positive light, which is accomplished in a number of ways and in a number of settings.

Management typically makes a formal presentation to each bidder's acquisition team during the initial stages of due diligence. This can be as informal as extemporaneous remarks but more often consists of formal presentations with a prepared script. It is critical that there is consistency in both the data and the message among the CIM, the actuarial appraisal, and the management presentation.

At the very least, the presentations should provide a summary of key investment considerations. Ideally, the presentation should provide an overview of the selling company's operating

[25] Confidentiality is particularly important if either of the companies has a publicly traded stock. Although public companies need not disclose preliminary M&A discussions regardless of materiality, the seller may be forced to make an announcement if there is a leak or an unusual trading in seller's stock occurs. See *Insurance and Investment Management M&A*, Debevoise & Plimpton, p. 5.

and management history, highlight the key selling points of the company, and perhaps briefly touch on future plans and projected financial results. Financial advisors typically assist management in preparing its presentation and coach them on style to ensure that the main selling points are effectively presented. The presentation is generally followed up by a question-and-answer period.

2.5.5.4 *Break-Out Session Strategy*

In addition to a general management presentation, it is helpful to both sides to organize small, sub-group meetings for the various disciplines. For example, there are typically finance, actuarial, underwriting, and legal breakout sessions. Line management should be prepared in advance and made aware of the types of questions that they will be asked in the interview process. It is critical that their line management's message is consistent with the CIM, which is in turn consistent with the actuarial appraisal.

2.6 EVALUATING THE OPPORTUNITY ON THE BUY SIDE

The majority of this chapter has focused on the M&A process from the seller's perspective. This emphasis is a function of the chronology and sequence of a fully marketed M&A transaction. Because the seller and its advisors begin preparations to sell the company months before potential buyers are contacted, the seller is the main protagonist at the beginning of the M&A process.

Of course, there are situations in which the buyer is the proactive party. It is not uncommon for a prospective acquirer to approach a potential target and initiate discussions regarding a strategic transaction. In addition to purely opportunistic approaches, some potential acquirers adopt a more methodical approach to an acquisition strategy. Often a company seeking growth will retain a financial advisor to proactively identify potential acquisition opportunities within certain parameters and to then approach selected targets.

In addition, certain companies will take a more aggressive approach and launch a hostile takeover. A hostile takeover is a takeover attempt that is strongly resisted by the target company's management and/or board of directors. While a hostile takeover bid is almost always good news for the company's shareholders in the short term, a "hostile" may be bad news for the company in the long term because the employee morale of the target firm can quickly turn to animosity against the acquiring firm.

As depicted in the movie *Wall Street* and the best-selling books, *Barbarians at the Gate* and *Den of Thieves*, the 1980s were the heyday of the hostile transaction. Spearheaded by the likes of Ron Perelman, Henry Kravis, Carl Icahn, and other "raiders," the infamous transactions during the 1980s were largely "bust ups," highly leveraged transactions financed by junk bonds and designed for short-term profit. As a result, most of the companies involved in such transactions had to be sold off, frequently in small "spare part" transactions.

Unfortunately, 1980s-style "raiders" gave the hostile transaction a bad name. In reality, a hostile transaction is generally launched after a target rebuffs an offer to buy the company. The shareholders of such companies may not be well served by entrenched managements and boards that are as interested in maintaining their jobs and perquisites as maximizing shareholder value. In the 1990s, the driving force behind takeovers was the scramble to stay big and strong enough to compete in an era of globalization and deregulation.

Upon receipt of an unsolicited bid, the owner or the board may have a fiduciary duty to solicit competing bids. The target company's board may also engage an investment banking firm to "defend" the target and, possibly, identify potential "white knights."[26]

[26] A company subject to a hostile take-over bid may invite another bid from a company it considers friendlier. The friendly company is known as a white knight.

In a seller-driven M&A process, there is a spasm of intense activity on the buy side once prospective buyers have been contacted. If a prospective acquirer is interested in pursuing an acquisition after reviewing the seller's CIM, the buyer's acquisition team prepares and submits an indication of interest to the board of directors (public company) or the target's owner (private company).

CRYPT 2.8

I Love The Night Life

You must, in this business, love the night life. Red eyes—planes that fly through the night—are all a part of this business. Traveling around the country and from country to country at night is the most efficient use of time. Heaven forbid travel should slow down a fast-moving transaction train.

My most memorable night flight involved traveling with two companions, and because the commercial airlines did not accommodate the CEO's time schedule, this time, for once, we got to fly with a private jet service. On schedule we showed up at the airport at 1 a.m. to catch the plane. No one was there to greet us at the private terminal. About a half an hour later, someone showed up to tell us that the pilots would not be there until 2:30 a.m. When they showed they found the plane had a problem that would not allow them to fly it; and they were not qualified to fly the other available plane. Pilots with those qualifications would show up at 6 am. Because it made no sense to travel home and back again, we stayed. If trying to get sleep in a plane is bad, trying to get sleep in an over-air-conditioned private terminal is not any better. The most senior executive got the primo spot—the dark stairwell—for his place to attempt to sleep. My other companion and I tried to make the most of the hard reception area floor (because the only alternative were hard chairs.)

The rest of the trip followed the revised departure schedule. We took off and landed, went to a hotel to shower, and attended our meetings—arriving late and compressing the full day's scheduled meetings into something less. We then left, and arrived back where we started—in the middle of the next night.

2.6.1 PRE-SCREENING THE OPPORTUNITY

The chief financial officer (at smaller companies) or the head of corporate development (at larger companies) on the buy side typically has authority to request a copy of the CIM if, based on the teaser, that individual deems the prospective acquisition worth exploring. Once that request is made, other individuals at the prospective buyer are drafted into service to assist with the process. The general counsel typically assists with the negotiation of the CA. Once the CA is executed and the CIM is received, copies of the CIM are distributed internally to the relevant operational, transactional, actuarial, and financial personnel for review. This group represents the nucleus of what will become the buy side deal team if there is a desire to proceed.

2.6.2 RETAINING A BUY SIDE FINANCIAL ADVISOR

A prospective buyer may want to hire a financial advisor, particularly if the buyer is inexperienced or if the seller has retained an investment-banking firm. The financial advisor is responsible for, among other things, pulling together the transaction team, facilitating an efficient review of the CIM, establishing a process to set deadlines and responsibility for key tasks, coordinating visits with sell side bankers, and managing expectations internally and externally.

Qualifications for retaining a financial advisor on the buy side are similar, but not identical, to qualifications for retaining a financial advisor on the sell side. Potential qualifications would include the ability to:

- build comprehensive financial models of companies' historical and future projections in the context of a change of control transaction
- value private companies

- prepare bids in the form of letters of intent
- negotiate the terms of purchase agreements on behalf of buyers
- prepare financing memorandums for raising capital for private companies going through a change of control transaction
- negotiate the terms of financing with sources of senior debt, subordinated debt, and equity
- negotiate shareholder agreements among the equity investors in a change of control transaction
- negotiate employment agreements for senior management of the target, if they are joining the combined company
- orchestrate the close of transactions.

2.6.3 FORMAL REVIEW OF THE OPPORTUNITY

If, based on the CIM and any additional information provided, the prospective buyer desires to submit a preliminary bid, the buy side work begins in earnest. The following are some of the major issues that management and the acquisition team should consider when trying to price, structure, and close an acquisition.

2.6.3.1 Market Analysis

The acquisition team should evaluate both the short- and long-term market potential for the combined company, including competitive pricing issues, which entails an analysis of the industry and competition, the forecasted demand for the combined company's services, and a review of its potential customers. This analysis should be integrated into the revenue section of the financial model that is included in the CIM.

A market or competitive analysis should also take into account the impact of any potential acquisition on each company's distribution relationships. The main risk here would be an acquisition that results in some type of real or perceived channel conflict. For example, an insurance company that relies on unaffiliated brokers and agents to sell most of its products may alienate this core constituency if it purchases an insurance company with a large captive agency force.

2.6.3.2 Preliminary Valuation of the Target

The foremost question in the minds of all parties involved will be how much should be paid for the acquisition. Before presenting a preliminary bid to acquire the target, valuation analysis must be done. There are many ways to value a company. Several methods are typically used to determine the purchase price, including:

- public company comparable valuation
- comparable transaction valuation
- discounted cash flow or dividend discount valuation
- financial buyer valuation[27]
- actuarial appraisal.

This valuation analysis provides a potential bidder with a general sense of the seller's stand-alone and change of control value. These metrics are merely a starting point for the construction of the seller's bid. As part of the valuation process, the acquisition team should evaluate whether synergies and/or cost savings will be required to achieve the investor's financial goals. If cost savings are necessary, the acquisition team should evaluate the potential areas where they can be attained as well as their impact on the new company and prospects for achieving them.

[27] A financial buyer encompasses most of the traditional valuation methodologies but does not include the synergy and/or cost saving assumptions that a strategic buyer would typically include. In addition, financial buyers would also factor in its "hurdle rate of return" (typically 30-35%) and may also examine "multiple" expansion or contraction sensitivities.

2.6.3.3 *Financial Modeling*

While valuation analysis guides the bidder in determining a price for the target, financial modeling shows if the acquisition makes sense within a range of potential offer prices given the buyer's financial objectives. The financial advisors construct the model based on information provided in the CIM, the buyer's view of the business, and the advisor's knowledge of the industry, projecting for up to five years the revenues, earnings, and cash flows of the combined company as well as any expense savings or revenue synergies that are expected to arise from combining the two businesses. The model provides an income statement, balance sheet, and cash flow statement, as well as a detailed set of assumptions consistent with the buyer's view of the transaction.

The model demonstrates the impact of different capital structures, how much debt (or equity) is prudent to finance the transaction, and whether the acquisition is accretive under different operating scenarios. The model is a tool to analyze the combined pro forma company's prospects for raising and/or generating enough capital to properly invest, service any debt, and provide a market rate of return to any equity needed to finance the acquisition. Particularly if the buyer is a public company, it will be vital for the buyer to assess if and when the acquisition is accretive to buyer's earnings. This analysis will assist management in assessing the optimal form of consideration from the buyer's perspective (cash, stock, or a combination thereof).

Similarly, it will be important to understand the relative contributions of each company to the pro forma company. Specifically, the buy side financial advisor generally prepares an analysis of relative contributions to the new company's revenue, earnings, and cash flow, as well as assets and liabilities.

2.6.4 PRELIMINARY DUE DILIGENCE OF THE SELLER: BUY SIDE PERSPECTIVE

From the seller's perspective, the goal of the marketing phase is to generate a high level of interest from a wide variety of qualified buyers. The interested and qualified bidders are then invited to participate in on-site or near-site due diligence with the seller. This typically involves a presentation by management of the seller, followed by a general Q&A period, "break out" meetings, and a data room review.

For the buyer's perspective, preliminary due diligence represents an opportunity to (a) decide whether to submit a bid, (b) ascertain information needed to formulate a meaningful bid, and (c) protect itself from potentially devastating downside risks. Depending on the size of the transaction, the level of complexity, and the resources available, a potential investor may dispatch a team of 10 or more professionals for a one- to three-day on-site due diligence exercise. It is important for buyers to identify individuals internally or contract externally a cross-section of talent with an appropriate skill-set to adequately perform a review of the company.

In addition to accomplishing the myriad tasks associated with vetting the seller, preliminary due diligence is an important opportunity for the buyer to present itself to seller's management. It is important to establish rapport and establish a collegial tone. It is important also to use this opportunity to better understand the goals of the various stakeholders within the seller's organization. For example, the seller's shareholders may only be interested in maximizing short-term profits whereas management may be more interested in saving its own jobs. As a result, it is important to send the appropriate message to each constituency.

Due diligence is a time-consuming process during a period when both sides are anxious and pressure to act quickly is intense. There is potential for disputes down the road over what was and was not provided. The provider may be tempted to deliver an information dump to the recipient without inventorying the documents being turned over. On the other end, the recipient may feel so pressured to get the documents into the hands of the appropriate reviewers that the opportunity to take stock of what has been received is lost, making it harder to piece together and interpret the results of the due diligence team's efforts.

Some of the following due diligence practices can help both sides stay organized and make intelligent decisions:

- The buy side team should work together to formulate a focused due diligence request list that addresses their specific areas of interest.
- Both buyer and seller teams should create and follow a system for memorializing and cataloguing both the information requested and the information delivered/received (this role is often handled by the financial advisors).
- The buyer's team should be large and experienced enough to efficiently analyze and communicate information about the seller to the buyer's decisionmakers to enable them to take action—action that might be as significant as renegotiating the deal or walking away from it.

Due diligence is treated in greater detail in Chapters 5 and 6.

2.6.5 FINAL BIDS

Following an analysis of the detailed information made available by the seller relating to both the economic potential of the target (the value of its book of inforce business, its marketing, and other business relationships and similar matters), as well as its potential liabilities, buyers will be expected to submit a more definitive expression of interest. In many auctions, bidders will be presented with the seller's version of a purchase agreement to mark up with comments. This is a strategy to move the process forward and quickly ascertain the interest level of the bidders, the major sticking points for each bidder, and the degree to which each bidder intends to haggle.

After due diligence, potential buyers have time (never enough) to review the results of their labor and make revisions to their preliminary valuations (typically downward) based on the team's findings. The buy side actuaries use this time to prepare their appraisal for management. They may create their own valuation model from scratch (a time-consuming process) or use the seller's appraisal model but run scenarios based on assumptions derived from the buyer's view based on the results of due diligence. GAAP pro forma financials of the stand-alone company are typically created using simplified tax assumptions, which will often serve as the basis for the actual reported financials of the purchased entity going forward. Purchase GAAP is treated in detail in Chapter 8.

As a result of the collective input of the due diligence team, management will decide whether to indicate an interest in continuing in the process or bowing out. The financial advisors will typically work with management to structure its bid and negotiate the letter of intent. These bids may be binding or non-binding as established by the seller. Typically, the winning bidder is given extended access to the company records and personnel in order to follow up on issues identified in the initial visit; although in some instances, more than one party may be invited back.

Buyers of public companies typically offer to pay an amount in excess of the then-per share stock price, the so-called control premium.[28] Why? The theory is that in addition to the value of the company's equity on a stand-alone basis, there is additional value associated with being able to influence or control the company's decisions. The control premium captures that value.

Control premiums are offered to induce the company's shareholders to vote in favor of the transaction and reflect the quantitative difference between transactions occurring under (and valuations prepared under) different *premises of value*. The first premise, controlling interest, represents the price per share paid for all of the equity of an acquired company (or a majority interest in the equity of that company). The second premise, marketable minority interest value, represents the value associated with minority interests in the equity of companies actively traded on the public exchanges. The difference in price derives solely from how the markets value a whole company versus a fractional interest in that company, or a majority interest versus a minority interest.[29]

---

[28] *Mergerstat Review* defines the "control premium" as the difference between the public market price of a minority interest in the stock of a subsequently acquired company five days prior to a buyout announcement and the actual buyout price.

[29] *Mercer Capital Management, Mercer Capital's BizVal.com—Vol. 11, No. 3, 1999.*

CRYPT 2.9

Fool Me Once

One aspect of the bidding process that I may have overlooked is the influence of financial advisors. It was possible that financial advisors were attempting to stimulate higher bids, which may have been attempted by encouraging bidders to raise their bids or by pressing the seller to pursue more aggressive bidding.

My suspicions were reinforced by a request from the seller to meet again. Our bidding group attended a meeting with the seller's two senior executives and the financial advisors.

The meeting started with the sell side's banker proposing that the value of the company had increased over the interval from initiating the potential divestiture up to the present day. This seemed somewhat unlikely given that all the top producers by this time had plenty of time to examine other marketing opportunities and to possibly even contemplate new destinations for existing business. I watched the person hypothesizing this position and he seemed to be serious. The other financial advisor reiterated this position, and I again noted it was done with a straight face.

A glance at the insurance company's two senior executives indicated that they did not seem pleased with the opening discussions. It seemed to me that this meeting was not starting on a positive note. My working with these two senior executives over the course of this potential transaction, as well as other dealings, had left me with an extremely high impression of both.

My bidding partners also felt uncomfortable with the hypothesis that announcing the sale would have a positive impact on the value of the business. The next 60 seconds decided the fate of the negotiations. One of the financial advisors then indicated that he had another interested buyer who was willing to offer more.

The chairman of our bidding group responded to this by indicating that because we were not interested in a higher price, the seller should pursue this opportunity with this willing buyer. If, at some future time, the seller wanted to reopen discussions, we would be willing to talk, but not at the higher price. The look on the faces of the seller's bankers accompanied by a significant amount of stuttering over the next two minutes demonstrated that this "selling technique" was a poor strategy.

As a consequence of this failed tactic, our bidding group walked away.

2.6.6 NEGOTIATION OF THE LETTER OF INTENT

If an indication of interest has been submitted and the parties wish to enter into a formal letter of intent (LOI),[30] the acquisition team will assist in negotiating the terms. Major negotiating issues include the financial terms, including the proposed purchase price, any deferred consideration, employment contracts, and the type of consideration offered. The letter is usually non-binding in the sense that neither party is bound to consummate a transaction until negotiation of all terms and completion of due diligence have been completed.

The letter of intent describes the ground rules for the buyer and the seller to negotiate in good faith to reach a final agreement. For example, the potential buyer may request an exclusivity period, the period of time in which the winning bidder is given to complete final due diligence and execute a definitive agreement without competition from other bidders. This letter can also be used to determine if there are any points that would be "deal-breakers" (i.e., points, such as indemnification limits or other matters, that no amount of negotiation would resolve). Making that determination prior to entering into the process of negotiating a definitive agreement can eliminate considerable expense and wasted effort for both parties.

In addition, the letter of intent may contain confidentiality provisions, timing limits (a

[30] It is important to note that public company buyers are cautious about entering into letters of intent in connection with transactions that would be "material" for the buyer because an obligation to publicly disclose the existence of the letter of intent may arise. Many buyers prefer to enter into a "memorandum of understanding" or other explicitly non-binding document so that there is no question that the discussions are preliminary and no "meeting of the minds" has occurred.

"drop-dead date"), "no-shop" clauses, agreements as to "break-up" or "termination" fees[31] or other penalties, "financing outs" or "due diligence outs,"[32] and other provisions that are meant to be binding, notwithstanding the fact that the parties have not reached an overall agreement. These provisions must be clearly addressed, and the legal ramifications of failure to observe these agreements should be made clear. In particular, the extent to which the letter of intent, or any provision of the letter, is to be binding must be explicitly stated in the letter, in order to avoid the possibility of a court imposing its interpretation of the effect of the letter.

In addition to negotiating the financial terms, negotiators should address potentially controversial "social" issues at this point. Issues such as management reporting, brand maintenance, and moving headquarters are often stumbling blocks to transactions. It is, therefore, vital for the seller to initiate full and frank discussion of these issues before committing to an exclusivity period. These issues will also be important drivers in the post-merger integration process.

UNUSUAL CONDITION

When I reacquired JKLCo from the company I had sold it to, one of the conditions of the purchase was that I agreed never to discuss any experiences regarding JKLCo during their ownership. There are very strong penalties if I do so. Accordingly, I can't share any of these experiences.

Management issues are typically a major social issue. Seller management typically seeks a significant post-transaction role as the buyer's employee. Related issues such as title, compensation, reporting responsibilities, and management succession are frequently deal-breakers. On the other hand, some management members may prefer to retire post-transaction. Other major stumbling blocks include whether the seller's corporate brand and related intellectual property will be used by the buyer and for how long, as well as whether the seller's management and employees will need to move physically to another location in order to work for the buyer.

In reinsurance transactions, the LOI is sometimes used as a fully negotiated, binding agreement, pending the preparation of a definitive reinsurance agreement, so that the reinsurance can be reflected on statutory financial statements for a particular reporting period. Letters of intent can have other legal effects. For example, in certain circumstances execution of a binding letter of intent may trigger reporting requirements for public companies under the securities laws. A letter of intent can also be used as the basis for filing under the federal Hart-Scott-Rodino Antitrust Improvements Act, which begins the running of a statutory waiting period.[33] Letters of intent can also be used in connection with finalizing financing arrangements for the transaction.

Following the execution of an LOI, the winning bidder begins a final, confirmatory due diligence process of the seller.

---

[31] A fee usually paid by the seller to the buyer if the seller opts to pursue a competing bid. This is usually reserved for the "purchase agreement," but may be a binding provision in a non-binding LOI in some circumstances.

[32] The right of the potential buyer to terminate the purchase process without penalty if financing is not available or if additional due diligence reveals problems.

[33] See NAIC Life and Health Reinsurance Agreements Model Regulation, sec. 5, which provides that no reinsurance agreement or amendment may be used to reduce any liability or establish any asset on a financial statement unless at least a binding letter of intent has been duly executed by both parties no later than the "as of" date of the relevant financial statement.

CRYPT 2.10

If You Don't Buy Local

Beware of buying a foreign-owned company. We were looking to buy a U.S. subsidiary of a foreign (non-U.S.) company. We'd done the due diligence, worked out our strategy, wooed the management of the subsidiary, and were in the process of putting together what we were sure was the winning bid.

Just as we were lighting the cigars, the parent company itself was purchased by a company in its home country, effectively taking the property off the market. Because we weren't licensed, and had no interest in doing business in the foreign country, we had no choice but to pack our bags.

When you are buying a foreign (non-U.S.) subsidiary, what currency should you think in? We spent an hour at a very high-level meeting discussing this issue. We resolved that all conversations and analysis would be in U.S. dollars. That didn't last long because we realized that all the data we received would be in the foreign currency and, more importantly, all the negotiations would be in the foreign currency. The only numbers our board was interested in were dollars. We had currency risk throughout the analysis.

2.6.7 CONFIRMATORY DUE DILIGENCE

Depending on the size of the transaction, the level of complexity, and the resources available, a potential investor may dispatch a team of 50 or more individuals on-site for a week or more, scouring the seller for potential issues ranging from actuarial and accounting to legal and regulatory to information technology and human resources. Any material issues identified during this period are usually addressed in one or both of two ways: by adjusting the bid price (upfront or earnout) to reflect any potential negative developments or by adding protection mechanisms into the transaction document.

2.6.8 DEAL FINANCING

Although having access to adequate capital to fund the deal is presumably a prerequisite for receiving the CIM, the buyer may not necessarily have cash on hand. If the buyer needs to establish financing for the transaction, the financial advisor will assist management in raising financing for the acquisition, including presentations to sources of senior debt, subordinated debt, and equity, and in negotiating with financial institutions over the terms of the financing. This will typically occur on a parallel path with the due diligence process. However, in order to execute a letter of intent, the seller often requires the financing to be in place. On the other hand, in order to formalize the financing terms, a LOI is typically required by the lender. The financial advisors will help resolve such difficulties. The structuring and financing of M&A transactions is treated in greater detail in Chapter 3.

2.6.9 RATING AGENCIES

It is important for buyer's management to meet with the appropriate rating agencies (S&P, Moody's, or Fitch for issuers of "rated" debt securities, and A.M. Best for all insurance companies) early in the process. If the buyer is serious about making a bid, management should advise the rating agencies of a possible transaction on a "no names basis" and solicit feedback. As the M&A process continues, buyer should continue to keep the agencies informed while being cautious about disclosing the name of the seller, particularly if the seller has publicly traded stock. After the LOI is signed, the buyer may want to provide the rating agencies with the name of the seller and the appropriate financial information requested. While the rating agencies cannot prevent a transaction per se, the threat of ratings downgrades is sometimes sufficient to scuttle a transaction.

2.7 NEGOTIATING THE DEFINITIVE AGREEMENT

Getting to "yes" involves the development and negotiation of terms and conditions acceptable to both the seller and the buyer.

2.7.1 NEGOTIATION

After a letter of intent has been executed and confirmatory due diligence has been completed, negotiations between buyer, seller, and their respective legal and financial advisors begin in earnest. Of course, for all intents and purposes, the buyer and seller have been negotiating from the outset of the process.

Final negotiations typically occur over the course of several weeks or months. Typical sticking points range from pricing to the form of consideration to indemnification provisions to the break-up or termination fee to shareholder lock-up agreements.[34] While many of these issues are addressed in the letter of intent, they are addressed in far greater detail, and are subject to more intense scrutiny, when negotiating the purchase and sale contract language.

The division of labor among the company (management, board members, and shareholders), the attorney, and the financial advisors during negotiations varies from deal to deal. As a general matter, representatives of both buyer and seller should not be involved in the day-to-day negotiations during the first phase of negotiations. It is generally recommended that the financial advisors and attorneys work together to negotiate as many of the key issues as possible.

Once the purchase and sale agreement has been drafted and the other side has reviewed the document and provided detailed written comments, it is worthwhile to collaborate on a memorandum setting forth the key substantive issues "on the table." This approach has the benefit of focusing each side on the issues that need to be resolved to effectuate a transaction. It also enables the advisors to begin discussions with their respective clients on the major issues, which can lead to suggested compromises where possible. This enables the parties to avoid a "paper war" in which each side seeks to make as many comments as possible without facilitating resolution of issues. Any additional drafting or purely stylistic differences of opinion are typically worked out in the ordinary course of negotiations between the attorneys.

There are many ways to resolve issues between willing buyers and sellers, including earnouts, straight price reductions, liability workout clauses, and pricing. The full range is limited only by the willingness of the two parties and the creativity of their advisors.

2.7.2 ANALYSIS OF NEGOTIATED TERMS

As negotiations progress, both buyer and seller (and their respective financial advisors) will invest considerable time and energy evaluating the impact of negotiated terms and conditions. This enables the parties to understand in "real time" the amount of latitude they have in further negotiations.

2.7.3 MANAGEMENT AND BOARD UPDATES

The financial advisor and attorney for each of the buyer and seller should also update their respective clients as the negotiations progress.

---

[34] If one party (usually the seller) has significant inside ownership, the other party (usually the buyer) may request that the inside shareholders enter into an agreement to agree to vote for the transaction. An "absolute lock-up" (without a "fiduciary out," which permits a party to terminate a merger in favor of a better deal) may be permissible so long as the net effect is not "preclusive" or "coercive." See *Omnicare, Inc. v. NCSHealthcare, Inc.*, 818 A.2d 914 (Del. 2003). But see *ACE Ltd. v. Capital Re Corp.*, C.A. No. 17488 (Del. Ch. Oct. 25, 1997), in which ACE sought an order restraining Capital Re from terminating their merger agreement to accept a competing higher bid from XL Capital.

2.7.4 PURCHASE AGREEMENT

The critical terms of the acquisition of an insurance company will be addressed in the purchase agreement (also known as the definitive agreement). While the outline of the purchase agreement has typically already been sketched out in the LOI, there are numerous legal, financial, and operational contingencies that have to be memorialized in the purchase agreement.

A standard stock purchase agreement will contain the basic agreements of the parties as to purchase price, the form of payment, the time of closing, and similar matters. The definitive agreement will also contain representations, warranties, and covenants of both seller and buyer, the purpose of which is to provide each counterparty with the comfort it needs to consummate the transaction, as well as protection against expected and unexpected problems.

2.7.4.1 Representations and Warranties

Counsel for each party will devote substantial amounts of time drafting and negotiating the representations and warranties. For example, the seller will provide the buyer with assurances that the target is properly formed and has the authority to carry on its business. The seller will also provide the buyer with assurances that the seller has the requisite power to sell the target. Other representations and warranties of the seller are intended to assure the buyer that it has a proper understanding of the property it is buying. The potential buyer will generally request the seller to represent and warrant that the target has no tax, business, employment, or other liabilities other than those disclosed in the due diligence process or in financial statements, although sellers sometimes try to limit representations and warranties to very basic items.[35] The buyer will provide representations and warranties that give the seller assurance that it can live up to its side of the transaction.

Both buyer and seller typically use disclosure schedules to specify the various issues that were previously revealed and that have been reflected in the sales price or by specific indemnification for losses arising from those disclosed items. Representations and warranties are generally made at the time of the signing of the purchase agreement and then are updated and restated (i.e., a "bring down") at the closing to account for any changes that may have occurred in the interim.

Sellers will typically try to limit their exposure to breaches of representations and warranties by providing for "knowledge" and "materiality" qualifiers and by limiting the period for which representations and warranties survive the closing. In the first instance, a representation will be inaccurate only to the extent that certain persons knew, or should have known, of a condition or event that makes the representation inaccurate.[36] In the second instance, the fact that a representation is inaccurate is relevant only if the potential loss is material.[37] Counsel for both buyers and sellers will spend considerable time negotiating the scope of the representations and warranties and their qualifiers.

Knowledge and materiality qualifiers can be a means of allocating risk between the parties. For example, if a representation subject to a knowledge qualifier is determined after the closing to have been inaccurate, the seller would be liable for losses only if it had knowledge (or should have had knowledge) of the facts giving rise to the inaccuracy either at the time of signing the

---

[35] It should be kept in mind that the seller of securities is obligated under federal securities laws to provide sufficient information to allow buyers to make informed investment decisions. Statements in offering memoranda, or representation or warranties, may not contain an untrue statement of a material fact nor may there be an omission of a material fact so as to make any document or representation and warranty misleading.

[36] If the seller makes an inaccurate representation of a fact, but had no knowledge of the inaccuracy, the seller will not have breached the representation. If the buyer becomes aware of the inaccuracy prior to closing, it can make the seller aware of the inaccuracy. As a result, the seller has knowledge, and unless it has the right to "cure" inaccurate representations by submitting revised disclosure schedules prior to closing, the representation will not be true at the time of closing, which may give the buyer the right to "walk away" from the contract—or to renegotiate the price or other matters.

[37] "Material" is generally not a specifically defined term.

agreement or at the time the representations and warranties are brought down. Thus, the risk of loss arising from an undisclosed liability is on the buyer. If there is no knowledge qualifier, any inaccuracy could give rise to liability for losses on the part of the seller. In the case of materiality qualifiers, the seller will not wish to have a deal not close because of minor inaccuracies in the representations and warranties. The buyer, on the other hand, will be concerned that although any one inaccuracy may not be material, a number of minor problems can add up to a major problem. The common resolution is to refer to matters that are not material individually or in the aggregate.

To the extent the target does have liabilities that have not been disclosed, there can be various ramifications. If the matter is discovered prior to closing, the buyer can refuse to close (and may seek damages if there is not a specific penalty provision in the agreement). If the matter is discovered subsequent to closing, the seller may be required to indemnify the buyer for any losses. These protections can be subject to a variety of limitations. For example, if the target is a widely held company, there may be no party to provide for post-sale indemnification. Similarly, if the seller is not financially strong, post-sale indemnification may be of limited value. Also, a seller may negotiate a limited survival period for representations and warranties; in such case even if there are undisclosed liabilities or breaches of other representations and warranties, there may be no remedy. Finally, sellers commonly negotiate a basket and/or a cap on indemnification liabilities, at some percentage of the purchase price. As was discussed with respect to representations and warranties, counsel for buyers and sellers will devote considerable resources to negotiating these matters.

In addition to the representations and warranties common to all industries, there are several representations and warranties that are specifically applicable to the insurance industry. First, there are certain representations and warranties regarding the seller's financial statements.[38] Second, it is common for the buyer to receive representations and warranties with respect to the adequacy of the seller's reserves.[39] A representation as to the "healthy" regulatory status of the seller is also commonly sought. Finally, there are a host of additional matters that can be subject to additional representations and warranties, ranging from market conduct and sales practices to compliance with anti-money laundering statutes.

2.7.4.2 Key Covenants

The stock purchase agreement will also contain various covenants relating to matters that will occur between the time the agreement is executed and the time of closing. It may also cover post-closing matters, such as competition and employment matters (for example, an agreement not to recruit a party's employees for an agreed period or matters relating to the termination of a business organization). Typical covenants relate to the conduct of the business, filing of tax returns, intellectual property matters, and the seeking of necessary approvals.

The agreement may also have a detailed indemnification section, pursuant to which the parties agree to indemnify one another for various matters, such as disclosed liabilities, as well as losses for undisclosed liabilities. The indemnification portion of the agreement will also specify which party controls tax contests or litigation involving third parties.

Both seller and buyer will be obligated to close the transaction unless there has been a breach of representations and warranties or a failure to perform a covenant, subject in each case to any materiality standards. Finally, many stock purchase agreements contain a "material

---

[38] Specifically there are representations and warranties regarding the accuracy of GAAP financials at the holding company level and the accuracy of the statutory financial statements for each insurance subsidiary. There are also representations and warranties regarding the accuracy and timeliness of state insurance department statutory financial statement filings for each insurance subsidiary. See *Insurance and Investment Management M&A*, Debevoise & Plimpton, p. 14.

[39] If an independent actuary has opined as to the adequacy of the reserves, the seller typically is asked to represent that it has supplied the actuary with all relevant information to form its opinion. *Insurance and Investment Management M&A*, Debevoise & Plimpton, p. 40.

adverse change" or MAC clause, pursuant to which a buyer is not obligated to close if there has been a material adverse change to the business or prospects of the target after the date on which the agreement was signed.[40]

2.7.4.3 Deal Protection

To protect the transaction against competing bids, the buyer typically bargains for a "fiduciary out" for seller's board of directors and a "no-shop" clause. A "no-shop" clause is a covenant that consists of two elements: (1) a "no-solicit" clause, which flatly prohibits the seller from soliciting additional bids and (2) a "no-talk" clause, which prohibits the seller from providing information to other prospective buyers.[41] A "fiduciary out" clause is an exception to the "no-shop" clause, which permits the board to take one of the prohibited actions if failure to do so would result in a violation of the board's fiduciary duties.[42] The price the seller generally pays for this flexibility is a "termination fee" in which the seller pays the prospective buyer a fee if the board exercises its fiduciary duty and then terminates the purchase agreement in favor of a competing bid.

When the transaction is an asset acquisition, the reinsurance agreement (or a combination of an asset acquisition agreement and a reinsurance agreement) will contain representations, warranties, and covenants similar to those contained in a stock purchase agreement, but relating only to the business that is being acquired. In addition, the agreements will address matters such as the responsibility of the assuming reinsurer to attempt to obtain novations from policyholders or ceding insurers and the assuming reinsurer's assumption of extra-contractual liabilities relating to the reinsured business.[43]

The agreements should address which party is liable for marketing or product design issues arising from the acquired book of business. For example, if the assumed business is life insurance, the agreements should allocate the economic cost in the event that the products failed to meet certain requirements set out in the Code (including, for example, Code Section 7702) at the time of the original issuance of the products. Intellectual property matters and transition service issues will also be addressed. In many cases the insurer or reinsurer selling a business desires to be freed of any responsibility for continued administration, often the driving force behind the sale. The assuming reinsurer will either bring the assumed business directly into its operating systems or bring in a third-party administrator to take over administration of the business.

2.7.5 EMPLOYMENT AGREEMENTS

Key members of seller management (and possibly other important non-management personnel) are typically offered employment contracts in connection with the transaction. The structure of such contracts may be a key determinant of the ultimate success or failure of the transaction, particularly in people-sensitive business such as in insurance brokerages. Typically such contracts have an element of "carrot" and "stick." The "carrot" is a generous financial package intended to compensate and provide incentives to key personnel with significant integration or transitional leadership roles. The "stick" is typically a non-compete/non-solicit provision, which prevents an exodus of talent to competitors.

[40] "Material adverse change" can be defined as a change, event, condition (financial or otherwise), or state of circumstances or facts with respect to the target that would have a materially adverse effect on its business, results of operations, assets, liabilities, financial conditions, or prospects.

[41] *Insurance and Investment Management M&A*, Debevoise & Plimpton, p. 14.

[42] Under Delaware law, a board of directors has no duty to maximize short-term value on a day-to-day basis. However, when a board is on the verge of selling, breaking up, or transferring control of the corporation, directors may not consider the interests of nonshareholders and have a narrow duty to maximize shareholder value. *Paramount Communications Inc. v. QVC Network Inc.*, 637 A.2d 34 (Del. 1994).

[43] *Insurance and Investment Management M&A*, Debevoise & Plimpton.

The Ink Must Be Dry

We owned a small consulting firm. It was time to get bigger or get smaller. We agreed to sell 50% of our shares to an investment advisory firm. The synergies would be fantastic.

The share purchase and subsequent employment agreements were lengthy. Our lawyers managed to agree, and we were ready to sign.

But the advisory firm couldn't wait to announce its growth. Much to my surprise, a page three article appeared in the National Underwriter *trumpeting the acquisition of my firm. My name wasn't even mentioned.*

With one call to them, the deal was off. But within a day, they were in our office, begging for reconsideration and mortified of perpetual embarrassment in front of their clients if the deal didn't complete.

We pondered for a day. We re-did the agreement, with substantially better terms at every juncture. They had no choice but to agree.

CRYPT 2.11

2.8 THE PATH TO CLOSING

For insurance deals, there is a long interlude from the executed purchase agreement to closing. This section addresses the events during this interval.

2.8.1 PRESENTATION TO THE BOARD OF DIRECTORS

Once the definitive agreement has been agreed to in principle, both seller (if it has minority shareholders) and buyer (if the transaction is material) typically present the transaction to their respective boards of directors for a vote. The financial advisor is usually asked to make a formal presentation regarding the proposed transaction to the board of directors. If shareholder approval is required, the board votes simply to recommend (or not) the transaction to their shareholders. If shareholder approval is not required,[44] the board votes to approve the transaction subject to regulatory approval or to disapprove the transaction.

The seller's board of directors will often request a "fairness opinion" from the financial advisor. The fairness opinion states that the consideration (in a cash deal) to be received (or the exchange ratio in a stock transaction) is fair, from a financial point of view, to the selling shareholders. The buyers' boards of directors also engage investment bankers to render fairness opinions.

2.8.2 REGULATORY ISSUES

Once the purchase agreement has been executed, there are several additional regulatory steps to be taken.

2.8.2.1 State Regulatory Issues

If the target is an insurance company, the buyer must seek the permission of the insurance regulator of the state of the target's domicile to take control of the insurer. The application for approval is filed on a standard document known as the "Form A," which is required under Insurance Holding Company System statutes.[45]

[44] Most state laws require that mergers involving SEC filing companies be approved by at least a majority of the company's shareholders (buyer and/or seller) if the merger will have a significant impact on the company. See Securities & Exchange Commission Web site at www.sec.gov.

[45] See NAIC Insurance Holding Company System Regulatory Act, sec. 3. "Control" is generally presumed if the buyer intends to own more than 10% of the voting securities of an insurer. As part of the Form A process, proposed buyers will be required to submit detailed biographical information with respect to directors and officers. A small number of states require non-domiciliary authorized insurers to make change of control filings, or to re-apply for insurance licenses. Some states require potential buyers of insurers that are commercially domiciled in the state to seek the regulator's permission for acquiring control.

State regulators will generally be required to approve any merger or other acquisition of control unless, after a public hearing, the regulator finds that: (a) after the change of control, the insurer would not be able to satisfy the requirements for the issuance of a license to write the line or lines of insurance for which it is presently licensed, (b) the effect of the merger or other acquisition of control would be substantially to lessen competition in insurance in the state or tend to create a monopoly, (c) the financial condition of any acquiring party is such as might jeopardize the financial stability of the insurer or prejudice the interest of its policyholders, (d) the plans or proposals that the acquiring party has to liquidate the insurer, sell its assets, or consolidate or merge it with any person, or to make any other material change in its business or corporate structure or management, are unfair and unreasonable to policyholders of the insurer and not in the public interest, (e) the competence, experience, and integrity of those persons who would control the operation of the insurer are such that it would not be in the interest of policyholders of the insurer and of the public to permit the merger or other acquisition of control, or (f) the acquisition is likely to be hazardous or prejudicial to the insurance-buying public.[46] It is important for buyers and sellers to obtain to the extent possible this approval in advance of submission.

CRYPT 2.12

Stick To Pianos

In the early 1980s I was involved in trying to extract value from a family of life companies on the brink of insolvency.

The life insurers' holding company had been in the musical instrument business until it decided it was qualified to acquire and manage life insurance companies. After a good start, fortunes soured.

The companies were selling single premium deferred annuities (SPDAs). At the time, the only accounting guidance was SFAS 60, instructing life insurers to report profit as a percent of premium. The companies took this literally and, of course, for SPDAs displayed very rosy earnings. The company was crediting at a very high rate of interest. It was investing the proceeds in its own or new subsidiaries. But it was tough to dividend up those GAAP earnings.

There were more forces at play. When interest rates fell below 13.25%, the surrender charge disappeared. Taxable gains couldn't be generated to offset losses on intercompany reinsurance. Eventually, all four wheels fell off the cart.

This company was obviously headed into rehabilitation and would soon be on the National Organization of Life and Health Guaranty Associations' (NOLHGA's) agenda.

I accepted an assignment by one of the states to investigate.

I was in the holding company's offices in New York and witnessed a last-ditch attempt to resurrect its financial situation. The parent needed extensions from its banks to avoid going into bankruptcy that night. Bank Nine, with its home office in Ohio, was the only bank that had not granted the time extension needed. Miraculously, just before midnight, after the governor of Ohio made a phone call, the bank granted the extension.

I got to see first-hand how the state governments can step in and influence the destiny of an insurance company.

The financing was too little and too late. The remnants of this conglomerate were soon on sale.

If the transaction is a reinsurance transaction, other regulatory filings may be necessary. For example, a number of states have enacted "bulk reinsurance" laws, pursuant to which regulatory approval must be sought if a company seeks to reinsure all or substantially all of its business. For example, the California Insurance Department requires permission to be sought if a licensed insurer desires to cede "substantially its entire property or business" (which is generally understood to be more than 50% of its insurance in force).[47] Similarly, New York requires the permission of the Insurance Department if a domestic insurer desires to cede reinsurance

[46] NAIC Model Insurance Holding Company System Regulatory Act sec. 3 D.

[47] Cal. Ins. Code §1011(c).

with respect to "whole risk" on any one life, or with respect to a "substantial portion" of its life insurance in force, and authorized companies desire to cede reinsurance with respect to its "whole risk" on any individual life or joint lives.[48]

2.8.2.2 Antitrust Issues

The parties may also be required to obtain antitrust clearance under the HSR Act and under state insurance laws by filing a Form E, which is required under state Insurance Holding Company laws when there is the potential for concentration in particular markets.[49] Also, assumption reinsurance transactions may be subject to Form E filing requirements.[50] If the transaction has cross-border impact, filing with foreign anti-trust authorities may be required as well. This filing is required regardless of whether the buyer or seller is a "public" or "private" company. To the extent possible, any potential hurdles regarding regulatory approval should be anticipated, identified, and mitigated in advance of the HSR filing.

2.8.2.3 SEC Review

In addition to federal anti-trust laws, the parties to an acquisition may have to make certain filings with the Securities and Exchange Commission pursuant to the Securities Act of 1933 and the Securities Exchange Act of 1934. If the buyer is a public company, the buyer will have to, at a minimum, file a Form 8-K[51] when the transaction is announced and file proxy materials (an information statement and voting materials), assuming the buyer's shareholders need to vote to approve the transaction.[52] A buyer's intent to issue shares to the seller's shareholders in connection with the transaction is considered a public offering, and a Form S-4 or the like will have to be filed with the SEC to register the transaction in which such shares are issues.

If the seller is a public company, the seller will have to, at a minimum, file a Form 8-K when the transaction is announced and file proxy materials, assuming that the seller's shareholders need to vote to approve the transaction.

The SEC reviews these submissions to ensure that the filings comply with federal securities law. With respect to the Form S-4, the registration statement relating to the securities is only deemed effective when the SEC declares it effective.

2.8.3 PRESENTING THE DEAL TO THE PUBLIC: ANNOUNCEMENT

Once the definitive agreement has been executed, the transaction is typically announced first to important constituencies (such as rating agencies, key shareholders, suppliers, brokers, and customers) and then to the general public. Because the transaction has not yet been reviewed by the regulatory agencies, the transaction is announced subject to shareholder and regulatory approval. Once the regulators approve the transaction, the transaction will formally close.

For public companies, the transaction is typically formally announced to the public in the form of a press release issued by the buyer. The press release announces the outline of the transaction, touts its major benefits, and directs readers to listen to an investor/analyst conference call within 24 hours. This conference call is usually accompanied by a formal presentation detailing the benefits of the transaction and addressing possible areas of concern. For private companies, the announcement may be delayed until closing or may take place in the context of a later marketing initiative.

---

[48] N.Y. Ins. Law § 1308(f).

[49] For purposes of filing the Form E, a "market" means direct written insurance premium in the state for a line of business as contained in the annual statement required to be filed by insurers licensed to do business in the state. Accordingly, the acquisition of a pure reinsurer typically will not require Form E filings. See NAIC Model Insurance Holding Company System Regulatory Act sec. 3.1 B(2)(e).

[50] See Model Insurance Holding Company System Regulatory Act sec. 3.1 A(1).

[51] Form 8-K is an interim filing to alert the public of a material corporate event.

[52] If the buyer is a public company, a shareholder vote is required if the transaction is significant.

Once the transaction of a company is announced, the transaction may attract competing bids. If the seller is a publicly traded company, a competing bid may take the form of a tender offer made directly to the seller's shareholders and thereby bypassing management.[53] As a result, buyer and seller typically structure acquisitions so that there is the shortest possible time lag between announcement of a proposed acquisition and consummation of that acquisition.

In insurance M&A, on the other hand, the time between announcement and closing is driven by a host of factors, mainly regulatory, that can delay closing for up to six months. Therefore, the best way for the buyer to protect itself against competing bids is to press for inclusion in the purchase agreement of the "no-shop" clause.

The key points analyzed by Wall Street include the following:

- magnitude of any control premium paid
- accretion/dilution (synergies and cost savings)
- strategic rationale
- financial implications (capital and leverage)
- ratings impact (financial strength and debt ratings)
- returns going forward.

2.8.4 SHAREHOLDER APPROVAL

M&A transactions generally require the majority of the seller's shareholders to vote in favor of the transaction. The extent of shareholder approval required is a function of state corporate law and of the individual company's governing documentation.

2.8.5 CLOSING

Assuming the state and federal regulatory bodies do not object to the proposed transaction, the transaction will generally "close" shortly thereafter. At closing, the purchase agreement is finalized and executed by all of the relevant parties, and the consideration is paid to the seller's shareholders.

2.9 CONCLUSION

This chapter provides a broad overview of the major tasks and milestones of the transaction process for insurance companies. Subsequent chapters are much more detailed and delve into great detail on financing, appraisal, due diligence, taxation, accounting, and integration.

[53] *Insurance and Investment Management M&A*, Debevoise & Plimpton, p. 3.

Chapter Three

Finance

3.1 INTRODUCTION

At its core, there are only two strategic questions facing a company's management team: how to raise capital and how to invest it. Working on behalf of the firm's owners, the charge of management is to increase the corporation's value, which is done by making decisions regarding the allocation of resources to particular projects. How to choose between competing projects is difficult and often requires some degree of subjectivity. This text assumes the process of deciding how to allocate capital between competing projects has been completed and the green light has been given to explore a potential acquisition.

The question then becomes how to pay for the investment. Before this question is addressed, some background in the basic tenets of finance theory, particularly as it applies to mergers and acquisitions, is needed to set the stage. A graduate level finance text will devote substantial time to the treatment of financial decision-making, valuation, risk, capital structure, and the characteristics of different financial instruments. Simplified assumptions as to the capital structure and efficient markets are typically assumed for illustrative purposes. This chapter addresses capital structure and financial instruments; other chapters addresses valuation (Chapter 4) and risk assessment.

3.1.1 EFFICIENT MARKET THEORY

Efficient market theory in its strongest form presumes that security prices instantaneously and accurately reflect all information available. Eugene Fama introduced the term "efficient market" in 1965 in his seminal paper "Random Walks in Stock Market Prices."[1] This assumption simplified the mathematics of financial theory and also assisted economists in developing several interesting hypotheses.

Economists now argue among three degrees of market efficiency, distinguishable by the amount of information that is assumed to be incorporated in securities prices: the weak form, the semi-strong form, and the strong form. The weak form states that current prices reflect all of the information contained in historical stock prices, which implies it should not be possible to earn excess returns simply by studying historical stock prices. Stated differently, changes in stock prices are random and are not correlated.

The semi-strong form of the hypothesis states that all publicly available information, in addition to historical price information, is already incorporated in prices. Prices are assumed to adjust immediately after announcements such as quarterly earnings statements or issues of stock, which implies it is not possible to make excess returns just by reading the paper or by looking at published financial statements.

Finally, the strong form of the hypothesis states that stock prices effectively incorporate all available information, public or otherwise. Prices reflect the best estimate of all micro- and macroeconomic information that could potentially impact the earnings of the company. Information that might give an investor an edge is difficult to find because he or she is in competition with thousands of other active investors whose efforts at buying and selling are accurately and fairly represented in the current stock price. The strong form implies that it would be impossible to find an investment manager who is able to consistently beat the market as a whole.

[1] E. F. Fama, "Random Walks in Stock Market Prices," *Financial Analysts Journal*, September-October (1965), p. 4.

3.1.2 CAPITAL STRUCTURE

The mix of securities issued by a firm is known as its capital structure. A firm's capital structure is the result of numerous choices made by the firm since inception, presumably with some degree of consideration and forethought.

The choice of capital structure is in one sense a securities marketing problem: the firm can issue dozens of distinct securities in countless combinations attempting to find the particular combination that maximizes its overall market value. Modigliani and Miller showed that, in perfect markets, financing decisions do not matter.[2] Their famous Proposition One states that a firm cannot change its total value merely by splitting its cash flows into different streams. The firm's value is determined by its real assets, not by the securities it issues.

Thus, according to Modigliani and Miller, capital structure is irrelevant as long as the firm's investment decisions are the same. However, in the real world, there are imperfections in the markets that do make a difference in financing choices. Some of these considerations will be discussed in this chapter.

3.1.3 COST OF CAPITAL

The cost of any capital investment has three components: the cost of funds, the cost of required capital, and the opportunity cost. The opportunity cost of an investment is conceptually the cost of not investing in another, potentially more lucrative and/or less risky project. The overall cost of funds is calculated using the weighted average cost of capital equation (basically the weighted average of the cost of equity and the cost of debt). The details of this calculation are presented in Chapter 4.

This cost of required capital for an insurance acquisition is captured in an actuarial appraisal in the following fashion. Given a particular project hurdle rate,[3] the cost of required capital for the transaction is the amount of capital times the difference between the hurdle rate and the after-tax earnings rate. The present value of this amount is calculated for the duration of the projection. The cost of required capital is examined in more detail in Chapter 4.

3.1.4 CASH FLOW RIGHTS VS. CONTROL RIGHTS

In any company there are two ownership issues: rights to a company's cash-flow stream and rights to control the firm's management and strategic direction. A firm's financial value is the stream of cash flows produced by its assets. When the firm is financed entirely by common stock, the cash flows and ownership rights belong to the stockholders. When a company issues both debt and equity, cash flows are split into two or more tranches: a (relatively) safe tranche that goes to the debt holders and a riskier one that goes to the stockholders.

In the classic textbook case, lenders have first claims to cash flows. Disputed claims between lenders arise based on the various contracts that have been entered into independently; these problems become more apparent during periods of financial distress. In the real world, the claims of policyholders, tax authorities, and employees come into play, further complicating issues.

Stockholders have claims to any residual cash flows after lenders are paid. In return for assuming a riskier position, control of the company accrues to stockholders. As discussed in Chapter 2, there is typically a control premium ascribed to a company for the right to control the firm's management and strategic direction.

---

[2] F. Modigliani and M.H. Miller, "The Cost of Capital, Corporation Finance and the Theory of Investment," *American Economic Review*, June (1958), pp. 261–297.

[3] The required return on a new investment. In order to attract capital into a particular project, the hurdle rate must exceed the company's weighted average cost of capital (WACC). The difference between the hurdle rate required for the project and the WACC will be a function of the amount of risk perceived in the project.

3.1.5 ROLE OF MANAGEMENT

Managers are hired by directors to act as agents on behalf of the firm's owners. Managers run the day-to-day operations and implement the board of directors' strategies. In addition to running the firm's day-to-day operations, managers have a significant public relations responsibility. The firm's financial managers are required to reassure markets, investors, and other stakeholders that there are no surprises on the horizon. Firms that have more stable earnings and manage information better typically get preferable rates when raising capital.

CRYPT 3.1

Shareholder Expectations

In September 2003, life insurer MONY agreed to be acquired by AXA at a price below its book value. In its regulatory filings, MONY stated its tangible book value to be $43 a share, yet it accepted a takeover bid of $31 a share. The following excerpts reveal reactions of MONY shareholders.

CONFERENCE CALL TRANSCRIPT

MNY - AXA Financial Agrees to Acquire MONY
Event Date/Time: Sep. 18. 2003 / 10:00AM ET

DAVID HELLER, ADVISORY RESEARCH: *I wonder if you could explain to me how I look at a financial statement that shows a tangible book value of $43 a share, which is represented by 60% in current assets and 40% of the assets are in a fixed income portfolio, and yet you're willing to sell those assets at 72¢ on the dollar. There may be something going on here that I just cannot grasp, and I certainly would be appreciative if you could explain to my associates and myself and possibly some other people on the phone how you have represented your assets as $43 a share. I assume you've attested to it. You've had an audit committee which has approved it, and yet you're selling those assets for 70¢ on the dollar.*

MICHAEL ROTH, MONY Group CEO: *Thank you for your question and certainly that is a question that people have been asking. First of all, our tangible book value is not $43 a share. Included in the $43 is about $17 a share of intangible deferred acquisition cost, so that is not viewed as a tangible asset.*

DAVID HELLER: *If that is true, then I want to tell you your balance sheet does not have any category for intangibles.*

MICHAEL ROTH: *Well it specifically refers to deferred acquisition cost, but let me comment on deferred acquisition cost from an accounting point of view. The question for our balance sheet is the valuation of deferred acquisition cost, and, when you look at the valuation of deferred acquisition cost, you look at it on the basis of a number of years. You don't look at it on a one-time basis. And this is standard accounting procedure, and it is reviewed by our outside auditors whenever they issue and comment on our financial statement. And it's based on protected earnings, interest rate assumption, cost over a period in excess of 1 years, so if you were to look at a snapshot on the valuation today, it includes $17 of an asset that will take a number of years to be realized. So therefore when you value an insurance company, you have to take into consideration the fact that this asset, although it's significant, is in fact an intangible asset.*

DAVID HELLER: *And how many companies did you open your books too and allow to be bidders on this transaction?*

MICHAEL ROTH: *...My response to that has always been that this company will always entertain discussions and opportunities that will enhance shareholder value. Throughout the almost five-year period of our de-mutualization, we've had numerous discussions with various companies on the potential transactions to enhance shareholder value.*

DAVID HELLER: *Let me restate the question. Can you quantify in the last two months how many companies have had an opportunity to look at your statements and prepare a bid?*

MICHAEL ROTH: *Everyone has an opportunity to look at our statements. We are a public...*

DAVID HELLER: *To the question. I'm asking you to quantify it. How many? Two, three, none?*

MICHAEL ROTH: *I cannot quantify specifically.*

DAVID HELLER: *I've been in this business a long time, Michael, and I've always had a list of the five most egregious transactions that I have looked at. I want to congratulate you because I knocked number three out, and you have just qualified for number three. I think this is absolutely a disgrace to the shareholders. I think it is marvelous to the management. All the synergies are terrific but you're not merging the companies. You are selling for cash. You're imposing a capital gains if people have profit, and I do want to congratulate you. You've qualified in my top five. Thank you.*

RICHARD GRUBMAN, Highfields Capital – Analyst: *Let me just make the observation that what your board and your management and your advisors think is fair is all very interesting, but your shareholders are going to vote against this transaction including this one. It's been five years of bad performance capped by this enriching transaction. On the eve of your takeover, defense is expiring. You know enough's enough. We're going to vote against it, and we're going to throw you out because, frankly, you know, the shareholders, your employees, your agents, and your customers couldn't possibly do worse without you.*

MANAGEMENT: *There was no response from management.*

DAVID HELLER: *Sorry to get back at you, but I'm here with two of my associates, Jim and Kip, who visited with you less than six months, and they called to my attention that you and your associates and your CFO who was there were asked whether the reflection on the balance sheet of deferred policy acquisition costs was a fair statement and the answer was positive. And I'm wondering why you would answer to my associates that that was a fair and positive representation and then on this telephone tell us that it's an overstatement of the asset.*

MICHAEL ROTH: *I'm sorry David, but I think you're misstating what I said. What I said was that the valuation of deferred acquisition cost is properly stated, and Rich, in that meeting where I attended, was correct in saying that every time we issue financial statements, we look at the carrying value of our deferred acquisition costs and get comfortable as to its realizability. What I was telling you on this call was that the realizability of the asset is over an extended period of time and that is proper GAAP accounting for valuation.*

DAVID HELLER: *Fine, let me say this Michael, so I can echo what High Fields Capital said. We will strongly vote against this acquisition, and we'll strongly vote to remove the directors and the present management of the company. Thank you.*

RICHARD GRUBMAN, HIGHFIELDS CAPITAL - Analyst: *Yeah, guys, let's try to not be too fast and loose with the facts. The annual return of the five years since you went public is less than 6 percent. The S&P mid-cap life index is up 28 percent annually over the same period, and telling people that the P/E is substantially higher than comparable transactions is merely an indictment of how poorly you've run the business, not where the comparables are actually valued, so cut the nonsense. We understand the math.*

STALEY KATES, SOUTHEASTERN ASSET MANAGEMENT: *Yes, thanks. This is Staley Kates, and we are not on a holders list on Bloomberg but we actually have 4.9 percent. so we'd be your largest shareholder. Kind of along of the lines of what we've heard from other shareholders and others who own the company, despite that very powerful endorsement by the investment banker, we think the price is ridiculously low and will certainly vote against it, and I guess I'd break this into one comment and two questions.*

The comment would be that book value is relevant and P/E ratio is not relevant. Just because the management team has underearned on the ROE basis does not make the book value irrelevant.

And then, as far as a question, I just do not understand why we would talk about how this is good for customers and AXA and not shareholders at the outset. Can you address that?

MICHAEL ROTH: *Well I think I did. I said in terms of the valuation that we went through in terms of the price, so it is in our judgment the best interest of our shareholders at this price.*

MASON HAWKINS, SOUTHEASTERN ASSET MANAGEMENT: *This is Mason Hawkins. I'm Staley Kates' partner and CEO and chairman of Southeastern Asset Management. We will vote against this transaction because we think it's one of the most ridiculous price-to-intrinsic-value appraisals we've seen. It gives no attribution for the closed book of business. It gives no value whatsoever for the distribution, for the brand name, and we have to also very much disagree with your portrayal of D PAC because over time people can use those assets that are there to earn significant assets.*

CURTIS GENSEN, THIRD AVENUE FUNDS: *I have a couple of items. And without talking out of both sides of your mouth, just for clarity, can you say again what percent of your shares do you need for approval of the transaction?*

MICHAEL ROTH: *We need a majority to approve the transaction.*

CURTIS GENSEN: *A simple majority?*

MICHAEL ROTH: *Yes. Yes.*

CURTIS GENSEN: *Since shareholders are getting their faces ripped off in this transaction, cashed out at a disgraceful number, I'm wondering if you considered taking AXA's stock, which among other things might have enabled us to enjoy some of the wonderful benefits you're talking about, and even perhaps get a better premium.*

MICHAEL ROTH: *Well, all I can comment on that is that in the proxy statement there will be discussion of the history of the transaction, and that issue I think would be addressed there.*

CURTIS GENSEN: *Well, I've got to say, in this day and age of corporate malfeasance and management enrichment, this one is right up there.*

LUCA IPPOLITO: *Thank you. Really a comment, and I don't want to beat a dead horse, but if you sell a company for cash, you are selling the company. In a situation like that, the only ethical and professional thing that you can do is to maximize value. I think it was very clear that here you were merely enhancing value and not maximizing value. That is simply not acceptable to shareholders. Thank you.*

The acrimony spilled over into the press. From the November 5, 2003, *Wall Street Journal:*

From Richard Grubman, chief executive of Highfields Capital, MONY's third largest shareholder: "I'm going to take you to court in Delaware, we're going to do a lot of discovery and a couple of years later you're going to owe me a lot more money with interest."

Addressing the third quarter 2003, "MONY's executives did little to soothe concerns yesterday during the company's quarterly earnings conference call. After going through the standard earnings presentation and discussing the current status of the merger, the executives allowed just two questions, both from Wall Street analysts. MONY's shareholders were cut off. "I calculated that I've done about 4,000 conference calls, and in 4,000 calls, I've never seen anything like this." says Staley Cates, president of Southeastern Asset Management.

There are certainly a few lessons learned from these exchanges.

At a time of heightened scrutiny of executives and increased shareholder activism, "golden parachutes" for underperforming management teams may not sit well with investors.

Do not assume that large shareholders of insurance companies are necessarily well versed in the differences between statutory and GAAP accounting.

The buy side and the sell side should be proactive and prepare an aggressive PR campaign before an announcement in connection with any potentially controversial transactions.

3.1.6 AGENCY THEORY

Agency theory is an important corporate finance concept to understand, particularly in the context of M&A. Shareholders are the owners of the firm, but in widely held organizations they are not the managers. Shareholders elect directors who in turn hire managers to act as their agents to oversee day-to-day operations with the objective (presumably) of maximizing the firm's value. One necessary condition of efficient markets is that managers always act in the best interest of the owners.

However, in the real world, managers do not always act in the best interests of their owners. Numerous academic papers have been written examining the relationships between owners and managers as their agents as well as the effect of incentives on manager behavior. The difference between the attainable value assuming owners' and management's interests are perfectly aligned and the actual value achieved by management as owner's agents is known as *agency costs*. Substantial agency costs are incurred when managers do not act to maximize firm value or when shareholders incur costs to monitor and/or influence the actions of managers. This is one of the arguments used for requiring management to have an ownership interest in the firm.

The potential for agency costs become exponentially complicated when additional types of ownership rights (i.e., rights accruing to lenders) are added to the mix. The fault lines among managers, owners, and lenders become increasingly apparent during periods of financial distress, mushrooming into potentially huge direct and indirect bankruptcy costs. In insurance, bankruptcy is further complicated by the claims of policyholders and the interests of the state in protecting its policyholders' rights.

One of the factors in more normal situations that increases agency costs and leads to difficulties in managing this complicated web of relationships is information asymmetries. Managers, owners, and lenders typically all have access to different information about firm finances. Information asymmetries play an important role throughout the M&A process; reducing information asymmetry is a primary goal of a potential buyer in order to reach optimal pricing. Reducing the information gap is also a real issue for suppliers of capital, whether a company is raising money through debt or equity. This is particularly true in insurance because it may be years, even decades, before the true financial return on a particular investment is revealed.

3.2 SOURCES OF FUNDS

There are numerous capital providers, including venture capital, private equity, commercial banks, insurers, and public funds. Each has its preferred structural tendencies, usually aligned with particular liabilities and desired risk-reward objectives. For example, banks prefer to provide the most senior, secured debt with floating rates to match with their floating-rate demand deposits, whereas insurers with longer-term liabilities prefer to issue subordinated, longer-term, fixed-rate debt.

All parties interested in providing capital to an organization or project will perform due diligence. The scope of the diligence will involve many aspects of the borrower's operations, including:

- a financial audit
- validation of customers and markets for the borrower's products
- legal diligence (contracts, bylaws, incorporation documents, etc.).

The borrower must provide assurances to the lender that the money will be well utilized. This typically is brought out in the due diligence process for the provider. If a project is not seen as providing sufficient return to pay the debt, lenders will not be attracted to it. This process of due diligence reduces the information asymmetry between borrowers and lenders, reducing the cost of funds.

A borrower may be presented with tailored financing proposals from capital providers. Lenders may wish to provide financing in stages, possibly upon the acquirer reaching pre-defined milestones, rather than a one-time payment. In addition, the capital provider may not guarantee its commitment in amount or cost, but rather request the option to provide additional funding at a price to be determined at the point the funding is to be considered. Moreover, capital suppliers providing funding earlier in a company's growth may desire a right of first refusal in future requests for capital or demand a re-valuation of the provisions for funding previously provided.

The rest of this section describes the characteristics of various sources of funds.

3.2.1 VENTURE CAPITAL

Startups typically generate no internal funds, only costs. Venture capital is often the first source of funds a growing organization taps when the need for capital outstrips the firm's ability to generate it internally. Venture capital is generally supplied to fund growth and capital investment rather than acquisitions. Venture capital is typically provided by specialized funds or wealthy individuals who are able to take a significant risk in return for an equity position in the fledgling operation. As such, venture capitalists may take an active role in managing the operation.

Venture capitalists want to see a strong business plan with a strategy that allows them to exit their investment in a defined timeframe with a hefty return. Returns on venture capital investments can be spectacular, but for every Google there are dozens of start-ups that fail to make it over the initial hump to long-term profitability. There may be several rounds of venture capital before the company generates enough cash internally to support growth.

3.2.2 INITIAL PUBLIC OFFERING

After one or more rounds of venture capital, a successful company may be ready to go public.

The first step in an IPO is choosing an underwriter. The selection process resembles the "beauty contest" described in Chapter 2. Relationships developed during the IPO may very well influence the choice of investment banker down the road. Sometimes, for particularly large offerings or offerings expected to generate a lot of interest, a group of underwriters known as a syndicate is chosen rather than a single firm. Syndicates may be formed to share the risk, increase distribution reach of the offering, or "share the wealth" among various banking relationships at the behest of the offering firm. Being chosen as sole underwriter or lead underwriter in a large, successful offering brings significant visibility and bragging rights on Wall Street (not to mention lucre), so there is significant jockeying for position around hot new issues.

The underwriters play three important roles in the IPO process:

1) They provide the company with strategic, financial, and procedural advice for all aspects surrounding the issuance of the security. The issuer has never done it before, whereas the underwriter does it regularly.

2) They typically buy the issue from the issuer at an agreed-upon price. This is known as "firm commitment" underwriting.[4]

3) They market (resell) it to the public. The underwriter serves as the initial market maker, standing ready to buy and sell regularly and continuously at a publicly quoted price. Unless alternate agreements are made, the underwriter keeps any unsold shares, a large potential liability during sudden shifts in market sentiment.

A registration statement providing detailed information about the firm's history, current operations, business plan, and use of the proposed financing must be filed and approved by the SEC. Part of this registration is a prospectus, a dense document that is provided to all potential investors. The underwriter also arranges for the listing of the security on the appropriate exchange.

The determination of the initial offering price uses some of the same financial alchemy described in Chapter 4 (comparison with competitors, analysis of price/earnings and price/book ratios, and the judgment of the underwriter). The underwriter and firm principals will take to the road to pitch the offering to large institutional investors, such as pension funds and mutual funds. Investor reaction coupled with non-binding indications of how much of the issue they are willing to buy provide a gauge of demand and send strong signals as to an appropriate price range for the issue. Ultimately, the price selected for a firm commitment underwriting issue must reflect the level the underwriter feels is necessary to attract the investing public to buy 100% of the offering.

The ongoing relationship between underwriters and institutional investors is particularly important. In the underwriter's role as intermediary and initial market maker there is the potential for conflicts of interest. While the issuing company wishes to maximize the funds obtained from the IPO, the underwriter needs to keep room for appreciation in the stock price in order make it attractive to investors. This also lowers the possibility of the underwriter losing money from an undersubscribed share offering. There are other reasons that cause markets to price equity offerings at below current market value, including information asymmetry. Studies show that while appreciation of IPOs provides above-average returns to investors initially, longer-term returns regress to the mean.

The costs of an IPO as a percent of capital raised are significant. Underwriters typically receive a spread of 5%-10% of the issue to cover their investment and assumed risks. The issuer's administrative overhead and opportunity cost of managerial time to the issuer are also

[4] An alternative to the firm commitment process described in this chapter is the "best effort" basis, where underwriters contract to sell as much of the issue as possible but do not guarantee to sell the entire amount. This approach might be taken with an offering that is perceived to be particularly risky, which itself sends a message to potential purchasers. The best effort approach is less commonly used.

high. A hidden cost to the issuer is the cost of underpricing the issue, which averages as much as 15%.[5]

3.2.3 PUBLIC SECURITY OFFERINGS

The process of a public security offering is very much like an initial public offering (except that it should be easier the second time). A lead underwriter is chosen (perhaps but not necessarily the same as the IPO), a statement is filed with the SEC, the underwriter buys the securities, and it re-sells them to the public.

Much of the same information is used or updated for the firm's current situation. Public offerings include debt or equity, whereas IPOs are almost always stock because the company does not typically have an earnings record with which to support debt payments. Barring a rights issue limited to existing stockholders, new stock issues typically have the effect of diluting firm ownership. As such, directors must make a case to existing shareholders that issuing new stock is in their long-term best interests.

Large companies may issue different classes of stock designed to appeal to different investors. When General Motors bought Electronic Data Systems, a tracking stock was created for investors interested in participating in the performance of this sector but not in the automobile giant as a whole. In other situations, companies offer different classes of stocks (often "A" shares and "B" shares), where one class has a component of privilege that the other lacks. In many cases, this has to do with voting rights, where those individuals with the secondary class status have less say in the company's management.

Debt raised in the public markets must comply with regulatory requirements, such as registration with the SEC and periodic reporting requirements. The selling price may not be par; the underwriter fixes the issue price in the same manner described for IPOs.

Raising capital in the public markets is intensive, costly, and time-consuming. The process involves investment bankers and underwriters, attorneys, senior management, and finance staff, among others. Because of friction inherent in the regulatory process, speed to market is an issue. Timing can be critical because a window of opportunity typically needs to be hit. Filing and marketing a new issue may take months without previous arrangements with the SEC or underwriting syndicates.

3.2.4 SHELF REGISTRATIONS

As a result of changes in SEC regulations, companies no longer have to register issues and issue them immediately. Delayed offerings are possible through a Section 415 "shelf registration." Companies may file a single registration statement good for up to two years. The issue or portions of it can then be sold with little extra paperwork when the company needs financing or if the company feels that the market is particularly attractive. This approach can be used for debt or equity issues.

Shelf registrations provide a great deal of flexibility and allow companies to have a war chest that they can dip into quickly should opportunities arise. Due to the nature of the process, which does not involve a lead underwriter from an investment bank, shelf registration is more often used for straightforward bond issues rather than riskier, more complex common stock or convertible securities.

[5] Clifford W. Smith, Jr., "Raising Capital: Theory and Evidence," *The New Corporate Finance*, Donald H. Chew, Jr. Ed. (New York: McGraw-Hill 2001), p. 289.

3.2.5 BANK MARKET

The bank market typically offers floating rate loans because its demand deposit liabilities are floating rate. While banks generally require the most restrictive financial covenants, asset-rich companies can borrow in excess of typical debt-to-cash-flow multiples. Maturities range from five to seven years, with a mandatory principal amortization for term loans. Transaction timing can be as little as three months.

Bank lenders have two focuses in determining availability of credit and its price: cash flow and assets. The focus of cash flow-oriented lenders is earnings before income tax, depreciation, and amortization (EBITDA). The debt capacity of a firm is calculated as a multiple of EBITDA, which can vary based on an interest coverage,[6] the company's current debt ratios,[7] overall credit availability, and market perceptions of the industry. For borrowers in cyclical industries, the resulting volatility in available credit can create potential problems.

Asset-rich companies may have more attractive alternatives, provided they are prepared to offer first priority security interest in assets. The amount bankers are willing to lend depends on the asset class. The basic measurement is the appraised net orderly liquidation value (NOLV). Maturities may be longer than under a traditional cash flow approach depending on the asset's useful life. Asset-backed loans generally have more flexible financial covenants than those deriving from the cash-flow lending market.

Over-leveraged or distressed companies may find attractive refinancing options in this market. Lenders are primarily U.S. banks and commercial finance companies. Commercial finance companies are more aggressive than traditional banks because bank regulations restrict banking activities.

3.2.6 PRIVATE PLACEMENTS

Private placements involve selling debt directly to a limited number of investors. Because they are negotiated privately, they may be priced without the constraints of public securities offerings. Private placements tend to be custom-tailored and may be structured to include future financings at fixed prices or at performance-based rates. Private placements are typically not rated by debt ratings agencies.

Private placements typically have a fixed-rate funding option, priced at a spread over U.S. Treasuries. Longer-term maturities are available with custom amortization schedules. The insurance industry is a significant purchaser in this market due to its size, financial sophistication, and appetite for long-term investments. Transactions of up to $500 million are not unheard of. Although private placements are typically not rated, an insurer must consider implications on its risk-based capital (RBC) requirements, which have a component to reflect asset risk (as typically measured by NAIC bond ratings). Although there can be flexibility in the financial covenants, due to the nature of the insurance liabilities limited prepayment flexibility is typically offered by insurance company issuers.

Regulation of private placements is significantly more flexible than placements in the public market. For example, in the United States, private domestic offerings and all foreign (Regulation S) offerings, whether public or private, are classified as restricted securities and are exempt from SEC registration. Rule 144-A allows large financial institutions to trade unregistered securities among themselves because the large institutions are sophisticated investors and can look out for their own interests. Therefore, they do not need the diligence and supervisory services that the SEC provides.

The intention of the rule is to increase liquidity and reduce issue costs for private placements.

[6] Interest coverage is a measurement of the number of times a company can cover its interest payments with EBITDA; the higher the ratio, the lower the company's burden for debt service.

[7] Debt/EBITDA or debt/total capitalization.

Rather than having to go into the public market, companies can issue private placements that can then be traded among qualified institutional buyers. These securities have proven to be popular with foreign issuers that wish to raise capital in the United States while avoiding the scrutiny of being a listed public company. There has been an increasing volume of secondary trading in Rule 144-A issues.

While insurers are dominant purchasers in this market, there are very few insurers that raise capital through private debt markets. Despite potential cost savings, there is a limited number of institutions interested in buying securities with limited liquidity in a heavily regulated industry.

3.2.7 MEZZANINE MARKET

The mezzanine market is a broad term used to describe the layer of financing between senior debt and pure equity. It is also referred to as subordinated or "junior" debt. The financing instruments used typically contain attributes of both debt and equity and are hence labeled hybrids.

Borrowers in the mezzanine market are usually private companies seeking growth capital. Issues are characterized by flexible financial covenants; there is no rating agency requirement. As with private placements, large insurance companies and specialized mezzanine funds dominate the marketplace. Credit analysis is typically focused on cash flows.

Maturities are up to 10 years, typically with no mandatory amortization but often with a sinking fund feature. Issues are usually structured as a coupon instrument with an equity participation. Equity features can be in the form of warrants, conversion rights, pay-in-kind, or cash flow participation. Coupons are higher than straight debt, but, due to the equity feature, expected total returns are in the same range as venture capital and private equity.

3.2.8 PRIVATE EQUITY

Private equity is essentially venture capital for established rather than start-up companies. Private equity financing is available for a wide variety of uses including recapitalizations, leveraged buyouts, acquisitions, capital investment, and distressed situations. The private equity marketplace is highly efficient, with capital available across a wide variety of industries including stable old economy businesses and high-growth environments. Both control and minority interest capital is available, but board of directors representation is typically required.

The private equity market is an alternate source for partially or fully meeting the capital needs for mid- to larger-size acquirers. It is often the only pure equity source for smaller acquirers.[8] Like venture capital, desired returns for private equity are significantly higher than for traditional funding mechanisms. Investors want a clear exit strategy in three to five years. The investment vehicle is usually in the form of preferred stock convertible into common shares.

3.2.9 SELLER FINANCING

In certain situations, to smooth negotiations and to help facilitate the transaction, a portion of the buyer's total consideration may be underwritten by the seller in the form of debt. The seller's note is usually subordinated to any other debt financing the buyer may carry but senior to equity. The note can be structured flexibly in terms of interest rates, prepayment, duration, etc., to address the concerns of both parties. The debt may also be reduced or eliminated by schedule or triggers based on the financial performance of the purchased entity.

For example, if the seller steadfastly maintains that the company is worth $100 million but

---

[8] In September 2003, Quanta Capital Holdings Ltd. of Bermuda completed a successful $550 million private equity placement.

the buyer cannot be convinced to pay more than $90 million, a seller's note may be used to bridge the gap. In this case, the value of the company would be pegged at $100 million, with $90 million consideration paid by the buyer at closing plus $10 million funded by the seller. The seller benefits by receiving the additional $10 million plus interim interest payments. The buyer benefits by deferring the additional $10 million, by using company cash flow to pay the $10 million over time, and by deducting the interest payments.

Seller financing becomes, in effect, a set of golden handcuffs linking the two organizations until the debt is worked out. Lending the buyer funds to consummate the deal can not only bridge valuation gaps but also provide the buyer leverage in the event of breaches in the seller's representations and warranties. In this case, the buyer is in a stronger position to negotiate a price abatement in the event that the buyer discovers representations in the purchase agreement that are false or if the seller fails to perform an act that it has covenanted to perform.

Buyers and sellers must recognize that seller financing adds an extra layer of complexity on top of an already difficult legal transaction. Long goodbyes are typically not recommended because even the best of relationships may become difficult if conditions deteriorate.

3.2.10 REINSURANCE

Reinsurance, particularly assumption reinsurance, will be discussed in greater detail in Chapter 4. Reinsurance can be used as an effective tool to finance transactions in a number of different, interesting, and creative ways. Insurance companies have far less access to capital than their counterparts in other industries, which is due to the strict approach regulators take to ensure solvency. Reinsurers have historically been able to find ways to work within the rules to enable direct writers to unlock some of the intrinsic value of their portfolio.

In the case of M&A, reinsurers can step in to provide much-needed financing options and liability restructuring to help finalize a deal. Reinsurance can be used to facilitate a large initial dividend through portfolio indemnity or assumption transactions or to improve future dividends through ongoing programs. In both instances, this may allow an acquirer to avoid bank debt or to repay debt more quickly.

3.3 FINANCING INSTRUMENTS

Financing instruments range from cash on hand to pure debt to pure equity to points in between. New instruments are regularly designed to meet the needs of borrowers, capital providers, and changing market conditions.

The key features that characterize a financing instrument are the repayment terms, the degree of ownership/control surrendered, the cost of financing, and its impact on capital structure. An increasingly important part of the value equation is the structure and potential cost of any options (puts, calls, and triggers) embedded in covenants and controls included in the contract.

The principal features of the more common financing instruments are described below, along with a brief discussion of advantages and disadvantages for use in acquisitions.

3.3.1 CASH AND CASH EQUIVALENTS

Cash and cash equivalents consist of uninvested funds and funds invested in liquid, short-term (generally fewer than 90 days), government-guaranteed securities such as money market funds, short-term bankers' acceptances, certificates of deposit, and treasury bills.

Companies with too much cash need to look for projects to invest in or they may become the subject of frustrated shareholder action or ultimately become takeover targets themselves. Various options for the use of cash include stock buybacks, extraordinary dividends, capital investments, or acquisitions. Management needs to examine these options and decide on a course of action appropriate to its particular circumstances.

In certain situations the use of cash in financing an acquisition may be indicated. For example, if cash on hand and/or future net cash inflows are anticipated to substantially exceed operational needs over a foreseeable period, the acquirer may feel confident in using a portion of cash on hand. This action would reduce overall borrowing costs for the acquisition while deploying underutilized capital in a (presumably) higher yielding investment. The drawback to using a significant portion of cash on hand for an acquisition is the opportunity cost of not having cash for another capital investment for which capital markets might be unwilling to provide funds and/or unexpectedly needing the cash at a later date.

3.3.2 DEBT

Debt financing involves borrowing money by selling interest-bearing instruments to institutions in a primary market or individuals through a secondary market. The borrower receives funds upon the sale of the securities. The use of the funds is typically unrestricted, although investors will examine the proposed use of the funds to evaluate the project's capacity to service the debt. The borrower services the debt with tax-deductible interest payments at scheduled intervals (occasionally with partial principal repayments) over a specified term with a final payment at the end of the term.

3.3.2.1 Structure and Control

Lenders want to make sure that their investment is as safe as possible with the highest return while borrowers want the lowest price with the most flexibility. There are various means of coming to a mutually satisfactory agreement, from contractual agreements to extra-contractual due diligence, which leave ample room for negotiations between the two parties.

A borrower may have bond issues with dozens of different lenders. Lenders want to make sure that their debt will be repaid but are willing to trade their place in line for a price. If a bankruptcy occurs, the more senior debt is first in line to be repaid. The junior debt is paid after all the senior bondholders are satisfied. However, all debt ranks ahead of preferred and common shareholders in receiving corporate assets in the case of a bankruptcy.

Lenders will also be concerned about additional future debt. While the company may currently have a strong balance sheet, conditions change over time. Therefore, some lenders put provisions in their contracts with specific limits on the capital structure of the company. If these conditions are violated, certain actions or options are available to the lender to remedy its situation.

Providers of funds exert control to protect their investment by way of covenants with requirements, such as the borrower maintaining particular levels of regulatory capital, rating agency ratings, and/or minimum profit levels. These clauses can be significant and have proven to be more than one company's undoing. The fate of General American was literally decided by a provision in a guaranteed investment contract that stated that if their rating fell below a certain level, contract holders could demand repayment. It happened and caused a liquidity crisis. The potentially devastating impact of these types of options was perhaps not adequately emphasized in internal company analysis or publicized beyond the corporate financing suite.

CRYPT 3.2

Two Halves Make A Hole

Bondholders can be at the mercy of creative corporate executives. In 1993, the Marriott Corporation split itself into two companies, Marriott International and Host Marriott. The entire debt for the original firm was transferred to one company with only a portion of the free cash flow to service it, while significant cash flow was spun off to the other company with no debt attached. First announced October 5, 1992, this restructuring was viewed favorably in the stock market. Bond markets, however, were thrown into turmoil. All of the due diligence and analysis that was performed by lenders in support of their original bond issues was suddenly obsolete. Markets were stunned and dismayed by the action, and rating agencies quickly moved to reduce what had been investment grade bonds to junk bond category.

Some say this was the work of corporate machinations at its best. Others suggest that bondholders had only themselves to blame for not demanding stronger covenants to protect themselves from restructuring tactics such as the one engineered by Marriott. Although bondholders were able to delay the eventual spinoff and win more favorable terms, they still suffered significant losses. In this instance, there was a significant wealth transfer from bondholders to stockholders. Taking into account both bond and stock markets, there was a measurable decline in total firm value following the restructuring announcement.

Options accruing to the borrower may be present in the debt agreement. For example, the debt may be callable by the borrower for redemption, most often only after some preset time. The option to prepay the outstanding balance at any time may or may not be offered.

Given the characteristics of debt instruments and financing considerations, pure debt financing (no rights to convert to equity) is well suited for use by entities with more predictable and larger absolute cash flows.

3.3.2.2 **Cost**

Debt cost varies with the types of features incorporated in the offering. Cost is lower for debt issues with:

- higher credit ratings
- more senior claims to assets
- more restrictive covenants
- fewer rights/options accruing to the borrower
- more rights/options accruing to the lender.

The cost for proposed financing also depends on the percentage and absolute amount of existing debt in the current capital base and debt term structure of the issue. Debt terms are classified as short (generally less than one year, such as a line of credit) or long. Interest rates may be at a fixed or floating rate.

Debt can be issued at various levels of seniority, classified broadly as senior and junior (subordinated to senior relative to claims on the borrower's assets and earnings, also known as mezzanine). Often the lender will include covenants (controls) restricting activities of the borrower to protect the lender's interests. The debt may be issued in unsecured or secured form via pledged assets (real property), although almost all debt issues by financial institutions are unsecured obligations.

In certain cases, an acquirer may desire or be required to issue securities at a higher rating than would otherwise be assigned to the particular security or entity post-financing. For example, purchasers of the securities may demand a higher rating in order to provide capital, or the acquirer may be seeking a lower cost of financing. Credit rating enhancement may be attained through financial guarantees, letters of credit, or surety bonds in the banking and insurance marketplaces. In exchange for the boost in credit rating, the acquirer pays a fee that covers the provider's perceived risk, expenses, and profit.

3.3.2.3 Advantages of Debt

Debt is flexible and has numerous attributes that make it useful as an acquisition financing tool. First, debt provides a lower-cost means of obtaining funds as measured on an after-tax basis. Second, debt allows the acquirer to lock in a fixed cost for several years, for example, in slow economic cycle/low interest rate environments. Third, it is hypothesized that companies prefer the use of debt versus equity due to information costs. Recognizing the information asymmetry between managers and investors, by issuing debt (with its fixed payment schedule), managers signal better prospects about a company's future to financial market than if they were to issue equity.[9]

The amount of funds made available by lenders is limited, being dependent on the projected cash flows and financial condition of the combined entity. In a debt-funded acquisition (leveraged buyout), the debt is typically secured by the assets of the firm (i.e., in the event of default, the bondholders become owners).

3.3.2.4 Disadvantages of Debt

Though debt has its advantages, it also has its drawbacks. First, the acquirer may not have sufficient taxable income to allow a tax deduction on interest payments. Second, the economy may be in a growth phase resulting in a high interest rate environment at the time financing is required and thus a relatively higher cost for debt financing. Although it may be possible to later refinance the debt should interest rates decline, the debt issue is likely to include prepayment and refinancing charges to protect the lender. Third, covenants in the debt issue may require periodic reporting and may restrict the form and amount of future financings. Finally, debt financing adds a financial burden to the existing operational leverage. The higher fixed costs of debt service may lead to changes in ratings, increase the probability of default, and increase the cost of future financings.

CRYPT 3.3

James Bond, Actuary

The time was in the early 1980s.

Acme Life Insurance Company was in a cash flow squeeze. The chairman had made a series of country-club investments,** whose deplorable performance was now haunting the company. Acme's chairman sought and found a supposedly friendly lender, Dr. Evil.*** Dr. Evil loaned Acme enough money to tide it over for six months, which everyone agreed would be ample time to turn some of these investments into cash, repay the "friendly" loan, and service debt. If Acme Life didn't repay the "friendly" loan in six months, then control of the company would pass to the lender, Dr. Evil.*

Acme wasn't worried, however, because the terms were easy and Dr. Evil was a nice guy.

Six months passed and Acme couldn't pay. Dr. Evil turned out to be not so nice and was salivating at the prospect of gaining control of the company.

The chairman decided to fight back. He hired "Good Guys," a white knight investment company, who in turn retained me.

We rode to rescue Acme from the clutches of Dr. Evil.

Day 1

The Good Guys team arrived at the front desk of Acme Life. After stating our names and business purpose, an armed guard approached, put his hand on his holster, and escorted us out of the door at gunpoint. Obviously shaken, my client still had the presence of mind to tell me that I would not receive combat pay.

* *not the real name*

** *investments made with anyone at the chairman's country club*

*** *not his real name*

[9] Michael Barclay and Clifford W. Smith, Jr., "The Capital Structure Puzzle: Another Look at the Evidence," *The New Corporate Finance*, Donald H. Chew, Jr. Ed. (New York: McGraw-Hill 2001), p. 201.

Day 2

After a series of legal moves and counter-moves, Good Guys got permission to perform due diligence under certain conditions. One of them was that we could not directly communicate with anyone from Acme. We entered a conference room. We sat on one side of the table and a team of Dr. Evil's lawyers sat on the other side. The rules for all requests were a) they must be in writing, b) they must include a full justification, and c) they must pass from us to the team of lawyers. One of the lawyers would then relay the request to the appropriate person at Acme, then back to the lawyers before getting to us.

Day 8

I was finally ready to do some number crunching when my associate arrived with my portable computer. Since personal computers had only been out for a year or so, and portables just weeks earlier, my 28 pound sewing machine look-alike drew everyone's attention. Hard drives had not yet made it to personal computers, so there was a lot of manual intervention as my associate swapped floppy diskettes in and out of the two drives.

We spent the next three days putting together the actuarial appraisal. Of course, everything was monitored so we spoke to each other in a cryptic actuarial tongue.

Day 11

After watching us for three days, Dr. Evil surmised we were up to something sinister. He could not figure out why two people spent all day in front of this sewing machine, uttering strange words like nonforfeiture, validation, and net present value. When his lawyers asked me what we were doing, my client told me that I didn't have to answer their question. Dutifully, I remained silent.

Day 13

We were completing our on-site work when the Good Guys struck a deal with the chairman. They were happy, but Dr. Evil wasn't. Due to the hostile conditions at Acme, we decided to finish our work at the hotel.

After completing our work at the hotel, we packed up our belongings and sewing machine-sized personal computer and headed down the elevator to go to the airport.

When we got off the elevator, the local sheriff and two deputies were there to greet us, again with firearms. The sheriff slapped me with a subpoena. Actually, the subpoena was not for me but for my computer. We were happy to oblige, not only because he had a gun but because I would have 28 fewer pounds to carry through the airport. I wouldn't have to buy a seat for the computer as I did on the way up.

We were safely home by the time the sheriff saw the "insert diskette 1 to continue" message.

Day 20: Epilogue

After all that effort, we were foiled by Acme's own actuary, who turned out to be one of Dr. Evil's henchmen. There was a small provision in Dr. Evil's loan agreement that allowed Dr. Evil to receive an extra payment of 50% of all new premiums written between the date of the loan and the date of the repayment. The actuary, wanting to please his new master, raised the interest rate on Acme's single premium deferred annuities to 15%! He also had reinsurer prospects lined up that could wire $1 billion of premium to Acme on a moment's notice. Some basic math, not exactly financial economics, revealed we could not afford the extra $500 million cost.

Foiled again. The flag we raised was white.

There are many morals of this story to pick from. Keep your eye on the details. Adhere to a written, formal investment policy. Try not to let the weapons distract you. If it seems too good to be true, it probably is.

3.3.3 EQUITY

Equity is a powerful instrument for acquisitions. The amount of capital that can be raised is not limited by cash flows of the combined entity. Additionally, equity may be used as currency in a stock swap and, through private markets, may be raised without diluting current ownership. The characteristics of equity make it well suited for use by entities with less stable or smaller but growing absolute cash flows. In addition to public markets, equity providers include banks, insurers, and private equity funds.

3.3.3.1 *Structure and Control*

Equity financing involves raising money by selling ownership rights to earnings and assets after the claims of debt, hybrid security holders, and other creditors. As an ownership vehicle, its term is expected to be for the life of the company. Common share ownership typically comes with voting rights. Owners control the company through their voting rights.

Each time a financing is undertaken, there is potential for dilution in ownership and possibly control, based on requirements of the funding providers. Issues to resolve in considering financing alternatives include the extent to which the current owners are willing and able to provide the financing needed, the degree of ownership dilution they are willing to accept, and the possibility of raising funds with non-voting shares.

3.3.3.2 *Advantages of Equity*

Pure equity financings provide a number of advantages. First, there is no requirement to repay the principal amount raised or to provide debt service, although dividends are typically paid out of retained earnings. Thus, the company has greater financial flexibility versus a debt financing. Second, rating agencies, with their eye on financial strength, view equity favorably. Third, ownership claims are limited to the residual amount after all other claims of the entity are paid. Fourth, for investors, interim cash flows received (dividends) may receive preferential tax treatment, whereas interim cash flows received by debt investors (coupon payments) may not receive preferential tax treatment.

3.3.3.3 *Disadvantages of Equity*

Despite its advantages, equity has several basic disadvantages. First, stock dividends are not tax deductible to the payor. Second, additional stock is potentially dilutive to earnings, reducing the P/E ratio, reducing ROE, and thus impacting valuation multiples described in Chapter 4. Dilution may also lead to a cession of control rights from current shareholders. Equity offerings are typically more costly than debt and consume significant management and staff time and resources.

Finally, equity offerings have a greater risk to the capital provider than debt as a result of information asymmetry between management and investors. While it may seem quixotic, the mere announcement that a firm is issuing stock to raise capital may reduce the share price by as much as three percent.[10] The reason for this phenomenon is not as simple as it might seem. It might appear that stock dilution would explain the reduction in share price, but this is not the full explanation.

Management's choice between debt and equity sends signals to markets. If managers feel that share prices are overvalued, then raising money through the equity market is more efficient than raising money through the bond market. If share prices were undervalued, it would be imprudent to issue stock to new investors who would stand to benefit from subsequent price gains at the expense of the prior ownership structure. Given the choices available to management, markets understand that if management feels that equity is the better choice

---

[10] Michael Barclay and Clifford W. Smith, Jr., "The Capital Structure Puzzle: Another Look at the Evidence," *The New Corporate Finance*, Donald H. Chew, Jr., Ed. (New York: McGraw-Hill 2001), p. 201.

than debt, management likely believes that the stock price is overvalued. The drop in value after the declaration of a stock issue quantifies the shareholders' estimate of the overvaluation.

Note that a similar phenomenon can be seen in the M&A market. Often when an acquisition is announced, the stock of the acquirer will decrease while the stock of the target will increase. Again, this phenomenon is explainable by the theory that management feels that the acquirer's stock is overvalued while the stock of the target is potentially undervalued.

3.3.4 HYBRID SECURITIES

Insurance companies were some of the first significant players in the market for hybrid securities. Using the broadest definition, hybrid securities are financing instruments having both debt-like and equity-like attributes. Thus, their seniority to claims on cash flow and control are between those of pure debt and pure equity, essentially providing unsecured subordinated loans in exchange for potential equity participation.

Several types of hybrids will be discussed. While they vary in their seniority, claims on assets, cost, tax benefits, capital treatment, and periodic payment requirements, they tend to have the common purpose of financing growth and acquisition goals.

3.3.4.1 Preferred Stock

In the beginning of debt-equity hybrids (the 1830s, as reported by Evans[11]), there was preferred stock. It was first issued in the transport sector and later by utilities and financial services companies. Like debt, preferred stocks have a face amount or "par" value, with a provision to make periodic payments (dividends) typically at a fixed rate. They may include a call option allowing the issuer to redeem the offering after an initial period, usually five years. Like equity, preferred stocks' claim on earnings and assets is subordinated to debt holder claims. The dividend may be deferred or not paid at all. However, most issues require that all cumulative preferred dividends be paid before any dividends on common stock are paid. Most importantly, preferred stock does not confer voting rights on shareholders.

Use of preferred securities in acquisition financing is more likely to occur with medium to large acquirers generating positive net cash flows consistently, because investors view preferred securities as income-producing securities. Advantages for the acquirer issuing preferred securities include attracting a new type of investor while not diluting control of existing equity-holders. Preferred securities offer some flexibility in cash management since dividends may be deferred without the acquirer being forced into bankruptcy. However, deferring payments is not a step to be taken lightly because it sends strong signals to the marketplace and will harm a firm's ability to raise capital in the future and raise its cost. Depending on the structure of the contract, this may confer additional rights upon preferred stockholders, including voting rights.

3.3.4.2 Trust Preferreds

Trust preferreds, whether single issuances or pooled vehicles, are largely confined to financial institutions like banks and insurance companies. Single issuer trust preferreds became prevalent in the early 1990s and are favored by larger companies with good credit. Pooled vehicles extend the availability of the structure to smaller issuers.

Trust preferreds are similar to preferred stock with some notable exceptions. The claims of trust preferred shareholders are senior to those of preferred stock owners. For issuers of trust preferreds, the net result is an improvement to both the balance sheet through the creation of equity capital and the income statement through tax savings (debt service on trust preferreds is tax deductible).

[11]Evans, G.H., "The Early History of Preferred Stock in the United States," *American Economic Review* (1929).

SUMMARY BENEFITS OF POOLED TRUST PREFERRED VEHICLES

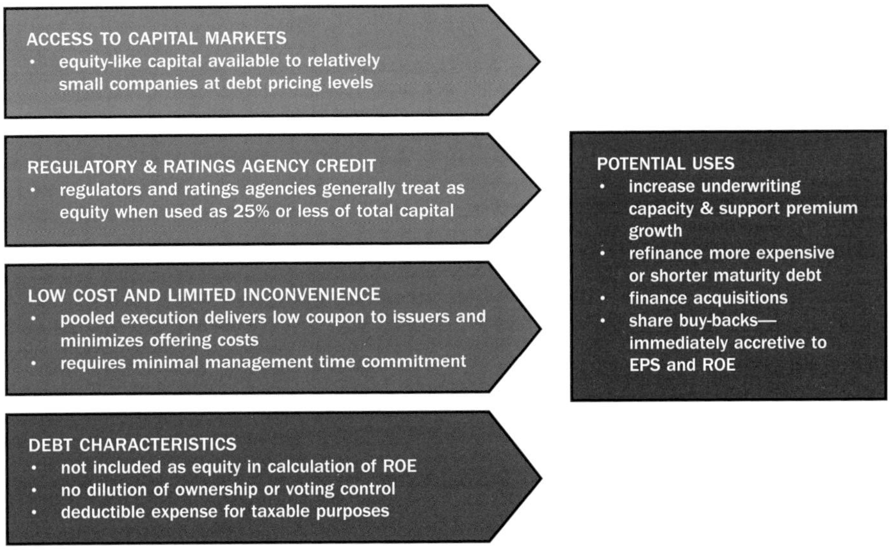

FIGURE 3.1

To achieve these financial benefits, the issuer, rather than offering preferred stock directly, creates a trust. Simultaneously, the trust issues preferred shares to capital providers and the issuing entity provides subordinated debt to the trust. The trust has raised equity, thus improving the balance sheet. Since interest payments are deductible but dividends are not, the operating company deducts the interest payments it makes to the trust, thus improving net income.

Since substantial benefits arise from tax deductibility of interest payments and funds being treated as capital instead of debt, trust preferreds issuers must monitor potential regulatory and accounting changes within the financial services industry. For example, a change to FASB's Interpretation Note 46 (FIN 46) requiring banks' special purpose entities to be included on an operating company's balance sheet may result in trust preferreds being disqualified as available capital, which would affect capital ratios.

3.3.4.3 Convertible Securities

Debt instruments that contain a provision to convert into common equity shares of the issuer have existed since the 1850s. Convertible securities can be either debt and interest-based or preferred stock and dividend-based. The securities agreement specifies a conversion ratio and premium at which a unit of the convertible changes to equity.

Convertibles provide rights to the investor and issuer. The investor has the right to convert the security (debt or preferred stock) to straight equity by paying the conversion price. The issuer has the right to call the offering, leading to the convertible being either redeemed by the issuer or converted by the investor. Some offerings may include a requirement to convert ("mandatory convertible").

Convertibles offer flexibility in design ranging from high coupon, high conversion premium (more debt-like, with greater debt burden and less earnings per share dilution effect) to low or zero coupon-low conversion premium (more equity-like). Convertibles are senior to common stock and junior to straight debt. Within convertibles, the more debt-like the offering, the higher the seniority. Thus, seniority is higher for convertible bonds over convertible preferreds, higher coupon versus lower coupon, and voluntary versus mandatory conversions.

Coupons and dividends on convertibles are lower than their non-convertible counterparts since convertibles provide upside potential from the underlying common stock.

Accounting treatment is more complex for convertibles due to rules for per share calculations and procedures that vary by type of convertible and nature of conversion, such as exercise by convertible holder, retirement by issuer, or conversion induced by issuer. Rating agencies differ in their classification of the various hybrids as debt or equity and have developed their own rules for evaluating convertibles and other hybrids. These rules are updated as new hybrids are created.

SIDE NOTE

EVALUATING HYBRID SECURITIES

Standard & Poor's outlined its methodology for evaluating hybrid securities issued by holding companies. S&P considers as equity those hybrids that:

(1) have maturities of 20 years or longer, or 10 to 20 years remaining to maturity based on aggressiveness of capital structure to current ratings
(2) are subordinated in claims to debt interest and principal and policyholder obligations
(3) will not force the issuer into receivership if it defaults on interest, dividends, or principal repayment
(4) are unlikely to be redeemed or refinanced with debt
(5) would maintain the equity component within 15% of total capital.

Certain preferred and hybrid securities that are mandatorily convertible to common stock within three years are considered outside of this 15% limit. However, they depress fixed-charge coverage until they convert because the issuer must pay preferred stock dividends on the securities.[12]

Convertibles tend to be issued at times when the overall market is exhibiting and/or expected to exhibit falling interest rates, rising equity valuations, and higher market volatility since the embedded option has greater value.

Convertibles offer several potential advantages to an acquirer. First, convertibles provide substantial flexibility in structure, meeting current and future financing needs by combining options and rights features. Second, the characteristics of a particular convertible offering may attract a new group of investors, thus expanding the investor base. Third, current investor control and rights are protected until a conversion occurs, at which time current investor control would be diluted. Fourth, coupon and dividend payments are likely to be lower than their non-convertible counterpart instruments. Fifth, to the extent conversion occurs, the borrower will not have to repay the capital raised.

Although convertibles offer several advantages, they are not without their drawbacks. First, convertibles have greater pricing and valuation complexity relative to other market securities, and the accounting treatment may distort economic results. Second, treatment of convertibles as debt or equity may differ from one rating agency to the next. Finally, convertibles impact the common stock price due to the anticipated dilution resulting from conversion.

3.3.4.4 Surplus Notes

Surplus notes are unique debt securities issued by U.S. insurance companies.[13] Capital notes are similar and are issued by banks as well as insurers. The two forms of notes are similar in

[12] Adapted from "Insurance Holding Company Analysis: Evaluating Debt, Hybrid, and Equity Instruments," Mark Puccia and Jacob Schlanger, March 1999. From the S&P Web site.

[13] In fact, they are the only debt-like security that can be offered by an insurance company (as opposed to a holding company) in the United States.

many respects including claim seniority being subordinate to all debt holders. The main difference occurs with the need for regulator approval of principal and interest payments. For surplus notes, regulatory approval is often required before a payment can be made. For capital notes, approval is usually not required if certain surplus level conditions are met. Other differences include minimum maturity (none for surplus notes and five years for capital notes) and statutory accounting treatment (capital notes do not count as statutory surplus).

Prior to the introduction of NAIC risk-based capital requirements in 1993, surplus notes were typically issued by relatively lower-rated companies. Since 1993, issuers have included large, highly rated insurers. Capital notes were first authorized for issue in 1996 by New York state regulators. The notes were developed so mutual insurers could benefit as banks and stock insurers had with trust preferreds. Specifically, the principal amount raised counted towards meeting the risk-based capital requirement, the interest expense was tax deductible, and these notes enjoyed a lower cost of capital versus straight equity.

The number of new issues of these notes declined dramatically in their first decade as several mutual insurers underwent reorganizations through either mutual holding company conversions or demutualizations. If such notes are being considered to finance an anticipated acquisition, significant lead time for regulatory approval at issuance is needed. While regulatory constraints limit the potential market for these securities, significant offerings have been floated in support of acquisitions, particularly by mutual companies whose sources of funds are limited.

3.4 M&A FINANCING CONSIDERATIONS

As discussed in Chapter 2, some companies have acquisitions incorporated as part of their strategic plan. For these "serial acquirers," management may earmark funds for acquisitions during the regular capital planning process or have contingency plans in place to quickly raise capital from existing relationships through public markets or private placements should an opportunity arise.

For other companies, capital must typically be raised for a deal of any significance. For those companies that have an existing track record and credibility in the marketplace, raising the capital necessary to fund a well-received deal is, while time consuming, a relatively straightforward process. However, for companies unaccustomed to raising capital, issuing securities while coping with the stress of an acquisition may prove to be an extraordinary strain on management resources.

3.4.1 GENERAL FINANCING CONSIDERATIONS

This section presents some of the general considerations in approaching financing decisions, structuring deal finance, and insurance-specific issues and constraints.

3.4.1.1 Economic Cycle

An entity in need of financing must start by assessing the state of the capital markets, which may be done independently or with the assistance of its financial advisor.

Capital markets are in a constant state of flux as thousands of buyers and sellers jockey for position, each searching for an edge. Capital may be in abundance or in tight supply. Spreads and relative costs among markets, sectors, and instruments are constantly changing as each new piece of information from the latest IPO, deal, bankruptcy, scandal, and regulatory action (enacted or proposed) is incorporated into prices. Certain financing instruments may or may not be available at an affordable price. Appetite for risk and spreads charged may be different between public and private markets.

These considerations are directly influenced by the economic cycle. The economic cycle refers to regular increases in economic activity, with rising output and employment, followed by a decrease in economic activity, with falling output and rising unemployment. The cycle is presumably managed, or at least influenced, by monetary policy. This in turn impacts price and availability of funds for capital investment and deal making.

In times of growth anticipated beyond that desired, the Federal Reserve (U.S. central bank) tends to tighten the money supply by increasing the interest rate financial institutions pay to borrow funds from the Federal Reserve. This has a ripple effect on other financing instruments, raising costs and reducing capital investment. Conversely, in times of slower growth or recession, the Federal Reserve tends to reduce interest rates to stimulate borrowing and capital investment.

In times of low growth, debt becomes more appealing relative to other points in the economic cycle. This is the point at which the burden of debt service is least attractive. As the economy enters a growth phase, the stock market typically increases, which may allow companies to raise funds at a lower cost through issuance of additional shares of common stock.

CRYPT 3.4

Buy Low, Sell High, But Make Sure You Sell

One March many years ago, with our parent company's stock trading about $20 per share, we were "in play" when we found out that another company had offered to buy all shares at $25. Although our board rejected that offer as inadequate, and the offering company did not counter, other bidders soon appeared on the horizon.

By July our board had accepted an offer of $47 per share from another bidder. That company began sending various key people to our company to go over the operation, personnel, products, procedures, and transition with a fine-tooth comb. Of course, while we had the additional headache of having to deal with this, we also had to continue doing our regular jobs.

One day in October, I was in the chief financial officer's office discussing some accounting issues. We finished the business at hand, and as I rose to leave, he began an unrelated conversation that went something like:

He: *"What are you doing about your options?"*
I: *"Selling them as fast as they vest. What about you?"*
He: *"The same."*
I: *"Just curious, but why do you ask?"*
He: *"Well, in talking to the other officers [of our subsidiary], they don't seem to be selling anything."*
I: *"So why are we selling and they aren't?"*

Pause. Another pause. Perhaps he was thinking what I was thinking—that each of us had tried to substitute facts for appearances and demonstrations for impressions in analyzing the other company's financial statements and observing what was happening in the economy and the financial markets. It looked like financing the deal would be a major stretch on the acquiring company's resources. Then both of us, almost simultaneously, said, "THIS DEAL ISN'T GOING THROUGH!"

The stock had gone up to a high around $45. I got out at $41, as had my boss.

Four weeks later, the deal collapsed. Interest rates had risen; the additional cost of financing (they were borrowing money to finance the buyout) caused the deal to collapse. The stock price fell back to $25. Within three months my boss and I had new jobs at other companies, not to mention the $41 per share that we pocketed.

3.4.1.2 Cost of Funds

The cost of financing is, naturally, a major consideration in capital decisions. Firms in stronger financial condition with lower anticipated fluctuations in earnings have more options and a lower cost of capital. Firms in weaker financial condition have fewer choices and ultimately a higher cost of funds.

For debt, the term of funding sought will affect the rate, form, and amount of funding offered as well as the market of potential capital suppliers. Generally, the shorter the term, the lower the cost of financing. For equity, there is no ongoing cost other than administration because dividends are not considered debt service per se (although investors typically do have implicit expectations).

There is far more to take into consideration in determining cost of funds than just the effective rate. Issuing securities incurs substantial transaction costs. In evaluating the total cost of various financing alternatives, registration fees, expenses paid to external parties, tax effects, impact on required capital, and the value of any options must be considered in addition to debt service. Economy of scale is an important driver. As the size of an issue goes up, costs as a percent of capital raised go down.

The expected present value of costs for different financing alternatives can then be compared in order to calculate the quantitative piece of the puzzle. But much more goes into financing decisions. Qualitative elements, such as time spent by management and staff, dilution of control, relationships with capital providers, and the opportunity cost of other projects that could be undertaken, must also be factored into the decision-making process.

3.4.1.3 Liquidity

Liquidity is an important element for any entity, in particular for insurers where a liquidity crisis can activate change of control provisions or regulatory triggers, jeopardizing interests of bondholders and shareholders alike. Acquisition activity adds another layer of uncertainty to liquidity needs and potential for volatility. If the current or anticipated post-acquisition liquidity position is less than desired, it may be addressed via the amount and form of financing chosen. In estimating liquidity needs for an acquisition, the buyer should be careful not to overlook potentially significant current items such as fees, deposits, professional service costs, and travel expenses.

An acquisition may lead to unanticipated outflows exceeding best estimates. Depending on the drivers, acquisitions may cause uncertainty among policyholders and agents alike. Insurance agents, uncertain about their status within the proposed post-acquisition entity, may switch their clients to another insurer, causing an increase in surrenders and reserve outflows. Similarly, policyholders concerned about the future performance of their policies may exercise their contractual rights to non-forfeiture options in greater numbers by surrendering or exchanging with another company. Should such actions persist for an extended period of time or are of significant magnitude, a liquidity crisis or "run on the bank" situation may unfold.

3.4.2 DEAL FINANCING CONSIDERATIONS

There are basically only two ways to pay for a deal (cash or stock) and only two ways to structure a purchase (company purchase or asset purchase). The deal financing and deal structure need not be related. A cash deal can be financed by the acquirer using any combination of retained earnings, debt, or equity. Asset purchases are typically handled in cash, whereas a company purchase can be executed using cash or stock. Deal structure and taxation implications are discussed in greater detail in Chapter 7.

3.4.2.1 *Seller Financing Considerations*

The form of the buyer's offer is a fundamental concern of the seller's board. Although there are exceptions, the typical offer consists of cash, the buyer's stock, or some mixture of cash and stock. The more competitive the auction, the more creative the components will become as bidders vie to sweeten the offer.

The structure of the offer may be more important to the seller than the absolute magnitude of the consideration. For example, if the selling shareholders are interested in cashing out and are prepared to incur a taxable event, a cash consideration is preferable. If, on the other hand, the selling shareholders view the buyer's stock as an attractive investment and wish to defer a taxable event, then the majority of the consideration offered should be in the form of the buyer's stock.[14]

The time needed to obtain the financing and to put the proceeds to work can be critical. In assessing acquisition offers, sellers will take into consideration the buyer's ability to close the transaction efficiently, including having sufficient financial resources. Once the seller has reached the stage of evaluating acquisition proposals that are relatively close in value, the seller will want to guarantee a smooth closing and will pass on buyers without sufficient access to capital.

CRYPT 3.5

What's In Your Wallet?

The 1980s were a wild time for corporate America. It was a time of corporate transactions involving equities, subordinated debt, and leveraged buy-outs. Through the '80s, however, although many mega-transactions were undertaken there were no major insurance company transactions that were anything like the leveraged buy-outs occurring in corporate America. Those were the times of Drexel, Milken, and RJR Nabisco.

Near the end of the decade, one of the giant Hartford companies indicated an interest in divesting of one of its major lines of business, individual life insurance. A likely price for this divestiture was going to be significantly over $500 million. Not too long after the prospective divestiture became public, investment bankers distributed various appraisal books for potential buyers interested in looking at the property. Industry response was not overwhelming; it seemed obvious that the handful that could write a check were not actively bidding.

So it seemed that people who might not have the ability to write a $500 million check but could raise the money could be well positioned to move forward. I suddenly developed a strong interest in this transaction.

I did recognize that there was a major negative factor with this transaction, which was the fact that my partners and I together would be hard pressed to raise even a fraction of the equity that was going to be needed to complete the transaction. In addition, this acquisition was in an industry where up until now no major leveraged buy-out had ever occurred.

Having virtually no money and needing to raise over half of a billion dollars to have any hope of succeeding, it seemed that the first place that would be a source of funds for this acquisition would be bank loans. After approaching several banks, we found out two things. First, it is hard to get money from banks. Second, insurance industry expertise was not the bank's strong suit. The banks' corporate finance areas were not aggressive participants in leveraged insurance transactions. After further discussion, it became clear that we would have to produce significantly more equity than we were considering (which was less than 1%). If we could raise substantially more equity, it appeared that we might be able to borrow, in the

---

[14] The percentage of consideration in stock that must be offered to effectuate an "A"—or tax free—transaction has changed over time. The rule of thumb is still that the majority of the consideration must be in stock. Typically, however, an individual shareholder is given the option of selecting whether to receive 100% stock or 100% cash, subject to limitations on aggregate stock or cash consideration. The bottom line is that one shareholder elects to receive only stock and another elects to receive cash and stock. This does not in any way obviate the tax-free status of the stock swap.

form of senior debt, 60-75% of the purchase price.

The next step was to find an additional unrelated source of money that could help us in our negotiations with the bank. We attempted to interest some insurance companies in participating with us in this acquisition. Although these were fairly substantial companies, they were not in a position to write a check for $500 million. However, we were able to interest at least a couple of insurance companies in the transaction. Eventually one committed to an interest in going forward with us. This company agreed to provide some preferred stock, which allowed us to significantly increase the total equity, including preferred, by several thousand percent.

Finally, in the best tradition of leveraged buy-outs in the 1980s, I was able to develop a method to use money from the target company itself.

When we finally tallied everything, we had raised approximately $550 million. Thus far, we were unaware of any other players with sources of capital placing a competing bid. We demonstrated to the bank that we now had a substantial amount of total equity. Hopefully this would allow us to go forward. Over the next several weeks we were able to solidify our relationship with our insurance company partner. The bank partner remained excited about doing the deal. We had structured the transaction in such a way that the risks to the bank were minimal while the opportunity to do well on their investment was not diminished. The small amount of common equity deal seemed not to be an issue. It looked like there was a reasonable chance that a purchase price of between $500 million and $550 million would allow us to make this transaction with less than five million dollars of common stock.

Sometime prior to the expected time for decision by the owner, I was invited to an outing by our bank partner. During the time of this outing we expected to hear the final decision regarding the target company. During the course of this golf outing, we would take a break and call the office to see where we stood.

Well into the day, a bombshell occurred. Another group had made an offer of more than $100 million in excess of our offer. We quickly compared what we had presented to what the other offer proposed. There was no sound way to equal, let alone exceed, the rival offer. We were very disheartened.

We discussed our options with our bank and our insurance company partners. We realized that we would not be able to counter with a more attractive offer. We were still licking our wounds when, some weeks later, we found that the rival group didn't close the deal. Why? They didn't have the money.

We could have doubled our offer if we didn't have to have any money. We were soon too busy with other opportunities to re-enter the fray. Next time we should find out what's in their wallet.

3.4.2.2 Buyer Financing Considerations

A buyer typically undertakes a high level analysis to determine what mix of consideration will enable it to offer the most competitive bid at the lowest cost. This analysis entails a review of the current cash position, the perceived value of the buyer's stock vs. the target's, available capital-raising alternatives, and the associated costs and timing issues. The buyer should also engage the seller in a dialogue as to the seller's willingness to help finance the deal by accepting notes, non-competes, and employment contracts as part of the purchase price.

If a prospective bidder lacks available cash (or stock currency) to make an acquisition, it must secure acquisition financing. Acquisition financing is simply a capital-raising event with the proceeds designated for use in the transaction. As with any project, acquisition financing can involve issuing equity, debt, or hybrid securities in either the private or the public markets.

The magnitude of the financing for the acquisition may materially alter the buyer's capital structure. It may result in too heavy a weighting of one type of capital, perhaps exceeding absolute or capital ratio limits set by the buyer's internal controls or as set by covenants in existing financing arrangements. A purchase contemplated to be financed by debt might exceed corporate debt limits, requiring board approval to exceed these limits. It is important to determine any restrictions or limitations on the type of financing as early as possible so that alternative financing instruments can be considered.

3.4.2.3 Debt Financing

The amount of debt that can finance an acquisition depends in large part on the projected cash flow of the combined company. Debt is typically less costly than equity because debt payments are tax deductible for the company. Debt, however, is temporary financing (i.e., it needs to be paid back), and the regular coupon payments a company must make, in good times and bad, can limit operational flexibility and, in the worst case, lead to default and bankruptcy. Large amounts of debt are more appropriate for mature companies with stable cash flows.

3.4.2.4 Equity Financing

Equity is more expensive than debt because it is riskier. Equity owners merely have a claim to the residual value of a company's cash flows after interest on debt and taxes have been paid. Acquisitions that have unstable cash flows, require capital for continued growth, or compete in turbulent industries often require a greater amount of equity financing.

Equity provides more financial flexibility because, unlike debt, it does not require scheduled payments. However, financing an acquisition with equity requires relinquishing some amount of ownership in the combined company. Additionally, private equity investors will often insist on some amount of representation on the board of directors. Private equity investors can take the form of leveraged buy-out funds, venture capital funds, or corporations.

3.4.2.5 Stock Swap

It is also possible to use the acquirer's stock to purchase all or some of the shares of the target. The stock of the buyer is either treasury stock (issued but not outstanding, typically bought back from the open market through a share repurchase program) or newly issued shares. Regardless of which option is used, the buyer typically has to file a registration statement because the stock swap is treated as a sale under Section T of the Securities Act of 1933.

Using stock as currency is common among companies whose stock is publicly traded. As discussed further in Chapter 7, stock transactions have tax advantages over cash. A stock swap is more difficult in private transactions because the stock is illiquid. However, if the owner of the target would like to retain a stake in the combined company, then exchanging shares is a sensible solution.

If the market is valuing the acquiring company higher than its industry and peers, its stock will have a higher P/E ratio. This premium in the market, due to perceived management expertise and expectations about future earnings, enables highly valued companies to acquire companies with lower multiples using a cheaper source of financing: stock currency.

Stock currency is an appropriate and instructive metaphor. Currency prices are set based on trading in open markets. Relative values of currencies fluctuate based on various external factors and are subject to intense speculation. Like countries attempting to support their currencies, companies may step in to purchase outstanding shares to prop up share prices or establish a war chest when they think it is a good investment to buy low and hold the stock in their treasury to reissue when the price is higher.

A stock swap often funds some portion of the purchase price in rollup acquisition strategy.[15] Financing a rollup strategy usually requires an initial equity infusion in the acquirer to position it for rapid growth. Subsequent acquisitions are then financed largely with stock currency, where stock in the combined company is used to execute the purchase. Many insurance company rollups (such as Conseco, ICH, and Penncorp) have failed to produce satisfactory results.

[15] Purchasing multiple companies as part of a consolidation process.

The Road Not Taken

CRYPT 3.6

*It's good to be known in the M&A world. But a major frustration is how difficult it is to get resumé credit for all the acquisitions that you **don't** do.*

When someone is hot to trot to make an acquisition and your price is so far from that of the leading bidder, your analysis is questioned. It's sometimes tough to stand up enough for your belief in your work, to keep a silly bid from being submitted. When I say tough, I don't mean that personal character strength is an issue, but when you look at the fact you are going up against so many others at once, you almost need to have a legal power of persuasion as well as financial analytical skills. But prevailing in these arguments is well worth it in the long run. However, five years later, when that winning bidder goes bankrupt, you don't get the "you were right" phone call from your co-workers. It was so bizarre, using overvalued stock for currency (the more overvalued stock being used to buy merely overvalued stock).

These incidents certainly add to one's experience in the M&A realm, but they don't get you much resumé credit since it's not what you did and succeeded at; it's what you didn't do, only to be proven successful much later, and by then, you are the only one who remembers or cares to talk about it.

In order to complete a stock swap, a value must be placed on the equity of both companies, and share prices must be determined. The financial advisor will be able to provide guidance in valuing both companies and developing a combined pro forma.

A stock swap is a valuable tool for retaining the involvement and expertise of the target's owner, if that is desired. If the owner is active in managing the target's operations, and his or her expertise is important to the success of the combined operation, offering stock in the combined company will ensure that the interests of the two parties are aligned.

3.4.3 INSURANCE-SPECIFIC CONSIDERATIONS

The insurance industry has a number of unique financing considerations. Key items for a potential acquirer to assess early on in the process are the post-transaction capital structure needed to satisfy statutory required capital and rating agency requirements for the combined entity.

3.4.3.1 Required Capital

Regulators impose capital requirements on the insurance industry to ensure solvency and protect policyholders' interests. Since their inception, state insurance commissioners have regulated for solvency, as noted by Patterson in 1927.[16]

The insurance solvency regime in the United States has evolved over time and consists of (1) early detection, (2) prompt action, and (3) guaranty funds. In 1993, 1994, and 1998, the NAIC introduced major regulatory changes with RBC requirements for life, property & casualty, and health lines of business, respectively. Early detection was enhanced and quantified by formulas. Prompt action was clarified for the regulators, specifying when to act and what action to take, eliminating potential loopholes that had troubled the system.

Having sufficient RBC implies having a large enough capital base to support the insurance, investment, and operational risks. For life insurers, an RBC ratio of at least 200% of the authorized control level must be maintained. Below that level a company must submit to its regulatory authority (the state insurance commissioner) a plan for increasing its RBC to at least 200%. If the company's RBC falls to 150% of the authorized control level, regulatory action is required, and if the RBC falls to 70%, regulatory action is mandatory. The formula itself is reviewed regularly by the NAIC and is updated periodically.

---

16 Patterson, Edwin W., *The Insurance Commissioner in the United States, A Study in Administrative Law and Practice*, Cambridge, MA: Harvard University Press, 1927.

3.4.3.2 *Rating Agency Implications*

Debt ratings and ratings of claims-paying ability by independent, private ratings agencies are critical to an insurance entity. These firms provide easily digested information to the public on the financial health of an organization in the form of a letter grade. Investor services firms such as Fitch, Moody's, and Standard & Poor's cover large swaths of financial markets. Due to its specialized nature, the insurance industry has dedicated agencies such as A. M. Best that focus solely on insurers.

Insurance industry participants, from capital suppliers to distributors to customers, will look to ratings in deciding whether to enter into a relationship with a firm. Targets and regulators will look to the ratings in assessing proposed acquisition offers. A downgrade or even the specter of one can be enough to shut down access to certain capital markets or start a run on the bank. Consequently, management takes these players and their views seriously. Rating agencies' views may differ, so it is common for an acquirer to meet with different rating agencies before finalizing a deal and its financing.

An investment banking firm developed guidance for insurance holding company optimal capital structures, reproduced in Figure 3.2 below, based on the Standard & Poor's methodology.

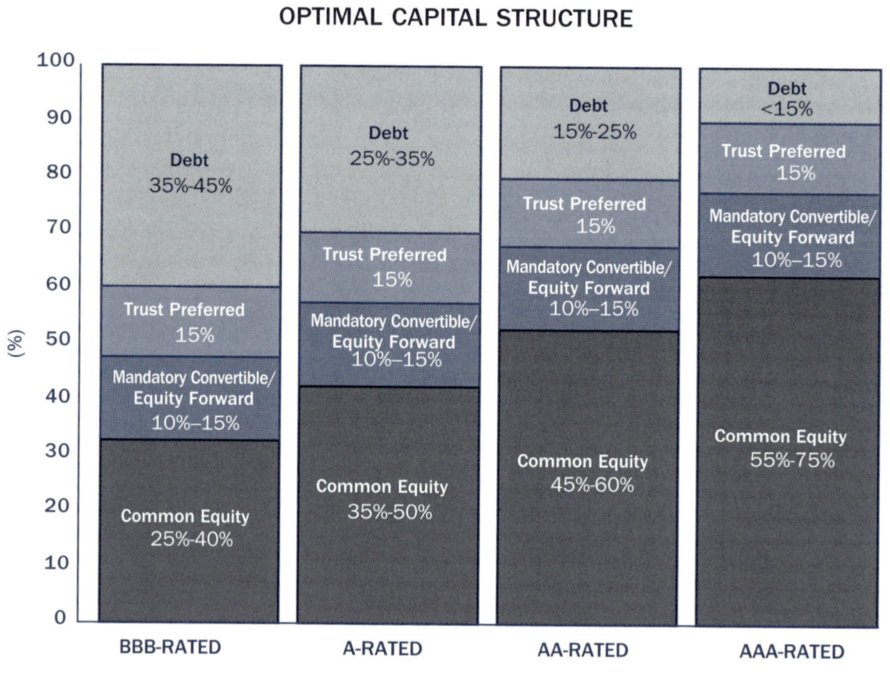

FIGURE 3.2 **Note:** Holding company senior debt ratings

3.4.3.3 *Holding Companies*

One manner in which capital structure issues may be resolved is through the use of a holding company structure. Holding companies permit greater financing and investment flexibility and reduce regulatory control over the group's non-insurance activities.

Holding companies may raise funds (usually in the form of debt) and pass the proceeds to a downstream operating company (usually in the form of equity). The operating company in turn needs to generate cash to repay the debt. Debt service typically takes the form of dividends or management fees to the parent. Rules for up-streamed dividends are determined by state law, but are typically limited in any calendar year to the higher of the operating company's prior year statutory earnings or 10% of surplus unless regulator approval is obtained.

Stat, GAAP... There Is A Difference

One acquired company was domiciled in a state with an insurance department that was very sensitive to paying upstream dividends to a parent.

When the new purchaser visited the department he was asked about its intentions. The reply was, "No more than 50% of earnings." The department was relieved because it understood this to mean that maximum stockholder dividends would be 50% of statutory earnings.

However, the acquirer's intent was to take out 50% of GAAP earnings, which were running considerably above statutory. The department never did detect it.

CRYPT 3.7

An acquirer may be either the holding company or an insurance operating entity, each of which has its own capital structure. Ratings agencies review their existing assessments of insurance operating companies in light of the financing activity with any affiliated insurance holding companies. Too much debt at the holding company level will at some point put downward pressure on the ratings of insurance subsidiaries.

Think Ahead

Many large, established companies making acquisitions were very bureaucratic. Often, some departments did not communicate with each other.

In one case, the acquirer's treasury department told the new insurance subsidiary that the parent needed $25 million of upstream dividends payable over the next five years. The subsidiary said we can do this. And they did.

However, what was overlooked was that investment income lost to the subsidiary due to these cash dividends made it impossible for them to reach their earnings targets—the same targets that the parent's board of directors relied on as a basis for making the purchase.

CRYPT 3.8

3.4.3.4 Mutual Companies

The corporate legal structure may limit the universe of available financing vehicles. For example, if the acquirer is a mutual insurance company, issuance of common stock is not an option. However, a mutual insurance company has alternatives. First, the mutual company itself may be able to issue surplus notes or capital notes. Second, if the mutual company is owned by a holding company, the funding needed may be raised by the holding company in the desired form, then provided to the mutual company in the form of debt. Third, a mutual company may form downstream holding companies.

3.4.3.5 Regulatory Requirements

In addition to the normal regulatory approval process associated with the SEC and federal antitrust laws, insurers must get approval from state regulators. The state's role is to protect the interests of the policyholder; hence, an emphasis is placed on solvency. State regulators may play an active role in the process and are not immune to political pressure, so public relations efforts and an open line of communication with regulators in the state of both the buyer and the seller are advisable.

Because of the regulatory environment and the need to protect the interests of policyholders, insurance company debt is far more restricted in liquidity and thus attracts less market interest than most corporate debt. Insurance companies are by far net providers of capital and rely more on retained earnings and equity than debt to finance growth.

3.5 SUMMARY

In many respects, an acquisition is no different than any other capital investment. Management picks a project that meets its strategic and financial objectives and then finds a way to fund that project. If the company does not have enough retained earnings, it will have to enter the capital markets and convince investors to entrust their capital with it by sharing vision and opening books. Depending on what potential investors see, they may be willing to provide their capital, but at a cost. Whether the investments on either side of this equation prove to be wise will play out over time in the capital markets.

CHAPTER FOUR

VALUATION TECHNIQUES

4.1 INTRODUCTION: VALUATION TECHNIQUES FOR INSURANCE M&A

In any M&A transaction, agreeing on the value of the selling company's stock or assets is typically the most challenging hurdle to overcome. The success or failure of a potential transaction hinges on whether both the buyer and the seller can agree upon a price. The buyer needs to be willing to pay the same price that the seller, and a majority of its shareholders, would be willing to accept in return for relinquishing control over the selling entity.

Valuing the common stock or the assets of a company is a difficult and inherently subjective process that is heavily dependent upon assumptions. The main valuation challenge is capturing the value of the selling company as a "going concern." A going concern is a self-sustaining company, a viable business enterprise that is worth more than the sum of its parts. A selling company is generally not purchased for its assets per se, but for the ability of those assets to generate a cash flow stream, ideally in perpetuity. If a company is being sold as a runoff business, it is generally worth less than it would be as a going concern.

A going concern valuation captures the value of certain intangible assets that are not reflected on the seller's balance sheet. Intangibles might include distribution relationships, geographic reach, customer loyalty, and market perception. As such, the financial advisors' job for both the buyer and the seller is to calculate a reasonable range of values within which a final price can ultimately be agreed upon by the two sides in the transaction. That agreed-to price is ultimately what the company is worth at that moment.

Mergers and acquisitions of insurance companies have typically involved some form of actuarial analysis due to the unique aspects of the insurance industry. In particular:

1) Insurance liabilities can extend over a very long period of time.
2) Insurance liabilities generally involve a great deal of uncertainty, requiring the application of actuarial techniques.
3) Statutory accounting and capital requirements form a unique set of rules governing the distributable earnings from an insurance company.

This chapter will address the approaches commonly used to value insurance companies. While it is generally written from the seller's perspective, most of the issues are applicable to a buyer's due diligence and certain items apply specifically to potential buyers. An extensive discussion of approaches to due diligence undertaken by potential buyers is provided in Chapter 5.

The majority of the chapter will focus on actuarial appraisals. The chapter will address the underlying theory for actuarial appraisals and, due to the importance of the underlying assumptions to appraisal results, will provide a fair amount of detail on the key assumptions and the bases for developing them. The assumptions are discussed at a general level first, in the broad categories of (1) mortality, (2) morbidity, (3) persistency, (4) investment returns and spread, (5) operating expenses, (6) determination of the appropriate discount rate, (7) cost of capital, and (8) taxes. The development of the three components of an actuarial appraisal value is described next: (1) adjusted book value, (2) value of existing business, and (3) value of future business. Specific issues related to lines of business are covered for (1) individual life and annuity business, (2) health and group life products, and (3) property and casualty (P&C) lines. A section is also included for specific issues related to a transaction structured as reinsurance instead of a company acquisition.

Before delving into the detailed discussion of appraisal methodologies and assumptions, the chapter will cover approaches typically used by investment bankers and other financial advisors that focus on market metrics, comparability of a given company to its peers, and recent M&A transactions. A list of major transactions (over $500 million purchase price) in the insurance industry is included at the end of the chapter.

4.2 GENERAL VALUATION TECHNIQUES

Value is, of course, in the eye of the beholder. There are many different ways to arrive at a company's reasonable value. At the simplest is a meeting of the minds culminating with a handshake. At the most complex is a valuation with the intricacies of a full-blown actuarial appraisal. In the remainder of this section, some of the techniques and rules of thumb in between these two extremes are presented.

4.2.1 INSURANCE COMPANY VALUATIONS

The task of valuing an insurance company is as much art as it is science. As a general matter, valuing an insurance company is more complicated than valuing companies in other sectors. The skill set required to gather, parse, and accurately analyze the relevant data is highly specialized. Given the complexities of the sector, a purely mechanical valuation is of limited utility. Because of the various financial, accounting, and regulatory factors unique to the industry, it is not possible to accurately value an insurance company without possessing an understanding of its particular dynamics. Some of the various challenges in valuing the industry sector include:

- long duration of liabilities (particularly for life insurance companies)
- the sensitivity to interest rate fluctuations and the performance of capital markets
- the inherently subjective and dynamic art of loss reserving
- the cyclical nature of P&C insurance and reinsurance
- the impact of reinsurance recoverables
- the challenges associated with non-market competitors (state funds and mutuals)
- the vicissitudes of state-by-state and occasional federal regulations
- the impact of statutory accounting on operational decision-making
- the influence of ratings agencies.

A variety of other factors unique to the sector also combine to make valuing an insurance company a treacherous and difficult job.

Nevertheless, with a few very important exceptions, the generic valuation techniques employed by investment bankers and other financial advisors to value an insurance company are typically analogous to the techniques used to value companies outside the industry.

4.2.2 VALUATION TECHNIQUES

In calculating the range of values of a selling company's common equity, financial advisors rely on a variety of valuation techniques. Generally, bankers consider the financial and stock market data of the seller compared to the same data for other similar, publicly traded companies, the financial terms of certain other business combinations and other transactions that have been effected or announced, and the seller's projected cash flows as a measure of its value.

In this regard, the three basic analytical tools of investment bankers are comparable company analysis, comparable transaction analysis, and discounted cash flow analysis. These are technical analyses informed by the qualitative judgments of the bankers as to the significance and relevance of each analysis and factor considered. Accordingly, the analyses must be considered as a whole. Selecting only portions of its analyses and factors without considering all assumptions could create a misleading or incomplete view of the processes underlying the analyses. Each of these methodologies will be explained in more detail.

In order to calculate a meaningful valuation range using these techniques, the financial advisors need to obtain (or create) a set of detailed financial projections for the seller. These projections are usually calculated and used by management to target specific goals for company performance in the future. The projections are dependent on numerous variables and assumptions, which are inherently uncertain, including factors related to general economic and competitive conditions. The selling company does not publicly disclose internal management projections of the type provided to its board of directors in connection with the review of a possible merger.

In most cases, management will provide the financial advisors with a "base case" forecast for that company on a stand-alone basis. It is also common for company management to develop certain adjustments to the base case forecast, typically to reflect a more optimistic or aggressive assessment of future financial results. In addition, adjustments are made to reported financials to more accurately reflect the seller's "core" operating results. Operating performance reflects basic pre-tax results before extraordinary events that are not core components of the company's activities and would not be expected to occur regularly. These projections are typically prepared for budgeting purposes and are adapted by the bankers for the purposes of the valuation exercise.

Finally, the bankers must take into account the effect of the merger itself. Specifically, the bankers should take into account purchase GAAP (PGAAP) adjustments that would not be available to the seller on a stand-alone basis. Income projections on a PGAAP basis should reflect the actuarial adjustments that would result from a purchase as described in Chapter 8.

4.2.3 COMPARABLE COMPANY ANALYSIS

The first of the three techniques used to generate a range of values for a selling company is commonly referred to as comparable company analysis. In the process, the financial advisor applies certain relevant financial statistics of the selling company to the appropriate "multiples" of companies that are deemed to be comparable and for which a valuation exists (i.e., generally public companies) to generate an implied range of values.

While this process appears to be fairly simple and mechanical, the impression is misleading. Because no company used in the banker's comparison analyses is identical to the seller, an evaluation of the results of those analyses is not entirely mathematical. Rather, the analyses involve considerations and judgments concerning financial and operating characteristics and other factors that could affect the acquisition, public trading, or other values of the companies, business segments, or transactions analyzed. Since the process is ultimately used to assist in determining the value of the seller, the banker must choose a group of comparable companies.

While peer group selection is dependent on judgment and experience, there are some general guidelines that are useful to bear in mind. First, the peer group must be large enough to be statistically significant. Second, companies that are subject to the same or similar regulatory, accounting, and tax rules should be selected. These distinctions may mask profound differences in results and are typically difficult to reliably adjust. Third, if the seller is a relatively diversified company, the financial advisor would be well advised to choose a peer group that is similar to the seller's core or dominant segments even if it neglects other segments. If the seller has sufficiently detailed segment information, the financial advisor may possibly do a "sum of the parts" valuation. Finally, assuming there is a sufficient number of potentially comparable companies, the bankers should devote much of their time and effort to analyzing the operations and finances of these companies in an effort to winnow down the group to companies that are similar performers in the same or fundamentally similar lines of business.

Bankers typically evaluate the comparability of the companies on a number of different axes, including financial and operational performance. With respect to operational comparability, the advisor looks at companies that provide some or all of the same or similar products and services. The banker evaluates geographical comparability, such as where the companies are located and where they sell their products and services. The financial advisor considers other important competitive factors, such as A.M. Best's ratings or whether the companies employ captive distribution or rely on independent agents. The banker may choose to eliminate certain companies that have, for any number of reasons, drastically different operating performance than the selling company. Finally, the investment banker may add or eliminate additional companies based on their judgment and experience.

With respect to financial and market performance measures, the investment banker further refines the search by eliminating companies that are significantly larger or smaller than the seller in terms of revenue and/or market capitalization. The financial advisor may also evaluate the risk profile of the company, including financial leverage (e.g., debt-to-total capitalization), debt servicing, operating leverage (e.g., net written premium to policyholders' surplus), and reliance on reinsurance (e.g., reinsurance recoverables-to-policyholders' surplus).

If the target company is publicly traded, the bankers also examine a host of factors related to how the respective stocks trade, including relative stock price performance, average daily volume, and liquidity. While dissimilar companies on an operational basis are not included in the analysis, otherwise similar companies may also be excluded from the group of comparables if the stock prices are, for example, not a reliable indicator of valuation due to insufficient liquidity or trading interest.

Once the comparable companies are chosen, the next step is to review the range of financial, operational, and market metrics and to choose the market multiples that are most significant for the sector in question. The advisor then analyzes the data and calculates median, mean, and quartiles to capture the group's performance. Market multiples are fractions generally calculated by taking a company's stock price (as measured by the stock market or another acceptable, public measure of the value of common equity such as a price actually paid by a third party) as the numerator and an actual or estimated financial statistic as the denominator. For example, for P&C insurance companies, advisors typically analyze per share stock price to the next period's earnings multiples (forward P/E) and per share stock price to common equity per share multiples (price/book).

Importantly, book value and tangible book value multiples are given considerable weight in the financial analysis of insurance companies, unlike many other industries. The general explanation for this difference is that an insurance company's profitability is largely a function of the magnitude of the balance sheet, balance sheet risk, and balance sheet management. As a general matter, the balance sheet drives ratings, which influence distribution and risk selection and impact the amount of premium that can be written and, therefore, profitability. In addition, because insurance company earnings, and particularly P&C insurance earnings, are volatile on a quarterly basis, book value multiples are assumed to be a more reliable indicator of value on any given date. Perhaps more significantly, the GAAP earnings in a certain period may be distorted by results from prior periods, as in the case of a significant reserve adjustment. In such cases, mistakes made years earlier and long since corrected may wipe out otherwise healthy current earnings. Similarly, certain types of companies such as P&C companies that write short-tail books of business, for example, property catastrophe, may post results in the short term that are inaccurate reflections of the core earnings power of the enterprise over time.

Once these data points are collected, the data set is grouped, and the analysis identifies high and low multiple values. Using a combination of the projections and actual company earnings, the financial advisor calculates an implied value range by multiplying the relevant value by both the high and low multiple derived from the comparable company data sheet.

Once a stand-alone range of values is established, bankers typically evaluate what buyers are willing to pay over and above the seller's stand-alone value. This is typically viewed as a premium paid to seller's shareholders over and above the fair stand-alone value of the seller in exchange for control. Therefore, if similar public companies generally sold at a 20% premium to the stock's trading value, and the seller's stock is trading at $10, the bankers will factor in a change of control premium of 20% with the result that the value of the company in an M&A transaction is $12. Alternatively, the change of control premium can be viewed as the percentage that the buyer must pay above the actual trading value of the stock in order to compensate the seller for relinquishing control of the company. The financial advisor generally selects a change of control premium or a range of change of control premiums based on comparable transactions and the advisor's own experience and judgment. To take into account natural volatility in a stock, as well as to adjust for any information about an impending transaction that leaks into the market and impacts the seller's stock price preannouncement, advisors generally look at one-day and 30-day premiums, and premiums to 52-week high and 52-week average share price paid in similar transactions.

For example, if the comparable company data set indicates price-to-book value multiples ranging from a low of 1.0 times to a high of 1.5 times, the financial advisor would multiply the target company's book value by 1.0 and by 1.5, respectively, and then add a change of control premium. Thus, if the seller's GAAP book value is equal to $10 million and the change of control premium in similar transactions is 20%, the range of values calculated would be $12 million to $18 million ($10 million x 1.0 x 1.20 = $12 million and $10 million x 1.5 x 1.2 = $18 million). A similar process is performed on several other meaningful metrics (i.e., per share stock price-to-trailing 12 months net income, etc.). While each metric will generate a different range of values for the seller, there is typically sufficient overlap in ranges to produce a general range of values that captures the implied valuation suggested by the totality of the metrics.

There is a distinction between leveraged and unleveraged financial metrics. The range of values produced using "above the line" financial metrics (pre-tax financial metrics such as earnings before interest, taxes, depreciation, and amortization, or EBITDA) reflect the value of the entire enterprise, factoring in debt and free cash. On the other hand, the range of values produced using "below the line" financial metrics (after-tax financial metrics such as net income) reflect the value of the seller's common equity. This is typically the value the shareholders and board of directors are interested in understanding.

4.2.4 COMPARABLE TRANSACTION ANALYSIS

The second technique financial advisors employ to value an insurance company contemplating a change of control is the comparable transaction analysis. The financial advisor reviews certain financial data relating to relatively recent insurance merger transactions of a similar size in terms of deal value and involving companies in similar sectors, subsectors, or lines of business.

The process is analogous to comparable company analysis in certain respects. For example, the financial advisor's goal in performing a comparable transaction analysis is to ascertain what buyers of companies similar to the seller have paid in arm's length transactions. Of course, simply looking at what the buyers paid in a vacuum is of limited use. As with comparable company analysis, meaningful data is generated by examining the deal value relative to pertinent metrics. Of course, with comparable transaction analysis, the advisor must sift through the "headline" deal value and ascertain the actual price paid for the common equity and understand the structuring implications of the other deals, such as whether it is an asset or stock transaction (and whether debt is assumed, repaid, or remains with the seller), the type of consideration paid (stock or cash), the accounting treatment, tax issues, and the time value of money when the consideration is deferred. In addition, contingencies such as performance-based, post-transaction purchase price adjustments must be taken into account.

Once these comparable transactions have been identified, the financial advisor will calculate the price multiples to the target's book or embedded value, estimated or trailing earnings, EBIT, EBITDA, or any other financial multiple metric that may be deemed significantly relevant. At this point, the same process that took place for the comparable company analysis will be repeated, only this time using the multiples identified from similar transactions rather than the multiples from comparable companies. Again, adjustments must be made to ensure that the deal value multiples are "converted" to common equity multiples. The financial advisor will again end up with a low and high dollar value for the company.

Table 4.1 illustrates the number of life and P&C insurer transactions from 1981 to 2003, along with the average for two important public GAAP metrics: price-to-earnings (P/E) ratio and price-to-book (P/B) ratio.

1981-2003 INSURANCE M&A DEVELOPMENT

Year	Tracked Number of Deals		Number of Deals Reflected In P/E Ratios		Number of Deals Reflected In P/B Ratios		P/E Ratios		P/B Ratios	
	Life	P&C	Life	P&C	Life	P&C	Life	P&C	Life	P&C
1981-2	11	7	N/A	N/A	N/A	N/A	12.7	10.2	2.0	1.7
1983-4	6	5	N/A	N/A	N/A	N/A	13.1	16.7	2.1	1.6
1985-6	9	4	N/A	N/A	N/A	N/A	13.2	10.4	1.5	1.3
1987	10	4	6	2	9	3	25.0	12.3	1.6	1.7
1988	13	8	0	5	9	7	N/A	10.6	1.2	2.0
1989	14	9	8	7	12	8	12.6	11.3	1.2	1.5
1990	16	12	11	7	14	11	16.6	16.0	1.2	1.8
1991	18	13	5	4	6	8	15.0	19.0	1.2	1.7
1992	20	12	2	2	3	7	14.0	16.0	1.8	1.2
1993	28	24	7	3	6	7	18.4	20.3	1.1	1.4
1994	49	40	10	6	11	6	16.3	12.9	1.3	1.3
1995	57	39	10	13	10	15	13.4	14.3	1.3	1.4
1996	77	39	14	9	16	11	19.1	19.2	1.4	1.7
1997	56	86	12	13	13	21	17.5	18.2	1.7	1.8
1998	47	65	6	10	8	17	22.6	23.0	2.3	1.9
1999	53	69	4	10	5	16	21.5	15.0	2.0	1.7
2000	40	39	6	4	5	8	17.0	18.0	2.5	1.6
2001	61	47	7	3	7	4	13.6	24.4	1.4	1.5
2002	49	55	3	0	5	4	14.3	N/A	1.7	0.8
2003	40	62	4	5	7	7	15.3	52.3	1.3	1.1

TABLE 4.1

Source: Publicly announced deals identified by The Shapiro Network, Inc., with assistance of others, most recently, P.W. Mattingly & Co. (starting with 1996).

4.2.5 DISCOUNTED CASH FLOWS

The final valuation technique that is heavily relied upon by investment bankers for determining the value of a target company involved in a merger or acquisition is discounted cash flow (DCF) analysis. This is a simpler variant of the DCF model used in the actuarial appraisal. The calculation estimates the present value of the future streams of after-tax cash flows that the target company could produce in the foreseeable future (generally five years). The financial advisor calculates the after-tax cash flows using management's financial forecast, subject to certain adjustments, plus an estimate of total cash flows produced after five years.

In general, a DCF analysis must factor in a projected dividend payout rate (assuming the company is public and either has historically paid dividends or plans on paying dividends in the near future), earnings estimates (which are derived from management's projections and might take into account adjustments as the acquirer sees fit), and an ultimate book value as of the terminal date that will be used in the projections. A terminal value is calculated for the final year by multiplying the seller's projected earnings for that year by a P/E multiple and/or by multiplying seller's GAAP book value by a P/B value multiple. These multiples are usually derived from the comparable transaction analysis multiples. The implicit assumption is that the seller remains a stand-alone company for five years and then sells for a market multiple at the end of year five.

Once the cash flow and terminal value data set has been calculated, a present value calculation is used to calculate a tangible value. At this point, an appropriate discount rate is needed to perform the present value calculation. For the DCF, the discount rate that is typically used is the weighted average cost of capital (WACC), which is an average representing the expected or target return on all of a company's securities. Each source of capital, such as stocks, bonds, and other debt, is weighted in the calculation according to its prominence in the company's capital structure. The projected cash flows and terminal value are then discounted to a net present value using the WACC. It is generally appropriate to provide a sensitivity analysis showing the range of discounted values that would result if discount rates were moderately increased and decreased. A high and a low dollar value will be identified from the range of sensitivities.

For insurance companies, the free cash flow reflected in the DCF analysis needs to be modified to reflect earnings that can be dividended out of the regulated insurance entity. Because insurance companies are established and regulated first and foremost for the benefit of policyholders, the departments of insurance of the various states and the laws of those states have a distinct bias toward keeping capital within the regulated insurance entity. Accordingly, in most states within the United States, insurance companies are subject to restrictions on dividending out capital to shareholders or other non-insurance entities (that are not under the domain of the department of insurance), such as a holding company. The general rule in most states is that no more than the lesser of 10% of statutory surplus or 100% of the prior year's operating (or net) income may be paid in the form of a dividend to shareholders (including upstream holding companies) annually without receiving special approval from the department of insurance. In addition, insurance companies will need to maintain sufficient capital to satisfy rating agency objectives.

4.2.6 OTHER CONSIDERATIONS

Bankers also consider other information and data, including:

1) the historical price performance of seller's common stock and the relationship between movements in seller's common stock and selected companies in the appropriate industry or sector, and
2) the one-day and 30-day premiums and premiums to 52-week high and 52-week average paid-in transactions with equity deal values greater than some amount in the relevant geographic jurisdiction (e.g., the United States) and in the relevant sector (e.g., life insurance) announced between certain dates, and the same premiums implied by the per share consideration in the merger in an effort to determine whether the premium implied by the merger considerations is comparable to the premium in the selected transactions.

Bankers generally:

1) do not assume any responsibility for independent verification of any of the information that they reviewed or considered and relied on that information being complete and accurate in all material respects
2) assume that the financial forecasts are reasonably prepared on bases reflecting the best currently available estimates and judgments of management as to the future financial performance of seller
3) assume that the proposed merger would be consummated upon the terms and subject to the conditions set forth in the merger agreement without amendment, modification, or waiver of any material terms thereof
4) do not include any actuarial determinations or evaluations, or attempt to evaluate actuarial assumptions
5) make no analyses of, and express no opinion as to, the adequacy of the policy and other insurance reserves of seller, and rely upon information furnished to it by seller as to such adequacy

6) do not make an independent evaluation or appraisal of the assets or liabilities, contingent or otherwise, of seller

7) do not address seller's underlying business decision to engage in the merger.

CRYPT 4.1

Know What You Don't Know

From time to time we hear about mega-mergers and acquisitions that involve armies of consultants and investment bankers on both sides of the transaction. However, there is a segment of the acquisition market that prefers to go it alone, without seeking the counsel of consultants. This can lead to a bargain environment for buyers.

A lot of companies have sold blocks of life insurance business over the years for many reasons (for example, a company may be exiting a line of business, a block of business does not have critical mass, or the company is trying to strengthen its balance sheet).

In an attempt to save on expenses, it is not uncommon for a seller of a small block of business to perform its own valuation of the business. This valuation may be performed using rules of thumb or by an internal actuary who may not be familiar with techniques for valuing blocks of business.

Even in a competitive bidding situation, we have seen instances of the purchase price being 20% to 40% less than what could have been achieved. When the purchase price is $8 to $10 million, this can be significant for a small company.

As a seller, it is important to understand when it is prudent to engage an outside consultant who deals with the issues daily for an appraisal process. Don't be penny-wise and pound-foolish.

4.3 THE ACTUARIAL APPRAISAL

The most in-depth analysis of an insurance company in support of the M&A transaction is the actuarial appraisal. In essence, an actuarial appraisal is a discounted cash flow (DCF) analysis, where "cashflow" is defined as the earnings and capital available to be distributed out of an insurance company, recognizing the insurance industry's unique statutory accounting and capital requirements.

Specifically:

Distributable Cash Flow = After-tax Earnings minus Increase in Required Capital

= Premium + Investment Income
– Benefits – Expenses – Commissions
– Increase in Statutory Reserves
– Taxes
– Increase in Required Capital

Actuarial appraisals are not done on the basis of US GAAP accounting. For public companies, the impact of a transaction on GAAP earnings and equity is usually an important alternative set of financial analysis. Nevertheless, statutory earnings and capital, not GAAP earnings and equity, define the cash flow available to be distributed to owners of a company in the regulated life insurance industry and therefore form the basis for a DCF analysis.

The development of an actuarial appraisal is described in Actuarial Standard of Practice No. 19, "Actuarial Appraisals[1]," which was adopted by the Actuarial Standards Board in October 1991.

[1] Actuarial appraisal typically refers to a complete report associated with the analysis, while actuarial appraisal value refers to the DCF present values resulting from the analysis.

4.3.1 COMPONENTS OF THE ACTUARIAL APPRAISAL VALUE

The actuarial appraisal value of a life insurance company is typically described in three components, as illustrated in Figure 4.1. The total value of a company in the marketplace will reflect adjustments for other items that are beyond the scope of the actuarial appraisal.

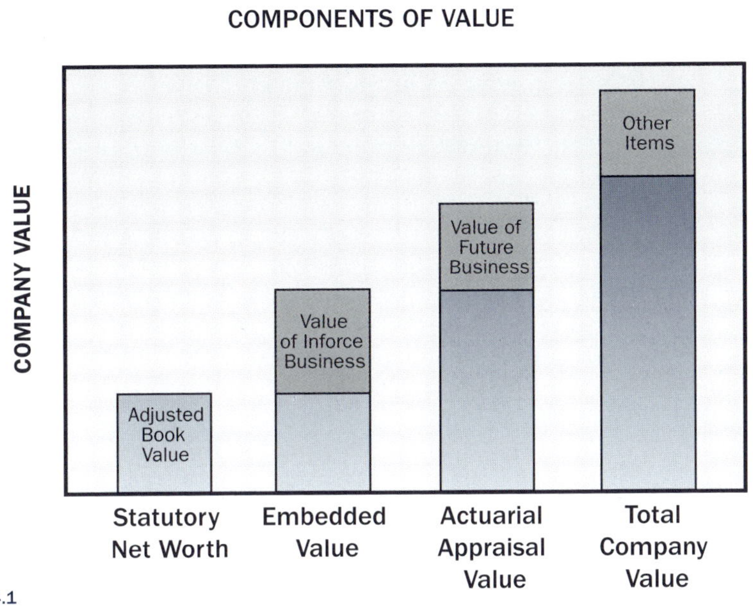

FIGURE 4.1

The three components of the actuarial appraisal value are:

1) Adjusted book value (ABV): The ABV is equal to the net worth of the insurance company on a statutory basis, i.e., the excess of statutory assets over statutory liabilities. In addition, certain adjustments are typically reflected for the economic values of certain miscellaneous assets or liabilities that are in the nature of surplus and that are not captured elsewhere in the valuation of the inforce business. For example, the asset valuation reserve (AVR) is typically included in ABV.

2) Value of inforce business: This component is equal to the present value of future profits arising from the business that is on the books of the company as of the valuation date. The projected profits are calculated on the basis of statutory regulatory accounting and reflect all future expected revenues of the business less benefits and expenses associated with the business. The projected profits are calculated reflecting best estimate assumptions. There is typically an adjustment made to reflect the opportunity cost of maintaining capital in the company to support the inforce business in order to meet regulatory and management requirements.

3) Value of future business capacity: This component is equal to the present value of future profits arising from the business that is projected to be written subsequent to the valuation date. Likewise, the projected profits are on the basis of regulatory reporting, reflect best estimate assumptions and reflect the opportunity cost of capital associated with the business. The value of future business is typically calculated for a certain number of years of new issues, for example 5, 10, or 20.

As discussed in section 4.3.2, the total value for a company in the open marketplace is not equal to a specific actuarial appraisal value, but rather will reflect adjustments for items outside the scope of the appraisal that increase or reduce value, such as value associated with branding or market position, a buyer's synergies, or general market conditions.

The appraisal value of a P&C company or a health insurance company may show a combined value for existing and new business due to the characteristics of that business. Considerations related to appraisal and other valuation techniques for P&C insurance companies are described later in this chapter.

The development of the actuarial appraisal values and basis for assumptions are described in detail later in this chapter. To illustrate actuarial appraisal values and projections, a sample company consisting entirely of universal life (UL) inforce and new business has been constructed. Table 4.2 illustrates sample actuarial appraisal values for the entity. Table 4.3 illustrates 10 years of a projected income statement for the entity on a statutory basis. The present value of the line item "distributable cash flow" in Table 4.3, over a 30-year period, is equal to the total actuarial appraisal value in Table 4.2.

UL SAMPLE COMPANY
Summary of Actuarial Appraisal Values
As of December 31, 2004
(in millions after tax and cost of capital)

Component of Value	Discount Rate		
	10.0%	12.0%	14.0%
1) Adjusted Statutory Book Value	100.0	100.0	100.0
2) Value of Business In Force as of December 31, 2004			
UL	212.1	185.0	163.1
Subtotal Pre-Tax Existing Business	212.1	185.0	163.1
Federal Income Taxes	(64.5)	(56.3)	(49.6)
Cost of Capital Based on 200% RBC *	(24.7)	(29.5)	(33.0)
Subtotal After-Tax Existing Business	122.9	99.2	80.4
3) Ten Years of New Business from December 31, 2004			
UL	226.9	174.4	135.8
Unallocated Expense	(7.9)	(7.8)	(7.7)
Subtotal Pre-Tax Future Business	219.0	166.6	128.2
Federal Income Taxes	(105.7)	(85.8)	(70.6)
Cost of Capital Based on 200% RBC *	(34.3)	(36.7)	(37.0)
Subtotal After-Tax Future Business	79.0	44.1	20.6
4) Total Actuarial Values with 10 Years of New Business			
(1) plus (2) plus (3)			
After-Tax	301.9	243.3	201.0

TABLE 4.2 * 200% of company Action Level Risk Based Capital is Illustrated for the purpose of this example.

UL SAMPLE COMPANY
Projected Statutory Operating Results
(in millions of dollars)

Baseline Growth
Ten Years of New Business

Year Ending December 31,	2004	2005	2006	2007	2008	2009	2010	2011	2012	2013	2014
Existing Business and 10 Years of New Business from December 31, 2004											
Premium Income		247.2	282.6	320.5	361.2	405.1	452.6	504.1	560.1	621.1	687.6
Investment Income		60.5	71.8	85.0	99.9	116.7	135.4	156.1	179.0	204.4	232.3
Total Income		307.7	354.4	405.5	461.1	521.8	588.0	660.2	739.2	825.5	919.9
Death Benefits		23.0	26.7	31.2	36.4	42.4	49.7	59.0	69.9	81.5	93.6
Annuity, Surrender, and Other Benefits		43.1	52.0	62.0	73.2	85.6	99.5	114.9	131.9	150.7	171.5
Premium Taxes		4.9	5.7	6.4	7.2	8.1	9.1	10.1	11.2	12.4	13.8
Reserve Increase		155.5	180.3	205.2	232.2	258.2	287.9	319.4	353.1	389.6	429.3
Other Expense		8.5	12.9	14.3	15.9	17.6	19.5	21.5	23.8	26.3	29.0
Commission		51.2	55.5	62.1	69.2	76.9	85.0	93.7	103.1	113.6	125.0
Total Benefits and Expenses		286.1	333.0	381.2	434.1	488.9	550.6	618.6	693.1	774.1	862.2
Statutory Profit on Existing and New Business		21.6	21.4	24.3	27.0	33.0	37.4	41.7	46.1	51.4	57.8
Unallocated Expense		5.5	1.8	1.1	0.3	0.0	0.0	0.0	0.0	0.0	0.0
Interest on Capital, Surplus, AVR		3.3	3.6	4.3	5.0	5.7	6.6	7.5	8.6	9.7	11.0
Total Pre-Tax Earnings		19.3	23.3	27.5	31.7	38.7	44.0	49.2	54.7	61.1	68.8
Federal Income Tax (35.0%)		(8.6)	(10.9)	(13.0)	(15.7)	(18.6)	(20.8)	(23.1)	(25.5)	(28.3)	(31.7)
After-Tax Earnings		10.7	12.4	14.5	16.0	20.2	23.2	26.2	29.2	32.8	37.1
Distributed Earnings	53.4	5.5	3.5	4.5	4.8	7.9	9.6	11.2	12.7	14.7	17.2
Balance Sheet											
Statutory Reserve	803.4	958.9	1,139.2	1,344.4	1,576.6	1,834.8	2,122.7	2,442.1	2,795.2	3,184.9	3,614.2
Capital, Surplus & AVR	100.0	51.9	60.8	70.8	81.9	94.2	107.8	122.7	139.2	157.3	177.2
Total Assets	903.4	1,010.8	1,200.0	1,415.2	1,658.5	1,929.0	2,230.5	2,564.8	2,934.5	3,342.2	3,791.4
Inventory Item											
Account Value	1,000.0	1,187.8	1,401.1	1,641.3	1,910.3	2,209.8	2,542.1	2,909.2	3,313.9	3,759.4	4,249.4
Cash Value	770.8	935.4	1,121.0	1,329.1	1,560.9	1,818.1	2,104.9	2,423.1	2,774.8	3,162.8	3,590.2
Tax Reserve	782.4	943.5	1,127.5	1,335.1	1,567.0	1,824.5	2,111.7	2,430.2	2,782.3	3,170.8	3,598.9
Proxy Dac Tax Asset	54.2	65.1	76.6	88.7	101.5	115.2	129.8	145.5	162.7	181.4	201.9
Inforce	10,000.0	11,613.6	13,356.5	15,242.8	17,288.2	19,509.7	21,925.8	24,555.9	27,422.3	30,550.3	33,967.9
Policy Count (Unscaled)	40,000	46,465	53,447	61,005	69,181	78,070	87,726	98,254	109,729	122,237	135,916
NAIC RBC at 100%	23.3	25.9	30.4	35.4	41.0	47.1	53.9	61.4	69.6	78.7	88.6
NAIC RBC Ratio	429%	200%	200%	200%	200%	200%	200%	200%	200%	200%	200%

TABLE 4.3 **Note:** Interest on Capital, Surplus & AVR is based on net earnings rate of 7.00%. The present value of Distributed Earnings in the above table is equal to the Total Value in Table 1.

4.3.2 USES OF AN ACTUARIAL APPRAISAL

The actuarial appraisal is a technique that is used widely to assist in determining the value of an insurance company. An actuarial appraisal report is typically prepared for the selling company, which is then used as part of the information to market the company or a block of business. In addition to the actuarial appraisal values, an appraisal report prepared by a seller typically includes:

1) Projection of statutory earnings and capital requirements: Along with DCF values, the appraisal report should illustrate the annual earnings and capital requirements of the business. This provides insight into patterns of profitability of the business. In addition, it will facilitate analysis regarding capital needs and financing alternatives. An important consideration to a buyer is the level of capital that it will initially need to set aside in order to support the business.

2) Sensitivity analyses: The importance of critical assumptions should be illustrated by showing the impact on results of reasonable deviations in those assumptions from expected levels. The sensitivity of results to changes in the underlying interest and/or equity environment is typically illustrated as well, unless the type of business is not significantly impacted by interest rates or changes in equity values. Sensitivity analysis may be illustrated either under deterministic scenarios or, for some types of risk, stochastic analysis.

Most potential buyers of insurance companies develop some form of actuarial appraisal as well, which may be based on the seller's actuarial appraisal report or may be based on independent analysis. A potential buyer typically will adjust the seller's analysis for the following:

1) A buyer will reflect its internal view of the appropriate discount rate.

2) A buyer may adjust certain experience and product management assumptions based on due diligence of the seller or based on its internal views.

3) A buyer may adjust new business values for its view of an appropriate goodwill premium[2] for future business capacity.

4) A buyer may reflect the benefits from anticipated synergies or cost savings, and from one-time acquisition costs, directly in the assumptions.

5) The specific structure anticipated by a buyer may have an impact on the appraisal values, including tax benefits or costs associated with the transaction and capital structure.

The buyer's actuarial appraisal analysis is typically a key element in establishing the opening balance sheet for purposes of purchase accounting under US GAAP. The conversion from actuarial appraisal values to VOBA under PGAAP is described in Chapter 8. Likewise, the actuarial appraisal can form the basis of alternative accounting methodologies resulting from cross-border transactions, such as Canadian GAAP or U.K. Achieved Profits.

Potential buyers frequently adjust the actuarial appraisal statutory income projections to calculate pro forma earnings projections on a US GAAP basis. While the cash flows are the same under either accounting system, a buyer would need to reflect the impact of the adjustments made to establish the opening PGAAP balance sheet, along with adjustments to new business earnings for GAAP accounting. GAAP earnings pro formas are the key driver for

[2] Under U.S. PGAAP accounting, "goodwill" is the balancing item in the opening balance sheet and equals the excess of the purchase price over the market value or fair value of all assets of the company, net of fair value of liabilities, after certain specified intangibles are recognized. As described in Chapter 8, when an actuarial appraisal is used to establish the value of business acquired (VOBA) for the acquired business, the amount of goodwill is roughly tied to the value associated with future business capacity, along with other items outside the scope of an appraisal.

accretion-dilution analysis and for the earnings multiples and other metrics described earlier in this chapter and in Chapter 2.

Finally, buyers may use the actuarial appraisal analysis as the basis for ongoing performance measurement after the acquisition. The appraisal provides measures of new business profitability, which can be used to set product pricing thresholds. Appraisal assumptions can establish a baseline for measurement of experience against expected mortality, morbidity, lapse, or spread targets. The projected earnings may provide a baseline for overall management profit expectations.

An actuarial appraisal value does not necessarily reflect the value of an insurance company's debt and equity in the open market. Rather, it is derived from a carefully constructed projection of future earnings and therefore reflects the value of a company's earnings potential under a specific set of assumptions and without regard to capital structure. Assignment of a value to any business enterprise is also a matter of informed judgment. Purchase or sales price is determined by the parties involved, based on their respective evaluations of all relevant factors, including:

1) the perspective of the buyer and the seller and the level of confidence regarding the assumptions underlying projected earnings
2) the desired rate of return and the associated cost of capital
3) the degree of urgency associated with the sale or acquisition
4) economies of scale and scope associated with the potential transaction
5) significant tax or other consequences/benefits, unique to a proposed transaction, which can have an effect on fair market value
6) value associated with branding or other intangibles, which may not be directly reflected in the appraisal values
7) one-time expenses associated with consummating a transaction and implementing the strategy, and
8) other assets or liabilities at the holding company level or otherwise outside the scope of the appraisal.

Additional discussion of market-based considerations that are typically outside the scope of the appraisal is in section 4.2.

4.4 BASIS FOR ASSUMPTIONS

The assumptions underlying the actuarial appraisal analysis are intended to be best estimate (that is, without margin for conservatism), based on the specific nature of the company's marketplace and the business itself. The discount rate used to develop a value from the projected earnings is intended to provide the necessary adjustment for risk. The assumptions are based on some combination of the following:

1) the company's own experience based on analysis of its historical performance
2) company management expectations, as reflected in, for example, management's internal plan, product pricing, or valuation actuary analysis
3) industry experience for comparable blocks of business, in particular where the company's own experience may not be available or may not be credible.

Certain key assumptions, notably future production levels and expense budgets, are typically based primarily on management's input as opposed to actuarial studies. In the case of an actuarial appraisal developed for a seller, the assumptions are typically based on the target company's management team, frequently as embodied in the target's near-term operating plan and long-term forecasts. The actuarial appraisal analysis developed by, or modified by, a potential buyer would reflect the buyer's perspective and may include potential synergies that a buyer would anticipate. For the management plan assumptions, it is difficult to view a single set of assumptions as "best estimate," because circumstances can vary considerably based on the specific situation of a potential acquirer.

The development of the assumptions requires considerable actuarial judgment. The determination of best estimates for some assumptions will be more difficult than for others. Assumptions for which historical experience is limited should be further analyzed and illustrated through sensitivity testing.

4.4.1 MORTALITY ASSUMPTIONS

Mortality assumptions are typically set based on company experience compared to an industry standard experience table, such as the 1975-80 Select & Ultimate table, or based on a company's internally developed mortality table. Considerations include the type of underwriting, sales distribution, and treatment of substandard risks. For life insurance business, typically multiples of the underlying table would vary by underwriting class and possibly by age or sex. Often a company's mortality experience may lack credibility due to an inadequate exposure base, in which case comparable industry experience is factored in.

The effect of reinsurance should be reflected. If there is a substantial amount of reinsurance, as is typical in many companies on competitive level term products, the reinsurance treaty terms are often modeled explicitly. If the use of reinsurance is limited, it may be appropriate to simply reflect the impact of the reinsurance in evaluation of the mortality experience of the retained business or through a simplified model of the reinsured business.

Mortality anti-selection is reflected to the extent that it is expected on lines of business with high lapse rates. For example, on competitive level term products that may exhibit lapse rates of 70% or higher at the end of the level period, mortality anti-selection can be incorporated based on a methodology such as Dukes-MacDonald or Becker-Kitsos.

The overall life insurance industry has exhibited mortality improvement in recent years. In some companies, current pricing or GAAP reporting of life insurance products may reflect some degree of mortality improvement assumptions extending into the future. Likewise, an assumption of future mortality improvement may be considered the best estimate assumption for purposes of the actuarial appraisal analysis. Due to the variety of views on this topic, it would be appropriate to include a sensitivity test regarding the impact of future mortality improvement.

4.4.2 MORBIDITY ASSUMPTIONS

Morbidity assumptions likewise are generally established based on a comparison of company experience to industry standard tables. Along with underwriting and distribution, product characteristics play an important role in establishing best estimate assumptions.

Certain health lines of business are re-rated annually, such as major medical and Medicare supplement. For these lines, it may be more appropriate to establish morbidity expectations in terms of loss ratio assumptions based on a company's demonstrated ability to meet target loss ratios. Medical inflation trend assumptions may need to be set as well.

4.4.3 PERSISTENCY ASSUMPTIONS

Persistency, or policy renewal, assumptions encompass voluntary surrenders, lapses without value, and premium suspension rates. Persistency can vary significantly by company and should be reviewed with regard to product type, specific product design, distribution system, and sales technique. For illustrated products such as universal life, it may be appropriate to review sample illustrations to set persistency assumptions in line with how the product was sold. Product features such as the end of the surrender charge period (on annuities) or large required premium increases (on term insurance or health insurance) typically exert a material influence on expected persistency rates.

The lapse assumptions on interest-sensitive products may incorporate a dynamic lapse component to reflect the relative competitiveness of the credited rate offered to the policyholder compared to general market conditions. This assumption is particularly important if various alternative interest rate scenarios are being tested, but may be reflected in a level interest scenario as well.

Depending on the specifics of a potential acquisition, it may be appropriate to consider any shock lapses expected as a result of a transaction. Typically deals are structured to have little or no direct impact on policyholders (e.g., company acquisitions or indemnity coinsurance), but situations involving troubled companies or assumption reinsurance may result in some additional lapsation.

4.4.4 INVESTMENT RETURNS AND SPREAD ASSUMPTIONS

Investment return assumptions may be based on either an assumed rate of return or on an explicit model of the existing asset portfolio along with future investments. Lines of business where the investment return is a significant component of overall profitability should reflect a complete model of the assets backing the liabilities. Short-term liabilities may reflect a fixed rate of investment return based on a review of the current asset portfolio and reinvestment strategy.

Explicit asset models reflect projections of the underlying asset portfolios, usually on a seriatim basis, based on coupons, maturities, and prepayment characteristics, and reflect statutory accounting principles for book values and book yields. Expected defaults reflect the underlying quality of the portfolio. Investment management expenses are generally incorporated as a reduction to gross yields. To the extent assets are projected to be sold or prepaid, capital gains or losses are capitalized into the interest maintenance reserve (IMR) and amortized under statutory guidelines.

Reinvestment strategies are generally based on the seller's or buyer's current practices or alternative strategies that are appropriate for the business. Reinvestment rates are set reflecting spreads available on new purchases based on general market data or the seller's actual purchases.

It is common for an actuarial appraisal to be based on a single underlying yield curve, which is assumed to remain constant. The yield curve may be set based on the valuation date or a more recent date closer to when the report is prepared. If the current yield curve is considered to be abnormally low or high, it may be considered best estimate to adjust the yield curve toward a long term expectation over time; however, this is more typically analyzed with sensitivity analysis.

The assumptions for setting future credited interest rates are set based on management strategy, either for the seller's current practices or reflecting changes anticipated by a buyer. The strategy should consider projected yields on the investment portfolio, external competitive pressures, and any policy guarantees, either explicit (embedded in policy language) or implicit (such as policy illustration language).

For interest-sensitive blocks of business, it is appropriate to include some analysis of the impact of interest rate movements on the actuarial appraisal values. ASOP 19 requires consideration of alternative scenarios where a level scenario may not adequately capture a product's dynamics. Typically, specific deterministic scenarios that illustrate a reasonable range of potential yield curve environments are illustrated.

Stochastic interest rate testing is occasionally reflected in actuarial appraisals on blocks of business that are particularly interest rate-sensitive, such as deferred annuities. Stochastic testing can provide useful information about the value of embedded options in products. For example, variable product guarantees can only be quantified through some type of stochastic testing. Even when stochastic testing is used, a level scenario set of results is typically illustrated as well in order to provide a baseline for projected capital needs and to facilitate management analysis.

CRYPT 4.2

Trumpeter's Delight—Acquisition Undervalues Options

Here is a case where an actuarial evaluation could have cushioned a huge settlement.

The story starts in 1962 in Los Angeles. Musician Herb Alpert and his partner formed A&M records, which evolved into Rondor Music. Rondor, owning the rights to 60,000 songs, was acquired in 2000 by Universal Music Group, which was owned by the Seagram Company.

The acquisition was funded with cash and stock. Alpert must have been wary of the value of the stock and secured an option from Universal. The terms stated that if the value of the stock fell below the price of $37.50 for 10 consecutive days at any time during the next five years, Alpert and his partner would receive an additional payment.

Shortly after this transaction, Seagram's Universal unit was sold to Vivendi and renamed Vivendi Universal. Soon thereafter, financing woes caused the value of Vivendi Universal's shares to plummet. During 2002, the shares fell below the trigger price for 10 consecutive days.

The trumpeter presented a demand of $200 million to Vivendi Universal. They sang his tune.

It would be interesting to know what, if any, liability was held on Seagram's and then Universal Vivendi's balance sheet prior to the payment date. Could it have been a Black-Scholes-driven amount? Could it be a binomial determination? Was it a conditional tail expectation? Was it the average of possible scenarios... or could it have been zero? An actuarial valuation would have been very appropriate in this situation.

4.4.5 OPERATING EXPENSES

Operating expense assumptions are generally determined based on one of the following alternatives:

1) Fully absorbed unit expenses: Under this approach, the budget of the target company is spread across the inforce and new business units. Projected expenses are based on applying the fully absorbed allowables to projected units.

2) Target unit expenses and an unallocated expense: Projected expenses are based on applying a set of target unit expense allowables to projected units. An unallocated expense is projected as well, equal to the excess of the company's total budget established by management over the total projected target expenses. This is the approach illustrated in the Sample UL Company example in this chapter.

3) Target unit expenses without an unallocated expense: Under this approach, no adjustment is made for the excess of the company's budgeted expenses over projected allowables. In this case, the total expenses of the company are not captured in the analysis; therefore, this approach tends to be followed primarily when a fundamental change in the business operations is expected subsequent to a transaction. For example, target unit expenses are typically reflected in illustrating the value of a runoff block of business being sold as a reinsurance transaction.

The projection of current fully absorbed unit expenses reflects an implicit assumption that unit expense reductions are not available under the normal growth of the business, i.e., that the company is already at its critical mass. Alternatively, fully absorbed unit expenses may be appropriate if any expense improvements that are realized are expected to be passed back to policyholders and therefore are often used for group lines of business or other blocks that are re-rated annually. Fully absorbed unit expenses may also be appropriate for companies that are large and mature in their markets and therefore are not expected to be able to improve efficiencies or dramatically increase scale on their own.

Target unit expenses, together with an unallocated amount, are the most common approach in actuarial appraisals. Target unit expenses may be based on some combination of:

1) company plan targets for fully allocated expenses at some point in the future
2) company assumptions used in their internal new business pricing analysis
3) representative industry levels of target expenses; typically "best practices" or some reasonable level of the expenses that can be achieved by the more efficient operators in the industry would be reflected, based on the expectation that those would be most relevant to a potential buyer
4) representative unit expense levels that would be charged by a third party administrator (TPA), with appropriate loading for non-TPA elements; TPAs have recently become an important factor in M&A, as potential buyers now have a low cost alternative to outsource the administration of an acquisition.

Under the approach of target unit expenses with an unallocated amount, it may be desirable to establish the target unit expenses such that the total unit expense allowables cross the budget (i.e., the unallocated expense goes to zero) over the medium term, for example, within 5 to 10 years. The projection of the amount and period of the unallocated expense is a key item that the target company's management will need to explain because potential buyers will scrutinize the expense items carefully.

Marginal unit expenses are another alternative for projecting cost levels. There is theoretical justification for this approach since a buyer in concept should analyze an acquisition based on the marginal costs incurred. Much as companies typically price new products with some allowance for fixed cost, it is general practice for buyers to analyze acquisitions by including some level of fixed cost and overhead allocation.

Expenses are an important aspect of buy-side analysis. Buyers typically will adjust an actuarial appraisal for unit expenses they believe to be appropriate, based on their internal cost structure and plans for the acquisition, along with provision for transition expenses over a period of time before the ultimate cost structure is realized.

4.4.6 DISCOUNT RATE DETERMINATION

There are a number of approaches for determining discount rates for use in valuing an insurance company or blocks of business as part of an M&A transaction. It is common practice in an appraisal prepared for the seller of a company to illustrate a range of reasonable discount rates, as opposed to implicitly providing an opinion that there is a single correct rate. ASOP 19 addresses the "risk-adjusted rates of return" as follows:

> The rates used for discounting future earnings should reasonably reflect risks inherent in the realization of such earnings, and should be representative of the returns desired by the buyer, seller, or owner of the enterprise. Since risks vary by product line and between in-force and new business, it is natural that risk-adjusted rates of return might vary similarly. Also, in the selection of risk-adjusted rates of return, the actuary should consider the actuarial methods and assumptions used.

There are both theoretical and practical approaches that provide input into establishing the discount rate. The discount rate reflected in appraisals is generally viewed as an unlevered discount rate, not an equity discount rate; that is, the discount rate is applied to distributable earnings before reflecting the impact of debt cost or other leverage. For example, an insurer with a capital structure of 30% debt and 70% equity (measured by market value) and required after-tax market return of 5% on debt and 15% on equity, would have a weighted average required return of 12%. For purposes of an appraisal, the aggregate rate of 12% would be used in order to separate the impact of the capital structure from the entity's economic value.

4.4.6.1 *Capital Asset Pricing Model*

The CAPM is described extensively in financial textbooks, including *Principles of Corporate Finance* by Brealey and Myers. The fundamental equation is:

FORMULA 4.1

$$r = r_f + \beta\,(r_m - r_f)$$

where

r = expected rate of return on the acquisition
r_f = risk-free rate of return
r_m = expected rate of return for the market as a whole
β = measure of risk of a company (both debt and equity) relative to the market as a whole.

Reflecting leverage explicitly in the CAPM results in:

FORMULA 4.2

$$r = r^D \times \frac{D}{D+E} + \frac{E}{D+E} \times \left(r_f + \beta^E\left(r_m - r_f\right)\right)$$

where

r = weighted average cost of capital (WACC)
r^D = required return on debt
β^E = beta of a company's stock
D = market value of a company's debt
E = market value of a company's equity.

Under CAPM, the WACC should be used as the discount rate. Theoretically, a company is creating shareholder value if an acquisition provides a positive value discounted at the WACC and destroying value if the acquisition is negative discounted at the WACC.

One implication of CAPM is that an acquirer should have a specific discount rate for the acquisition of business comparable to its own that is determined by the market through the company's beta and debt cost. The uncertainties in the acquisition should be captured in the underlying cash flows, as opposed to adjusting the discount rate for an acquisition that is more or less risky. A second implication of CAPM is that discount rates should float with movements in the risk-free rate. In practice, a number of factors in addition to risk-free rates have influenced acquirers' discount rates.

4.4.6.2 *Internal Company Targets*

Most insurance companies have internal hurdle rates that are used as minimum benchmarks for pricing internally generated new business or for pricing acquisitions. The target hurdle rates may vary by line of business based on the perceived risk in the business or based on market conditions. Companies may have long-term targets as well, which could vary from current hurdle rates due to market conditions. Both current hurdle rates and long-term targets may be used to establish a minimum discount rate to price an acquisition.

4.4.6.3 *Cost of Funds for Transactions*

A potential buyer may have a specific cost of funds for a given transaction, which will then be the appropriate discount rate for its analysis. For example, a private equity concern will typically have specific target rates for the various tiers of debt, mezzanine, and equity financing of a transaction. The overall WACC of the financing, including the expected return on the equity, equals the discount rate to price the transaction.

A potential acquirer may have excess capital trapped in the company that is currently earning a low return and is not needed for its other operations. In this case, the cost of funds is a low rate. The company may temporarily have an advantage in pursuing acquisitions until the trapped excess capital is fully used.

4.4.6.4 *M&A Marketplace Discount Rates*

There are enough actual or potential M&A transactions among insurers taking place for market participants to have a sense of the discount rates currently being used by buyers. Along with the active acquirers, the investment bankers, actuaries, and other advisors who specialize in insurance M&A generally have a sense of current market conditions. In practice, discount rates have varied over time, reflecting:

1) supply and demand of sellers and buyers
2) nature of buyers and the cost of financing, including public debt markets
3) type of business being sold.

Transactions in the 1980s and early 1990s were generally priced at 15% or higher discount rates, although the inconsistency in treatment of cost of capital during that period may make comparisons to later transactions difficult. Transaction pricing in the late 1990s was at lower discount rates, in the 10% to 12% range, although some transactions were at single-digit discount rates. Discount rates in the 2002-2003 period have seen a slight increase, in part due to a reduction in demand as some of the major European market participants stopped pursuing transactions.

CRYPT 4.3

Discount Rate—More Than Picking A Number

My holding company was emerging from bankruptcy. We hired advisors to help determine the value of the underlying insurance entities. I, as the valuation actuary, was involved with helping the consultants prepare the appraisal values by supplying the bases for key assumptions. Everyone (the lenders, other creditors, the preferred stockholders, the common shareholders, the management, the auditors, the bankruptcy court, etc.) was eager to see the value of the underlying insurance companies. This appraisal would determine the amount, if any, that the creditors and investors would receive.

I was close to the discussions that determined the discount rate, a topic that has always fascinated me. I've always been on the valuation side and, until this most recent appraisal, I never got much of a view into the choice of discount rate. It always seemed a bit of a mystery to me. I finally saw one as it came together.

Not too long before our bankruptcy, we performed an SFAS 142 goodwill recoverability test. For the discount rate, our advisors came up with a 12% rate. It was a WACC type of rate, the weighted average being an average of two rates. One is what we would likely incur for debt financing, and the other what we would likely incur for equity financing. In our case, the debt rate was taken at 7.9%. That was a BAA grade corporate bond rate. The equity rate was developed using the CAPM approach starting with a risk-free rate. Our advisors chose a 20-year Treasury, which was 5.7%. Adding in an equity risk premium, they picked a 30-year average, which was 7.8% at that time. Then they applied a company-specific beta to it, 75% in our case, implying that our stock price movements might be 75% of the stock market as a whole. Finally they added a 1% premium for the size of the company and our competitive positioning. Those components got them to the equity rate of 12.6%. Our debt and equity makeup at that point gave them the weighted average rate of 12%. So, 12% was used on the insurance cash flows for the test.

There were just a couple of intangibles—trademarks and trade names—for which they bumped the rate up and valued those at 14%, thinking that those were even riskier than our insurance business.

That was for goodwill recoverability purposes. Shortly after that we headed into bankruptcy and began to look at the study in a new light. Amazingly, the 12% survived, but how we got there became really interesting because all components of the formula became moving pieces during bankruptcy. The whole process took almost a year. During that year, the BAA rate dropped a 100 basis points and, of course, only in our wildest dreams were we still BAA.

The Treasury rates fell. Our competitive posture certainly changed. If a 1% risk premium was appropriate then, what was appropriate now? Also, the debt-to-equity mix was still being debated.

It became a circular argument as to what this discount rate should be. The creditors were looking ahead to see what they were willing to do, what the company would look like at emergence, and what the WACC ought to be for that company. At the same time, given that it took us a year to get through bankruptcy, there were a number of insurance industry acquisitions going on, most of which used discount rates higher than 12%. There was a natural resistance to going below 12% at that time. However, groups like the preferred stockholders were pressing the issue. Going to 11% would have made an incredible difference in their recovery, and going to 10% might have given them a full recovery. It was a very dicey issue. In our case, it was a compromise in the end.

The bondholders received the lion's share of the new company's common stock. All of their recovery was in common stock. The creditors next in line were the preferred shareholders. They ended up receiving only a small amount of common stock. During the negotiations, they would advance ideas for improving the value, frequently suggesting lowering the discount rate. Fortunately we had a theoretical basis for anchoring into this assumption that played such a major role in determining value.

4.4.7 COST OF REQUIRED CAPITAL

As discussed in Chapter 3, insurance companies are required to maintain a level of capital in addition to reserves in order to absorb adverse experience without threatening the company's solvency. The amount of capital targeted by management is influenced both by regulatory requirements and rating agencies. Actuarial appraisals in the late 1990s to early 2000s typically reflected required capital in the range of 200% to 250% RBC-CAL (risk based capital—company action level), although companies and lines of business vary considerably and higher or lower levels may be appropriate. The NAIC RBC formula has a co-variance adjustment factor that varies depending on the size and type of business for a buyer.

The requirement to maintain capital in an insurance company creates an opportunity cost associated with the required capital, which is described as "cost of required capital" or "cost of capital." The opportunity cost is equal to the difference between the target return (discount rate) that could be generated if the capital could be used elsewhere and the rate the capital can earn if it is trapped with the block of business:

$$\text{Cost of Capital}_t = \text{Required Capital}_{t-1} \times (\text{discount rate} - \text{after-tax earnings rate}_t)$$

$$\text{Appraisal Cost of Capital} = NPV\,(\text{Cost of Capital}_t)$$

where

NPV = net present value at the discount rate.

Actuarial appraisals typically show the present value of after-tax earnings on the business prior to interest on capital, along with a separate deduction for the opportunity cost of capital as described above, to produce the total actuarial value.

Distributable earnings equal the after-tax earnings of the business, including interest on capital, adjusted for the change in required capital. Distributable earnings, therefore, equal the actual cash flow that can be distributed from an insurance company or is available to the enterprise for other uses such as new business or other acquisitions, while maintaining its targeted capital position. The actuarial appraisal value can likewise be defined as the present value of distributable earnings. The two approaches to appraisal value are equivalent as demonstrated below:

NPV (Distributable Earnings$_t$) = Excess Capital$_0$ + NPV (After-tax Earnings$_t$ − Increase in RC$_t$)

= NPV (After-tax Earnings on the Business$_t$)
+ Excess Capital$_0$ + NPV (After-tax Earnings on Capital$_t$)
− NPV (Increase in RC$_t$)

= NPV (After-tax Earnings on the Business$_t$)
+ Excess Capital$_0$ + NPV (RC$_{t-1}$ $\times$ i$_t$) − (NPV (RC$_t$) − NPV (RC$_{t-1}$))

= NPV (After-tax Earnings on the Business$_t$)
+ Excess Capital$_0$ + NPV (RC$_{t-1}$ $\times$ i$_t$) − [(1+d) NPV (RC$_{t-1}$) - RC$_0$ - NPV (RC$_{t-1}$)]

= NPV (After-tax Earnings on the Business$_t$)
+ Excess Capital$_0$ + RC$_0$
− NPV (RC$_t$ $\times$ (d - i$_t$))

= Value of Inforce and Future Business
+ Adjusted Book Value
− Cost of Required Capital

where

i_t	=	after-tax investment earnings rate on capital
d	=	discount rate
RC_t	=	required capital

The cost of required capital for the UL Sample Company is illustrated in Table 4.4.

UL SAMPLE COMPANY
Cost of Capital
(in millions of dollars)

Baseline Growth
Ten Years of New Business

Year Ending December 31,	2004	2005	2006	2007	2008	2009	2010	2011	2012	2013	2014
Existing Business as of December 31, 2004											
Required Capital at 200% RBC	46.6	46.5	49.4	51.8	53.9	55.5	56.7	57.6	58.2	58.4	58.3
After-Tax Interest on Required Capital		2.1	2.1	2.2	2.4	2.5	2.5	2.6	2.6	2.6	2.7
Cost of Capital (12% Hurdle Rate)		3.5	3.5	3.7	3.9	4.0	4.1	4.2	4.3	4.3	4.3

Year Ending December 31,	2004	2005	2006	2007	2008	2009	2010	2011	2012	2013	2014
Future Business as of December 31, 2004											
Required Capital at 200% RBC		5.4	11.4	19.0	28.1	38.7	51.0	65.1	81.0	99.0	118.9
After-Tax Interest on Required Capital		0.0	0.2	0.5	0.9	1.3	1.8	2.3	3.0	3.7	4.5
Cost of Capital (12% Hurdle Rate)		0.0	0.4	0.9	1.4	2.1	2.9	3.8	4.8	6.0	7.4

Year Ending December 31,	2004	2005	2006	2007	2008	2009	2010	2011	2012	2013	2014
Existing and Future Business as of December 31, 2004											
Required Capital at 200% RBC	46.6	51.9	60.8	70.8	81.9	94.2	107.8	122.7	139.2	157.3	177.2
After-Tax Interest on Required Capital		2.1	2.4	2.8	3.2	3.7	4.3	4.9	5.6	6.3	7.2
Cost of Capital (12% Hurdle Rate)		3.5	3.9	4.5	5.3	6.1	7.0	8.0	9.1	10.4	11.7

Present Value of Cost of Capital	12%
Existing Business	29.5
Future Business	36.7
Existing and Future Business	66.2

TABLE 4.4 **Note:** Interest on Capital, Surplus & AVR is based on net earnings rate of 7.00%.

4.4.8 TAXES

The actuarial appraisal is based on distributable cash flows, which reflect a deduction for U.S. federal income taxes. The tax characteristics of a company are often complicated and unique to the specific situation. As a result, tax experts are typically involved in the M&A process. Nevertheless, there are a number of basic tax adjustments that are a characteristic of most companies and that account for the large majority of tax attributes reflected in actuarial appraisals.

Federal income taxes are calculated as the tax rate (currently 35% for U.S. companies) times taxable income, where taxable income equals statutory pre-tax income adjusted for the following items:

1) Differences between statutory and tax reserves: Tax reserves are based on minimum statutory reserve standards and a federally prescribed interest rate. Statutory deficiency reserves do not qualify as tax reserves. Certain blocks of business such as LTC or level term insurance may generate large differences between statutory and tax reserves. Tax reserves cannot exceed statutory reserves.

2) DAC proxy tax: Under Internal Revenue Code Section 848, premiums generate a proxy DAC asset for tax purposes equal to 7.7% of individual insurance premium, 2.05% of group life insurance premium, and 1.75% of non-qualified annuity premium. The proxy DAC is capitalized and amortized straight-line over 10 years (5 years for small companies) for taxable income purposes.

3) Interest maintenance reserve (IMR): Capital gains or losses are taxed as realized. For statutory purposes, the after-tax gain or loss is capitalized into IMR and amortized over the remaining life of the security. The capitalization and amortization of IMR is not reflected in taxable income.

4) Asset basis differences: Differences between statutory and tax bases for invested assets may arise from a number of items such as write-downs of troubled securities, differences in depreciation rules, or differences in treatment of accrual of discount. Typically the differences are small, but to the extent these differences are material, the impact should be reflected in the actuarial appraisal values.

5) Dividends received deduction (DRD): Companies with blocks of variable business may receive a taxable income deduction for a portion of the dividends that accrue to policyholders in separate account funds.

The tax strain from timing differences between statutory and tax reserves and the DAC proxy tax often result in effective tax rates on future business that are well in excess of 35%. Likewise, the embedded tax benefits on an inforce block often result in effective tax rates for existing business that may be well below 35%. An example of the tax adjustments to statutory income is illustrated in Table 4.5.

UL SAMPLE COMPANY
Taxes
(in millions of dollars)

Baseline Growth
Ten Years of New Business

Year Ending December 31,	2004	2005	2006	2007	2008	2009	2010	2011	2012	2013	2014
Existing and Future Business as of December 31, 2004											
Pre-Tax Statutory Income		19.3	23.3	27.5	31.7	38.7	44.0	49.2	54.7	61.1	68.8
+ Increase in Statutory Reserve		155.5	180.3	205.2	232.2	258.2	287.9	319.4	353.1	389.6	429.3
- Increase in Tax Reserve		161.1	184.0	207.6	231.8	257.6	287.1	318.5	352.1	388.5	428.0
+ Increase in Proxy DAC Tax Asset		18.1	18.8	19.4	19.9	20.3	20.7	20.9	21.2	21.3	21.4
+ Other Statutory - Tax differences		0.0	0.0	0.0	0.0	0.0	0.0	0.0	0.0	0.0	0.0
- Existing Proxy DAC Tax Asset Runoff		7.2	7.2	7.2	7.0	6.7	6.1	5.2	4.0	2.6	0.9
Taxable Income		24.5	31.1	37.1	44.9	53.0	59.3	65.9	72.8	81.0	90.5
Taxes at 35%		8.6	10.9	13.0	15.7	18.6	20.8	23.1	25.5	28.3	31.7

TABLE 4.5

When a company sells a wholly owned subsidiary, an important aspect of tax analysis is the potential benefit from a Section 338(h)(10) election. This analysis is described in Chapter 7. When a block of business is sold via a reinsurance transaction, there are a number of tax implications that are described later in this chapter.

4.5 COMPONENTS OF THE ACTUARIAL APPRAISAL

The components of an actuarial appraisal consist of (1) the company's adjusted book value, (2) the value of the earnings from existing business in force at the company, and (3) the value of the earnings from the future business to be written at the company going forward. The assumptions described in the previous section form the basis for the projections of future statutory earnings, which are then discounted to determine the values of existing business and future business. This section will describe certain considerations in developing each of the components of the actuarial appraisal.

4.5.1 ADJUSTED BOOK VALUE

The adjusted book value (ABV) is the first component of an actuarial appraisal value. The ABV represents the net worth of an insurance company on a statutory basis with certain adjustments for liabilities or non-admitted assets that are in the nature of surplus. The major items that comprise the ABV are the following:

1) Capital and surplus: The statutory capital stock, contributed surplus, and retained earnings of the company make up the capital and surplus.

2) Asset valuation reserve (AVR): The AVR liability is determined based on the distribution of the asset portfolio by type and quality rating. The AVR is generally considered surplus because (a) changes in AVR flow through the surplus account, not net income and (b) the AVR counts as capital for purposes of RBC ratios, both for the NAIC formula and independent rating agencies.

3) Interest maintenance reserve (IMR): The IMR liability represents past interest-related capital gains that have not yet been amortized into income. The IMR is usually presented as a component of existing business value because the liability is intended to support inforce policy liabilities. In some cases, however, it is treated as a component of ABV, for convenience or because it may be difficult to determine a precise allocation to blocks of inforce business. If the IMR is included in ABV, it is presented on a discounted basis because the IMR liability represents trapped capital that can only be released over time.

4) Deferred tax asset: The admitted portion of the statutory deferred tax asset is typically deducted from ABV in order to be consistent with a direct recognition of tax attributes in the projection of cash taxes as described in section 4.4.8. For most life insurers, the admitted portion of the deferred tax asset is limited to a small portion of the total amount of deferred tax balances, i.e., the tax-affected differences between statutory and tax carrying values, and therefore it is more appropriate to reflect cash taxes directly. The annual change in deferred tax asset is an adjustment to the surplus account and is not reflected in income.

5) Non-admitted assets: It is appropriate to recognize in the actuarial valuation the realizable value of assets that have been non-admitted for statutory purposes to the extent these will contribute to earnings over time. This is typically treated as an adjustment to ABV. The most common adjustments are the estimated realizable values of amounts due from agents and for furniture and equipment.

6) Surplus notes and other debt: Debt may exist in several ways on a life insurer's balance sheet:

- Debt at the holding company level: Most U.S. public life insurers carry debt principally outside of the regulated entity. The actuarial appraisal is typically of the regulated life insurer, so this would not impact the appraisal directly.

- Internal surplus notes: Surplus notes within a life insurer that are payable to the holding company would cancel out in consolidation. Typically the surplus notes are valued as part of the surplus of the life insurer, and likewise are not reflected as an asset of the holding company.

- External surplus notes: Surplus notes within a life insurer that are payable to an external party may either be included in the appraisal, in which case the appraisal value is for the entity as a whole, or deducted, in which case the appraisal value is for the equity only. Usually the appraisal is designed to reflect the value for the entity in total.

Because there are alternative ways to treat surplus notes and other debt, it is imperative for the actuarial appraisal to be clear on the approach used in order for any necessary adjustments to be made in looking at consolidated value.

7) Mark-to-market on assets allocated to ABV: An important component of the ABV is the after-tax mark-to-market on assets supporting ABV. In general, riskier assets, such as equities and real estate, and troubled assets, including NAIC 5 or 6 bonds, are allocated to ABV. Most companies think of these assets as backing surplus rather than backing liabilities. Given that ABV is considered a current (i.e., immediately distributable) cash flow as opposed to a projected and discounted value, it is appropriate to reflect the market value of the assets backing ABV. For consistency, the after-tax yield on assets backing required capital, which is used to develop cost of capital, reflects a current market yield.

The ABV is determined as of a particular date, which then defines the "as of date" or "appraisal date" for the complete appraisal. The majority of items comprising the ABV can be determined directly by referring to a target company's published statutory financials. Therefore, the ABV is almost always determined as of a quarter end, coinciding with a public statement, although intermediate dates are possible if a company maintains internal statements more frequently. Frequently a buyer or seller will "roll forward" the appraisal value to the projected closing date. Each of the components of the appraisal value can be rolled forward on an estimated basis using the projected earnings and growing the future discounted earnings at the discount rate in order to produce an estimate of the value as of the actual acquisition date.

4.5.2 EXISTING BUSINESS VALUE

The value attributable to the business in force at a company on the appraisal date is the second component of an actuarial appraisal value. The existing business value can make up a substantial portion of the total appraisal value due to the long tail on insurance policies written in the past, along with generally conservative capital and reserve requirements under statutory accounting that tend to push profits into the future.

The value of existing business is determined by developing detailed models of all of the material business that is in force as of the appraisal date. The development of the models is a complex exercise requiring both a detailed understanding of the characteristics of the business along with a considerable amount of data detailing product structure, policy charges, reserving requirements, etc. For some lines of business, it is typical to develop detailed model offices starting with seriatim listings of a company's inforce policies. For other lines, aggregate approaches may be taken. The development of assumptions to project the future profitability of the business was described generally in the previous portion of this chapter. Specific issues related to the major types of business are described later in this chapter.

CRYPT 4.4

100 Cents On The Dollar

Most sales agreements are based upon a fixed price, but the statutory equity and assets to be transferred (which are based upon statutory reserves) are subject to review by the buyer. The buyer does due diligence and usually finds numerous statutory reserve "errors." Somehow, these errors always result in reserve increases. It is sometimes difficult for the sellers to refute these reserve differences under the terms of the sales agreements. This is especially true if the errors are dependent upon the interpretation of new or evolving statutory reserve requirements.

In most of the cases in which I have seen this occur, the consulting actuaries for the seller had noted reserve discrepancies when reconciling opening balances in their appraisal model. Because these validation differences were immaterial to total reserves, they had been ignored. In general, I believe the consulting actuaries have used what were believed to be the "correct" statutory reserves. However, they have not attempted to resolve the reserve differences between their model and the liabilities actually booked with their client.

Although the reserve differences are usually immaterial to the total modeled reserves, they are worth 100 cents on the dollar when settling up the purchase price. These reserve errors can be very material when compared to the purchase price. Even if the appraisal sales price is based on the "correct" reserves, the seller feels blindsided because its actual gain (especially when computed on a GAAP basis) can be significantly less than it had projected.

In a recent version of this story, the buyers hired a team of consulting actuaries to comb through the booked statutory reserves for "errors" as part of the due diligence process. I wonder if this shouldn't be a best practice for the sellers prior to the bidding and negotiation process begins. At the same time, there might be some way to modify the standard sales agreement so these types of disputes are minimized. Perhaps the buyer and seller get a third party to establish the appropriate level of reserves or agree upon statutory reserve methodologies during the early stages of the sales process.

The models of the existing business are used to project statutory earnings over the lifetime of the business. The projection period is intended to cover the time period until all but a small amount of business has run off the books, so that extending the period further would not materially affect the appraisal. The typical projection period for individual life and annuity business is 30 years. Short-tail blocks such as some group coverages may use a shorter projection period. For some long-tail blocks such as long-term care or structured settlements a projection period greater than 30 years may be appropriate.

Minor blocks of business or ancillary coverages may be reflected in an aggregate manner instead of by developing refined models. For example, the value of miscellaneous blocks of liabilities may be determined by applying runoff trend factors to historical earnings or by developing an estimate of the redundancy in the reserves as of the appraisal date. The value of minor rider coverages may be determined by applying a profit margin to a runoff trend projection of rider premium.

An important step in the development of a model is to review the ability of the model to validate historical experience. This includes validating both balance sheet amounts (statutory and tax reserves, inforce amounts, account values, etc.) and income statement amounts (premium, policy charges, death benefits, surrenders, etc.). Often the development of a model follows an iterative process, whereby certain elements of both the model structure and assumptions are refined in order to produce adequate validations. Often a buyer will spend a significant amount of time reviewing model validations and detailed projections as part of a due diligence process in order to gain comfort that the model appropriately reflects the characteristics of the business and to develop an understanding of how assumptions are applied. This process is discussed in detail in Chapter 5.

CRYPT 4.5

Extreme Appraising

Actuarial appraisals are important components of most M&A transactions. Typically the seller engages an independent actuary to provide an actuarial appraisal of the business to be sold. The buyers are then given this appraisal as a part of the information provided to assist them in developing an acquisition proposal.

In this case, the process began normally. The seller had put together a descriptive memorandum and had engaged an independent actuarial firm to provide an appraisal. This material was provided, along with other information, to potential buyers. The intermediary working for the seller was unaware that, in several places, significant adverse experience (e.g., a recent loss of a major source of business) was ignored in the appraisal report.

When buyers began their due diligence, differences between the assumptions used in the appraisal and what the company's experience suggested were quite troubling to the readers. Buyer concerns reflected themselves in a more intense effort to look for other flaws or areas where the values could be discounted. Because of the heightened concern of buyers that there might be other aggressive assumptions employed in the appraisal, the search for negative adjustments was intense, with no counter-balancing search for potential pockets of profits that hadn't been reflected in the appraisal.

The end result was that the company was pulled off the market and ultimately, several years later, sold at a significant discount to what it might have been sold for had the original work been done professionally. The moral is that the actuarial appraisal should be credible and transparent because buyer confidence in the appraisal will generally lead to a positive outlook and a more attractive proposed price. An actuarial appraisal that becomes suspect will be the catalyst for significant buyer negativity and, ultimately, either a low proposed price or disappearing interest.

4.5.3 FUTURE BUSINESS VALUE

The third primary component of an actuarial appraisal value is the economic value of business to be written in the future. While the same techniques are used to value future business as to value inforce, the valuation of future business is considerably less certain due to (a) uncertainty over new business volumes to be produced in the future and (b) uncertainty over expected profit margins that will be embedded in future pricing of products.

4.5.3.1 New Business Production

The level of new business production, mix of products, and future growth rates are typically based on marketing forecasts by the target company's management. Frequently insurance company management will have a formal plan for three to five years into the future, which would be the starting point for the analysis. Growth rates subsequent to the plan period should reflect expectations for the overall growth rates in the specific markets and lines of business the target company is in, as well as potential for market share expansion. It may be appropriate to have alternative production scenarios for either external shocks (economic changes, tax law changes) or internal changes specific to a company.

Company ratings are extremely important in certain lines of business. Various production scenarios may be illustrated based on assumptions should there be a ratings upgrade or downgrade. An acquirer should also consider the impact on production levels of any changes expected to be made as a result of the transaction directly to the distribution system or the potential ramifications of a transaction on agent retention.

4.5.3.2 Profitability of Future Business

Future business projections can be developed based on assumptions comparable to those used to value the inforce business, adjusted for any issues unique to new sales. In addition to recent experience, the actuarial assumptions are typically reviewed in comparison to the assumptions currently used in pricing new products. In general, pricing assumptions are viewed as representing management's current best estimates for future experience. For product lines where a company has significant experience, future business assumptions for the appraisal are generally set both on experience and current pricing expectations. For new lines of business or new markets, greater reliance would typically be placed on pricing assumptions or general industry experience.

The results of appraisal analysis of future business profitability can be compared directly to internal company pricing targets. For example, if a company prices for a 12% internal rate of return (IRR), then the value of future business under comparable assumptions at a discount rate of 12% should be approximately zero. Differences from that result should be able to be determined by isolating the impact of any assumption or model differences.

The profitability of future business in an appraisal also can be compared to general market conditions and profitability expectations. In competitive markets, for example, a buyer may conclude that a return above 12% is not sustainable due to market pressures on product margins. On the other hand, a company may be able to maintain above-market returns if it has some form of competitive advantage such as lower expenses or a particular market niche.

4.5.3.3 Value of New Business

The actuarial value of future business is determined based on the combination of the profitability of new business, the amount of annual production, and the number of years the production is assumed to continue. The value has traditionally been reflected in actuarial appraisals in one of two ways:

1) The actuarial value of future business is reflected under a given production plan for a specified number of years. The production plan is typically the company management's plan for as long a period as that continues, together with a long-term growth rate assumption beyond

the plan period. The specified number of years the production is assumed to continue is most typically 10 years although alternatives of 5 years, 20 years, or in perpetuity may be illustrated. Advantages of this approach include:

- It explicitly reflects management's plan over the planning period, including any business shifts among products or distribution systems.
- It allows for certain assumptions to change over time, such as the absorption of any unallocated expense as the company grows.
- It produces a projected statutory income statement, facilitating analysis such as dynamic validations and capital funding determination. A further by-product is an earnings projection under PGAAP, as described in Chapter 8.

This approach is typically followed in appraisals provided by sellers in the United States.

2) The actuarial value of future business is illustrated for just one year of issue. Various multipliers are then illustrated, representing the present value of $1 of production based on assumptions for growth rate, discount rate, and number of years of new business. The total value of future business is then the product of the multiplier times the value of one year of new business. The advantages of this approach are:

- It allows the user of the report to easily adjust for different growth rates, years of new business, etc.
- It provides a straightforward basis for comparison of prices paid in transactions. For example, the goodwill premium may be described as "a multiplier of eight on one year of new business value."

This approach is often used in emerging markets, where growth rates may be uncertain and buyers may wish to look at a number of production scenarios and periods. This approach is also used by analysts in the United Kingdom and other markets where companies publicly report an estimate of the value of new business produced over the past period.

Under the same assumptions for growth rate, discount rate, and years of new business, the two approaches provide the same result, as illustrated in Table 4.6.

VALUE OF FUTURE BUSINESS
(in millions)

	10.0%	10.0%	10.0%
Actuarial Value 1 Year of New Business Production	$11.47	$8.33	$5.94
Multiplier: 10% growth rate, 10 years of production	10.00	9.23	8.56
Total Future Business Value	114.7	76.9	50.8
Actuarial Value 10 Years of New Business Production	114.7	76.9	50.8

TABLE 4.6

Assumptions regarding production growth rates and the number of years of production vary considerably by market segment, company, geographical region, and general market conditions. The pricing of the largest life insurance transactions in the United States have reflected 10 or more years of new business value. By contrast, acquisitions of smaller companies or troubled situations have typically reflected value from 10 years or less of future production. The number of years of new business production, or the new business multiplier, can be viewed as the largest component of goodwill premium associated with a life insurer acquisition. Troubled situations have generally resulted in transactions with little goodwill premium, while acquisitions of high quality companies with a strong market presence have typically resulted in substantial goodwill premiums.

As an example of how multipliers used for new business may vary over time based on business outlook, as well as vary by company and region, the following Table 4.7 illustrates sample multipliers taken from published analysts' reports in the United Kingdom, where companies provide an estimate of the value associated with one year's new business production.

SAMPLE NEW BUSINESS MULTIPLIERS

COMPANY		Morgan Stanley[1] Fall 2000	Fall 2001	February 2002	October 2002	December 2003	UBS Warburg[2] 7/02 – 9/02	
Aviva (CGNU)	UK	18.0	17.8	18.0	14.9	9.1	UK Life	10.0
	Non-UK	16.0	24.7	16.0	14.9	9.1	Europe Life	13.0
							Other Life	10.0
							Other Business	12.0
Legal & General		22.0	20.0	20.0	14.0	7.9	US	13.0
							UK Life	12.0
							UK Mgd. Funds	10.0
Prudential Plc	UK	15.8	12.0	18.0	12.4	9.7		8.0
	US	21.7	12.0	13.0	12.4	9.7		11.0
	Asia	45.5	26.0	22.0	12.4	9.7		15.0
	Europe	26.7	19.0	16.0	12.4	9.7		13.0
Aegon		40.0	32.0	32.0	9.4	9.2	N/A	
ING		30.0	20.0	20.0	14.6	12.7		11.4
AXA					10.0	13.3	US	9.8
							UK	9.4
							France, Germany	10.2
							Japan	12.0

TABLE 4.7

1 UBS Warburg report dated October 15, 2002.

2 Morgan Stanley reports dated November 15, 2001, February 7, 2002, October 2002, and December 2003.

4.6 INDIVIDUAL LIFE & ANNUITY PRODUCT LINE ISSUES

The sections below describe issues of particular importance with respect to modeling and valuing individual life insurance and annuity lines of business. Specific issues related to the individual lines change over time along with the general economic environment and the insurance marketplace, so inevitably new issues will arise as the environment evolves.

4.6.1 LIFE INSURANCE

There is a fair amount of actuarial literature on techniques for developing models of life insurance blocks of business. Typically, life insurance projections are developed with commercially available actuarial projection software and reflect a representative model consisting of model points covering major plans, issue years, major underwriting classes, males and females, and a range of issue ages.

Models of flexible premium UL and variable universal life blocks of business often reflect different funding levels in order to capture the dynamics of alternative premium patterns. Possible funding buckets in the model include the following:

1) Premium-paying vs. non-premium-paying: The model may distinguish between policies that have received any premium contribution over the prior 12 months versus those that have not.

2) Funding level split based on target premium: High-funded, medium-funded, and low-funded policies may be distinguished by the current account value as a percent of cumulative target premium or some other benchmark measure.

3) Funding level split based on projected charges: Funding level may be distinguished by the length of time a policy would continue in force, covering future cost of insurance (COI) and other policy changes, without any additional premium payments.

The importance of funding level will vary by block of business. The economics of some blocks of UL business are extremely sensitive to funding level while other blocks of UL were designed to be largely insensitive to premium patterns.

The general approach to developing assumptions was described earlier in this chapter. Certain assumptions that are of particular importance to life insurance business include the following:

1) Mortality improvement: The U.S. insurance industry has seen general mortality improvement over time, both from population improvement and improved underwriting. During the 1990s, the overall level of population mortality improvement exceeded 1% per year. Companies vary in the degree that they include future anticipated mortality improvement in best estimate assumptions for pricing and US GAAP financial reporting. For purposes of an actuarial appraisal, the actuary should consider whether future improvement is appropriate in light of the characteristics of the block, experience, and management expectations. Typically, if the impact were material, a sensitivity test would quantify the impact of future mortality improvement on the results.

2) Reinsurance: If material, the impact of reinsurance should be reflected in the actuarial values of life insurance business. In the mid-1990s it became common for life insurers to reinsure the majority of their competitive level term insurance business, both to manage mortality risk and because the pricing of the business often improved after reflecting the financial benefit of reinsurance. The appraisal should consider recapture provisions, the likelihood of the reinsurers to change rates, or other items that may affect the value of the block.

3) Reserve issues: The statutory reserves for life insurance are calculated according to a defined set of state regulations and are generally predictable for purposes of financial projections. Reserves related to long-term guarantees and secondary guarantees, including Actuarial Guidelines XXX and AXXX, may be more complex to model and can have a material impact on both projected earnings and value. In addition, life insurers frequently reinsure the deficiency reserves related to term insurance and secondary guarantees on UL.

4) Low interest rate environment: The low interest rate environment seen in the early 2000s raised considerable concern over the potential cost of the guaranteed interest rates in life insurance contracts. Sensitivity tests related to the potential cost of the interest guarantee should be prepared and reviewed. It may be important to consider as well the reinvestment risk as policyholders realize the value of the guarantees with respect to both potentially lower lapses or increased funding of contracts.

5) Non-guaranteed elements: Crediting strategies and any changes to loads or COIs in UL products are generally based on management's strategies, either for the seller or the buyer (reflecting changes a buyer might make). In addition to contractual guarantees, it is important to reflect any potential non-contractual implied guarantees that may be in place, such as sales literature, illustrations, or past company practice.

4.6.2 FIXED DEFERRED ANNUITIES

Actuarial values for blocks of individual deferred annuities are typically developed from a model office in the same manner as life insurance blocks. For blocks of fixed (general account) annuities, the risks causing the most concern tend to be disintermediation and reinvestment risk and the ability to achieve required spread between earned and credited rates. As interest rates fell in the early 2000s, many annuity carriers were able to take advantage of the interest environment to lower crediting rates on inforce blocks more quickly than portfolio yields fell, thereby widening spreads. As interest rates rise, companies will face the question of whether credited rates will need to increase more quickly than portfolio yields in order to remain competitive with alternative investments. If not, they risk increased lapsation and potential capital losses from liquidating low yielding investments in a higher interest rate environment. The crediting rates and guarantees in a contract may also have an impact on increasing or decreasing premium flows into flexible premium (FPDA) contracts, although for most blocks of deferred annuity business the anticipated renewal premium flow is small. The actuarial appraisal should follow management's expectations for credited rate strategies in alternative yield curve environments.

If a company has a sizable block of fixed deferred annuity business or other interest-sensitive business, the actuarial appraisal will often include an analysis of the impact on the economic value of alternative interest scenarios. This may be illustrated either via deterministic scenarios, such as "an immediate increase in the yield curve of 1%" or "a gradual decrease of 2.5% over 10 years," or stochastic scenarios where a large number of alternative scenarios are projected under stochastically generated interest rates and summarized based on mean, various percentiles, etc. ASOP 19 states that:

> ...in many areas, such as evaluating interest-sensitive and variable life insurance and annuity products, deterministic approaches may be inadequate for properly evaluating and projecting financial results. The actuary needs to examine each assumption critically in this regard, and apply stochastic analysis where the tools exist and where stochastic analysis is deemed material to the appraisal.

For both deterministic and stochastic analyses, the interest scenarios should represent a reasonable range of results since the actuarial values should continue to reflect best estimate assumptions. For example, the standard seven scenarios used for appointed actuary analysis may be viewed as somewhat extreme scenarios, which, while appropriate for purposes of establishing reserves with a certain degree of conservatism, may reflect interest movements that are too large to provide a reasonable range of results for an appraisal. Certain characteristics of deterministic and stochastic analysis are:

1) Deterministic analysis may point to specific interest exposures in blocks of business that would be buried in a stochastic analysis. Deterministic scenarios that reflect immediate up or down yield curve shocks provide an indication of the movement in actuarial value subsequent to the yield curve date that formed the basis for the appraisal.

2) Stochastic analysis may do a more complete job at valuing options in products. Some buyers view the appropriate best estimate economic value as the mean value under a set of stochastic interest rate projections.

Assumptions regarding lapse rates are an important driver of the actuarial values on fixed deferred annuities. Lapse rates can vary widely based on product features, including surrender charges, market and distribution, relative competitiveness of the crediting rates, and other factors. Deferred annuity policyholders frequently exhibit a significant shock lapse in the year following the expiration of the surrender charge. Partial withdrawal features are actively utilized in fixed deferred annuities. Partial withdrawal amounts may range from 1% to 2% or more of account value annually. For annuities written as tax-qualified business, the impact of minimum withdrawal rates after age 70 and a half should also be considered.

4.6.3 FIXED IMMEDIATE ANNUITIES

The liability cash flows for fixed immediate annuities are quite predictable because the products are non-surrenderable and generally are not impacted by the economic environment. For these liabilities it is common to use a seriatim (policy by policy) projection since statutory and GAAP valuation systems can provide the projection of expected cash flows and reserves on a precise basis and the liability model generally does not need to be dynamic. The economic environment may substantially affect asset cash flows, of course, and the primary risk for fixed immediate annuities is reinvestment risk. On blocks of structured settlements, cash flows may extend for beyond 30 years so that a cash flow match between assets and liabilities is not possible, leaving the company exposed to some form of reinvestment risk (for example, credit spread risk) even if the block is matched durationally.

Mortality assumptions for fixed immediate annuities are usually based on standard statutory valuation tables or U.S. population tables. The mortality risk on substandard immediate annuities may lack credible experience, and sensitivity testing is appropriate if the impact of this assumption is material. Projected future mortality improvement should be considered.

4.6.4 VARIABLE ANNUITIES

The primary risk for variable annuities (VAs, or separate account annuities) relates to future policyholder investment returns. VA business typically has monthly fees that are specified contractually, but the revenue is highly dependent on funds under management. Since maintenance expenses are relatively fixed, the earnings on VA business have a high degree of operational leverage. In addition, most VA contracts feature some form of guaranteed minimum death benefit, and some blocks have guaranteed minimum income and/or withdrawal benefits. The cost of these features increases substantially as separate account returns fall, so that the value of the business is highly dependent on equity and other market movements. A best estimate separate account return usually reflects a combination of management expectations, such as GAAP or pricing long-term return assumptions, and historical returns for market indices consistent with the underlying fund distribution. The risk associated with market movements should be illustrated in sensitivity analysis, either through deterministic or stochastic scenarios. Seriatim projections may be required to appropriately reflect the cost associated with the guarantees.

Many of the leading VA carriers have either implemented, or are in the process of implementing, some form of hedging to limit their exposure to market movements. In part this has been driven by the market declines subsequent to 2000 and in part reflects NAIC required capital guidelines that result in substantial increases to required capital for most VA business that is not hedged. Both the costs and benefits of a company's hedging program should be reflected in an appraisal analysis. Likewise, the impact of any reinsurance a company may have on guaranteed benefits should be reflected, including the costs, benefits, and impact on reserves and capital requirements.

Embedded options or guarantees in variable contracts may be separately valued through option pricing techniques. For example, the cost of a guaranteed death benefit in a VA contract can be determined by calculating the theoretical cost of the benefit under an option pricing model. Alternatively, the cost of the guarantee could be set based on the actual cost of fully hedging the guarantee by directly reflecting what an investment bank would charge for the hedge, or reflecting the cost of a series of over-the-counter options that would replicate the benefit. Option pricing techniques can be applied to non-variable blocks of business as well, such as determining the theoretical cost of a guaranteed interest rate in a fixed deferred annuity.

The general account option in VAs requires similar considerations to those described in the prior section on fixed deferred annuities. In addition, consideration should be given to the option policyholders have to move funds from separate accounts to the general account, particularly in low interest environments where the fixed account guarantee may be relatively attractive.

4.7 HEALTH AND GROUP LIFE COVERAGES

In this section, a wide range of coverages is discussed, including individual, group, and various situations with aspects of both group and individual coverages. The coverages have been categorized based on the similarity of their general modeling techniques in the following five coverage groupings:

- Traditional group term coverages are one-year term coverages issued by insurance companies. They contain few, if any, guarantees on rates or renewability. Typical products include group life, accidental death and dismemberment (AD&D), long-term disability (LTD), short-term disability (STD), indemnity medical, dental, and medical stop loss. The bulk of group life and health premium sold falls into this category.
- Guaranteed elements within group term coverages create the need for special modeling techniques. These features include portability options, extended rate guarantees, conversion options, and other special benefits.
- Voluntary and worksite coverages cover a broad spectrum from traditional group policies with additional underwriting and guarantees to individual policies with limits on rates, renewability, and underwriting. Benefits under these coverages are often highly unique and customized; however, from a modeling perspective, similar principles apply.
- Group life coverages containing individual life-type guarantees include group universal life, group variable universal life, corporate-owned life insurance, and similar coverages.
- Traditional individual health products span a wide range of benefits provided and rating structures. Typical products include individual disability income (DI), long-term care (LTC), medical, hospital indemnity, dental, critical illness (CI), accident coverages, and others.

The analysis excludes other health-related organizations, such as managed care providers, TPAs, health services providers, pharmacy benefit managers (PBMs), and vision care networks because actuarial methodology is typically not applied in these situations.

4.7.1 TRADITIONAL GROUP TERM INSURANCE PRODUCTS

Traditional group is one-year term and contains few, if any, guarantees on rates or renewability. Typical products include group life, AD&D, LTD, STD, indemnity medical, dental, and medical stop loss.

4.7.1.1 Nature of Group Term Insurance

Group term coverages are driven by considerably different factors than individual life and health products, which have long-term guarantees. The projection models used for group term appraisals should be consistent in structure with the way that the group business is managed. In particular, group term coverages generally can be re-priced or non-renewed annually.

Pricing of group risks is done at the case level, based on a large number of factors, including:

- industry
- underwriting basis (e.g., guaranteed issue amounts, plan maximums, pre-existing conditions, exclusions)
- case size
- plan design (e.g., benefit options, plan parameters)
- prior experience
- underwriters' judgment
- competitive discounting.

As a result, the pricing of each case (group) is unique. Manual rates are often the starting point, not the ending point, for pricing. Pricing is also dynamic in that rate guarantees are generally limited to two years on new business and one year on renewals. The underlying risk profile (census) of each case can change each year. A substantial amount of judgment and discounting can take place. Group insurance is re-priced at each renewal by adjusting rates for the differences in the actual-to-expected loss ratios (e.g., morbidity or mortality assumptions), at either the case or the block level. This is contrasted against individual products, which have long-term guaranteed prices set at issue.

Group term insurance operates in a commodity-like environment that sets practical limits on the pricing flexibility open to an insurer. The factors that go into setting appraisal assumptions for group projections include:

- experience loss ratios (e.g., morbidity or mortality)
- pricing targets (target loss ratios and profit margins)
- pricing strategy and tactics
- external benchmarks (competitive limitations).

If a company's recent morbidity experience is worse than its target loss ratio, it usually has a plan to raise rates on renewal. To the extent that the plan is explicit and the company has a track record of successful implementation of rate increases, it is reasonable to build expected rate increases into the projection assumptions. However, competitive pressures restrict the amount of rate increase that is practical to achieve. External benchmarks should be used to validate that level. In group insurance, the external environment is as important as the company's internal environment in determining appropriate projection assumptions.

4.7.1.2 General Modeling Issues for Group Term Products

Due to the nature of group term products, there are certain modeling issues that need to be addressed. Some of these considerations are discussed below.

4.7.1.2.1 Projection Period

Group term business is annually renewable; renewals have to be re-sold each year. Therefore, the projection period is generally more limited than that for individual products. A 10-year projection period is common; however, there are no fixed rules.

Another common approach in sellers' appraisals is to set the projection period to be the same for all products (i.e., the longer period used for individual products). However, potential buyers might ignore any incremental value produced by such a longer projection period.

Runout of existing and future claim reserves is guaranteed; thus, projecting the full runout period for long-tail claim reserves (e.g., group life waiver of premium (WP), LTD disabled lives reserve (DLR)) is appropriate. For practical considerations, the claim reserve runout is generally cut off after 20 or 30 years.

4.7.1.2.2 Definitions of Inforce and Sales

In group insurance, a high proportion of a company's business commonly has a January 1 effective date. "Sold date" is often reported as the date of quote or the date the quote is accepted rather than the effective date. Therefore, for a 12/31 appraisal date, a potentially significant amount of business that has been sold may not be reported in the 12/31 inforce listing. However, trying to model these situations exactly could complicate the modeling process without adding materially to the overall utility of results. Group appraisals generally try to incorporate reasonable approximations to address these types of issues.

It is common to limit sales projections to five or 10 years of new business. Techniques include both the multiple years of issue and the one-year of issue methods mentioned in section 4.5.3.3.

4.7.1.2.3 Acquisition vs. Maintenance Expenses

Group writers vary widely regarding the expenses they classify as acquisition versus maintenance. The critical distinction is to differentiate between expenses that are truly one-time and those that are ongoing. This split can have a material impact on appraisal values. External benchmarks should be consulted regarding the reasonableness of the seller's expense assumptions.

4.7.1.2.4 Value of Renewals and the Impact of Ownership of the Distribution System

If the seller's distribution system does not move to the acquirer, the producer will likely try to re-establish his or her relationships with the case through a new insurance company. Thus, it is critical in "buyer's" appraisals to understand the buyer's distribution strategy and what will happen with any acquired sales capabilities and to adjust the projected lapse rates accordingly.

Blocks of group business are likely to suffer additional shock lapses following the announcement of the sale as competitors try to exploit any uncertainty in the minds of employers or brokers. In particular, this can be a problem when the buyer plans to re-write the group business from the selling company's paper to the buyer's paper. This re-write process generally results in shock lapses as clients are confronted with a decision point they would otherwise not face. The level of shock lapse is often higher for voluntary coverages.

4.7.1.2.5 Reserves and Reserve Margins

A substantial portion of the value of group term business may be implicit in statutory claim reserve margins. Claim reserve margins can also have a substantial and sometimes misleading impact on profitability. Thus, it is critical to understand the dynamics of claim reserves and to reflect them in the model.

For many group term coverages (e.g., AD&D, STD, Life Death Benefit (DB)), claims are short tail and reserves are based on simple IBNR claim triangles. However, individual company practices vary widely, and it is important to analyze historical claim reserve adequacy tests to understand the seller's specific situation and model it consistently. When buyers make their adjustments to appraisal model results, they often assume they will convert the seller's reserve base to their own (if the difference is material).

Medical, dental, and similar group term coverages also have relatively short-tail claims and use IBNR triangles; however, the situation is more complex than for AD&D. Medical trends, utilization, backlogs, seasonality, and other factors have a material impact on reserve margins. Recent loss ratios (and profitability) can be distorted, which could have a material impact on starting model assumptions. It is important to look at accident year as well as calendar year experience.

Life WP and LTD DLR are long-tail claim reserves; their statutory reserves often contain substantial margins. However, reserving methodologies and assumptions and actual claim run-out experience can vary significantly from company to company. It is not uncommon for claim reserve margins to be much higher in early claim durations relative to later claim durations. This can distort apparent profitability; for instance, a company whose sales growth has slowed can show a dramatic increase in apparent profitability. One way to adjust for this potential problem is to project "no-margin" claim reserves and paid claims, then calculate the statutory, GAAP, and tax reserve margins separately.

Interest margins may be a substantial component of claim reserve margins. Also, tax-to-statutory reserve differentials can have a material impact on value and should be modeled explicitly.

Group term coverages seldom have contract reserves. An exception is when there are extended rate guarantees with inadequate rates. The insurance company should recognize these situations and should hold reserves; however, industry practice in this area is inconsistent. Other situations requiring contract reserves are described in section 4.7.2.

4.7.1.2.6 Investment Income Assumptions

In general, models of group term products assume that premium rates will be adjusted on new and renewal business to react to future changes in interest rates. Thus, other than for potential rate guarantees, the values of new business and future premium renewals are relatively insulated from future interest rate changes. However, life WP and LTD DLR claim reserve interest rates do represent long-term interest commitments, and potential mismatches between asset and liability flows must be reviewed. Also, in cash transactions, the new assets will likely have significantly different yield rates than the seller's assets, and reserves may need to be adjusted.

4.7.2 SITUATIONS WITH ASPECTS OF BOTH GROUP AND INDIVIDUAL COVERAGES

Special modeling considerations within group term coverages include guaranteed elements such as portability options, extended rate guarantees, conversion options, special benefits, etc.

Voluntary and worksite coverages cover a broad spectrum, from group policies with additional underwriting and guarantees to individual policies with varying degrees of flexibility in rates, renewability, and underwriting. The coverages and benefits are often highly unique and customized; however, from a modeling perspective, the principles are similar.

4.7.2.1 Special Modeling Considerations in Group Term Coverages

There are several considerations for modeling group term coverages.

- Portability and ported lives. Portability provisions vary widely. Ported lives generally have substantially higher mortality or morbidity than active lives. Often, companies overlook or underestimate potential past and future liabilities.
- Group conversions. Similar to portability, conversions contain guarantees or options not found in traditional group contracts; corresponding liabilities may be understated.
- Beneficiary checking account. Asset spreads on a group life beneficiary checking account represent a potential source of value.
- Association, affinity, or other special purpose groups. These types of groups often rely on special relationships, the likely continuance of which must be identified and evaluated by the actuary to validate any value.
- Other specialty coverages. Specialty accident, travel, and other unusual or non-standard coverages require specific expertise and careful investigation to avoid overlooking potential values or liabilities.

4.7.2.2 Voluntary and Worksite Coverages

As mentioned above, there is a considerable overlap between voluntary and worksite benefits, underwriting, rating, etc. The actuary must decide which type of modeling platform (i.e., group or individual) is most suitable based on the characteristics of the specific coverage.

Individual-type modeling is most suitable when individual lives have rights to renew the coverage separately from the rest of the group or if the policy has issue age-based premiums or individual-level nonforfeiture values. This includes most individual policies as well as many group policies such as group universal life (GUL), group variable universal life (GVUL), and group LTC.

Group modeling platforms are most appropriate when the attained rates are age-based and the coverage ceases when the group policy terminates. This generally includes coverages linked to an underlying group term policy as well as some stand-alone voluntary group or community-rated coverages.

4.7.3 GROUP LIFE COVERAGES THAT INCLUDE INDIVIDUAL-LIFE-TYPE GUARANTEES

This category includes GUL, GVUL, corporate-owned life insurance (COLI), bank-owned life insurance (BOLI), trust-owned life insurance (TOLI), group whole life (GWL), and similar group products. These products have guarantees and other features (e.g., cash values) that require individual modeling techniques.

In general, these types of coverages use individual life modeling platforms and entail similar considerations as described in section 4.6. These products may have considerations worthy of reflecting in the modeling, such as testing that GVUL contracts have not exceeded permitted funding levels or identifying potential tax considerations of COLI, BOLI, and TOLI-type contracts.

4.7.4 INDIVIDUAL HEALTH COVERAGES

This section addresses individual health products issued by insurance companies. These contracts can include a wide range of rate and renewability guarantees. Typical products include DI, LTC, medical, hospital indemnity, dental, CI, and accident coverages. This section also applies to group health coverages, such as group LTC, that utilize an individual-type modeling platform.

4.7.4.1 Morbidity Assumptions

The structure of individual health morbidity assumptions can span a wide range. DI and LTC products tend to use claim incidence and termination rates. Medical and dental coverages tend to use claim costs.

Health morbidity experience can vary widely from company to company and situation to situation. A variety of methods can be used to set appraisal assumptions. Often adjustment factors are applied to industry experience tables to match to recent company experience. Other times the seller's pricing assumptions are adjusted as appropriate. When selecting appropriate adjustment factors, attention should be given to the credibility and volatility of the seller's data, and the results compared against industry benchmarks.

Sometimes improvements in morbidity are anticipated based on recent or projected changes in claim management or underwriting practices. These should be carefully evaluated and quantified by the appraising or reviewing actuary. Likewise, assumptions for trend can be critical and should be supported by experience reports and comparisons to external benchmarks.

4.7.4.2 Rate Guarantees, Rate Increases, and Renewability

Individual health coverages vary widely as to the contractual provisions and policyholder expectations regarding rate increases and renewability. For some products, rate increases are common and accepted. For most coverages, rate increases are rare and unpopular. Non-cancelable products may not increase rates. When projecting any rate increases, the following factors should be considered:

- company's history of rate increases, including timeliness and percent of target achieved
- regulatory approval process, including potential delays and reductions
- lapse and antiselection on lapse
- impact of potential bad publicity on reputation and sales
- lawsuit potential.

Many potential buyers are apprehensive about future rate increases and may discount much of the value generated by them.

4.7.4.3 Reserves and Reserve Margins

Individual health coverages generally have both contract and claim reserves. Considerations related to claim reserves are generally similar to those described under group term products described in section 4.7.1.2.5.

Considerations related to contract reserves are generally similar to those described for individual life contracts in section 4.6. One major difference is that morbidity experience tends to exhibit significant variations from company to company and situation to situation, much more so than individual life mortality experience tends to do. Thus, it is critical to examine or perform experience studies and appraisal assumptions accordingly.

4.7.4.4 Lapse Rates

In general, individual health lapses are modeled using techniques similar to individual life products; however, the impact can be much different. Individual health pricing is often lapse-supported; this is particularly true for DI and LTC coverages. DI and LTC contracts commonly have steep claim costs by age and no nonforfeiture values. If ultimate lapse rates are lower than pricing, the value of the business can disappear or even turn negative.

Experience and modeling assumptions must be examined closely. Comparison to external benchmarks is critical. Models frequently have to be refined to adequately capture the variety of coverages and variations in experience within blocks of DI and LTC.

4.7.4.5 Investment Income

In most respects, considerations for the modeling of investment income are consistent with those for individual life products. There are a few significant differences, however:

- DI and LTC contracts have long coverage periods and long-tail claims. Combined with the fact they commonly do not have cash values, the average duration of liabilities is very long.
- Some companies try to lock in yields on future premium flows through hedging vehicles, which must be evaluated and modeled. For long-tail health coverage, which can extend beyond 30 years, it may not be possible to match cash flows; instead, companies will manage durations and, potentially, partial durations over time.
- Some companies do not hedge or match future liability durations closely; the potential reaction of a buyer to the related volatility of future earnings or the cost of restructuring the asset portfolio should be considered.

The combination of high renewal premium flow, steep claim curves, and low lapse rates can make the earnings on the long tail health liabilities highly sensitive to investment earnings. Therefore, this assumption is typically analyzed further through sensitivity testing with respect to future economic environments.

4.8 ISSUES RELATED TO SALE OF A BLOCK OF LIFE OR HEALTH BUSINESS

In addition to the M&A market of insurance companies, there is an active market in the purchase and sale of blocks of business. In general, the motivations of buyers and sellers of blocks of business are the same as for transactions involving entire companies. However, the sale of a block of business is often driven by the desire of an insurance company to exit a particular line of business while retaining the corporate entity to pursue its remaining business lines. This section primarily relates to the sale of 100% of a line of business, although comparable analysis would apply to a quota share sale of a portion of a block. For reinsurance transactions, the seller is referred to as the ceding company and the buyer as the assuming company.

4.8.1 REINSURANCE APPROACHES

The sale of a block of business is accomplished through a reinsurance mechanism. The primary alternatives are the following:

1) Assumption reinsurance: Under assumption reinsurance, the underlying policyholder contracts are transferred from the seller's books to the buyer's books. In order to accomplish this, policyholder notification is required. In a number of states, affirmative consent by the policyholder is necessary to transfer the policy; in the majority of states, lack of non-consent is sufficient. Assumption reinsurance is the cleanest approach, since the ceding company is no longer part

of the structure. However, due to the legal and regulatory complexity, assumption reinsurance is relatively uncommon. In addition, there are some tax disadvantages to assumption reinsurance, discussed later in this section.

2) Indemnity coinsurance: Under an indemnity coinsurance structure, the financial interest in the contracts is transferred to the assuming company but the policies remain as policies of the ceding company. While the purchaser may choose to notify the policyholders, there is not a requirement to do so. The advantage to a coinsurance structure is that it can be accomplished quickly with no disruption to policyholders other than potential service-related disruptions if policy administration is transferred. Coinsurance generally requires more limited regulatory approval than assumption reinsurance or a company acquisition, although some states require significant approval processes. The disadvantage is that the ceding company remains in the middle of the transaction, which may be an issue if there are concerns about the ceding company's credit. The assuming company's credit is important as well because the original writing company (ceding company) retains the contractual obligation to the policyholder. Trust accounts may be used to limit the credit exposure to buyer or seller. Coinsurance structures are typically used for the sale of a block of business.

3) Modified coinsurance: A mod-co structure is similar to indemnity coinsurance but the assets backing the liabilities remain with the ceding company. Typically the assets under a mod-co structure would be put into a trust so that the assuming company can retain control over the portfolio. Mod-co structures are relatively uncommon for the sale of a block but may be used in some situations, such as the reinsurance of variable products.

Until the early 1990s, assumption reinsurance was the favored means of acquiring a block of business because policyholder approval was not required and because the tax treatment of the purchase price was favorable. However, the change in law to require policyholder approval for assumption reinsurance, together with tax law changes, subsequently tilted the balance in favor of coinsurance as the predominant mechanism for acquiring a block.

4.8.2 REGULATORY AND TAX ACCOUNTING

The basic financial analysis and valuation of a coinsurance transaction follows the same procedures as the actuarial appraisal of a company. Typically, no capital, surplus, or AVR is transferred with the business. In addition, due to the structure, there are several key adjustments that are made in the development of appraisal values:

1) The asset portfolio that is transferred is marked-to-market as a result of the transaction. The IMR related to the business, as well as IMR associated with the mark-to-market, is also transferred.

2) There are several adjustments to taxes. In particular, the ceding commission (on a tax basis) is deductible by the purchaser.

3) From the seller's perspective, the gain on the transaction on a statutory or GAAP basis is deferred and amortized into income over time.

These items are discussed further in the remainder of this section.

4.8.2.1 Mark-to-Market and Transfer of IMR

Under a reinsurance structure, statutory liabilities are generally transferred to a purchaser on the same basis as was held by the seller. In particular, the statutory liabilities are not updated to current year minimum statutory valuation rates and tables, although a buyer may have the opportunity to reduce any reserves that are in excess of statutory minimums. An exception might be on structured settlements or other payout annuities sold in an interest rate environment that resulted in valuation rates no longer consistent with the yields on the underlying assets. Assets, on the other hand, are transferred at market value as of the date of the transaction. As a result of this mismatch, NAIC model regulations for reinsurance transactions require that a new IMR be established on the books of the purchaser as if the portfolio had actually been liquidated and a capital gain or loss were realized. In addition, the model regulations require that any historic IMR associated with the business on the books of the seller be transferred.

The mark-to-market of the asset portfolio and establishment of IMR does not affect the actual coupon and principal cash flows from the investment portfolio. In fact, the net effect of the mark-to-market of the asset portfolio and the establishment of the IMR is that investment income will continue to reflect the historic book yields of the seller, with two exceptions. First, there is an economic loss from paying tax on the gain in the portfolio immediately, rather than as the investment income is earned. Second, if there were an unrealized loss in the portfolio that exceeds any positive IMR on the books of the purchaser, there would be an economic loss since total IMR is not allowed to fall below zero for statutory accounting purposes.

4.8.2.2 Reinsurance Taxes

There are several adjustments to taxable income as a result of a reinsurance transaction. From the purchaser's perspective, the following adjustments are made:

1) The DAC proxy tax is based on the ongoing net consideration received by the assuming company. For coinsurance, this would typically be premiums less claims and commissions. In addition, DAC proxy tax is payable based on the initial net consideration paid, i.e., the assets transferred backing liabilities less ceding commission. For assumption reinsurance, DAC proxy tax continues to be paid based on premium because the policyholders merely switch to become direct policyholders of the purchaser.

2) The mark-to-market on the asset portfolio creates an immediate taxable gain or loss to the purchaser.

3) The excess ceding commission on a tax basis is deductible. The excess tax ceding commission can be calculated as follows:

Excess Tax Ceding Commission = Purchase Price (statutory ceding commission)
- (Statutory Reserve - Tax Reserve)
- Mark-to-Market of Assets
- DAC Proxy Tax on Initial Consideration.

The period over which the excess tax ceding commission is deductible varies based on structure and type of business. In addition, companies may take different approaches in filing with the IRS. General approaches used are:

- For assumption reinsurance, the entire amount is deductible straight-line over 15 years.

- For coinsurance, amounts associated with new business or goodwill are deductible straight-line over 15 years.

- For coinsurance of inforce business subject to DAC proxy tax, the excess tax ceding commission associated with inforce business is deductible immediately.

- For coinsurance of inforce business not subject to DAC proxy tax, for example qualified annuities, the amount is deductible over the life of the business.

Table 4.8 illustrates the appraisal value for the UL business in the UL Sample Company under a reinsurance structure.

UL SAMPLE COMPANY
Tax Benefit Under Coinsurance
As of December 31, 2004
(in millions)

Component of Value	Discount Rate		
	10.0%	12.0%	14.0%
Initial Statutory Liability	803.4	803.4	803.4
Initial Tax Liability	782.4	782.4	782.4
After Tax After Cost of Capital Value of EB	122.9	99.2	80.4
After Tax After Cost of Capital Value of FB	79.0	44.1	20.6
DAC Proxy Tax on Initial Consideration	51.7	54.0	55.7
Mark-to-Market on Asset Portfolio	0.0	0.0	0.0
Excess Tax Ceding Commission on EB	59.1	27.4	3.2
Tax Benefit from 338 (h) (10) Election :			
DAC Proxy Tax on Initial Consideration	11.1	10.7	10.2
Elimination of Exisiting DAC Proxy Tax Balance	(12.7)	(11.9)	(11.1)
15-Year Deduction on EB	10.5	4.3	0.5
15-Year Deduction on FB	17.0	8.3	3.4
Total Tax Benefit	25.9	11.5	3.0
Adjusted Book Value	100.0	100.0	100.0
Total Value of Inforce	131.8	102.4	79.9
Total Value of New Business	96.1	52.4	24.0
Total Actuarial Value	327.8	254.8	204.0

TABLE 4.8

4.8.2.3 Amortization of Ceding Commission for Selling Company

Under a coinsurance transaction, for statutory purposes the ceding commission (purchase price) results in an immediate gain in surplus. For statutory income purposes, however, the gain is amortized into income over the life of the business, i.e., the expected future profits of the business, with an equal offset in surplus.

For purposes of US GAAP reporting, the ceding commission from a coinsurance transaction results in a deferred gain presented as a liability on the balance sheet. The deferred gain is amortized into income, and therefore equity, over the life of the business.

4.9 P&C INSURANCE COMPANY VALUATION ISSUES

For P&C insurance companies, the sell-side actuarial appraisal has not always been a staple among the financial information available in the data room. Property and casualty insurance products have two distinct features that increase the complexity of the actuarial appraisal and the uncertainty of the resulting sell-side actuarial appraisal value.

First, the renewal assumptions have greater uncertainty than for life and health insurers. Almost all P&C insurance products are one-year contracts. Due to the competitive nature of the personal lines market and the distribution system prevalent for the commercial markets, the persistency and new business assumptions have a greater uncertainty than those for life and health companies.

Second, the timing and amount of the liabilities for P&C insurance products have significantly more variability than life insurance or group health insurance products. In general, P&C insurance liabilities are paid out over a shorter time than for life insurance liabilities. Each type of P&C exposure has a different claim reporting and loss payment pattern. The resulting cash flows for property casualty loss and loss adjustment expenses may differ significantly for two insurance companies writing the same exposure due to diverse claim handling philosophies. As a result, the selling company's P&C actuary typically devotes a significant amount of time gathering data to support the company's estimated loss and loss adjustment expense (LAE) reserves and the implied historical loss ratios. The differences in opinion relating to the estimate of the liabilities for property casualty insurers significantly reduce the certainty of the appraisal value.

In the 1980s and 1990s there were far fewer P&C insurance company transactions than life company transactions. The majority of the P&C acquisitions were strategic acquisitions as opposed to financial acquisitions, which may have led to a greater divergence between the actuarial appraisal value and the purchase price. The actuarial appraisal value represents the economic value of the company being sold. The purchase price, or the amount the buyer is willing to pay, includes numerous factors including the added value from synergies and embedded options, less any transition costs. For strategic buyers, the value of embedded options and synergies may significantly enhance the value of the P&C insurer. Therefore, the economic value developed for the sell-side actuarial appraisal may understate the potential market value of the company.

While sell-side actuarial appraisals are not always readily available, transactions are very rarely consummated without the principals involved having determined the company's value. The purchase price must allow the buyer to meet its target return on investment, and the seller should not be willing to accept an offer significantly below the economic value. Due to the uncertain nature of the liabilities, the most important components for determining the value of a P&C insurer are assessing the adequacy of the loss reserves and estimating the historical and prospective accident year loss ratios.

The Casualty Actuarial Society (CAS) has published many papers regarding issues relating to the valuation of P&C insurance companies, which include valuation techniques to address the unique nature of P&C insurance products and the variability inherent in the cash flows. The following sections highlight some of the valuation issues that are unique to P&C insurance companies including valuation models, loss and LAE reserving techniques, cash flow assumptions, management assumptions, and other P&C valuation issues. These sections provide a summary of the key issues.

4.9.1 DISCOUNTED CASH FLOW VS. ECONOMIC VALUE ADDED METHODS

The uncertainty of the P&C insurance exposure creates significant challenges when developing an actuarial appraisal. During due diligence, the investor's actuary will develop an independent estimate of the loss and LAE reserves. Many times the investor's estimate is materially different than that presented by the selling company due to differences in methods used, selection of key parameters, and differences in actuarial judgment. This is especially true for long-tailed commercial lines of business. Given the difficulty in reaching agreement on the estimated value of the unpaid losses and loss ratios for accident years that have already expired, actuarial appraisals for P&C insurers that include long-term projections of future earnings on business yet to be written can be met with skepticism.

Property and casualty actuaries often use the economic value added (EVA) method in an actuarial appraisal. Traditional discounted cash flow (DCF) determines the value of the firm as the present value of distributable cash flows, which is defined as after-tax earnings minus the increase in required capital measured on a statutory accounting basis. Under the EVA model, the value of the company equals the adjusted statutory book value (ABV) plus the present value of future earnings less the cost of capital. Blackburn provides examples to show that both methods produce the same results for an infinite time horizon under either static or constant growth assumptions.

The most significant difference between the DCF and the EVA approaches relates to the terminal value. The terminal value is the remaining value added after the initial forecast period. Under the DCF approach the terminal value is a significant portion of the appraisal value because it includes the remaining capital value of the company that will eventually flow back to the investor in perpetuity. Therefore, the terminal value increases as the initial forecast period decreases.

Under the EVA approach, the initial capital requirement is immediately recognized, and the terminal value represents only the portion of earnings that exceeds the investor's cost of capital. Under the simplifying assumption that the target company's long-term returns will equal the investor's cost of capital, the terminal value under the EVA approach is zero. Due to the uncertainty in estimating the amount and timing of unpaid loss and LAEs, investors tend to be more comfortable with the short-term projections. Since the terminal value of the EVA method is much smaller, it allows the investor to gain a better understanding and have more control of the assumptions relating to late emerging profits.

4.9.2 ADJUSTMENTS TO BOOK VALUE

For P&C insurance companies, many of the adjustments made to the statutory capital and surplus for life insurers as discussed in section 4.5.1 are equally applicable to the P&C insurers, including deferred tax assets and non-admitted assets. For P&C insurance company valuations, the following additional adjustments to statutory capital and surplus should be considered:

Adequacy loss and LAE reserves—The most significant adjustment to the statutory capital and surplus for P&C insurers usually relates to differences in the estimated adequacy of the recorded loss and LAE reserves. The methods and issues relating to estimating these liabilities are discussed in detail in section 4.9.3. The book value adjustment equals the difference between the recorded reserves and the valuation actuary's best estimate of the loss and LAE reserves, on an undiscounted basis, with no additional margin for risk. The economic value of these liabilities will be captured in the valuation model cash flows. The risk inherent in estimating loss and LAE liabilities is implicitly considered by discounting these cash flows at the selected cost of capital. Statutory reserves that are deemed to be in excess of the best estimate indications should also be included as a book value adjustment.

Goodwill—Under the Code, P&C insurers are allowed to carry goodwill and an admitted asset, subject to certain limitations. The value of goodwill is eliminated for the purposes of a valuation.

Market value of bonds—Statutory accounting requires that bonds in good standing be recorded at amortized cost for P&C insurers. For the purposes of determining the adjusted net worth, bonds should be valued at their market value.

Schedule F penalties for reinsurance—Statutory accounting imposes a Schedule F penalty for P&C insurers that have ceded balances with unauthorized reinsurance companies and other reinsurers that present a collectibility risk. A liability is established on the balance sheet for cessions that are not secured with a letter of credit or other collateral. Many times the collectibility of the ceded balances is not impaired. Therefore, adjustments should be made to reflect the probable recoveries.

Unearned premiums reserve adjustments—Certain P&C insurance policies may require additional reserve provisions. Two common types of policies are retrospectively rated policies and long-duration contracts (see section 4.9.6.2). Differences in the best estimate for the reserve relating to these policies should also be included as a book value adjustment.

4.9.3 LOSS AND LOSS ADJUSTMENT EXPENSE RESERVES

The estimates of the amount and timing of the unpaid loss and LAEs is the most critical aspect of the P&C insurance company valuation. The CAS has published a vast amount of research regarding the models, methods, and techniques used to estimate loss and LAE reserves. Certain loss reserving methods and techniques are applicable to most P&C lines of business, while other methods have been developed for specific types of exposure. In addition, a number of tests have been developed to detect unusual conditions or circumstances that may require the actuary to perform special procedures.

A comprehensive discussion of the various tests used to evaluate P&C loss reserves is beyond the scope of this book. In this section, a brief description of the most common P&C loss and LAE reserving methods is presented. The data considerations, techniques used to estimate key parameters, and the strengths and weakness of the common reserving methods are addressed. The purpose of this section is to allow the reader to develop a better understanding of how changes in claim handling procedures, underwriting decisions, legislative action, judicial interpretation, inflation, and other economic factors impact the estimates of ultimate losses and resulting reserve estimates suggested by the common reserving methods. This is particularly important when performing reserve estimates for an acquisition since these changes are more prevalent for companies being sold. The methods discussed in this section apply to insurance companies as well as to corporations with self-insured P&C exposure.

Valuation models for P&C insurance companies use the best estimate of loss and LAE reserve on a statutory basis. The estimate of the P&C self-insured liabilities for a corporate acquisition and the estimate for purchase price accounting may be made on a "fair value" basis. The CAS Fair Value task force has published a White Paper[7] on Fair Valuing Property/Casualty Insurance Liabilities. This document also serves as a reference on issues relating to purchase price accounting under GAAP. In addition to addressing FASB developments, the paper also addresses fair value of property casualty liabilities under International Accounting Standards #39 (ISA 39). While the valuation techniques for estimating the fair value of property casualty liabilities will be addressed in section 4.9.3.6, the accounting issues are covered in Chapter 8.

4.9.3.1 Data Considerations for Estimating Loss and LAE Reserves

There are several elements of the process by which loss and LAE liabilities are estimated: type of exposure, data, methods, and parameters. Based on the type of exposure, the actuary may choose to apply a method to various types of data, including paid losses, reported losses (paid plus case basis claim reserves also referred to as incurred losses), claim counts, frequency, severity or other loss, and LAE ratios. Similarly, the actuary will consider more than one method for application to a particular data set.

The various methods applied to alternate data sets will likely give rise to a wide range of preliminary reserve estimates. Based on the strengths and weakness of the particular method, for the particular exposure and accident year being estimated, the actuary will select the best estimate. The actuarial judgments inherent in the loss reserving process will naturally lead to differences in opinion of the value of the unpaid losses. The casualty actuarial profession, in its Statement of Principles Regarding Property and Casualty Loss and Loss Adjustment Expense Reserves,[8] has acknowledged that a range of estimates of the liabilities can be considered reasonable.

---

[7] CAS Task Force on Fair Value Liabilities (2001) Casualty Actuarial Society Forum; Vol: Winter: White Paper on Fair Valuing Property/Casualty Insurance Liabilities. Pages 439-570; Arlington, VA.

[8] CAS Yearbook—Statement of Principles Regarding Property Casualty Loss and Loss Adjustment Expense Reserves, adopted May 1998.

Due to the provision for risk, these principles recognize that the estimate of the unpaid losses may differ based on the purpose for which the estimate is being performed. For the purpose of estimating the unpaid losses and cash flows used in a valuation model, the best estimate should be used, without a margin for risk. The margin for risk is intrinsic in the discount for the cost of capital used in the valuation model. The fair value estimate of the self-insured loss and LAE reserves may be the more appropriate estimate for a corporate acquisition when the liabilities are valued on a GAAP basis and the cash flows are not being used in a cash flow valuation model.

Due to the diverse nature of the risk, exposure, and loss development patterns, the loss and LAE reserves are reviewed by line of business. Property and casualty lines of business include fire, earthquake, homeowners, farmowners, commercial multiple peril, mortgage guaranty, ocean and inland marine, medical malpractice, workers' compensation, general liability, product liability, financial guaranty, private passenger auto, commercial auto liability, aircraft, fidelity and surety, burglary and theft, boiler and machinery, and credit.

The segregation of the data used in the analysis of loss and LAE reserves differs for each company based on the amount of business written in each line of business. The two basic principles in evaluating the proper segmentation are homogeneity and credibility. Conforming to the homogeneity principle entails analyzing types of losses that are expected to have similar development patterns. The credibility principle requires a sufficient volume of data to establish stable development patterns. These two principles oppose each other because the former suggests separating the data into refined groups while the latter suggests grouping data for stability.

The 21 lines of business reported in Schedule P of the P&C insurance company statutory annual statement typically form the basis for the data segmentation. However, the claim data is typically segmented into additional detail, such as type of loss, type of product within a line, or geographical regions. For example, personal automobile liability loss reserves may be calculated separately for bodily injury and property damage claims because the former type of claims take significantly longer to settle.

The data used in the loss reserve analysis is typically arranged in a triangular format. The inception to date paid losses, reported losses, reported claim count, and closed claim count data are shown for each accident period, at uniform intervals of valuation. Annual (12-month intervals) and quarterly valuation intervals are most common. The claim data may also be segregated by policy year, report year, or other fiscal year ending period. Accident-year data is the basis for the statutory reporting in Schedule P. Policy-year data is commonly used for corporations with self-insured exposure. Report-year data is commonly used to estimate the reserves for claims-made insurance policies.

In general, the objective for most loss-reserving techniques is to project an estimate of the ultimate losses for each period under review. The total indicated reserve is then determined by subtracting the loss payments made inception to date. When calculating the outstanding liabilities for corporate self-insureds, it is important to distinguish between the claims paid by the third-party claims administrators and the loss payments made by the company being evaluated. Sometimes corporate self-insureds establish prepaid loss fund deposits and other times they are billed subsequent to the administrator paying the claim. The difference in the indicated liability for these two processes may be material.

The total required reserve is made up of two components: the case basis reserves and the incurred but not reported (IBNR) reserves. Case basis reserves are established on an individual claim case basis by the claims adjusters settling the claim. IBNR reserves typically include a provision for claims that have not been reported, pipeline claims (those that have been reported but are not recorded in the insurer's claim system), development on known claims, and the additional cost for claims that have closed but may reopen at a later date. The provision for loss reserves should only include amounts for claims that have been incurred to date. As noted in section 4.9.6.4, the equalization and catastrophe reserves allowed in many European countries are provisions for claims that have not been incurred. These are not considered loss reserves for statutory accounting and should therefore be included as an adjustment to book value.

4.9.3.2 Common Actuarial Techniques for Estimating P&C Loss Reserves

There are numerous actuarial loss reserving techniques for P&C exposure, some specifically designed for unique exposure, and others that are common to most types of insurance. When estimating P&C liabilities, multiple techniques should be applied to the claim data. Most methods begin by projecting the ultimate losses and determine the required reserve by subtracting the payments made to date. The weights assigned to each technique are usually based on actuarial judgment, considering the strengths and weakness of the method and data to which it is being applied. The methods and techniques described below are staples in most actuarial reserve studies for the common lines of business. However, even these methods are considered but disregarded by the reserving actuary under certain circumstances.

4.9.3.2.1 Loss Development Method

The loss development method (LDM) is the most common method used to estimate loss reserves and is a staple in most actuarial reserve studies for P&C lines of business. This method may be applied to the paid or reported losses to project the ultimate losses and is also applied to claim counts to estimate the ultimate number of claims that will be reported for each accident period. This method projects the preliminary estimate of ultimate losses by applying loss development factors (LDFs) to the recent valuation of losses for that accident period (Table 4.10).

PC SAMPLE COMPANY
Workers' Compensation
Summary of Selected Ultimate Losses
as of December 31, 2004

	Estimate of Ultimate Losses ($000)					
Accident Year	(1) LDM Paid Analysis	(2) LDM Reported Analysis	(3) BF Paid Analysis	(4) BF Reported Analysis	(5) Selected Estimate of Ultimates	(6) Weights Used
1991	9,609	9,462	9,597	9,460	9,536	(.5, .5, 0, 0)
1992	13,183	13,155	13,149	13,139	13,169	(.5, .5, 0, 0)
1993	15,851	15,350	15,875	15,378	15,601	(.5, .5, 0, 0)
1994	17,935	18,192	17,935	18,182	18,063	(.5, .5, 0, 0)
1995	20,533	19,939	20,351	19,883	20,236	(.5, .5, 0, 0)
1996	19,930	20,042	19,867	20,008	19,986	(.5, .5, 0, 0)
1997	21,512	20,619	21,206	20,535	20,913	(0, .5, .5, 0) a
1998	17,917	17,706	17,923	17,721	17,812	(.5, .5, 0, 0)
1999	15,377	14,712	15,701	14,888	15,244	(.8, .2, 0, 0) b
2000	19,852	19,664	19,748	19,637	19,814	(.8, .2, 0, 0) b
2001	18,393	17,322	18,477	17,449	18,179	(.8, .2, 0, 0) b
2002	16,894	14,709	17,181	15,029	16,457	(.8, .2, 0, 0) b
2003	16,347	14,845	16,556	15,118	16,185	(.4, 0, .4, .2) c
2004	17,417	15,120	17,582	16,006	17,267	(0, 0, .8, .2) d
Total	240,750	230,838	241,149	232,432	238,461	

a - Paid LDM distorted due to large claim settlement
b - Reported loss development given less weight because of case reserve weakening (see Table 4.17)
c - BFM given more weight to adjust for late emerging large losses that may not be reflected in claim data
d - BFM given more weight due to immaturity of accident year

	Estimate of Ultimate Losses ($000)					
Accident Year	(7) Paid Loss	(8) Reported Loss	(9) Case Reserves	(10) IBNR	(11) Estimate of Total Reserve	(12) Estimate of Ultimate
1991	9,157	9,237	81	298	379	9,536
1992	12,426	12,779	353	390	743	13,169
1993	14,750	14,836	87	764	851	15,601
1994	16,474	17,495	1,021	568	1,589	18,063
1995	18,581	19,080	499	1,155	1,654	20,236
1996	17,788	19,083	1,295	903	2,198	19,986
1997	18,888	19,535	648	1,377	2,025	20,913
1998	15,484	16,692	1,209	1,119	2,328	17,812
1999	12,996	13,773	777	1,471	2,248	15,244
2000	16,131	18,226	2,096	1,588	3,683	19,814
2001	14,230	15,801	1,571	2,378	3,949	18,179
2002	11,784	13,208	1,425	3,249	4,673	16,457
2003	8,899	12,784	3,885	3,401	7,286	16,185
2004	4,728	9,813	5,085	7,454	12,539	17,267
Total	192,315	212,345	20,030	26,116	46,146	238,461

Notes:
(1), (2) From Table 4.10
(3), (4) From Table 4.13
(5) - Actuarial Judgment: Weighted average of (1) - (4) using (6) as weights.
(7), (8) Company Data.

(9) = (8) - (7)
(10) = (5) - (8)
(11) = (9) + (10)
(12) = (5)

TABLE 4.9

PC SAMPLE COMPANY
Workers' Compensation
Loss Development Methods
As of December 31, 2004

	Paid Loss Development			Reported Loss Development		
	(1)	(2)	(3)	(4)	(5)	(6)
Accident Year	Paid Loss Amount ($000)	Paid LDF	Indicated Ultimate Loss	Reported Loss Amounts ($000)	Reported LDF	Indicated Ultimate Loss
1991	9,157	1.0494	9,609	9,237	1.0244	9,462
1992	12,426	1.0609	13,183	12,779	1.0295	13,155
1993	14,750	1.0747	15,851	14,836	1.0346	15,350
1994	16,474	1.0887	17,935	17,495	1.0398	18,192
1995	18,581	1.1050	20,533	19,080	1.0450	19,939
1996	17,788	1.1204	19,930	19,083	1.0502	20,042
1997	18,888	1.1389	21,512	19,535	1.0555	20,619
1998	15,484	1.1571	17,917	16,692	1.0608	17,706
1999	12,996	1.1832	15,377	13,773	1.0682	14,712
2000	16,131	1.2307	19,852	18,226	1.0789	19,664
2001	14,230	1.2925	18,393	15,801	1.0963	17,322
2002	11,784	1.4337	16,894	13,208	1.1136	14,709
2003	8,899	1.8369	16,347	12,784	1.1612	14,845
2004	4,728	3.6840	17,417	9,813	1.5408	15,120
Total	192,315		240,750	212,345		230,838

(1), (4) Company Claim Data
(2) - From Paid Loss Development Factor Analysis (see Table 4.11)
(3) = (1) x (2)
(5) - From reported loss development factor analysis - not shown
(6) = (4) x (5)

TABLE 4.10

The paid loss development method assumes that the future pattern of loss payments will be consistent with historical payment patterns. Paid loss development factors are estimated by analyzing the percentage change in paid losses between successive valuation periods (Table 4-11). These ratios are commonly referred to as link ratios. For example, if, on average, paid losses at 24 months after the start of the accident year were 150% of losses paid at 12 months, the link ratio from 12 to 24 months is 1.50. The process to estimate the link ratio from 24 to 36 months, 36 to 48 months, etc., is continued until a level of maturity is reached, at which point no change is expected. To estimate the development beyond the experience period, curves are sometimes fit to the development patterns to determine an appropriate tail factor. The tail factor and link ratios are then cumulated backwards from the oldest age of development to determine the LDF needed to project the losses from each age of valuation to its ultimate settlement value. The same process is used for reported losses.

The LDFs are the key parameters in the LDM. Ideally, the LDFs are calculated using historical claim data from the specific segment of business being valued. When sufficient historical claim data is not available or fully credible, industry benchmarks are sometimes used in lieu of, or to supplement, the LDFs derived from actual company data. The benchmark LDFs should be obtained from a peer group of companies that have a similar mix of business and claim handling philosophy. Various tests may be performed to ensure that the benchmark LDFs represent a reasonable estimate of the expected claim development patterns. Otherwise, errors in the reserve estimates may result.

PC SAMPLE COMPANY
Workers' Compensation
Loss Development Methods
As of December 31, 2004

Paid Loss Amounts ($000)

Accident Year	12	24	36	48	60	72	84	96	108	120
1991	2,578	4,972	6,448	7,195	7,876	8,083	8,416	8,500	8,770	8,890
1992	3,130	6,369	8,136	9,580	10,491	10,969	11,217	11,480	11,662	11,948
1993	3,781	7,988	10,785	12,459	13,079	13,516	13,780	13,932	14,139	14,320
1994	4,581	9,414	12,423	13,947	14,889	15,266	15,609	15,787	15,988	16,230
1995	5,122	10,374	14,164	15,972	16,990	17,747	17,865	18,060	18,513	18,581
1996	4,495	9,970	13,603	15,365	16,101	16,876	17,301	17,544	17,788	
1997	5,240	11,323	14,800	16,773	17,567	18,008	18,586	18,888		
1998	5,242	10,440	12,781	14,210	14,672	15,181	15,484			
1999	4,347	8,583	10,939	11,824	12,484	12,996				
2000	5,040	10,778	13,846	15,281	16,131					
2001	4,886	9,960	12,796	14,230						
2002	4,462	8,713	11,784							
2003	4,442	8,899								
2004	4,728									

Age-to-Age Factors

Accident Year	12-24	24-36	36-48	48-60	60-72	72-84	84-96	96-108	108-120	To Ult.
1991	1.929	1.297	1.116	1.095	1.026	1.041	1.010	1.032	1.014	
1992	2.035	1.277	1.177	1.095	1.046	1.023	1.023	1.016	1.025	
1993	2.113	1.350	1.155	1.050	1.033	1.020	1.011	1.015	1.013	
1994	2.055	1.320	1.123	1.068	1.025	1.022	1.011	1.013	1.015	
1995	2.025	1.365	1.128	1.064	1.045	1.007	1.011	1.025	1.004	
1996	2.218	1.364	1.130	1.048	1.048	1.025	1.014	1.014		
1997	2.161	1.307	1.133	1.047	1.025	1.032	1.016			
1998	1.992	1.224	1.112	1.033	1.035	1.020				
1999	1.974	1.274	1.081	1.056	1.041					
2000	2.138	1.285	1.104	1.056						
2001	2.038	1.285	1.112							
2002	1.953	1.352								
2003	2.004									
2004										

Averages

	12-24	24-36	36-48	48-60	60-72	72-84	84-96	96-108	108-120	To Ult.
Simple Avg.										
All Yrs	2.049	1.308	1.125	1.061	1.036	1.024	1.014	1.019	1.014	
Latest 5	2.022	1.284	1.108	1.048	1.039	1.021	1.013	1.016	1.014	
Latest 3	1.998	1.307	1.099	1.048	1.034	1.026	1.014	1.017	1.011	
Medial Avg.										
Latest 5x1	2.005	1.281	1.109	1.050	1.040	1.023	1.012	1.015	1.014	

Paid Loss Development Factor Selection

	12-24	24-36	36-48	48-60	60-72	72-84	84-96	96-108	108-120	Tail Factor*
(1) Industry	2.186	1.259	1.110	1.058	1.034	1.025	1.018	1.017	1.015	1.168
(2) Prior	2.019	1.275	1.112	1.049	1.036	1.021	1.015	1.015	1.015	1.105
(3) Selected	2.005	1.281	1.109	1.050	1.040	1.023	1.016	1.016	1.014	1.105
(4) Paid LDF	3.684	1.837	1.434	1.293	1.231	1.183	1.157	1.139	1.120	1.105
(5) Percent of Ult	0.271	0.544	0.698	0.774	0.813	0.845	0.864	0.878	0.893	0.905

Notes:
Age-to-Age Factors determined by dividing successive valuations:
For AY 2003, 2.004 = 8,899 / 4,442

(1) Industry from NCCI 5-year averages
(2) From the prior loss reserve analysis
(3) Based on actuarial judgment
(4) Cumulating selected factors from oldest period
(5) = 1.00 / (4)

* Tail Factor - based on special study of payments beyond 120 months

TABLE 4.11

A comparison of the net paid and reported LDFs based on information published in the 2003 annual statements of a sample of insurance companies is shown in the table below.

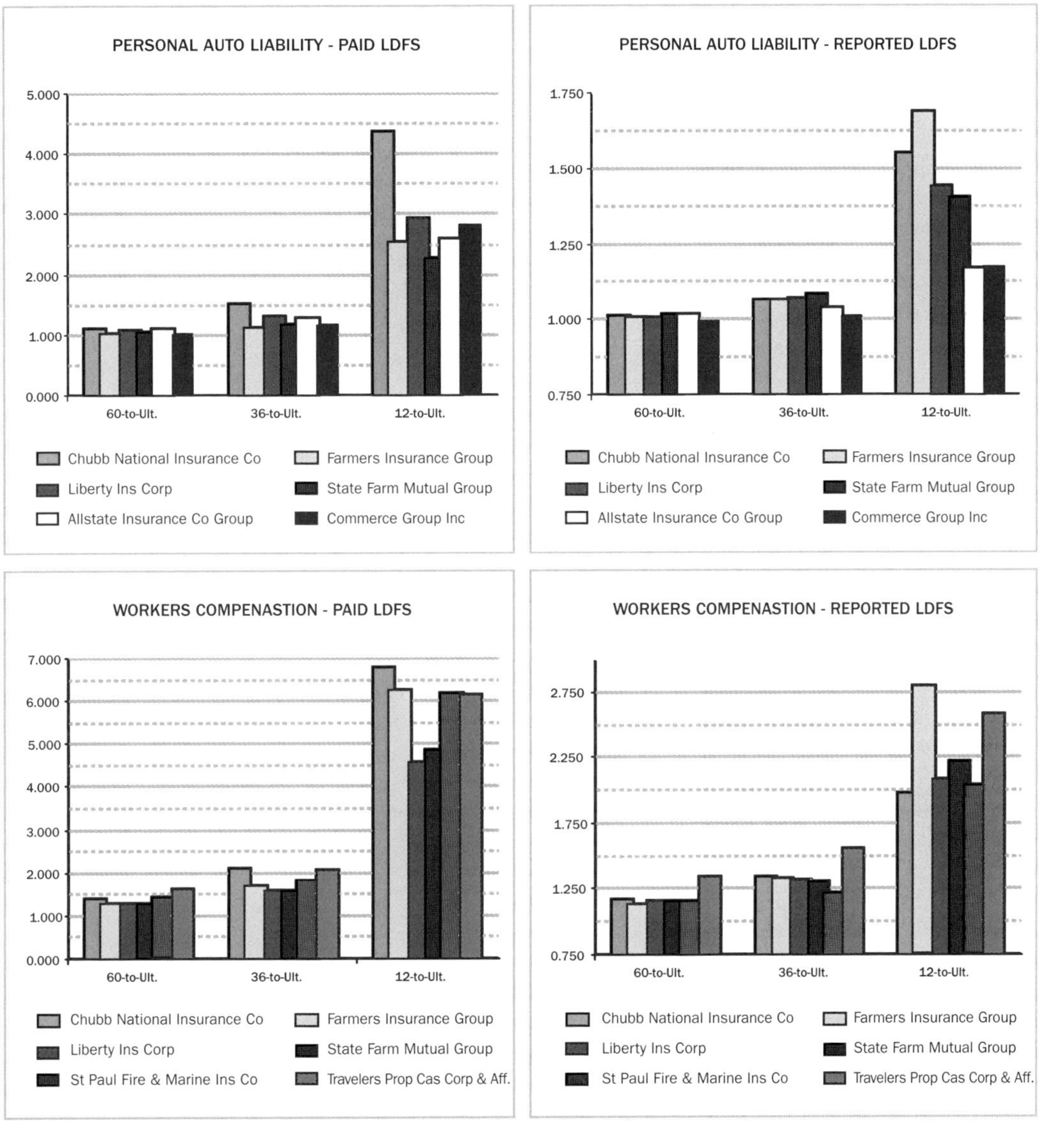

EXHIBIT 4.1

The various claim processes established by these companies result in significantly different development patterns. It is evident that the use of benchmark LDFs from an inappropriate peer group of companies will result in materially different indicated loss reserves. For example, the data above suggest that if one were to use the Travelers loss development factors as a benchmark patterns for workers' compensation, the reported loss development method would indicate 71% more IBNR than the indications produced using the St. Paul factors. Similarly, the Travelers paid development factors would produce 29% more total indicated reserves than the St. Paul factors.

Loss development patterns will also differ by retention level. The lower the retention, the quicker the losses will reach their final settlement value or retained limit.

There are three weaknesses of the LDM. First, for immature accident years, the LDFs may become very large, especially for long-tailed lines of business. As a result, variations in claim experience during the early valuation periods, such as the absence or presence of a large loss, may materially distort the indicated reserve. Second, for long-tailed lines of business, the tail factor selection (the factor for development beyond the review period) has a leveraged effect on the indicated reserve. The additional development assumed by the tail factor applies to all years in the reserve analysis. Third, a change in a company's claim reporting patterns and loss payment patterns may produce an indicated change in IBNR reserve that moves in the wrong direction. For example, if a company begins to pay off claims quicker and/or strengthens its case reserves, the indicated LDFs will increase and then be applied to higher claim values. The LDM will therefore suggest that additional reserves are needed, when the opposite may be true.

4.9.3.2.2 Expected Loss Method

The expected loss method is used for incomplete policy years, for new exposures, or where the limited historical experience does not provide credible information for projection purposes.

The expected ultimate loss for the accident period is estimated by multiplying the forecast exposure by the a priori estimate of the expected ultimate loss rate. The unit of exposure for P&C insurance is the basis from which insurance premiums are developed and represents a relative measure of loss expectation. For P&C insurance, the exposure unit varies by line of insurance. The a priori expected ultimate loss rate is developed from industry loss costs or derived as an average of the company's historical adjusted loss rates, as shown in Table 4.12.

PC SAMPLE COMPANY
Workers Compensation
Initial Expected Ultimate Loss Analysis

Policy Year Ending	(1) Payroll ($10,000)	(2) Prior Estimated Ultimate Loss ($000)	(3) Large Loss	(4) Limited Loss (2) - (3)	(5) Net Trend & Benefit Adjustment	(6) Trended Limited Loss (4) x (5)	(7) Limited Loss Rate (6) / (1)	(8) Expected Loss ($000)
1991	9,093	9,192	-	9,192	1.078	9,912	1.090	9,353
1992	12,182	12,725	766	11,959	1.073	12,831	1.053	12,593
1993	15,458	15,184	-	15,184	1.059	16,083	1.040	16,188
1994	16,911	17,799	680	17,119	1.046	17,899	1.058	17,940
1995	17,334	20,140	2,235	17,905	1.032	18,481	1.066	18,627
1996	17,907	19,890	1,435	18,455	1.027	18,954	1.058	19,339
1997	17,513	20,967	2,756	18,211	1.022	18,610	1.063	19,008
1998	16,308	17,727	663	17,064	1.007	17,180	1.053	17,966
1999	16,097	14,974		14,974	1.022	15,306	0.951	17,467
2000	17,699	19,664	1,203	18,461	1.017	18,775	1.061	19,302
2001	17,118	17,775	-	17,775	1.012	17,988	1.051	18,761
2002	16,085	16,894	-	16,894	1.000	16,894	1.050	17,841
2003	15,229				0.995			
2004	15,750				1.010			
Total '91-'02	189,705	202,931	9,738	193,193		198,913	1.049	
latest 7							1.041	
'91-'02 ex hi/lo							1.055	
(9) Selected Average Loss Rate as of 2002							1.055	
(10) Average Large Loss Load			0.051					
(11) 2003 Expected Loss ($000)								16,807
(12) 2004 Expected Loss ($000)								17,644

Notes:
(2) From prior loss reserve analysis
(3) Company data - claims over $500,000
(5) Excess loss over premium trend plus cumulative benefit level changes based on NCCI 2003 statistical report.
(8) = (1) x [1+(10)] x (9) / (5)
(9) Based on averages of (7)
(10) Based on total (3) / Total (1)
(11), (12) = (1) x ([1+(10)] x (9) x (5)

TABLE 4.12

When determining the adjusted loss rate using historical loss data, the historical losses are usually adjusted for future development, inflation, trend, unusual large loss experience, and changes in policy provisions. Similarly the historical exposure is adjusted for inflation and company growth. The purpose of the adjustments is to bring the historical experience on-level with the current conditions. The adjusted historical adjusted losses are divided by the adjusted exposure to determine the adjusted historical adjusted loss rates from which the a priori expected ultimate loss rate is selected.

Alternatively, the expected ultimate loss is determined by multiplying the company's estimated earned premium by an expected loss ratio. The expected loss ratio may be derived from a pricing study or be selected based on an average of the company's historical adjusted loss ratios. The process to adjust the historical losses when calculating the adjusted historical loss ratios is similar to the process used to develop the historical loss rate. Historical premiums must be adjusted for prior rate changes to bring premiums on-level with the current average rates.

The primary weakness of the expected loss method is that the indicated ultimate loss produced by this method is not responsive to changes in actual loss activity during the year. As a result, the indicated reserves will decrease proportionally to an increase in paid losses and the indicated IBNR decreases when reported losses increase. Using the expected loss method, the resulting change in IBNR reserves may move in a direction that is intuitively opposite from what the actual loss experience might suggest. As a result, the expected loss ratio method should only be used in circumstances where the actual experience provides little or no additional predictive value in estimating the ultimate losses.

4.9.3.2.3 Bornheutter-Ferguson Method

The actuarial technique described by Bornheutter and Ferguson (Table 4.13) is a combination of the LDM and the expected loss method. In this method, the actual loss experience will affect the indicated ultimate losses, but it does not alter the expectation of the remaining unpaid (or unreported) losses. This technique determines the unpaid losses based on an initial estimate of expected ultimate loss and an assumed development pattern. The initial expected losses for each accident period are derived from the expected loss method. The remaining development for each year is determined using loss development factors from the LDM. The indicated reserve is derived as the unpaid (or unreported) portion of the expected loss.

PC SAMPLE COMPANY
Workers' Compensation
Bornhuetter-Ferguson Methods
As of December 31, 2004

Paid Bornheutter - Ferguson Method ($000)						
	(1)	(2)	(3)	(4)	(5)	(6)
Accident Year	Initial Expected Ultimate Loss	Expected Percentage Paid	Expected Total Reserve Factor 1.00 - (2)	Actual Paid Loss	Expected Paid (1) x (3)	Indicated Ultimate Loss (4) + (5)
1991	9,353	0.953	0.047	9,157	440	9,597
1992	12,593	0.943	0.057	12,426	723	13,149
1993	16,188	0.930	0.070	14,750	1,125	15,875
1994	17,940	0.919	0.081	16,474	1,461	17,935
1995	18,627	0.905	0.095	18,581	1,770	20,351
1996	19,339	0.893	0.107	17,788	2,079	19,867
1997	19,008	0.878	0.122	18,888	2,318	21,206
1998	17,966	0.864	0.136	15,484	2,440	17,923
1999	17,467	0.845	0.155	12,996	2,705	15,701
2000	19,302	0.813	0.187	16,131	3,618	19,748
2001	18,761	0.774	0.226	14,230	4,246	18,477
2002	17,841	0.698	0.302	11,784	5,397	17,181
2003	16,807	0.544	0.456	8,899	7,658	16,556
2004	17,644	0.271	0.729	4,728	12,855	17,582
Total	238,835			192,315	48,834	241,149

Reported Bornheutter - Ferguson Method ($000)						
	(1)	(7)	(8)	(9)	(10)	(11)
Accident Year	Initial Expected Ultimate Loss	Expected Percentage Reported	Expected IBNR Factor 1.00 - (7)	Actual Reported Loss	Expected Unreported (1) x (8)	Indicated Ultimate Loss (9) + (10)
1991	9,353	0.976	0.024	9,237	222	9,460
1992	12,593	0.971	0.029	12,779	361	13,139
1993	16,188	0.967	0.033	14,836	542	15,378
1994	17,940	0.962	0.038	17,495	687	18,182
1995	18,627	0.957	0.043	19,080	802	19,883
1996	19,339	0.952	0.048	19,083	925	20,008
1997	19,008	0.947	0.053	19,535	999	20,535
1998	17,966	0.943	0.057	16,692	1,029	17,721
1999	17,467	0.936	0.064	13,773	1,115	14,888
2000	19,302	0.927	0.073	18,226	1,411	19,637
2001	18,761	0.912	0.088	15,801	1,647	17,449
2002	17,841	0.898	0.102	13,208	1,820	15,029
2003	16,807	0.861	0.139	12,784	2,334	15,118
2004	17,644	0.649	0.351	9,813	6,193	16,006
Total	238,835			212,345	20,086	232,432

Notes:
(1) From Expected Loss Method, Table 4.12
(2) = 1.00 / Paid LDF, see Table 4.11, Paid Loss Development Factors
(4), (9) Company data
(9) = 1.00 / Reported LDF

TABLE 4.13

This method estimates the unpaid losses by applying the following formula to the paid loss data:

FORMULA 4.3

$$Total\ Reserve = \{1-1/PLDF\} \times Expected\ Loss$$

where PLDF represents the paid loss development factor.

Alternatively, the IBNR reserve may be estimated by applying the Bornhuetter-Ferguson Method (BFM) method to the reported loss data using the formula:

FORMULA 4.4

$$IBNR\ Reserve = \{1-1/RLDF\} \times Expected\ Loss$$

where RLDF represents the reported loss development factor.

The Bornhuetter-Ferguson technique is particularly useful for the most recent accident years that have huge loss development factors and for low frequency, high severity lines of business that exhibit significant variability. Paid loss development factors, in particular, may be huge for immature accident years; a relatively small change in the paid losses may have a significant impact on the indicated loss reserve. This method adds stability to the projected loss reserves since only the expected development is added to the actual loss experience to date to estimate the ultimate losses.

The weakness of this method is that it is slower to respond to changes in claim activity than the LDM.

4.9.3.3 *Common Actuarial Techniques for Estimating P&C LAE Reserves*

The CAS literature also has a plethora of methods and techniques for estimating LAE reserves and resulting cash flows for the various P&C insurance exposures. For P&C insurers, there are two types of loss adjustment expenses included in Schedule P of the financial statements: defense and cost containment (DCC) expense and adjustment and other payment (AOP) expense.

4.9.3.3.1 Defense and Cost Containment Reserves

DCC expenses are sometimes referred to as allocated loss adjustment expenses[9] (ALAE) because they are typically recorded on a claim-by-claim basis. DCC expenses share many of the same development characteristics as the losses. The duty to defend an insured may in fact have a longer duration than the actual loss payments and for some lines of insurance the cost to defend is a significant portion of the total claim cost. Therefore, special actuarial techniques have been developed to contemplate both the long-term nature of these costs and the variability inherent in the experience.

Due to the similar nature of the DCC expenses, many of the methods used to estimate loss reserves may also be used to estimate DCC expense reserves. For some lines of business, the loss and DCC experience is analyzed on a combined basis and a DCC expense analysis is used to allocate the total reserves. The LDM and BFM methods are also used to project the ultimate DCC expenses using DCC data. Some DCC actuarial reserving methods attempt to estimate the ultimate paid DCC-to-paid loss ratio. The ultimate paid-to-paid ratio is then applied to the best estimate of the ultimate loss to determine the ultimate DCC cost. The LDM method may also be applied to the paid-to-paid ratios at each age of development (Tables 4.14 and 4.15).

[9] ALAE was also the term used prior to 1998 when the NAIC modified the classification of LAE reserves for property and casualty insurance companies.

PC SAMPLE COMPANY
Workers' Compensation
Selected Ultimate Defense and Cost Containment Expense
as of December 31, 2004

	Ultimate DCC Expense and Indicated DCC Reserve ($000)									
	Paid-to-Paid Method					LDM Method			Indicated reserve	
Accident Year	(1) Paid DCC to Paid Loss Ratio	(2) Paid-to-Paid Development Factor to Ultimate	(3) Indicated Ultimate Pd-to Pd Ratio	(4) Estimated Ultimate Loss	(5) Indicated Ultimate DCC Expense	(6) Paid DCC	(7) Paid DCC Development Factor to Ultimate	(8) Indicated Ultimate DCC Expense	(9) Selected Estimated Ultimate DCC	(10) Estimated DCC Reserve
1991	0.0514	1.024	0.053	9,536	502	471	1.072	505	504	33
1992	0.0515	1.029	0.053	13,169	698	640	1.089	697	697	57
1993	0.0508	1.035	0.053	15,601	820	749	1.105	828	824	75
1994	0.0578	1.040	0.060	18,063	1,085	952	1.124	1,070	1,078	126
1995	0.0567	1.045	0.059	20,236	1,198	1,053	1.145	1,206	1,202	149
1996	0.0658	1.051	0.069	19,986	1,382	1,170	1.170	1,368	1,375	205
1997	0.0624	1.058	0.066	20,913	1,381	1,179	1.196	1,411	1,396	216
1998	0.0648	1.068	0.069	17,812	1,233	1,003	1.225	1,228	1,231	227
1999	0.0632	1.122	0.071	15,244	1,082	822	1.318	1,084	1,083	261
2000	0.0573	1.143	0.066	19,814	1,299	925	1.401	1,295	1,297	372
2001	0.0577	1.240	0.072	18,179	1,301	821	1.593	1,308	1,304	483
2002	0.0611	1.445	0.088	16,457	1,452	719	2.091	1,504	1,478	759
2003	0.0448	1.971	0.088	16,185	1,429	399	3.766	1,502	1,465	1,067
2004	0.0256	3.469	0.089	17,267	1,533	121	13.282	1,607	1,570	1,449
Total				238,461	16,395	11,024		16,612	16,504	5,479

Notes:
(1), (2) From Table 4.15
(3) = (1) x (2)
(4) From Table 4.9, Column 5
(5) = (3) x (4)
(6) = Company Data
(7) From DCC development factor analysis - not shown.
(8) = (6) x (7)
(9) Actuarial judgment - average of (5) and (8)
(10) = (9) - (6)

TABLE 4.14

PC SAMPLE COMPANY
Workers' Compensation
Paid DCC to Paid Loss Ratio Development
as of December 31, 2004

	Paid DCC to Paid Loss Ratio									
Accident Year	12	24	36	48	60	72	84	96	108	120
1991	0.0109	0.0250	0.0322	0.0380	0.0421	0.0457	0.0480	0.0488	0.0494	0.0495
1992	0.0119	0.0289	0.0368	0.0432	0.0461	0.0488	0.0491	0.0498	0.0505	0.0507
1993	0.0131	0.0282	0.0402	0.0454	0.0490	0.0491	0.0496	0.0496	0.0495	0.0503
1994	0.0128	0.0320	0.0460	0.0546	0.0554	0.0548	0.0556	0.0570	0.0573	0.0578
1995	0.0145	0.0326	0.0452	0.0494	0.0503	0.0494	0.0551	0.0556	0.0562	0.0567
1996	0.0181	0.0350	0.0406	0.0473	0.0544	0.0585	0.0652	0.0657	0.0658	
1997	0.0223	0.0318	0.0447	0.0529	0.0600	0.0613	0.0617	0.0624		
1998	0.0155	0.0347	0.0463	0.0598	0.0623	0.0634	0.0648			
1999	0.0151	0.0297	0.0528	0.0609	0.0623	0.0632				
2000	0.0206	0.0318	0.0470	0.0531	0.0573					
2001	0.0223	0.0433	0.0497	0.0577						
2002	0.0266	0.0477	0.0611							
2003	0.0299	0.0448								
2004	0.0256									

	Age-to-Age Factors									
Accident Year	12-24	24-36	36-48	48-60	60-72	72-84	84-96	96-108	108-120	To Ult.
1991	2.289	1.287	1.181	1.106	1.088	1.049	1.016	1.013	1.002	
1992	2.441	1.273	1.173	1.066	1.058	1.006	1.015	1.015	1.004	
1993	2.161	1.424	1.131	1.077	1.003	1.010	0.999	0.998	1.016	
1994	2.504	1.439	1.186	1.015	0.988	1.016	1.025	1.005	1.008	
1995	2.252	1.384	1.095	1.017	0.982	1.115	1.010	1.011	1.008	
1996	1.931	1.162	1.164	1.150	1.075	1.115	1.007	1.002		
1997	1.424	1.407	1.184	1.133	1.022	1.006	1.012			
1998	2.243	1.332	1.293	1.041	1.018	1.021				
1999	1.961	1.781	1.153	1.022	1.015					
2000	1.541	1.479	1.129	1.081						
2001	1.942	1.149	1.160							
2002	1.797	1.279								
2003	1.496									
2004										

	Averages									
	12-24	24-36	36-48	48-60	60-72	72-84	84-96	96-108	108-120	To Ult.
Simple Avg.										
All Yrs	1.999	1.366	1.168	1.071	1.028	1.042	1.012	1.007	1.008	
Latest 5	1.747	1.404	1.184	1.085	1.023	1.055	1.011	1.006	1.008	
Latest 3	1.745	1.302	1.148	1.048	1.019	1.047	1.010	1.006	1.010	
Medial Avg.										
Latest 5x1	1.760	1.364	1.166	1.085	1.019	1.051	1.010	1.006	1.006	

	Paid Loss Development Factor Selection									
	12-24	24-36	36-48	48-60	60-72	72-84	84-96	96-108	108-120	Tail Factor*
(1) Benchmark										
(2) Prior	1.811	1.385	1.184	1.073	1.017	1.052	1.010	1.008	1.007	1.043
(3) Selected	1.760	1.364	1.166	1.085	1.019	1.051	1.010	1.006	1.006	1.045
(4) Paid DCC LDF	3.470	1.971	1.446	1.240	1.143	1.122	1.068	1.058	1.052	1.045
(5) Percent of Ult.	0.288	0.507	0.692	0.806	0.875	0.891	0.936	0.945	0.951	0.957

TABLE 4.15

Notes:
Paid to paid DCC ratios developed by dividing paid DCC development triangle (not shown) by paid loss triangle (Table 4.11)
Age-to-Age factors determined by dividing successive valuations: For AY 2003, 1.496 = .0448 / .0299
(2) From prior loss reserve analysis
(3) Based on judgment
(4) Cumulating selected factors from oldest period
(5) = 1.00 / (4)
* Tail Factor - based on special study of payments beyond 120 months

4.9.3.3.2 All Other Payments

All other payments (AOP) expenses are also referred to as unallocated loss adjustment expenses (ULAE). This category of LAE includes the claim department costs and other adjustment expenses incurred in the process of settling claims that are not recorded on an individual claim basis. The claim administration expenses typically represent between 5 and 10 percent of the total loss and LAE costs.

The most common approach for estimating the AOP reserves is the calendar year paid-to-paid ratio method. For this method, the historical ratio of paid AOP to paid losses is calculated for prior calendar periods. To determine the unpaid cost to settle the remaining claims, it is usually assumed that one-half of the expense to handle a claim is incurred when the claim is established and the remaining half is incurred over the life of the claim. Therefore, the selected paid-to-paid ratio is applied to the IBNR reserve, and one-half of the selected paid-to-paid ratio is applied to the case reserves. As noted above, the IBNR reserves reported in statutory financial statements also include development on known claims. To adjust for this, the IBNR reserve is sometimes separated into its components for this calculation. Alternatively, an adjustment may be made to the 50/50 rule to reflect the potential conservatism resulting from applying the paid-to-paid ratio to the total reported IBNR.

The calendar year paid-to-paid method is one of the more common methods used to estimate AOP reserves because it is the most efficient method to apply. Other methods using time studies, claim counts and the average settlement cost per claim may produce more accurate results.

For corporate self-insureds, the AOP reserves are calculated using the contract provisions from third-party claim administrators. Some third-party claim administrators collect all fees up front to cover the cost to settle claims from the time they are reported until they close, commonly referred to as "cradle to grave." Some claim administrators charge on a per claim basis when the claim is reported and others charge as a percentage of paid loss as payments are made.

4.9.3.4 Loss Reserving Diagnostics

The underpinning of most actuarial loss reserving techniques is the assumption that the historical claim emergence and claim settlement patterns will be a valid predictor of future loss development patterns. Most actuarial projection techniques perform well in a stable claims environment. However, changes in company underwriting and claim handling philosophies, as well as changes in the legal system and regulatory environments, may significantly impact claim activity. Companies being sold are also more likely to have undergone recent operational changes. Therefore, the loss reserve analysis performed in conjunction with an actuarial appraisal should also include reserving diagnostics to determine whether there has been a change in claim development patterns that may distort the indicated reserves. Generally there are three diagnostic tools actuaries use.

1. assessing the convergence of the various loss reserving techniques
2. analyzing various reserving statistics, and
3. testing the runoff of prior reserve estimates.

4.9.3.4.1 Convergence of Reserving Methods

The actuarial loss reserve analysis for property casualty exposure should include multiple actuarial loss reserving techniques to project the preliminary estimates of the ultimate losses. The various actuarial reserving techniques use diverse data sets and assumptions. When the indications produced by the various methods diverge, it may be a sign that there has been a change in claim development.

A reconciliation of the various indications may allow the actuary to associate the divergence with certain business or environmental changes that are not contemplated by the various actuarial projection techniques. The reconciliation process allows the actuary to determine which method or technique will produce the best indication for the particular line of business and accident year being forecasted. Based on this assessment, the actuary will either explicitly or implicitly assign weights to the various indications when selecting the best estimate.

4.9.3.4.2 Analysis of Reserving Statistics

There are various reserving statistics that are developed to test the underlying assumptions or key parameters used in each loss reserving method. To assess the reasonableness of the loss development factors derived in the LDM, development triangles displaying historical settlement rates and the average case reserve per outstanding claim are analyzed (Tables 4.16 and 4.17). The settlement rate represents the percentage of the ultimate number of claims that have been closed at each age of development. This statistic is used to evaluate changes in payment patterns. The average case reserve per outstanding claim is used to identify changes in case basis claim reserving practices that affect the reported loss development patterns. When a measurable change in the claim data has occurred, loss development methods may produce erroneous results. Under these circumstances actuaries may need to rely on other techniques or use methods such as those described by Berquest & Sherman to adjust the historical data so that a valid estimate of future development patterns may be determined. Other important diagnostic statistics of the historical data include:

1. development patterns of average claim size, paid loss ratios, and reported loss ratios,
2. indicated ultimate frequency, severity, and pure premium (Table 4.18),
3. open claim duration, or the average number of days claims remained open, and
4. reporting lags, or the number of days between accident date and the date the claim was entered into the claim system.

PC SAMPLE COMPANY
Workers' Compensation
Settlement Rate
as of December 31, 2004

	Closed Claim Count									
Accident Year	12	24	36	48	60	72	84	96	108	120
1991	3,662	5,240	5,393	5,476	5,530	5,553	5,564	5,582	5,594	5,597
1992	4,620	6,158	6,397	6,461	6,520	6,532	6,545	6,567	6,573	6,576
1993	4,675	6,767	7,030	7,095	7,143	7,182	7,201	7,214	7,231	7,231
1994	5,194	6,954	7,210	7,295	7,354	7,405	7,430	7,437	7,442	7,445
1995	5,231	6,942	7,227	7,311	7,360	7,384	7,411	7,417	7,422	7,419
1996	5,012	6,944	7,185	7,313	7,350	7,370	7,387	7,401	7,397	
1997	5,526	7,108	7,322	7,422	7,491	7,508	7,533	7,532		
1998	4,897	6,406	6,583	6,692	6,743	6,760	6,758			
1999	4,973	6,428	6,643	6,721	6,758	6,762				
2000	5,729	7,226	7,432	7,537	7,560					
2001	5,130	6,281	6,494	6,545						
2002	4,491	5,585	5,714							
2003	4,402	5,162								
2004	4,666									

	Settlement Rate - Closed Count / Ultimate Count									
Accident Year	12-24	24-36	36-48	48-60	60-72	72-84	84-96	96-108	108-120	To Ult.
1991	0.653	0.935	0.962	0.977	0.986	0.990	0.992	0.996	0.998	0.998
1992	0.702	0.935	0.972	0.981	0.990	0.992	0.994	0.997	0.998	0.999
1993	0.646	0.934	0.971	0.980	0.986	0.992	0.994	0.996	0.998	0.998
1994	0.696	0.932	0.966	0.977	0.985	0.992	0.996	0.997	0.997	0.998
1995	0.703	0.932	0.971	0.982	0.988	0.992	0.995	0.996	0.997	0.996
1996	0.675	0.936	0.968	0.985	0.990	0.993	0.995	0.997	0.997	
1997	0.730	0.938	0.967	0.980	0.989	0.991	0.995	0.994		
1998	0.720	0.942	0.968	0.984	0.991	0.994	0.994			
1999	0.730	0.944	0.975	0.987	0.992	0.993				
2000	0.749	0.944	0.971	0.985	0.988					
2001	0.766	0.937	0.969	0.977						
2002	0.754	0.938	0.960							
2003	0.776	0.910								
2004	0.770									

TABLE 4.16

Notes:
Settlement rates developed by dividing the closed claim count triangle above by the ultimate claim counts in Table 4.18, Column 4. Settlement rates have been relatively consistent, potential drop off during latest year.

PC SAMPLE COMPANY
Workers' Compensation
Average Case Reserve
as of December 31, 2004

	Case Basis Reserves ($000)									
Accident Year	**12**	**24**	**36**	**48**	**60**	**72**	**84**	**96**	**108**	**120**
1991	4,971	4,343	3,513	2,486	1,427	597	633	513	333	35
1992	7,162	7,071	4,757	2,793	2,366	1,640	1,392	886	653	580
1993	7,466	6,559	3,756	2,350	1,467	1,008	739	536	371	297
1994	8,087	7,033	4,127	2,967	1,783	949	1,499	1,495	1,323	1,178
1995	8,754	7,810	4,082	2,655	1,653	1,081	601	1,033	692	499
1996	7,566	5,989	3,615	2,323	2,449	1,052	832	613	1,295	
1997	8,185	6,679	4,173	2,438	1,223	1,063	647	648		
1998	6,621	5,924	3,787	2,381	1,739	1,310	1,209			
1999	5,438	4,289	2,271	1,436	1,162	777				
2000	8,371	5,997	3,661	2,319	2,096					
2001	6,398	4,861	2,166	1,571						
2002	4,248	3,060	1,425							
2003	4,032	3,885								
2004	5,085									

	Open Claim Count									
Accident Year	**12-24**	**24-36**	**36-48**	**48-60**	**60-72**	**72-84**	**84-96**	**96-108**	**108-120**	**To Ult.**
1991	1,574	354	208	125	74	52	41	25	13	10
1992	1,584	405	178	118	60	49	36	16	11	8
1993	2,013	457	205	141	95	58	40	28	11	11
1994	1,854	497	248	164	106	56	31	25	21	18
1995	1,736	488	211	130	82	59	34	29	25	27
1996	1,962	456	230	103	69	49	32	20	25	
1997	1,527	437	246	151	82	65	41	41		
1998	1,435	375	214	108	58	42	41			
1999	1,449	366	160	85	50	46				
2000	1,597	414	214	113	90					
2001	1,316	400	200	153						
2002	1,273	351	235							
2003	1,026	494								
2004	1,143									

	Average Case Reserve per Open Claim									
Accident Year	**12-24**	**24-36**	**36-48**	**48-60**	**60-72**	**72-84**	**84-96**	**96-108**	**108-120**	**To Ult.**
1991	3,158	12,268	16,889	19,888	19,284	11,481	15,439	20,520	25,615	3,500
1992	4,521	17,459	26,725	23,669	39,433	33,469	38,667	55,375	59,364	72,500
1993	3,709	14,352	18,322	16,667	15,442	17,379	18,475	19,143	33,727	27,000
1994	4,362	14,151	16,641	18,091	16,821	16,946	48,355	59,800	63,000	65,439
1995	5,043	16,004	19,346	20,423	20,159	18,322	17,676	35,621	27,680	18,482
1996	3,856	13,134	15,717	22,553	35,493	21,469	26,000	30,665	51,808	
1997	5,360	15,284	16,963	16,146	14,915	16,354	15,773	15,793		
1998	4,614	15,797	17,696	22,046	29,983	31,179	29,482			
1999	3,753	11,719	14,194	16,894	23,242	16,881				
2000	5,242	14,486	17,107	20,525	23,284					
2001	4,862	12,153	10,828	10,267						
2002	3,337	8,718	6,062							
2003	3,930	7,865								
2004	4,449									

TABLE 4.17

Notes:
Observation: Average case reserve has been reduced during the past 18 months, discuss with claim managers. Reported loss development methods will understate true ultimate losses in 1998-99 and 2001-2004.

PC SAMPLE COMPANY
Workers' Compensation
Ultimate Claim Count Analysis
as of December 31, 2004

				Estimated Ultimate Claim Count					
Accident Year	(1) Open Claims	(2) Reported Count	(3) Claim Count LDF	(4) Estimated Ultimate Count	(5) Estimated Ultimate Loss	(6) Estimated Severity	(7) Payroll ($10,000)	(8) Adjusted Payroll	(9) Adjusted Frequency
1991	10	5,607	1.000	5,607	9,536	1,701	9,093	12,535	0.45
1992	8	6,584	1.000	6,584	13,169	2,000	12,182	16,383	0.40
1993	11	7,242	1.000	7,242	15,601	2,154	15,458	20,282	0.36
1994	18	7,463	1.000	7,463	18,063	2,420	16,911	21,648	0.34
1995	27	7,446	1.000	7,446	20,236	2,718	17,334	21,648	0.34
1996	25	7,422	1.000	7,422	19,986	2,693	17,907	21,818	0.34
1997	41	7,573	1.000	7,574	20,913	2,761	17,513	20,817	0.36
1998	41	6,799	1.000	6,801	17,812	2,619	16,308	18,912	0.36
1999	46	6,808	1.000	6,810	15,244	2,238	16,097	18,212	0.37
2000	90	7,650	1.000	7,653	19,814	2,589	17,699	19,536	0.39
2001	153	6,698	1.001	6,701	18,179	2,713	17,118	18,434	0.36
2002	235	5,949	1.001	5,955	16,457	2,764	16,085	16,899	0.35
2003	494	5,656	1.003	5,672	16,185	2,853	15,229	15,610	0.36
2004	1,143	5,809	1.043	6,061	17,267	2,849	15,750	15,750	0.38
Total	2,342	94,706		94,991	238,461		220,684		

Notes:
(1), (2), (7) – Company Data
(3) – From claim count development factor analysis (not shown)
(4) = (2) x (3)
(5) From Table 4.9
(6) = (5) / (4) x 1000 *Observation:* Ultimate severity changes relatively consistent with historical inflation
(8) – Column (7) adjusted for 2.5% annual payroll trend
(9) = (4) / (9) *Observation:* Frequency of claims is consistent after adjusting for inflationary effect on payroll

TABLE 4.18

4.9.3.4.3 Runoff Analysis

A runoff analysis is a comparison of the selected ultimate losses from the most recent valuation to those selected in prior reviews. Schedule P, Part 2 of the P&C statutory annual statement displays the results from a one-year and two-year runoff of the company's selected ultimate losses. The one-year runoff represents the difference in the estimated ultimate losses from the current period to those selected in the prior year. The two-year runoff compares the current ultimate loss selections to those in the penultimate year.

The runoff analysis provides two important pieces of information during the valuation process. First, when the current best estimate of the ultimate losses is compared to those underlying the recorded reserves from the prior accounting period, the resulting runoff represents the impact to the current year's earnings due to changes in reserves relating to prior accident years. This is one of the more significant quality of earnings adjustments required when performing a valuation using comparable multiples.

A runoff analysis may also be used by the actuary to determine whether the reserving model, method, or assumptions are biased optimistically or conservatively. If a similar reserving process has been used in prior loss reserve reviews, and there has consistently been unfavorable runoff in the ultimate losses, it might indicate that one of the key assumptions in the model is optimistic. The actuary performing the reserve analysis should be able to reconcile material runoff amounts by identifying assumptions in prior loss projections that did not materialize as expected and quantifying the impact of the differences.

While this test is a valuable tool for an actuary to assess the appropriateness of the reserve model and the assumptions used in prior reviews, this test should not be used to assess the adequacy of the current reserves. The actuary's best estimate of the ultimate losses must be selected for the current period for this test to provide meaningful results. Otherwise, it will be impossible to discern whether the unfavorable change in ultimate losses was due to an optimistic bias in the prior reserving assumptions or conservative assumptions selected in the current review.

4.9.3.5 Loss Reserve Cash Flows

The loss development factors derived from the paid LDM are used to determine the paid loss cash flows. The inverse of the paid LDF (1/PLDF) represents the expected portion of losses paid at each valuation period. It is generally assumed that the loss reserves will run off proportionally to the paid development pattern (Table 4.19). A more detailed discussion of loss and LAE cash flows is included in section 4.9.4.2.

PC SAMPLE COMPANY
Workers' Compensation
Cash Flow Analysis
as of December 31, 2004

Paid Loss Development Patterns

	12-24	24-36	36-48	48-60	60-72	72-84	84-96	96-108	108-120	120-132**
(1) Percent of Ultimate	0.271	0.544	0.698	0.774	0.813	0.845	0.864	0.878	0.893	0.905
(2) Percent Unpaid	0.729	0.456	0.302	0.226	0.187	0.155	0.136	0.122	0.107	0.095
(3) Incremental Paid	0.271	0.273	0.153	0.076	0.039	0.033	0.019	0.014	0.014	0.012

Future Loss Payments

Accident Year	(4) Total Reserve	(5) Precent Paid	24-36	36-48	48-60	60-72	72-84	84-96	96-108	108-120	120-132**
1991	379	0.047									
1992	743	0.057									
1993	851	0.070									
1994	1,589	0.081									
1995	1,654	0.095									
1996	2,198	0.107									255
1997	2,025	0.122								240	207
1998	2,328	0.136							237	248	214
1999	2,248	0.155						276	201	210	181
2000	3,683	0.187					640	374	272	285	245
2001	3,949	0.226				679	569	332	241	253	218
2002	4,673	0.302			1,177	601	504	294	214	224	193
2003	7,286	0.456		2,449	1,218	622	521	304	221	232	199
2004	12,539	0.729	4,698	2,635	1,311	670	561	328	238	249	215
Total	46,146										

Future loss payments distributed proportional to incremental payment pattern = (4) x (3) / (5)
Each diagonal represents a future calendar year, as shown below.
** Table extends beyond 132 months

Future Cash Flow - Expected Calendar Year Payments

Accident Year	(4) Total Reserve	2005	2006	2007	2008	2009	2010	2011	2012	2013	2014
1991	379	97	97	97	89						
1992	743	130	156	156	156	143					
1993	851	148	123	148	148	148	136				
1994	1,589	235	235	196	235	235	235	216			
1995	1,654	244	209	209	174	209	209	209	192		
1996	2,198	255	286	245	245	204	245	245	245	225	
1997	2,025	240	207	232	199	199	166	199	199	199	183
1998	2,328	237	248	214	240	206	206	171	206	206	206
1999	2,248	276	201	210	181	203	174	174	145	174	174
2000	3,683	640	374	272	285	245	275	236	236	197	236
2001	3,949	679	569	332	241	253	218	244	209	209	174
2002	4,673	1,177	601	504	294	214	224	193	216	185	185
2003	7,286	2,449	1,218	622	521	304	221	232	199	224	192
2004	12,539	4,698	2,635	1,311	670	561	328	238	249	215	241
(6) Total	46,146	11,505	7,160	4,748	3,679	3,125	2,637	2,357	2,097	1,834	1,591

Notes:
(1) From Table 4.14
(2) = 1 - (1)
(3) Developed from subtracting two successive factors in Row (2) Incremental Factors not shown:

132-144	144-156	156-168	168-180	180-192	192-204	204-216	204-216
0.014	0.012	0.012	0.010	0.012	0.012	0.012	0.011

(4) Table 4.9
(5) From (2), also Table 4.12, Column 3
(6) Calendar year total payments

TABLE 4.19

4.9.3.6 Discounted Loss Reserves and Fair Value Liabilities

Section 4.9.2 described a number of adjustments that are made to the capital and surplus to determine a company's adjusted book value. The purpose of most adjustments is to restate the value of assets at their current market value. Under statutory accounting principles, P&C liabilities must be recorded at the nominal value, without discounting these liabilities to reflect the time value of money. Because statutory accounting is the basis used to determine distributable earnings, the nominal value of loss reserves is used in the valuation models. However, fair value liabilities are used for purchase price accounting under GAAP and may be required for valuing self-insured liabilities for corporate acquisitions.

The embedded value in the loss and LAE reserves must be determined for purchase price accounting under GAAP. The fair value reserves for GAAP purposes represent the expected value of the reserves, reduced by a discount for the time value of money plus the market value margin for risk associated with an uncertainty of the loss payment stream.

There are various approaches to estimating the fair value reserves for P&C loss reserves. The CAS White Paper discusses 10 approaches, including the strengths and weaknesses of each method. Some methods determine the fair value reserves directly using a risk-adjusted discount rate. For these methods, the challenge is to determine the appropriate risk-adjusted discount rate to use for the various property casualty cash flows. Capital asset pricing model methods, internal rate of return models, and single period risk-adjusted discount methods fall in this category.

Other methods to calculate the fair value reserves determine the discount and market value margin separately. For methods that determine the fair value as the sum of two components, the discount is determined using duration-matched yield curves. Once the cash flows relating to the loss and LAE payments are determined using the techniques discussed in section 4.9.3.3, the present value is determined using standard discounting techniques (Table 4.20). Various methods are then used to determine the market value margin. These include stochastic simulation, loss development modeling, aggregate probability distribution methods, and market values determined from reinsurance transactions.

PC SAMPLE COMPANY
Workers' Compensation
Loss Reserve Discount Analysis
as of December 31, 2004

Reserve Discount											
	(1)	(2) Calendar Year Payments									
	Total Reserve	2005	2006	2007	2008	2009	2010	2011	2012	2013	2014
(2) Cash Flow	46,146	11,505	7,160	4,748	3,679	3,125	2,637	2,357	2,097	1,834	1,591
(3) Years Before Payment		0.5	1.5	2.5	3.5	4.5	5.5	6.5	7.5	8.5	9.5
(4) Discount Factor (5.0%)		0.9759	0.9294	0.8852	0.8430	0.8029	0.7646	0.7282	0.6936	0.6605	0.6291
(5) Discounted Reserve	38,047	11,228	6,655	4,203	3,101	2,509	2,016	1,717	1,454	1,211	1,001

Notes:
(1), (2) From Table 4.19 (Note: Not all calendar years shown)
(3) Assumes payments made uniformly during the calendar year
(4) [1/1.05]*(3)
(5) = (2) x (4) (Note: Present value of expected payments made during 2015-2021 included in total.)

TABLE 4.20

The method selected by the actuary is based on the strengths and weaknesses of the method, the lines of business written by the company, the data available for the calculation, and ease of explanation.

4.9.4 P&C CASH FLOW ASSUMPTIONS

For P&C insurance valuations, significant attention is given to the adequacy of the loss reserves and the loss ratio assumptions used in the valuation model. However, as Witcraft documented in her 1989 paper, the assumptions relating to the timing of the cash flows also present significant risk to the valuation. The claims processes used by P&C companies create significantly different claim payment patterns as noted in the discussion on loss development methods in section 4.9.3.2.1. Therefore, an analysis of the direct payment patterns and reinsurance recoveries is needed to assess the timing of cash flows for the target company.

4.9.4.1 Investment Returns

The issues relating to investment returns are similar to those for life and health insurers discussed in section 4.4.4. Due to the variability in payment patterns for property casualty losses, property casualty insurance companies do not always develop investment strategies to match cash flows. While developing the valuation model, specific attention should be given to the mix and duration of the assets supporting the liabilities. If the assets supporting the loss reserves are not properly matched to the expected loss payment stream, the insurer may be forced to liquidate high yielding bonds or sell equities during inopportune times.

4.9.4.2 Loss and LAE Cash Flow

The LDFs from the loss development method define the payment patterns and percentage of unpaid loss at each age of development. It is generally assumed that the selected outstanding losses for each accident year will be paid in subsequent periods proportional to the reduction in unpaid losses implied by these development patterns.

The selected reserves may not be based on the paid LDM when other methods produce more reliable results. When the selected reserves are similar to that indicated by the paid LDM, or when the differences are due to random variation, it is reasonable to assume cash flows will follow the paid LDM patterns. When the paid LDM produces indicated reserves that are materially different from the selected reserves, adjustments to the cash flows derived by the paid LDFs may be necessary. Berquest & Sherman techniques to adjust the historical paid loss data for changes in settlement rates may be used to develop revised payment patterns. Alternatively, a payment pattern may be derived by fitting a curve through the percentage of unpaid losses selected for each accident year.

The number of lines of business or segments used to determine the loss and LAE cash flows is usually consistent with the analysis performed to assess the adequacy of the reserves. However, lines of business are sometimes combined to simplify the cash flow assumptions.

When non-homogeneous lines are combined, the historical composition of the consolidated lines should be evaluated to ensure that there has not been a significant change in the mix of business that would alter the expectations for future payment patterns.

Many of the comments relating to P&C losses apply to the LAE cash flows. The amount and duration of the defense and medical cost containment expense cash flows will depend, in part, on the company's claim settling philosophy. However, since many P&C insurance policies require the insurer to defend the insured, the tail for these costs is usually larger than the tail for losses.

For other adjusting costs, statutory reporting requirements require insurance companies to assume that 50% of the AOP expense is allocated proportional to claim payments, 45% is allocated to the current accident year, and 5% is allocated to the prior year. Models based on reported and closed claim counts will generally produce a better estimate of actual cash flows.

4.9.4.3 Reinsurance Cash Flow

Property and casualty insurance companies use various forms of reinsurance to reduce risk and provide surplus relief. To properly account for the cash flows, the valuation model should include direct and ceded assumptions for premiums and losses. For proportional reinsurance contracts, such as quota share and surplus share agreements, the reinsurer assumes a predefined percentage of the premium and loss. Ceded cash flows for proportional reinsurance follow the insurance company's assumptions.

For excess reinsurance contracts the insurer remits the ceded premium during the contract year but only receives reimbursement when the insurer's loss payments exceed a certain limit. Excess reinsurance may be written on a per occurrence basis, a per event basis (for catastrophes), or an annual aggregate basis. The terms and conditions of reinsurance policies are custom designed to meet the needs of each insurer. Therefore, these contracts must be reviewed carefully to understand the coverage that has been extended and the resulting cash flows for the ceded premium and losses.

4.9.4.4 Premium Cash Flow

The length of the policies issued by the insurer, the type of billing plans used, and the collection process will affect the premium cash flows and the accrual of unearned premium reserves. Most P&C insurers write annual policies, but it is not uncommon for personal automobile policies to be written on a six-month basis. Property and casualty premiums may be paid annually, or billed monthly, quarterly, or semiannually. Some companies that use the independent agent distribution system offer agency-billing options, whereby the insurance agent or broker collects the premium and remits balances to the insurance company. Other P&C insurance companies use direct billing, electronic fund transfers, and credit card billing options.

Special attention should be given to the premium cash flows on retrospectively rated policies and other commercial policies with loss-sensitive adjustment provisions. Under these plans, an initial premium deposit is collected and annual premium adjustments are made based on the insured's loss experience until all losses have been settled.

4.9.5 MANAGEMENT PLAN ASSUMPTIONS

When the actuarial appraisal is being performed by the selling company, the management assumptions used in the valuation model should be consistent with those used in the pro forma financial statements. For P&C insurance valuations, detailed forecasts are usually only made for short periods of time (5-7 years) and simplifying assumptions are made for longer forecasts. Appraisals prepared for the investor may include alternative assumptions to determine the economic value of assumed synergies, embedded options, and transaction costs. This section contains issues relating to the management assumptions that should be considered for P&C insurers.

4.9.5.1 Premium Projection

The premium projections for P&C insurance companies have greater uncertainty than those in the life and health insurance industry. Property and casualty insurance products are usually sold as annual contracts without guaranteed renewal provisions.[10] Insurance companies often re-underwrite their policyholder upon renewal and have the option to cancel coverage or charge a significantly higher premium when there has been an increase in risk of loss. The P&C insurance market is highly competitive, and policyholders often change insurance carriers. In the personal insurance market, policyholders or their insurance agents often shop the market for competitive prices. In the commercial lines market, company risk managers keep constant pressure on their brokers

[10] It should be noted that for personal lines insurance, some state insurance regulations place nonrenewal restrictions on insurance carriers.

to place insurance coverage at the most competitive rates. As a result, the persistency for P&C insurance companies is significantly lower than those for life and health insurance companies.

Premium projections are usually made on a written premium basis, and the premium is earned proportionally during policy term. Written premium for the prospective period should consider:

Written premium during previous periods
- \- Less a reduction for nonrenewed policies
- \+ Plus new business exposure
- \+ Plus increases from inflation sensitive exposure base (i.e., payroll and revenues)
- +/- Plus impact of planned rate changes
- +/- Plus flexible pricing modifications (experience modifications, schedule modifications, pricing tiers, and other subjective discounts).

Many times the new and renewal components are combined in a P&C valuation model. However, it may be necessary to develop separate projections of these components to determine the value of intangible assets for SFAS 141 (see Chapter 8). The intangible value of renewals for short-term contracts and the intangible value of distribution relationships are sometimes estimated separately using historical renewal rates and new business assumptions.

A common investor complaint regarding P&C valuation models is the amount of subjectivity underlying the key parameter used in the model. Models that incorporate a constant change in forecasted premiums, without contemplating changing market conditions, are subject to investor skepticism. By forecasting the premium impact from each of the components above, the actuary is able to validate the reasonableness of the assumptions using the company's historical results, the company's marketing plans, and anticipated changes in the underwriting cycle. Furthermore, many of the components used to project premium are also used to forecast future losses.

4.9.5.2 Loss and Loss Ratio Assumptions

Losses for the prospective accident periods may be forecasted directly or by estimating future loss ratios that will be applied to management's forecasted premiums. Regardless of which method is used, an analysis of the components underlying the forecast should be performed to validate the assumptions. The expected losses or loss ratio derived for the loss reserve analysis described in section 4.9.3.2.2 is typically the base from which the forecast is made.

Forecasted losses are then projected by adjusting the base year expected loss (or loss ratio) for:

- \- Reduction in exposure for nonrenewed policies
- \+ Increase for new business exposure
- \+ Increase for loss inflation
- +/- Adjustments for frequency and severity trends
- +/- Impacts from underwriting changes.

When using the loss ratio approach to forecast losses, changes in exposure are not needed because they are implicit in the forecasted premium. In addition, only inflation net of premium inflation is used to modify the expected loss ratio.

Forecasted changes in losses from underwriting come from two sources: modifications to policy provisions that expand or reduce insurance coverage and changes in the company's mix of business. When the loss ratio approach is used to forecast losses, revisions to policy provisions may have no impact on forecasted loss ratios if they are introduced with a corresponding change in rate levels.

Material modifications in the expected loss ratio from changes in the mix of business should be justified with a reasonable business plan. Underwriting changes in the company's mix of business occurs when the quality of the new business differs from the business lost at policy renewal. Premium growth assumptions should be consistent with the other underwriting assumptions. For example, loss ratio improvements resulting from the elimination of an unprofitable segment of business should be accompanied by a corresponding reduction in exposure. Conversely, significant growth assumptions are typically coupled with loss ratio deterioration since new business loss ratios are generally assumed to be higher than those from a stable book of renewal business, and premium reductions are usually required to attract new business. The P&C underwriting cycle should be considered when developing the loss ratio assumptions.

4.9.5.3 *Expenses and Expense Ratios*

The issues for developing management plan assumptions for expenses are similar to those for life and health insurers. Agent commissions, taxes, and a portion of the general and other acquisition expenses are considered variable expenses and are forecasted as a percent of written premium. The remainder of the general and other acquisition expenses are forecasted using CPI inflation or other reasonable business plan assumptions.

4.9.5.4 *Reinsurance*

In the sell-side appraisal, the reinsurance assumptions for the forecasted period are typically consistent with the current program. However, the investor should also consider the reinsurance underwriting cycle and the profitability of the reinsurance program (from the reinsurer's perspective) when assessing the reinsurance assumptions selected for the forecast. If the ceded experience has historically been unprofitable for the reinsurer, the forecast should include anticipated increases in the cost for reinsurance and increases in anticipated retention levels. When the buy-side appraisal is being performed for an investor that will consolidate the target into its existing operations, the appraisal may also be performed using the assumptions consistent with the investor's reinsurance program. The difference in the two estimates represents the value of the embedded reinsurance option or an additional integration cost for the acquisition.

4.9.6 OTHER UNIQUE PROPERTY CASUALTY VALUATION ISSUES

There many other issues associated with P&C insurers that go beyond the methods and assumptions used in the valuation model for an actuarial appraisal. Some of the more important issues are summarized in this section.

4.9.6.1 *Adjustments for Market-Multiple Valuations*

As noted above, actuarial appraisal values using discounted cash flow techniques are not always available for P&C insurance companies. Under these circumstances, investors may rely on market multiples of comparable companies to determine a reasonable bid price pending a more thorough analysis of the economic value. This method attempts to determine a company's market price (as opposed to its economic value) by applying a factor to key financial statistics, such as:

1. earnings before income tax (EBIT),
2. earnings before income tax, depreciation, and amortization (EBITDA),
3. revenues,
4. cash flows,
5. assets, and
6. book value.

The ratios of price (or total invested capital) to each of the financial statistics above are calculated for all recent acquisitions and evaluated to select the appropriate multiple to apply to the financial statistics for the target company.

When using the market-multiple approach for P&C insurance companies, there are two important issues that should be considered. First, market multiples will be most appropriate for peer group companies, companies that are most similar to the target company. Second, certain adjustments to the financial statistics may be needed before calculating the market-multiples or before applying the benchmark multiples to the target company's data.

Property and casualty insurance companies are not homogeneous. The mix of business written, the type of insurance product sold, the size of the company, the distribution channel, and the geographical location of the markets create significant differences in the risk of the business. Theoretically, the companies with less risk will command higher market multiples. Therefore, when using a market-multiple approach, the market-multiples from companies that are reasonably similar to the target company represent the best benchmarks. However, the number of P&C acquisitions is limited, and the diverse nature of property casualty operations makes it difficult to find multiple peer group acquisitions. Under these circumstances, one may adjust the multiples of relatively similar companies for any perceived differences in risk.

Certain financial statistics are subject to significant variability due to the risk inherent in the P&C exposure. Others are subject to distortions from the loss reserving process. When applying the market-multiple approach, it is sometimes necessary to make adjustments to both the benchmark multiples and the target's earnings (or other base) to which they are being applied. The two most common adjustments are distortions caused by catastrophes and changes in reserve adequacy. The absence or presence of catastrophe losses may significantly alter the earnings multiples. Similarly, changes in the reserve adequacy or distortions in the calendar year earnings from prior accident year activity may distort market-multiples based on book value or earnings. Therefore, adjustments to the financial statistics to normalize for these and other variations may produce a better set of market-multiples for the peer group companies and reduce errors when they are applied to the target's statistics.

4.9.6.2 Unearned Premium Reserves for Multi-Year Policies

Many P&C insurers offer commercial insurance products that have retrospective premium provisions. These policies allow for the collection of additional premium and return of excess premium based on an insured's actual losses. Retrospectively rated policies may be written on a paid loss basis, reported loss basis, or a developed loss basis. Policies written on a paid loss basis provide the insured with the most favorable cash flow terms. To eliminate the credit risk, these policies usually require the insured to post security for the unpaid premiums in the form of an irrevocable letter of credit. Retrospective premium adjustments are earned as written. Therefore, an actuarial reserve must be calculated to properly accrue for expected additional or returnable premium.

Some P&C insurance products cover an exposure over a multiple-year period, sometimes referred to as long-duration contracts. Coverages such as residual value insurance, title insurance, and warranty insurance are examples of this type of product. Under most long-duration contracts, the premium is paid at policy inception and earned during the exposure period. Losses may be incurred at any point during the coverage period with no specific accident date. Therefore, the accounting principle of matching may be applied to allocate these losses over the years during which the premium is earned.

When a book of business is significantly underpriced, the unearned premium may not be sufficient to cover all of the losses that may emerge during the remaining coverage period. Therefore, for long-duration contracts, it is also necessary to test the adequacy in the unearned premium reserve and establish a reserve for any deficiencies that may emerge.

4.9.6.3 Environmental Liability/Asbestos/Mass Tort

For some actuarial appraisals, the unpaid losses relating to environmental liabilities, asbestos exposure, or other mass tort claims are recorded on a best estimate basis, and the risk associated with this exposure is included in the selection of the investor's required cost of capital. However, due to the significant risk inherent in this exposure, the economic value of these liabilities is often treated separately. Actuaries that specialize in this product are retained to evaluate the remaining exposure, estimate the indicated reserves, and develop assumed cash flows. Many times the indicated range of reserves resulting from these exposures is extremely large. Therefore, a separate risk-adjusted discount rate may be selected to estimate the economic value of these special exposures, and special purchase and sale provisions are developed to mitigate the risk.

4.9.6.4 Catastrophes and Concentration of Risk

The catastrophic risk associated with property insurance should be considered in the selection of prospective loss ratios and the required cost of capital. Property and casualty insurance companies commonly use catastrophe models to determine their risk and exposure from windstorms, earthquakes, and other events. The results of these models are usually reported to insurance company rating agencies. A common catastrophe model will develop the expected loss for a 100-year event. These statistics may also be useful for an investor in assessing the relative risk for the target company compared to others in the peer group when using the market multiple approach.

In the United States, insurance companies are not permitted to establish loss reserves for catastrophe losses that have not occurred. The NAIC has made proposals for establishing tax-deferred reserves to protect the solvency of property insurers. In essence this reserve would be considered a segregation of surplus in an actuarial appraisal.

In other countries, insurers may be allowed to (or may be required to) establish equalization reserves for this exposure. For the purposes of determining the appraisal value of P&C insurance companies in the United States, elimination of the equalization reserve is included as a book value adjustment.

4.9.7 SCENARIO VS. STOCHASTIC RISK EVALUATION

The limited time frame to perform the valuation may prohibit a detailed analysis of the key variables required for stochastic modeling. Most nontechnical executives and investment bankers prefer scenario testing to assess the risk of the various assumptions. Using this approach, different valuations are produced under a range of scenarios, varying key assumptions such as loss ratios, discount rates, and premium growth rates. Key parameters are sometimes varied, holding other variables constant to test the sensitivity of particular parameters on the appraisal value. While technical shortcomings may exist, this approach allows the actuary to focus the decisionmaker's attention on the key assumptions, providing a measure of how a change in those assumptions will impact the appraisal value.

When discussing the valuation risk, it is important to distinguish the different types of risk that exist. Certain risks may already be considered in the valuation through the selected cost of capital or risk-adjusted discount rate. As discussed in section 4.4.7, the cost of capital used in many sell-side valuations is derived using a capital asset pricing model (CAPM) approach and an insurance industry beta. The insurance industry beta reflects the relative risk for the insurance industry. An appraisal using a hurdle rate derived in this manner would only incorporate the market risk (systematic risk that cannot be eliminated through diversification) with no additional provisions for the specific risk of the target company. Many financial experts argue that this is the appropriate hurdle rate to use in the valuation model. However, from the investor's point of view, the specific risk of the target company should also be considered.

The cost of capital should be increased if the target company has unusually high underwriting risk, asset risk, or parameter risk. Underwriting risk is generally related to long-tailed liabilities or a material exposure to catastrophe losses. In pricing P&C products, the underwriting risk is typically reflected through higher profit loads and through the cost to transfer the risk to the reinsurance markets. A company that retains the underwriting risk is expected to receive higher profits as compensation for assuming this risk. Similarly, adjustments to the required cost of capital may be needed if the target company has a relatively risky investment portfolio supporting its liabilities. Finally, if there is significant uncertainty in estimating key parameters for the valuation model, the investor may reduce the appraisal value by increasing the required cost of capital to reflect this risk.

4.10 SUMMARY

With the range of values derived using the various techniques described in this chapter, deciding the ultimate value of the target company is in the hands of the management of both the seller and the buyer. Due to the complexity of insurance entities, there are many factors that could be weighted differently in the eyes of the parties involved. The financial advisors' job is to provide management of both sides with a range of reasonable values. Once this range has been identified, the price ultimately paid by the buyer will be decided in the negotiation process.

The tables on the following pages identify the major public life and P&C insurance transactions that have occurred over the past 25 years with a purchase price in excess of $500 million, and that include a North American buyer or seller. Along with the purchase price, the tables display the resulting GAAP P/E and P/B ratios. Table 4.21 lists life company transactions while Table 4.22 shows P&C company deals.

INSURANCE M&A ACTIVITY
Selected 1987-2003 Announced Life Transactions
Deals $500 Million or More

Buyer	Unit To Be Bought	Price (in $millions)	GAAP P/E	GAAP P/B
1987				
1988				
1989				
GE Capital	FGIC	642.0	9.9	1.2
Zurich Insurance	Maryland Casualty	740.0	9.9	0.8
1990				
1991				
AMEV (Fortis)	Mutual Benefit Group	500.0	10.0	NA
1992				
UNUM	Colonial Companies	570.0	15.0	1.9
Conseco	Bankers L&C	600.0	NA	2.8
1993				
GE Capital Corp.	Great Northern Ins. Annuity	525.0	18.0	1.4
GE Capital Corp.	United Pacific Life	550.0	10.0	0.8
UNUM	Colonial Companies	656.0	15.0	1.9
1994				
Torchmark Corp.	American Income Holding Inc.	563.5	14.4	2.8
American General Corp.	Western National (40%)	724.0	8.3	1.1
American General Corp.	Franklin Life	1,170.0	14.6	0.9
American General Corp.	Unitrin	2,611.0	27.5	1.3

TABLE 4.21

INSURANCE M&A ACTIVITY (Continued)

Buyer	Unit To Be Bought	Price (in $millions)	GAAP P/E	GAAP P/B
1987				
1988				
1989				
GE Capital	FGIC	642.0	9.9	1.2
Zurich Insurance	Maryland Casualty	740.0	9.9	0.8
1990				
1991				
AMEV (Fortis)	Mutual Benefit Group	500.0	10.0	NA
1992				
UNUM	Colonial Companies	570.0	15.0	1.9
Conseco	Bankers L&C	600.0	NA	2.8
1993				
GE Capital Corp.	Great Northern Ins. Annuity	525.0	18.0	1.4
GE Capital Corp.	United Pacific Life	550.0	10.0	0.8
UNUM	Colonial Companies	656.0	15.0	1.9
1994				
Torchmark Corp.	American Income Holding Inc.	563.5	14.4	2.8
American General Corp.	Western National (40%)	724.0	8.3	1.1
American General Corp.	Franklin Life	1,170.0	14.6	0.9
American General Corp.	Unitrin	2,611.0	27.5	1.3
1995				
Jefferson-Pilot Corp.	Alexander Hamilton Life	575.0	11.3	
Humana Inc.	Emphesys Financial Group	650.0	10.4	2.3
GE Capital	Life of Virginia sub of AON	960.0		1.2
Zurich & Insurance Partners	Kemper Corp.	1,744.0	15.0	1.9
1996				
Conseco Inc.	Life Partners Group	600.6	21.2	1.4
Conseco Inc.	Capital American Financial Corp.	650.0	12.7	2.2
American General	Home Beneficial Corp.	665.0	17.8	1.3
Conseco Inc.	American Travelers Corp.	774.0	22.2	2.8
Provident Companies	Paul Revere Corp. (merger)	1,200.0	13.7	0.9
GE Capital	First Colony Corp.	1,782.0	14.6	1.4
1997				
American General Corp.	Western National Corp. (55% not owned)	1,178.0	19.0	2.2
Lincoln National Corp.	Cigna Corp.'s life insurance and annuity business	1,400.0	17.5	
American General Corp.	USLIFE	1,684.1	21.6	1.5
ING Group NV	Equitable of Iowa	2,200.0	18.8	2.7
Great West	London Insurance Group	C$2,940.0	18.8	1.9
American United Life Insurance Co.	Indianapolis Life Insurance Company	merger		
1998				
Fortis	John Alden	575.9	26.8	1.6
Lincoln National Corp.	Aetna Inc.'s U.S. Individual Life insurance business	1,000.0	14.4	
Swiss Reinsurance Co.	Life Re Corp.	1,956.0	38.4	2.6
UNUM Corp.	Provident Cos.	4,800.0	16.3	1.7
American International Group Ins.	SunAmerica Ins.	18,200.0	35.6	5.4

TABLE 4.21

INSURANCE M&A ACTIVITY (Continued)

Buyer	Unit To Be Bought	Price (in $millions)	GAAP P/E	GAAP P/B
1999				
Allstate Corp.	American Heritage Life Investment Corp.	1,094.1	24.3	3.3
Aegon NV	Transamerica Corp.	10,688.9	14.3	1.7
2000				
Royal Bank of Canada	Liberty Life Insurance Co. & Liberty Insurance Services	578.7	16.1	
Hartford Financial Services	Hartford Life Inc. (20% not owned)	1,308.0	15.1	3.1
ING Groep NV	Aetna Financial Services & Aetna International	5,000.0	13.3	
ING Groep NV	ReliaStar Financial Corp.	5,011.2	18.9	2.4
AXA	AXA Financial (39.7% not owned)	9,400.0	29.6	3.9
2001				
American International Group Inc.	Chiyoda Mutual Life Ins. Co.	513.5		
GE Capital Corp.	National Mutual Life Assurance Society	524.1		
Old Mutual Plc	Fidelity and Guaranty Life Insurance Co. (sub. of St. Paul Cos.)	635.0	10.8	1.1
Hartford Financial Services	Fortis Financial Group	1,120.0		
Nationwide Financial Services Inc.	Provident Mutual Life Insurance Co.	1,560.0	14.5	1.5
AEGON NV	J.C. Penney Direct Marketing	1,600.0		
Sun Life	Keyport Life Insurance Co. and Independent Financial Marketing Group	1,702.0		
Swiss Reinsurance Co.	Lincoln National Reassurance	2,000.0	16.0	
American International Group Inc.	American General	23,400.8	17.5	2.7
Sun Life	Clarica Life Insurance Co.	C$7,339.5	19.5	2.4
2002				
MetLife Inc.	Aseguradora Hidalgo S.A.	966.8		3.0
Nationwide Financial Services Inc.	Provident Mutual Life Ins. Co.	1,120.0		
Prudential Financial Inc.	American Skandia Inc.	1,150.0		0.7
ManuLife Financial Corp.	Canada Life Financial Corp.	3,817.6	16.8	1.7
2003				
Bank One Corp.	Zurich Financial Services Group (most of U.S. life ins. group)	500.0		
Hartford Financial Services Group Inc.	CNA Group Life Assurance Co.	500.0		0.7
United Health Group	Golden Rule Financial Corp.	500.0		
AXA	MONY Group Inc.	1,482.0		0.7
Prudential	Retirement Business of Cigna	2,100.0	10.5	1.9
Great-West Life Co.	Canada Life Financial Corp.	4,800.0	19.4	2.0
Manulife Financial Corp.	John Hancock Financial Services	10,400.0	12.4	1.3

TABLE 4.21 **Source:** The Shapiro Network, Inc., with assistance of others, most recently, P.W. Mattingly & Co. (1996 – on).

INSURANCE M&A ACTIVITY
Selected 1987-2003 Announced P&C Transactions
Deals $500 Million or More

Buyer	Unit To Be Bought	Price (in $millions)	GAAP P/E	GAAP P/B
1987				
1988				
1989				
G.E. Capital	FGIC	642.0	9.9	1.2
Zurich Insurance	P&C sub of American General	740.0		0.8
1990				
Winterthur Swiss Insurance	General Casualty Cos.	630.0		2.9
Allianz AG	Fireman's Fund Ins. Co.	3,300.0	17.0	1.7
Investor Group	Home Insurance Co.	970.0	19.0	8.0
1991				
1992				
KKR (with Am. Re. Mgt.)	American Re-Insurance Corp.	1,400.0	131.0	1.3
1993				
Primerica Corp.	Travelers Corp.	4,600.0		0.9
1994				
Commercial Union Plc.	Group Victoire	2,310.0		
CNA Financial	Continental Corp.	1,100.0		
General Re	Cologne Re (50.1%)	595.0		
1995				
Berkshire Hathaway	GEICO (remaining 49%)	2,329.0	21.3	3.0
Travelers	Aetna Property Casualty Operations	4,000.0		
1996				
ACE Ltd.	Tempest Reins. Co. Ltd.	976.0	2.2	
Aetna L&C Co.	U.S. Healthcare Inc.	8,900.0		
American Financial	Allmerica Property/Casualty	700.0		
General Re	National Re Corp.	940.0	17.3	2.4
Munich Reinsurance Co.	American Re Corp.	3,178.0		3.8
Scor US Corp.	Allstate Reinsurance (U.S. operations)	500.0		
Swiss Re	Mercantile & General Re (from Prudential UK)	2,650.0		
1997				
American International Group	American Bankers	2,200.0	21.0	2.7
AON Corp.	Alexander & Alexander Services	1,200.0		
Credit Suisse Group	Winterthur Insurance Co.	9,510.0		
Exel Ltd.	GCR Holding Limited	645.1	8.3	1.6
G.E. Capital Corp.	Colonial Penn Group	950.0		
General Motors Acceptance Corp.	Integon Corp.	518.8		3.0
MBIA Inc.	CapMac Holding Inc.	652.5	19.6	1.9
Partner Re Ltd.	Societe Anonyme Francaise de Reassurances	972.2		
Partner Re Ltd.	Swiss Reinsurance Co.	950.0		
Safeco	American States Financial Corp.	2,822.4	15.6	2.3
TRG Holdings Corp.	Resolution Group - sub of Xerox	612.0		

TABLE 4.22

INSURANCE M&A ACTIVITY (Continued)

Buyer	Unit To Be Bought	Price (in $millions)	GAAP P/E	GAAP P/B
1998				
Ace Ltd.	CAT Ltd.	711.5		1.5
Assoc. 1st Capital Corp.	Northland Co.	600.0		
Berkshire Hathaway	General Re Corp.	22,300.0	22.9	2.7
CMAC Investment Corp.	American Corp.	646.4		
Exel Ltd.	Mid Ocean (73% not owned)	2,143.5	12.6	2.1
Fairfax Financial	Crum & Forster Holdings sub of Xerox	565.0		0.5
General Electric Co.	Kemper Reins. Co.	500.0		
Guardian Royal Exchange	Netherlands Insurance Cos. (Sub ING Groep NV)	1,150.0		2.0
Hannover Re	Clarendon Ins. Group	500.0	18.3	1.9
Nationwide Mutual	Allied Group	1,488.9	26.9	4.0
Norwich Union Plc.	London & Edinburgh Insurance Co.	523.9		
Partner Re Ltd.	Credit Swisse Group (Reinsurance operations)	781.0		
St. Paul Cos.	USF&G	2,670.8	13.0	1.4
1999				
ACE Ltd.	Cigna Corp. - P&C Business	3,450.0	17.4	1.5
Chubb Corp.	Executive Risk Inc.	902.3	20.0	2.5
Farmers Insurance Exchange	Foremost Corp. of America	814.0	15.0	2.9
Fidelity National Financial	Chicago Title Corp.	1,139.6	10.4	2.4
Fortis	American Bankers Insurance Group	2,600.0	9.7	2.5
Liberty Mutual	Guardian Royal Exchange PLC (U.S. operations)	1,465.0		
Markel Corp.	Terra Nova Holdings Ltd.	886.4	12.1	1.6
Metropolitan Life Insurance Company	St. Paul Cos. (personal lines insurance operations)	600.0		
Royal & Sun Alliance Insurance Group	Orion Capital Corp.	1,400.0		2.2
Swiss Reinsurance Company	Underwriters Re Group Inc.	725.0		
XL Capital Ltd.	NAC Re Corp.	1,185.4	11.6	1.4
2000				
American International Group	HSB Group Inc.	1,203.8	31.3	3.1
Citigroup	Reliance Group Holdings' surety business	580.0		3.6
Dexia SA	Financial Security Assur. Holdings	2,649.2	18.1	2.1
Radian Group Inc.	Enhance Financial Services Group	549.8	12.2	0.8
2001				
White Mountains Insurance	CGU Corp.	2,170.0		
XL Capital Ltd.	Winterthur International Ins. Co. (sub of Credit Suisse)	598.5		
2002				
2003				
AIG	GE Edison Life (Japan) & U.S. auto & home ins.	2,150.0		
Liberty Mutual Insurance Group	Prudential Financial (property & casualty business)	540.0		0.8
PMI Group Inc. + Investors	Financial Guaranty Insurance Co. (sub of G.E.)	1,835.0	8.2	1.0
St. Paul Cos. Inc.	Travelers Property Casualty Corp.	16,138.5	56.3	1.4

TABLE 4.22 **Source:** The Shapiro Network, Inc., with assistance of others, most recently, P.W. Mattingly & Co. (1996 – on).

Chapter Five

Due Diligence

Chapter 5 discusses the complex process known as due diligence. The purpose of due diligence is straightforward: to ensure that the target is in the condition in which it was represented by the seller and that there are no "holes," unfunded liabilities, or other problems. A massive undertaking in normal circumstances, it is further complicated by the long-term nature of some insurance product liabilities. All the members of the buyer's team have an important role to play, and their roles are laid out in this chapter. In addition, the special concerns and considerations of the actuary are examined, as well as why they are critically important.

5.1 INTRODUCTION

M&A transactions can be looked at from several different perspectives, for example:

- Acquisitions vs. mergers
- Bidding situations vs. private negotiations vs. public tender offers
- Buyer viewpoint vs. seller viewpoint.

In this chapter, discussions will be directed at acquisitions (as opposed to mergers) conducted through a bidding process. Similarly, issues will be presented from the buyer's viewpoint unless specified otherwise. However, the principles underlying the discussions should reasonably apply to the other M&A situations.

Due diligence is presented in the following sections:

- Objectives of due diligence—what needs to be accomplished and why
- Due diligence team—who is involved and their roles
- Due diligence process—the key steps involved
- Due diligence implementation—a comprehensive review of the overall process
- Actuarial due diligence—a detailed review of the actuaries' roles.

This discussion is limited to acquisitions of insurance risk-related entities. Although the principles embodied herein apply equally to other entities, those acquisitions would involve their own specific considerations.

Finally, a single, specific acquisition scenario has been chosen to illustrate the principles and practices applicable to due diligence. Exhibit 5.1 outlines a sample sequence of events for an M&A transaction based on a bidding process. Actual M&A transactions could encompass a wide range of potential scenarios.

ILLUSTRATIVE STEPS FOR TYPICAL M&A TRANSACTION

	BUYER	SELLER
1	Develop business strategy, analyze options; consideration of buying	Analyze selling options
2	Retain advisors	Retain advisors
3	Identify potential targets	Develop seller's actuarial appraisal
4		Market valuation
5		Go/no-go decision
6		Develop offering memorandum
7		Identify potential buyers
8	Respond by indicating interest	Solicit preliminary bids
9	Sign confidentiality agreement	Distribute confidentiality agreement
10		Start to prepare data room
11		Distribute bid specifications, actuarial appraisal, and offering memorandum

EXHIBIT 5.1

ILLUSTRATIVE STEPS FOR TYPICAL M&A TRANSACTION (Continued)

	BUYER	SELLER
12	High-level questions	Respond to high-level questions
13	Develop preliminary bid based on seller's data	
14	Submit preliminary bid	Review bids and select finalists
15	Submit initial data request	
16	On-site due diligence and data room; get copies of data for additional review	Host management presentations and data room; Q&A
17	Review seller-supplied data and other info	
18	Follow-up Q&A; request additional information	Provide responses, additional data, additional sensitivities
19	Develop buyer's actuarial appraisal and PGAAP projections	
20	Distribute purchase agreement	
21	Prepare final bid, closing conditions, representations and warranties	
22	Submit final bid	Review final bids
23	Negotiate price and terms	Negotiate price and terms
24		Select winning bid
25	Closing	Closing
26	Transition	Transition
27	Integration; Sarbanes-Oxley	

EXHIBIT 5.1

5.2 OBJECTIVES OF DUE DILIGENCE

This chapter addresses the buyer's full due diligence process, which is kicked off by the seller's invitation to a few preliminary bidders to proceed to the final bidding round. The preliminary bidding process has been described in Chapter 2; the number of bidders invited to the next round can vary widely.

The objectives of due diligence are to validate and quantify the explicit and implicit assumptions (financial and strategic) that are used to value the deal. In addition, the due diligence process should include preparation of an integration plan, which should begin to be implemented immediately after closing. Generally, due diligence occurs under very tight deadlines, often over as little as one to four weeks.

As part of the preliminary bid development, the buyer may have performed some rudimentary due diligence; however, heavy reliance is generally placed on the seller's offering memorandum and actuarial appraisal. Practices can vary widely from situation to situation.

For the purposes of this chapter, formal due diligence should be considered as the buyer's in-depth analysis of the target, whenever it occurs. Due diligence generally encompasses the activities outlined in steps 14-19 above.

The result of the due diligence process is the final bid. Winning bids reflect that most deals are done for strategic as well as financial reasons.

Due diligence is a complex process, with a large number of sophisticated and potentially conflicting perspectives. In order to help organize the process for the reader, five major objectives of due diligence have been identified:

- Confirm strategic value
- Confirm financial value
- Confirm operational value
- Construct appropriate bid
- Prepare for successful integration.

Addressing the first three objectives involves an intensive review of the target company's operations, financials, and risk exposures; it includes identifying and assessing the material risk factors that could reduce value. These efforts make up what most people regard as "due diligence." Satisfying the last two objectives, however, is just as critical to a successful acquisition.

Each objective emphasizes specific due diligence practices. Sections 5.2.1 through 5.2.5 describe each of the objectives in more detail. The due diligence practices associated with these objectives are described in sections 5.4 through 5.6.

5.2.1 CONFIRM STRATEGIC VALUE

One purpose of emphasizing the above objectives is to stress that successful M&A bids most often occur when the restructuring creates more value following the acquisition than existed prior to the deal. This means that a key objective of the seller's due diligence process is to identify opportunities, synergies, and potential additions to value beyond the strict financial value of the acquired business. Higher perceived value translates into a higher bid and the highest bid usually wins. Thus, the due diligence process is much more than just "getting the numbers right."

Some examples of value-adding strategies include:

- Increase in market share
- Derivation of synergies through complementary markets, products, or distribution
- Exploitation or leveraging of superior technology
- Increase in scale and ability to leverage existing resources better
- Preventing a new entrant from gaining a foothold in the market.

In due diligence, the buyer must evaluate how well its strategies will be achieved. Ultimately strategic value must be translated from a qualitative situation into a quantified expression of value (i.e., the bid amount).

CRYPT 5.1

Due Diligence Detects Dress-Up

Prairie Casualty Assurance Company (PCAC) was a personal lines property casualty insurance company, writing mostly personal automobile insurance. The company had $200 million annual premiums; reported earnings for the past two years were an impressive $23 million and $27 million. PCAC's principal owner and chief executive was nearing retirement and decided to sell the company.

PCAC's seller's document presented a favorable outlook. It attributed improvements in recent years' loss ratios to enhancements in the company's underwriting model. The company touted its growth during the past two years which was achieved by appointing new agents, obtaining book transfers, and increasing new business from existing agents. The presentation of the loss reserves highlighted a conservative reserving philosophy, citing favorable development in Schedule P for the one- and two-year runoff studies. Could things be any rosier?

I was on the due diligence team for my buyer. I had to dig into the financials as, typical with casualty companies, there was no actuarial appraisal. The company asserted several inconsistent items, such as improving loss ratios and conservative reserves. My guard was up.

I looked at the development of reserves during the last two years. I ascertained that PCAC made two significant changes in its reserve assumptions: tail factors were reduced and the expected loss ratios were lowered. The current estimates were based on an average of historical results with a slight improvement to reflect the enhancements to the underwriting model.

I then uncovered that PCAC had lowered its explicit margin for conservatism from 8% to 1%.

Further, I determined that the improvement in loss development factors was driven by backlogs in the claim department. With slower processing, there were fewer dollars paid.

I concluded these facts alone overstated reported earnings by $6 million each year.

I then switched gears to look at the portrayal of future issues. I found that no adjustments were made to the expected loss ratios to account for the higher proportion of new business. Also, the transfers from the new agents were not of the same high quality as PCAC's renewal book.

Based on these due diligence findings, my investor lowered its offer significantly. At that price, he was unsuccessful in the bid to acquire the company.

This gave us a hollow feeling. But, for each of the two years following the attempted sale, we saw reported earnings of zero. The reserves did prove short and the loss ratios were four percentage points above that projected.

My client still thanks me.

5.2.2 CONFIRM FINANCIAL VALUE

The buyer's final bid is a function of a number of strategic and financial considerations. These include, but are not limited to:

- Scarcity of the target
- Value of the target to potential bidders, especially competitors of the buyer
- Number, financial strength, and financial resources of other bidders
- Aggressiveness of other bids.

The buyer's financial consideration begins with the seller's actuarial appraisal, which is then modified based on the market value of the target (stand-alone and transactional), as well as actual and projected financial performance. Most important is the effect the target's financial performance will have on the buyer's earnings, leverage, capital position, ratings position, and whether the target's financial performance is likely to exceed the buyer's cost of capital (otherwise the transaction destroys value).

Two critical goals of the buyer's due diligence efforts are to:

- Establish there are no "holes" in the seller's financials, such as:
  - Reserve inadequacies
  - Unreserved (or previously unknown) liabilities, including off-balance sheet liabilities
  - Overvalued assets (in particular whether impairments meet the buyer's normal criteria)
  - Contingent or undervalued future obligations (e.g., change of control clauses), including off-balance sheet assets
  - Inadequate reserves for embedded options or guarantees.
- Develop the assumptions needed to support the buyer's actuarial appraisal, GAAP pro forma projections, and other financial calculations. This generally takes the form of reviewing the assumptions presented in the seller's actuarial appraisal, confirming or adjusting those assumptions, or developing new assumptions as appropriate. Steps include, but are not limited to:
  - Reviewing the seller's actuarial appraisal documentation
  - Reviewing the seller's claim, lapse, and other experience reports

- Discussing the assumptions with the seller's management
- Projecting the buyer's future unit costs (often done on a marginal basis)
- Assessing future investment returns and interest spreads
- Quantifying synergies and other strategic values.

The due diligence process is used to identify and quantify items that affect value. In particular, the buyer should assign conservative estimates of value to areas it does not fully understand. Thus, the ability of the buyer's team to gain confidence regarding potentially material issues may drive the winning bid.

5.2.3 CONFIRM OPERATIONAL VALUE

A major driver of value is the quality of the operations to be acquired. As will be seen in the sections on due diligence implementation, a major component of the due diligence process is to identify:

- Whether there are any weaknesses in any of the seller's operational areas
- What it will take to fix those weaknesses from a financial or resource point of view
- What the impact will be on financial performance while any fixes are occurring
- What the strengths are in the seller's operational areas that may be used to improve the buyer's unit costs.

The buyer's team may also have to determine how effectively the acquired operation can be integrated into the buyer's operation. Issues would include:

- Is the acquired business's culture consistent with the buyer's culture? If not, what steps will need to be taken? What are the implications of those steps? Will fundamental changes be necessary?
- What are potential systems integration issues and how will that affect expense efficiency?
- How will retention of key staff be addressed? What about severance and change-in-control costs, etc.?
- How will agency and distribution functions be integrated?

Again, it will be the actuaries' role to translate these operational findings into financial values.

5.2.4 CONSTRUCT APPROPRIATE BID

The main deliverable of the due diligence process is the final bid. The bid needs to appropriately recognize the key components of value if it is to be high enough to win the bidding process. At the same time, it must generate returns sufficient to satisfy the expectations of the buyer's management and ultimately its shareholders.

Both financial and non-financial aspects must be considered, including:

- The amount of the bid. The buyer is responsible for developing its own view of financial worth, generally described as the buyer's actuarial appraisal. In most cases, the starting point for the buyer's work is the seller's actuarial appraisal, which is generally provided with the offering memorandum. However, the buyer must adjust the seller's value or calculate its own value by confirming or adjusting key assumptions or other parameters.

- Issues, concerns, or unknowns identified during due diligence. These will need to be accounted for in the final bid through a combination of price adjustments and bid structures (i.e., conditions).

The bid price must reflect the risk inherent in the assumptions used to develop the appraisal values and pro forma financial statements. The buyer will discount or reduce the bid price for assumptions that are not sufficiently supported or are not fully understood.

- Appropriate bid construction. For example, the level of the bid price is important, both in terms of its impact on the buyer (it could dilute earnings going forward or cause a ratings downgrade through excessive leverage) and on the seller (it impacts how attractive the offer will be). If the buyer is offering its stock, it must demonstrate to the seller that the stock will remain a strong performer post-acquisition. The anticipated reaction of the stock market to the announced deal will be critical.

5.2.5 PREPARE FOR SUCCESSFUL INTEGRATION

There is a huge gap between the potential value inherent in the target business and actually capturing that value. The due diligence process is the time to plan specific steps to protect or improve value. Some of these steps will take place at the public announcement of the deal, some between then and the closing, and others post-closing.

CRYPT 5.2

Actuarial Precision, Or Should We Bang On The Table?

A few years ago, as a member of a buyer's due diligence team, I attended a last-ditch negotiating session with the seller. Both sides were represented by company executives, investment bankers, accountants, actuaries, and attorneys. Each side lined up on opposite sides of a long table. This was going to be a big meeting.

The selling company had a block of disability income business whose claim reserves were generally acknowledged to be short. The question, of course, was by how much.

The seller's actuaries had provided an analysis that indicated a deficiency based on a one-year test as performed in Schedule H. It was clearly a "back of the envelope" analysis. Further, we received this information only the day before, very late in the game.

I had done a more thorough calculation, based on the present value of future benefits, revealing a much larger estimate of the deficiency. There was a large difference to be resolved, with only a few hours to go! While the discussion started with a technical description of the issue, our side nevertheless interpreted this as stonewalling. The two opposing attorneys started arguing (all the actuaries were dumbstruck) as to the timeliness and quality of the information. Voices were raised, the two lawyers stood up, yelled, literally banged on the table, and one stormed out for a while. "You can't give us this c___ the day before closing!!"

It was a scene straight out of a movie.

Finally, after considerable huffing and puffing, the issue was resolved. The final numbers, however, were not based primarily on actuarial calculations but rather on a negotiated amount. The discussion was much closer to "why don't we split the difference" rather than technical precision.

In this example, actuarial calculations helped to influence negotiations, but the final numbers were based on many other factors. As actuaries go about their work, they should keep in mind their role as technical advisors, but also realize that business issues may take precedence over apparent precision.

5.3 DUE DILIGENCE TEAM

As described above, the objectives of the due diligence process include identifying and anticipating all of the key issues that could materially affect the viability or attractiveness of the deal. This requires an extensive team of experts, representing all areas of both the insurance operations and the M&A process.

The buyer's due diligence team consists of both internal and external experts. However, it is important to note that the internal team has to "own" the due diligence process. The external experts are primarily advisors; at the end of the day, the internal team will live with the results.

5.3.1 EXTERNAL EXPERTS

External experts are generally specialists in M&A transactions. Most buyers retain external investment bankers, accountants, attorneys, and actuaries. In some cases, buyers retain other external experts with situation-specific skills. This is especially common when the buyer's board of directors wants an independent opinion in a specific area. Examples of situation-specific experts include integration specialists, human resource specialists, and technology experts.

Outside professionals generally fill two roles in the due diligence process. The first is to provide expertise and experience specifically related to M&A transactions (e.g., to provide structure and guidance to the process). The second is to assist with operational due diligence efforts. Outside professionals generally bring extensive experience and expertise derived from many M&A transactions. They can provide a broad perspective for evaluating the target business; in addition, they can supplement internal expertise in any areas new to the buyer.

5.3.2 INTERNAL EXPERTS

Internal experts include staff with operational expertise in the businesses to be acquired, as well as corporate functions. Some buyers also have internal staff that specializes in M&A transactions. The operational and corporate functions represented on the internal team generally include underwriting, tax, human resources, legal, sales, marketing, accounting, actuarial, compliance, administration, claims, investments, information systems or technology, and enterprise risk management.

Where the needed expertise is product-specific (e.g., actuarial or claims), experts are generally required from each product area.

The primary role of the internal team members is to provide operational expertise. The internal team is most effective when the staff who will manage the acquired operations participate directly in the due diligence process.

5.3.3 PROJECT MANAGEMENT

Due diligence teams (internal and external combined) often involve a large number of participants. Teams of 20 to 30 people are common; and teams of 50 to 80 people are not unheard of. Coordinating the work of such a large team, and producing reliable results in such a short time frame, is a project in itself.

Successful acquisition generally requires the direct involvement of the senior management of the buyer, plus effective project management staff. The investment banker and other external experts often act as joint project managers and provide valuable expertise and resources based on experience with many M&A transactions.

5.4 DUE DILIGENCE PROCESS

In this section, the due diligence process is discussed from the buyer's perspective. At the end, key aspects from the seller's perspective are discussed.

5.4.1 BUYER'S PERSPECTIVE

In section 5.2, the buyer's objectives of due diligence were summarized in five categories:

- Confirm strategic value
- Confirm financial value
- Confirm operational value
- Construct appropriate bid
- Prepare for successful integration.

Addressing the first three objectives requires an intensive review of the target company's operations, financials, and risk exposures, which includes identifying and assessing the material risk factors that could reduce value. It is what many people consider "due diligence." However, the last two objectives will be ineffective if the first three are not addressed soundly and thoroughly.

As noted above, due diligence generally takes place under an extremely tight time frame, often as little as one to four weeks. Access to data and key staff is usually limited as well because most deals are highly confidential, and few staff on the seller's side will be "in the know." As a result, the buyer's due diligence team is required to develop informed decisions under very challenging circumstances. These constraints require a decision-making process that differs greatly from the buyer's day-to-day business processes. The buyer's team has to identify and focus on the critical issues quickly and limit the depth of its analyses accordingly.

As discussed in section 5.1, the illustrative scenario assumes that the buyer has received a seller's offering memorandum and actuarial appraisal, has submitted a satisfactory preliminary bid, and is now ready to prepare a final bid.

To get started, the buyer's team will construct an initial data request, which identifies the key information that the buyer wants to support its evaluation and bid development.

Meanwhile, the seller should have prepared a data room, which contains the information the seller deems appropriate for the buyer's review. An on-site visit will generally be scheduled for the buyer's team to peruse the material in the data room.

5.4.1.1 On-Site Visit

During the on-site visit, presentations will be made by the seller's management, advisors, and staff regarding key aspects of the business. Q&A (breakout) sessions will also be held to address key operational areas. Generally, copies can be made of some, but not all, materials. The team can usually make notes regarding items that cannot be copied.

The on-site visit is essential to confirmation of value. Not only is the "hard" data exchanged, but much of the chemistry of the deal becomes apparent. The potential buyer will contemplate:

- Can you envision working with target's people?
- Do they have confidence in the data they are providing? Are they credible?
- Can you tell who and what makes the operations successful?

All these pieces of information will need to be factored into the valuation equation.

The data room and presentations will address many of the items on the buyer's initial data request list, and the seller will generally try to provide the remaining items. At the same time, due diligence is a cyclical process; each round of data and discussions will generate new requests for clarifications, explanations, and additional data.

Each of the operational areas is interrelated (e.g., underwriting and claims affect experience; reserving affects financials). Similarly, although the operational review will be divided up among the members of the team for efficiency, the information and findings must be shared effectively if the team members are to make their assessments. This is often accomplished through nightly meetings of the entire team where each member debriefs the rest of the group on his findings and the implications.

If appropriate, the buyer also assesses how well the target can be integrated into the buyer's operations. Due diligence teams will assess key areas, such as distribution, systems, product management, and claims. The teams will identify and quantify the value added from potential synergies as well as the costs of integration that could reduce the value.

Box Lunch

CRYPT 5.3

*What ever happened to the **Gentlemen's Agreement**?*

A standard reinsurance agreement + poor reporting + a large claims settlement request + lots of name-calling = ARBITRATION.

It was not pretty, certainly not the way gentlemen should act. We requested information from the client as our right set in the reinsurance treaty. What we received was something straight out of a TV lawyer show. Two thousand dusty boxes of information were packaged up and waiting for us at the client's place of business. It was a ruse. Their strategy was to give us so much information that we couldn't possibly look at all of it.

Well, our CEO was not going to be intimidated. He sent 12 senior employees, about 10% of the entire company, to the client for three weeks straight to read through the boxes in the discovery phase of the arbitration. I was one of them. When we first arrived, the client put us into a room with no air conditioning and no working windows. This particular room was under construction because of leaks. The windows were covered with thick plastic and when it rained, buckets collected the water flowing down the plastic.

So we were in this very small room with no air, no windows, and 2,000 dusty boxes to review. So what did we do? We rolled up our sleeves and dug right in!

We opened up each box in succession and documented our findings. We found all kinds of stuff in these boxes, such as people's shoes, Rolodexes, and rolls of tape. In other words, they just went up to a desk and told the employee to put everything in these boxes. They put it in and we looked through it. When we completed our review, they brought it back to that person. You would never believe that it is possible for any professional to act this way.

*So, what did we find besides some interesting magazines (this is a good reason for you not to keep those magazines at your desk)? We found no fewer than seven copies of the **smoking gun**, the memo which basically said let's keep all this information from the reinsurance companies and they will never know. Another interesting piece of literature that we discovered was the client company's arbitration strategy. It seems that they boxed up the Chief Council's desk too! Other fun items were salary lists, confidential human resources files, and internal sniping memos. Of course, we didn't read these because they weren't pertinent to the case.*

*The final outcome of the arbitration was a victory for us, mainly based upon the information in the **smoking gun** memo. Our CEO gambled and won big. Their box strategy failed; we ate their lunch.*

5.4.1.2 Post-Visit Due Diligence

Following the on-site visit, the team-based review of identified due diligence issues will continue intensively. At this point, the team members also start to work with the actuaries and investment bankers to translate their findings into assumptions that will drive the appraisal and financial projection models. The team members also continue to report their findings to the due diligence management team, who assemble an integrated, qualitative assessment. Because of the volume of work involved, these steps generally occur concurrently, with updates to the actuarial models and qualitative assessments occurring on a real-time basis.

The intensive review process prepares the information necessary to accomplish the final two objectives of due diligence: construction of an appropriate bid and preparation for successful implementation.

5.4.1.3 Construct Appropriate Bid

As mentioned in section 5.2.4, the construction of the buyer's bid relies heavily on the following items of information:

- The buyer's actuarial appraisal (described in section 5.6.2.3 below)
- The buyer's purchase GAAP (PGAAP) pro forma projections (described in Chapter 8)
- Other financial and non-financial issues evaluated during due diligence.

The buyer may have concerns about specific issues relating to certain items, such as:

- Key assumptions or representations by the seller that the buyer has been unable to validate
- Exposures to liabilities that have not been quantified
- Known litigation or tax exposures.

As a result, the buyer may seek some protection for these concerns. As will be discussed in more detail in section 5.5.4, protections can take the form of closing conditions, representations and warranties, post-closing true-ups, amounts held in trust for loss reserve deficiencies, or other types of provisions that could be included in the purchase.

The process and strategies involved in bid construction are discussed in more detail in Chapter 2.

CRYPT 5.4

Good Assumptions, Good Bid, Good Bye

When we buy, we always get confidence in the assumptions before we formulate our bid. We present our case and then stick with our convictions, no matter how the seller re-shapes the facts.

The intimidation tactic is used frequently in the negotiation process by both buyers and sellers. I have been professionally "attacked" on the poor choice of assumptions I have made in my valuations, by both the buyer and the seller. I generally look beyond the tone of the message and listen to the claim of the individual questioning my work. There may be some good information I can use to improve my position. I have never changed an assumption because of "bullying" tactics. One of my favorite cases involved a common carrier risk. As I discussed the peril, the individual on the other side of the table said to me, "Well, THAT will never happen!"

We always dig deep. A few years ago my company considered purchasing a small block of accident insurance from a small insurer. We made a reasonable bid and sent a team of professionals to complete due diligence. As we went through this process, we verified many of our assumptions.

One key assumption confirmed was that a third party had significant contractual control over the block. This control was long term and impacted a significant portion of the value, which significantly depleted our valuation of the business.

We affirmed our originally submitted bid to the broker. The broker accepted the bid, but was discouraged by its amount. He explained that he had received several bids much more aggressive than what we had submitted. The broker gave several arguments to increase our bid, but could not adequately address the issue of the third party control.

The broker went silent for weeks. By now we didn't expect to be the victor, but we were interested in the details of the winning bid. What a surprise it was for us to open a publication several weeks later and find that the book was sold to a competitor for over four times our bid!

This exercise wasn't a winner for us, but it did illustrate one point. While there may be one right answer for a seller's valuation, there is a different right answer for each buyer's valuation.

5.4.1.4 *Prepare for Successful Integration*

There is a huge gap between the potential value inherent in a final bid and actually capturing that value; the issues associated with successful integration are discussed in Chapter 9. Due diligence is the time to anticipate and plan appropriate integration steps. Some of these activities will take place at the public announcement of the deal, some between then and the closing, and others post-closing. Integration activities can include:

- Protection of value during the transition of the business. Activities may include:
  - Joint buyer and seller communications plans
  - Transition services agreements
  - Key employee stay-on bonuses
  - Ownership/access to key systems or licenses.
- Establishment of positive relationships with key seller staff during the due diligence process is very useful to encouraging their retention.
- Anticipation of stock analyst and rating agency meetings. Rating agencies and stock analysts will expect explanations from the buyer for its decisions, including:
  - How price was established and what return it represents
  - Projected impact on GAAP earnings per share
  - How due diligence was conducted (e.g., reserve adequacy analyses).

  The initial meetings will occur at the time of public announcement; however, the buyer will also need to report on the progress of integration and the impact on financial results on an ongoing basis. Stock analysts' views have a significant impact on the public perception and, ultimately, on the buyer's stock price.
- Anticipation of Sarbanes-Oxley reporting requirements. The buyer's CFO and CEO will be required to sign off on integrated financials for the first quarter following the sale.
- Development of a preliminary integration plan. The plan needs to be constructed during due diligence so it may be implemented on closing. Critical items must be identified so they can be included in the closing conditions or purchase/sale agreement.

5.4.2 SELLER'S DUE DILIGENCE

So far, this chapter has discussed due diligence from the buyer's perspective; however, sellers also have a tremendous interest in facilitating an effective and efficient process.

- The seller's primary interest is in receiving maximum value for the business it is selling. To the extent the buyer's due diligence process leaves unanswered questions or weak support for key assumptions, the bid price will be reduced. Clear and complete preparation, organization of the seller's data room, and responses to potential buyers' questions will result in the best price. Solid preparation also tends to enhance any value the buyer attributes to intangibles.

- The seller risks significant loss of value just by putting its business up for sale. Even when trying to keep deals confidential, rumors of sales are likely to emerge, affecting customers, agents, and staff. Franchise-building opportunities are deferred and key employees can leave; the value of the franchise can drop.
- The seller should anticipate the buyers' key questions and concerns and should have answers prepared. For instance, if there is a doubt as to reserve adequacy the seller may wish to have an independent reserve adequacy report prepared to answer such questions.

A clean, efficient, and satisfying due diligence accelerates the overall process and minimizes those risks. The seller's investment banker generally plays an integral role assisting the seller to set up and manage the due diligence process.

The seller's role in due diligence generally includes the following functions:

- Preparing the data room
- Hosting on-site visits
  - Preparation, coordination, and ground rules
    - Who does what
  - Selling team presentations
    - External experts
    - Seller's management
    - Target company staff
  - Q&A sessions
- Responding to seller's data requests and questions
- Coordination and control of process.

The most important aspect of seller's due diligence is to be thoroughly prepared. It is critical for the seller to understand all-important information early in its evaluation process to have a complete grasp of the seller's appraisal calculations and underlying assumptions. The seller must present the supporting information effectively in the data room.

The seller must approach the due diligence process with the understanding that bid prices will be reduced for perceived risk and uncertainty. Supporting key assumptions and assertions with consistent, high-quality data will increase bid prices. Most important, the seller wants to avoid finding "holes" in value, or any other surprises, late in the process.

5.5 DUE DILIGENCE IMPLEMENTATION

This section provides a comprehensive overview of issues that need to be covered during the buyer's due diligence implementation. In particular, these issues address the objectives of confirming strategic, operational, and financial values, which will be used to support the qualitative and quantitative aspects of the final bid.

In practice, the seller's operations are summarized into several functional areas; subsets of the buyer's team are assigned to review each of these functional areas. As described in section 5.3, the buyer's team consists of a combination of internal and external experts.

A typical categorization of functional areas would be:

- Financial
- Investments
- Tax
- Legal and compliance

- Marketing and distribution
- Systems
- Human resources
- Product management
- Claims
- Reinsurance
- Risk management
- Actuarial.

The first 11 of these areas are described in sections 5.5.1 to 5.5.11 below. Due to this book's emphasis on actuarial issues, an entire section (section 5.6) is devoted to actuarial due diligence.

The sections below identify major issues that commonly need to be addressed for each of the areas; no attempt has been made to identify every potential key issue. In particular, specific seller situations, product lines or other factors might require research and analysis into issues not mentioned here.

Un-Credible

My company was being acquired. As they should, my senior management performed due diligence on not only the people behind the acquisition but the assets they planned to use to acquire us.

Management discovered the main figure had pleaded "nolo contendere" to a felony. The suitor was confronted with this fact, but he was clever and explained it away to the satisfaction of the insurance department.

Management reviewed the principal assets to be used to fund the acquisition. They turned out to be a nearly vacant and mortgaged office building, a bunch of unproved oil leases, and a large collection of first mortgages on unbuilt home-building lots. An independent appraisal was performed, and the report was clean.

The deal went through. I left.

Ninety days later, from a safe distance, I read that the first mortgages were really second mortgages and the oil leases were dry. The company was liquidated and people went to prison.

I was disappointed that the review my management performed was superficial. You really need to dig during due diligence.

CRYPT 5.5

5.5.1 *Financial*

Financial analysis is the crux of due diligence in that it either directly sets the appraisal value or defines the parameters that drive value. It is a broad category; analysis requires teamwork from the buyer's accountants, actuaries, investment bankers, and other financial specialists. This generally includes review and analysis of financial statements (both SAP and GAAP), supporting worksheets, data listings and interpretations, and financial processes and controls. Typical areas include:

- Review of recent statutory and GAAP financials and underlying worksheets (including independent auditor's workpapers), business plans, internal management reports, rating agency presentations, etc.
  - Are there any potentially significant liabilities not fully accounted for or that may be subject to contingencies?
  - Are there any potential contingent liabilities that should be subjected to stochastic analysis or scenario testing?

  - Does the data reconcile to published financials?
  - Are there any off-balance sheet liabilities?
  - Are there outstanding issues or queries from any of the state insurance departments?

- Review of lease commitments, receivables and payables, intercompany transactions, parent company cut-through agreements, etc.
  - Are there any commitments that need to be honored or replaced?
  - What is the quality of any claimed receivables (e.g., reinsurance recoverables)?

- Review of expenses by function
  - What expenses are allocated for parent-supplied services and how will these services be replaced?
  - Will the buyer's appraisal be based on marginal expenses? If so, how are they defined and measured?

- Review of financial systems and controls, including audit reports and regulatory issues
  - Are there any known or potential issues? Are there potential implications for reliability of past and future financials, Sarbanes-Oxley requirements, etc.?
  - What are the potential systems and process integration issues?

- Review the asset side of the balance sheet (see section 5.5.2)
  - What is the worth of nonadmitted and intangible assets?
  - How has asset impairment testing been conducted?

This section is intended to provide a high-level perspective on the types of issues subject to financial due diligence. In an actual due diligence, the list of financial areas to be subject to review often covers many pages (see checklist in the Appendix for a sample list of questions).

5.5.2 INVESTMENTS

Analysis of investments is generally performed by the buyer's investment team, often with help from the investment bankers. In stock deals, the buyer will acquire the seller's investment portfolio and must review everything. In reinsurance (asset) deals, the buyer generally receives cash; investments and investment income must be modeled using the buyer's investment strategy. Investment due diligence includes:

- Review of asset type, quality, and potential impairments
- Review of seller's investment strategies and guidelines, such as use of derivatives and other financial instruments
- Asset-liability matching policies and issues
  - Hedging and swap strategies
  - Often the buyer performs its own investment cash flow projections under different scenarios
- Review of seller's investment policies and internal control environment
- Assessment of any changes needed to conform to buyer's strategies, policies, quality standards, or asset-liability matching standards.

In cash transactions, the buyer must determine the appropriate investment returns and scenarios to incorporate into the buyer's appraisal.

Check and Double Check Your Data

CRYPT 5.6

When doing due diligence in the process of purchasing a life insurance company or block of business, it is always imperative to do a thorough due diligence of the actuarial models that are used to form a basis for the purchase price.

We were involved in the due diligence of a small company in which the company's financial models were relied on to determine the purchase price. In the process, we were able to "tick and tie" various control totals in the model to the company's annual statement workpapers. However, we still felt that something was wrong with the investment income that was being developed in the company's financial model.

After detailed investigation, we determined that the par values of certain bonds in the portfolio were incorrect in the company's annual statement. The company's auditors subsequently told us that the par values do not have a financial impact on the balance sheet or income statement, so they were audited with less scrutiny than other items.

For modeling purposes, the use of the correct par value is necessary in order to develop projected cash flows and implied yields. In this situation, the incorrect values caused the model to ascribe a yield rate of over 30% to this block of bonds and overstated the overall yield in the model by about 25 basis points.

Corrections were made to the data in the model, at our request, and the modeled value of the business decreased by about $10 million. This decrease, along with the implied inaccuracies in the models, enabled us to have a winning bid that was significantly less than the seller's original expectations.

5.5.3 TAX

Tax due diligence addresses the potential impact of the seller's positions regarding the broad array of tax issues. Buyers' tax strategies in acquisitions are discussed in Chapter 7. In tax due diligence, the necessary homework is performed to adequately validate the tax strategies and quantify various options open to the buyer.

5.5.4 LEGAL AND COMPLIANCE ISSUES

The role of the legal due diligence team is critical. Just as the fundamental purpose of actuarial due diligence is to determine the ultimate value of the target property (whether the target is an insurance company or just a book of business), the fundamental purpose of legal due diligence is to determine that there are no legal impediments or hidden liabilities that could prevent a buyer from realizing the value of the target.

5.5.4.1 Overview

A buyer is entitled to fair disclosure by sellers as to various matters that could influence the bid. Relying on disclosure is not sufficient, however; the buyer must carefully examine the target to determine if there may be potential liabilities or other problems that may only manifest themselves after the transaction has closed. Although buyers may attempt to obtain contractual protections from the seller, generally in the form of representations, warranties, or covenants, if the target is a widely held company or is not credit-worthy, or if the indemnification provided is limited in duration or amount, contractual protections against unrevealed losses may be unavailable or insufficient to make the buyer whole.[1]

[1] As discussed in Chapter 4, it is quite common for indemnification provisions under stock purchase agreements to include limitations on the seller's liability for losses; the relative bargaining power of the buyer and the seller may make it difficult to achieve meaningful protection for a buyer.

The due diligence process is also an opportunity for the buyer to identify exposures to future problems. Demonstrating that appropriate due diligence has occurred provides protection to officers and directors when the buyer is a public company. Mistakes may be inevitable, but if the buyer's officers and directors have properly exercised their fiduciary duties by making efforts to ensure that their decisions were reasonable in light of the facts known at the time, their decisions will be subject to the "business judgment rule," which means that the directors and officers, as well as the corporation that they manage, will be protected from shareholder lawsuits.[2]

In the course of legal due diligence, the legal team will review a wide variety of matters, including:

- Proper formation and authorization of the target
- Corporate structure and ownership of subsidiaries
- Existence of prior acquisitions
- Compliance with applicable laws, including, but not limited to, securities laws, tax laws, and insurance laws
- The results from the most recent market conduct exam and financial examinations
- In the case of life insurance companies, compliance of products with statutory and tax requirements
- In the case of reinsurance companies, compliance with state laws and regulations with respect to giving or receiving credit for reinsurance
- In the case of property casualty companies, the types of risks (e.g., asbestos) covered by contract forms
- Exposure to regulatory problems or lawsuits (e.g., market conduct issues, class actions)
- Material financing arrangements and any defaults thereunder
- Ownership of assets, including but not limited to intellectual property and real property
- Employee liabilities
- Other material contracts or agreements of any type.

CRYPT 5.7

Quick Action Deters Derailment

Earlier in my career my company was being acquired. Halfway through the process, I was asked to respond to due diligence questions.

As I became involved, I sensed that the commitment to buy had been made. However, one important item had been discovered late in the due diligence process that needed research. The item was absolutely critical and central to our annuity company—whether or not an inadvertent dropping of some policy language several years earlier meant our annuity policies no longer complied with Section 72(s). Specifically, for several years our policies did not include the language that outlined how policies would be handled at the death of the owner. As the due diligence process was drawing to a close, the acquiring company noticed that our older policies contained the necessary language, while our more recent contracts did not. This created a very serious situation as our company had issued literally thousands of policies without the 72(s) language.

It was at this point that we kicked off a project to quickly and completely identify all death claims that could have resulted in either a five-year distribution after death or a life expectancy settlement commencing within one year of death. While the size of this list was rather large,

[2] The "business judgment rule" has been described as follows: "directors' decisions are presumed to have been made on an informed basis, in good faith and in the honest belief that the action taken was in the best interests of the company." *Cede & Co. v. Technicolor, Inc.*, 634 A.2d 345, 360-61 (Del. 1993). In cases in which the traditional business judgment rule applies, directors' decisions are protected unless the plaintiff is able to carry its burden of proof in showing that the board has not met its duty of care or loyalty. *Smith v. Van Gorkom*, 488 A.2d 858, 893 (Del. 1985).

we determined that only one claim had been paid over a period longer than life expectancy.

Our actions had clearly been within the requirements of 72(s). However, the acquirer was not confident that compliance was sufficient. They believed that the IRS would potentially judge thousands of our annuity contracts to not be eligible for tax-deferral, thus putting the company into a crisis situation where we would have unhappy customers and possible lawsuits. In order to be proactive and reduce or eliminate the potential financial ramifications of the situation, the new owner decided to strike an anonymous deal with the IRS, assuming they would be willing to do so. The parent company utilized their tax counsel to approach the IRS in Tulsa, an office with absolutely no relationship with our company or the parent company. Counsel notified the IRS that they were representing an annuity insurer that had issued a number of contracts without the language needed to support 72(s). In exchange for an absolution of wrongdoing, the new owner agreed to pay fines in the neighborhood of $1 million. While this was obviously a large sum of money, it was minimal compared to individual fines for each violating contract and possible class action lawsuits, plus damage to the company's reputation. The attorneys were successful in crafting an agreement where the IRS accepted our payment and issued an anonymous absolution, relieving us of any future legal problems.

The deal got back on track and was consummated. So what did I learn from this experience?

- *It is imperative that you evaluate a potential acquisition not just from a financial perspective but also that you make certain the essence of the business is free of problems and legal issues.*
- *Identify problem situations that are basic to the operation of the business as early as possible. By doing so, you can either scrap the deal or begin to formulate solutions.*
- *Be prepared to act quickly to remedy problem situations. While some issues may not be significant enough to end a deal, they may still be serious enough that failure to resolve them soon after the acquisition could lead to serious problems. In this case, in the absence of the 72(s) problem, the acquisition presented an excellent opportunity to grow the parent company. However, not capping the potential legal and financial liability associated with this problem could have resulted in this being a terrible acquisition. The parent acted early to ensure they resolved the problem before someone else detected it.*

5.5.4.2 Corporate Due Diligence

When the transaction is the acquisition of one or more corporate entities, one of the primary tasks of legal due diligence is reviewing the corporate structure and the compliance of the target with corporate formalities. The legal team will review the documents by which the corporation was formed (the corporate charter and bylaws) in order to determine that the target is properly empowered to carry on its business. The team will also review such things as minutes of meetings of the board of directors to determine whether the company's actions have been subject to proper oversight, including whether the transaction has been properly authorized.

The buyer must also review and understand the effects of any special provisions in the organizational documents that may be triggered as a result of the acquisition. For example, the target may be subject to anti-takeover provisions, such as a "poison pill" (also known as a "shareholders' rights agreement," which authorizes the board to issue more shares to current stockholders if there is an unapproved acquisition of shares by a prospective buyer). The target company (or its holding company) may be subject to limitations on its ownership in order to avoid having it become a "controlled foreign corporation" for U.S. federal income tax purposes.[3]

[3] If a company is a "controlled foreign corporation" (CFC), U.S. persons who own 10% or more of the voting control of the company may be subject to tax on the CFC's income, whether or not distributed. The organizational documents of many corporations that have been formed outside the United States, but that have significant U.S. ownership (including companies listed on the New York Stock Exchange), have provisions in their organizational documents that limit ownership by U.S. taxpayers and also have provisions that cut back voting rights in the event that a U.S. person does come to own more than 10% of the shares of the foreign corporation.

Other agreements or interests, such as outstanding convertible debt securities, warrants, or options may affect the rights of the prospective buyer with respect to the target or its subsidiaries. The legal team should determine what rights dissenting shareholders may have.[4]

For public reporting companies, the legal team must determine the degree to which the company has complied with reporting requirements under federal and state securities laws. Of particular interest will be a review of the various certifications required for public companies under the Sarbanes-Oxley Act, including the internal control systems and support procedures.

For buyers that are public companies, the ability to provide internal control certification by the buyer's CEO and CFO after the closing requires in-depth internal control assessments prior to closing. Also, the Sarbanes-Oxley Act prohibitions on personal loans, as well as off-balance sheet disclosure rules, dictate thorough due diligence on those issues. Waiting until closing is not a viable option in light of reporting timetables.

Not only do inadequate filings expose the buyer to future financial penalties; they can also indicate inadequate administrative or risk management practices, which can be much more costly.

5.5.4.3 Regulatory Due Diligence

This phase of due diligence begins with a review of insurance annual and quarterly statements, as well as the various annual or periodic filings required under state insurance holding company system statutes and regulations. For example, the legal due diligence team must determine whether the company has obtained necessary consents for material transactions with affiliates. An important part of the inquiry may be to determine if the target company has the capacity to pay intended dividends.

The legal team must look into whether the target company holds the necessary certificates of authority to write its business in the various jurisdictions, as well as its history of enforcement actions by regulators. When the target operates in the direct market, another important inquiry is into the nature of the company's relationship with the insurance public. For example, are there any pending or prospective market conduct issues? Not only should the legal team review legal and complaint files, but it should also review marketing materials and products to determine whether the company is open to "mis-selling" or similar charges that might expose the target to class action lawsuits.

With respect to both life and non-life companies, the legal team must review the target's claims-paying history to determine whether there has been a pattern of violations of state laws intended to protect the insurance-buying public. Other regulatory issues include whether the target participates in assigned risk pools, rating organizations, or similar state-sponsored organizations. The legal team must review any obligations to state-sponsored guaranty funds.

Finally, in certain lines of business, premiums are subject to state regulation. The legal team must review state laws governing the target's lines of business and determine (with the actuaries) whether the target is in compliance. The most recent filings for rates and forms should be reviewed to determine if any were rejected or modified. Are there any rate or form regulations that would impact the value from a strategic value perspective?

---

[4] Under the laws of a number of states, including Delaware, shareholders who do not desire to participate in a transaction may have "appraisal rights" or "dissenter's rights," under which the shareholder can bring an action to require the corporation to buy out the shareholder's interest based on the appraised value of the corporation. For example, under Delaware law, shareholders of corporations that are not publicly traded or otherwise widely held can petition the Delaware Chancery Court to determine the value of the shares and direct the corporation to redeem the shares for cash, in lieu of receiving stock in a merger. Del. Code Ann. tit. 8, § 262 (2003).

5.5.4.4 *Insurance Product Issues*

If the target is engaged in the life insurance business, the legal team (usually working in conjunction with product actuaries) must review the target's insurance products. A significant issue is whether life insurance and annuity contracts comply with the detailed provisions of the federal income tax laws, as well as various qualified retirement plan provisions of ERISA.[5] Failure of compliance with tax laws or ERISA can raise significant financial issues because it is generally the responsibility of the insurer to ensure that policyholders receive the tax benefits they expected in buying the products.

The legal due diligence team must also review compliance of variable contracts with federal and state securities laws and determine whether separate accounts with respect to variable contracts or pension plans have been properly established under state laws.[6] In this regard the team will review compliance by the target and its distribution force (including any investment advisors or broker-dealers) with rules and regulations of the U.S. Securities and Exchange Commission and the National Association of Securities Dealers arising under the Securities Act of 1933, the Investment Company Act of 1940, and the Investment Advisors Act of 1940.

5.5.4.5 *Legal Issues Specific to Reinsurance*

When the target is a direct writer, the legal due diligence team must review the company's reinsurance agreements to determine the degree of protection that they afford legally. The team must examine reinsurance agreements to determine their enforceability in general and more specifically to determine whether the contracts comply with various regulatory requirements, such as risk transfer and credit for reinsurance regulations, so as to ensure that the target has properly reported the agreements on its GAAP and statutory financial statements (FAS 113, SSAP 61 and 62).

Another part of the review is to determine the extent to which the target may have acquired reinsurance from unauthorized reinsurance companies, and whether the assuming reinsurer has established the security devices (such as letters of credit or trusts) required under insurance laws and regulations relating to the target's credit for reinsurance on its financial statements. If the target is itself a reinsurer, the legal team must examine assumed reinsurance agreements to determine whether the target's reinsurance contracts provide ceding insurers with the benefits they expect from such contracts.

As part of this review, the legal team must be cognizant of the financial strength of counterparties to reinsurance agreements. For example, if one of the target's assuming reinsurers is financially troubled, what are the target's rights in a delinquency proceeding?[7] Will the target be able to draw on trusts or letters of credit posted by the assuming reinsurer to secure the reinsurer's liabilities to the target?

Conversely, when the target is a reinsurer, the legal due diligence team must determine the rights of ceding insurers in the event of their impairment. For example, can a ceding insurer draw on assets or letters of credit posted by the target? Finally, in the case of a reinsurer, will a change of control, or other events, allow ceding insurers to recapture reinsurance agreements or terminate them as to new business?

---

[5] The Employee Retirement Income Security Act of 1974.

[6] Under state laws, assets held in properly established separate accounts underlying specified insurance products are not available to the general creditors of an insolvent insurer. See, e.g., National Association of Insurance Commissioners (NAIC) Model Variable Contract Law 260 § 1.E.

[7] An impaired U.S.-based insurance company is not a "debtor" that is subject to the provisions of the U.S. Bankruptcy Code. See 11 U.S.C. § 109(b) ("A person may be a debtor under . . . this title only if such person is not . . . . a domestic insurance company."). Accordingly, financially impaired domestic insurers are subject to delinquency proceedings (generally, supervision, conservation, rehabilitation, or liquidation) under state insurance laws. See, generally, NAIC Insurers Rehabilitation and Liquidation Model Act.

5.5.4.6 *Financial Arrangements and Other Material Contracts*

The legal team must also review various financial arrangements in order to understand their legal and financial risks. One area of concern is the target's use of derivatives. In some states (New York in particular), derivatives can only be used for certain purposes, and only after an insurer has filed a "derivative use plan." All investment advisory agreements and similar contracts must also be reviewed. Financing agreements must be reviewed to reveal any loan covenants that might restrict the operations of the target after the acquisition. The legal team must review any "off-balance sheet" financing transactions.

The legal team must also review the target's ownership of real property or rights and obligations under material leases. Does the target have clear ownership of property? Are its lease agreements enforceable? A particular area of concern is the target's exposure to liability under environmental laws. For example, the team must determine not only whether the target has any such liability as a result of real property that it owns or leases, but also whether any of its investment properties could give rise to environmental issues (for example, as a result of a foreclosure on a mortgage).

5.5.4.7 *Business Due Diligence*

Contracts relating to the target's distribution system must also be reviewed. Does the target have an agency force or an independent distribution system? If the system is independent, the legal due diligence team should determine the target's exposure under distribution agreements to which it is a party. If the target has recently altered its distribution system, the team should determine whether there is any remaining liability to the agency force or whether there is any significant exposure to lawsuits as a result of the change. One important inquiry is whether a change of control could result in the loss of significant distribution channels.

5.5.4.8 *Due Diligence in Asset Acquisitions*

When the acquisition relates only to books of business, many of the concerns outlined above become moot. For example, corporate governance concerns are generally of little concern to a buyer in a reinsurance transaction, as long as the seller has the necessary corporate and regulatory authorization to consummate the transaction. The legal due diligence team must, however, understand the nature of the exposures under the business being acquired, so that the buyer can obtain contractual protections, if necessary. For example, if the acquisition relates to a book of business and corresponding distribution contracts are to be transferred, the legal team must review those contracts to, first, determine that all pre-acquisition liabilities are retained by the seller and, second, to understand what liabilities could arise under those agreements after the buyer has taken over the business.

5.5.5 MARKETING AND DISTRIBUTION

A critical area of due diligence is an analysis of the target's marketing capabilities in general, and distribution channels in particular. Marketing, and more specifically the distribution channels, hold the key to the value of new business. They can also significantly impact the value of existing business.

The person who will be responsible for integrating the distribution channels of the two companies should participate directly in due diligence and should interpret the findings into sales and profitability projections for the buyer's appraisal. This requires a thorough analysis of the various components of production capacity as well as the cultural drivers that are embedded in them.

Actuaries typically think in terms of the numbers: commission rates, production costs, total compensation. However, certain critical aspects of distribution are harder to quantify. The cultural differences between the distribution channels of the two companies are simultaneously the most important to manage and the most difficult to quantify. The cultural challenges to integrating distribution are typically far more difficult than those for other operational areas.

Certain decisions will need to be made. Will the acquirer consolidate everything into a single brand, or will it build a "fleet" of separate company brands that leverage back-office efficiencies? If the two companies have the same type of distribution channel, how will they be integrated? If they are different, how will channel conflict be avoided? "Turf conflict" will need to be resolved, as much to prevent confusion in the marketplace as among the producers.

The buyer must plan producer compensation from a strategic value perspective. Sales representatives' reactions to changes in compensation must be anticipated. There will be a cost associated with changing commission or contingent commission schedules. Existing producers will not willingly accept a new group receiving higher commissions; no one will accept a reduction in his or her compensation without fallout. Cultural differences must be taken into account, particularly as regards compensation drivers, systems integration, underwriting authority, and distribution channel compatibility.

The buyer must also estimate the degree of agent turnover and the effect of existing agents leaving and taking future sales and existing business with them. Specific plans for securing agent loyalty may be necessary to achieve the value assumed for new sales.

The buyer needs to ascertain the extent of any special deals, in either compensation or services, provided to agents. Also, during due diligence, the nature of agents' retirement plan commitments and funding should be affirmed. If the company is not being bought as a going concern, any existing termination agreements should be sought and reviewed.

Due diligence should include a plan to communicate with the target company's sales management and representatives before they can be approached by other carriers. As discussed in Chapter 9, successful integration of the distribution channels should build on relationships established during due diligence.

5.5.6 SYSTEMS

Review of the target's systems and information technology (IT) capabilities is a critical aspect of due diligence.

An insurance company has many systems. Some are generic and serve all areas, such as payroll, e-mail, word processing, spreadsheets, and database managers. Others are product-specific, including policy administration, new business processing, policy illustrations, commissions, claims, valuation, experience analysis, pricing, investment accounting, and general ledger. Operating efficiency, proper licensing, and ongoing costs should be ascertained for all of these.

The due diligence process should look at the entire IT spectrum, including hardware, networks, committed upgrades, ongoing support agreements, disaster recovery plans, third-party providers, in-house-developed software, and vendor relationships to determine the potential cost of either continuing or discontinuing certain operations of the target. IT due diligence also needs to include the integration of home office financial systems with the policy processing systems used by producers, customer service centers, and the claim systems used by brokers and claim service centers.

If the target's site is to be closed, its IT capabilities should be reviewed to see if they could provide more value than the acquirer's own systems or hardware. Also, any service agreements need to be studied to ascertain how termination can be achieved.

If the target's operations will shift to the buyer's systems, or vice versa, a data conversion may be required. This is potentially a very large cost. In addition, planning for future IT support of the surviving system should be done during due diligence to evaluate future costs or anticipated savings. Costs and timing of conversion are often underestimated.

5.5.7 PERSONNEL, COMPENSATION, AND BENEFITS

The effectiveness of an organization is a function of effective staff. Often, a few key staff occupy the critical roles. People-related costs, e.g., benefits and severance policies, can have a material effect on the value of the deal.

Required due diligence steps include the review of:

- Schedules of personnel by function, salary, job grade; also turnover and hiring plans
- Employment contracts, severance policies, special severance agreements (e.g., golden parachutes), stock options, bonus plans, loans to staff, etc.
- Health, disability, retirement, and other benefit programs; retiree pension and health liabilities; benefits budgets and projections
- Benefits administration systems, use of vendors or consultants
- Comparison of seller's benefits to buyer's benefits, integration plans, and potential costs
- Potential liabilities that may be triggered by the transaction
- Whether any pension or health liabilities are underfunded
- Any cultural differences that need to be addressed.

Another key consideration is that the valuation of pension benefits under SFAS 87 requires many assumptions; these are unlikely to be consistent between buyer and seller. The seller's liabilities may need to be revalued using the buyer's assumptions.

In most deals, the human resource benefits programs of the two entities will be merged. As discussed in Chapter 6, this is a complex process with potentially significant costs.

5.5.8 PRODUCT MANAGEMENT

An important aspect of due diligence is the review of the target's product management. The due diligence team needs to affirm what the target's practices actually are and, if appropriate, plan how they will be integrated into the buyer's operations. Product management due diligence is often specific to the product lines being acquired.

Some key considerations for property casualty (P&C) coverages include:

- Product design—Insured perils and policy sub-limits, endorsements and exclusions
- Underwriting processes—Manual or automated underwriting, authority levels, exception processes
- Pricing strategy—Classifications, rating tiers, discounts, profit margins
- Renewal strategy—Re-underwriting philosophy, persistency, policy loan provisions
- Product risk management—Policy limits, deductibles, exclusions, use of reinsurance, concentration of risk limits
- Claim settlement practices—Authority levels, service centers, use of independent adjusters, defense strategies.

The specific issues within the key product management categories above are specific to the type of P&C insurance products sold and are addressed in more detail in section 5.6.

The following are some key considerations for life and annuity coverages:

- Underwriting philosophy and practice set the tone for good product management; determine if the formal guidelines are liberal or conservative. See whether the rate classifications align with the buyer's classes. If not, there might be opportunities for consumers to "arbitrage." If there are a plethora of classes, check how the company promotes its products and what percentages of applicants actually qualify for the advertised premium rates. Investigate how frequently the target grants exceptions to its guidelines. No practice is bad per se, as long as it has been priced accurately.

- Underwriting and issue are no longer performed once in a policy's lifetime; the target's handling of changes to inforce policies must be ascertained. Those changes include converting from smoker to nonsmoker, dropping a substandard rating, increasing face amounts, or scheduling re-entry at favorable rates.

- In a multi-product line company, costs for corporate functions and external company-wide capital requirements must be allocated somewhere. Determine how the target assesses product lines for corporate services and for risk-based capital (RBC). What other intra-company charges and credits are there and how are they allocated? Generally, the buyer uses its own or marginal overhead expenses and RBC covariance factors.

- The target's pricing philosophy is only as good as the results achieved. The company's defined profit goals may vary by product or market. Certain segments might subsidize other segments. This could result from competitive pressures or philosophical considerations. Finally, the target should have an effective system for measuring how profit goals are being met relative to pricing standards.

  Profitability depends upon allocations of expenses and investment income. These allocations can be part art and part science. Methods used in pricing and how well they correlate to the actual reporting by product line should be investigated. Allocation of capital gains and losses and asset defaults to product lines and policyholders should be reviewed.

  The pricing process does not stop at issue, especially if the products contain non-guaranteed elements, such as credited interest, mortality charges, expense charges, or current premiums. The methods and philosophies the target employs to manage these should be identified. The nature of how competitive pressures affect the process should be determined. Other factors, such as avoiding shock lapses, could affect the process.

- Reinsurance may have been integral to the target's ability to achieve a desired position in the market. If so, the quality of the target's relationships with its reinsurers is critical. Consider if the reinsurers will remain supportive of the target's efforts or if new reinsurers might augment what already exists. Also, the buyer's current relationship with the target's reinsurers should be considered to assure that the buyer will not have a concentration risk to one reinsurer.

- Claims adjudication processes must be reviewed in depth, especially whether they are cost-effective. Confirm that they are appropriate for the product line; for example, disability income, accidental death, and basic life insurance are radically different in their nature of claims. Confirm that legitimate claims are paid in a timely manner.

- The days when an applicant bought a policy and stuck it in his or her safety-deposit box until death are long gone. Increased policyholder sophistication, the transparency introduced by universal life, and the need for agents to find new sources of income have affected premium persistency and policy loan activities. The target's management mechanisms from both a processing and profitability standpoint should be identified.

- Finally, distribution channels may have a much greater effect on some products than on others. Agents' and policyholders' reaction to the change of ownership should be estimated, especially if adverse pricing changes will be made.

The above considerations are intended to be high level. Actual due diligence will need to address many issues not discussed above. It is not an easy task. Sometimes appearances and impressions get substituted for facts and demonstrations. Nevertheless, due diligence is aptly named—it requires a lot of diligence to uncover the necessary facts to ensure a smooth transition.

CRYPT 5.8

Vanished Premiums Vanquish Deal

After having reached tentative agreement on coinsuring a block of seasoned universal life policies, we visited the seller's offices for some final due diligence. We first asked for and received sample copies of all of the policy forms. A review of the forms and sample policy schedule pages turned up no problems.

Then, on a whim, we asked to see 100 randomly selected actual policy files. We found that a lot of the policies had an endorsement attached to them, mysteriously saying that "The premium for this policy has been vanished." The word "vanished" was not defined in either the policy or the endorsement.

The company told us that the policies had been sold under a "vanishing premium" concept during the 1980s. The endorsement had been added after the number of premiums that had been called for in the original policy illustration had been paid. Literally thousands of individual policies had been endorsed to say that their premiums had "vanished."

We knew that interest rates declined significantly during the 1990s. Many policies that were sold as "vanishing premium" policies in the 1980s had required additional premium payments to keep the policies in force.

After looking up the word "vanish" in the dictionary (meaning—"to disappear; to pass completely from existence; to assume the value zero"), we came to the conclusion that the policyholder could argue that he or she had no legal obligation to pay any more premiums to us. Additionally, since the original illustration showed that the policy would stay in force indefinitely after the "vanish" date, we felt that we could be obliged to keep the policy in force indefinitely, even if no additional premium were paid and even if the cash value were run down to zero.

Needless to say, the seller didn't agree with our interpretation of the language in the endorsement. Since we couldn't reach agreement on the meaning of the undefined term "vanished," we gladly walked away from the transaction.

5.5.9 CLAIM MANAGEMENT

For P&C and health products, due diligence of claim settlement practices is an integral part of assessing the operational and financial value of the company. In addition, claim due diligence is the primary area for identifying certain material risk factors that may affect the value of the target. The risk assessments that occur during claim due diligence may lead to adjustments in the bid price or special considerations in the purchase and sale agreement.

Operational review of claim management includes the claim intake, validation, and settlement. Claims intake may be through agents, claim service centers, or directly to the company. Studies have shown that, for P&C insurance, claim savings are directly related to the insurer's response time and the expertise of its claims adjusters. Therefore, due diligence assesses both the infrastructure and expertise of the claims function. In addition, the potential costs of integration into the buyer's claim systems must be considered. Contracts with independent claim adjusters or retained counsel should be evaluated for potential changes in defense costs and other adjustment expenses.

Claims due diligence should include an investigation of any changes in settlement practices during the past three to five years. A change in defense strategy from rigorously defending liability claims to quick settlements will change the loss development patterns and thereby loss and loss adjustment expense reserves. The actuaries performing loss reserve analysis must be aware of any operational changes to understand prior reserve changes.

Finally, claim due diligence may uncover potential risks that the buyer may not have contemplated in its initial bid. Claims is the first area to learn of newly emerging exposures that may impact reserve adequacy and future earnings. Reviewing timeliness of claims payment or complaints to insurance departments may provide insight into the effectiveness of the target's claim practices. Unfair claims practice could expose the operation to triple damages under many state laws.

5.5.10 REINSURANCE

Insurers frequently use reinsurance to achieve financial or risk objectives on a short- or long-term basis. Consequently, reinsurance is likely to be present at the target.

In conducting due diligence, it is common to focus attention on a cross-section of the target's key reinsurance arrangements. This selection could represent:

- The larger net income and balance sheet items, such as reinsurance receivables/payables and letters of credit
- Different plans of reinsurance, such as coinsurance, modified coinsurance, financial reinsurance, stop-loss, or risk layer transactions
- Various underlying product or risk types
- Intra-group or affiliated company transactions
- All transactions with reinsurers not authorized, licensed, or accredited by the target's domicile state.

Legal considerations relating to reinsurance are addressed in section 5.5.4.

Strategic and operational issues include:

- Review functions that the reinsurer is responsible for managing, yet for which the target company is at risk. These include asset management, policy administration, claims management, or underwriting.
- Ascertain the retention levels, rights, and options of the target company, such as the right to recapture existing business or increase retention amounts on new or existing business.
- Identify the effect of reinsurance on the combined entity. For each major risk category, the extent of buyer and target coverage overlap should be ascertained. If there is substantial overlap, and the retention level of the combined entity remains unchanged, the net business acquired may be less than expected.
- Identify the overall exposure to certain risks. If there is limited reinsurance market capacity for a particular type of risk, the combined entity could potentially end up with more risk than it desires.

When the target is a reinsurance company, the same principles apply. Reinsurance-specific considerations include the following:

- Acquisition of coverage on similar risks may result in total risk exposures exceeding the buyer's current retention levels or retrocession market capacity.
- Ceding companies may seek to recapture their risk or exercise other options triggered by sales.
- A specific type of reinsurance exposure includes passive stakes in reinsurance pools. A particular risk is the potential lack of alignment of economic interests of all parties.
- A key risk of financial reinsurance relates to letters of credit. The cost and volume available are based on the creditworthiness of the insurer. Letters of credit are renewed each year, yet the corresponding reinsurance contracts may be long term. If the buyer is not able to obtain the desired cost of letters of credit, profitability or availability could be greatly affected.
- Evaluation of reinsurance arrangements may be complicated by complexities in accounting for embedded derivatives within reinsurance arrangements.

5.5.11 RISK MANAGEMENT

Most buyers and sellers will have a formal enterprise risk management (ERM) structure in place, usually under a chief risk officer (CRO) or risk committee. (For simplicity, this discussion assumes a CRO.) Actuaries are generally heavily involved in risk management functions.

Due diligence interacts with risk management operations in two ways. The first addresses the seller's ERM structures, analyses, and reports as a due diligence resource. A robust risk management function should focus on precisely the types of exposures and concerns that the due diligence team is trying to analyze. Thus, the target's ERM practices and documentation can provide highly efficient analysis tools given the limited time frame due diligence allows.

The second main aspect of due diligence is that the seller's ERM practices, policies, and standards need to be integrated into the buyer's practices, policies, and standards. The buyer's CRO needs to identify and anticipate any differences in philosophy and scope of approach. Staffing issues may also need to be addressed. The ERM functions may also play an integral role in supporting Sarbanes-Oxley requirements following the acquisition.

5.6 ACTUARIAL DUE DILIGENCE

In section 5.2, the objectives of due diligence were summarized into five categories:

- Confirm strategic value
- Confirm financial value
- Confirm operational value
- Construct appropriate bid
- Prepare for successful results.

The actuary has a role in addressing each of these.

5.6.1 INTRODUCTION

Perhaps the most important role of the actuary is to translate the data and information developed by the due diligence team into quantified expressions of value. This takes place in the course of developing the buyer's actuarial appraisal.

The development of supporting data is the result of the entire team's due diligence work in addressing the first three objectives above. However, it is the actuary's responsibility to translate all that information into quantified assumptions that will drive the buyer's actuarial appraisal. The sources of the information the actuary uses include:

- Information and opinions developed by the buyer's team during due diligence efforts
- Information provided by the seller
- External industry benchmarks
- General industry knowledge and experience.

Validation of the strategic issues that drive value is generally a team process. However, the actuary generally has the specific responsibility to translate the findings and opinions of the team members into explicit assumptions (e.g., expense reductions).

Actuaries and accountants usually take the lead with financial due diligence. This includes validating the seller's income statement, balance sheet, and experience reports, and making adjustments as appropriate. The adjustments made are often based on analyses performed by others on the due diligence team (e.g., adjustments to asset values based on the investment team's analysis). The financial due diligence process is the primary driver of assumptions for the buyer's appraisal.

Many team members have roles in operational due diligence. The actuary has primary responsibility for reviewing the seller's actuarial functions (e.g., pricing, product management) and reflecting these in appraisal assumptions. The actuary may also have primary responsibility for due diligence on the target's risk management practices. In particular, P&C actuaries take the lead to identify and assess the material risk factors for P&C targets.

The primary driver of bid price is the buyer's actuarial appraisal. PGAAP and earnings per share projections can also be key factors; these are generally driven by the same assumptions and actuarial models as the appraisal. However, equally as important as the numbers is the buyer's degree of confidence in the assumptions and projections underlying them. The buyer's appraisal model uses risk-adjusted discount rates to determine the present value of book profits; as the uncertainty of the underlying book profits increases, so should the rate used to discount the book profits. This translates to lower appraisal values. Alternatively, the buyer may give a substantial haircut to its bid if it has gaps in knowledge or confidence regarding assumptions or data. A major objective of due diligence is to minimize those gaps.

Although the objectives for P&C acquisitions generally parallel those for life company acquisitions, P&C acquisitions tend to emphasize strategic and operational values over financial values. Since P&C contracts contain few long-term guarantees, projections of future profits tend to be more subjective than for life. As a result, sellers' actuarial appraisals are not always performed by P&C sellers.

Another aspect of P&C companies is that claim reserves can be very volatile. P&C claim reserve valuations play a key role in developing bid prices. Finally, the volatility inherent in certain P&C insurance products may present risks the buyer is not willing to assume. P&C due diligence must identify and assess the critical material risk factors.

Health insurance lines reflect aspects of both life and P&C and, in fact, may be written in either type of company. Individual health products tend to be similar to individual life products, while group health products tend to be more similar to P&C products. However, since most health products are written in life companies, the due diligence process for health products tends to follow the life insurance model.

To better handle these distinctions, the actuarial due diligence is presented in separate discussions for life and health companies versus P&C companies. Although the same principles apply, the approaches used are different.

Also, in the following discussions, no distinction is made between the roles of internal and external actuaries because practice varies widely from situation to situation. Generally, when external actuaries are retained, their expertise and experience are relied upon in every phase of the due diligence process. Reliance is generally heavy as regards review of financials, development of buyer's appraisal, PGAAP pro formas, and construction of bid. Reliance is often less as regards reviewing target company operations and preparing for closing and implementation.

5.6.1.1 *Working with Insufficient Time and Incomplete Data*

For many actuaries, the most disconcerting aspect of due diligence is having to work with insufficient time and incomplete data. This is the norm within the environment of mergers and acquisitions. It is critical that actuaries deal with this by identifying and prioritizing the most critical issues and by recognizing that less critical issues will have to be addressed quickly, if at all.

Actuarial Standard of Practice No. 19 "Actuarial Appraisals," recognizes this in its introduction:

> Often this work must be done under extreme time pressure and in the absence of complete data. In order to frame properly the project approach and documentation, the practicing actuary needs to address carefully the following questions:
>
> 1. What is the context of the assignment?
> 2. What are the needs, areas of expertise, and expectations of the user?
> 3. Are there users of the report beyond the client?

4. How much will the user rely on the work product of the actuary?
5. Will the actuary be functioning as an advocate?
6. How much time was provided to complete the assignment?
7. How much access to data was provided?
8. What assumptions are appropriate?
9. What methods are appropriate?[8]

It is critical that the actuary identify the areas addressed versus those not addressed. The potential implications of areas not addressed must be quantified for management (and any other users) in a way that allows them to make practical decisions regarding a bid. In some cases, it may be practical and advisable to propose specific closing conditions to address particularly important issues.

5.6.2 ACTUARIAL DUE DILIGENCE FOR LIFE AND HEALTH

For ease of discussion, the actuarial due diligence for life and health operations has been summarized into the following areas:

- Review of financials
- Review of operations (including risk management practices)
- Development of buyer's appraisal and PGAAP pro formas
- Support of bid development and negotiations
- Preparation for closing and integration.

5.6.2.1 *Review of Financial Statements*

5.6.2.1.1 Balance Sheet

Actuarial due diligence will usually include a review of the actuarial components of both the statutory and GAAP balance sheets for compliance with applicable standards, potential exposure to any proposed new standards, accuracy of computation, and completeness. The specific items that may be reviewed include the following:

- Reserve adequacy or margins (under statutory, tax, or GAAP). Statutory balance sheets are reviewed for accuracy and completeness as well as for compliance with regulatory standards. The actuarial items in the GAAP balance sheet are also reviewed for compliance with statements and appropriateness of assumptions. This gives a better understanding of experience and potential margins. Given the short time frame and limited access to information that is common in due diligence, it is important to focus on areas that have the potential to have a large financial impact.

- Statutory reserve methodology. A review of a company's reserve methodologies should be performed to determine any areas where a company may have disputes with regulators or is following procedures that may be controversial. If there are any concerns about the target's valuation system, the due diligence may include sample checking of reserves for individual policies. Due diligence should also include a review of areas for potential conservatism of reserves, as well as for deficiencies.

- Tax reserve methodology. Similarly, due diligence should include a review of a company's tax reserve calculations. Generally, changes to tax reserves grade in over a 10-year period instead of having an immediate impact on taxable income.

- Adjusted net worth. The balance sheet requires analysis and confirmation of several items that will go into the adjusted net worth component of the seller's actuarial appraisal. The actuary generally works with the investment banker and other teams to value these items.

[8] Actuarial Standards Board. Actuarial Appraisal Task Force. *Actuarial Standard of Practice No. 19, Actuarial Appraisals*. Washington, D.C.: Actuarial Standards Board, 1991.

5.6.2.1.2 Income Statement and Management Metrics

A review of the patterns of income statement items over the past several years can reveal potential issues:

- Fluctuations in earnings can indicate unusual volatility or exposures.
- Recent earnings used to initiate actuarial projections may not represent longer-term trends.
- Nonrecurring adjustments to earnings can generate concerns about underlying business fundamentals or the integrity of internal accounting/actuarial practices or controls.

Both GAAP and statutory statements should be reviewed, as well as any internal management reporting bases.

Just as important as the income statements are the earnings analyses and management metrics that the seller uses to manage its businesses. These often include:

- Breakdowns of earnings to product or line of business
- Explanations of earnings variances (to plan or pricing) in terms of operations (e.g., claims frequency and severity)
- Patterns of key indicators over time (e.g., actual-to-expected mortality or lapse)
- Embedded value (EV) statements, especially change in EV and the associated explanations
- DAC recoverability testing, which may introduce issues not seen in other earnings projections and which can provide additional perspectives on the quality of earnings.

The review of management reports on earnings is critical from a multitude of perspectives. It should address:

- How well seller's management has managed its business. Are there fundamental or endemic problems that will need to be overcome?
- Have these situations been accounted for in the seller's appraisal projections?
- Are there gaps or inadequacies in management's explanations that would affect the buyer's confidence in the assumptions underlying the actuarial appraisal?

In addition to historical earnings, the actuary should review the seller's recent business plan projections.

- Are they based on sound methodologies, assumptions, and experience data?
- Have they been overly optimistic or pessimistic?
- Are they consistent with the seller's actuarial appraisal? In particular, has the seller historically set lower goals for itself than are reflected in the appraisal?

5.6.2.1.3 Experience Reports

Review of experience reports is critical to actuarial due diligence from a number of perspectives:

- Experience reports are generally used as the primary basis for the assumptions underlying the seller's actuarial appraisal.
- Experience reports generally drive the key management metrics and explanations of earnings described above. They should be considered in that light for consistency.
- The seller's experience should be compared to the buyer's and the differences analyzed. This can lead to insights into the seller's operations, especially as regards specific operational areas for the due diligence team to investigate in more detail. Correspondingly, such insights can represent opportunities for the buyer to generate additional value by introducing improvements to the seller's operations or by leveraging seller-specific competencies into its own operations.

- The quality and utility of the seller's experience reports also reflect on the quality and competency of the seller's actuarial staff and product management.

Key areas of experience analysis include mortality, morbidity, lapses, spread (for annuities), and expenses. In particular, analysis of seller's expenses is the starting point for defining and quantifying potential expense synergies in the buyer's appraisal.

5.6.2.2 *Review of Operations*

Section 5.5 identified due diligence efforts regarding 11 non-actuarial functional areas. This section addresses the 12th functional area, actuarial operations. This section also discusses in more detail the actuary's role in supporting the review of first 11 functional areas.

5.6.2.2.1 Review of Actuarial Operations

The actuary has the responsibility for performing an operational review of the seller's actuarial functions for effectiveness and potential impact on financial results. In the course of reviewing the effectiveness of the actuarial operations, the actuary will also identify the quality of the methodologies, assumptions, and practices used by the target's actuaries, including:

- Pricing and profitability management
- Product development, including coordination with underwriting and sales
- Valuation
- Business plans
- Setting non-guaranteed elements
- Experience monitoring.

Obviously, there is a major overlap between understanding the quality of the actuarial operations and evaluating the impact of those operations on the buyer's appraisal assumptions (e.g., adequacy of pricing on projected profit margins).

In a related issue, actuarial staff often falls into the category of "corporate" functions, which may be subject to consolidation in an acquisition. As a result, the actuarial operations review may have to anticipate:

- Is consolidation appropriate in this case?
- Are there specific skills or experience that will be required going forward?
- How does the quality of the seller's actuarial staff measure up against the buyer's standards?

5.6.2.2.2 Review of Risk Management Functions and Exposures

It is particularly important to identify potentially unaddressed risks, especially in light of how the buyer evaluates those risks. The actuary often has primary responsibility for risk management. Even if the buyer has a separate risk management function, the actuary will still have primary responsibility regarding areas of specific risks or exposures. For example:

- Determining the approaches followed by the target company to manage long-tail exposures, such as structured settlements or long-term care. These liabilities typically extend well beyond 30 years, and therefore can't be matched on a cash flow basis. Some companies make active use of financial derivatives for these lines.

- Determining the approaches to manage book value surrender exposure on fixed annuities or other lines potentially subject to substantial disintermediation risk. On blocks of fixed annuities that include equity index-linked or market value adjusted (MVA) products, the management of these exposures should also be reviewed.

- Reviewing exposures of variable annuity (VA) blocks to guaranteed minimum death benefit or withdrawal benefit options. A number of VA companies are dynamically hedging these exposures; a review of a target's procedures in this area is a key component of due diligence.

- Evaluating the exposure to falling or rising interest rates. Low interest rates can have a devastating impact. Examples of such include minimum accumulation rate guarantees in interest-sensitive and par products and long-term guarantees in fixed benefit products, such as payout annuities and long-term care. Historically, increases in the interest rate environment have also led to disintermediation concerns. The target company's approach to managing interest rate exposures should be reviewed.

5.6.2.2.3 Support Other Due Diligence Subteams

- The actuary often assists other subteams to evaluate operations, in particular, as regards underwriting, sales, accounting, and investment issues.
- The actuary generally works with each subteam to translate their findings into quantified assumptions for the buyer's actuarial appraisal. Examples include:
  - Underwriting effectiveness
  - Claims management effectiveness
  - Sales projections
  - Potential tax issues and strategies.
- Other issues should be considered during due diligence in order to determine potential economic exposure. The following items may not be specifically included in financial projections, but a determination of the potential for loss may fall within the actuary's scope of analysis.
  - Policy administrative systems. Along with a general review of the adequacy of the admin systems, it's important to determine the ability of the systems to appropriately administer all aspects of the inforce polices. Items such as UL policyholder bonuses, shadow fund accounts, and changes to par dividend scales may be difficult to administer.
  - Sales practice litigation. The potential for future policyholder litigation over past sales practices, changes to policy features, premium mode loadings, or other aspects related to the inforce business should be reviewed.
  - In group insurance, certain actuarial functions, such as pricing, are implemented by the underwriters, who utilize a significant degree of discretion and judgment. Thus, it is critical for the actuary to coordinate his or her work with the operational review of underwriting in order to get a complete picture of pricing. Similar issues exist with claim management and P&C or health pricing.

5.6.2.3 DEVELOPMENT OF BUYER'S APPRAISAL AND PGAAP PRO FORMAS

The buyer has to develop its own financial basis for its bid. The main tool for this is generally the buyer's actuarial appraisal. Usually, the buyer has a seller's appraisal as a starting point. However, the buyer must develop its own perspective on the business, in particular as regards the key assumptions.

Another key financial tool used to determine the attractiveness of the acquisition is the GAAP pro forma financial projection. The seller's appraisal package generally includes statutory pro forma projections. Sometimes GAAP financial projections are available from the seller as well.

During the due diligence process the buyer will perform its own review of the target's experience, adjust that for actions the buyer will take, and develop its own appraisal and projection assumptions.

Often the buyer does this by adjusting the values generated by the seller's appraisal, using sensitivities to key assumptions (which are provided as part of the seller's appraisal). However, especially in group life and health, it is also common for a buyer to perform its own appraisal, including the underlying projections.

It is critical for the buyer to understand the inner workings of the models ultimately used (for instance, the impact of key buyer assumptions on the financial projections). This is particularly important for the projections used to support the GAAP pro forma projections of earnings.

The buyer must also closely analyze seller's experience in the period following the "as of" date of the seller's actuarial appraisal and offering memorandum. It is common for the subsequent data to be provided by the seller in a format that is significantly less detailed and structured than the original data. It is critical that the buyer identify whether material changes in experience or other issues have occurred.

5.6.2.3.1 Buyer's Actuarial Appraisal

The first step in developing the buyer's actuarial appraisal value is to determine the validity of the model underlying the seller's appraisal. This review usually encompasses the following issues:

- Develop an understanding of the model. The actuarial due diligence of the model would include developing an understanding of (a) the robustness of the model; (b) the level of refinement of the cells; (c) the steps taken to develop the model; and (d) the level of access to the target company provided in order to answer questions about the underlying business.
- Static model fit. A key validation criterion is the ability of the model to reproduce initial balance sheet items and inventory amounts, including inforce amounts, statutory and tax reserves, account values, cash values, and policy counts. Typically the model fit would be expected to be very tight; to the extent differences exist, the causes of those differences should be determined.
- Dynamic model fit. This refers to the ability of the model to reproduce recent experience as shown in statutory or GAAP income statements. A comparison of actual reported amounts to amounts projected in the model should be performed for each of the key income items including premiums, investment income, claims, surrenders, commissions, expenses, and change in reserves. On interest sensitive business, it is helpful to compare against certain GAAP income items as well, such as collected charges and interest credited. Due to the changing nature of the business in force, as well as fluctuations in experience, dynamic validations are generally viewed as having a higher tolerance than static validations. To the extent there are significant differences between actual and projected amounts, however, the causes of the differences should be reviewed.
- Policy illustrations. To the extent the target runs illustration software on its business, a useful validation of the policy specifications reflected in the model is to compare illustrated amounts against model projections for a selection of specific cells. Note that this will only test input related to policy specifications, not to experience assumptions.
- Review of experience assumptions. The experience assumptions underlying the financial projections should be reviewed for consistency with the target's historical experience studies, along with industry experience for the target's competitors in similar lines of business and similar distribution systems. Sensitivity tests should be reviewed to develop an understanding of which assumptions are critical and the dependency of the economic values to reasonable deviations in those assumptions.
- Review of management plan assumptions. The key management assumptions underlying the target's financial projections, primarily production levels and expense levels, should be reviewed for consistency with its historical results, its ability to meet its plan in the past, and the buyer's comfort level with the assumptions in the context of overall industry size, growth rates, and expectations. Typically a buyer will have due diligence teams focused on (a) marketing and production objectives and (b) expense planning, including expectations for expense reductions as a result of consolidation or efficiencies the buyer brings to the table. The

buyer's assumptions for these items should be incorporated into the buyer's due diligence analysis, and typically a number of sensitivities are performed.

- Review of new business profitability. The profitability of new business reflected in the actuarial appraisal and financial projections should be compared against the selling company's internal pricing targets, as well as profitability achieved by the company's competitors. While the profitability underlying the financial projections may be justifiably different than internal pricing, it can be instructive to reconcile the two approaches.

CRYPT 5.9

Pocket Picked

I joined Consolidated Holding as group actuary. I did the pricing and the valuation. We soon entered a down cycle for the group business. The company then lost its appetite for this line and put the block out for sale.

In doing the reserves, I inherited a reserve that seemed to be a contingency reserve for the monthly group term life line. It wasn't a claim reserve. It wasn't an unearned premium reserve. It wasn't an experience refund reserve. It was something like a potential premium deficiency reserve. I never got a good handle on exactly what it was for. But since it added some conservatism to the balance sheet, I left this $3,000,000 alone. It had been in the annual statement for at least three years. It's always good to have something for your back pocket.

When Consolidated decided to exit this line, I wasn't real happy, but what could I do? In helping prepare for the sale, I informed management how I felt about the nature of this liability, that it didn't correlate to any precise liability, but could be viewed more in the nature of surplus. Oddly enough, management didn't want to tinker with anything; they just wanted to get out of this line. So it stayed as a reserve.

Several buyers passed through. The most astute one turned out to be the winner. This winning buyer had suggested that perhaps a 10% profit margin existed in this block, so Consolidated only had to transfer $2,700,000 rather than the full $3,000,000. Consolidated was happy with that.

The deal went through. Since I found another area of the company to work in, I was still in town when an interesting story made the local paper. Via public information, a reporter had come across some details of this transaction and reported on bonuses distributed by the buyer. The buyer distributed $2,700,000 in bonuses to the senior members of the in-house due diligence team, for work well done.

The buyer did release the reserve. It was no coincidence that the amount of bonus paid was equal to the amount of reserve released.

Watch your pockets or someone else will.

The second step in determining appropriate buyer's appraisal assumptions is to compare the internal consistency of assumptions across various sets of "best estimates." In particular, it can be informative to compare the seller's appraisal assumptions to the following:

- Business plan assumptions. The business plan often ties to historical experience over the near term (one to three years), due to trending or other techniques. The business plan would generally reflect management's best estimate, in particular with respect to production amounts and expenses.

- Pricing assumptions. The assumptions underlying new business pricing typically reflect the product manager's best estimate for long-term experience. The assumptions may or may not be applicable to inforce business, due to changing mix of product, distribution changes, or other changes. In addition, new business pricing is often looked at a number of ways (e.g., varying premium deposit patterns, marginal vs. fully allocated expenses), which may make composite assumptions difficult to determine.

- Cash flow testing assumptions. The assumptions underlying cash flow testing are generally the best estimate for future experience as determined by the appointed actuary. The degree of refinement of cash flow testing models and assumptions varies by company. In addition, assumptions underlying cash flow testing may tend to be on the conservative side, due to the nature of the exercise in establishing a regulatory minimum reserve level.
- US GAAP FAS 97 assumptions. For FAS 97 products, assumptions are to be best estimate at each point in time.
- Embedded value assumptions. For companies that determine embedded values, either for internal use or for external release, the EV analysis and assumptions can be very useful to validate appraisal analysis and financial projections. The EV assumptions generally reflect management's best long-term estimates. Certain regulatory restrictions, however, may detract from best estimate, such as disallowing future mortality improvement or setting limits on separate account growth rates.

None of the above sets of assumptions necessarily provide a "pure" best estimate on the part of management for future experience. Nevertheless, a comparison across the different sets may highlight key issues that are worth further review.

The last step in determining appropriate buyer's appraisal assumptions is to compare against external industry benchmarks. These are particularly important for group and P&C products, which are subject to competitive re-rating each year.

5.6.2.3.2 GAAP Pro Forma Projections

It is generally the role of the actuary and accountant to produce financial projections to support the pro forma income statements and balance sheet projections using PGAAP accounting rules. The approaches and formulas for these are described in Chapter 8. The actuary generally uses the same assumptions and models as were used to generate the statutory projections underlying the actuarial appraisal. The buyer's internal and external accountants usually select the accounting approach to be used.

GAAP pro forma projections are used to estimate the accretion (or dilution) to future earnings per share expected from the deal (see Chapter 8). Accretion estimates have a major impact on how the deal will be viewed by the investment community. Buyers should anticipate that they will be questioned closely on this issue by investment analysts and rating agencies upon announcement of the deal.

5.6.2.4 Support of Bid Development and Negotiations

The actuary may support the bid development and negotiations in several areas:

- During the financial review and development of the buyer's actuarial appraisal, the actuary identifies areas of potential concern or high variability. The actuary will work with the bid management team to determine if these need to be specifically addressed in the bid, and if so, the best method and parameters to use. Potential approaches (discussed in Chapter 2) include:
  - Exclusion of certain blocks of business
  - Closing conditions (e.g., additional true-up calculations between bid and closing)
  - Post-closing true-up or run-out calculations (if selling entity survives)
  - Reinsurance
  - Representations and warranties (if selling entity survives)
  - Representations and warranties insurance (if selling entity does not survive).
- The bid negotiations also can involve proposals and counterproposals regarding the structure of the deal; e.g., tax structure, which employees are retained by the buyer, and who pays severance. These issues can have a significant impact on both the bid price and the pro

forma projections. Actuaries may be called on to estimate the impacts of various options on a real-time basis during the negotiations.

- There is generally a significant gap in time between the date of the bid and the date of the financial records and appraisal provided by the seller. Generally, the final bid is "rolled forward" to the closing date, using aggregate adjustments based on relatively few parameters (see Chapter 2). The actuary supports the negotiation of these formulas by identifying critical parameters, confirming that the buyer's interests are adequately protected, and suggesting modifications or additions to formulas or approaches, as appropriate.

5.6.2.5 *Preparation for Closing and Implementation*

Successful M&A transactions involve a lot more than just the right price and conditions. To achieve the goals of the transaction, the buyer and seller must present the deal successfully to stockholders, rating analysts, and the investment community. The buyer must then follow that up with effective merger integration. There are a variety of issues that will have a material impact on ultimate value; these must be anticipated practically and quantitatively during the bid development period. Also, since performing the tasks associated with successful integration requires preparation and lead time, that process must also be started during the due diligence period.

This section discusses the actuary's role in certain aspects of that preparation.

Rating agencies, stock analysts, and the investing public are generally skeptical regarding the value of acquisitions. As a result, they require explanations of both the price paid and the value received from a strategic perspective. Explanations are demanded from both the buyer and the seller. Unsatisfactory responses can hurt stock prices, or even lead to shareholder lawsuits. Equally as important as price and value is the projection of GAAP earnings over the first few years. Some potential deals never get done because GAAP earnings would not be sufficiently accretive.

The values determined by the actuary are at the center point of these disclosures. Buyer's management can expect critical examination, not only of the values, but also of the processes used to calculate or confirm those values; for instance, how the buyer's actuary confirmed adequacy of reserves, or what internal rate of return he or she expects from the acquired business.

5.6.2.5.1 Sarbanes-Oxley

Since 2003, Sarbanes-Oxley has required that the buyer's CEO and CFO certify the financials and underlying internal controls of the surviving operation at the end of the first quarter following the transaction. There is generally insufficient time to perform the required independent review from scratch. The due diligence period is the time for the actuary to make sure he or she will be prepared to support the requirements for sign-off. The requirements imposed by Sarbanes-Oxley affect all aspects of financial reporting; the actuary's role is usually a supporting one. Issues that will be reviewed include:

- Assessing internal audit functions
- Reviewing risk management policies and practices
- Reviewing any relevant audit committee comments or concerns
- Reviewing the use of estimates for reserves or actuarial liabilities
- Reviewing potential contingent liabilities; e.g., potential guaranteed minimum death benefit (GMDB) exposure
- Assessing data quality and internal controls.

CRYPT 5.10

Head For The Exit

I was doing due diligence for a health insurer on the possible acquisition of a workers' compensation division of a giant P&C group. After a couple of days reviewing the loss reserves, I found a huge deficiency, about $500 million. I went to the subsidiary division's local actuary and confronted him with it. He told me that $500 million was about equal to the difference between what he reported to the home office and what they reported in his division's annual statement.

My client, the investment banker, the auditor, and I then met with the executive vice president of the parent company and told him we thought the division reserves were short by $500 million. He said, "That sounds about right."

My client ran for the exit. Soon thereafter, another company bought the division without due diligence. Within two years, both the division we had looked at and the buyer were in rehabilitation.

5.6.2.5.2 Staffing and Transition Issues

In Chapter 9, staffing, culture, and people issues in merger integration are discussed. In section 5.6.2.2.1, some of those issues are identified as they relate specifically to actuarial staff.

Due diligence is the time for the actuary to start considering these issues and to make sure he or she is prepared to take the appropriate steps. Quick and decisive post-merger implementation is critical to capturing potential value.

5.6.3 ACTUARIAL DUE DILIGENCE FOR P&C COMPANIES

In this section, four areas of P&C insurance due diligence are described:

- Drivers of strategic and operational value
- Evaluating P&C loss reserves
- Buyer's actuarial appraisal
- Assessing the material risk factors.

To address these areas, the actuarial team needs a complete understanding of the key operational areas that drive financial results. As a result, the P&C actuary takes an active role in many facets of operational due diligence. These can include marketing and distribution, underwriting and pricing, loss and LAE reserves, and claim settlements.

5.6.3.1 Overview

In section 5.6, it was indicated that P&C due diligence may emphasize due diligence objectives differently than a life insurance transaction would. Since most life insurance company transactions involve long-term financial commitments, the primary focus is often on financial value, and the actuarial appraisal is paramount.

P&C insurance contracts are generally underwritten annually and involve short-term commitments. The future financial value of the business acquired is largely under the control of the buyer. As a result, P&C transactions typically emphasize strategic value, and P&C due diligence tends to focus on identifying and quantifying the drivers of strategic and operational value. These drivers may be in the form of strategic options that will result from the merger or operational synergies that will emerge from the combination. Quantifying these value drivers must also recognize the costs of integration. The resulting adjustments to the value can make or break the deal.

P&C insurance contracts can have high variability in the timing and amount of loss payments; products with long-tail claims may have a great deal of uncertainty. P&C contracts also contain few long-term guarantees, so the buyer can generally change the terms and conditions upon which future business can be written or renewed. Therefore, projections of future book profits are inherently more subjective than those for life insurance contracts. As a result (i.e., due to the perceived inability to produce a narrow enough range of value), sellers' actuarial appraisals are not always developed by the P&C insurance company. However, existing claim liabilities are contractually guaranteed and P&C claim reserve valuations are virtually always performed.

Sometimes the buyer develops a buyer's actuarial appraisal to help determine a bid price; other times the bid price is estimated using a market multiple approach. In that case, the actuary assists with development of the appropriate benchmark multiples, and helps determine the quality of earnings adjustments needed to properly apply this technique.

It is standard in P&C due diligence for the actuary to identify and assess the key material risk factors associated with the potential acquisition. Generally, the risk factors are categorized by type of risk (i.e., obligation risk, asset risk, interest risk, and parameter risk). The actuary's role includes assessing the material risk factors and associated volatility. The actuary and other members of the due diligence team can then evaluate options to mitigate or transfer undesirable risks. Finally, the uncertainty inherent in certain P&C insurance products may present the buyer with a level of risk it is not willing to assume.

5.6.3.2 Drivers of Strategic and Operational Value

In Chapter 4, several methods for determining the economic value of P&C insurance companies were discussed. These methods are based on the thesis that the economic value of a company is based on economic adjustments to net worth, plus the present value of expected future earnings, less the cost of capital. The buyer's appraisal value of the target company is based on the economic value, plus value added by synergies and embedded options, less anticipated integration costs. Due to the cyclical nature of the P&C underwriting cycle, the perceived value of the potential synergies sometimes drives the market price for P&C insurers well above the economic value.

The value drivers for an acquisition are the attributes that create worth beyond the strict economic value of the existing business. These can take many forms, including:

- Operating structure or location of the target
- The states where the target is licensed to write business
- The target's distribution channels, products, underwriting expertise, claim operations, or systems capabilities.

Value is created when the target's operations complement the buyer's business objectives. Because of the diverse nature of P&C insurance products and company operations, the value drivers for one buyer can differ significantly from other buyers. To effectively identify and evaluate value drivers, the due diligence team must understand the buyer's business operations and strategic motivations for the acquisition.

Buyers' strategies will significantly influence the due diligence work plan. At one end of the spectrum is the purchase of an insurer as a financial investment; the target company may remain intact as a stand-alone operation. At the other end, a strategic acquisition may involve integrating the target's operations into the buyer's existing operations, taking advantage of specific synergies and reducing future expenses.

If the acquisition is a financial investment that will remain intact, quality of earnings may be the primary value driver. For many financial acquisitions, buyers look to recoup their investment in a relatively short period of time, which may result in a five- to seven-year time horizon for the financial projections. If the deal is to be financed with debt, due diligence should include evaluating whether the earnings and projected book profits will cover debt servicing. For financial acquisitions, the due diligence team will focus its attention on the key financial assumptions in the pro forma business plan. The due diligence team will also evaluate the target's management team to assess their ability to execute the business plan. In this case, the goal of operational due diligence is primarily to identify any shortcomings that present a risk to achieving the financial goals.

There are many potential rationales for a strategic acquisition; the specific strategy will define the value drivers. Examples of strategies include:

- Vertical growth—writing more of the same type of business
- Horizontal growth—opening up new products to existing distribution channels or new channels for existing products
- Acquiring technology or intellectual capital—more efficient to buy than to build.

In a strategic acquisition, the buyer is hoping to leverage value through synergies. Therefore, a detailed review of the operational and integration issues becomes a critical aspect of due diligence. The evaluation of the target's management team will be less important if the buyer intends to integrate those responsibilities under its existing management. The bid decision will be driven by an assessment of how the target's operations complement the buyer's long-term plan. However, it is also important to assess the short-term implications of the deal, as well as the stock market's perception of the acquisition.

Due to the diverse range, it is not feasible to identify all potential strategies and possible value drivers. The following sections address a select few of these as well as potential integration costs for the major operational areas of a P&C insurer.

5.6.3.2.1 Marketing and Distribution Strategies

Value drivers relating to marketing and distribution address horizontal growth and the ability to leverage effective marketing techniques across both operations. The buyer may have products that will be sold through the target's producers or cross-sold to the target's insureds. The buyer could have a successful direct marketing program that can utilize the target's operations to enhance market share. Similarly, the buyer may be purchasing intellectual capital or infrastructure to better market its own products. Expense synergies may result from the buyer's excess operating capacities. For example, if the buyer has underutilized call centers or service centers, the marginal cost to process additional policies and endorsements may be significantly less than the target's existing cost.

Integration costs for distribution-related acquisitions are often underestimated. They include the cost of integrating the target's distribution operation plus the value of business lost due to market disruption. If the target uses a different policy administration system or communication technology with its agents, the cost of converting to the buyer's systems might be considerable.

Differences in agent commission and profit-sharing plans may impact agent retention or future expense levels. Differences in underwriting philosophies may create market disruptions. For example, if the target offers products that the buyer will not retain, the cost to divest those products must be quantified as an integration cost. The cost should also include the value of any lost affiliated business.

Finally, market overlap must be considered if the strategic acquisition involves the merger of two firms. Agents currently producing business for two separate insurance carriers may feel that the resulting concentration of their business with a single insurer would be too high.

5.6.3.2.2 Underwriting and Pricing Strategies

Underwriting and pricing value derives from leveraging the best practices from either company to improve the underwriting results for the combined entity. The acquisition of underwriting intellectual capital may be the primary strategy for the deal. If the buyer's strategy is to enter new markets or enhance its underwriting expertise, an analysis of the cost "to buy" vs. "to build" should be considered.

The underwriting models used by successful personal lines companies are considered trade secrets; they utilize a variety of factors such as an individual's claim history, credit report, family status, and motor vehicle records. The underwriting formulas, as well as the technology to implement the model within a specific distribution channel, may add significant value to an acquisition. Similarly, acquiring products, underwriting expertise, and a diversified, profitable book of business is typically less expensive than attempting to develop a new market from scratch.

While underwriting and pricing intellectual capital and infrastructure can present great opportunities, they can also present the highest integration costs. While P&C insurance products are similar, companies customize products using slight variations of covered perils, exclusions, and endorsements. The buyer needs to consider the integration costs required to either make products consistent or maintain multiple product offerings. Re-underwriting a book of business may improve the profit margin, but it also creates market disruption and lost business.

To achieve the desired synergies, policy terms and conditions may need to be consistent. Costs for more favorable terms or expanded coverage will either be passed along to policyholders, creating market disruption, or absorbed as an integration cost. The introduction of new products or enhanced underwriting models may also require systems changes.

5.6.3.2.3 Impact of Loss and LAE Reserves on Value Drivers

Generally, there is little strategic value inherent in the establishment of loss and LAE reserves. There may be a financial value adjustment relating to differences in opinion between buyer and seller relating to the specific liabilities. Outstanding liabilities can sometimes be sold for less than the recorded reserves; however, the difference usually represents only the discount for investment income.

However, it is important to consider the due diligence findings relating to the adequacy of the loss reserves when assessing value drivers. The adequacy of the loss reserves may distort the reported earnings and ultimate loss ratios by year and line of business. Similarly, when the best estimate of the loss reserves includes a provision for risk, it is important to identify the risk load so that underwriting trends are not distorted.

Due diligence should assess the company claim database, processes, and systems used to develop loss reserves. Integration costs may result from the need to improve or maintain inefficient old systems. Costs can also result from the need to upgrade to actuarial best practice methods and procedures.

5.6.3.2.4 Impact of Claim Settlement Practices on Value Drivers

P&C insurance companies employ a variety of claim settlement practices. The infrastructure of an insurance company's claim department may add to or detract from the economic value of the firm. Some companies primarily use their own claim adjusters, in-house attorneys, fraud detection, and special investigation units. Others outsource a significant amount of this work. Strategic due diligence includes an assessment of the claim management resources the target company maintains. A strategic acquisition may allow a smaller insurance company to gain sufficient volume to bring more of the claim processes in-house. Efficiencies of scale may be attained when the consolidated firm is sufficiently large to operate claim service centers or call centers.

For some lines of P&C insurance, studies have shown that claim severity is directly related to the time lag to the first contact. Therefore, the estimated synergy resulting from a more efficient claim operation may include both expense savings and improved underwriting results.

There are a number of claim systems used for processing claim data. Many P&C companies allow their agents and brokers to have access to these systems; some are even granted authority to settle claims on behalf of the insurer. While the claim infrastructure of a target company may represent a potential value driver, different claim settlement processes and systems may also lead to significant integration costs.

5.6.3.3 *Evaluating P&C Loss Reserves*

P&C loss reserve analysis is a critical element of the due diligence process. This section addresses the importance and components of loss reserve review.

5.6.3.3.1 Importance of P&C Loss Reserves

Invariably, uncertainty in the recorded loss and LAE reserves represents the most significant financial risk in P&C acquisitions. The loss reserves are typically the largest liability on the target's balance sheet. Due diligence of the target's loss reserves should provide the potential buyer with three key pieces of information:

- A best estimate of the liability for unpaid losses to use in the actuarial appraisal
- Insight into the loss ratios used to project future earnings
- A measure of the risk (variability) inherent in those estimates.

The adequacy of the loss and LAE reserves materially impacts the actuarial appraisal or key data used in a market multiple valuation estimate. Loss reserves have both a direct and indirect influence. As explained in section 4.9.2, the difference between the recorded reserves and the buyer's "best estimate" is a direct adjustment to the value of the target. The adequacy of the loss reserves also influences the projected loss ratio assumptions used to estimate future profits.

The buyer's best estimate reserve often differs from that recorded by the target company. Actuarial Standard of Practice No. 36, regarding P&C loss and LAE reserves, does not define a "best estimate" reserve. It acknowledges that "the most appropriate reserve within the range of actuarially sound estimates depends on the relative likelihood of estimates within the range and the financial reporting context in which the reserve is presented." The reserves recorded by the target company may include a "provision for uncertainty" to take into account the degree of variability inherent in the projection of ultimate losses. The best estimate of reserves used in an actuarial appraisal should exclude any "provision for uncertainty" because provision for risk should be addressed by the cost of capital discount.

Buyers may rely on relative valuation methods to determine the bid price for a P&C insurance company even when actuarial appraisals are available. Prior to applying the earning multiples, adjustments to the book value and reported earnings are made to reflect the adequacy of the loss reserves. Adjustments to the net worth are made to reflect the current reserve position. A change in the adequacy of the carried loss reserves from one accounting period to the next distorts the earnings reported in the financial statements. Therefore, an assessment of the adequacy of the carried loss reserves from prior accounting periods is also necessary to determine the quality of earnings adjustment to be made before applying the market multiples. An important aspect of P&C actuarial due diligence is a reconciliation of the reported fiscal year loss ratios with the most recent accident year results.

The calculation of the present value of future earnings is typically based on a forecast of the expected ultimate loss ratios. In many sellers' appraisals, the average loss ratio during the most recent few accident years is used to forecast future results (i.e., to reflect the "underwriting improvements that have occurred in the recent past"). While this is a desirable objective, it must be also recognized that the ultimate loss ratios for the recent accident years are primarily driven by estimated loss reserves and, therefore, contain the most uncertainty. Consequently, the loss ratios selected for the projection period should also be tested using historical loss ratios adjusted for rate changes, underwriting improvements, and inflationary trends.

CRYPT 5.11

Asbestos Attacks Actuary

***Buyer** retained **Team** to perform the due diligence of **Target**, a mid sized P&C insurer specializing in commercial insurance. I was a member of **Team**. Due to the significant asbestos and environmental (A&E) liability exposure, **Team** recommended that **Buyer** retain **Expert**, a well-known actuary who had published articles on the topic and had performed A&E liability reviews for many large insurers.*

*The **Team** and **Expert** finished their work at the 12th hour. **Buyer** had been anxiously awaiting **Expert's** results since the assessment of the environmental liability reserves was a critical component of the purchase price. At the final debriefing meeting, **Team** presented the results of the other loss reserves and provided some input on the level of the recorded A&E reserves in relationship to those held by other companies. Then **Expert** presented his results. The first exhibit presented was a range of reserves based on a range of reasonable assumptions. **Expert** concluded that the range of unpaid A&E liabilities was between $65 million and $90 million. The $25 million difference represented 20% of the purchase price.*

***Buyer** pressed **Expert** to provide his single best estimate. When **Expert** refused to do so, **Buyer** threw **Expert** out of the room and chastised **Team** for the $95,000 fee they incurred to retain **Expert**.*

*We sat stunned. The **Team** felt **Expert** had done a very professional job and that it was not **Expert's** call to decide on which assumption set would be used as the best estimate and which risks **Buyer** was willing to assume by using these assumptions. **Experts** are good at modeling the financial effects of various potential scenarios, but that doesn't mean they know which one will come true.*

5.6.3.3.2 **Reserving Due Diligence**

The actuarial due diligence of P&C loss reserves extends beyond a simple review or audit report. To adequately assess the reserve position for an acquisition the actuary must integrate the review of loss reserving principles, appraisal principles, and pricing principles. The review of reserves by product is essential to assess value drivers and develop the loss ratio assumptions used in the buyer's actuarial appraisal. The review of reserves by accident year is critical to understand underwriting trends and forecast future earnings. During loss reserve due diligence, the actuary identifies risks that may lead to adverse development of existing liabilities, as well as future underwriting results. The basic steps of loss reserve due diligence include:

- Obtaining the necessary information
- Evaluating the target's reserving methods and assumptions
- Preparing independent estimates
- Calculating reserving diagnostics
- Reconciling findings with claim settlement practices.

5.6.3.3.3 **Obtaining the Necessary Information**

The primary source of reserve information is the actuarial statement of opinion and the supporting actuarial report. State insurance regulations require P&C insurance companies to issue an actuarial loss reserve opinion annually. The actuarial opinion letter contains statements regarding the adequacy of the recorded loss and LAE reserves, identifies any material change in the methods or assumptions used to estimate the reserves, and discloses the risk of material adverse deviations. A report prepared by the appointed actuary is provided to the seller's board of directors and must be retained by the company for seven years.

An actuarial analysis is also performed by the seller's auditor. The auditor's actuaries must evaluate the methods and assumptions used by the company to estimate its reserves, and must attest to the reasonableness of the recorded reserves. To accomplish this, the auditor's actuaries typically produce an independent estimate of the reserves. The indications produced by the auditor should be reconciled to those produced by the target company.

State insurance departments perform financial examinations every three to five years. These examinations include an independent actuarial analysis of the loss and LAE reserves. This review may serve as an additional resource.

The actuarial opinion and audit reports attest only to the reasonableness of the total recorded reserves. It should be noted that the company's recorded reserve is *management's* best estimate, which may differ from its actuary's best estimate. The actuarial opinion and audit reports are silent on the adequacy of reserves by accident year and line of business. For most companies, the recorded loss reserves are based on the indicated reserves from the most recent actuarial study. However, for some companies, the incurred but not reported (IBNR) reserves recorded in the financial statements are based on a predetermined allocation formula. As a result, the buyer's actuary needs to develop independent reserve estimates to assess the target's strategic and financial value.

In addition to obtaining the standard actuarial reserving information, information gathered from due diligence of the claims, marketing, underwriting, and pricing areas should also be factored into the reserve analysis.

5.6.3.3.4 Evaluating the Target's Reserving Methods and Assumptions

The CAS has published a vast amount of research regarding models, methods, and techniques for estimating loss reserves. Certain loss reserving methods and techniques apply broadly to most P&C lines of business; other methods apply only to specific types of exposure. The actuary should assess the methods used by the target company to assure that the techniques being applied are considered best practice. The company's use of non-standard methods may be indicative of data availability issues.

Standard actuarial reserve reviews use a range of methods and techniques to develop multiple preliminary estimates of the ultimate incurred loss (see section 4.9.3). The best estimate is usually a weighted average of these preliminary estimates; the indicated reserve is determined by subtracting the losses paid to date from the selected ultimate loss. For a particular projection period, the relative weight assigned to each method should be based on the strengths and weakness of that method for that particular situation.

The various methods often produce significantly different preliminary estimates of the ultimate loss. These different estimates should not be disregarded; the actuary should attempt to reconcile the various preliminary estimates to gain an understanding of the critical drivers of results. Many times, this reconciliation process will uncover changes in the underlying experience.

5.6.3.3.5 Preparing Independent Estimates

Even if the buyer's actuary feels that reserve adequacy could be sufficiently tested by reviewing the target company's actuarial analysis and the auditor's work papers, an independent reserve estimate should still be performed. A vast amount of information can be gained by performing a review in the detail necessary to assess the strategic issues of the buyer. The issues relating to performing independent reserve estimates are addressed in Chapter 4.

5.6.3.3.6 Calculating Reserving Diagnostics

Most actuarial loss reserving techniques are based on the hypothesis that past experience is appropriate to predict future results. Changes in underwriting and claim settlement procedures may invalidate this hypothesis and present a significant risk to the estimation of loss reserves. As a result, a number of tests have been published in actuarial literature to detect unusual conditions or circumstances. Due diligence of the loss reserves should include a variety of diagnostic procedures to assess the consistency of the data used in the analysis. These may include:

- Claim reporting patterns
- Claim settlement rates
- Average case reserve per outstanding claim
- Paid-to-incurred ratios

- Loss reserve runoff analysis
- Frequency, severity, and pure premium trend analysis
- Large loss analysis.

Other actuarial procedures and techniques have been developed to adjust historical data or accommodate the changes in the ultimate loss estimate.

The due diligence findings from the underwriting and claims subteams should be incorporated into the reserve analysis; the statistics produced by the loss reserve diagnostics should be consistent with these findings. Finally, the due diligence of loss reserves should include an analysis of the actuarial reserves for the prior two years and the consistency of the methods applied and the key parameters selected. Reviewing multiple years is important, since a change in the reserve margins from one to the next may have a material impact on earnings, even if the reserves for all years are considered within range of reasonable estimates for accounting standards.

5.6.3.3.7 Reconciling Findings with Claim Settlement Practices

Actuaries need to develop a comprehensive understanding of the target's claim department operations to appropriately interpret claim statistics and predict future losses. Interviews with claim managers provide insight into claim frequency and severity trends, settlement rates, newly emerging types of claims, and strategies used to mitigate losses. Anecdotal information should always be substantiated with objective data. Claim department management reports are an excellent source of information and usually contain information not typically reviewed by actuaries. For example, most claim departments produce workload statistics, such as the number of open cases per claim adjuster or the average number of days before first adjustment. These may provide insight into reporting patterns and claim settlement rates. Statistics from the "Significant Change in Reserve Report" may be useful in validating a change in case reserving philosophy. Claim departments may also maintain claim settlement benchmarking statistics to manage claim severity. The management statistics developed by the claim department should be reconciled with the diagnostic statistics produced as part of the loss reserve review.

P&C insurance companies employ a variety of claim settlement procedures and case reserving philosophies. Some companies settle claims slowly to take advantage of interest float; others believe a quick resolution reduces claim severity and legal fees. Some companies use an average claim value to quickly establish an initial case reserve; others may wait until specific claim information is obtained to set the initial case reserve. Some companies may employ a stair-step procedure to adjust the case reserve upward, while others attempt to immediately establish the maximum potential loss. Some companies use their own claim adjusters and in-house attorneys, while others outsource a significant amount to independent adjusters and retained counsel. During the claim department due diligence, the actuary needs to identify any recent changes in procedures that may alter historical development patterns or the relationship between types of reserves (case vs. IBNR or loss vs. expense).

Claim adjusters are the first to identify new types of emerging claims or trends by type of loss. In the early stages, a new exposure may not be detected in loss reserving statistics or underwriting results. Information from the claim department regarding these claims may allow the actuary to identify this activity and evaluate whether the current loss development sufficiently contemplates this new exposure. The buyer's actuary should also assess whether a newly emerging exposure is contemplated in the projected loss ratios and, if appropriate, consult with the team's underwriters to develop an integration plan to mitigate future losses.

5.6.3.4 P&C Actuarial Appraisals

When a seller's actuarial appraisal is available, the actuary must assess the key management assumptions used to ensure they are consistent with the findings from the buyer's due diligence team. The actuary also estimates adjustments to convert the economic value included in the appraisal into a bid price. For a strategic acquisition, the actuary works closely with other team members to estimate the value drivers and the expected integration costs.

To accomplish this, the actuary must coordinate activities with other members of the due diligence team, including accounting, marketing, underwriting, claims, reinsurance, investments, information technology, and taxes. The findings of any of these areas can have significant implications for the actuarial valuation of a P&C insurance company. For example, any recent changes in the target company's underwriting practices, claim procedures, or reinsurance programs may have a material impact on the actuarial loss reserve analysis. Findings relating to the target company's distribution channels, marketing programs, underwriting, or product mix may impact the projected loss ratios or renewal rates. Due diligence of marketing, claims, reinsurance, and tax is required to validate the underwriting profits and investment returns underlying the appraisal assumptions.

Due diligence tests are intended to ensure that the parameters and variables used in the appraisal model are reasonable and appropriate under current and projected economic conditions. The buyer's actuary evaluates all of the data and information presented by the selling company to determine a best estimate (buyer's) appraisal value that represents the central tendency in the range of estimates. Material differences between the buyer's and seller's appraisal values may be subject to later negotiations.

5.6.3.4.1 Buyer's Appraisal—Market Issues

The present value of future profits is a key component of the economic value of a company. Two of the key assumptions driving future earnings are renewals (measured by a persistency rate) and anticipated new business growth. It is important to measure these two components separately since it is generally recognized that new business loss ratios will be higher than the loss ratios for renewal business.

For the seller's appraisal, it may be reasonable to assume historical persistency rates and an assumed growth rate for new business. This may also be a reasonable assumption for certain P&C acquisitions, in particular, for a financial acquisition of a stable P&C insurer. These situations represent the minority of the P&C insurance industry acquisitions.

Strategic acquisitions are far more common. There, historical persistency and growth rates are a starting point from which the buyer's actuary will make adjustments. During due diligence, the actuary must gain an understanding of how the seller's markets will react to the acquisition and develop assumptions to reflect any anticipated changes. Sometimes the market is aware of the potential for a transaction months in advance of the sale. If so, a review of the most recent data may afford the actuary valuable insight into the market's reaction.

Monthly marketing trend reports can be a valuable tool to assess the current market conditions. Reports showing persistency and new business activity by producer can be used to determine if agents may have started to move their business. For agency companies, marketing data pertaining to new agent appointments and terminations can be leading indicators for new business and renewals. To assess growth potential for direct writers, reports displaying response rates and conversion rates provide valuable insight on the effectiveness of their marketing efforts and the ability to penetrate certain markets. Extraordinary growth may also signal rate adequacy concerns.

The buyer's actuary will typically produce various scenarios of new business growth and renewal rates to assess the economic value. Alternative scenarios are also produced to determine the value of embedded options and to measure goodwill.

5.6.3.4.2 Buyer's Appraisal—Pricing and Underwriting Issues

The underwriting and pricing of personal lines products are highly regulated, and company changes are easily identified. During the due diligence, actuaries evaluate the changes in the filed rates and the distribution of written premium by underwriting tier to determine if there has been a material change in pricing. Changes in the distribution of business by geographic region, class, and product are reviewed to assess whether there has been a change in underwriting philosophy.

The premium and historical loss ratios for various segments of the business are analyzed to evaluate whether a change in the mix of business will affect the forecasted profitability. Significant changes in premium volume are evaluated to assess whether an increase or decrease was driven by a modification to the pricing strategy, marketing efforts, or from the appointment of new producers.

A funnel approach is the best way to describe the due diligence of the underwriting and pricing for commercial insurance products. The efforts begin with an overview of the underwriting process to identify the operational issues, lines of business, and market segments that present the most significant risk, as well as opportunities to create value to the buyer. An analysis of the exposure, premium distribution, profitability, and growth will be required for each product. During the initial assessment, the actuary considers the consistency of the results.

Interviews with the lead underwriter for each product line will allow the due diligence team to assess how the material underwriting risks are being mitigated and how underwriting philosophy may have changed over time. An analysis of filed rate levels, combined with flexible pricing modifications, will provide an indication of changes in premium levels and rate adequacy. Companies that do not maintain adequate information on the use of flexible pricing may not be effectively managing their business. Because of the diverse nature of the exposure, product line experts should be used to performing a detailed review for any product line deemed to present a material risk.

5.6.3.4.3 Buyer's Appraisal—Forecasted Loss Ratio Issues

The actuarial appraisal includes an estimate of the present value of future profits, usually based on a forecasted ultimate loss ratio. The forecasted loss ratio is typically based on an average of adjusted historical results. The number of years used to determine the appropriate loss ratio must balance the conflicting goals of stability and responsiveness. The period used should be sufficiently long to eliminate distortions from random variation and to encompass the expected variations from a full underwriting cycle. At the same time, the forecast should incorporate any recent changes in the expected future book of business.

Actuarial adjustments to the ultimate loss ratios from prior accident years are sometimes made to reflect changes in price levels, economic conditions, and other underwriting differences between the current book of business and that written in older years. Making actuarial adjustments to the historical results is sound in principle, especially when making short-term forecasts. However, when assessing the adjustments used to develop the expected loss ratio used in a long-term forecast, consideration must be given to the cyclical nature of the underwriting results. Actuarial due diligence of the underwriting area will allow the actuary to evaluate the forecasted loss ratios and any "actuarial adjustments" made to the historical results.

5.6.3.4.4 Reinsurance (Including Pools and Associations)

P&C insurance companies use reinsurance to stabilize underwriting results and to increase their capacity to grow. Catastrophe reinsurance is used to protect the company from a single event. The results from the target's most recent catastrophe models and its assessment of concentration of risk should be used to evaluate the target's catastrophe program.

Excess reinsurance is used to limit the adverse variation in underwriting results relating to multiple large claims. The discount rate used in the appraisal model must be commensurate with the level of risk the buyer is willing to assume; otherwise, additional reinsurance must be incorporated as an integration cost. For strategic acquisitions, the reduction of risk from geographic diversification and the ability to retain larger losses may be a value driver.

Quota share reinsurance is used by companies that do not have sufficient capital to retain all of their direct business written. Under a quota share reinsurance contract, a reinsurance company assumes a pro rata portion of the premium and underwriting risk. Potentially eliminating the cost for this reinsurance could be a value driver.

The reinsurance contracts must be examined carefully during due diligence. Reinsurance contracts are sometimes custom-designed to achieve certain business objectives and may intentionally change the amount and timing of premiums and earnings. Financial reinsurance contracts are designed to provide surplus relief with less than a commensurate reduction in risk.

Sometimes reinsurance terms and conditions are not finalized until well after the effective date. These programs are designed to allow the primary insurer to "rent" the reinsurer's capital at a cost below the expected underwriting profits. Catastrophe and excess reinsurance contracts may have provisions that modify the ceding commission based on actual experience.

Under FAS 113, reinsurance contracts must pass two risk transfer tests to be considered reinsurance:

1. The reinsurer must assume significant insurance risk (timing and underwriting) under the reinsured portion of the contract.
2. It must be reasonably possible that the reinsurer may realize a significant loss from the transaction.

Contracts that do not meet these criteria are required to use deposit accounting for these contracts. The tests to meet these criteria are subjective. Many accounting firms and insurance departments are taking a closer look at creative reinsurance agreements.

P&C insurance companies may also be required to participate in involuntary reinsurance, (e.g., pools, associations, and other residual market mechanisms). This is primarily an issue for personal lines and workers' compensation insurance; the risk is greatest in states with difficult regulatory environments. The participation obligations for the various residual market mechanisms are usually related to the business written voluntarily, but the associated costs are not always proportional. The actuary's due diligence should include an assessment of the involuntary pools to assess whether participation obligations could materially reduce future profits.

5.6.3.4.5 Buyer's Appraisal—Relative Valuation Approach

Sellers' appraisals are not always provided for P&C insurance companies and, because of the complexities of the insured exposure, there may not be sufficient time or information to prepare a buyer's actuarial appraisal during the due diligence period. Under these circumstances, the buyer may determine the bid price using a relative valuation approach. The indicated market value is developed based on a multiple of earnings, book value, or revenue. Even though these methods rely primarily on accounting ratios, the actuary plays an important role in converting the ratios to a purchase price. Even when a buyer's appraisal is developed, it is very common to benchmark its reasonableness using relative valuation approaches.

The multiples used in the relative valuation methods are compared to recent sales of other P&C insurers; however, the insured exposures for two P&C insurance companies are rarely alike. Therefore, it is important to use benchmark ratios for comparable types of companies. The historical database of relative multiples maintained by some investment bankers is generally segmented by personal vs. commercial writers, by distribution channel, and by premium volume. The actuary can provide valuable assistance in selecting a set of homogeneous comparables or by making adjustments to develop an apples-to-apples comparison.

Multiples from the most recent transactions should provide the best indication of current market values. By comparing the multiples from a number of similar transactions, the relative valuation method provides an indication of the market value of the target. Due to the low number of P&C insurance companies sold and the diversity of products across P&C insurance companies, it may be necessary to consider comparable transactions over a number of years. However, if there has been a material change in the market conditions, prior years' multiples may no longer be appropriate. Using the relationship between the market value and the underwriting cycle, the actuary can make adjustments to the historical benchmark multiples to bring them on-level to the current market conditions. Once the benchmark multiples are selected, they are applied to the target's financial data to determine an indication for the bid price.

Actuarial adjustments may also be made to the target's financial data prior to applying the benchmark multiples. The purpose of these adjustments is to eliminate any anomalies that would not be contemplated in the ratios calculated for the benchmark acquisitions. Since the earnings multiple will magnify any distortion in earnings, quality of earnings adjustments are made to restate the target's actual historical earnings to a "normalized" prospective run-rate basis. Quality of earnings adjustments are made for large or unusual loss activity, reinsurance transactions, and recent underwriting or pricing changes that could have a material impact on future earnings. As discussed in section 5.6.3.3, a quality of reserves adjustment may also be necessary for changes in the book value.

5.6.3.5 *Assessing the Material Risk Factors*

One of the key elements of the P&C actuary's due diligence is an assessment of the target's material risks. The risk characteristics of P&C insurance companies are diverse and a buyer may perceive certain risks as deal breakers.

The variability of the parameters used and the sensitivity of the value to changes in those parameters need to be tested to allow the buyer to assess the level of risk. As a result of perceived high variability in potential value, sellers' appraisals are not always calculated. When a seller's appraisal is available, the range of best estimates typically does not reflect the full range of risk inherent in the target company's operations. The cost of capital used in a seller's appraisal is typically formula-based and also may not reflect the risk characteristics specific to the buyer's operations.

The buyer generally reflects the perceived level of risk through the selected discount rate. This requires an assessment of the material risk factors that could cause future earnings to deviate from those assumed in the appraisal. Material risk factors are the key parameters, assumptions, or events that drive the future earnings and economic value of the target.

Technically, stochastic modeling, which defines a probabilistic distribution of valuation estimates or a confidence interval around a best estimate, is the best method for evaluating risk. However, as noted in Chapter 4, stochastic modeling is rarely used in practice. Instead, scenario testing is generally used to assess risk. The following types of risk are evaluated:

- Obligation risk
- Asset risk
- Interest risk
- Parameter risk.

Obligation risk is generally related to underwriting risk. It includes the potential economic impact of long-tailed liabilities, changes in experience relating to the underwriting cycle, or material exposures to latent or catastrophe losses. Scenario testing of the economic impact of long-tailed lines may lead to revisions to the adjusted net worth and present value of future earnings sections of the actuarial appraisal.

Obligation risk also includes exposure to economic changes, such as high medical inflation, and can materially impact the ultimate value of unpaid losses for long-tail lines of business, leading to revised estimates of loss reserves. These revisions can flow directly to the adjusted net worth calculation and can similarly impact loss ratios used to estimate the expected value of future earnings.

Similarly, the actuary must assess asset and interest risk under various scenarios. In the seller's actuarial appraisal, assets are marked to market during the adjustment to net worth calculation. Therefore, scenario tests for asset risk may only impact the future investment earnings and the cost of capital calculations. However, if the mix of the target's assets does not meet the risk appetite of the buyer, any transaction costs to modify the asset portfolio should be included as an integration cost.

For P&C insurance companies, the most extensive scenario testing will assess the parameter risk. Typically, there is significant uncertainty underlying the key parameters selected to estimate the loss reserves and project future earnings. These include the loss development factors, expected loss and LAE ratios, renewal premium rates, and sales assumptions. Various scenarios are produced to assess the variability of appraisal results. In some situations, specific stress tests are developed to determine circumstances under which the value of the company would fall below a predetermined threshold.

During due diligence, material risk factors that could significantly impact the level or variability of the appraisal are identified and quantified. The material risk factors are discussed among the buyer's entire team at debriefing meetings and mitigation strategies are developed. For some risk factors, the mitigation strategy may include conditions to the purchase and sale agreement. For example, if the indicated loss reserves have a significant amount of uncertainty and the buyer and seller cannot reach a consensus on the value of the liabilities, the purchase and sale agreement may include a true-up provision, based on a more mature valuation performed in the future.

For other material risk factors, a mitigation strategy may become a critical component of the integration plan, with the additional integration costs factored into the bid price. For example, if the exposure to catastrophe loss exposes the company's capital to more risk than the buyer is willing to assume, additional catastrophe reinsurance may be planned after the acquisition. An estimate of additional cost for the reinsurance is determined and included as one of the integration costs within the buyer's appraisal.

Examples of due diligence considerations to assess the company's material risk factors are described below for three key operational areas: marketing, underwriting, and claims.

5.6.3.5.1 Marketing Risk Factors

Marketing risk factors result from the market's perception of the acquisition and overlapping markets. For direct writers, if the acquisition creates significant market disruption, a reduction in policyholder retention will most likely result. Policyholders tend to shop their coverage in times of change. Similarly, for agency companies it is imperative to assess the producers' perception of the buyer because independent agents are not required to renew their business with the buyer. Any changes in compensation, workflow, or technology connecting the insurance company with the producer may result in the agents moving their business.

Failure to consider overlap in markets is one of the most common mistakes in evaluating future business assumptions. For direct writers, only one pricing basis will eventually survive, potentially affecting retention. Independent agents who currently represent both the buyer and the target may be reluctant to have a high concentration of business with one company. Competitors will try to exploit any market disruption to recruit new agents and seek profitable book transfers.

5.6.3.5.2 Underwriting and Pricing Risk Factors

Underwriting and pricing risk factors include rate competition, the underwriting cycle, rate regulation, participation in residual markets, natural catastrophes, and exposure to new types of losses that had not been contemplated.

The risk of severe rate competition varies by product line and is one of the elements creating the underwriting cycle. For personal lines insurers, competition from electronic marketing and direct writers with low-cost delivery systems may limit future profits. A material risk to future rate adequacy may result from the regulatory environment and the associated costs from the residual markets.

The P&C underwriting cycle is a well-known phenomenon. Little effort is typically spent during due diligence to predict the underwriting cycle within an actuarial appraisal. However, when evaluating the projections for future earnings, it is essential to understand whether the assumptions used in the actuarial appraisal were developed using historical averages from a hard market, soft market, or an average over the cycle. Anticipated changes in the underwriting cycle may provide valuable insight to a financial buyer with a relatively short investment horizon.

A risk for P&C insurers is an exposure that was not contemplated when the product was designed and underwritten. Environmental and asbestos liabilities are the most common examples. Other examples include carpal tunnel syndrome, construction defects, mold, and terrorism exposure. Examples exist for each P&C insurance product.

5.6.3.5.3 Claim Risk Factors

The most obvious claim risk factors are environmental liability, asbestos, mass tort exposure, catastrophes, and large losses. During due diligence, the lead actuary's role includes identifying and providing an initial assessment of potentially unique risks presented by the target. Some of these issues may be more appropriately handled by actuaries with specific subject matter expertise.

Assessing environmental and asbestos liabilities is clearly an area for subject matter experts. The methods used and benchmark statistics developed by expert actuaries (who perform this analysis for multiple companies) are invaluable.

The lead actuary works with the buyer and the subject matter experts to establish clear expectations for performing the claims review and presenting results. The expert should identify the risk inherent in the best estimate by presenting a sensitivity analysis regarding the key assumptions. In order to establish a best estimate or reduce the range of reasonable estimates, the buyer may need to select certain assumptions, and then make an adjustment for the variability this causes by adjusting the discount rate.

The actuary should also investigate contagion exposure not adequately represented in historical experience. Product liability, contractor's liability, workers' compensation, employee benefits liability, professional liability, employment practices liability, and directors' and officers' liability are examples of P&C contracts where a successful claim or court decision may give rise to multiple claimants filing similar suits. Construction defect, toxic mold, carpal tunnel syndrome, and product liability claims are examples of these exposures.

Increased claim activity may not initially be apparent in the actuarial data, and potential future losses may not be anticipated using the usual actuarial techniques. The claim department is usually the first area to recognize a potential exposure. Claim managers sometimes establish a specific loss code to identify these claims. Special procedures are then used to estimate the total exposure and future emergence patterns. These claims are a particular concern when the resulting exposure occurs over multiple years and the exposure affects multiple policies. Due diligence regarding the potential for mass tort claims extends to the underwriting department because future losses may be mitigated by modifying coverage, such as offering policies on a claims-made form.

The risk of catastrophe loss is inherent in most lines of P&C insurance. The risk may arise from a single event creating numerous claims or multiple events giving rise to extraordinary losses. Actuaries have developed tools to measure the risk of catastrophe claims, such as hurricane and earthquake models. Some companies use geo-coding to assess concentration of risk. During the due diligence for a strategic acquisition, the actuary should analyze concentration of risk to determine if the target's business adds value through diversification of exposure or increases the concentration risk. The insurance company's risk from large and catastrophe loss may be mitigated by purchasing reinsurance.

For strategic buyers, certain risks that were considered material to the selling company may no longer be material once the two operations are consolidated. The associated costs to mitigate these risks may potentially be eliminated and included among the acquisition synergies.

5.7 SUMMARY

The major activities of due diligence revolve around confirming the strategic and financial values that drove the buyer's interest and preliminary bid. A critical part of that process involves validating the quality of the seller's operations and whether the operations are capable of producing the value implied in the preliminary bid. This validation requires the coordinated efforts of a large, multi-talented due diligence team, concentrated into a minimal time frame. The buyer's actuary and other advisors then translate the broader team's findings into a final bid. Finally, the buyer's team also plans for the integration implications of actually winning the bid.

Actuaries have perhaps the most pervasive role in this process in that they are integrally involved in each step. They have critical roles in the confirmation of financial value and the quantification of strategic issues. They lead the review of actuarial operations and provide support in the review of other operational areas. They quantify the findings of the other teams and use that information to construct the buyer's appraisal and support the GAAP pro forma projections. They support the development of the bid conditions and negotiations. Finally, they prepare for their role in integration, assuming a winning bid.

If due diligence has overlooked some critical drivers of value, the buyer's final bid may be too high. Reasons could include undervalued liabilities, under-performing segments of the business, or operational shortcomings that require unanticipated time and money to fix. Conversely, the buyer's financial evaluation may be too conservative or not fully recognize potential strategic values or synergies, resulting in an uncompetitive bid

Other problems may surface following a winning bid. At closing, rating agencies may feel the buyer has accepted too much risk, triggering a downgrade. Stock analysts may feel the buyer's explanations or projections do not support sufficient value and influence stock price downward. Shareholders may feel the price was too high, which can lead to shareholder lawsuits. This is especially true if inadequate due diligence results in earnings surprises or integration problems from any number of perspectives. Stock analysts and buyers will generally show little patience for unexpected problems, because their skepticism has been fueled by an industry record of limited success. Finally, inadequate preparation for transition may result in an environment of uncertainty, in which key members of the seller's staff look for other opportunities.

If due diligence has been done well, the buyer will have either identified strategic sources of value that fund a competitive bid or determined why the target is not a good fit. Assuming the bid is successful, due diligence will have laid the groundwork for successful merger integration. The buyer's shareholders, stock analysts, and rating agencies react favorably to well-prepared explanations. There are few earnings and operational surprises following the closing, none of them major. The seller's staff has been impressed with the professionalism and interest shown by the buyer's staff during the due diligence process, and the key staff view working with the new organization favorably.

CRYPT 5.12

Subpoenaed From The Hotel Bar

My client was a small life company owned by a mutual health organization. The life company had been given the green light and cash to grow.

The life company's astute CFO took the lead. He identified a likely target, a struggling life company that was entertaining offers. After initial review of the appraisal report and public information, the CFO hired me to go in and perform due diligence. The two of us flew down to the small town where the company was located for a three-day visit. We checked into the only hotel and went to meet the management.

The company was publicly traded but family controlled. There were many entities being operated out of this home office.

I spent the first day with the local actuary. After listening to his account, reviewing forms

and treaties, and inspecting the financials, I concluded the right-hand side of the balance sheet appeared in order. But the CFO, probing the left-hand side, asked me to sit in on a meeting.

It was there I met the company president. I got uncomfortable when he wouldn't maintain eye contact. My CFO probed on the nature and ownership of several unusual investments, illiquid items with limited opportunity for appreciation. We had stumbled into a spider web of commingled family and corporate assets and service contracts.

We had smelled enough. On the second day we announced our departure and, having missed the last flight out of town, returned to our hotel.

During that second day, we had also learned that the state insurance department was in the midst of an examination that was evolving into an investigation. The state insurance department had heard we were there and was aware that we had open access to all the books. They had asked how long we were going to be in town.

Having left the company, my CFO and I were now sitting in the hotel bar. It was about 4 p.m. and we were the only customers there. The quiet was interrupted when the phone rang and the bartender answered it. He looked up at us and asked if one of us was Ed Greenbriar. Sure enough, that was my CFO. Ed took the call, listened in silence and said, "I'll call you back."

He returned to our table. He said it was the state insurance department. They had tried to contact us late in the day at the company and heard we had pulled out. They too knew the plane schedules and the hotel landscape, so the chief deputy figured we would be in this hotel bar commiserating. He was right on.

The deputy wanted to talk to us before we left. He asked if we would come down and tell us what we encountered during due diligence. The deputy said he understood that we had signed confidentiality agreements, so he asked if we would like to be subpoenaed rather than volunteer. We phoned back and said, yes, that would be a good idea. Shortly thereafter the hotel clerk brought two faxed subpoenas to the bar. We continued chewing peanuts. The next morning we were chewing with the state insurance department.

Having no surprises during due diligence would be a surprise.

Chapter Six

Corporate Benefits & Insurance Programs

6.1 OVERVIEW

This chapter focuses on the actuarial elements of due diligence for non-insurance companies, which typically include the review of the current property and casualty risk management program, employee benefits, and other financial obligations. As noted in previous chapters, the actual work performed will depend on whether the actuary is representing the buyer, the seller, or a third party. The objective in these reviews is to understand the other financial contingencies that may exist due to these corporate obligations. Although it is not within the scope of this chapter to discuss the roles of other professionals on the due diligence team, many of the same principles from Chapter 5 apply.

A key objective of a corporate due diligence process is to identify any liabilities that can make, break, or shape a deal. This chapter focuses on the actuary's roles in understanding the liabilities that are in other parts of the corporation. These roles traditionally involve the review of property and casualty risk and insurance and employee benefits.

The chapter is split between human resource and corporate property and casualty issues. The key issues to be covered are outlined in the next two subsections.

6.1.1 HUMAN RESOURCE ISSUES

The human resource (HR) issues are generally viewed as the softer aspects of any merger or acquisition. Many of the financial concerns in this area are dwarfed by the company's business operations. However, a thorough review of HR objectives and long-term strategies can be revealing because the benefit program designs offered employees are generally consistent with the overall company culture. For example, generous company-provided benefits, including low-cost medical programs and above-average financial security programs, indicate a paternalistic environment. Average benefit programs, including only a profit-sharing plan (i.e., no defined benefit plan) and health care plans with average employee contribution requirements and cost-sharing provisions, generally indicate a more egalitarian environment and promote an internal entrepreneurial atmosphere.

There are several significant HR issues in which actuaries may become involved. These include:

- Executive compensation
- Employee and sales compensation
- Organization and staffing
- Labor relations
- Human resource information systems (HRIS) and payroll systems
- Employee communications
- Employee benefits.

6.1.2 CORPORATE PROPERTY AND CASUALTY ISSUES

Companies have a variety of corporate risks and exposure that are managed through various forms of risk avoidance, risk assumption (uninsured, self-insured, or captive insurance), and risk transfer (insurance). Because many of these risks are long-term, it is important to understand how they have been managed and accounted for on the corporate books. The key issues involve understanding the insurance arrangements and in particular any self-insured exposures or risks insured through affiliated companies or captive insurance companies. Other risk management issues include:

- Reinsurance and excess covers
- Surety bonds, letters of credit, and other financial guarantees supporting the liabilities
- Product warranty and product recall

- Acquisitions, divestitures, and discontinued operations
- Latent injury and environmental risks
- Business interruption.

6.2 EMPLOYEE BENEFITS

From a high level perspective, the evaluation of employee benefit plans can make, break, or shape deals. Although the overall business aspects and value are the traditional financial focus, a comprehensive benefits due diligence can isolate significant liabilities, opportunities, and drivers in a deal.

SIDE NOTE

MAKERS, BREAKERS AND SHAKERS

Deal Makers In an analysis of the target company's health plan operation, it was noted that they made extensive use of their own clinical and technology staff to improve their own employee benefit program. This led to a higher valuation of the target company's capabilities and how they could be leveraged in the total company's programs.

Deal Breakers A review of a company's overall benefit program suggested that the culture of the target company was paternalistic while the buyer promoted greater employee independence and financial involvement. Both companies became concerned with the culture clash that was raised because of the benefits review.

Deal Shapers In a due diligence review of unfunded benefit programs (executive retirement and retiree health care), significant concessions were made by the seller to adjust its original selling price to reflect a more realistic assessment of the future obligations.

In the end, employee benefits rarely make or break a deal. Employee benefits, however, can disrupt the financial and cultural aspects of a merger or acquisition. The key findings that may be uncovered in a due diligence of a target company's benefit programs are:

- The liabilities and costs of programs are often calculated differently and inconsistently with the buyer's financial standards.
- When purchasing a portion of a larger company, the allocation methodologies may be simplified and may not reflect the true costs of the target entity.
- The design and delivery of benefit programs may provide a better understanding of the company's culture that should be taken into account in the overall business integration strategy.
- Plan designs may contain controversial provisions, or the plan operation may reflect lapses in fiduciary oversight—in either case suggesting potential legal issues or regulatory compliance problems.
- Employee benefits often have significant transition and integration issues that should be reviewed during the due diligence.

6.2.1 KEY PLANS TO REVIEW

This chapter will review specific considerations that should be addressed for:

- U.S. qualified plans
  - Defined benefit (e.g., pension)
  - Defined contribution (e.g., savings, profit-sharing, and 401(k) plans)

- Nonqualified programs
  - Retirement
  - Deferred compensation
  - Executive contracts
- Group benefit programs
  - Health plans
  - Life and disability plans
  - Severance programs.

The review of each of these programs requires a different focus. In addition, the structure of the deal may also affect the key issues underlying the scope of the review. If the target company has foreign operations, a review of comparable programs should be made. The actuary should also consider the varying accounting treatments that employers may have, including:

- Financial accounting
- Tax accounting, and
- Cost accounting (in particular the special rules for government contractors).

In the 1960s through the 1980s, qualified retirement plans were reviewed to assure adequate funding levels. In the 1990s, defined benefit plans were often viewed as potential hidden cash when many of the plans became over-funded due to conservative contribution strategies and strong market performance of assets. In the 1990s, retiree health care plans were discovered as significant hidden liabilities that were almost always unfunded. In the 2000s, defined benefit plans again became a key focus. Low market returns meant that companies now had required contributions for plans that had not paid any contributions for a long time. And new contribution requirements had been significantly affected by funding rules under the Employee Retirement Income Security Act of 1974 (ERISA) that have led to volatile contribution requirements.

Throughout this period various management and executive benefits have fallen in and out of favor. The employment contracts and other agreements that have been entered into with key employees may have implicit costs that are not readily apparent.

6.2.1.1 Qualified Plans

Qualified plans primarily include retirement programs offered by the target company including defined benefit (DB) plans (primarily pension plans) and defined contribution (DC) plans (savings, profit-sharing, and 401(k) plans for taxable companies and 403(b) plans for tax-exempt organizations).

DB plans are characterized as retirement programs that provide a specified benefit at retirement (e.g., 50% of pay at retirement will be continued to the employee after retirement). DB plan benefits are commonly based on the years of service that an employee has at retirement (e.g., the benefit is equal to 2% of pay times years of service at retirement).

DC plans provide a set contribution to an account during an employee's working career. For example, a savings plan may include an employer contribution equal to 2% of pay during the year. These contributions are invested in individual accounts, and often the employee has an opportunity to specify the fund types (e.g., bonds, growth stocks, real estate) in which their accounts are invested. A 401(k) plan is another type of DC plan that allows employees to make pre-tax contributions to a fund while they are working. Employers usually match an employee's contributions up to a certain amount (e.g., the employer matches $0.50 for every $1.00 contributed by employees up to a maximum 3% of the employee's pay).

The review of tax-qualified plans includes an analysis that the plan complies with all current laws. An operational compliance review is especially important if the acquiring company will inherit a plan, either directly or indirectly, as a result of either the taking over of the target's plan or a spin-off from the target to the buyer. The type of sale (purchasing assets or stock of the company) may be a key indicator of the plan treatment. An asset sale typically will leave much of the past obligations with the selling company. Under a stock deal, the buyer typically takes over all obligations—past and future.

If the buyer finds significant operational defects, it can utilize one of the voluntary programs offered by the Internal Revenue Service to correct the defects. Using the IRS correction program will significantly reduce the exposure to the buyer for compliance defects. If the IRS discovers defects on audit at a later date, it could result in significant liabilities.

The indemnification contained in the purchase agreement may have a limited time span. As a result, unless these issues are identified and corrected by the buyer, the ability to approach the seller for redress on a breach of representation and warranties will be lost.

6.2.1.2 *Nonqualified Plans*

Nonqualified plans are typically unfunded plans providing retirement benefits to a select group of management or highly compensated employees. They can be either DB or DC plan designs. The unfunded nature of these benefits makes them an important benefit to understand their long-term financial obligations.

The actuary should review the liability calculations for the plans so that they may be taken into account when determining the purchase price. If the nonqualified plan is not being transferred in whole as part of the transaction (e.g., the plan will be maintained by the seller and the target company is a subsidiary), a clear understanding of the allocation methodology must be made. The buyer may want to require the seller to fully vest all target company employees in their accrued nonqualified benefits or to consider post-closing vesting and eligibility service with the buyer when determining benefits for the seller's employees who transfer with the target company.

In addition to retirement-type programs, there may be other types of executive contracts that the actuary should review. The details of the contracts are beyond the scope of this textbook but include termination contracts, executive medical, and other special contracts that preserve the executive's employment rights. A review of all senior-level executives included in the transaction should be undertaken to determine any financial obligations after a sale. For example, an executive's contract may stipulate that a stream of payments be made if the company is ever sold. This may or may not be conditional on his or her continued employment. Such a contract is an ideal actuarial present value calculation involving present values of contingencies of termination, mortality, and other probabilities.

6.2.1.3 *Group Benefit Programs*

Group employee benefit programs constitute a significant portion of overall labor costs, primarily due to health care costs. The most significant issues tend to be the future obligations of retiree health care, broad-based severance programs, and other group benefit reserves and liabilities primarily for long-term disability programs and potential COBRA (discussed in section 6.2.1.3.3) liability. These reserve and liability exposures could be significant. It is imperative that the buyer identify these issues and make appropriate allowances in the purchase price.

6.2.1.3.1 Retiree Life and Health Insurance Obligations

These obligations are typically unfunded and can therefore imply significant additional liabilities. Most of these obligations will be accounted for on the financial statements but allocations to subsidiaries are often done in a simplified manner (e.g., per employee). These allocations may not represent the true cost of the benefits to the target company's population.

Accounting rules require appropriate aggregate accounting and therefore some of the liabilities will already be reflected in the financials. However, separate calculations are often desirable to fully understand the future obligations and the sensitivity of these obligations to assumptions used to project benefits.

A significant issue that is often raised is whether the plan can be amended or terminated and, if the buyer is to assume the liabilities under the plan, how those liabilities should be apportioned. The potential amendment of retiree coverage is frequently a litigated issue. Most plans have a reservation of rights clause that allows them to amend or terminate the plan at any time in the future. However, these clauses cannot prevent future litigation.

CRYPT 6.1

Widget Wedgee

The ABC Widget Company had been buying smaller widget companies for the past 15 years. Like ABC itself, many of these companies started right after World War II. Their owners were now retiring and looking to sell their businesses. ABC had found that this acquisition strategy was a successful way to grow its widget revenues. In fact, ABC had three full-time acquisition specialists on board whose sole function was to find widget companies to buy.

ABC had grown tremendously. The acquisition specialists were very successful. In fact, the CEO of ABC was so encouraged by the growth prospects of their acquisition model that he instituted a significant bonus program based on the number of companies the specialists successfully brought into the company.

The benefits department of ABC noted that many of the acquired companies had a retiree health care benefits program. For the size of companies that were being bought, this seemed unusual because this benefit was usually only offered by much larger employers. In fact, it was only two years ago that ABC established a policy that if an acquired company had retiree health care benefits at the time of acquisition, they would maintain it after the acquisition. Before then, it had not been an issue because none of the acquired companies had the benefit.

The CEO asked the benefits director to review the recently acquired companies to see if there were any patterns. Why did some companies offer retiree health care and others did not? Was it common in certain regions of the country or was it due to size of the acquired company? The investigation did find a pattern. Every one of the companies brought in by acquisition specialist #1 had retiree health care. Only one company from the other two specialists had retiree health care.

The CEO interviewed the former owners for all the companies that had retiree health care coverage. The former owners said that ABC's top gun acquisition specialist had offered health care for them after they retired but their plan had to be amended before the sale.

The specialist felt that he was helping the former owners and their employees with a much needed retirement benefit—even though they didn't have it before. By showing these prospects that he was indeed on their side when negotiating this important benefit, for the other parts of the deal the owners gave him their full trust.

As everyone knows, retiree health care is an expensive benefit. ABC Widget is still paying the price, even though it is now saving salary costs for one less acquisition specialist.

What are the morals of the story? Don't overlook employee benefits in your due diligence. Further, be careful how much authority rests in one person. Finally, provide appropriate pay incentives.

6.2.1.3.2 Broad-Based Severance Programs

Broad-based severance programs (i.e., available to employees below the executive level) are typically unfunded programs that may have significant liabilities. Review of whether the transaction will trigger the benefits of this program should be performed. This will be of particular concern if the buyer is considering significant headcount reductions after closing.

6.2.1.3.3 Other Group Benefit Reserves and Liabilities

The seller may have other reserves and liabilities for group benefit programs. The three most common are reserves for disabled employees under their long-term disability (LTD) program, claim liabilities for amounts that have been incurred but unpaid (IBU) under the health plans, and reserves for workers' compensation benefits.

The LTD reserves should be reviewed for appropriateness. They are usually established for self-funded plans but the seller may have a contract with its insurer for a fully insured program that allows the seller to maintain the reserves on its books. The IBU liabilities are generally for the self-funded plans only.

Internal Revenue Code (IRC) Section 4980B requires employers to provide continued medical coverage to an employee and their covered dependents who lose coverage under a group health plan. This requirement is included in the Consolidated Omnibus Budget Reconciliation Act of 1985 (COBRA). The penalties for failing to comply with COBRA continuation requirements can be significant. Under certain circumstances, the buyer may be considered a "successor employer" and therefore would be subject to the seller's COBRA obligations. Therefore, the parties should clearly allocate the responsibility for COBRA obligations for individuals who become entitled to COBRA coverage after the closing date of the sale.

Companies are required by state statute to provide workers' compensation benefits to employees. These required benefits provide medical expense and lost wages to workers injured on the job. Actual benefits vary by state. Workers' compensation benefits are the most common property and casualty insurance exposure retained by corporations. Companies will often retain a portion of the costs for these benefits and purchase an insurance policy to limit their exposure. Therefore, the due diligence team should request copies of any policies to assess whether any exposure is self-insured.

In the instance where only a portion of the liabilities is being transferred to the buyer, it is important to understand the cost implications of the portion being transferred. For example, if the group being sold is older than the others, its costs are generally higher for most benefit programs.

6.2.2 DUE DILIGENCE PROCESS

While the due diligence process will vary for every situation, common elements include:

- Identify target company programs
  - The report to the buyer should provide enough detail so that its HR staff can understand what benefits are available from the target company to its employees.
  - A comparison of key provisions for each plan to the buyer's plan may help with the understanding (and will be used in the integration process if the sale progresses).
  - Oftentimes it is difficult to assess the value of the target company's plans compared to the buyer's plans; thus, a value comparison is helpful. This comparison will use actuarial value calculations for each program.
- Understand the target population
  - Active employee demographics
  - Any legacy plans for retirees or disabled former employees
- Consider financial implications of alternative designs
  - Preliminary design alternatives may be considered
    - Integrate into buyer's plans
    - Move to seller's plans
    - Modify both target and seller plans
    - Receive the best of both worlds
  - Determine the financial impact of each alternative
- Identify reserves and liabilities
  - Show reserves and liabilities under the target company and acquiring company methods and assumptions
  - Determine which obligations, if any, will stay with the seller
  - Determine if changes in the adequacy of the recorded reserves or funding process have resulted in a quality of earnings adjustment

- Understand current utilization of programs
  - Identify employees participating in each of the programs and those who are not
  - Understand what drives participation in the programs, for example
    - Demographics
    - Location
    - Contribution requirements
    - Communication
- Anticipate how utilization may change under alternative benefit designs and participant contribution structures
- Identify synergies or integration costs related with the combination of the buyer and the target populations and programs
  - Greater negotiation leverage with insured health maintenance organizations (HMOs)
  - Consolidation of plans (e.g., HMOs, life insurance, multinational pooling)
  - Spread certain fixed costs over larger number of employees
  - Consolidate functions (internal and external).

Note that any considerations made on reviewing plans will have to consider the sales agreement and the cultures of all parties. For example, the sales agreement might require the acquiring company to maintain substantially the same benefits to the employees who are being acquired that they had with the seller's program. Or, if an alternative on the table is to simply integrate all of the target company's employees in the buyer's plans, consideration will be needed for human resource issues such as loss of coverage due to freezing prior company benefits or the fact that the buyer's plans may be less rich than the seller's plans.

The following sections focus on specific analyses that may be done for different benefit programs. The Appendix section includes a more detailed checklist of considerations for each.

6.2.2.1 *Qualified Plans*

The compliance review mentioned requires access to legal documents, including the plan document, trust documents, and any amendments to either document. Any IRS determination letter should be reviewed as well as required government filings for the last three years. These documents should be used to identify any compliance issues that may need to be discussed with the seller. Early detection may help reflect the cost of defects in the sale price or require the seller to fix them prior to sale.

For DC plans (e.g., savings and 401(k) plans), a review of current administration processes will help assess the work required during integration.

If there are assets backing up the obligations, the review needs to identify how they will be handled after the sale. The range of possibilities includes anything from being retained with the seller to being entirely transferred to the buyer's plans. If the target is selling a portion of the company, the evaluation of appropriate assets to be transferred is subject to calculations that the reviewing actuary should analyze. If there are any assumptions that are subjective, these details should be reconciled during this process.

By their very nature, DB plans require significant actuarial review. Since these benefits are payable in the future, contingent-type calculations are required to appropriately evaluate the liability. In addition, the funding rules are complex and require specific calculations.

The expertise of an actuary becomes particularly critical when only buying a portion of a company because the buyer will likely only get a portion of current assets that have been funded. Understanding of approximate financial implications can be assessed before final calculations are made to make the buyer aware of potential issues.

Reviewing both the funding and the accounting reports will provide some understanding of the financial decisions being made by the seller. It is important to recast the numbers using the buyer's methods and assumptions to understand the likely financial impact of the acquisition.

6.2.2.1.1 Specific DC Plan Review

The DC review will focus primarily on plan design and compliance issues. The due diligence team will need to develop potential strategies to integrate the target company's plans into the buyer's organization in order to assess potential integration costs.

The target company's plan should be reviewed to see if it has an annuity form of benefit. This may impact a plan-to-plan transfer if the acquiring company does not offer annuities. This is a philosophical design question and may likely mean that assets will not be transferred and employees will either need to maintain money in the seller's plan or roll them over to an IRA if they are considered legally terminated from the seller after the sale.

The target company's annual employer contribution determination method should be reviewed. If it is a variable amount (e.g., based on profit) the buyer should request to see a history (say, five years) of contributions.

The potential issues, synergies, and transition costs relating to the plan administration should be reviewed. In particular, if outside vendors are used to administer the plan, the due diligence team must develop an understanding of how the acquisition will impact the administration agreements. If the current vendors cannot or will not continue administering the plans, the costs to transfer the plans to alternative administrators should be determined. The due diligence team may also need to assess whether or not the buyer is able to administer the plans with its current arrangements.

It is important to understand whether the target company's program covers a controlled group or only the company's employees (and former employees). If it covers a larger group than the target group being acquired, an understanding of final accounting should be gained to determine if the allocation of costs represent a fair estimate of the target group's costs.

The plan investment vehicles must be reviewed to determine if they can be changed (particularly any termination provisions). In particular, the following investment provisions should be reviewed to note any inconsistencies with the provisions of the buyer:

- Guaranteed investment contracts
- Employee self-directed accounts
- Company stock.

In addition, the assets should be reviewed for any liquidity concerns, especially if any of the assets are being transferred to the buyers's plans.

Qualified retirement programs have various nondiscrimination tests that must be passed in order for the plan to remain "qualified" under ERISA. In general, a plan cannot discriminate in favor of highly paid employees with respect to who's covered or the level of benefit provided. Specifically, IRC Section 410(b) provides objective tests of coverage, and IRC Sections 401(a)(4), 401(k), and 401(m) include tests on assuring that contributions to DC plans are not discriminatory. In addition to these objective tests, a plan must be designed to not discriminate as to the level of targeted benefit. The IRS reviews those provisions when plan sponsors submit their legal documents for approval. The purpose of these rules is to assure that the plans provide both benefits and coverage to a broad range of employees and are not principally for the benefit of high-paid employees. A review of how the plan has passed the applicable nondiscrimination tests (IRC Section 410(b) and IRC Sections 401(a)(4)/401(k)/(m)) should be made. If nondiscrimination documentation cannot be found, a determination should be made as to why not and a request should be made that a test be performed prior to closing the sale.

The plan designs should be reviewed to see how they qualify under IRC Section 401(a)(4), which provides for either design-based "safe-harbors" or demographic based "general testing." There should be a review of any integration issues that these plans may have on the buyer's basis for testing their plans under Section 401(a)(4).

Plans with 401(k) savings features will present annual testing issues, such as refunds to or limits on amounts contributed by highly compensated employees. Such issues could have negative consequences for the buying company.

An often-missed test is whether the plan has met the contribution limits under IRC Section 415 (the maximum benefit and contribution limits imposed by the Code).

6.2.2.1.2 Specific DB Plan Review

Besides plan design and compliance issues, a DB review will include a financial review due to the variety of funding strategies employed by plan sponsors.

Key demographic data should be collected for each DB plan including:

- Number of active participants in each plan
  - Average age
  - Average service
- Number of terminated vested participants
- Number of retirees.

If little financial data is available, this information will help to better understand the magnitude of the seller's obligations for each plan by making cost estimates relative to the buyer's demographics. It will also help make better program cost estimates after plan decisions have been finalized.

A review of key financial measures should include:

- ***Current cash contribution requirements.*** The buyer should get the detailed components of the calculation including normal cost (current year's cost allocation), amortization total, and percentage of pay. Also, the current liability will help the actuary understand potential funding implications in the short-term.

  The actuary can test these numbers for reasonableness. If the target company is a portion of the seller and the seller uses "charge-backs" to each operating company, the charge-back methodology should be reviewed. If all numbers are simply allocated as a percent of payroll, a separate evaluation of the target company alone should be performed to better understand the true costs. For example, if the target company has lower turnover or has an older workforce than the total company, a charge-back based on payroll may significantly understate its real costs.

  U.S. funding rules allow the use of an "actuarial value of assets" that dampens market movements in plan assets, which in turn tempers contribution volatility. The particular method for smoothing market changes will pass to the buyer and will need to be evaluated in the buyer's funding policy context.

  Given the above information, the actuary can assess the likelihood that contribution requirements will increase substantially in the future. Because most qualified DB plans are well funded with assets close to liabilities, small changes in assets and liabilities (driven by required assumptions) can have a significant effect on contribution requirements. They should not surprise the buyer.

- ***SFAS 87 expense (the financial statement expense).*** Statement of Financial Account Standards No. 87 is entitled "Employers' Accounting for Pensions." The pension expense should be provided by component—service cost, interest cost, expected return on assets, amortizations, and the total and the assumptions used to calculate these amounts. The actuary can review these amounts for reasonableness and carefully review any asset smoothing reflected in the expected return. If the acquisition is to be accounted for under the purchase method under Accounting Principles Bulletin (APB) 16, all amortized amounts will be eliminated, often making for drastically different expense amounts after the transaction.

- ***Key financial statement disclosure information.*** This is often easily found in the financial statements, but, if only a portion of the seller is being considered, the specific target company values should be requested. The components that should be analyzed are the vested benefit obligation, the accumulated benefit obligation, the projected benefit obligation, plan assets, unrecognized transition obligation, unrecognized prior service cost, unrecognized gain or loss, and accrued or pre-paid pension expense. All of these values should be as of a stated measurement date. A detailed list of assumptions should also be requested so that a rough estimate may be done to evaluate the reasonableness of the numbers. These assumptions should be compared to the buyer's assumptions.

If the seller has had any settlements or curtailments in the past, details of the events along with all of the financial statement calculations per SFAS 88, Employers' Accounting for Settlements & Curtailments of Defined Benefit Pension Plans and for Termination Benefits, should be requested. SFAS 88 is the accounting standard that provides guidance in the financial treatment of pension obligations after they have been settled (usually when the obligations have been transferred to a third party, such as the purchase of an annuity from a life insurance company) or curtailed (when future benefits are reduced). In general, it accelerates or adjusts the recognition of pension costs to bring the liabilities closer in line with the current obligations. This information will help to better understand the plans' current financial condition, as well as the seller's financial and policy decisions.

The valuation review should include a complete examination of all of the key assumptions, including:

- Demographic assumptions (e.g., mortality, retirement, and turnover)
- Economic assumptions (e.g., discount rate and salary increase).

In particular, the individual assumptions for the financial statement calculations (i.e., SFAS 87) should be compared to those used for IRS funding purposes. SFAS 87 defines how retirement plans are accounted for in an employer's financial statements. These calculations determine the expense used in their income statement and the liabilities to be shown on their balance sheet. They are completely different from the funding rules established and defined in the IRC. However, the key assumptions are usually the same, so deviations should have rational reasons for why they are different.

The expected long-term rate of return assumption for SFAS 87 is oftentimes the same as the interest rate used for IRS funding requirements. If they are different, they should be reconciled. There are valid reasons why they may be different. For example, investment expenses may be implicitly included in the rate of return while they may be explicitly shown under the funding assumptions. Setting the two rates the same could be used to estimate the sensitivity of this important assumption.

All the seller's assumptions should be compared to the buyer's. There may be philosophical reasons why they differ (e.g., financial conservatism), and the seller's costs and liabilities should be estimated under the buyer's assumptions to the extent they are reasonable for the plans being transferred.

Finally, if any assumptions are different, an estimate should be made to determine what the target company's obligations would look like if the buyer's assumptions were used. A pro forma financial statement should be developed to illustrate how these amounts will be reflected on the buyer's books after the sale.

If the target company participates in any multiple employer or multi-employer plans, there are several items to consider. For example, the actuary should identify the current costs, determine whether or not there are scheduled increases, and ascertain if the plan is fully funded. If the plan is not fully funded, the actuary will need to determine if there any withdrawal liabilities that may need to be paid up on sale or what risks may be passed on to the buyer.

The investment strategy of the seller's trust fund should be reviewed, which will help assess volatility implications and perhaps better understand historical returns. If there is an investment policy statement, it should be compared to the buyer's statement.

There are a variety of administrative issues regarding qualified plans that an actuary may be involved with, including:

- Plan qualification issues. All plan documents should have been properly filed in a timely manner. The plan should cover the appropriate employees. The plan administrator should be using the correct compensation base (e.g., total annual pay instead of base pay only). It must be assured that the plan meets any applicable nondiscrimination rules.
  - The plan is designed to qualify under either the "safe harbor" provisions of IRC Section 401(a)(4) or to qualify under the "general test." If the latter is used, a copy of the general test (Demo 5 or 6 from the most recent determination letter submission) should be requested. It should be determined if testing is performed annually or less frequently (such as triennially).
  - It should be determined how the plan passes the nondiscrimination tests of IRC Section 410(b), and assess whether there may be issues with passing these tests in the post-closing environment.
- Tax liability issues. Tax filings should be reviewed for propriety and tax deduction appropriateness. It should be ascertained that excise taxes are not due. The excises taxes are penalties for things such as engaging in prohibited transactions, failing to fund the plan as required, making nondeductible contributions, or receiving refunds from excess assets.
  - A prohibited transaction is a very broad transaction between the qualified plan and what ERISA calls "parties in interest." Parties in interest include persons connected with the plan, such as plan fiduciaries, employers of employees covered by the plan, owners of the company, and company officers.
  - ERISA includes minimum funding requirements for defined benefit plans. Failure to fund may also highlight the seller's other financial problems.
  - There is a 10% excise tax on any contributions paid in excess of the maximum tax-deductible contribution. A review of all contributions should be made to assure that this excise tax is not due upon sale.
  - There is a non-tax-deductible excise tax of 50% on excess assets returned to the company. This basically implies that any asset reversion from terminating a pension plan is not accessible by the company. If there were any recent plan terminations, there should be a review to assure that there are no excise taxes due. Prior to the law change in 1991, companies would commonly acquire another company that had an overfunded pension plan, terminate the plan, and recover the excess assets. With the imposition of the excise tax, the pension plan is no longer a source of windfall income, except in somewhat limited and specialized circumstances.
- PBGC filing. Most DB plans are subject to the ERISA requirement that guarantees benefits by the Pension Benefit Guaranty Corporation (PBGC). Filings should be reviewed to assure that all of the PBGC premiums have been timely paid and properly determined, and that the disclosure of reportable events under ERISA has been properly made.
- Employee notice requirements. Depending on plan funding levels, employees covered by poorly funded plans must receive a notice of the plan's funded status. Other notices may also be required, for example, when benefits are reduced prospectively.

6.2.2.2 Nonqualified Plans

Since nonqualified plans are typically unfunded, they are often sources of significant liabilities. If the plans are funded, the due diligence team needs to determine how they are funded (e.g., rabbi trust or corporate-owned life insurance[1]) and whether a portion of these assets will also be provided with the matching liabilities.

The plan documents should be reviewed to see if any of the benefits increase or trigger required contributions due to the sale (e.g., a springing rabbi trust that may require automatic funding upon an action such as an acquisition). If so, clarification will need to be made as to who will pay for these increases.

The due diligence team should evaluate all information relating to the benefit design and participants covered by non-qualified plans. This will allow the team to assess the program's potential costs and implications after the sale.

6.2.2.3 Group Benefit Programs

Much of the due diligence for the group benefit programs involves understanding and comparing the benefits offered by the target plan relative to the buyer's plans, which can be difficult for the layperson to adequately determine because of the variety of design alternatives that an employer may use. For example, for a prescription drug plan, is a $20 copay per prescription a more or less valuable plan than one that requires 25% coinsurance? Is a sick pay plan that allows 10 days of pay better or worse than a short-term disability plan that pays 60% of pay from the eighth day of sickness or the first day if the disability is due to an accident? Nevertheless, a structured comparison of plan designs and an analysis of the value of each plan is an important exercise.

6.2.2.3.1 Retiree Life and Health Insurance Obligations

These obligations are often the company's largest unfunded liability. Because there are no funding requirements for retiree life and health insurance benefits, large obligations with no offsetting assets are common.

The due diligence team should request the information necessary to determine whether the target company has any employees or retirees eligible for retiree life or health insurance benefits. If these benefits exist, a specialist should evaluate a description of the program, eligibility rules, demographics of the eligible employees and retirees, any applicable grandfather provisions (e.g., retired before 1991), ability of the plan sponsor to change or terminate benefits, and retiree contribution policy.

The due diligence team will need to evaluate all information related to the various SFAS 106 values. SFAS 106, Employers' Accounting for Postretirement Benefits Other Than Pensions, contains the financial accounting rules for retiree life and health plans, which is equivalent to the pension rules under SFAS 87 and SFAS 88.

- The valuation assumptions should be assessed for reasonableness and should be compared to the buyer's assumptions. There is a wide variation of assumptions that would be considered reasonable and, consequently, a wide range of results. Understanding the target company's assumptions relative to the buyer's will help estimate the financial effect to the buyer on its financial statements. The claim costs used in the SFAS 106 valuation enables evaluating the reasonableness of the projections. For example, are they close to the budget rates used for budgeting the current year's costs or are they adjusted through a smoothing methodology to reflect longer-term expected costs?

[1] A rabbi trust is one type of non-qualified funding vehicle often used to fund executive benefits. It provides an element of security for the participants but may still be subject to bankruptcy creditors. A corporate-owned life insurance (COLI) policy is a whole life insurance policy issued to help prefund benefits that allow tax-favored asset build-up though insurance reserves.

- The SFAS 106 expense for each plan should be collected. The information collected should include the cost components, including service cost, interest cost, expected return on assets, and each component of amortization amounts. These values can be used to estimate the potential financial effect on the buyer's statement.
- The reconciliation of the funded status should also be requested, including the accumulated postretirement benefit obligation for retirees, actives eligible to retire, and actives not eligible to retire; unrecognized transition obligation; unrecognized prior service cost; unrecognized net gain or loss; and accrued or prepaid plan cost. Comparison of these amounts to the buyer's statements can help estimate the impact of inheriting the new plans.
- The historical cash flow experience, coupled with retiree counts, should be compared to the rates used in the SFAS 106 valuation. If they do not match, a reconciliation of the differences needs to be made prior to accepting the seller's numbers.
- Interviews with management or the HR manager in charge of the plan may be necessary to assure that any known events that will affect future cash flows or liabilities are reflected in the valuation. For example, if senior management approved a change in the program but it has not yet been communicated to employees, it may not be included in the valuation results until employees understand the change.
- The plan documents and other communication pieces should be reviewed to determine if the plans have sufficient reservation of rights to amend or terminate the plan. If not, any reductions attempted after the sale closing are probably not possible.
- The common assumptions[2] between the SFAS 87 and SFAS 106 calculations should be compared. For example, it is common to use an average retirement age assumption in SFAS 87 valuations but an average should not be used for SFAS 106 valuations due to the high costs of health care coverage prior to Medicare-eligibility age in the United States. Understanding of any differences may help explain some differences in estimates between the pension plans and the retiree life and medical plans.
- The assumed health care cost increases should be reviewed to determine how realistic they are relative to the buyer's short- and long-term expectations. Consideration of the historical difference between the discount rate and the ultimate health care trend rates should be made because this difference is the key driver in the SFAS 106 results. If there is a 300 basis point difference or greater, it indicates that management assumes that high quality fixed income securities will earn more (by at least three percentage points) than health care cost increases. Most experts do not believe that such a difference is a reasonable long-term assumption.
- The source of the SFAS 106 claim costs should be determined. They should be based on actual retiree claims but may be estimated from active claims, theoretical claims (i.e., a manual rate[3]), or a combination of the above. Average claim rates may be based on gross claims or net claims (i.e., gross claims less retiree cost-sharing). The actuary should determine the cost estimate reasonableness.

---

[2] Common actuarial assumptions include demographic assumptions such as rates of turnover, mortality, disability, and retirement. The economic assumptions should also share common inflationary expectations.

[3] A rate produced from an actuarial model that accounts for plan design, demographics, geography, and other risk factors, but does not consider the specific group's experience.

CRYPT 6.2

Short Cuts Don't Pay Off

It was coming to the end of long and grueling summer of working through details of a major acquisition. Besides sweating due to the intolerably humid weather, my buy-side team added to the perspiration of the selling company's consulting actuary because of all the simplified assumptions he had used for his client's retirement programs. He argued that they were all reasonable assumptions and were selected following all professional guidelines. There was no argument there, but they happened to all favor his client.

At every turn, we agreed that more sophisticated techniques would yield higher liabilities for the division being sold than his calculations. These shortages amounted to several millions of dollars. We negotiated them into the sales price.

As we were leaving the soaked actuary, we asked him what he himself knew about his client's retiree medical plan. He looked up over his glasses to just say that he made the calculations correctly. In fact he said it was easy because it's a "capped" plan. That means the company's contribution to the plan was fixed and retirees paid actual costs above the fixed amount. We agreed that any trained monkey should be able to do that calculation and had a laugh together.

However, as we left the room, the benefits manager for the seller looked confused with that verbal exchange. We were puzzled by her body language. She asked us to explain what we meant by a capped retiree medical plan. After the explanation, she shook her head and said, "That's not how our plan works!" After further investigation, we found that the only place where a capped plan was documented was in the actuary's report. There were no letters to retirees and no legal documents. Not a single other benefits person could confirm a cap to the program. Needless to say, the value of the plan was severely understated because of the actuary's misunderstanding of the program.

We didn't misunderstand and again adjusted the bid offer. The costs of this employee benefit program had been severely underestimated. Fortunately, we had done our homework.

6.2.2.3.2 Other Group Benefit Reserves and Liabilities

The key areas that should be reviewed closely for the other group benefit programs are their administrative and financial liabilities.

All of the plan documents for the other group benefit programs should be reviewed. Self-funded plans often do not have legal plan documents but the summary plan descriptions generally provide enough program detail to suffice. All of the insurance contracts for the various insured programs (HMOs, life insurance, disability plans) should be collected. These documents will be the source of plan comparisons and evaluation.

Both the legal plan document and the communication to employees should be reviewed. If differences exist, they should be resolved prior to closing the sale. For example, the legal plan document may indicate that only base pay be used to determine life insurance amounts but employee communication may state that total pay (base pay plus bonuses) be used. The legal plan document may have indeed expressed management's agreement to use base pay but if it hasn't been used in practice and employees' understanding is total pay, it would be difficult to enforce the legal document.

The plan documents should be checked against employee communications to assure that the documents are current and consistent. It is important to assess the potential litigation issues that may arise due to the employees' understanding or misunderstanding of the benefits.

Each plan should be reviewed to uncover any problems that the sale may pose for the transfer of administrative functions (e.g., payroll, claims certification, enrollments, status changes, coordination of benefits (COB) rules, maximum benefit limits). An immediate assessment should be made to understand whether the buyer will have to change carriers or administrators on the closing date. This preliminary assessment will help determine the required timing and even plan offerings that will be considered during the integration process.

If employee contributions for any welfare plans are paid on a pre-tax basis, the buyer needs to determine if its administrator can handle any differences from its current plans. For example, some LTD plans allow the employee to elect to make contributions on either a pre- or post-tax basis so that benefit payments are taxable or non-taxable, respectively. Because not all administrative systems can handle such elections, it is important to uncover this type of design.

The review team should check that all of the required forms have been filed. For example, each ERISA plan should have filed an annual information form (Form 5500) and any plans funded in a welfare benefit fund (e.g., voluntary employees' beneficiary association (VEBA) trust fund[4]) should file a tax return (Form 990 or 990T, if unrelated business income tax is payable).

Necessary plan reserves (e.g., medical claim liabilities or LTD disabled life reserves) should be objectively evaluated to determine the adequacy of the funding levels. The actuary should determine whether or not the buyer will be assuming the reserves.

A review of health care claim liabilities should be made. For example, a special analysis of liabilities for incurred but unreported health care claims should be undertaken. This type of analysis is typically not done in most situations because on an ongoing basis the results are seldom significant. However, for a larger group, an understanding of these potential future claims is important to better understand the obligations the buyer is assuming. The responsibility of this liability will need to be established prior to the sale.

Under certain situations, the IRS or the Department of Labor (DOL) may impose a liability on the seller or the target company under COBRA. In addition, it should be determined whether the seller or the target company has ever experienced COBRA compliance issues.

The funding arrangements for each welfare plan should be determined.[5] For self-funded plans, stop loss insurance contracts should be identified. Specific insurers need to be identified as well as any claim limits or restrictions on transfers and termination.

The financial statements should be reviewed to determine whether the seller has recognized costs for other post-employment benefits in accordance with SFAS 112, Employers' Accounting for Postemployment Benefits. The buyer needs to determine which benefits (e.g., LTD, workers' compensation, severance) are included.

6.2.3 REPORTING THE RESULTS

The report to the client will vary depending on findings. As outlined in the process section above, a review of plan designs should be provided with enough detail so that the buyer's employee benefit staff can understand similarities and differences between the buyer's and seller's benefits. Table 6.1 provides an example of a typical grid of plan design information comparing and contrasting the buyer's benefits to the seller's benefits.

[4] A VEBA is a trust fund qualified under IRC §501(c)(9). It allows plan sponsors to generally make tax-effective contributions to an outside fund and offers certain tax-favored asset treatment.

[5] Group insurance programs may be fully insured (i.e., an insurance company is responsible for the full risk of the benefit) or self-insured (the plan sponsor assumes the full risk) with other financial arrangements that blend these two arrangements.

CONTRAST OF EMPLOYEE BENEFIT PLAN DESIGNS

BENEFIT	ABC – BUYER	XYZ – SELLER
Pension		
Eligibility	Immediate	No plan
Pension Formula	1.25% FAP-5 plus 0.25% FAP-5 over Social Security covered compensation (year of birth) x service (maximum 35 years	
Covered Pay Definition	Total	
Vesting	5 years	
Employee Contributions	None	
Early Retirement	Age 55/10; reduced 3% per year below age 62; 5% per year below age 60	
Supplemental Nonqualified Pension Plans		
Normal Payment Form	Allows lump-sum distribution ERISA restoration plan covering maximum benefit and pay limits for all plan participants	No plan
Savings		
Eligibility	Immediate	Immediate
Employee Contributions	Up to 15% pre-tax only	Up to 15% pre-tax only
Employer Contributions	75% match up to 6% of pay (pre-tax only), up to 9% unmatched (pre-tax only)	60% of first 6% of pay
Pay Definition	Total	Total
Vesting	20% per year	Immediate
Investments	Bond, Various Equity Funds, Money Market, Asset Allocation, Company Stock	Bond, Various Equity Funds, Money Market, Asset Allocation, Company Stock
Loans	Yes	Yes
Stock Purchase		
Eligibility	Immediate	Immediate
Employee Contributions	Up to 10% after tax	Up to 15% after tax
Pay Definition	Total	Total
Purchase Price	85% of market	85% of market
Supplemental Nonqualified Savings Plans		
	ERISA restoration plan covering maximum benefit and pay limits for all participants	
Company-Paid Life and AD&D		
Eligibility	Immediate	Immediate
Employee Contributions	None	None
Benefit	2 x pay	1 x pay
Age Reduction	Reduces 10% per year to 50% at age 70 (first reduction is at age 66)	Reduces 10% per year to 50% at age 70 (first reduction is at age 66)
Retirement Reduction	.75 x base pay (maximum $20,000)	100% - no retiree life

TABLE 6.1

CONTRAST OF EMPLOYEE BENEFIT PLAN DESIGNS (Continued)

BENEFIT	ABC – BUYER	XYZ – SELLER
Optional Life Insurance		
Eligibility	Immediate	Immediate
Employee Contributions	Age-graded (100% of cost)	Age-graded (100% of cost)
Benefit	1x, 2x, 3x, 4x, 5x pay	1x, 2x, 3x, 4x, 5x pay
Dependent Life	Spouse: $10,000 to $100,000 Children: $5,000 to $10,000	Spouse: $10,000 to $100,000 Children: $5,000 to $10,000
AD&D	1x, 2x, 3x, 4x, 5x Base Pay	1x, 2x, 3x, 4x, 5x Base Pay
Business Travel Accident	2x company paid life amount	
	ERISA restoration plan covering maximum benefit and pay limits for all plan participants	No plan
Short-Term Disability		
STD BENEFIT Sick Days	5 work days	PTO – see vacation/sick days
Disability beyond Sick Days	Service 100% 50% <2 yr 6 19 2<5 yrs 8 17 5<10 yrs 10 15 10<15 yrs. 12 13 15<19 yrs. 20 5 20+ yrs. 25 0	Service 100% 60% All 4 21
Long-Term Disability		
Eligibility	Immediate	Immediate
Employee Contributions	For additional 10% only	For additional 10% only
Benefit	50% (employee receives credits) 60% company-paid 70% (employee pays for 10%)	50% company 60% (employee pays for 10%)
Reduces For:	Primary Social Security	Primary & Family Social Security
Pay Definition	Base Salary	Base Salary
Waiting period	Six months	Six months
Benefit Period	ADEA 1	ADEA 1
Maximum Monthly Benefit	$25,000 for each option	$15,000 for each option
Definition of Disability	24 months own occupation	24 months own occupation
Mental/nervous, drug, alcohol	24 months of LTD benefits	24 months of LTD benefits
Preexisting condition limitations	None	3 mos. prior to, or 12 mos. of employment

TABLE 6.1

CONTRAST OF EMPLOYEE BENEFIT PLAN DESIGNS (Continued)

BENEFIT	ABC – BUYER	XYZ – SELLER
Medical—Indemnity Plan		
Eligibility	No plan	Immediate
Employee Contributions		20%
Deductible		$500 per person, $1,000 per family
Preventive Care		Covered
Out-of-Pocket Limit		$1,500 per person, $3,000 family
Lifetime maximum		$1,000,000
Prescription Drug		80%
Inpatient Services		80% after deductible
Outpatient Treatments		80% after deductible
Medical Managed Care— POS, or PPO	**POS**	**PPO**
Eligibility	Immediate	Immediate
Employee Contributions	Emp. only: $15/month Emp. + Sp: $30/month Emp. + Ch: $25/month Emp. + Fam.: $60/month	Emp. only: $10/month Emp. + Sp: $60/month Emp. + Ch: $50/month Emp. + Fam.: $100/month
Benefit In-Network Out-of-Network	$15 copay office visits 70% after deductible	$20 copay office visits 70% after deductible
Lifetime maximum	Unlimited	Unlimited
Deductible In-Network Out-of-Network	None $300/$900	$100/$200 $300/$900
Out-of-Pocket Limit In-Network Out-of-Network	 None $3,000/$9,000	 None $3,000/$9,000
Inpatient Services In-Network Out-of-Network	 90% 70%	 90% 70%
Outpatient Treatments In-Network Out-of-Network	 $15 per visit 70% after deductible	 $20 per visit 70% after deductible
Prescription Drugs Retail Mail	 $20 copay ($10 if generic, $25 if non-formulary) $40 copay ($20 if generic, $50 if non-formulary)	 $15 copay, $5 if generic $30 copay , $10 if generic

TABLE 6.1

CONTRAST OF EMPLOYEE BENEFIT PLAN DESIGNS (Continued)

BENEFIT	ABC – BUYER	XYZ – SELLER
HMO/EPO	**HMO**	**HMO**
Eligibility	Immediate	Immediate
Copay	$10 per visit	$15 copay per visit
Deductible	None	None
Coinsurance	100%	100%
Out-of-Pocket	None	None
Employee Contributions	Emp. only: $5/month Emp. + Spouse: $20/month Emp. + Children: $15/month Emp. + Family: $30/month	Emp. only: $12.50/month Emp. + Spouse: $50/month Emp. + Children: $35/month Emp. + Family: $70/month
Prescription Drug		
Retail	$20 copay ($10 if generic, $25 if non-formulary)	$20 copay ($10 if generic)
Mail	$40 copay ($20 if generic, $50 if non-formulary)	$40 copay ($20 if generic)
Dental Plan – Indemnity		
Eligibility	Immediate	Immediate
Benefit	Diagnostic and preventive: 100% Restorative: 80% Major: 50% Orthodontia: 50%	Diagnostic and preventive: 100% Restorative: 80% Major: 50% Orthodontia: 50%
Deductible	$25/$50 (waived for diagnostic and preventive)	$50/$150 (waived for diagnostic and preventive)
Maximums	Annual: $1,500 Ortho: $1,500/person/lifetime	Annual: $1,500 Ortho: $1,500/person/lifetime
Employee Contributions	None	$4, $8, $12
Dental Plan – (D) HMO		
Benefit	Diagnostic and preventive: 100% Restorative: 100% Major: 60% Orthodontia: 50%	Diagnostic and preventive: 100% Restorative: 100% Major: 60% Orthodontia: 50%
Deductible	$0	$0
Maximums	Annual: Unlimited Ortho: 1 treatment/person/lifetime	Annual: Unlimited Ortho: 1 treatment/person/lifetime
Employee Contributions	None	None
Vision		
Employee Contributions	None	$2, $4, $6
Exam	$10 copay	$10 copay
Eyeglasses (frames and lenses)	$25 copay; limited 1 pair each 24 months	$25 copay; limited 1 pair each 24 months
Contacts	$0 copay; $125 maximum each 24 months	$0 copay; $125 maximum each 24 months

TABLE 6.1

CONTRAST OF EMPLOYEE BENEFIT PLAN DESIGNS (Continued)

BENEFIT	ABC - BUYER	XYZ - SELLER
Flexible Spending Accounts		
Health Care	$3,000 maximum per year	$3,000 maximum per year
Dependent Care	$5,000 maximum per year	$5,000 maximum per year
Employer Contribution	$500—HC and DC Not matched	$200—HC, DC Matched $1/$1
Work Life Benefits		
Holidays	12 fixed	10 fixed plus 4 floating holidays
Vacation	SERVICE / SCHEDULE 6 mos. / 5 days 1-4 years / 10 days 5-14 years / 15 days 15-19 yrs. / 20 days 20-24 yrs. / 25 days 25+ yrs. / 30 days	SERVICE / SCHEDULE 0 – 4 years / 15 days 5 – 19 years / 20 days 20+ years / 25 days plus 1 week sabbatical every 5 years PTO - combined sick and vacation days
Flex work hours	Included	Included
Tuition Refund	$6,000	Maximum $10,000 per year
Casual dress	Fridays	5 days per week
Wellness / Fitness programs	On-site facilities	On-site facilities
Adoption Assistance	Up to $2,500 per child	Up to $2,500 per child
Elder Care Assistance	Included	Included
Group Purchasing	Group auto and home ins., payroll deductions available	Group auto and home ins., payroll deductions available
Van Pooling	Provided	Provided
Parking Initiatives	Subsidized	Subsidized
Work/Life Manager		Yes
Work/Life Library		Yes
Diversity Training	Included	Included
Child Care Referral	Included	Included
Sick Child Care		
Back-up Child Care		
Convenience Services	Dry Cleaning pick-up on-site	Dry Cleaning pick-up, ATM
Financial Planning		
Family Care Resource Program	Not available	Not available
Career Counseling (Employee)	Available (outsourced)	Available (outsourced)
Career Counseling (Dependents)	Available (outsourced)	Available (outsourced)
On-site Meals	Subsidized	Free

TABLE 6.1

CONTRAST OF EMPLOYEE BENEFIT PLAN DESIGNS (Continued)

BENEFIT	ABC - BUYER	XYZ - SELLER
Eligibility Rules, Categories, and Classifications:		
Active Employees, spouse, children	First of month following 30 days employment	Immediate for most coverages
LTD and Leave of Absence (LOA)	Coverage is continued for 6 months, at same cost as active employee	Coverage is continued for 6 months, at same cost as active employee
Retirees	Covered for health and welfare benefits	Not covered for health and welfare benefits
Surviving Spouse	Not covered for health and welfare benefits	Not covered for health and welfare benefits
Domestic Partner	Excluded	Included
Child of Same Sex Domestic Partner	Excluded	Included
College Student	Included to age 23	Included to age 28
Grandfathered dependents	Covered	None

TABLE 6.1

Descriptions of benefit plan designs provide the client with information to decide potential issues that may need to be dealt with during the integration process. Due to the variety of plan design components, it may not be evident which design has a higher value and by how much. That is why it is often helpful to provide a table of relative value differences between the buyer's plans and the seller's plans. Table 6.2 provides an example of such an analysis.

SUMMARY OF RESULTS

COMPANY	ABC–ACQUIRER		XYZ–SELLER	
	Employer-Paid Value	Total Value	Employer-Paid Value	Total Value
Defined Benefit Pension	100.0	100.0	0.0	0.0
Defined Contribution	100.0	100.0	90.3	90.3
Defined Benefit Pension + Defined Contribution	100.0	100.0	49.2	49.2
Group Life	100.0	100.0	50.3	50.3
All Preretirement Death	100.0	100.0	73.0	50.3
Postretirement Death	0.0	0.0	0.0	0.0
All Death	100.0	100.0	73.0	50.3
Short-term Disability	100.0	100.0	88.6	88.6
Long-term Disability	100.0	100.0	71.4	63.6
All Disability	100.0	100.0	83.6	83.3
Medical Composite (w/o HMO)	100.0	100.0	99.4	85.9
Medical Composite (w/ HMO)	100.0	100.0	99.4	85.3
Dental	100.0	100.0	94.4	90.0
All Preretirement Health Care	100.0	100.0	98.2	86.6
Postretirement: Pre-65	0.0	0.0	0.0	0.0
Postretirement: Post-65	0.0	0.0	0.0	0.0
All Postretirement Health Care	0.0	0.0	0.0	0.0
All Health Care	100.0	100.0	98.2	86.6
All Security Benefits	100.0	100.0	80.9	73.6
Holidays	100.0	100.0	116.6	116.6
Vacations	100.0	100.0	96.6	96.6
Total Time Off with Pay	100.0	100.0	105.3	105.3
All Benefits	100.0	100.0	88.1	83.9
All Postretirement Benefits	100.0	100.0	49.2	49.2
All Preretirement Welfare Benefits	100.0	100.0	97.0	93.0

TABLE 6.2

Table 6.2 provides two key relative value numbers, each value relative to the buyer's plan. One value is based on the total value of the particular benefit plan. The other value is based on the portion paid by the employer (the employer-paid value). Simply, it's the comparison of the relative value of the seller's benefit plan compared to the buyer's benefit plan. If the seller's employer-paid value is less than the total value, it implies that the seller's employee contributions to the plan are greater than the buyer's.

Based on the above analysis, the seller's plan benefits are less generous overall than the buyer's. The retirement benefits are in particular much lower, primarily due to the lack of a DB plan and lower DC plan employer contributions. This type of analysis will help the integration team to understand where to strengthen communications in order to offset potential negative employee feedback. It can also be used to identify areas of focus in the financial analysis.

The additional financial analysis that will be done for a company will highlight key areas of concern because of specific funding levels. For example, in the above example, there would be no worry about any unfunded liability for the retiree medical and life insurance program that is often found in larger companies. The report will provide all such comparisons.

An analysis of the cost impact of varying alternatives may also be shown depending on discussion with the buyer's M&A team. The relative value analysis above can be used to estimate potential financial impact of various decisions. For example, if the team wants to understand what the added medical plan costs would be if the seller were added to the buyer's program, a first-step answer would be equal to their current employer costs divided by 0.853 (the employer provided relative value under "Medical Composite (w/ HMO)").

6.3 CORPORATE INSURANCE & RISK MANAGEMENT PROGRAMS

Due to the potential harm to their operations, small to mid-size companies typically insure their property and casualty risks using traditional insurance products. The claim experience for large corporations and conglomerates, on the other hand, may be sufficiently stable to allow them to absorb the cost of most property and casualty claims with little distortion to earnings. Instead of transferring this risk, large corporations may finance their exposure as a self-insurer (or establish a captive insurance company) for direct losses and purchase excess insurance to cover catastrophic losses.

When a large corporation self-insures, the corporate finance and risk management departments usually manage the risk, make the financial decisions relating to the annual accrual and reserve levels, and allocate the cost of the exposure to the various operating divisions. Third-party claim administrators are usually retained to handle claims for most exposure. However, in-house counsel may manage the high-risk liability claims. For some lines of insurance, such as workers' compensation, the self-insured company must meet certain eligibility and other requirements established by the state insurance departments. These requirements may involve the posting of a surety bond or other financial instrument to secure the corporation's self-insured obligations.

While acting as a self-insurer eliminates much of the cost associated with risk transfer, being self-insured may not be efficient from a tax perspective. Companies that self-insure the exposure must accrue the liability for unpaid losses but are only allowed to deduct losses that are paid as an expense for income tax purposes. As a result, many large corporations establish a captive insurance company to finance their property casualty exposure.

6.3.1 DUE DILIGENCE ISSUES

The property casualty actuary may play an important role in the due diligence for a non-insurance corporate acquisition, particularly in evaluating the impact of insurance and risk management programs in place. The valuation techniques used by investment bankers for non-insurance entities are based on the same principles discussed in Chapter 4 for valuing insurance entities. As a result, the actuary's goals and objectives for the corporate due diligence are basically the same as those for insurance companies:

- Evaluate any balance sheet items relating to insurance to determine if there are adjustments to the company's net worth
- Identify quality of earnings adjustments; quality of earnings adjustments are any expenses, or lack thereof, included in prior year earnings that do not belong in the run-rate assumptions used to project future earnings[6]
- Identify the target's material risk factors; for non-insurance entities the material risk factors are assumptions or events that materially impact the net worth or future earnings of the company.

For property casualty insurance companies, claim reserves represent the largest entry on the liability side of the balance sheet. Consequently, the actuary's findings relating to the loss and LAE reserves are often a "deal shaper or deal breaker." However, for corporate acquisitions,

[6] Run-rate earnings are the adjusted earnings before income tax, depreciation, and amortization (EBITDA). Adjustments are made to "normalize" anomalies to earnings from unusual events.

the liabilities relating to property casualty risk and exposure may be less significant in relation to revenues and capital. Therefore, before commencing a corporate due diligence of the property casualty risk and insurance, the actuary must have a clear understanding of the levels of materiality for the balance sheet adjustments and quality of earnings adjustments. The materiality levels and type of risk management programs in place will dictate the scope of the review performed on the property casualty insurance accounts.

The balance sheet adjustments relating to self-insured property casualty liabilities could be a deal breaker for non-insurance acquisitions. In particular, it is important to evaluate the unpaid liabilities and assess the risk of future claim activity. The risks associated with certain exposures, such as environmental liability, asbestos, and product liability are material and can be a deal breaker when not properly accrued for. For other acquisitions, the uncertainties relating to the self-insured property casualty liabilities require special purchase provisions. The savvy chief executive officer or investment banker will consider an actuarial analysis of the property casualty exposure prior to closing a deal.

For corporate acquisitions there are several areas where the actuary's due diligence report will include quality of earnings adjustments. Quality of earnings adjustments tend to be more important to investment bankers than balance sheet adjustments because bankers often assess the acquisition price in terms of a multiple of run-rate earnings. Therefore, earnings distortions from self-insured property casualty exposure have the potential to create significant purchase price adjustments. For example, a change in the reserves for self-insured exposure or the failure to properly accrue certain liabilities will distort the company's earnings. In addition, the company's recent claim activity or a change in the underwriting cycle may indicate a significant increase in the future cost to manage the company's property casualty risk. Due to the frequency and magnitude of the potential adjustments, many investment bankers retain property casualty actuaries to assess the self-insured exposure for all corporate acquisitions.

One of the key elements of a corporate due diligence is the assessment of the material risk factors and an evaluation of the company's risk management program. The process used by corporations to manage the property casualty risk varies by size and type of organization. Conglomerates usually have a corporate risk management department and a chief risk officer responsible for establishing corporate policies and risk management procedures. Larger companies may have a corporate risk manager responsible for these duties and may retain outside consultants to perform an enterprise risk management assessment and assist in developing a strategy to manage the operational and financial risks.

The property casualty risk management program for large corporations is often complex and difficult to evaluate. Some conglomerates have captive insurers. Sometimes companies within the conglomerate may have separate plans for some coverages but share risk management programs for other exposure. However, the level of materiality for the purchase of a large corporation is also significantly higher, allowing the actuary to reduce the scope of due diligence to only issues that may have a material impact to the economic value. The due diligence becomes significantly more complex for a carve-out acquisition of certain operating divisions of a large corporation due to the need to discern which costs have actually been incurred and which costs have been allocated to the division through a corporate program.

For mid-size or smaller firms, the chief financial officer (CFO) may assume the risk management functions. Since many of the significant risks are exposures covered by property casualty insurance products, the CFO may depend on an insurance broker to perform the company's risk assessment and develop an insurance program to transfer this risk. The risk assessment services are usually provided for "free" because the insurance agent is compensated with commission from the insurance policies. However, the limited assessment performed by insurance brokers typically excludes exposure not covered by insurance products, such as the risk of production delays due to reliance on a single supplier of materials.

To perform the due diligence relating to the property casualty risk and exposure, the actuary should request the following items:

1. Copies of any risk assessments performed during the past three years
2. A schedule of insurance and a summary of all changes in the insurance program for the past five years
3. The most recent claim experience reports
4. Copies of all actuarial studies performed on the self-insured exposure, and
5. Access to the officer in charge of risk management.

It is assumed that other members of the team have access to the financial data relating to the property casualty insurance accounts. Additional information, such as copies of all existing insurance policies, will always be needed to complete the "phase two" due diligence of the property casualty accounts. However, it is far more efficient to review items one to four above and have a discussion with the risk manager to identify the other areas where additional diligence is required. For most acquisitions, there is limited time to perform the review and the number of requests being made by potential investors is enormous. By interviewing the risk manager, the actuary will identify the salient risks and determine the information required and readily available for review. The risk manager is usually the actuary's best resource for additional data, and the company will appreciate the shorter list of essential data needed to evaluate the material risks. For other acquisitions, access to company personnel may be limited, and all requests are submitted through a central clearinghouse. For these acquisitions, a comprehensive data request list may be necessary.

The following sections discuss the due diligence issues for the various types of risk management programs for insurable risk. In addition to the insurable risks, the actuary should also evaluate other operational risks, such as those related to economic conditions, distribution channels, and supply chains to assess the future earning potential. The operational risks are unique to the type of corporation being acquired and will not be discussed in detail in this chapter.

6.3.2 PROGRAM DESIGN FOR INSURABLE RISKS

The company's risk management program typically includes a number of techniques to manage risk. These include risk transfer, risk avoidance, risk financing, and mitigation strategies for retained risk. Insurance products are the most common technique to transfer risk. Mid-sized companies typically manage insurable risk using a combination of risk transfer and risk financing techniques. Many commercial insurance products include a self-insured component using insurance products with a large deductible or retrospective premium adjustment endorsement. Large companies and conglomerates typically underwrite risk as a self-insurer or through a captive insurer. In practice, due diligence will uncover a myriad of policies for the various types of exposure within the same company.

The first step in the due diligence of property casualty risk and exposure is to evaluate the seller's most recent risk assessment (if one exists) and review the schedule of insurance. A sample of the schedule of insurance, including the essential data elements, is provided in Table 6.3. Other information may be needed, such as the insurance broker's contact information and the expiration dates. However, the information in Table 6.3 combined with the company's most recent risk assessment will allow the actuary to identify uninsured, underinsured, and self-insured exposure.

INSURANCE SUMMARY FOR ABC CORPORATION

All policies effective July 1, unless noted

COVERAGE	INSURER	POLICY LIMIT	RETENTION	CM*	EXPOSURE	PREMIUM
Workers' Compensation and Employer's Liability	Zurich (January 1, renewal)	Statutory 1,000,000	500,000 500,000		$11,270,000 Payroll	135,250
Auto (owned/non-owned)	Liberty	1,000,000	250,000		198 Vehicles	119,000
Commercial GL	CIGNA	2,000,000	250,000		$66.5 Million Revenue	133,000
Products, Completed Operations		2,000,000	250,000			included
Advertising Liability		2,000,000	250,000			included
Employee Benefits Liability		2,000,000	1,000	CM		included
Media Liability	National Casualty	1,000,000	50,000	CM	Revenue	117,271
Foreign Liability/DIC	Ins. Co of Penn	1,000,000	None		$9.3 Million Foreign sales	24,237
Property	FM Global	$2.4 Billion	350,000		Insured value	406,000
Business Interruption		included				included
Earthquake/Flood		None				
Umbrella	Zurich / CNA Federal et al.	100,000,000	Underlying $50,000**		Insured limits	165,756
Errors and Omissions (claims made)	National Union	2,000,000	100,000	CM	Revenue	48,650
Crime/Employee Dishonesty	Travelers	1,000,000	500,000		Assets	46,468
Fiduciary/ERISA	National Union	25,000,000	100,000	CM	See IRS Form 5500	65,000
Directors & Officers (claims made)	CNA, ACE	50,000,000	2,500,000	CM	Assets/sales	344,183
Employment Practices (claims made)	CNA	2,000,000	100,000	CM	246 Employees	35,000
Ocean Marine	Federal	20,000,000	100,000		Transported Revenue	150,000
Domestic Transportation	Affiliated	1,000,000	100,000		Shipped Value	27,500
Environmental Impairment Liability		None				
Non-Owned Aircraft/Aviation	USAIG	5,000,000	10,000		1 Unit	6,890

* CM – Denotes policies written on a claims-made basis, otherwise coverage on an occurrence basis.
** A $50,000 corridor deductible applies before Umbrella attaches.

TABLE 6.3

In addition to evaluating the current insurance program, it is also necessary to evaluate any historical changes that modified the company's retained exposure. Companies that are currently insured may have self-insured liabilities from prior years. Many companies modify their program as the commercial insurance underwriting cycle changes. During the soft market, risk managers typically purchase additional guaranteed cost insurance to take advantage of the low premiums. In the hard market, insurance companies have limited capacity, insurance coverage may not be available, and premiums are significantly higher. Risk managers typically avoid high-risk transfer costs during the hard insurance market cycle by retaining additional exposure.

Additionally, companies may have purchased long-tailed coverage from insurers that are no longer solvent. Protection from state guarantee funds may be limited or, in the case of surplus lines companies, non-existent.

Finally, in the phase two due diligence, a thorough review of all property casualty insurance policies should be performed. For smaller companies the policies are usually written on standard industry forms. Therefore, particular attention is given to the policy endorsements that may include retrospective premium adjustment provisions, contain exclusions, or otherwise limit coverage. The larger companies may have manuscript insurance policies containing specific provisions and exclusions required by the underwriters. Therefore, a detailed review of the insured exposure, limitations and exclusions contained in the policy is essential to evaluate the insurance coverage provided. The information obtained from the policy review will be needed by the integration team to place the insurance coverage prior to the close.

6.3.3 INSURED EXPOSURE

Small corporations primarily transfer their risk by purchasing guaranteed cost insurance products. These businesses are too small to absorb the variability in earnings that results from the random nature of property casualty losses. When the insurance markets turn hard, these companies must either absorb the increase in premium or reduce coverage. The most significant risk for small corporations relates to how management responds to the changing costs of insurance. In an effort to meet expense budgets, company management may reduce policy limits or decide not to purchase certain insurance protection. Uninsured and under-insured exposure creates significant risk for the investor, especially since many casualty claims are not reported and paid until many years after they have occurred.

During due diligence, the uninsured and underinsured exposure is identified by evaluating changes in the insurance program, reviewing the most recent renewal proposal, reviewing the policies, or performing an independent risk assessment. Since many smaller firms rely on their insurance broker to perform a business risk assessment and recommend the appropriate coverage, the renewal proposal is an excellent source to identify uninsured and underinsured exposure. The insurance broker has a professional obligation and economic incentive to recommend insurance coverage for all insurable risk.

There are no hard and fast rules to evaluate whether the policy limits will adequately protect the firm from all claims. Benchmarking studies, such as those published by Risk Insurance Management Society (RIMS) Benchmark Surveys, are sometimes used to compare the seller's policy limits to other companies in the same industry. Loss distributions may also be used to evaluate the probability of a claim exceeding the limits of protection purchased. The actuary must also consider other loss control techniques used by the target when evaluating the prospective emergence of uninsured losses. A reserve estimate is calculated for all uninsured and underinsured exposure, and any unfunded liabilities represent a balance sheet adjustment. The additional cost to fully insure the risk may also be included as a quality of earnings adjustment.

The risk from the changing underwriting cycle and changing premiums due to the company's recent loss experience must also be considered. Major catastrophes create abrupt changes in the insurance markets. For example, premium increases ranging from 30% to 60% for workers' compensation and property insurance were not uncommon following the incidents of September 11, 2001. Significant premium increases also occur when new types of loss emerge or a company has had poor claim experience. Adjustments to experience modifications and audit premiums should also be considered when assessing the future insurance expense. For some acquisitions, even the largest premium change will not exceed the materiality threshold, but for others the insurance premium represents a significant portion of the operating expenses, and changes may be sufficient to warrant a quality of earnings adjustment.

For some acquisitions, synergies result when the insurance program is integrated into a larger portfolio. The combined risk portfolio may allow the investor to self-insure a portion of its exposure, reducing the risk transfer costs. However, some of the value may diminish if the investor requires higher limits of liability due to the size of the combined entity.

6.3.4 SELF-INSURED EXPOSURE

To reduce the costs associated with transferring risk through insurance products, risk managers of larger companies often retain a portion of their exposure, thereby assuming responsibility for paying a portion of losses. For most companies, the retained exposure is the first layer of coverage that can be reasonably predicted. The most common retention amounts for the primary layer are $50,000, $100,000, $250,000, and $500,000 per occurrence. Lower amounts are sometimes available for smaller companies. Corporations that have the ability to retain more than $500,000 per claim typically consider other risk-financing arrangements, such as captive insurers or acting as a true self-insured.

Retaining the first layers of insurance is typically accomplished by purchasing insurance policies with large deductibles or by endorsing the insurance policy to include a retrospective premium adjustment provision. Some companies also retain a corridor deductible in the excess layer. A corridor deductible requires the company to retain a layer of losses above the primary policy limits, before the excess insurance coverage pays or "attaches."

6.3.4.1 Large Deductibles

For large deductible policies, an insurance company insures the exposure, but the insured is responsible for all losses under the selected deductible limit. The insurance company or a third-party claims administrator typically provides loss settlement services for all claims and seeks reimbursement for claim payments below the deductible. To facilitate reimbursement, a pre-funded loss account is sometimes established, allowing the claims administrator to withdraw funds as claim payments are made. The LAE paid to claim administrators may be a flat annual fee or vary based on the number of claims or amount of losses paid. The flat fee may be paid in advance to cover all settlement services until claims are closed, or it may be paid each year for the services rendered. Variable fees are paid concurrently with claims payments.

The cost to settle the remaining claims may materially increase the required reserves and is often an unrecorded liability. It is common for claims administrators to collect fees concurrently with claim payments as a multiple of the paid losses, usually between 107% and 112%. This multiple is referred to as the loss conversion factor. When the insurance company is providing the loss adjustment services, a portion of the cost for the excess insurance coverage may also be included in the loss conversion factor, resulting in multiples as high as 118%.

Corporations using large deductible insurance products are required to accrue a liability for the unpaid loss and LAE. The required accrual is the best estimate of the ultimate loss and LAE payments less any payments made to date. The payments made to date may not necessarily be the actual claim payments made to date but the amount the insured has paid to date. There is often a reporting lag between the times the administrator pays the claims and the company reimburses the administrator; the latter payments should be considered in lieu of the paid losses in the loss experience reports. Payments made by the company include all deposits into the pre-funded loss account, unless the company has recorded these deposits as an asset on its balance sheet.

Under US GAAP, companies should record the estimated value of all unpaid losses as a liability and record a receivable asset for the anticipated insurance recoveries. In practice, property casualty liabilities are not always recorded in this manner. Many companies establish a liability only for the unpaid losses net of insurance. Companies are permitted to discount self-insured property casualty loss reserves as long as it can be shown that the payment pattern is reasonably stable and predictable. For PGAAP accounting, the fair value of these liabilities is used, representing an amount that an independent objective market participant would pay in a cash exchange. For tax purposes, only the actual loss payments may be deducted as an expense; loss reserves affect GAAP earnings but are not used to determine taxable earnings.

Many companies with self-insured exposure do not discount loss reserves for the time-value of money. The difference between the discounted loss reserves and the nominal value may represent a value driver for the investor. However, as discussed below, the required provision for risk may offset the investment income that would be earned before losses are paid. Furthermore, it should be recognized that many companies that do not explicitly discount the loss reserve do so by recording a reserve below the expected value.

6.3.4.2 *Retrospective Premium Policies*

For policies with a retrospective premium adjustment provision, the insured pays a deposit premium at inception. For a set period after policy inception (typically 18 months) and every year thereafter, the insurer evaluates the loss experience and uses a predefined formula to recalculate the retrospective premium. The formula terms are established in the policy, differ for each insured, and may change each policy period. Basically, the retrospective premium is equal to the sum of the limited losses, a provision for expenses, loss settlement services, an insurance charge, and premium tax. Sometimes the formula includes maximum and minimum premium provisions. Paid or incurred losses may be used in the retro formula, and losses entering the formula may be limited by the insured's selected retention. The insurer continues to recalculate the premiums until all losses are closed or both parties agree to a final settlement.

Corporations using insurance products with retrospective premium adjustment features are required to accrue a liability for the unpaid retrospective premium. To estimate the required accrual, the best estimate of the ultimate losses is used in the retro formula to determine the ultimate premium. The ultimate premium is reduced by premiums paid to date to determine the required accrual. For PGAAP, the fair value of these liabilities is recorded. For tax purposes, only the paid premiums may be deducted as an expense, not the accrual for unpaid retrospective premium adjustments.

6.3.4.3 *Due Diligence Issues for Self-Insured Exposure*

The actuary needs to develop an estimate of the ultimate retained losses in order to evaluate the economic value of the required reserve. Loss development methods described in Chapter 4 are typically used to project the ultimate losses. However, for many self-insured companies the loss histories are not available or sufficiently credible to determine company-specific loss development factors. Changes in retention levels or claim administrators may significantly distort the company's loss development patterns. As a result, the actuary must complement the company-specific data with industry benchmark factors to estimate the required reserves.

Benchmark factors are available from a number of public sources, including the Insurance Services Office (ISO), the National Council on Compensation Insurance (NCCI), Reinsurance Association of America (RAA), and from A.M. Best, which publishes statistics from insurance company financial statements. However, most of these sources do not maintain loss development patterns at the various retention levels used by self-insureds and as a result must be adjusted in order to reflect the target's specific program.

Many times the due diligence report includes findings that the loss development factors being used by the self-insured to estimate its required reserves are not reasonable based on the target's exposure. When selecting development factors, the actuary should consider the company's exposure, the retention levels, and the reserving and settlement practices used by the claims administrator.

For corporate due diligence the actuary should evaluate the economic value of the property casualty reserve and the best estimate of the reserve required for financial reporting purposes. These two estimates are rarely the same. As discussed in Chapter 5, the Casualty Actuarial

Principles suggest that the most appropriate reserve depends on the financial context for which the estimate is being calculated and that the reserve estimate may include a provision for uncertainty. For the investor acquiring the liabilities, the economic value of the reserves must include a provision for risk inherent in the estimate. For GAAP accounting, a provision for risk is not recorded. Differences in these two reserve estimates create an adjustment to the economic value of the firm, which is usually reflected as a balance sheet adjustment and may result in a quality of earnings adjustment.

The provision for risk is sometimes reflected by using a risk-adjusted discount rate to evaluate the economic value of loss reserves. Under GAAP, loss reserves may be discounted if the payment patterns are reasonably stable and predictable. When the risk-adjusted discount rate is near zero, the undiscounted loss reserves may represent the economic value to the buyer. Most times, the provision for risk is based on the investor's judgment or the price the market would charge for a loss portfolio transfer.

CRYPT 6.3

Let's Get Real

Target had retained the first $500,000 of its product liability exposure for each of the past three years. To date, it had no paid losses and had only one reported incident. No reserve had been established for the incident because the company believed the injury was the result of product misuse, not a product defect. Target argued that no reserve was required because an estimate could not be reasonably determined based on experience.

Investor's actuary estimated the economic value of all unpaid losses, including IBNR. The actuary noted that there was a reasonable expectation of a claim based on the claim history prior to the self-insured experience period, thus requiring a reserve to be established. The actuary determined the expected annual losses from industry loss costs and the company's exposure, producing an expected loss of $290,000. Using the estimated expected loss and applying benchmark development patterns, Investor's actuary calculated $675,000 to be the required reserve for the three years of exposure.

Investor noted that the type of products produced by Target do not give rise to losses until they begin to wear. Due to the type of exposure and claim history, Investor thought the actuary's estimate of $675,000 was not adequate to cover the $1,500,000 for three years of self-insured exposure, even considering the investment income that would be earned before claims are paid. Investor judgmentally added a $75,000 provision to adjust for risk and adjusted the book value of the firm by $750,000 before applying market multiples.

The difference in the accrued liability for each of the past three years also created a quality of earnings adjustment. To determine the appropriate quality of earnings adjustment, Investor considered the $290,000 expected annual loss that was developed for the reserve estimate and the annual premium for a guaranteed cost insurance policy of $350,000. Based on this range of estimates, Investor selected a quality of earnings adjustment of $300,000 before applying the market multiples.

There are several ways to resolve differences in unpaid liability estimates. Many times the difference is only one of many potential purchase price adjustments that are negotiated. Indemnification agreements or true-up provisions are sometimes included in the purchase agreement. When commercial markets exist, the tail (longer-term) liabilities are sometimes sold to third parties.

In evaluating the quality of earnings adjustments, the actuary should also consider the investor's willingness to absorb fluctuations in earnings resulting from retained exposure. The actuary's assessment of the variability of losses and investor's risk utility function will be used to determine the retention limit after the acquisition. Strategic buyers may be able to absorb a high retention, while financial buyers that are more concerned with stability of earnings may desire lower retention levels. If additional insurance is required after the acquisition, the net cost to transfer the risk should be considered as a quality of earnings adjustment.

Security requirements may also be an important consideration for the investor. Insurance companies that issue large deductible and retrospective premium policies assume the credit risk relating to the insured's ability to meet their obligations. To eliminate this risk, many insurers require security in the form of a surety bond or a letter of credit. The amount and terms of the security requirements for all prior policies should be identified for the investor during due diligence. The cost and amount of the security requirements may significantly change after the acquisition. This is especially true when an investor is purchasing a division within a conglomerate and the investor poses a greater credit risk than the conglomerate. These requirements may place additional capital strain on the investor.

6.3.5 CAPTIVE INSURANCE PROGRAMS

A captive insurance company is a wholly owned subsidiary of a corporation that has been established for the primary purpose of financing the company's insurable risk. The captive must maintain the capital requirements and abide by other regulations established by the insurance department in the state or country of domicile. The primary advantages for establishing a captive insurer are:

- Favorable tax treatment of the premiums (if certain conditions are met)
- Ability to create unique insurance coverage forms, and
- Access to the commercial reinsurance markets for difficult-to-place coverage.

Many offshore captive insurers are domiciled in Bermuda and the Grand Cayman Islands due to the favorable insurance regulations and tax treatment. Vermont and South Carolina are popular states to establish captive insurers for similar reasons.

The role a captive insurer plays in the property casualty risk management program is as unique and creative as those designing the program. Most captives only insure the exposure from its parent and other affiliated companies. However, some captives also assume some third-party exposure or may be used by smaller companies to administer reciprocal agreements, in essence sharing unaffiliated exposure among similar types of companies. The corporate risk manager and chief financial officer are usually the executives of the captive insurer or members of the board of directors. Therefore, the parent corporation controls all financial decisions for the captive. The corporate risk manager also decides which risks the captive insurer will insure. The risk not insured by the captive may be retained at the corporate level or placed in the commercial reinsurance market.

Access to the reinsurance and surplus line markets is one of the key advantages for establishing a captive. Large corporations may have billions of dollars of property, liability, and time loss exposure. Primary insurance markets do not have the capacity to underwrite potential losses of this magnitude. Due diligence of the target's captive should include an assessment of the reinsurers and Lloyd's syndicates to validate that they are still financially sound because reinsurers and syndicates may become insolvent or unable to meet their full obligations for insured losses.

The administration of the risk management program for firms with a captive insurer is similar to that when the company acts as a self-insured. The primary difference is the premiums for the insured risks are sent to the captive insurance company, which then acts as a clearinghouse for claims and other insurance-related expenses. Most corporations use third-party captive managers to perform administrative and accounting duties.

6.3.5.1 Coverage Gaps

Identifying coverage gaps is extremely challenging in the short amount of time provided for the due diligence. One of the more difficult aspects of due diligence for large corporations is identifying all of the self-insured exposure for which an accrual is required to be established. The risk management program and financial accounts relating to risk exposure differ by company and may differ further for different divisions within a company. In addition, some companies may have multiple captive insurers and/or use multiple types of policies to manage the various property casualty risks. Further complicating matters, operations or divisions within a company may have been bought and sold with or without their retained self-insured losses. Certain exposure may be retained because the cost to transfer the risk is prohibitive, the risk is not understood, or the company does not have a risk manager responsible to assess and mitigate the exposure.

The first step of the due diligence is to take inventory of all applicable exposure to identify risk retention limits and excess policy limits. The risk and exposure covered by the standard insurance products in Table 6.3 form a basis for the inventory. This list is supplemented with any unique exposures for the target company. The purpose of the inventory is to identify how the loss experience flows through the financial statements, determine how the accrual for the unpaid exposure is established, and document where the liabilities are being recorded. Audit workpapers are a valuable resource to identify the accounting used for certain segments of exposure.

For companies using a captive, the inventory must specifically identify the terms and conditions of the policies issued by the captive insurer. A comprehensive inventory will ensure that the coverage provided by the captive complements the exposure retained at the corporate level and division level. Because the corporate risk manager creates these contracts, they may contain unique provisions to accomplish certain business objectives. The due diligence should identify any gaps in the captive insurance program to ensure they are properly accounted for at the corporate or operating division level.

A review of all financial accounts relating to the property casualty exposure is performed to validate the inventory of exposure and insurance. For smaller companies, reviewing loss reports produced by the claims administrator and reconciling these amounts to the paid loss accounts will validate the self-insured exposure. However, for large corporations, the reconciliation of the accounts may be significantly more complex due to the structure of the company and the design of the risk management program. The most common source of unfunded liabilities results from gaps in coverage among the parent, its subsidiaries, and a captive insurer. However, the threshold for materiality for large transactions is usually much higher than unfunded liability and only a cursory review of some accounts may be necessary due to the limited risk inherent in the exposure. Thus, the primary goal is to identify the high-risk exposures that require a significant accrual or that have the potential to create significant distortions to earnings.

Large corporations also have in-house counsel or staff within the risk management department that handle claim activities for certain exposures. These earmarked claims are sometimes those that pose the greatest risk to the company. These claims are difficult to find in the financial statements because they are sometimes expensed through miscellaneous accounts. The best approach is to interview the risk manager and question the treatment of special exposures. Many times the claim database maintained by the target company will not include point-in-time data needed to evaluate loss development patterns. Special actuarial techniques may be required to properly account for this exposure.

Large corporations also acquire and divest operating divisions more often than smaller companies. Understanding the terms of these transactions and evaluating which entity is responsible for the incurred losses prior and subsequent to the transaction is essential. The acquisition of a company with no indemnification for prior incurred losses may add significant liabilities to the balance sheet and reduce future earnings. Similarly, the divestiture of a division may not eliminate the parent company's liabilities if the purchase agreement included an indemnification provision. Furthermore, the divestiture of a subsidiary company may not insulate a self-insured parent company from future liabilities if the divested company becomes insolvent. Therefore, any recent divestitures of operating divisions with mass tort exposure should be considered a material risk factor.

Any unpaid loss exposure that has not been properly accrued will create balance sheet adjustments. Uninsured liabilities may also create quality of earnings adjustments when the annual payments charged to earnings are significantly different from the expected annual losses that should be accrued each year.

6.3.5.2 Captive Premiums

The corporate risk manager or officer in charge of managing the captive typically determines the premium paid to a captive insurer. Any differences between the premium paid to the captive and the actuarially calculated required premium may distort earnings. The required premiums usually include the present value of the expected losses incurred during the year, anticipated LAE, captive administrative expenses, and any additional costs for reinsurance. However, other business considerations may influence the actual premiums paid to the captive. For example, a provision may be included in the premium to strengthen loss reserves or increase the captive's capital. The excess premiums will lower the consolidated corporate earnings when they are retained in the captive's loss reserves. Likewise, if the premiums paid to the captive are less than those required, the reverse is also true.

Evaluating the appropriateness of the captive premiums becomes more important in a carve-out, when the entity being acquired is only one of the various operating divisions that the captive insures. Due diligence should be performed to validate the reasonableness of the total premium as well as the process used to allocate the premiums to the operating units. For some large corporations the captive premiums are allocated to the operating units using revenue or some other basis that may have little relationship to the actual loss experience for that division. Whether the acquired entity will become a stand-alone operation or be integrated into another conglomerate, the cost of the insurance program on a run-rate basis may be significantly different than the premiums paid to the captive insurer.

6.3.5.3 Valuation Issues

The valuation of a captive insurer presents many of the same challenges faced when valuing property casualty insurance companies. The general valuation principles and techniques for property casualty insurance companies will still apply. However, in practice, since a captive insurer is simply a risk-financing mechanism and not usually considered a profit center, a number of simplifying assumptions are usually made. The actuary should use the same framework and formulas advanced in Chapter 4 to estimate the economic value of the captive, with adjustments for synergies, embedded options, and integration costs as discussed in Chapter 5.

While the valuation framework allows the actuary to develop an estimate of the economic value and think through the risks and value added through the captive, for many corporate acquisitions, simplifying assumptions are made by the investor that eliminate the need to perform a detailed valuation. A captive insurer is usually established by large corporations to better manage its property casualty risk and exposure, to provide the corporate risk manager additional markets for excess insurance, and to accelerate the tax deduction for financing the losses. The use of a captive insurer will create few synergies for non-insurance entities, and only in rare instances will there be embedded options that will add value for the investor. Integration costs are usually below the materiality threshold for most corporations that use third-party claim administrators and captive managers to administer the program.

The economic value of a property casualty insurance company is based on economic adjustments to net worth, plus the present value of expected future earnings, less the cost of capital.

In determining the economic value for a captive insurer, it is generally assumed that there will be no material earnings from future premium. Insurance premiums paid by the captive each year are established by the corporate risk manager such that the premiums and the investment income credited to the captive are sufficient to pay future loss obligations. The exception is when the captive needs to increase capital in future years to meet minimum regulatory capital requirements, and the planned additions to capital are funded through captive earnings. Typically, the parent company will capitalize the captive with a surplus note, and the costs associated with the note may be included in the valuation of the parent corporation. Under these simplifying assumptions, the primary focus in assessing the value of the captive boils down to determining the adjusted net worth resulting from differences between the recorded reserves and the fair value of these liabilities.

To determine the fair value of the loss reserves, the standard actuarial techniques discussed in Chapter 4 are used to develop the best estimate. These reserves are loaded for the market value of risk and discounted for the time value of money at market rates of return.

Assessing the appropriate provision for risk requires a more detailed understanding of the parent corporation's underlying risk and the historical changes to the insurance program. For an insurance company, the diversity in the insured exposure, the stability in the claim handling process, and greater control over the reinsurance program reduce the variability in the net loss reserve estimates. A captive insurer typically has only one insured. The absence of a spread of risk implies that insured events may not be independent. In addition, the parent corporation (the insured) may have significant control over the claim process, increasing the parameter risk.

To assess this risk, the actuary needs to obtain a clear understanding of the historical changes in the insured program and claims administration. Changes in insured exposure, coverage terms and conditions, deductibles, retention limits, and third-party claim administrators will have a material effect on loss development patterns. When evaluating the loss development histories, the actuary should investigate any unusual changes in loss development patterns or recent unexpected development in mature accident years to gain a better understanding of the potential future development. A recent spike in liability or workers' compensation claims may indicate the emergence of a new type of exposure that may impact the future development on all prior accident years. The actuary should investigate the cause of loss for all large claims or a surge in the claim frequency.

The recorded value of the loss reserves for a captive insurer may be a discounted estimate of the indicated reserves. In practice, the discount rate is usually based on the company's invested assets, on an internal rate of return, or selected to match its SFAS 106 calculation, without a provision for adverse deviation. US GAAP accounting guidance suggests that a duration-matched, risk-free rate of return, is the appropriate discount rate, but the fair value of liabilities from an investor's perspective should include a provision for risk. Methods discussed in Chapter 4 can be used to quantify the risk provision objectively. However, for some corporate acquisitions, the provision for risk is negotiated as the difference between the captive's recorded loss reserves and a more conservative estimate produced by the investor's actuary. When differences in opinions cannot be resolved, a provision is sometimes included in the purchase agreement to hold some loss reserves in escrow, to be released pending a later re-valuation of the unpaid losses.

6.3.5.4 *Creative Contracts Issued by the Captive*

One of the more interesting aspects of the captive due diligence is reviewing the unusual contracts that are sometimes created to achieve the parent company's specific business objectives. The company's risk manager and chief financial officer create the insurance contracts between the captive insurer and its parent. The business objectives for these contracts are as varied as the financial issues facing the organization, and the insured exposure may be as creative as the executives who craft the contracts. Therefore, a detailed review of the insured exposure is an essential aspect of the due diligence.

The business objective for these contracts may be to change the amount or timing of the cost required to finance self-insured exposure. However, in some instances the business objective extends beyond risk financing. For example, the business objective may be to take advantage of tax preferences offered to offshore captive insurers or to manage expenses at a division level. An example of a contract that has been used to reshape the profile at the division level is a business interruption policy that includes provisions to reimburse any of the company's operating divisions for lost earnings caused by specified insured events. At the corporate level, these policies may have no significant impact on earnings. However, at the operating division level, claim payments for this coverage may significantly impact earnings.

Unusual contract provisions usually have one or more of three elements that will allow the actuary to identify their existence. The first is premiums that are not proportional to the exposure. When this exists, there may be a distortion in earnings between years or between divisions. The second is a significantly large first party claim payment. As noted above, the cause of loss should be investigated for all large claims. The third is special policy endorsements. This may indicate that the cause of loss is not one that is typically insured by the regular or surplus lines markets. These contracts should be reviewed closely to ensure that they meet the risk transfer requirements of SFAS 113 (Accounting and Reporting for Reinsurance of Short-Duration and Long-Duration Contracts), and the insured event should be assessed as to whether the surplus lines markets would assume this risk.

6.4 OTHER P&C RISK MANAGEMENT ISSUES

Property casualty actuaries add significant value to a corporate due diligence beyond providing the loss reserve analysis of self-insured exposure and the actuarial valuation of captive insurers. The actuary's risk management skills are valuable in identifying other areas of concern for the investor that may not be insurable. For example, the insurance products may include significant business interruption coverage for loss of use of a property or piece of equipment related to an insured event. However, if the company is dependent upon a single supplier, distribution channel, or a piece of equipment, there may be uninsurable risk of lost earnings. The actuary or other risk management specialist should evaluate both the insurable risk and uninsurable risk in his or her diligence report.

There are other areas where a property casualty actuary should assist with the corporate due diligence relating to risk and insurance. A short description is included in the following sections.

6.4.1 CARVE-OUTS

Large corporations may divest operating divisions that no longer fit their business model. During the sell-side due diligence, pro forma financial statements are produced for investors to evaluate during the bid process. The cost for the risk and insurance typically incorporated in the pro forma financial statements is usually an allocation of the overall cost for the corporate risk and insurance program. When the actuary is involved on the sell-side due diligence, the actuary can assist in preparing the pro forma financial statements by ensuring that the costs associated with insurance policies are allocated based on the appropriate exposure base. The provisions for the risk and insurance expenses in a pro forma financial statement should represent the estimated cost to adequately insure the division on a stand-alone basis. Therefore, the actuary should consider any adjustments in the coverage required for the smaller company. The actuary should also evaluate the division's actual self-insured loss experience and make it available for review.

When the actuary is performing the buy-side due diligence for a carve-out of a large corporation, the actuary evaluates the estimated cost for the risk and insurance program for reasonableness. In doing so, the actuary needs to consider the financial structure of the company after it is acquired by the investor when evaluating the risk management program. Changes in the program design, the self-insured retention, claims administration, and excess policy limits that were previously in force may no longer be appropriate. As a stand-alone company, it may no longer be feasible to self-insure a significant amount of the exposure and, therefore, the pro forma allocations are replaced by the estimated cost for the appropriate risk program. When the investor is another large corporation that anticipates integrating the acquired company into its own operations, the costs in the pro forma statements are compared to the marginal costs to include the additional exposure from the acquisition into its own insurance programs. These costs include an estimate of the expected losses at the investor's self-insured retention.

The issues and procedures to assess the balance sheet liabilities are consistent with those discussed previously. However, in practice, the company divesting its operation will usually decide to retain the prior liabilities, which maximizes the cash flow to the seller and allows the seller to eliminate any risk charge that an investor would require to assume these liabilities. When the prior liabilities are included in the acquisition, there will typically be a difference in opinion in the proper estimate of these unpaid losses due to the risk charge required by the buyer that is not included in the selling company's estimates. The buyer's position is best supported with a market analysis of the prices required for a loss portfolio transfer.

6.4.2 SURETY BONDS AND LETTERS OF CREDIT

Technically, there is a difference between being self-insured and having self-insured exposure. A self-insured retains the risk and purchases excess reinsurance. If the company does not survive, any unpaid claims are included in the bankruptcy proceedings. Some states have regulations that require self-insureds to post security to ensure that the self-insured will meet its obligations. This security is usually in the form of cash, a surety bond, or a letter of credit.

Other companies in effect self-insure a portion of their exposure through large deductible policies or insurance policies with a retrospective premium adjustment provision. In the latter case, if the corporation is unable to meet its obligations, the insurance company issuing the retro policy is required to pay these losses. In order to eliminate the credit risk, insurance companies usually have security requirements in the form of cash deposits, a pre-funded loss account, a surety bond, or an irrevocable letter of credit. Replacing or funding these security instruments needs to be considered by the investor. Letters of credit will increase the investor's debt ratio. The cost for surety bonds, if available, may be significantly greater than the price paid by the existing entity due to the increased credit risk of the acquiring entity.

6.4.3 PRODUCT WARRANTY/PRODUCT RECALL

During due diligence, the actuary should review the provisions for product warranty claims. Most products being sold today have some protection against defects. For many products, the warranty period is sufficiently short that the costs for warranty claims are paid out of earnings. However, companies should have a balance sheet provision adequate to cover all future warranty claims. The size of this provision may be material when the products are subject to wear and sold with a relatively long warranty period. The principles for assessing the adequacy of the warranty provision are similar to those for evaluating self-insured loss reserves. During due diligence, the actuary also reviews the recent warranty claim experience to identify new types of claims that may not be adequately represented in the historical results or that may indicate a product defect.

The actuary should assess the risk and protection for product recall. Insurance coverage may be available to protect against the cost associated with a product recall. However, insurance policies may not protect against lost earnings resulting from the reduction in market share that typically follows a high-profile product recall.

6.4.4 CLAIMS-MADE POLICIES

For certain exposure, such as product liability, professional liability, errors and omissions, and director's and officer's liability, the exposure to loss and the claim reporting period spans many years. Insurance companies mitigate their exposure to long-tail risks by issuing claims-made insurance policies. Claims-made insurance policies only cover claims made during the policy period. Companies that use claims-made insurance policies should record a provision for the tail liabilities. In practice, only hospitals, medical professional organizations, and a few other businesses that commonly use claims-made policies maintain a provision for the tail liabilities. Sometimes, captive insurers issue claims-made policies that are not typically found in the insurance market. When this is done the insured affiliates should accrue the liability for the tail liabilities. When the frequency of claims for the exposure is low, many corporations that have claims-made insurance coverage do not record a provision for the tail liabilities.

When an investor buys a corporation that is covered by a claims-made insurance policy, the purchase agreement should include an indemnification clause for the tail liability, or the purchase price should include compensation for claims that were incurred prior to the purchase date but reported subsequent to the transaction. The amount of the purchase price adjustment should be equivalent to the cost to purchase a policy for tail coverage. Depending on the type coverage, a policy covering a six-year tail reporting period usually costs 1.5 to 3.5 times the annual premium for a mature claims-made policy.

6.4.5 MASS TORT/LATENT INJURY/ASBESTOS AND ENVIRONMENTAL

Some property casualty risks are so significant they have the ability to deplete the strongest corporation's net worth. Many of these same exposures have also cost the insurance industry so much capital that insurers are no longer willing to provide coverage for this risk at any price. Asbestos and environmental liability exposures are the well-known examples, but there are a number of other mass tort and latent injury exposures. A sick building or a risk that exposes an entire workforce may devastate even a company that has a relatively low retention on a per occurrence basis. Similarly, products that expose consumers to risk over a number of years may destroy a company with a relatively low annual aggregate retention.

The two characteristics that create this risk involve mass tort and latent injury claims. Mass tort exposure relates to risks that have the ability to result in multiple claimants but be sufficiently independent to be considered multiple occurrences under the company's self-insured retention. Latent injury claims are those that take a number of years to manifest into injury and are usually the result of exposure to the risk during a number of years. The actuary is not responsible for foreseeing new types of future claims. However, during due diligence the actuary should investigate new types of claims that have been recently reported to assess the risk of future claim activity.

When this exposure exists, the actuary should provide an estimate of the expected cost and some measures of the risk of future reported claims. The methods and techniques used by actuaries to quantify these costs are specific to the type of risk and beyond the scope of this book. In many instances the actuary performing due diligence will use actuaries with specific expertise to evaluate this exposure.

6.4.6 STRUCTURING THE DEAL

During due diligence the number and variety of issues that arise resulting from the actuary's efforts are often extensive. Many of these issues will require the assistance from one of the many interdisciplinary members of the due diligence team. During due diligence, the actuary maintains constant communications with the other team members in an effort to identify, evaluate, and resolve any issues that may be impediments to a successful transaction.

The property casualty actuary may play an important role in developing the structure of the deal or the final terms of the purchase agreement. When there are differences of opinion relating to the outstanding liabilities for self-insured exposure, the actuary may take an active role in developing the data necessary for selling these liabilities to insurers and reinsurers. The actuary's knowledge of the exposure and negotiation skills are valuable assets when liquidating these liabilities. Alternatively, the actuary may assist in developing the terms of a "true-up" provision, whereby the differences of opinion are resolved by a revaluation of the liabilities at a later date. The actuary will be able to determine amounts to be held in trust and the timing of the revaluation. Finally, when the liabilities are to be retained by the seller, the actuary should review the terms in the purchase agreement to ensure that the intentions are fulfilled. Many times, the lawyers writing these agreements may not have an extensive understanding of insurance.

CRYPT 6.4

Watch Your Language

In a carve-out acquisition of a division of the ABC corporation, ABC agreed to provide the buyer with indemnification for all claims incurred prior to the closing date. However, the language in the purchase agreement provided reimbursement for all claims reported prior to the closing date. This "slight" difference resulted in a purchase price adjustment of $4.3 million estimated post sale IBNR claims.

After discussing this issue in more detail with its advisors, the buyer demanded indemnification for future claims relating to products sold prior to the closing date. Based on the actuary's forecasts, the indemnification for this additional exposure was re-negotiated and settled with an additional $1.2 million purchase price adjustment. The actuary's review of the purchase agreement netted the buyer a total purchase price adjustment of $5.5 million.

Chapter Seven

Taxation

7.1 OVERVIEW

This chapter focuses on the tax aspects of mergers and acquisitions, in particular those involving insurance companies. Several significant federal income tax issues arise in connection with M&A transactions involving insurance companies.

In order to appreciate how tax issues can affect acquisitions, it is important for members of a transaction team to have at least a general understanding of certain unique aspects of the taxation of both life insurance and non-life insurance companies, including the unique consolidated federal income tax return rules applicable to life insurance companies.

Moreover, both sellers and buyers will need to understand the impact of taxes on various structuring decisions. For example, the seller may desire to structure a transaction as a tax-free reorganization, thus deferring the recognition of gain or loss with respect to the disposition of its property. The buyer, on the other hand, must understand how the tax-free reorganization rules can have an effect on its after-tax cost of acquiring the target insurance company or its business.

A tax-free structure may not, however, be feasible or desirable for either business or tax-planning reasons, thus necessitating a taxable form of transaction. In some circumstances a taxable stock sale may be more economically beneficial for the seller on an after-tax basis, while in other circumstances an asset sale will be more beneficial.

From the buyer's perspective, a taxable asset purchase will often be the most tax-efficient form of transaction because the buyer may be able to "step up" (i.e., increase) the basis of depreciable or amortizable assets to current values and take corresponding deductions, which will have the effect of reducing the after-tax cost of the acquisition. When the parties' business goals necessitate the sale of a company in a stock transaction, the tax law does allow certain elections to treat the stock purchase as an asset purchase for federal income tax purposes.

When acquiring the stock of an insurance company, the buyer must also have an understanding of certain post-acquisition tax issues. For example, if the target has net operating losses, the buyer must understand the extent to which those losses will be usable in the future. Finally, the buyer must use the due diligence process to obtain an understanding of the pre-acquisition tax history of the target and how that history can affect future values.

7.2 TAXATION OF INSURANCE COMPANIES—IN GENERAL

Insurance companies are subject to tax under specialized rules contained in Subchapter L of Chapter 1 of the Internal Revenue Code of 1986, as amended (Code). A business enterprise will be subject to tax as an insurance company only if more than half of its business during the taxable year is issuing insurance or annuity contracts or engaging in reinsurance of risks written by insurance companies. If an enterprise is organized under local insurance laws or possesses one or more insurance licenses, but it does not meet the "more than half the business" test, it will not be treated as an insurance company for federal income tax purposes.[1]

[1] See Code §§816(a) (which applies to life insurance companies for taxable years beginning after 1983) and 831(c) (which applies to insurance companies other than life insurance companies for taxable years beginning after 2003). Under prior law, an entity would be treated as an insurance company if its "primary and predominant" activity had been issuing or reinsuring insurance contracts. See Treas. Reg. §1.801-3(a)(1). See also *Interamerican Life Insurance Company v. Commissioner*, 56 T.C. 497 (1971), *aff'd*, 469 F.2d 697 (9th Cir. 1971). Code §7701(a)(3) provides that the term "corporation" includes "associations, joint-stock companies and insurance companies." See also Treas. Reg. §301.7701-2(b) (which provides that "for federal tax purposes" the term "corporation" includes insurance companies). Accordingly, any entity that is engaged in the insurance business and meets the "more than half the business" test will be treated as corporation that is an insurance company for all purposes under the Code. See Revenue Ruling 83-132, 1983-2 C.B. 270 (a non-corporate entity that is primarily engaged in issuing insurance contracts is an insurance company for federal income tax purposes even if it was not organized as such under local law).

The Code provides two sets of provisions for insurance company taxation: one for life insurance companies and another for insurers that do not qualify as life insurance companies. An insurance company will be treated as a life insurance company for federal income tax purposes if its reserves with respect to life insurance, annuity, and non-cancellable accident and health insurance contracts, and its unearned premiums and unpaid losses with respect to non-cancellable accident and health contracts that are not included in life insurance reserves, exceed 50% of its total reserves.[2]

Life insurance companies are taxed under the provisions of Part I of Subchapter L (Code Sections 801 to 818 and the regulations thereunder). If life insurance reserves do not exceed 50% of the reserves of an insurance company, the company will be taxed as an "insurance company other than a life insurance company" (referred to in this chapter as a "non-life insurance company") under the provisions of Part II of Subchapter L (Code Sections 831 to 835 and the regulations thereunder).[3] The reserve test is applied without regard to an insurer's status for regulatory purposes; thus, an insurance company that is licensed as a life insurance company, but that also writes substantial amounts of health insurance other than non-cancellable accident and health insurance, may be subject to tax as a non-life insurance company.

The taxation of insurance companies is generally based on their role as financial intermediaries (i.e., insurance companies receive premiums and earn investment income), but with the expectation that a major portion of such receipts will be paid out in the form of future benefits. Both life and non-life insurance companies generally base the determination of their taxable income on the items of income and expense reported on the annual statement prescribed by the National Association of Insurance Commissioners (NAIC), to the extent that the Code and the regulations do not provide otherwise.[4]

Life insurance companies are required to include premiums and investment income, as well as decreases in reserves, in "life insurance gross income" for federal income tax purposes, but then are permitted deductions for expenses, plus increases in reserves, in computing "life insurance company taxable income" (LICTI).[5] For this purpose deductible reserves include "life insurance reserves," which include reserves for "future unaccrued claims."[6] The Code also

---

[2] Code §816 defines the term "life insurance company" for federal income tax purposes.

[3] Part III of Subchapter L (Code §§841 to 848) sets out provisions generally applicable to insurance companies. For example, Code §843 requires insurance companies to use the calendar year for tax accounting purposes, subject to certain exceptions for consolidated groups.

[4] See Code §811(a) ("To the extent not inconsistent with [provisions of the Code] all such computations shall be made in a manner consistent with the manner required for purposes of the annual statement approved by the [NAIC]"), and Code §832(b)(1) ("the combined gross amount earned during the taxable year, from investment income and from underwriting income . . . computed on the basis of the underwriting and investment exhibit of the annual statement approved by the [NAIC]"). Treas. Reg. §1.832-4(a)(2) provides that "The underwriting and investment exhibit is presumed to reflect the true net income of the company, and insofar as it is not inconsistent with the provisions of the Code will be recognized and used for that purpose."

[5] Code §801(b).

[6] Under Code §807(c), life insurance companies may deduct increases in "life insurance reserves" as well as certain other reserves. "Life insurance reserves" are defined by Code §816(b) as reserves that are set aside to mature or liquidate, either by payment or reinsurance, future unaccrued claims under life insurance, annuity, and non-cancellable accident and health insurance contracts involving life, accident, or health contingencies, if such reserves are computed or estimated on the basis of recognized mortality or morbidity tables and assumed rates of interest, and are required by law. Other reserves include: unearned premiums and unpaid losses; amounts (discounted at the appropriate rate of interest, but not less than cash surrender values) necessary to satisfy obligations under insurance and annuity contracts, but only if such obligations do not involve (at the time with respect to which the computation is made) life, accident, or health contingencies; dividend accumulations, and other amounts, held at interest in connection with insurance and annuity contracts; premiums received in advance and liabilities for premium deposit funds; and reasonable special contingency reserves under contracts of group term life insurance or group accident and health insurance that are established and maintained for the provision of insurance on retired lives, for premium stabilization, or for a combination thereof.

contains special "proration" rules designed to prevent life insurance companies from obtaining double tax benefits by using tax-advantaged investments to fund life insurance reserves.[7]

For taxable years beginning before December 31, 2004, mutual life insurance companies were also subject to a so-called "add-on tax" or "equity tax," under which deductions for otherwise deductible policyholder dividends were disallowed in part, on the basis that some portion of mutual life insurance company dividends were being paid to policyholders in their capacity as owners of the enterprise, rather than purely as customers. The goal of Code Section 809 was to equalize a perceived competitive advantage for mutual life insurance companies with respect to stock companies. This provision has been controversial since its enactment, and efforts to bring about its repeal have been underway for some years.[8]

For non-life insurance companies, gross income consists of investment income and underwriting income, as well as gains from the sale of property and other items of gross income.[9] Both life and non-life insurance companies are permitted deductions for incurred losses (both reported claims and incurred but not reported (IBNR) claims, based on reasonable estimates of the ultimate liability), plus loss adjustment expenses, reduced by reinsurance recoverables and, when appropriate, by salvage and subrogation recoverables; for non-life insurance companies, incurred losses reduce underwriting income, which, as noted above, is a component of gross income.[10] Unpaid losses of non-life insurance companies are included in losses incurred, but are subject to discounting, using discount factors published by the Internal Revenue Service based on industry-wide loss experience (unless a company elects to use its own experience).[11]

Moreover, deductible losses of non-life insurance companies are subject to reduction when the insurance company receives tax-exempt interest or dividends subject to the dividends received deduction.[12] In addition, both life and non-life insurance companies are allowed deductions for reserves for the portion of premiums that have been received but that have not yet been earned; as is the case with losses incurred, reserves for unearned premiums of a

---

[7] Code §§807(a)(2)(B) and 807(b).

[8] Code §809 was repealed by sec. 205(a) of the Pension Funding Equity Act of 2004, P.L. 108-218. Prior to its repeal, stopgap measures to render Code s809 ineffective had been enacted. For example, Code §809(j) effectively nullified the application of this provision for the 2001, 2002, and 2003 tax years, by treating a key component of the calculation as zero. The legislative history of the Pension Funding Equity Act of 2004 states, however, that S809 is intended to be effective for 2004. See H.R. Conf. Rep. No. 108-457, 108th Cong., 2d Sess., 52 (April 1, 2004).

[9] Under Code §832(a), a non-life insurance company determines its taxable income by deducting allowable amounts from gross income. Code §832(b)(1) provides that gross income includes underwriting income and investment income.

[10] Underwriting income for a non-life insurance company consists of premiums received, less deductions for annual increases in unearned premiums, as well as "losses incurred" and related expenses. Code §832(b)(3). For life insurance companies these items are allowable as deductions from life insurance gross income in the computation of LICTI. Code §805.

[11] See Code §846 and the regulations thereunder. Code §846(e) permits a company to use its own loss payment patterns in certain circumstances. Code §846(f)(6) further provides that unpaid losses under disability insurance business (other than credit disability insurance) are to be discounted by reference to the rules of Code §807(d) applicable to accident and health insurance contracts, subject to certain modifications. Other accident and health insurance business is discounted on the assumption that claims are paid in the middle of the year following the accident year. Code §807(c) applies Code §846 principles to unpaid losses (other than losses under life insurance contracts) of life insurance companies. It should be noted that non-life insurance companies are allowed deductions for estimated loss adjustment expenses, but for life insurance companies such expenses are deductible only to the extent they meet the "all events" test generally applicable to deductions under Code §461. See Staff of the Joint Comm. on Tax., 99th Cong., 2d Sess. General Explanation of the Tax Reform Act of 1986, 614 (Comm. Print 1987).

[12] Losses incurred by non-life insurance companies are subject to reduction for 15% of such items. Code §832(b)(5)(B).

non-life insurance company are reflected in the determination of underwriting income.[13]

Finally, both life insurance and non-life insurance companies are subject to the so-called "DAC tax" (for "deferred acquisition costs") under Code Section 848 (which is discussed in section 7.4.3) to the extent such companies write life insurance, annuity, or non-cancellable accident and health insurance business.

Life and non-life insurance companies are generally subject to tax at rates applicable to corporations, although there are a number of exceptions to the general rule.[14] Code Section 806 provides for a "small life insurance company deduction" equal to 60% of a qualifying life insurance company's "tentative LICTI" up to $3,000,000, subject to a phase-out for tentative LICTI between $3,000,000 and $15,000,000.[15]

There are also special rules for non-life insurance companies. "Small" non-life insurance companies can elect to be taxed on their investment income only if their net written premiums (or direct written premiums, if greater) are not more than $1,200,000.[16]

Code Section 833 provides special rules for Blue Cross/Blue Shield companies and similar organizations, and Code Section 835 provides special rules for non-life insurance companies that are organized as interinsurers or reciprocal underwriters.[17] In many other respects, however, both life and non-life insurance companies are subject to the same tax rules applicable to all other corporate taxpayers.[18]

---

[13] Unearned premiums reflect the fact that premiums are treated as being earned, and thus includible in gross income, ratably over the life of the contract to which the premium relates. For non-life insurance companies, Code §832(b)(4) effectively allows a deduction for 80% of the annual increase in unearned premiums. The 20% that is not deductible (referred to as the "haircut") is intended to reduce the double benefit of allowing a full deduction for expenses incurred in generating the unearned premiums. Note, however, that life insurance reserves of a non-life insurance company are treated as unearned premiums that are not subject to the 20% "haircut." See Code §§832(b)(4) (flush language) and 832(b)(7). For life insurance companies, Code §807(c)(2) generally allows a full deduction for annual increases in unpaid losses and unearned premiums; Code §807(e)(7) applies the "haircut" only to deductions relating to insurance contracts that are not described in §816(b)(1)(B) (i.e., contracts other than life insurance, annuity, and noncancellable accident and health insurance contracts involving life, accident, or health contingencies). See Code §807(e)(7).

[14] Code §§801(a) and 831(a) subject insurance companies to tax based on the rates set out in Code §11, which are: 15% for the first $50,000, 25% for the next $25,000, 34% for the next $9,925,000, and 35% for taxable income above $10,000,000. The benefit of the lower graduated rates is offset by additional taxes at the 38% and 39% rates, so that a corporate taxpayer with taxable income in excess of $18,333,333 is taxed at a flat 35% rate. Life insurance companies are subject to an alternative tax under Code §801(a)(2) in the event such companies have a certain level of capital gains; net capital gains are taxed under Code §1201(a) if the result would be a lower tax liability than under the regular tax.

[15] The small life insurance company deduction is not allowable if a life insurance company has assets of $500,000,000 or more. For purposes of the asset test, all members of a group of controlled corporations, as defined by Code §1563(a), that includes one or more life insurance companies, as well as companies that are not life insurance companies, are treated as a single company. In addition, all life insurance companies that are members of the controlled group are treated as a single life insurance company, and any allowable deduction is allocated based on each company's tentative LICTI. Code §806(c). Tentative LICTI is defined by Code §806(b) as a life insurance company's LICTI without regard to the small life insurance company deduction. Code §806(b)(3)(C) also contains a provision limiting a life insurance company's deductions for losses arising from a non-insurance business.

[16] Code §831(b)(1). Taxable investment income is determined under Code §834. For purposes of this election, premiums are determined on a controlled group basis, but the definition of control is based on greater than 50% ownership, rather than at least 80%. Code §831(b)(2). If a non-life insurance company's net written or direct premiums, if greater, are less than $350,000, the company can qualify as a tax-exempt entity under Code §501(c)(15).

[17] Code §833 provides that Blue Cross/Blue Shield and similar organizations are subject to tax as stock non-life insurance companies, but also provides special rules for such organizations that had been tax-exempt organizations prior to 1987. Code §835 allows a reciprocal to elect to take into account the income and taxes of the attorney-in-fact that manages the reciprocal's business in computing its income. Other provisions of the Code allow special treatment for factory mutual insurance companies (Code §832(b)(1)(D)) and certain perpetual policies (Code §832(b)(1)(C) and (D)). Finally, tax-exempt organizations that offer commercial-type insurance are subject to tax on their insurance income under the "unrelated business income tax" rules (see Code §§501(m) and 513).

[18] See, e.g., Code §§803(a)(3) and 832(c).

Moreover, insurance companies are permitted to carry net operating losses to other taxable years. A non-life insurance company may carry net operating losses back for two years, and forward for 20 years, while a life insurance company may carry its "operations loss deductions" back for three years and forward for 15 years.[19]

7.3 CONSOLIDATED FEDERAL INCOME TAX RETURNS

There are several provisions that limit the consolidation of life insurance companies with other companies (insurance and non-insurance) for federal income tax purposes. From an M&A perspective, significant concerns center on (i) certain time restrictions as to how soon a newly acquired life insurance company can join in the filing of a consolidated federal income tax return and (ii) limitations on the use of losses generated by members of the group that are non-life insurance companies against income generated by life insurance company members.

A corporation can join in the filing of a consolidated federal income tax return only if it is an "includible" member of a group of affiliated corporations. Such "includible" corporations are all corporations (with certain exceptions, including a special rule for life insurance companies) owned under (and including) a common parent corporation, when there is an 80% ownership connection (by both voting power and value, but without regard to certain preferred stock).[20]

As a general proposition, non-life insurance companies and non-insurance companies are "includible" corporations. Thus, when a non-life insurance company is newly acquired by a group that files (or intends to file) a consolidated federal income tax return, it will automatically be included in the group filing, and its income and losses will be included in determining consolidated income.

A life insurance company, however, can join in the filing of a consolidated return only in two circumstances:

(i) A life insurance company can be treated as an includible corporation if it is a member of a group consisting of only life insurance companies as long as there is the requisite direct 80% parent-subsidiary ownership connection, in which case the companies can file a "life/life" consolidated return;[21] or

(ii) A life insurance company can be treated as an includible corporation in a group that includes non-life companies, but only if the life company is "eligible."[22]

A life insurance company is not "eligible" until it has been a member of the group of affiliated corporations for a five-year period.[23] Until a life insurance company becomes "eligible" (often referred to as being "seasoned"), it and any companies owned by it will be excluded from

[19] Compare Code §§172(b) (net operating losses of corporations generally, including non-life insurance companies) and 810(b) (operations loss deductions of life insurance companies).

[20] Code §1504 defines the term "affiliated group" for purposes of determining whether a group of corporations may file federal consolidated income tax returns.

[21] See Treas. Reg. §1.1502-47(f)(3).

[22] Under Code §1504(b)(2), life insurance companies are generally not "includible corporations," but §1504(c)(1) provides that life insurance companies can be treated as "includible corporations" in an affiliated group including only life insurance companies, and Code §1504(c)(2) permits life insurance companies to join in filing consolidated returns with other corporations pursuant to regulations, which are set out in Treas. Reg. §1.1502-47. The insurance industry has for many years attempted to obtain repeal of these limitations.

[23] Treas. Reg. §1.1502-47(d)(12) defines an eligible corporation as one that has been in existence, and a member of the group, for five years, is engaged in an active trade or business, and has met certain other criteria. The five-year period is measured by reference to the taxable years of the parent of the group; accordingly, unless the acquisition of a life insurance company is made on the first day of the acquiring parent's taxable year, the year in which the acquisition was completed is not included in the five-year period.

any consolidated return of the acquiring group.[24]

Once the new members of the life/non-life group become includible in a group, there are limitations on the use of losses between life and non-life companies. The regulations require treating all life insurance companies as one subgroup (the "life subgroup") and all other members of the group as a different subgroup (the "non-life subgroup").

Consolidated taxable income is determined for each subgroup, and any available operating losses must be carried back, to the extent ordinarily allowable, within each subgroup. If, after giving effect to carrybacks, either subgroup then has an unused net loss for the year, the loss can be carried over and used to reduce the other subgroup's consolidated subgroup taxable income.

Losses generated by the non-life insurance company subgroup may be used in full to reduce non-life subgroup income, but such losses may be used to reduce life subgroup consolidated taxable income in any year only to the extent of the lesser of 35% of life subgroup income or 35% of non-life subgroup losses for such year.[25] Life subgroup losses can be used to reduce non-life subgroup consolidated taxable income in any year without limitation. After allowable losses have been used to reduce subgroup consolidated taxable income to the extent allowable, life subgroup taxable income and non-life subgroup taxable income for the year are combined, and the result is the amount on which the group pays tax.

7.4 FEDERAL INCOME TAX CONSIDERATIONS IN ACQUISITIONS OF INSURANCE COMPANIES

In structuring an acquisition, buyers and sellers have a variety of tax and non-tax goals. In some transactions, a seller will wish to avoid the recognition of gain on a sale and will thus desire to structure the transaction as a tax-free reorganization. In other circumstances, however, a tax-free transaction may not meet the non-tax and/or tax goals of the parties, in which case the transaction will be structured on a taxable basis. Both tax-free and taxable transactions can be structured as stock sales or asset sales.

7.4.1 TAX-FREE TRANSACTIONS

Tax-free transactions can be structured as follows:

[24] Treas. Reg. §1.1502-47(d)(13). Even though the ineligible life insurance companies cannot join in the life/non-life group, they generally would be able to file a life/life return in the interim period, if they are structured as a group of corporations with an ineligible life insurance company as the parent.

[25] Code §1503(c)(1).

1. Statutory mergers or consolidations ("A reorganizations")[26]

CODE SECTION 368(a)(1)(A) – MERGER

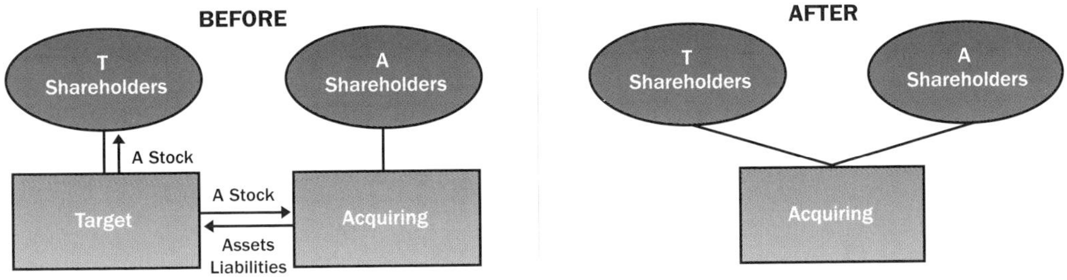

FIGURE 7.1 Acquiring ("A") and Target ("T") are domestic insurance companies, each of which is widely held (by shareholders if A and T are stock insurance companies, or by policyholders if they are mutual insurance companies). A desires to acquire T in a tax-free transaction. The companies enter into a merger agreement, with A as the surviving corporation. All assets and liabilities of T are transferred to or assumed by A pursuant to state insurance or corporate laws. The transaction will qualify as a tax-free A reorganization as long as at least 45-50% of the consideration received by the T shareholders is A stock (or policyholder interests if A is a mutual insurer); cash or other consideration could be received as well, but gain would be recognized to the extent thereof. For all tax-free reorganizations, A must either continue T's historic business or use a significant portion of T's assets in a business.

2. Stock-for-stock reorganizations ("B reorganizations"), in which the transferor solely receives voting stock of the acquiring entity (or its parent) and the acquiring entity has control of the acquired entity immediately after the acquisition[27]

CODE SECTION 368(a)(1)(B) – STOCK ACQUISITION

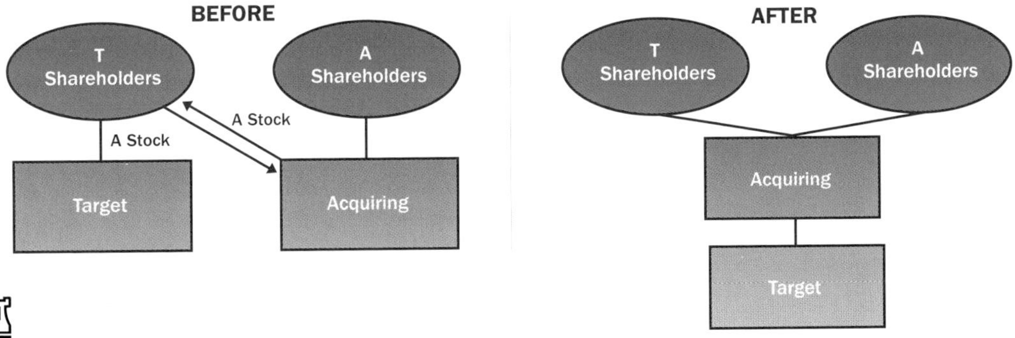

FIGURE 7.2 A desires to acquire T in a tax-free transaction, but does not wish to expose A to T's liabilities. A will acquire the stock of T from T's shareholders. The transaction will qualify as a tax-free B reorganization only if the T shareholders receive solely voting stock of A, and after the transaction, A owns at least 80% of the voting stock and 80% of each class of nonvoting stock of T (a "controlling interest"). If Parent ("P") has a controlling interest in A, P stock may be used in lieu of A stock. T may redeem dissenting shareholders for cash, as long as A does not directly or indirectly fund the redemptions.

26 Code §368(a)(1)(A). Statutory mergers include only mergers under the laws of a state, the District of Columbia, or the United States. In A reorganizations, as well as in certain other tax-free reorganizations, property other than stock or securities can be transferred, but such other property (referred to as "boot") will result in the recognition of gain, but not loss.

27 Code §368(a)(1)(B). "Control" for this purpose is defined as ownership of at least 80% of the total voting power of all stock entitled to vote and at least 80% of the total number of shares of all other classes of stock. Code §368(c). In a B reorganization, no property other than voting stock can be used.

3. Asset acquisitions ("C reorganizations"[28] or "non-divisive D reorganizations"[29]), in which the transferor receives voting stock of the acquiring entity (or its parent) in exchange for substantially all of the target's assets

CODE SECTION 368(a)(1)(C) - ASSET ACQUISITION

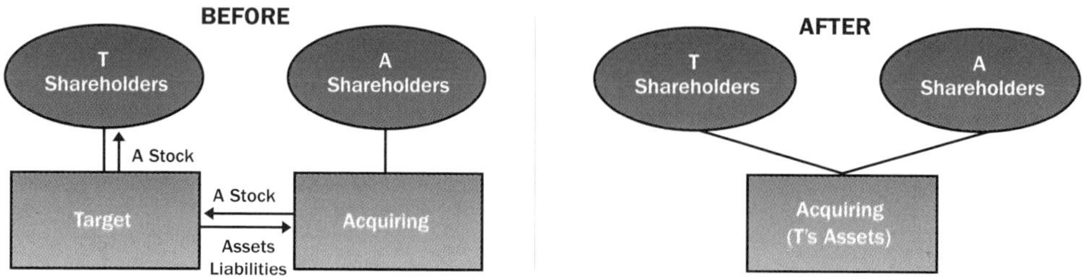

FIGURE 7.3 A, which is a stock insurance company, desires to acquire the insurance business of T, which is either a stock or mutual insurer. In order for this transaction to qualify as a tax-free C reorganization, T will transfer its insurance assets and liabilities to A, and T shareholders will receive A voting stock (or P voting stock if P has a controlling interest in A). In this transaction, A must acquire "substantially all" of T's assets (for purposes of obtaining a ruling from the IRS, 90% of the fair market value of net assets and 70% of the fair market value of gross assets must be acquired by A). Generally, T must be liquidated after the transfer is complete. In a C reorganization as much as 20% of the consideration to T may consist of money or property other than voting stock of A (or P), but if any consideration other than voting stock of A or P is used, the liabilities of T assumed by A must be treated as money.

NON-DIVISIVE - CODE SECTION 368(a)(1)(D) REORGANIZATION

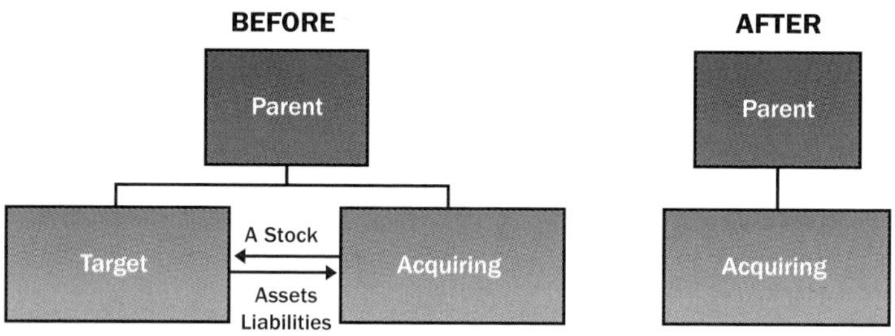

FIGURE 7.4 Parent desires to eliminate overlapping business and insurance licenses of A and T. In order to do so in a tax-free non-divisive D reorganization, A will acquire "substantially all" of the assets of T (90% of net assets, and 70% of gross assets) in return for additional shares of A stock. T must then transfer the A stock it acquired to P in complete liquidation. In a non-divisive D reorganization, the former T shareholders must control at least 50% of either the value or voting power of P after the transaction. In practice, because the issuance of additional shares of A stock would be a meaningless gesture, that step is often ignored. A transaction that could qualify as either a C reorganization or a D reorganization must meet the D reorganization requirements. It is possible to preserve the corporate shell and licenses of T for future sale. See discussion in section 7.4.4.

[28] Code §68(a)(1)(C). In a C reorganization the buyer must receive "substantially all" of the target's assets, and the target generally must be liquidated. The term "substantially all" is not defined, but is generally considered to be 90% of the target's net assets by value and 70% of the target's gross assets by value. See Rev. Proc. 77-37, 1977-2 C.B. 568, §3.01. In a C reorganization, the transferor company can receive up to 20% of the consideration in the form of money or property (i.e., boot) in addition to voting stock of the buyer or its parent. Code §368(a)(2)(B) provides, however, that if other consideration is used, all liabilities of the transferor that are assumed in the transaction must be treated as money paid to the transferor. This rule will strictly limit the use of consideration other than voting stock when insurance business is transferred in a C reorganization.

[29] Code §368(a)(1)(D). The stock received in these types of reorganizations must be distributed (either actually or deemed) in a transaction qualifying under either §§354, 355, or 356.

4. Corporate spin-off transactions ("divisive D reorganizations"), in which a corporation contributes a business (not constituting all or substantially all of the assets of the contributing corporation) to a new subsidiary and distributes the stock of the subsidiary to its shareholders[30]

CODE SECTION 368(a)(1)(D) – DIVISIVE REORGANIZATION

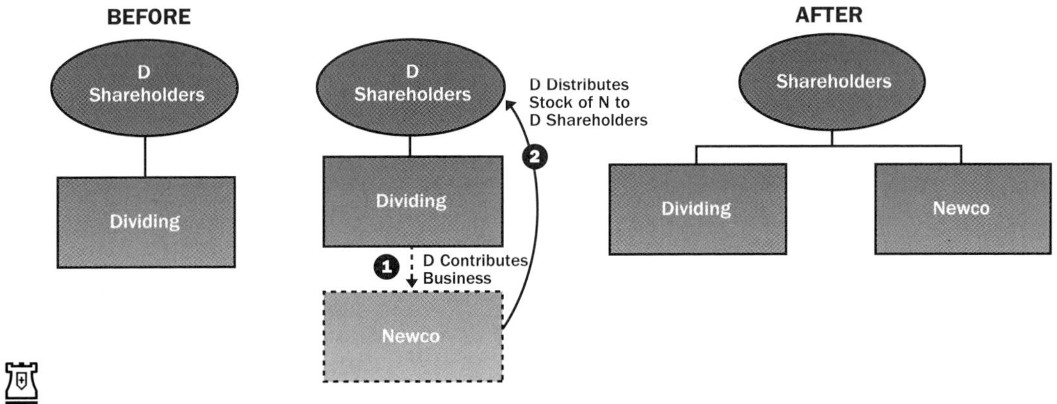

FIGURE 7.5 Dividing Insurance Company ("D") desires to spin-off one of its two lines of insurance business. D will create a new insurance company, Newco ("N"), and obtain the appropriate licenses. D will then transfer the part of its assets and liabilities that make up one line of business, to N. D will immediately distribute the stock of N to the D shareholders. Both D and N must conduct an active business after the spin-off, and the D shareholders must have controlling interests in both D and N following the transaction; accordingly, the D shareholders will be subject to certain restrictions as to subsequent transfers of D or N stock. In addition, several other highly technical requirements must be satisfied in order for the transaction to be treated as a D reorganization.

[30] The stock received in a divisive D reorganization must be distributed pursuant to §355 of the Code, which imposes significant and complex requirements for transactions to qualify for tax-free treatment. In addition, §355 imposes restrictions that will not allow certain distributions of stock to qualify as tax-free if the stock of either the distributing corporation or the "spun-off" corporation was acquired within specified periods of time. Certain other restrictions apply to distributions that are part of a plan that also involves the acquisition of a more than 50% interest in the stock of the distributing or the distributed corporation.

5. Tax-free reorganizations are also commonly structured as forward and reverse triangular mergers, utilizing merger subsidiaries[31]

CODE SECTION 368(a)(2)(D) - FORWARD TRIANGULAR MERGER

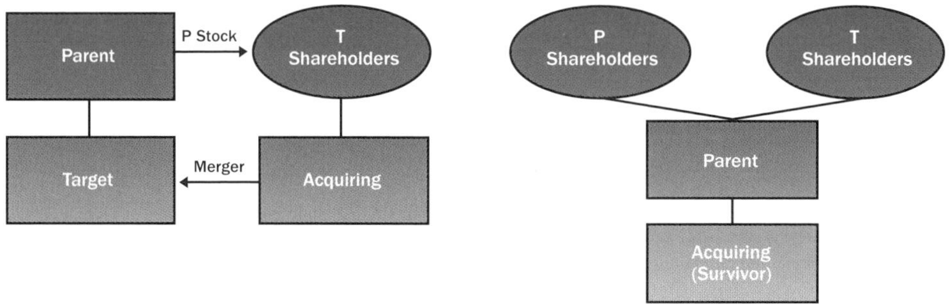

FIGURE 7.6 A triangular merger is a merger in which the stock of P, which has a controlling interest in A, is used as consideration. In a forward triangular merger, A is the survivor, and therefore must hold all licenses necessary to act as an insurer. Substantially all (90% of net/70% of gross) of T's assets and liabilities must transferred to A, and at least 50% of the consideration given to T's shareholders must be stock (although not necessarily voting stock) of P. Stock of A cannot be used as consideration.

CODE SECTION 368(a)(2)(E) - REVERSE TRIANGULAR MERGER

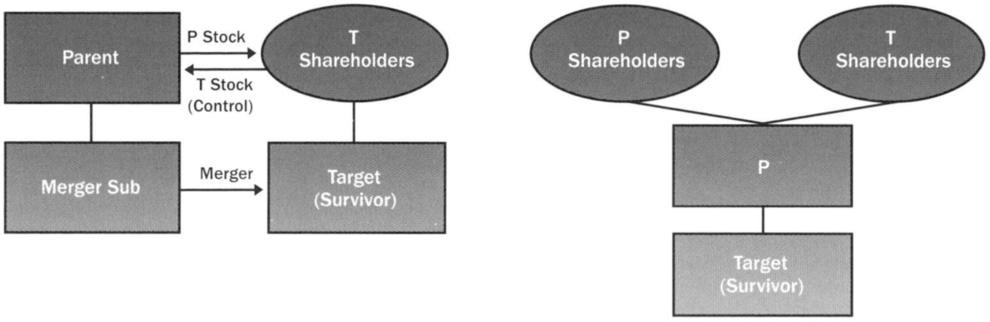

FIGURE 7.7 A reverse triangular merger is an acquisition in which stock of P, which has a controlling interest in A, is used as consideration, but T, rather than A, is the surviving entity in the merger. Following the merger, T must hold substantially all (90% of net/70% of gross) of both T's and Merger Sub's assets. In a reverse triangular merger, P must also receive a controlling interest in T.

[31] See Code §368 (a) (2)(D) and (a)(2)(E). In a forward triangular merger, the target corporation is merged into a merger subsidiary, with the merger subsidiary as the surviving corporation, and with the transferor receiving stock of the buyer's parent. This structure is substantially similar to an asset acquisition. In a reverse merger the target survives and thus can be viewed as a stock acquisition. The rules for triangular mergers are somewhat more restrictive, in that "substantially all" of the assets of the acquired entity must be transferred to the acquiring entity, and voting stock of the buyer must be used to acquire control of the target corporation.

6. Other forms of reorganizations are recapitalization of a single corporation (an "E reorganization"); a change of identity, form, or place of organization (an "F reorganization"); and certain insolvency reorganizations (a "G reorganization").[32]

SECTION 368(a)(1)(E) – RECAPITALIZATION

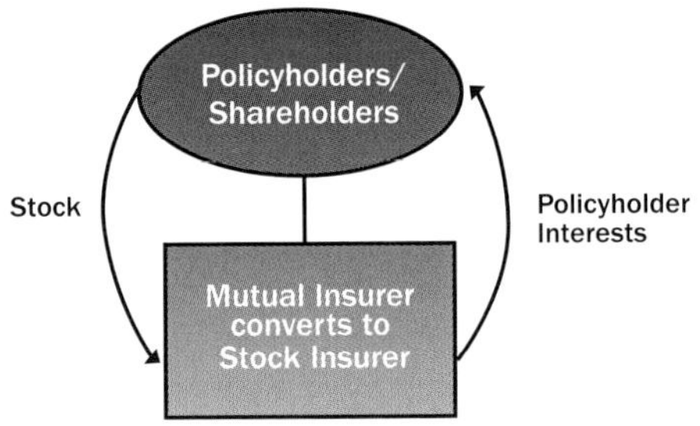

FIGURE 7.8 An E reorganization may only involve one insurance company. Insurance company demutualizations are typically treated as E reorganizations. Policyholders are deemed to exchange their interests in the mutual company (which are treated as the equivalent of stock) for stock or other property of the demutualizing company. Policyholders must recognize gain to the extent that they receive cash or property, as they are deemed to have a zero basis in their interests in the mutual company.

An E reorganization can also include situations which shareholders of one class (e.g., preferred) exchange their stock for another class (e.g., common), although certain E reorganizations involving preferred stock may result in the realization of gain or income.

CODE SECTION 368(a)(1)(F) – CHANGE OF IDENTITY, FORM, OR PLACE OF ORGANIZATION

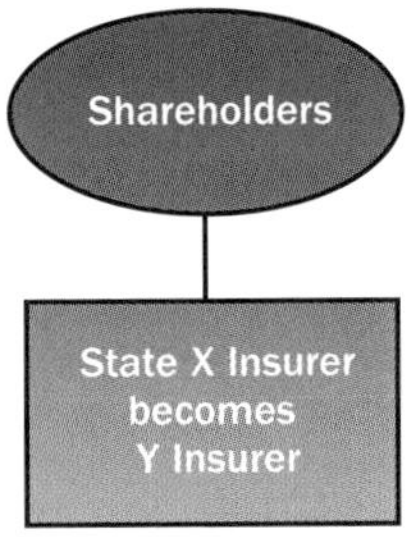

FIGURE 7.9 An F reorganization only involves one operating corporation. The most common form of F reorganization is a redomestication in a new state.

[32] Code §368(a)(1)(E) and (F), respectively. Insurance company demutualizations have commonly been structured as E reorganizations or F reorganizations. At least one demutualization has been structured as a triangular merger under Code §368(a)(2)(D). See Private Letter Ruling 9717026 (a mutual insurer formed a holding company as a parent of a new insurance company, after which the mutual merged with and into the new insurance company, with the mutual policyholders receiving holding company stock).

There are separate non-statutory requirements for tax-free reorganizations: the "continuity of interest" requirement, the "continuity of business enterprise" requirement, and the "business purpose" requirement. The "continuity of interest" requirement is satisfied, in general, if the exchanging shareholder receives approximately 45% to 50% stock in the reorganization. The "continuity of business enterprise" requirement is satisfied if the acquiring corporation either continues the target corporation's historic business or uses a significant portion of the target's historic business assets.[33] There must also be a non-tax business purpose for structuring the transaction as a tax-free reorganization.

In a tax-free asset acquisition, many of the acquired corporation's tax attributes, including loss carryforwards (subject to limitations discussed below) are carried over to the acquiring corporation.[34] As a general rule, the historic basis in assets is also carried over.[35] As a result of the latter rule, tax-free reorganizations are frequently less desirable to buyers than certain types of taxable transactions, in which the buyer will be permitted to "step up" the tax basis of assets and then achieve tax benefits by taking depreciation or amortization deductions or by selling the assets after the acquisition.

In addition to the categories of Code Section 368 reorganizations described above, tax-free acquisitions can also be accomplished utilizing the provisions of Code Section 351. Under Code Section 351, a transfer of property (including stock) to an acquiring corporation is tax-free provided the transferor or transferors "control" the transferee corporation "immediately after" the transfer (i.e., the transferor owns 80% of the voting power and 80% of the number of all non-voting classes of stock following the transfer). In general, both the shareholders of the target corporation and the acquiring corporation must transfer their stock to a new holding company in order to create the "control group" necessary to qualify the transaction as tax-free under Code Section 351. The chief advantages of this structure is that it permits greater flexibility in structuring the consideration provided to the target shareholders (i.e., more cash and non-voting stock is possible) and there are no "continuity of business enterprise" or "continuity of shareholder interest" requirements (although the "immediately after" requirement may restrict the ability of shareholders to transfer their shares for a period of time).[36]

7.4.2 TAXABLE TRANSACTIONS—STOCK SALE VS. ASSET SALE

If it is determined that a taxable structure will be used, the buyer and the seller must decide whether the transaction will be a stock purchase or an asset purchase. If the transaction is structured as a stock purchase (and the election permitted by Code Section 338(h)(10) (discussed more fully at section 7.4.5), which effectively treats a stock sale as an asset sale for federal income tax purposes is not made), the seller will recognize gain or loss to the extent the amount of consideration received exceeds the seller's basis in the stock. Generally, stock constitutes a capital asset in the hands of a seller, and thus the gain or loss will be capital in nature.[37] The buyer will receive the stock with a cost basis.[38] Because stock is not a depreciable or amortizable asset, and the basis of assets owned by the target will not be affected by the sale, the buyer in a stock purchase will

[33] Treas. Reg. §1.368-1(d)(1). Generally, one-third of the target's historic business assets are considered to constitute a "significant portion" of the assets.

[34] Code §381(c). Code §381(c)(22) provides special rules for the carryover of certain tax attributes unique to insurance companies in tax-free reorganizations.

[35] Code §362(b).

[36] Code §351 can also be useful in creating a holding company structure in connection with a demutualization or other restructuring transactions.

[37] Code §1221 defines the term "capital asset."

[38] Code §1012.

generally obtain no immediate tax benefits.[39] The acquired company will, however, retain its historic tax attributes, such as loss carryforwards, that may have value.

Accordingly, both the buyer and the seller should consider the relative tax advantages and disadvantages that arise from an asset sale rather than a stock sale. From a buyer's perspective, an asset purchase may be the most tax-efficient acquisition structure because the buyer will be permitted to step up the basis of assets for depreciation or amortization purposes, although the buyer should weigh this factor against the loss of the acquired company's historic tax attributes.[40]

From the seller's perspective, an asset sale may be advantageous or it may be disadvantageous. For example, if the target company's basis in its assets is greater than a corporate seller's basis in the target stock, the net tax liability may be lower in an asset sale.

7.4.3 ASSET ACQUISITIONS—REINSURANCE

An asset purchase in the insurance industry has typically been achieved through an assumption (or "bulk") reinsurance transaction, which is viewed for tax and regulatory purposes as the purchase of a block of business.[41] Generally, in an assumption reinsurance transaction, the ceding insurer is released from direct liability to policyholders and the assuming reinsurer becomes solely liable.[42] In order to release the ceding insurer from liability, however, it is necessary to obtain each policyholder's actual consent or establish their deemed consent to the substitution of one insurer for another (a "novation").[43] In light of the practical difficulties in obtaining such consents, reinsurance transactions are frequently structured so that the ceding company maintains at least residual liability to policyholders; for example, it is now common to structure a transaction as 100% coinsurance, with the assuming insurer taking on the responsibility for obtaining consents.

For federal income tax purposes, the ceding company will report income to the extent it releases reserves and will be allowed a deduction equal to the fair market value of assets transferred to the reinsurer.[44] For this purpose, the reserves that are treated as being released are tax reserves, rather than statutory reserves. The ceding insurer also reports any ceding commission as ordinary income. Finally, assets are deemed to have been disposed of at fair market

---

[39] See Code §§167, 197(e)(1) (interests in corporations not amortizable).

[40] The buyer may also have non-tax reasons for preferring an asset acquisition. For example, the buyer may have concerns about various liabilities at the corporate level.

[41] Mergers and certain similar corporate reorganizations that do not meet the requirements for tax-free reorganization treatment can be treated as taxable asset acquisitions. See, e.g., Revenue Ruling 69-6, 1969-1 C.B. 104.

[42] See, e.g., Treas. Reg. §1.809-5(a)(7) ("the term 'assumption reinsurance' means an arrangement whereby another person [the reinsurer] becomes solely liable to the policyholders on the contracts transferred by the taxpayer [the ceding insurer]. Such term does not include indemnity reinsurance or reinsurance ceded.").

[43] The NAIC Assumption Reinsurance Model Act sets out detailed rules for effectuating assumption reinsurance transactions. Under the Model Act, if a policyholder has neither objected nor consented to the transfer, it is possible to obtain a deemed consent and novation by sending out various notices over a period of more than two years.

[44] In an assumption reinsurance transaction involving life insurance companies, the ceding insurer reports income equal to the reserves released pursuant to Code §803(a)(2) and is allowed a deduction for consideration paid under Code §805(a)(6). See Treas. Reg. §1.817-4(d)(3) Example 1, which applies to assumption reinsurance transactions. In the case of 100% indemnity reinsurance, the ceding insurer would also report the decrease in reserves ceded to the reinsurer as income under Code §803(a)(2), but would treat the amount paid to the reinsurer as a reduction in premiums otherwise includible in life insurance company gross income under Code §803(a)(1). See also Treas Reg. §1.809-4(a)(1)(iii). Although Treas. Reg. §1.817-4 directly applies only to life insurance companies, the IRS applies these concepts to non-life insurance companies as well. A non-life insurance company would reduce its premiums written by the amount of reinsurance premiums paid pursuant to Code §832(b)(4)(A), and would adjust its deduction for losses incurred under Code §832(b)(5).

value, and thus the ceding company may report capital gain or loss. The assuming reinsurer will report premium income to the extent of the fair market value of assets (both tangible and intangible assets) received and will deduct the reserves it establishes.[45] Generally, the excess of the tax reserve over cash or investment assets received by the reinsurer is treated as a ceding commission paid by the reinsurer with respect to the intangible assets acquired.

When the transaction is more than the simple acquisition of a book of insurance business, but rather is the acquisition of a line of business, the basis of the assets acquired by the assuming company would in certain cases be determined under Code Section 1060.[46]

In an assumption reinsurance transaction, as well as in 100% coinsurance transactions that are applicable asset acquisitions, the basis of the transferred assets in the hands of the reinsurer is determined by allocating the consideration received under the "residual method" (i.e., first to cash and general deposit accounts ("Class I assets"), and then to actively traded personal property ("Class II assets"), certain debt instruments and assets that are marked-to-market ("Class III assets"), and the value of intangible assets ("Class VI or VII assets")).[47]

Intangible assets received in an assumption reinsurance transaction, such as the value of the business being acquired, may be subject to amortization under Code Section 197 over a period of up to 15 years.[48] An assumption or indemnity (coinsurance) reinsurance transaction involving life insurance, annuity, or non-cancellable accident and health insurance contracts is also subject to the DAC tax rules of Code Section 848.[49]

Under these rules, as a "proxy" for requiring insurers to capitalize actual policy acquisition expenses, a portion of otherwise deductible "general" expenses of the assuming insurer must be treated as "specified policy acquisition expenses" that are capitalized and amortized over a 10-year period. The amount that must be capitalized and amortized is based on varying percentages of premiums received by the company with respect to "specified insurance contracts," which are life insurance, annuity, and non-cancellable accident and health insurance contracts. The percentages are 1.75% for annuity contracts, 2.05% for group life insurance contracts, and 7.7% for life insurance contracts and non-cancellable accident and health insurance contracts, subject to certain exceptions and special rules.[50]

Under the DAC tax regulations, the ceding insurer can usually reduce its unamortized DAC balance by the amount of DAC attributable to business ceded to a reinsurer that is itself subject to the DAC tax. On the other hand, the assuming reinsurer must capitalize all

---

[45] The assuming reinsurer in a life reinsurance transaction is required to report the premium received in gross income under Code §803, and is allowed a deduction for the increase in reserves assumed under Code §805(a)(2). In a non-life reinsurance transaction, the reinsurer would report the reinsurance consideration in premiums written and would be allowed a deduction for any increase in incurred losses under Code §832(b)(5).

[46] Code §1060 applies to an "applicable asset acquisition," which is defined as assets that constitute a trade or business. In Prop. Reg. §1.1060-1 the IRS proposes to apply Code §1060 allocation methods to both indemnity and assumption reinsurance transactions that constitute applicable asset acquisitions, which the proposed regulation describes as the acquisition of assets to which going concern and goodwill attach. For transactions that are not applicable asset acquisitions, basis of assets, including intangible assets acquired, is generally determined by allocating consideration received over the assets received based on market values.

[47] Treas. Reg. §1.1060-1(c) uses the allocation methods set out in Treas. Reg. §1.338-6. Class IV assets are generally stock in trade and inventory. Class V assets are all assets other than Class I, II, III, IV, VI, and VII assets. See also Prop. Reg. §§1.1060-1(c)(5) and 1.338-11.

[48] Code §197(f)(5) provides that the amortization rules apply to any "section 197 intangible" asset resulting from an assumption reinsurance transaction.

[49] Code §848(d)(4).

[50] See Code §848(e), which excepts certain pension plan contracts, flight insurance contracts, qualified foreign contracts, and Archer MSA contracts. It also provides special rules for group life contracts, combination contracts, and reinsurance contracts.

outstanding DAC attributable to the assumed business.[51] When an assumption reinsurance transaction involves the types of policies subject to the DAC tax, only the excess of the ceding commission over the DAC amortization amount is amortizable over 15 years.[52]

7.4.4 SALE OF CORPORATE SHELLS

In some instances, the acquiring corporation might be interested in acquiring a book of business but the seller is unwilling to structure the transaction as a reinsurance transaction. A transaction of this nature can be structured so that the target insurance company is purchased directly by an insurer having similar licenses. The newly acquired subsidiary insurer can then transfer its insurance liabilities to the parent, leaving behind a shell corporation with its valuable licenses, which then can be sold.[53]

Similarly, a corporate group may determine that it no longer needs all of the insurance entities in its group that are licensed in overlapping jurisdictions. In this case, virtually all of the company's assets and insurance liabilities will be transferred to an acquiring affiliate, and the insurance charter and licenses will be retained by the target company, or "shell," which can then be sold. The IRS has issued guidance indicating that transactions of this nature can be structured as tax-free subsidiary liquidations or D reorganizations, followed by a taxable sale of the shell.[54]

7.4.5 THE SECTION 338 ELECTION

Under Code Section 338, an election may be made to treat a stock transaction as an asset sale and purchase for federal income tax purposes. If the election is made, the sale of stock is ignored and the corporation to be acquired ("old target") is treated as having sold all of its assets to a newly formed corporation ("new target") for a price equal to the price paid for the stock, plus the corporation's liabilities assumed. The advantage of the election to the buyer is significant; it is allowed to "step up" and amortize the basis of intangible and other amortizable or depreciable

---

[51] The amount of specified policy acquisition expenses subject to the DAC tax is limited by the insurer's general deductions. See Code §848(c)(e). The DAC tax regulations require consistent treatment by parties to a reinsurance transaction. Treas. Reg. §§1.848-2(f) through (j) set out rules applicable to reinsurance transactions. Treas. Reg. §1.848-2(g)(8) permits those parties to elect to have the assuming insurer report positive consideration for DAC tax purposes, even if when its general deductions limitation would otherwise limit the amount of positive consideration, thereby allowing the ceding insurer to report negative consideration. It should be noted that in a coinsurance transaction, the DAC tax is imposed on a "cash flow" basis; premiums, return premiums, benefit payments, and other amounts enter into the determination of negative and positive consideration for DAC tax purposes over the life of the reinsurance treaty.

[52] Under Code §848(g), the "excess" ceding commission is not subject to capitalization and amortization if the transaction is subject to the DAC tax, and is not subject to Code §197. This treatment would appear to apply to 100% coinsurance transactions involving life insurance, annuity, or non-cancellable accident and health insurance contracts because Code §197 does not apply when the ceding insurer remains liable to policyholders. See Treas. Reg. §1.197-2(g)(5)(A). A ceding commission with respect to coinsurance of other types of insurance would appear to be capitalizable and amortizable, presumably over the life of the business reinsured. See Treas. Reg. §1.848-2(j).

[53] See Rev. Proc. 89-50, 1989-2 C.B. 631, in which the IRS set out procedures by which an insurance company could be turned into a shell. Under this procedure, all of the assets of the subsidiary are deemed to be distributed to the parent in a tax-free liquidation, but the capital and surplus and licenses are deemed to be contributed to a "new" insurance subsidiary.

[54] See Rev. Proc. 89-50, 1989-2 C.B. 631 and Rev. Proc. 90-52, 1990-2 C.B. 626. See also, Private Letter Ruling 9306014. Before it will issue a private letter ruling, the IRS requires representations that the target will transfer all of its business and assets to its parent (in a subsidiary liquidation) or to another affiliate (in a D reorganization) other than its insurance licenses and statutory minimum capital and surplus (which are deemed to be contributed to a "new" shell insurance company). The shell must then be sold to an unrelated purchaser or be dissolved with in 12 months. The charter and licenses of an insurance company are not transferable and will disappear if the target company is merged out of existence.

assets of the target company at no tax cost to itself, thereby reducing the after-tax acquisition cost. The buyer may unilaterally elect this treatment for a transaction, by making the election under Code Section 338(g) only.

Unless the special election under Code Section 338(h)(10) (which is discussed below) is also made by both the buyer and seller, however, the full value of intangible assets, such as the insurance in force in the case of insurance companies, and any gain inherent in the investment portfolio, is subject to tax on a special one-day federal income tax return that must be filed by the target company, without regard to any consolidated group of which the acquired company might be a member (either selling or buying).[55] Thus, only the current or carryover losses of old target can be used to shelter the income and gain resulting from the election, which, because of the recognition of the value of intangible assets, could be significant.[56]

Moreover, the selling shareholder must recognize gain on the sale of the stock. As a result, even though new target has a "stepped up" basis in its assets, a "regular" election under Code Section 338(g), without an accompanying election under Code Section 338(h)(10), is rarely made.[57]

Code Section 338(h)(10), which allows for a special joint election by a buyer and a seller to have the income and gain resulting from the election reported on the seller's return, has potential advantages for both parties. As noted above, the buyer is permitted a basis step-up. From the seller group's perspective, the sale of the stock is ignored; rather, the corporation to be sold (old target) is treated as if it sold its assets to new target, after which old target is liquidated, and the purchase price distributed to shareholders.[58] The seller reports any income or gain resulting from the deemed asset sale.

Current losses or loss carryforwards can reduce or eliminate the tax from the deemed asset sale. Even if losses are not available, if the target's basis in its assets (the "inside basis") is greater than the seller's basis in old target's stock (the "outside basis"), seller's gain will be reduced as a result of the Code Section 338(h)(10) election. This situation frequently arises when the seller's outside basis is negative, as a result of the use of losses generated by the corporation to be sold on the seller's consolidated federal income tax return.[59]

In 2002, the Treasury Department proposed comprehensive regulations for insurance companies subject to a Section 338(h)(10) election.[60] When the corporation for which the election is being made is an insurance company, the deemed asset sale is treated in part as an assump-

---

[55] The §338 rules provide that the gain is reported on a special one-day return. Code §338(h)(9). If an affiliated group that has been filing a consolidated return, or members of such a group, is acquired in a single transaction, consolidation of those companies may be allowed under Code §338(h)(15).

[56] As will be noted below, there is a special rule to prevent the new rules with respect to the carryover of losses in an acquisition from eliminating the target's losses prior to the recognition of the §338 gain.

[57] The election under Code §338(g) may be useful when the both the seller and the target company are non-U.S. taxpayers. Although the interaction of the Code §338 rules and the foreign tax provisions of the Code is beyond the scope of this chapter, a Code §338(g) election with respect to the sale of a foreign target corporation may create certain tax benefits or detriments depending upon the tax position of the seller or buyer. See Treas. Reg. §1.338-9. For example, a buyer may be able to reduce a target foreign corporation's future earnings and profits (resulting from increased depreciation/amortization or less gain recognition in connection with an asset sale) thereby potentially reducing the income subject to tax in the hand of a domestic owner of an interest in a "controlled foreign corporation" or generating a higher foreign tax credit.

[58] Code §338 (h)(10)(A).

[59] Under Treas. Reg. §1.1502-32, the basis in the stock of a subsidiary is reduced when losses of the subsidiary are used on the consolidated return, when there is a deficit in that company's earnings and profits, or when distributions are made. A "negative basis" is reflected in an "excess loss account." Treas. Reg. §1.1502-19. If the subsidiary is sold, and no election under Code §338(h)(10) is made, the excess loss account is included in income as gain from the sale of stock.

[60] Prop. Reg. §1.338-11 (REG.-118861-00, published in the Federal Register March 8, 2002).

tion reinsurance transaction.[61] Under the proposed regulations, old target is treated as receiving income equal to the reduction in its tax reserves and a deduction for the amount deemed paid as a reinsurance premium in the deemed asset sale, and new target has income and offsetting reserve deductions when it is deemed to have assumed the business. The portion of the purchase price that is allocated to the value of intangible assets is determined under the "residual" method. All tax attributes of old target are either transferred to the selling parent corporation in the deemed liquidation of old target under Code Sec. 332, or are terminated; thus, credits, loss carryforwards, and other items of old target are not available to new target.[62]

7.5 ACQUISITION OF A MUTUAL INSURANCE COMPANY

A mutual insurance company can acquire another mutual insurance company in a tax-free merger (an "A reorganization"). A mutual insurer cannot generally be acquired in a taxable transaction without a revision of the ownership structure of the mutual company. Conversions of mutual companies to stock companies can be structured as tax-free recapitalizations ("E reorganizations") or mere changes in corporate form ("F reorganizations"), followed by the creation of an "upstream" holding company, which can be sold to a buyer in a taxable transaction.[63]

There are also taxable alternatives available to convert mutual companies to stock companies. Historically, these alternatives have consisted of statutory mergers that do not satisfy the continuity of interest requirement or assumption reinsurance transactions followed by liquidation of the mutual insurer. In these transactions the mutual insurance company policyholders are subject to tax on the cash or other property received in exchange for their proprietary interests in the insurance company, and, as discussed in section 7.3.3, the transferor insurance company will typically recognize gain or loss with respect to appreciated property transferred in the reinsurance transaction and may be subject to tax on net consideration it receives from the assuming reinsurer.[64]

---

[61] Treas. Reg. §§1.338-1(a)(2); 1.338(h)(10)-1(d)(4).

[62] See Prop. Reg. §1.338-11. The proposed regulations raised a number of issues that may be subject to change before they become final. For example, for life insurance companies, an existing policyholders surplus account (commonly known as a "Phase III account," which is discussed at note 72, below) would be brought into income and cannot be offset by losses. For non-life insurance companies, certain increases in loss reserves in the first four years following an acquisition would not be deductible but rather would be capitalized and amortized as part of the cost of the acquired assets. Industry representatives have filed comments on the proposed regulations stating that both of these provisions produce unwarranted results. It is likely that the provision relating to the Phase III account will be included in final regulations; the provision regarding loss reserves may be changed prior to the adoption of final regulations.

[63] In Revenue Ruling 2003-19, 2003-7 I.R.B. 468, the IRS set out the federal tax consequences of three different scenarios involving the reorganization of mutual insurance companies. The scenarios range from the mutual insurer authorizing the issuance of capital stock and having its policyholders exchange their membership interests in the mutual company for stock to more complicated fact patterns involving the creation of various mutual and stock holding companies to effect the transaction.

[64] Code §336 also requires gain or loss to be recognized by the liquidating corporation when appreciated property is distributed to its owner in a liquidation.

7.6 USE OF LOSSES IN INSURANCE COMPANY ACQUISITIONS

As previously noted, corporations, including life and non-life insurance companies, are permitted to carry losses forward to future taxable years. Although loss carryforwards are generally considered valuable assets of a corporation, the Code limits the use of loss carryforwards after a corporation undergoes any significant ownership change. Moreover, the rules relating to the filing of consolidated federal income tax returns contain other limitations, as discussed more fully in sections 7.6.1 and 7.6.2.

7.6.1 STATUTORY LIMITATION ON LOSSES

Code Section 382 imposes limits on a company's use of pre-acquisition losses to reduce its post-acquisition taxable income. The section 382 limitation prescribes the amount of an acquired company's post-acquisition income that can be offset by pre-acquisition losses in any year.

This limitation generally is determined by multiplying the value of the stock of the company that has the losses by a federally prescribed long-term tax-exempt rate in effect at the time of the ownership change.[65] If the acquired company does not either continue its historic business or use a significant portion of its assets in a business, the Code Section 382 limitation is zero.[66] Any pre-acquisition losses that cannot be used because of the Code Section 382 limitation are carried forward to be used in the future (subject to a maximum 15- or 20-year life, depending on whether the company is a life or a non-life insurance company).

The Code Section 382 limitation applies when the company with losses has undergone an ownership change. In order to determine if there has been an ownership change, the ownership interests of each 5% shareholder are examined during a testing period, generally the three years preceding the acquisition or, if less, the time since the last ownership change.

Although the rules in this area are exceedingly complex, in general, all shareholders less than 5% are aggregated and treated as a single 5% shareholder. Thus, the acquisition of a company with losses will generally trigger the application of the Code Section 382 limitation.[67]

Code Section 382(h) also limits recognition of "built-in losses" after an ownership change. If the fair market value of an acquired corporation's assets is less than the aggregate cost basis of those assets, it will have a net built-in unrealized loss that will increase the amount of pre-acquisition losses that are taken into account in calculating the Code Section 382 limitation for a five-year period after the ownership change.

Conversely, if the loss corporation has unrealized built-in gain with respect to its assets for a five-year period after the ownership change, the Code Section 382 limitation is increased by the amount of such gain that is recognized in a taxable year, up to the amount of unrealized built-in gain that existed on the date the change in ownership occurred. Application of the built-in gain or loss rules is subject to a threshold, however: if the net built-in gain or loss is not greater than the lesser of 15% of the difference between the value and basis of the company's assets or $10,000,000, the net built-in gain or loss will be zero.

Code Section 384 also limits the use of pre-acquisition losses of a corporation that acquires the assets of or files a consolidated return with a newly acquired corporation. Thus, for example, if a company with a pre-acquisition loss acquires the assets of a corporation in a transaction in which gain is not recognized (e.g., a tax-free reorganization), the losses may not be used to reduce built-in gains realized with respect to the acquired assets by the acquiring company unless more than 50% of the stock of the acquired company had been held for five or more

[65] See Code §382(b).

[66] Code §382(c). The requirement is similar to the "continuity of business enterprise" requirement for corporate reorganizations. See sec. 7.3.1. above.

[67] Code §383 contains similar rules for tax credits.

years by the acquiring company.

Similarly, pre-acquisition losses of a newly acquired member of a consolidated group cannot be used to reduce the built-in gain of another member of the group (unless the 50% rule applies).

7.6.2 CONSOLIDATED RETURN LIMITATIONS

If a group of corporations files a consolidated return, the Code Section 382 limitation, subject to certain rules beyond the scope of this chapter, is calculated as if the consolidated group were a single entity. This rule can be very helpful because the inclusion of all members of the group in the calculation may increase the amount of the Code Section 382 limitation.

The general consolidated return regulations also limit the use of losses in acquisitions. The separate return limitation year (SRLY) provisions of the regulations limit the use of a group member's pre-acquisition losses in any year to the income contributed by that member to consolidated taxable income (unless the loss company is the common parent company of the group).[68] An overlap rule, however, provides that in most acquisitions, if both SRLY and Section 382 would limit losses, only Section 382 will apply.[69]

If an insurance company with a loss carryforward is acquired, it can join in filing a consolidated return (subject to the life/non-life rule discussed in section 7.3); indeed, if any domestic company other than a life insurance company is acquired by a group already filing on a consolidated basis, it must join the consolidated group. Before losses of the acquired company can be used against consolidated income, however, the losses are subject to the Code Section 382 limitation, and, if not, they are most likely subject to the SRLY limitations.

If a corporation that is the common parent corporation of a consolidated group has loss carryforwards and acquires profitable subsidiaries, however, the losses should be available to reduce the consolidated group's taxable income, subject to Code Section 384, as described above, because the SRLY rules do not apply to the losses of the parent. Also, the Code Section 382 limitations should not apply because the loss corporation (the parent) will not have undergone a change of ownership.[70]

7.7 TAX-BASED VALUATION AND DUE DILIGENCE CONCERNS

Tax concerns, such as the availability of loss carryforwards, are ultimately reflected in the acquisition price; in some cases, tax issues will have a significant impact on the decision as to whether to proceed with an acquisition. Moreover, other more specific tax-related issues can have a significant bearing on the value of an insurance company.

7.7.1 LIFE INSURANCE COMPANIES

Whether a life insurance company's products meet relevant requirements of the Code must be considered. Life insurance contracts must meet the requirements of Code Sections 7702 and 7702A, and annuities must generally meet either the requirements of Code Section 72(s) or specific requirements for "tax-qualified" arrangements, such as the requirements of Code Sections 403(b) (tax-sheltered annuities) or 408(b) (individual retirement annuities). All non-qualified variable contracts must meet the diversification requirements of Code Section 817(h) and the regulations thereunder.

---

[68] The SRLY rules are set out in Treas. Reg. §1.1502-21(c). Under these rules, losses generated by a target corporation when it filed a separate return, or was a member of another consolidated group, will be subject to the SRLY rules and thus will be usable only against income generated by the target after the acquisition.

[69] Treas. Reg. §1.1502-21(g).

[70] Treas. Reg. §1.1502-1(f)(2).

A failure to comply with provisions of the Code relating to insurance products can frequently be "cured," but the cost is usually that the insurance company that issued the failed products must pay a "toll charge" to the IRS that is based on the tax the policyholders would have paid.[71] If the company does not "cure" the contracts, it is exposed to possible policyholder lawsuits to recover lost tax benefits. In addition to product compliance issues, another tax concern relates to the accuracy of the company's reserves for insurance products.

7.7.2 PHASE III ACCOUNTS

An additional tax concern that is unique to stock life insurance companies is the Phase III account.[72] All Phase III accounts, which reflect certain untaxed profits of stock life insurance companies prior to 1984, were frozen at 1983 levels; they cannot be increased, but they can be decreased when certain events occur. When they are decreased, the amount of the decrease must be included in gross income.

Two frequently encountered triggering events for a Phase III account are (i) an insurance company's failure to continue qualifying as a life insurance company for two consecutive years, or (ii) termination of a company's status as an insurance company for one taxable year. A tax liability resulting from the reduction of the Phase III account can also be triggered when reserves are reduced to certain levels or by the payment of dividends.[73] As noted above, certain acquisition techniques may have the effect of triggering the Phase III account into income.

7.7.3 NON-LIFE INSURANCE COMPANIES

Loss reserves, which in reality are estimates of reported but unpaid and unreported losses and LAEs for the year, net of salvage and subrogation and reinsurance recoverables, are commonly adjusted by the IRS on audit. These estimates may sometimes take into account losses for unrecoverable reinsurance, which can involve significant amounts.

7.7.4 CONSOLIDATED RETURN ISSUES

Under the consolidated return regulations, every member of the consolidated group is severally liable for the entire group tax.[74] Thus, if a company is acquired from a group filing a consolidated return, the assets of the acquired company are theoretically exposed to any unpaid tax liability of the prior group for years in which the acquired corporation participated in the filing of the consolidated return.

It is thus important to understand the tax positions taken by any affiliated group of which the target corporation is a member. Treas. Reg. Section 1.1502-6(b) provides a procedure by

[71] Code §7702(f)(8) permits the IRS to waive "reasonable" failures to comply with Code §7702 requirements; other failures can be cured, subject to the toll charge procedure. In Rev. Proc. 92-25, 1992-1 C.B. 741, the IRS provided a procedure by which an issuer of variable contracts that fail the diversification requirements of Code §817(h) can obtain relief. See also Rev. Rul. 91-17, 1991-1 C.B. 190, in which the IRS addressed the consequences to an insurance company when its contracts failed to comply with the provisions of Code §§7702 or 817(h). In Rev. Proc. 2001-42, 2001-2 C.B. 212 the IRS set out a procedure for curing "inadvertent nonegregious" failures to comply with the requirements of Code §7702A.

[72] Code §815(a). Prior to the Deficit Reduction Act of 1984 (DEFRA), life insurance companies were subject to tax under a highly complex "three phase" tax system. Phase I, which covered investment income, was the tax base for mutual life insurers. Phase II, which covered investment income plus 50% of net underwriting income, was the tax base for stock life insurance companies. The remaining 50% of underwriting gains, plus certain "special deductions" were recorded in the tax-deferred policyholders surplus account (the "Policyholders Surplus Account" or "Phase III account").

[73] Code §815(f), which incorporates various provisions of pre-DEFRA Code §815.

[74] Treas. Reg. §1.1502-6(c). This liability will carryover in a transaction for which a §338(h)(10) election has been made. See Treas. Reg. §1.338(h)(10)-1(d)(2). Note that Treas. Reg. §1.1502-6(c) makes clear that the joint and several liability of each member of a consolidated group cannot be reduced by intercompany agreements.

which the exposure of a newly acquired subsidiary to the consolidated tax liability of the selling group can be limited to the subsidiary's allocable share of such liability, but as a practical matter this procedure is dependent upon an agreement with the IRS and is rarely used.

7.8 STATE TAXES

State tax issues can also arise in the context of the acquisition of an insurance company. A relatively small number of states subject insurance companies to income taxes. Of those that do, some conform their taxes to the federal income tax, while others set out their own free-standing income tax.[75] Some states allow insurance companies to join in filing consolidated returns, while others tax insurers on a "stand-alone" basis. Some states do not allow for loss carryovers, and others do not recognize a Code Section 338(h)(10) election. Obviously, state tax laws must be examined in any acquisition.

7.9 TAXES ON VALUATION

Federal income tax issues have an important impact on actuarial appraisal values or other valuation techniques. The valuation of an insurance company is almost always performed on an after-tax basis. Some structures, such as reinsurance, may allow for the deduction of the purchase price, as discussed in section 7.9.2, but even in these situations the timing of tax deductions causes an economic drag compared to pre-tax values.

7.9.1 SALE OF A COMPANY STOCK

The sale of a company's stock generally results in no impact to the company's tax basis. The discussion of actuarial appraisal value technique in Chapter 4 includes a section on federal income tax issues encountered in the normal course of business, which would impact projections of distributable earnings. In addition, the descriptions earlier in this chapter regarding consolidation for tax purposes may have a material impact on value.

7.9.2 TAXES ON REINSURANCE TRANSACTIONS

There are a number of adjustments to taxable income as a result of a reinsurance transaction. From the purchaser's perspective, the following adjustments are made:

1) The DAC proxy tax is based on net consideration received by the assuming company. For coinsurance, this would typically be premiums less claims and commissions. For assumption reinsurance, DAC proxy tax continues to be paid based on premium because the policyholders simply switch to become direct policyholders of the purchaser. In addition, DAC proxy tax is payable based on the initial net consideration paid (i.e., the assets transferred backing liabilities less ceding commission).

2) The mark-to-market on the asset portfolio creates an immediate taxable gain or loss.

3) The excess ceding commission on a tax basis is deductible. The excess tax ceding commission can be calculated as follows:

   Excess Tax Ceding Commission = Purchase Price (statutory ceding commission)
   – (Statutory Reserve – Tax Reserve)
   – Mark-to-Market of Assets
   – DAC Proxy Tax on Initial Consideration

[75] Twenty-nine states (plus District of Columbia) impose no corporate income tax on insurance companies. The balance of the states imposes a form of an income tax; such taxes are sometimes offset and sometimes augmented by premiums taxes.

The period over which the excess tax ceding commission is deductible varies based on structure and type of business. In addition, companies may take different approaches in filing with the IRS. General approaches currently utilized are:

- For assumption reinsurance, the entire amount is deductible straight-line over 15 years.
- For coinsurance, amounts associated with new business or goodwill are deductible straight-line over 15 years.
- For coinsurance of inforce business subject to DAC proxy tax, the amount is deductible immediately.
- For coinsurance of inforce business not subject to DAC proxy tax (for example, qualified annuities), the amount is deductible over the life of the business.

Certain other tax attributes of the business may remain with the ceding company under an indemnity coinsurance or modified coinsurance (mod-co) transaction. For example, the dividends received deduction on variable business will remain a benefit to the ceding company if the sale is structured as mod-co, which is typical for variable business transactions.

Table 7.1 illustrates the appraisal value for the universal life (UL) business in the UL Sample Company under an indemnity coinsurance structure.

UL SAMPLE COMPANY
TAX BENEFIT UNDER COINSURANCE
As of December 31, 2004
(in millions)

Component of Value	Discount Rate		
	10.0%	12.0%	14.0%
Initial Statutory Liability	803.4	803.4	803.4
Initial Tax Liability	782.4	782.4	782.4
After Tax After Cost of Capital Value of EB	122.9	99.2	80.4
After Tax After Cost of Capital Value of FB	79.0	44.1	20.6
DAC Proxy Tax on Initial Consideration	46.7	49.9	52.5
Mark-to-Market on Asset Portfolio	0.0	0.0	0.0
Excess Tax Ceding Commission on EB	129.8	84.5	47.9
Tax Benefit from Coinsurance:			
DAC Proxy Tax on Future Net Consideration	19.1	16.7	14.7
DAC Proxy Tax on Initial Consideration	10.0	9.9	9.6
Immediate Deduction on EB	45.4	29.6	16.8
15-Year Deduction on FB	17.0	8.3	3.4
Total Tax Benefit	91.6	64.5	44.5
Adjusted Book Value	0.0	0.0	0.0
Total Value of Inforce	197.4	155.4	121.4
Total Value of New Business	96.1	52.4	24.0
Total Actuarial Value	293.5	207.8	145.5

TABLE 7.1

7.9.3 ACQUISITION OF A COMPANY UNDER SECTION 338(h)(10)

As described in section 7.4.5, Code Section 338(h)(10) allows for a joint election by buyer and seller to convert the acquisition of a company's shares into a deemed asset acquisition. The result from a buyer's perspective is that the tax basis of the acquired entity is stepped up to the full purchase price. One criterion of a 338(h)(10) election is that the target company is a wholly owned subsidiary of the selling corporation; the election is not available if the target is a publicly traded entity.

Under a 338(h)(10) election, the tax treatment is identical to assumption reinsurance from the buyer's perspective. Therefore, the buyer's tax benefit of the step-up in basis can be calculated based on the following adjustments:

1) There is an immediate DAC proxy tax asset based on the initial net consideration transferred to the buyer (i.e., the market value of assets transferred backing liabilities less ceding commission). The existing DAC proxy tax in the company is eliminated.

2) The tax basis of the asset portfolio is reset to market value at time of closing.

3) The excess tax basis ceding commission, if positive, is deductible over 15 years. The excess tax ceding commission is calculated as described above in section 7.9.2.

4) If the excess tax basis ceding commission is negative, other tax assets are reduced until the excess ceding commission is zero. In this case, the seller's tax benefits on the sale may be limited.

The economic value of the step-up in basis is dependent on the mark-to-market of the target's asset portfolio. In some cases, the tax benefit of the 338(h)(10) could become negative if interest rates move enough. Since closing typically occurs a minimum of several months after a deal is agreed to, the buyer may choose to have a purchase price adjustment to protect against deterioration in the value of the tax benefit due to market movements in the asset portfolio value. Alternatively, a buyer could hedge the tax benefit with financial instruments over the period until close.

Table 7.2 illustrates the appraisal value for the UL Sample Company under a 338(h)(10) election.

UL SAMPLE COMPANY
TAX BENEFIT UNDER 338(h)(10) ELECTION
As of December 31, 2004
(in millions)

Component of Value	Discount Rate		
	10.0%	12.0%	14.0%
Initial Statutory Liability	803.4	803.4	803.4
Initial Tax Liability	782.4	782.4	782.4
After Tax After Cost of Capital Value of EB	122.9	99.2	80.4
After Tax After Cost of Capital Value of FB	79.0	44.1	20.6
DAC Proxy Tax on Initial Consideration	51.7	54.0	55.7
Mark-to-Market on Asset Portfolio	0.0	0.0	0.0
Excess Tax Ceding Commission on EB	59.1	27.4	3.2
Tax Benefit from 338 (h) (10) Election:			
DAC Proxy Tax on Initial Consideration	11.1	10.7	10.2
Elimination of Exisiting DAC Proxy Tax Balance	(12.7)	(11.9)	(11.1)
15-Year Deduction on EB	10.5	4.3	0.5
15-Year Deduction on FB	17.0	8.3	3.4
Total Tax Benefit	25.9	11.5	3.0
Adjusted Book Value	100.0	100.0	100.0
Total Value of Inforce	131.8	102.4	79.9
Total Value of New Business	96.1	52.4	24.0
Total Actuarial Value	327.8	254.8	204.0

TABLE 7.2

Chapter Eight

Accounting

8.1 INTRODUCTION

This chapter focuses on pronouncements for business combinations under generally accepted accounting principles (GAAP) in the United States. It contains some interpretations of these pronouncements, as well as practical examples to help the reader better understand the application of these rules and how they apply to insurance acquisitions.

Also presented are accounting rules under U.S. statutory accounting principles (SAP). SAP constitutes an accounting basis for statutory financial statements filed by insurance companies with state insurance regulators.

8.2 US GAAP PURCHASE ACCOUNTING

Financial Accounting Standards Board (FASB) Statement No.141, "Business Combinations" (Statement of Financial Accounting Standards (SFAS) 141), addresses the financial accounting and reporting for business combinations and requires that all business combinations be accounted for by the "purchase method" of accounting for all transactions initiated after June 30, 2001. SFAS 141 superseded Accounting Principles Board Opinion No. 16, "Business Combinations" (APB 16) and amended or superseded many of the interpretations included in APB 16. Also, SFAS 141 superseded FASB Statement No. 38, "Accounting for Preacquisition Contingencies of Purchased Enterprises" (SFAS 38), but carries forward the guidance from SFAS 38 without reconsideration.

SFAS 141 does not change many of the provisions of APB 16 and SFAS 38 related to the application of the purchase method. Examples of provisions remaining the same include: (a) determining the cost of an acquisition, (b) allocating the cost of the acquisition to assets acquired and liabilities assumed (except intangible assets), (c) contingent considerations, and (d) preacquisition contingencies. As a result, the new guidance is not a radical change from the way purchase price has historically been determined and allocated. However, the most significant changes reflect the elimination of the "pooling-of-interests" method and the establishment of criteria for identifying and recognizing more intangible assets separately from goodwill in a business combination.

SFAS 141 does not address the accounting for the formation of joint ventures, combinations of two or more mutual enterprises, combinations of two or more not-for-profit organizations, or the acquisition of a for-profit business entity by not-for-profit organizations. The accounting for these types of transactions is beyond this chapter's scope. In addition, SFAS 141 does not address techniques for determining actuarially derived values.

Effective December 15, 2001, FASB Statement No. 142, "Goodwill and Other Intangible Assets" (SFAS 142), superseded APB Opinion No. 17, "Intangible Assets." The major provisions of SFAS 142 include the following: (a) elimination of goodwill amortization, (b) prohibition of amortization of certain identifiable intangible assets with "indefinite useful life," and, (c) requirement of amortization of an *identifiable* intangible asset if it has a "finite useful life."

SFAS 142 also requires rigorous impairment testing of goodwill and other intangible assets. Later sections address in detail the amortization of goodwill and identifiable intangible assets.

8.2.1 BUSINESS COMBINATION

SFAS 141, paragraph 9, states, "a business combination occurs when an entity acquires net assets that constitute a business or acquires equity interests of one or more other entities and obtains control over that entity or entities." Business combinations can include the combination of two or more enterprises, the transfer of equity interests by owners of one enterprise to owners of another, the transfer by one enterprise to another of net assets, and the transfer by all parties in the transaction of either their net assets or equity interests to a newly formed enterprise. The formation of a joint venture is not considered a business combination, and transactions in which control is obtained through means other than an acquisition of net assets or equity interests are not covered by SFAS 141.

A common strategy in the insurance industry is to make acquisitions of net assets through either indemnity or assumption reinsurance. Reinsurance transactions should be evaluated to assess what has been acquired and if they meet the definition of a "business" and thus follow SFAS 141 accounting.

Emerging Issues Task Force Issue No. 98-3, "Determining Whether a Nonmonetary Transaction Involves Receipt of Productive Assets or of a Business" (EITF 98-3), provides guidance in determining whether a transferred set of assets constitutes a business. EITF 98-3 states, "a business is a self-sustaining integrated set of activities and assets conducted and managed for the purpose of providing a return to investors."

If all of the elements necessary to sustain normal operations are transferred, the transferred set is a business, and the acquisition would follow SFAS 141 accounting. In essence, if technology and employees are acquired in the reinsurance transaction, it could lead to the determination that a "business" has been acquired. If not, FASB Statement No. 113 "Accounting and Reporting for Reinsurance of Short-Duration and Long-Duration Contracts" would be followed.

The majority of business combinations in the insurance industry involve the purchase of common stock of an insurance company and/or a holding company that owns insurance companies, the acquisition of net assets through indemnity and assumption reinsurance, and the combination of mutual insurance companies.

8.2.2 IDENTIFYING THE ACQUIRING ENTITY

Business combinations accounted for under the purchase method require that an acquiring entity be identified in every combination. SFAS 141 eliminates the prior presumption of APB 16 that the acquiring entity is the one whose owners as a group retained or received the larger portion of the voting rights in the combined entity, but relies instead on the evaluation of all pertinent facts and circumstances.

SFAS 141, paragraph 17, provides a detailed listing of pertinent factors that should be analyzed when identifying the acquiring entity. However, judgment will be required whenever two or more factors conflict. SFAS 141 provides no hierarchy to rank these factors. The pertinent factors included in paragraph 17 are:

(a) The relative voting rights in the combined entity after the combination. Consideration should be given to the existence of any unusual or special voting arrangements.

(b) The existence of a large minority voting interest in the combined entity when no other owner or organized group of owners has a significant voting interest. SFAS 141 does not define the terms "large minority interest" or "significant voting interest." As a result, judgment will be necessary when analyzing this factor.

(c) The composition of the governing body of the combined entity. Factors that should be considered include: (i) what will be considered the governing body of the combined entity, (ii) how the governing body will be elected or appointed, and (iii) whether any statutory requirements exist that will impact any agreement in place governing such election or appointment.

(d) The composition of the senior management of the combined entity. Factors in determining who dominates include: (i) positions considered to be "senior management" (because job titles are likely to vary by entity) and (ii) positions jointly held or subject to scheduled rotation or transition.

(e) The terms of the exchange of equity securities. All else being equal, the acquiring entity is the combining entity that pays a premium over the market value of the equity securities of the other combining entity or entities.

SFAS 141, paragraph 16, states, "in a business combination effected solely through the distribution of cash or other assets or by incurring liabilities, the entity that distributes the cash or other assets or incurs liabilities is generally the acquiring entity."

8.2.3 PURCHASE ACCOUNTING

The purchase method follows the principle that an acquired business should be recorded at the historical cost paid by the acquirer. Hence, any and all consideration paid for a "business" becomes the acquirer's new "historical cost" for the acquired business and should appropriately be reflected in the acquirer's financial statements. The costs should then be allocated to the identifiable individual assets (including intangible assets) acquired and liabilities assumed based on their fair market values. The residual amount should be recorded as goodwill. There are three basic steps to purchase accounting: determination of the acquisition date, determination of the purchase price, and allocation of the purchase price.

8.2.3.1 Acquisition Date

Ordinarily the acquisition date is the date that consummates the transfer of ownership or the date that assets are received and consideration is distributed. Generally, for insurance acquisitions, the acquisition date is more complex because it is affected by the timing of governmental and/or regulatory approval.

8.2.3.2 Determination of Purchase Price

The cost of an acquired entity includes: (i) cash and other assets distributed, (ii) fair value of securities issued unconditionally, (iii) direct costs of the transaction, and (iv) amounts of contingent consideration that are determinable beyond a reasonable doubt as of the date of the acquisition. Direct costs and amounts of contingent considerations need to be evaluated to determine it they represent purchase price or operational expense.

8.2.3.2.1 Cash and Other Assets Distributed

According to SFAS 141, paragraph 20, "a cash payment by an acquiring entity shall be used to measure the cost of an acquired entity. Similarly, the fair values of other assets distributed as consideration, such as marketable securities or properties, and the fair values of liabilities incurred by an acquiring entity shall be used to measure the cost of an acquired entity."

8.2.3.2.2 Fair Value of Securities Issued Unconditionally

EITF Issue No. 99-12, "Determination of the Measurement Date for the Market Price of Acquirer Securities Issued in a Purchase Business Combination," requires that the value of the acquirer's marketable equity securities to effect a purchase business combination be determined based on the market price of the securities over a reasonable time before and after the terms of the acquisition are agreed to and announced.

Based on past consideration of SEC registrant matters, the SEC has experienced diversity in the application of this guidance due in part to an undefined period of time (i.e., a "reasonable period" before and after). The SEC presumes that reasonable period before and after requires registrants to use a period beginning two days before and ending two days after the date that the terms of the acquisition are agreed to and announced to determine the fair value of the securities issued.

The above discussion relates to equity securities in which market value is readily available. If market value is not readily available (i.e., common stock issued by closely held enterprise with no quoted market price or preferred stock issued with no quoted market price, etc.), significant judgment is required to determine market value, which can include considering the fair value of the acquired entity in determining fair value of shares issued or characteristics of the preferred shares issued (i.e., dividend rate, redemption features) to other comparable securities. Independent valuation specialists can offer advice in these situations.

8.2.3.2.3 Direct Costs of the Business Combination

Acquiring Entity

The direct costs of a business combination are included in the cost of the acquired entity. These include direct "out-of-pocket" or incremental costs that are directly related to a business combination. Examples are finder fees or fees paid to outside consultants for accounting, legal, or appraisal work. Indirect and general expenses to the acquirer related to a business combination are expensed as incurred, which include the acquiring entity's cost to maintain an internal mergers and acquisition department. Direct costs incurred in connection with unsuccessful attempts to acquire an enterprise should be charged to expense in the period in which the plans to acquire the enterprise are abandoned.

Acquired Entity

Indirect acquisition costs incurred by the acquiree should be expensed as incurred. In addition, direct acquisition costs incurred by the acquiree also should be expensed as incurred, except in limited situations where there is a preexisting agreement between the acquirer and the acquiree that authorizes the acquiree to incur the costs and provides that the acquiring company will reimburse the costs, in which case recognition of the receivable from the acquirer would appear to be appropriate.

8.2.3.2.4 Contingent Considerations

Contingent consideration can be used to resolve conflicts between buyers and sellers regarding the value of the company being acquired and provide additional consideration to the seller. There are generally two types of contingent consideration, security prices and future earnings.

8.2.3.2.4.1 Based on Security Prices

An acquirer may guarantee the attainment or maintenance of a specified security price. If the market price of the security is not attained or maintained, the acquirer is required to issue additional consideration to make the current value of the total consideration equal to the specified amount. As a result, the acquirer has guaranteed the purchase price of the acquired entity. Therefore, the guaranteed amount should be included in determining the cost of the acquired entity at the date of the acquisition.

When the contingency is resolved and additional consideration is issued, the acquirer should record the current fair value of the additional consideration issued or issuable. However, the amount previously recorded for securities issued at the date of acquisition simultaneously should be reduced to the lower current value of those securities. In effect, the resolution of the contingency is a transfer of the par value of the additional shares from paid-in capital to capital stock.

Example of contingency based on security price

Company XYZ acquires Company ABC by unconditionally issuing one million shares of common stock at the date of acquisition. At the date of acquisition, the market price of this stock is $50 per share. Company XYZ also provides a guarantee to Company ABC that it will issue additional stock to Company ABC if the market price of the stock is less than $100 per share at the end of five years. The purchase price of Company ABC is $100 million (one million shares times $100 per share).

At the end of five years, Company XYZ's stock is $80. As a result, Company XYZ issues an additional 250,000 shares representing $20 million (250,000 times $80 per share) with the corresponding reduction of the amount reported previously for the stock issued to effect the combination. The net effect of these changes is a reclassification from additional paid-in capital to common stock for the par value of the additional shares issued. The $100 million to acquire Company ABC does not change due to the issuance of the additional $20 million in stock.

8.2.3.2.4.2 ***Based on Earnings***

Additional consideration in a business combination that is contingent on maintaining or achieving specified earnings levels in future periods (often referred to as an "earn-out" arrangement) generally is not recorded until the contingency is resolved and the additional consideration is distributable, unless the outcome of the contingency is determinable beyond a reasonable doubt. When the contingency is resolved or the contingency outcome is determinable, the acquiring enterprise should record the current fair value of the additional consideration as additional cost of the acquired entity. The fair value of the consideration is allocated to assets acquired, generally goodwill. Unless contingent considerations are determinable beyond a reasonable doubt, they are merely disclosed and not recorded as a liability (or outstanding securities).

However, if the initial purchase price (excluding the contingent amount) is below the fair value of the net assets acquired prior to resolution of the contingency (giving rise to an excess over cost referred to as "negative goodwill"), and resolution of the contingency will result in additional purchase price, SFAS 141, paragraph 46, requires the acquirer to establish a liability in purchase accounting. The liability will represent an amount equal to the lesser of the excess of net assets over purchase price (excluding the contingent amount) and before pro rata allocation or the maximum amount of the contingent consideration to be recognized.

Example of contingency based on earnings

December 31, 2002, Company XYZ purchases Company ABC for $5 million in cash and $5 million of common stock in Company XYZ. The purchase agreement requires Company XYZ to provide an additional payment of $1 million to the former shareholders of Company ABC if Company ABC's operating income is at least $4 million by December 31, 2003 (FY03). The FY03 operating income is $4.5 million. Therefore, Company XYZ would record this additional payment as additional purchase price and record the offset to goodwill.

8.2.3.2.4.3 ***Compensation in Contingent Agreements***

The SEC maintains that contingent consideration is actually compensation to selling shareholders who remain employees of the ongoing entity. The substance of the agreement for contingent consideration dictates whether contingent payment is compensation or purchase price. EITF No. 95-8, "Accounting for Contingent Consideration Paid to the Shareholders of an Acquired Enterprise in a Purchase Business Combination," states that any additional consideration that represents compensation should be recognized as expense. Each situation must be examined before making a determination.

Example of compensation in contingent agreements

Company XYZ purchased a small property and casualty (P&C) insurance company (Company ABC) in which all of the shareholders were senior management. The purchase agreement requires additional payments to the shareholders if the loss ratios of Company ABC are below 65% for the next three years. However, the additional payments are only paid if the shareholders remain with Company XYZ for the next three years. Based on these facts, Company XYZ would treat these payments to the former shareholders of Company ABC as compensation expense because the payments are contingent upon the former shareholders' continued employment with Company XYZ.

8.2.3.3 *Purchase Price Allocation*

The acquiring entity must allocate the cost of the acquired entity to the assets acquired and liabilities assumed. The allocation is based upon their estimated fair values at the date of the acquisition. However, the acquiring entity should first ensure that all consideration has been identified in determining the cost of the acquired entity.

Second, the acquiring entity should ensure that all assets acquired and liabilities assumed, including all identifiable intangible assets that meet the requirements of SFAS 141, paragraph 39, are recognized. Any excess purchase price over net assets acquired (at fair value) is recorded as goodwill.

Appendix F of SFAS 141 defines fair value as the amount at which an asset or liability can be exchanged (or settled) in a current transaction between knowledgeable unrelated willing parties when neither is acting under compulsion. Therefore, market prices, where available, are considered to be the best evidence of a fair value. Accordingly, assets and liabilities should be recorded using the following hierarchy:

(a) Level 1—Observable market prices for *identical* assets or liabilities at or near the measurement date should be used
(b) Level 2—Observable market prices of similar assets, if identical assets or liabilities are not available should be used
(c) Level 3a—If level 1 and level 2 are not available, valuation techniques using market-based assumptions may be used
(d) Level 3b—If market-based assumptions are not available without undue cost and effort, an entity may use its own assumptions.

8.2.4 MARKET VALUE OF INVESTMENTS (INCLUDING DERIVATIVES) AND OTHER ASSETS

The following describes a general guideline for determining the fair value of assets acquired and liabilities assumed in purchase accounting:

- Marketable securities, such as publicly traded bonds, mortgage-backed securities, options, swaps, other derivative items, cash, and other cash equivalents, are recorded at current net realizable value on the acquisition date. At the date of acquisition, investment securities acquired should be classified as held-to-maturity, available-for-sale, or trading securities based on the intent and ability of the acquiring entity rather than the historical classification of the acquired entity.

- Other invested assets, including mortgage loans, nonmarketable securities, and properties are recorded at appraisal value developed using discounted cash flows or other reasonable financial model results.

- Receivables are recorded at present values of amounts to be received determined at appropriate current interest rates, less allowances for uncollectibility and collection costs, if appropriate. However, discounting may not be necessary when the receivables are to be recovered within a short period of time, such as within several months, provided that the difference between the present values and the gross amounts of the receivables is not significant.

- Plant and equipment are recorded at the current replacement cost for similar capacity unless the expected future use of the assets indicates a lower value to the acquiring entity.

- Identifiable intangible assets (for example, the value of business acquired resulting from the acquisition of a life insurance company, known as "VOBA"; brand name; distribution channel; etc.) that meet the requirements of SFAS 141, paragraph 39, are valued and established in purchase accounting.

8.2.5 DEFERRED TAXES

SFAS 141, paragraph 38, indicates that an acquiring entity shall not recognize deferred income taxes recorded by an acquired entity before its acquisition when allocating the purchase price. A new deferred tax liability or asset will be recognized under purchase accounting for the difference between the relative fair value of assets acquired and liabilities assumed in the business combination (the "net assets") and the tax basis of the net assets acquired. The tax basis will change if an IRS Section 338 election is made (stock acquisition treated as an asset acquisition and a step-up in basis for purchased assets).

8.2.6 LIABILITIES AND RESERVES

Product classification determines both reserve methodology and type of valuation assumptions to be used to compute GAAP reserves and related liabilities both before and after the date of acquisition. As a result, it has been common practice to compute purchase GAAP (PGAAP) reserves based on the same methodology and type of assumptions that will be used for valuations subsequent to the date of acquisition.

The most common practice for traditional products covered by SFAS 60 is that reserves are restated based on current assumptions with provision for adverse deviation at the date of acquisition. For other products with policyholder account value balances covered by SFAS 97, the most common practice is basic reserves continuing to be policyholder account values.

This practice may initially appear to be in conflict with the requirement of SFAS 141 that reserves be stated at fair value. However, in section 8.2.7.5.2.6, a discussion of fair value liabilities is provided that shows how conventional PGAAP reserves in combination with the VOBA can satisfy the fair value definition.

8.2.6.1 SFAS 60 Traditional and Group Contracts

SFAS 60, "Accounting and Reporting by Insurance Enterprises," was effective for fiscal years beginning after December 15, 1982. SFAS 60 classified insurance contracts as short-duration or long-duration, depending on whether contracts were intended to remain in force for an extended period. A short-duration contract "...provides insurance protection for a fixed period of short duration and enables the insurer to cancel the contract or to adjust the provisions of the contract at the end of any contract period, such as adjusting premiums charged or coverage provided." Examples of short-duration contracts include most property and liability insurance contracts, group term life, major medical and disability, credit life, and credit disability.

A long-duration contract "...generally is not subject to unilateral changes in its provisions, such as a non-cancelable or guaranteed renewable contract, and requires the performance of various functions and services (including insurance protection) for an extended period." Examples of long-duration contracts include whole life, limited pay life, guaranteed renewable term life, endowments, life contingent payout annuities, and title insurance.

8.2.6.1.1 Short-Duration Contracts

In general, PGAAP reserves for short-duration contracts (sometimes called active life reserves to distinguish from claim reserves) are unearned premium reserves. Such reserves are generally computed the same way as those prior to the date of acquisition. PGAAP adjustments would be required only where discounting is involved or re-estimation is necessary, as for claims reserves.

8.2.6.1.2 Long-Duration Contracts

SFAS 60 defines the reserve to be the present value of future benefits and policy maintenance expenses less the present value of future net premiums. Valuation assumptions, such as investment yields, mortality, morbidity, terminations, and expenses, are based on best-estimate assumptions at the time of issue. Valuation assumptions include a provision for adverse deviation (PAD), where appropriate. The assumptions used at issue remain unchanged unless the reserve proves to be inadequate at a later date (lock-in concept) or the liabilities are subsequently purchased.

There is little guidance for computing PGAAP reserves for SFAS 60 long-duration contracts. APB Opinion 16 (APB 16), "Business Combinations," and Opinion 17 (APB 17), "Intangible Assets," issued in 1970, were the predecessors to SFAS 141 and SFAS 142. Numerous AICPA and FASB interpretations, SEC Staff Accounting Bulletins, and Accounting Series Releases have been issued to deal with these opinions.

In 1992 the FASB Emerging Issues Task Force issued EITF 92-9, "Accounting for the Present Value of Future Profits Resulting from the Acquisition of a Life Insurance Company." While the task force did not deal directly with PGAAP reserves, documents contained in the EITF 92-9 Minutes/Issues Summary did provide some guidance.

A second document that attempted to provide specific guidance to actuaries is the American Academy of Actuaries (AAA) Interpretation 1-D: Purchase Accounting, adopted in 1977. The concepts of Interpretation 1-D have been illustrated in a paper, "Purchase Accounting: A Fresh Look," appearing in the 1983 *Transactions of the Society of Actuaries*. Although not authoritative guidance, Interpretation 1-D has been applied extensively in practice.

Another resource is an AICPA Draft Issues Paper, "Accounting For the Purchase of a Life Insurance Enterprise," dated November 30, 1983, which delivered thorough illustrations of PGAAP situations, but was never published in final form. The AICPA draft included references to Interpretation 1-D and other PGAAP implications of APB 16.

At the date of acquisition, SFAS 60 reserves would continue to be the present value of future benefits and policy maintenance expenses less the present value of net premiums. However, the date of acquisition replaces the date of issue for assumption-setting purposes. Hence, valuation assumptions are reset as of the date of acquisition and include appropriate PAD. Subsequent to purchase, net valuation premiums and PGAAP valuation assumptions remain locked-in unless reserves subsequently prove deficient, triggering loss recognition.

At the date of acquisition, there are three components to consider: the reserve, the present value of future benefits and expenses, and the present value of future net premiums. Of the three, only the present value of future benefits and expenses can be directly computed with the revised valuation assumptions.

With respect to the other two components, if one is set, the other can be derived, as addressed in Interpretation 1-D. Under one method, the defined initial reserve method (DIRM), an initial reserve is selected and the net premium is derived. Under the defined valuation premium method (DVPM), a net premium is selected and the PGAAP reserve is derived.

Although Interpretation 1-D was intended for traditional non-par contracts covered by SFAS 60, the principles of DIRM and DVPM can provide a basis of logic for valuing other contractual provisions and policy features on contracts covered by SFAS 97, SFAS 91, SFAS 113, SFAS 120, and SFAS 133.

8.2.6.1.2.1 ***Defined Initial Reserve Method***

Many forms of the PGAAP reserve have been deemed acceptable in practice. These include use of the historical GAAP (HGAAP) reserve, the statutory reserve, or other basis in setting the initial (at purchase) PGAAP reserve. Once the initial PGAAP reserve is set, net valuation premiums are derived using revised valuation assumptions appropriate to the business, which include choosing valuation interest rates based on then-current market values, not on prior book value rates of return. For post-purchase valuations, net valuation premiums, along with locked-in valuation assumptions (with PAD, as appropriate) established at purchase, are used to compute reserves.

Given this methodology, one of three types of valuation premium will emerge, influenced by the level of the initial reserve, the revised valuation assumptions, and the level of gross premium. If the derived net premiums are less than the gross premiums for a line of business or major block of business, no adjustment is needed. If the net premiums exceed gross premiums, the PAD may be reduced to allow the net premiums to equal gross premiums.

However, if valuation premiums derived with then-current best-estimate assumptions (excluding any PAD) still exceed gross premiums, the gross premiums should be used as valuation premiums, and a revised initial PGAAP reserve should be derived using such best-estimate assumptions as of the date of acquisition. This revised result is consistent with the gross premium valuation methodology described in actuarial literature.

For contracts beyond the premium-paying period (e.g., paid-up policies, extended term insurance, or paid-up additions), net valuation premiums do not apply. The post-purchase reserve is the present value of future benefits and policy maintenance expenses using the same valuation assumptions that produced the PGAAP reserve.

8.2.6.1.2.2 ***Defined Valuation Premium Method***

In applying the DVPM, Interpretation 1-D indicates that valuation premiums are taken as gross premiums less a reasonable profit allowance for risk taking. Reserves are then computed as the present value of future benefits and policy maintenance expenses less the present value of the defined valuation premiums, using assumptions appropriate to the business that include PAD.

The valuation assumptions are based on revised assumptions at the date of purchase, including then-current market interest rates. The valuation premium will include a provision for post-purchase deferrable commissions (mainly heaped renewal commissions) and deferrable acquisition expenses (i.e., expenses in excess of maintenance expenses expected to be incurred by the acquiring entity).

In selecting a reasonable profit allowance, reference is made to consistency with the allowance on then-current new business of either the acquiring or acquired entity. An example of considerations for such calculation follows.

A new business product has the following profile:

- gross premium (GP) is 100
- net valuation premium for benefits and maintenance expenses is 60
- net valuation premium for deferrable acquisition expenses is 30.

The resultant profit margin is 10 (i.e., 10% of GP). A reading of Interpretation 1-D suggests that the DVPM valuation premium would be 90 (100 less a typical profit allowance of 10% of GP). However, at the date of acquisition, inforce policies are generally beyond the period of significant acquisition costs. Also, at purchase the HGAAP deferred acquisition cost (DAC) is eliminated. Hence, little or none of the portion of gross premium normally needed to amortize deferred acquisition expenses (30% in this example) would be required. Assuming that no post-purchase acquisition costs will be incurred on inforce business, the entire 30% of gross premium would be expected to release into profits in the future. This makes a case for setting the net valuation premium equal to 60% of GP.

With valuation premiums of 60% of GP, it is true that the resulting PGAAP reserve would be higher than had 90% of GP been chosen. However, a higher reserve results in a higher VOBA (an asset discussed in section 8.2.7.5), producing a similar net GAAP liability (reserve less VOBA). As a result, the choice of level of net valuation premium is not as critical as it might appear.

8.2.6.1.2.3 *Summary*

In summary, the DVPM valuation premium for benefits and policy maintenance expenses should be consistent with what is typical for new business. The PGAAP reserve can then be computed as the present value of future benefits and maintenance expenses less the present value of DVPM valuation premiums.

Whether applying DVPM or DIRM, acquisition expense valuation premiums should be computed by discounting (present-valuing) all post-purchase deferrable acquisition expenses (mainly heaped renewal commissions) to the date of purchase and dividing by the present value of gross premiums at the date of purchase. By definition, the PGAAP DAC asset will be zero at purchase because the present value of post-purchase acquisition expenses will exactly equal the present value of acquisition expense valuation premiums.

Another way to view opening DAC as zero is that acquisition costs were incurred by the seller, not the buyer. Under both DIRM and DVPM, profit margins, defined as the difference between gross premiums and the sum of net valuation premiums (for benefits, maintenance expenses, and post-purchase acquisition expenses), are expected to release into gross income (or unearned revenue for limited-pay contracts as subsequently discussed). In addition, if actual experience follows best-estimate assumptions, releases of PAD can be expected as an additional source of gross income.

8.2.6.2 *Liability for Unpaid Claims (Claims Reserves)*

The liability for unpaid claims (or claims reserve) should represent management's best estimate of future claims costs, including associated claims expenses, discounted to present value. The liability should include all incurred claims, both reported and unreported (IBNR). For PGAAP purposes, revised estimates of claims costs, associated expenses, and interest rates for discounting should be based on current assumptions as of the date of acquisition. While there is a wide range of estimates used in practice, SFAS 60 indicates that there should be no PAD placed on assumptions.

8.2.6.3 *SFAS 60 P&C Liabilities*

P&C company liabilities may be classified into one of two categories: claim liabilities or unearned premium reserves.

8.2.6.3.1 Claim Liabilities

Prior to SFAS 141, separate valuations of P&C reserves to determine the fair value of these liabilities were rare in practice. Under SFAS 141, actuaries and accountants are required to value these liabilities more consistently with their fair value. Staff Accounting Bulletin 100 requires that receivables, liabilities, and accruals be recorded at their fair value in the allocation of purchase price. The SEC's view that claim liabilities should be remeasured at fair value in purchase accounting is consistent with the general guidance in APB 16 and SFAS 141 that liabilities assumed be recorded at fair value.

Due to the lack of guidance on the topic, there are multiple approaches considered acceptable in determining the fair value of P&C liabilities. In response to a FASB fair value project and increased activity by the IASC on fair valuing P&C liabilities, the Casualty Actuarial Society (CAS) issued a White Paper on the Fair Value of Property/Casualty Insurance Liabilities. This paper discusses various methods that are considered reasonable to determine the fair value of P&C liabilities.

The underlying principle is that one needs to evaluate the value of these obligations in a cash exchange using valuation assumptions that are consistent with those used by the typical marketplace participant. The key components for the valuation of P&C liabilities include the expected value of the liabilities, the expected payment pattern for these liabilities, and a discount rate that is commensurate with the risk of variability in the cash flows.

Three general approaches have emerged to determine the fair value of P&C liabilities. The first method, the direct method, is to discount the expected value of the loss and loss adjustment expense reserves using a risk-adjusted discount rate. The risk-adjusted discount rate is one that the market would require to assume the cash flows and the risk inherent in the timing and amount of the payments inherent in the expected loss reserve.

Due to the inherent risk in some property casualty exposure, the direct method usually results in a risk-adjusted discount rate less than market investment yields. Furthermore, in some instances the implied discount rate may be negative if the risk premium associated with the potential variability in cash flows exceeds the assumed investment earnings rate.

The diverse nature of property casualty insurance exposure presents significant challenges for actuaries to determine the appropriate risk-adjusted discount rate. Due to the differing risk inherent in the various lines of P&C insurance, the risk-adjusted discount rate would vary by line of insurance, adding to the complexity of the calculation.

The second method, the indirect method, is to determine the discount for the time value of money and market value margin in two separate steps. For this method, the market discount for the time value of money is determined using duration-matched yield curves. Various methods are then used to determine the market value margin that would be required by a typical marketplace participant to assume the risk inherent in the assumed cash flows. These methods include: stochastic simulation, loss development modeling, aggregate probability distribution methods, and market values determined from reinsurance transactions.

The use of the indirect method sometimes seems to be in conflict with the SFAS 60, which suggests that no PAD be placed on assumptions used for claim reserves. One argument is that the market value margin is calculated for process risk (variability in claim payments) and does not include parameter risk (variability in the assumptions). Therefore, this method is consistent with the PADs. In theory, both the direct method and the indirect method are attempting to estimate the market discount commensurate with the underlying risk of the assumed liabilities.

The third method for determining fair value liabilities is the market comparable approach, whereby the fair value of the liabilities is based upon the pricing of recent similar market reinsurance transactions. Comparability of the transaction must exist, but it is difficult to determine without detailed information on the attributes of the blocks of business that were reinsured.

Two common accounting approaches are used to determine the post-purchase value of these claim liabilities. One approach is to continue to calculate the present value of the remaining payment patterns using the risk-adjusted discount rate from the direct method or by using an implicit interest rate from the indirect method. The implicit interest rate from the indirect method would be calculated by determining the rate of return required to obtain the fair value liabilities given the payment patterns underlying the undiscounted expected losses. This method would require P&C insurers to determine the payment patterns of the remaining liabilities at each measurement date.

A second approach is to amortize the difference between the fair value and undiscounted expected claim payments in relation to undiscounted expected claim payments used in the fair value calculation.

8.2.6.3.2 Unearned Premiums

Similar to loss and loss adjustment expense reserve estimates, the unearned premium reserve (UPR) must also be recorded at fair value under FAS 141. The same principle applies; the fair value is the amount at which the liability could be settled for in cash at the purchase date in an unbiased, third-party exchange.

Generally, such fair value would be based on the book value of UPR adjusted for projected distributable earnings discounted at a market discount rate commensurate with the risk of variability in cash flows, using the discounted cash flow techniques described in Chapter 4. However, due to the short-term nature of most property casualty insurance contracts, premiums will be earned, and the policy administration expenses will be paid in less than one year. Therefore, the fair value of the unearned premium is sometimes determined as the sum of the unpaid policy administration expenses plus the fair value of the expected loss and loss adjustment expense inherent in the UPR.

Using pricing information, the actuary is able to determine the expected loss and loss adjustment expense inherent in the UPR. The methods described in the loss reserve discussion are used to determine the fair value of these costs. The market risk load and the risk-adjusted discount rate used to fair-value the expected loss payments from the UPR will differ from that used to fair-value the loss reserve liabilities. The losses inherent in the UPR have not been incurred, and therefore have greater uncertainty than those for which loss reserves have been established. Therefore, the market value margin should be relatively higher and the risk-adjusted discount rate should be relatively lower, than that used for similar loss reserve liabilities.

A common practice that has been used is to account for the difference between the fair value and gross amount of unearned premium through a contra-liability. The contra-liability would be amortized ratably over the remaining coverage period at the purchase date as a reduction of earned premiums.

8.2.6.4 SFAS 97—Deferred Profit Liability for Traditional Limited Pay Contracts

The deferred profit liability (DPL), a post-purchase issue, is based on PGAAP components. The standard profit margin associated with SFAS 60 traditional products is the difference between the gross premium and the sum of net valuation premiums.

Before SFAS 97, "Accounting and Reporting by Insurance Enterprises for Certain Long-Duration Contracts and for Realized Gains and Losses from the Sale of Investments," such margins were recognized in income as gross premiums were earned. SFAS 97 recognized that a limited-payment contract subjects the insurer to risks over a period that exceeds the premium payment period.

As a result, SFAS 97 requires such margins to be deferred and amortized into income as a uniform percentage of either insurance in force or expected annuity payments, for life insurance and annuities, respectively. The post-purchase premium margins will be the difference between the gross premium and the sum of the valuation premiums, where valuation premiums cover benefits and maintenance expenses, post-purchase acquisition expenses, and VOBA amortization (if VOBA is amortized as a uniform percentage of gross premiums). At the date of acquisition, the DPL is zero.

8.2.6.5 SFAS 97—Universal Life Contracts

SFAS 97 applies to an array of long-duration insurance contracts with terms that are not fixed and guaranteed, called universal life-type contacts. Such contracts provide either death or life-contingent annuity benefits and are characterized by any one of the following features: one or more amounts assessed by the insurer are not fixed and guaranteed, amounts that accrue to the benefit of the policyholder are not fixed and guaranteed, and premiums may be varied by the policyholder. Examples include universal life, variable universal life (VUL), most corporate-owned life insurance (COLI) and bank-owned life insurance (BOLI), and private placement variable universal life (PPVUL). These products come with both fixed and flexible premium features. In most cases UL-type products have an explicit policyholder account value (AV).

Common practice has been to set the PGAAP reserve equal to the AV at the date of acquisition. However, some believe the PGAAP reserve should be recomputed based on then-current market assumptions. That is, projected best estimate cash flows to and from the policyholder account would be present-valued using then-current credited rates. The result would be an initial PGAAP reserve that could be higher or lower than the actual AV. The process is analogous to computing the market value of a corporate bond or mortgage based on updated market assumptions.

8.2.6.5.1 Unearned Revenue and Accrued Liabilities for Bonuses

SFAS 97 requires unearned revenue to be deferred and redistributed over the life of the underlying contracts. The same applies to charges taken from policyholder account values, such as front-end loads on UL-type contracts. For example, front-end loads are quite often charged to compensate the insurer for acquisition expenses. Since acquisition expenses are deferred and amortized as a uniform percentage of gross profits, SFAS 97 requires similar treatment for front-end loads (i.e., capitalization and amortization into income as a uniform percentage of gross profits).

Since the PGAAP balance sheet eliminates existing DAC at the date of acquisition, consistent treatment would call for the elimination of existing unearned revenue liabilities. However, not all such liabilities should receive similar treatment. Those liabilities established to spread revenue over the life of the contracts, such as the liability for unearned profit margins on SFAS 60 limited pay contracts or the liability for unamortized front-end loads, should be eliminated. However, those established to accrue a liability that the insurer is likely to incur after the acquisition date should be retained. An example of the latter type would be an accrued liability for the payment of a persistency bonus.

While guidance for establishing a PGAAP bonus liability is scarce, the following describes practices commonly in use. An accrued liability for future contract-holder bonuses can be established analogously to either DIRM or DVPM in principle. For example, if the principles of DIRM are employed, the HGAAP liability for accrued bonuses can be carried over to the PGAAP balance sheet. A uniform percentage of post-purchase estimated gross profits (accrual percentage) can then be solved for such that an appropriate bonus can be accrued by the expected date of bonus payment.

A variant of this method is to set the initial PGAAP liability to zero, requiring a higher uniform percentage of future gross profits than would be the case with a positive initial PGAAP liability. Best-estimate assumptions at the date of acquisition would be used to project gross profits and expected bonus payments.

Similarly, if DVPM principles are employed, the typical percentage of estimated gross profits (EGPs) necessary to accrue the bonus liability on new business is chosen. The PGAAP liability is then derived as the present value of bonus payments less the present value of the chosen percentage of post-purchase future gross profits. Consistent with SFAS 97 principles, all present values and accumulations (accruals) are computed using credited rates of interest, not earned rates of interest.

The above methods treat the purchased business as a new cohort. Although less common in practice and more difficult to implement, if historical gross profits are obtained for each issue cohort, an accrued bonus liability can be derived for each cohort as a uniform percentage of historical and projected gross profits. The sum of accrued bonus liabilities at the date of purchase constitutes the PGAAP liability.

8.2.6.5.2 Universal Life with No-Lapse Guarantees

Statement of Position 03-1, discussed in section 8.2.6.7, addresses UL contracts with no-lapse guarantees. Typically, such guarantees stipulate that as long as prescribed minimum premiums are paid, the contract will not lapse even if the AV balance is depleted. The SOP requires that reserves for this contingency be held in addition to the policyholder account value.

Principles of DIRM and DVPM can be applied to establish the PGAAP reserve consistent with requirements of the SOP. In addition, some might set the PGAAP reserve to zero, requiring future contract-holder assessments to fund expected benefits.

The above approaches treat the acquired business as a new issue cohort. If historical data is available, the PGAAP reserve can be derived from historical and projected contract-holder assessments by issue cohort, consistent with the SOP.

8.2.6.6 *SFAS 97—Investment Contracts*

SFAS 97 indicates that investment contracts issued by an insurance enterprise do not incorporate significant insurance risk as contemplated in SFAS 60. Examples of investment contracts include single and flexible premium deferred annuities, guaranteed investment contracts (GICs), market value adjusted (MVA) annuities, two-tiered deferred annuities, variable annuities in the accumulation phase, and payout annuities without life contingencies (annuities certain).

Investment contracts issued by insurance entities are accounted for in a manner consistent with interest-bearing or other financial instruments. Equity-indexed annuities (EIAs) are a special case of investment contracts that contain embedded derivatives as defined by SFAS 133, "Accounting for Derivative Instruments and Hedging Activities."

Common practice has been to establish the basic PGAAP reserve for investment contracts as the contract-holder AV, where an AV exists. However, some believe the PGAAP reserve should be recomputed at the purchase date based on then-current market assumptions. Projected best-estimate cash flows to and from the contract-holder AV would be discounted at then-current credited rates. The resulting initial PGAAP reserve might be higher or lower than the actual AV. The process would be analogous to computing the market value of a corporate bond or mortgage.

Under (historical) GAAP, reserves for payout annuities without life contingencies (annuities certain), the SFAS 91 constant yield method is applied at issue to solve for a constant yield rate that links the premium less deferrable acquisition expenses to the guaranteed annuity payments and related expenses. That is, the present value of annuity payments and related expenses at the constant yield rate will exactly equal the premium less acquisition expenses. For post-issue valuations, the present value of annuity payments and related expenses is computed with the valuation interest assumption equal to the constant yield rate derived at issue.

By analogy, the PGAAP reserve for payout annuities should be recomputed as the present value of annuity payments and related expenses based on revised best-estimate assumptions at the date of acquisition, including a revised constant yield rate. Consistent with a DIRM approach, the PGAAP reserve can be chosen to equal the HGAAP reserve, and a constant yield rate that links the present value of future payouts with the reserve can be derived. Likewise, if a DVPM approach were taken, a constant yield rate would be selected, consistent with then-current market conditions and appropriate for similar new business. The PGAAP reserve would then be derived as the present value of future payouts and related expenses. In either case, for post-purchase valuations the PGAAP constant yield rate should continue to be used because assumptions are locked in.

8.2.6.7 *Liabilities Required by SOP 03-1 for MGDB, GMIB, Two-Tiered Annuities, and Sales Inducements*

AICPA Statement of Position (SOP) 03-1, "Accounting and Reporting by Insurance Enterprises for Certain Nontraditional Long-Duration Contracts and for Separate Accounts," requires liabilities for certain minimum guaranteed death benefit (MGDB) and guaranteed minimum income benefit (GMIB) contract features. Such liabilities are held in addition to the contract-holder account value. The SOP also requires a liability for sales inducements.

Regarding variable annuities in the accumulation phase (deferred stage), several MGDB designs are encountered in practice. MGDB features include return of premium, account value at a particular previous anniversary, return of premiums accrued at a minimum interest rate, and highest account value balance. The SOP addresses the determination of whether mortality risk is significant, causing an investment contract to be classified as a UL-type contract. For variable annuities with significant mortality risk, the SOP may require a reserve to be held in addition to the account value.

The SOP defines contract-holder assessments as the aggregate of all charges, including those for mortality, administration, and surrender (and, for fixed account products, investment spreads). For variable annuities with significant mortality risk, if the pattern of expected periodic contract-holder assessments for the benefit feature less expected claims exhibits profits followed by losses, a reserve is required in addition to the account value. The SOP defines a reserve methodology based on a uniform percentage of contract-holder assessments.

At each valuation date, a benefit ratio (BR) is computed as of the contract issue date as the present value of actual and projected claims divided by the present value of actual and projected contract-holder assessments. The MGDB reserve is the BR times the accumulated value of contract-holder assessments less the accumulated value of claims. The interest rates used to compute present values and accumulated values are the credited rates of interest, the rates used for DAC amortization and/or discounting EGPs. The same concepts apply to mutual funds with significant MGDB features.

A GMIB in variable annuities typically provides a minimum income benefit that is only available upon annuitization, but applies regardless of fund performance. The value of the guaranteed income may be in excess of what the expected account value balance would be able to provide. The SOP requires a liability to be accrued for the excess of the present value of expected guaranteed annuity benefits at the expected date of annuitization over the expected AV balance. The liability should be accrued as a uniform percentage of contract-holder assessments using the same BR methodology described for MGDB.

While the SOP does not demand the use of stochastically generated scenarios to compute reserves, it is likely that at each valuation date multiple scenarios would be needed to adequately quantify the present value of MGDB and GMIB benefits, which depend on projections of fund performance and vary by scenario.

The SOP also addresses two-tiered annuity contracts. Two-tiered annuity contracts typically have two AV balances, one (the lower-tier) available in the event of surrender and the other (the higher-tier) available only upon annuitization. The SOP clarifies that the basic benefit reserve is the AV supporting the cash surrender value (the lower-tier account value). However, the SOP requires a liability to be accrued for the excess of the present value of the annuity benefits guaranteed to be purchased with the expected higher-tier AV over the expected lower-tier AV at the expected annuitization date.

Similarly, an additional liability might be required for insurance and investment contracts that contain guaranteed annuity purchase rates. All such additional reserves are to be accrued from a uniform percentage of contract-holder assessments. Computation of the BR and GMIB reserve is analogous to the method described for MGDB.

The principles of DIRM and DVPM can again be applied to derive the PGAAP reserves for contract features such as MGDB, GMIB, and two-tiered annuity benefits.

If DIRM is employed, the initial PGAAP reserve is set equal to the HGAAP reserve at the date of acquisition. Subsequently, a PGAAP BR, a uniform percentage of post-purchase future contract-holder assessments, must be derived. As with all PGAAP computations, the PGAAP BR would be derived with revised best-estimate assumptions at the date of acquisition, including credited rates of interest required for discounting. In addition, some might set the initial PGAAP reserve to zero, requiring future contract-holder assessments to fund expected benefits.

If DVPM principles are applied, a reasonable BR, consistent with that for new business, is assumed. Then the PGAAP reserve, defined as the BR times the accumulated contract-holder assessments less the accumulated claims, is derived based on then-current best-estimate assumptions at the date of acquisition. Consistent with SFAS 97 principles, computations of present values and accumulated values are performed at credited rates of interest.

Considering the date of acquisition to be similar to a contract re-issue date allows the acquired inforce business to be aggregated and represented by a single new issue cohort. Future unlocking to recompute the benefit ratio will involve only post-purchase actual and future expected claims and contract-holder assessments. Alternatively, if historical claims and contract-holder assessments are available, the PGAAP reserve can be derived from historical and projected best estimates of claims and contract-holder assessments by issue cohort, a methodology consistent with the SOP.

Finally, SOP 03-1 addresses sales inducements, including those in the form of persistency bonuses. As previously discussed, the principles of DIRM and DVPM can be employed to accrue a liability in addition to the contract-holder account value. However, certain persistency bonuses meeting the criteria of the SOP may qualify for deferral. While there would be no PGAAP impact, the deferral and subsequent amortization would be similar to the treatment of post-purchase DAC.

8.2.6.8 SFAS 120—Participating Contracts

SFAS 120, "Accounting and Reporting by Mutual Life Insurance Enterprises and by Insurance Enterprises for Certain Long-Duration Participating Contracts," was published in January 1995. SFAS 120 specifies two conditions pertaining to participating life insurance contracts. The first is that contracts are long duration and are expected to pay dividends based on actual experience of the insurer. The second is that annual dividends follow the contribution principle.

Mutual companies with contracts meeting both conditions are required to account for such contracts in accordance with SOP 95-1, "Accounting for Certain Insurance Activities of Mutual Life Insurance Enterprises." Stock companies with contracts meeting both conditions are permitted, but not required, to adopt SOP 95-1. Participating contracts not meeting the two conditions are to be accounted for in accordance with SFAS 60 or SFAS 97.

SOP 95-1 defines methodology and assumptions for required reserves, estimated gross margins (analogous to SFAS 97 EGPs), and DAC amortization. The basic reserve for death and endowment benefits is the net level premium (NLP) reserve, based on mortality and interest underlying the dividend fund (typically the guaranteed cash surrender basis). In addition, if payment of terminal dividends is probable and reasonably estimable, a terminal dividend liability (TDL) should be accrued as a uniform percentage of gross margins.

Because SOP 95-1 applies post-purchase, and guarantees are not changed at the date of acquisition, the PGAAP benefit reserve usually equals the HGAAP NLP reserve. With respect to the TDL, the principles of either DIRM or DVPM can once again be employed. For DIRM, the PGAAP TDL should be set equal to the HGAAP TDL. Subsequently, a uniform percentage of post-purchase estimated gross margins (EGMs) must be derived, such that the PGAAP reserve plus the uniform percentage of post-purchase EGMs will accrue to amounts necessary to pay terminal dividends when due. Some might set the PGAAP TDL to zero, requiring the liability to be wholly funded from post-purchase gross margins.

To apply concepts of DVPM, a typical TDL accrual percentage is selected based on new business. The PGAAP reserve is derived as the present value of expected terminal dividends less the accrual percentage times the present value of post-purchase EGMs.

The above approaches treat the acquired business as a single new issue cohort. Alternatively, if historical gross margins are available, the initial PGAAP TDL can be derived from historical and future gross margins by issue cohort. These approaches are entirely analogous to SFAS 97 approaches for accruing bonus liabilities from EGPs previously discussed.

8.2.6.8.1 Closed Block Contracts—SOP 00-3

When mutual companies convert to stock companies (demutualize), some state insurance departments require that a closed block be established to protect adjustable policy features and dividend expectations of participating policyholders from the competing interests of stockholders. SOP 00-3, "Accounting by Insurance Enterprises for Demutualizations and Formations of Mutual Insurance Holding Companies and for Certain Long-Duration Participating Contracts," addresses restrictions on stockholder income imposed by closed blocks.

In particular, net favorable deviations in closed block performance from that assumed in the original closed block funding will be available for future distribution only to closed block policyholders and not to stockholders. As a result, as such favorable experience emerges, to avoid acceleration of stockholder income and to recognize restrictions on distributions, a policyholder dividend obligation (PDO) must be maintained.

The SOP requires an actuarial calculation to project NLP reserves and closed block assets from the date of demutualization (establishment of the closed block) to the time when closed block assets are depleted. Projected closed block assets that are classified as available for sale under SFAS 115 should exclude the fair value adjustment required by SFAS 115. The actuarial calculation is based on best-estimate assumptions at the date of demutualization and is locked in.

The projected net closed block liability (the NLP reserves less the closed block assets) forms the basis for a glidepath. The glidepath is used for future (post-demutualization) determination of the PDO. At any future valuation date, the PDO will emerge as the excess (if any) of the glidepath net closed block liability over the actual net closed block liability. The PDO can only be positive or zero. If the closed block is charged with federal income tax, the excess is an after-tax PDO, which would need to be grossed up to a pre-tax basis for balance sheet purposes.

A recurring theme for PGAAP has been to eliminate any assets (DAC) or liabilities (unearned revenue liabilities) that have been established as a result of pre-purchase deferral. However, liabilities should continue to be accrued to honor future obligations (such as the SFAS 97 accrued liability for bonuses or the SFAS 120 TDL).

Because the PDO represents a future dividend obligation that must be met from closed block funds, a PGAAP liability should be established equal to the HGAAP PDO with an adjustment for restatement of assets to fair value. More specifically, at the date of acquisition, all closed block assets are reset at fair value, which becomes the new cost basis going forward. Any net increase (decrease) in closed block assets resulting from fair value restatement would cause a corresponding decrease (increase) in the actual net closed block liability. Hence, the PDO should be increased (decreased) accordingly (subject to the constraint that the PDO can never be less than zero).

One point of view is that the glidepath can be unlocked and reset at the date of acquisition. A literal reading of SOP 00-3 implies that the glidepath is permanently locked in. However, it is the closed block assets, not the mechanics of the glidepath, that determine amounts to be ultimately paid to policyholders. Policyholders are still protected by the mere existence of a closed block.

The glidepath is intended to control the speed of amortization of DAC and recognition of shareholder income. Because DAC is eliminated upon acquisition, and a new group of shareholders emerges, the benefits of retaining the original glidepath are less certain. While a case can be made for unlocking the glidepath, another point of view is that SOP 00-3 should be interpreted literally, requiring the original glidepath to be retained.

8.2.6.9 SFAS 133—Embedded Derivatives

SFAS 133, "Accounting for Derivative Instruments and Hedging Activities," covers both free-standing and embedded derivatives in assets and liabilities. A derivative is a financial instrument or contract with an underlying to which its value is tied and a notional amount. At inception, any investment in the contract will be zero or smaller than that required to purchase the underlying.

The contract may require or permit net settlement. For example, one party is required to deliver an asset that can be readily converted to cash or is itself a derivative. Alternatively, neither party is required to deliver an asset associated with the underlying, as is the case with most interest rate swaps. Or, one party is required to deliver an asset, but there is a market mechanism that facilitates a sale or entry into an offsetting contract, such as an exchange that offers such opportunities.

Derivatives are reported at fair value on the balance sheet with changes in fair value recognized in income. However, SFAS 133 allows for special hedge treatment for fair value hedges, cash flow hedges, and foreign currency hedges. In such cases, the change in value of the derivative can be matched with the change in value or cash flow of the hedged asset or liability.

However, the rules are complex, requiring extensive documentation and continuous demonstration of hedge effectiveness. The complexity of SFAS 133 caused the FASB to create the Derivatives Implementation Group (DIG) to deal with implementation and practice issues and advise the FASB. In addition, SFAS 138, "Accounting for Certain Derivative Instruments and Certain Hedging Activities, an Amendment of FASB Statement No. 133," and SFAS 149, "Amendment of Statement 133 on Derivative Instruments and Hedging Activities," further clarify SFAS 133 and incorporate a number of conclusions that have arisen as a result of the work of the DIG.

Freestanding derivatives are exchange-traded or over-the-counter contracts, which include stock options (e.g., European, American, and Asian puts and calls), options on stock indices, forward and futures contracts, interest rate floors and caps, currency options, interest rate swaps, currency swaps, swap options, credit default swaps, collateralized debt obligations, energy and weather derivatives, warrants, and convertibles. SFAS 133 requires such identifiable freestanding derivatives to be held at market. In addition, SFAS 133 requires that embedded derivatives also be identified and prescribes accounting treatment.

Embedded derivatives in insurance and annuity contracts are less obvious than their freestanding counterparts. However, most can be identified by comparison of the characteristics of the host contract with its embedded derivative candidate. In general, if the characteristics of the host contract differ substantially from those of the derivative candidate, an embedded derivative exists.

For example, if the host contract is a variable annuity contract, it will have equity-like characteristics because fund performance can result in gains or losses to the contract-holder. However, if the variable annuity contract contains a minimum guaranteed interest rate, the interest guarantee would resemble a debt instrument. A contract that mixes equity and debt characteristics contains an embedded derivative. Even if only return of premium is guaranteed in a variable annuity, that feature of the contract is similar to a debt instrument with an interest guarantee of zero percent. Hence, the zero percent floor guarantees on an equity host (the variable annuity contract) would constitute an embedded derivative.

Another example is a general account deferred annuity contract that guarantees a specified interest rate for *n* years, but not less than *x*% of the increase in the S&P 500 stock index over the period. Such products, coming in a variety of forms, are also known as EIA contracts. The host contract would be a deferred annuity with debt-like characteristics (guaranteed interest). The equity portion of the contract, tied to performance of an external equity index, would not be clearly and closely related to the debt-like general account deferred annuity host contract. Hence, the equity-linked portion of the contract would be an embedded derivative.

Examples of contracts with embedded derivatives include variable annuities with guaranteed interest or return of premium upon surrender or maturity, EIAs, equity-indexed life insurance with equity-indexed cash surrender values, European medium term notes (EMTNs), modified coinsurance (mod-co) and coinsurance funds withheld contracts (embedded credit derivatives), and reinsured GMIBs that settle in cash at annuitization.

SFAS 133 requires a contract with an embedded derivative to be bifurcated into a host contract and an embedded derivative unless the entire contract is already being carried at fair value on the balance sheet. An embedded derivative is to be held on the balance sheet at its fair value, with changes in fair value going through income.

If the acquired company is publicly traded in the United States, SFAS 133 will most likely have already been operative. In this case, embedded derivatives will have already been identified. The PGAAP liability for embedded derivatives is the restated fair value at the date of purchase. The embedded derivative would continue to be held at fair value for post-purchase valuations. The purchaser would continue to account for the host contract in accordance with the underlying SFAS (e.g., SFAS 97 AV liability for a variable annuity or SFAS 91 constant yield method account value for the EIA host).

8.2.6.10 SFAS 113—Ceded Reinsurance

SFAS 113, "Accounting and Reporting for Reinsurance of Short-Duration and Long-Duration Contracts," requires an asset or liability to be set up for the projected cash flows between the reinsurer and ceding company. The cash flows include all reinsurance premiums, expense allowances, reinsurance claims payments, and related expenses. For clarity of presentation of concepts, reinsurance mechanics will first be discussed in the context of reinsurance ceded by the acquired company.

The reinsurance contract can result in an asset or a liability to the ceding company, depending on whether the present value of net reinsurance cash flows at inception is positive to the ceding company (an asset representing inflows) or negative (a liability representing outflows). From the ceding company's perspective, the projected cash flows are computed based on assumptions consistent with the valuation of underlying contracts.

For example, if SFAS 60 long-duration contracts are reinsured, net reinsurance cash flows (amounts to and from the reinsurer) should be projected and present-valued with assumptions that include a PAD. Valuation assumptions for reinsurance are locked in, as are those for valuing underlying contracts. The present value of net reinsurance cash flows would be amortized as a uniform percentage of gross premiums, consistent with amortization of DAC on the underlying contracts.

Net reinsurance cash flows for SFAS 97 UL contracts would be projected with best-estimate assumptions, without PADs. The present value of net reinsurance cash flows, using the credited rates of interest, would be amortized as a uniform percentage of EGPs, similar to the DAC treatment.

PGAAP would follow the principles of SFAS 113 as to the use of best-estimate or conservative assumptions (i.e., with PADs), based on the underlying contracts reinsured. However, revised assumptions at the date of acquisition would be used to project the post-acquisition net reinsurance cash flows and present values. The principles of DIRM and DVPM can once again be employed.

For long-duration SFAS 60 contracts, if the PGAAP reinsurance asset (or liability) is set equal to the acquired company's HGAAP value, net reinsurance premiums can be derived based on revised assumptions with PADs. If a net reinsurance premium is chosen to be consistent with reinsurance of new business, the PGAAP reinsurance asset (or liability) is revalued at the date of acquisition. The PGAAP asset (or liability) is the present value at the date of acquisition of net reinsurance cash flows less the present value of net reinsurance premiums.

For SFAS 97 contacts, in most cases the acquired reinsured inforce contracts would represent a new issue cohort. The post-purchase net reinsurance cash flows would be discounted to the date of purchase at credited rates of interest. The same principles of DIRM and DVPM can be applied.

If the PGAAP asset (liability) is set equal to the HGAAP asset (liability), a uniform percentage of EGPs can be derived. Some might set the initial PGAAP reinsurance asset (liability) to zero and solve for a uniform percentage of post-purchase EGPs.

Alternatively, if a uniform percentage of gross profits is selected to maintain consistency with reinsured new business, the PGAAP reinsurance asset (liability) is recomputed. The PGAAP asset (or liability) equals the present value of net reinsurance cash flows at the date of acquisition less the present value of a uniform percentage of post-purchase EGPs, with all discounting performed at credited rates of interest.

Finally, although a less common approach, if historical data is available, a reinsurance asset (liability) can be derived for each issue cohort, with the initial PGAAP reinsurance asset (liability) equal to the sum of the cohort values.

In summary, SFAS 113 applications should follow the principles implied by the product classification of underlying reinsured contracts (e.g., SFAS 60 short-duration, SFAS 60 long-duration, SFAS 97 UL-type contracts, and SFAS 120 participating contracts). Product classification will also determine whether unearned premium reserve principles apply or whether valuation assumptions should be used, and whether such assumptions should be best-estimate or with PAD. Finally, principles of DIRM and DVPM can be applied to accept or restate the HGAAP reinsurance asset (liability).

8.2.6.10.1 SFAS 133 Embedded Derivatives in Reinsurance

Application of SFAS 133 to reinsurance calls for attention to two situations.

In the event that GMIB contracts are reinsured, if a lump-sum settlement is required at the date of annuitization, an embedded derivative exists. SFAS 133 does not apply to a contract that provides guaranteed annuity payments. However, if such a contract is net settled (such as by lump-sum payment), it qualifies as an embedded derivative.

Many reinsurance agreements call for net settlement (lump-sum payment from the reinsurer to the ceding company) at the time of annuitization. This qualifies the reinsured GMIB option as an embedded derivative that must be valued at fair value on the books of both the reinsurer and the ceding company. Typically, the result of the fair valuation is an asset to the ceding company and a liability to the reinsurer.

A second situation that might require recognition of an embedded derivative is the presence of a coinsurance funds withheld contract or a mod-co contract. DIG Issue No. B-36 concluded that if the investment performance of a designated asset portfolio (or portion of general account assets) is passed on from the ceding company to the reinsurer, a credit derivative is most likely present. Such derivatives must be carried at fair value by both the reinsurer and the ceding company.

For PGAAP, as under HGAAP, embedded derivatives arising from reinsured GMIB, mod-co, and coinsurance funds withheld contracts are valued at fair value at all times, including the date of acquisition.

8.2.6.11 Fair Value Liabilities Required by SFAS 141

Some of the methods previously described might appear to be in conflict with the fair value requirements of SFAS 141. Such an apparent inconsistency can be resolved as in the following example.

For this example, assume there are no taxes, no required capital (RC), and no difference between GAAP and statutory reserves. Further assume the product in question is covered by SFAS 97 and carries an AV balance of $1,000. Hence, the statutory and GAAP reserves both equal $1,000. Assume a prospective buyer were to use the actuarial appraisal method to derive the value of inforce business as described in Chapter 4. Based on a projection of distributable earnings and an appropriate risk discount rate, assume the buyer arrived at a fair value purchase price of $100. An argument can be made that the fair-value liability (FVL) would be $900. This is because, in order to assume liabilities of $1,000, the purchaser would demand assets of $900. That is, net assets of $900 (reserves of $1,000 less purchase price of $100) would be transferred from the seller to the buyer. Establishing a PGAAP reserve of $1,000, as opposed to $900, would appear to be in direct conflict with fair value requirements.

The conflict is more apparent than real and emerges only when one examines one side of the balance sheet in isolation. As will be subsequently discussed in detail (see, for example, the discussion beginning at 8.2.7.5), at acquisition a PGAAP identifiable intangible asset equal to the VOBA is generally established. In this example, VOBA would be set at $100. This makes the net GAAP liability (PGAAP reserve less VOBA) equal to $900. While the PGAAP reserve of $1,000 would most likely not approach an FVL, the net GAAP liability of $900 would. Hence, compliance with fair value principles of SFAS 141 would be achieved. In short, the PGAAP reserve less VOBA serves as a surrogate for an FVL.

8.2.7 IDENTIFICATION OF INTANGIBLE ASSETS

SFAS 141, "Business Combinations," requires that acquired intangible assets be separately recognized at the date of acquisition. In addition, SFAS 141 requires the cost of an acquired entity to be allocated to assets acquired and liabilities assumed. Furthermore, SFAS 141 defines goodwill as the excess of the purchase price over net assets acquired (including any intangible assets), with net assets computed at fair value.

SFAS 142, "Goodwill and Other Intangible Assets," requires that goodwill be allocated to reporting units and subsequently be tested for impairment. Goodwill will not be amortized unless impairment tests are failed. Intangible assets, on the other hand, must be amortized over their useful life unless that life is determined to be indefinite. The different treatment of goodwill and intangible assets places heavy emphasis on identifying and establishing all intangible assets.

According to SFAS 141, paragraph 39, an identifiable intangible asset must be segregated and recognized as an asset separate from goodwill if it meets either of the following criteria:

- The asset arises from contractual or other legal rights, regardless of whether these rights are transferable or separable from the acquired entity or from other rights and obligations (contractual-legal).
- The asset shall be recognized apart from goodwill only if it is separable; that is, it is capable of being separated or divided from the acquired entity and sold, transferred, licensed, rented, or exchanged (regardless of whether there is an intent to do so). An intangible asset that cannot be sold, transferred, licensed, rented, or exchanged individually is still considered separable if it can be sold, transferred, licensed, rented, or exchanged in combination with a related contract asset or liability (separability).

In insurance company acquisitions, typically, the most significant identifiable intangible asset is the VOBA. It represents the fair value of inforce business at the date of acquisition. Due to its significance and relative value, after a discussion of other intangibles, the development of VOBA is addressed in detail in section 8.2.7.5.

8.2.7.1 Value of Renewals and Other Intangibles

Trademarks, trade names, Internet domain names, noncompetition agreements, customer lists, customer contracts and related customer relationships, noncontractual customer relationships, lease agreements, servicing contracts, employment contracts, and computer software are examples of common identifiable intangible assets listed in Appendix A of FAS 141 that might apply to insurance company acquisitions.

In addition to the above, identifiable intangibles for insurance companies frequently include renewal rights for short-duration insurance contracts, distribution relationships, and insurance licenses, which are discussed in sections 8.2.7.2 through 8.2.7.4.

8.2.7.2 Value of Renewals for Short-Term Contracts

For property casualty insurers, the value of renewals for short-term contracts is considered an identifiable intangible asset that should be recorded at fair value. The underlying principle to determine the value of the renewal rights should be the amount for which the rights could be sold for at the purchase date in an unbiased, third-party exchange.

Generally, such fair value would be based on projected distributable earnings discounted at a market discount rate commensurate with the risk of variability in cash flows. To determine the value, the valuation models discussed in Chapter 4 are produced using two sets of assumptions. First, the model is run using no new or renewal business subsequent to the purchase date. This value is then compared to the model under normal persistency assumptions for a relatively short duration, usually about five years. The difference represents an estimate of the value of renewals.

Under FAS 142, the fair value of renewals should be amortized over their useful life in relation to the economic benefits or on a straight-line basis if the economic benefits are not reliably determinable. Therefore, two reasonable methods for amortization would be in relation to expected distributable earnings used to derive the fair value estimate or based on the expected premiums from future renewals.

8.2.7.3 ***Distribution Relationships***

Another identifiable intangible asset that should be considered in purchase accounting is the fair value of distribution relationships. For property casualty insurers that distribute their products through a network of independent agents and brokers, the value of the distribution network has a significant economic value. Many of these agents have contingent commission arrangements and an infrastructure to process business on behalf of the company.

The value of these intangibles is typically determined by valuation specialists considering discounted free cash flows, comparable market transactions, and replacement cost, as appropriate in the circumstances. Using the valuation models discussed in Chapter 4, the value of this intangible asset may also be determined by comparing the model produced under no new business assumptions and one produced using the expected new business produced by agents under contract at the purchase date, including assumptions for agent withdrawals and terminations. For property casualty companies that rely exclusively on the independent agent system, the value of the distribution relationship may also include the value of renewals because most agency agreements stipulate that right of renewals belong to the agent, not the company.

The intangible should be amortized in relation to economic benefits or on a straight-line basis when the timing of the economic benefits is not reliably determinable. Therefore a reasonable amortization basis would be the projected distributable earnings expected to arise from future new business, as determined by the valuation model. When other methods are used to determine the fair value, distributable earnings patterns from historical existing business or proportional to new business premiums are reasonable alternatives. In addition, estimates of distributable earnings used as a basis for amortization should be evaluated regularly. Also, total amortization recorded to date should be retrospectively adjusted by a charge or credit to amortization expense if actual experience or other evidence suggests that earlier estimates should be revised.

8.2.7.4 ***Insurance Licenses***

The value of insurance licenses is another common identifiable intangible asset in insurance purchase accounting. The fair value of licenses acquired may be established by using market comparables of recent sales of clean shells, insurance companies where existing inforce business has been novated so that the only remaining assets are certain invested assets and insurance licenses. These clean shells usually are bought or sold for the fair value of their invested assets plus a stated amount per state for each line of business it is licensed to do business.

Insurance licenses are typically considered to be indefinite life intangible assets because these licenses can generally be maintained indefinitely without a substantial cost. Accordingly, insurance licenses are not typically amortized, but rather, are subject to review for impairment. These reviews may be performed annually or when certain triggering events occur.

If the fair value of insurance licenses decline to less than their carrying amount, an impairment loss is recorded for the excess of the carrying amount over the current fair value. Previously recorded impairment losses cannot be reversed if the fair values of insurance licenses subsequently increase.

8.2.7.5 Value of Business Acquired

In insurance company acquisitions, typically, the most significant intangible asset is the VOBA. Some have interpreted VOBA to be a financial asset or a contraliability as opposed to an intangible asset. Because it has been common in practice to treat VOBA as an intangible asset, the remainder of this chapter treats VOBA as an intangible asset and briefly addresses the consequences of an alternative interpretation.

A number of other acronyms have been used to represent VOBA, such as PVP (present value of profits, used in EITF 92-9), VIF (value of inforce), IBV (insurance business value, usually used in embedded value reporting), and CIP (cost of insurance purchased). This section describes methodology for computing the value of the VOBA asset at the date of acquisition, its subsequent amortization, and loss recognition testing.

A common method used to compute the initial VOBA at acquisition is the actuarial appraisal method (AAM), which was introduced in Chapter 4. While some valuation methods, such as stochastic and option pricing methods, use multiple scenarios to reflect risk, AAM reflects risk through use of the risk discount rate (RDR). Although not the only available valuation method, the AAM has been used extensively in practice for life insurance company valuations. The rationale behind this method will be discussed, and alternative methods of VOBA computation will be subsequently presented (see section 8.2.7.5.2.6).

8.2.7.5.1 VOBA and DAC

At the date of acquisition, all existing DAC is eliminated and, in essence, replaced with VOBA. VOBA can be considered the PGAAP counterpart to HGAAP DAC. The initial amount of capitalized DAC represents the cost to acquire new business (usually from a company's own distribution system). VOBA, on the other hand, represents the cost to acquire a block of inforce policies (usually originating from the selling company's distribution system). Conceptually, they are similar. In practice, the DAC asset on the seller's books is replaced with VOBA on the purchaser's PGAAP balance sheet. It is useful to link VOBA to DAC because rules for amortization and loss recognition testing are well established for DAC but almost non-existent for VOBA.

8.2.7.5.2 VOBA via the Actuarial Appraisal Method

VOBA has sometimes been defined as the present value of GAAP book profits. While this definition has been accepted in practice, there are other definitions that might more stringently adhere to the fair value requirements of SFAS 141 and SFAS 142.

One definition of VOBA, believed to be consistent with fair value principles, can be obtained from the AAM. To allow AAM to be initially introduced in its basic form, some simplifying assumptions are made. First, assume that statutory reserves, GAAP reserves, and net tax reserves (tax reserves less proxy DAC, discussed more fully in section 8.2.7.5.2.7) are equal. Also assume that book value, market value, and tax basis of assets are equal. Subsequent sections will discuss the necessity to reflect cost of capital, offer an embedded value alternative, and deal with those complexities temporarily avoided by having made simplifying assumptions.

8.2.7.5.2.1 Components of AAM

The AAM, discussed in Chapter 4, describes a common practice for valuing life insurance companies. Actuarial Standard of Practice No. 19 (ASOP 19), "Actuarial Appraisals," indicates that the value of an insurance company is often made up of the following three components:

- Adjusted net worth
- Appraisal value of existing business
- Appraisal value of future business capacity.

Adjusted net worth (ANW) is statutory capital and surplus, adjusted to include certain liabilities that are, in essence, allocations of surplus (e.g., asset valuation reserve) and non-admitted assets that have realizable value. In addition, invested assets supporting ANW are generally marked to market and are tax-effected.

The second bullet might serve as an initial candidate for VOBA. However, practice varies regarding what is included in the value of existing business. Some appraisals reflect only the present value of statutory book profits. Others reduce the present value of book profits (PVBP) for the cost of capital (discussed in section 8.2.7.5.2.3). Still others allocate required capital to inforce business and include the present value of releases of required capital, producing the present value of distributable earnings. In practice, any impact of RC not included in the appraisal value of existing business is included in ANW.

The geography of RC is irrelevant for valuing an entire company because the sum of the components remains unchanged. However, to the extent that ANW includes any RC necessary to support inforce business, the entire ANW could not be immediately distributed to shareholders. This would suggest that it would be more appropriate to remove RC from ANW and allocate it to inforce business. This would allow inforce business to be valued based on distributable earnings.

8.2.7.5.2.2 Distributable Earnings

Distributable earnings can be thought of as the maximum dividends that can be distributed to shareholders while still maintaining statutory solvency and meeting capital requirements. Assets equal to statutory liabilities plus RC are assumed to be assigned to the block of inforce business. No surplus beyond required surplus (i.e., no free surplus) is assigned to inforce business. The main driver of the value of inforce business is a best-estimate projection of distributable earnings. Defining distributable earnings in formula form,

Let:

- t = accounting period
- RC = required capital
- i_A = after-tax investment return on required capital
- BP_t = after-tax statutory book profit [after-tax statutory income assuming surplus is reset to zero at the beginning of each period in the projection].

Then, distributable earnings are defined as follows:

FORMULA 8.1

$$DE_t = BP_t + i_A \cdot RC_{t-1} - (RC_t - RC_{t-1})$$

In addition to earning investment income on assets supporting statutory reserves, after-tax investment income will be earned on assets supporting RC (the second term in the above formula). Typically, RC is defined in terms of minimum regulatory capital. However, RC would not be interpreted to be the absolute minimum required to avoid intervention by regulatory authorities. Rather, RC should be defined at a level that would satisfy regulatory authorities, allow a company to conduct normal operations, and maintain its ratings.

RC for most U.S. companies would be at least 200% of the NAIC company action level risk-based capital (RBC). RC for most Canadian companies would be at least 150% of the minimum continuing capital and surplus requirement (MCCSR). The exact level of RC will depend on the targeted credit rating defined by the buyer. The statutory earnings for a block of inforce business consist of the statutory book profit plus the investment earnings (after tax) on RC (the first two terms in the above formula).

However, these statutory earnings do not represent amounts that are immediately distributable to shareholders. This is because distributions might be constrained (or enhanced) by minimum capital requirements. Hence, to compute potential distributions to shareholders, any increases in RC must be subtracted from the statutory earnings, whereas releases of RC would be added to statutory earnings (hence, the necessity for the third term in the above formula).

Statutory Book Profits

The statutory book profit, the first term in Formula 8.1, is the after-tax net income achieved by setting invested assets at the beginning of each modeled accounting period exactly equal to the net statutory liabilities (for simplicity, statutory reserves). The elements comprising statutory book profits are those found in statutory income statements. An abbreviated list would include the sum of premiums, investment income, capital gains, and fee income less the sum of claims, surrenders, maturities, commissions, expenses, dividends, experience refunds, the increase in statutory reserves, and taxes.

It is possible that assumptions chosen to support a purchase price might not match assumptions prevalent in the market. To the extent possible, market-based assumptions should support VOBA. For example, to support an offer, the purchase price might reflect the buyer's unique tax position or ability to achieve certain expense synergies. If the acquired company were immediately put up for sale, market-based assumptions for tax and expenses would likely determine the company's fair value. In short, best-estimate assumptions consistent with market conditions should be used to compute fair value elements such as VOBA.

Some actuarial models do not reset assets to equal statutory reserves at the start of each accounting period in the projection. Instead, such models project self-generated assets, allowing surplus to accumulate. This is common among pricing models. However, book profits can be routinely derived from such models using an equivalence as follows:

FORMULA 8.2

$$BP_t = Surplus_t - Surplus_{t-1} \cdot (1 + i_A)$$

The interpretation is intuitive. If the book of business were to contribute zero profit, surplus would be expected to grow at the after-tax rate of return on assets supporting surplus (i_A in the above formula). Consequently, to the extent ending surplus exceeds the after-tax accumulation of prior surplus, such excess must have come solely from the book of business (hence, the term "book profit").

For models that do not reset assets at the beginning of each accounting period in the projection, the above concept can also be applied to directly derive distributable earnings. Distributable earnings can be thought of as modified book profits. In this case, it is free surplus that is expected to grow at the after-tax rate of return on assets supporting free surplus. Free surplus is simply surplus less RC, as can be seen in formula form:

FORMULA 8.3

$$DE_t = (Surplus_t - RC_t) - (Surplus_{t-1} - RC_{t-1}) \cdot (1 + i_A)$$

Present Value of Distributable Earnings
Assume the actuarial appraisal value of inforce business is the present value of distributable earnings (PVDE), computed at a risk discount rate (RDR). In theory, PVDE represents the price a willing buyer would pay a willing seller for the block of inforce business, where inforce business includes assets supporting required reserves as well as RC.

When neither buyer nor seller is forced to enter into the transaction, PVDE can be interpreted as the fair value of inforce business. However, as discussed later, GAAP income does not reflect releases of RC. Hence, VOBA should include the cost of having to hold RC, but should not include RC itself. As a result, a type of statutory based-VOBA is obtained by subtracting RC from PVDE. (This will be further discussed in section 8.2.7.5.2.4.)

8.2.7.5.2.3 RDR—Adjusted WACC
Some valuation techniques use option pricing models or models that stochastically generate economic scenarios. Risk is reflected in projected cash flows, the probability weighting of scenarios, the RDR, or some combination of these factors.

If risk is fully reflected in the projections on a market-consistent basis, it may be appropriate to discount projected cash flows at risk-free rates of return. However, the AAM typically projects a single best-estimate scenario, which is generally a single deterministic scenario (although it can be an average of multiple scenarios). As a result, risk needs to be reflected in the discount rate.

If there were an active, complete, and efficient market for buying and selling blocks of insurance and annuity inforce business, an appropriate RDR could be derived directly from then-current market transactions. However, such a market does not exist. The RDR, however, can be derived based on principles of economics and finance theory.

The RDR, commonly encountered in finance theory, is based on the cost of capital, which is dependent upon an entity's capital structure (e.g., mix of equity and debt), and the relative cost of each source of capital. An RDR that is based on a blended rate of the cost of equity capital and the cost of debt capital is referred to in finance theory as the weighted average cost of capital (WACC).

The cost of equity capital (to be subsequently discussed) reflects the inherent risks associated with the acquired company. The cost of debt reflects the purchaser's credit rating and debt capacity. The weighted average would be based on the acquiring entity's capital structure.

Due to supply and demand and other market conditions, a company or block of business might sell at a higher or lower price than that obtained using WACC as the RDR. As a result, WACC might have to be adjusted to better match then-current market conditions before becoming the final choice for the RDR.

Because WACC serves as a reasonable starting point for the derivation of the RDR and because the concept of WACC is frequently used in fair value computations, including goodwill impairment testing (discussed at section 8.2.9.1.2), the balance of this section is devoted to the development of WACC.

Let:

E = equity capital
D = debt
r_E = cost of equity capital (expected return on equity)
d = after tax cost of debt

Both debt (D) and equity (E) are assumed to be market values. Firms issue stocks and bonds at market values, not at book values. Hence, an individual company's WACC would be based on the market value of its debt and equity. In this regard, E is the market capitalization (market value of the company's outstanding stock) and not 'shareholder' equity, which is a book value concept and irrelevant to cost of capital.

Once the capital structure is decided, the RDR can be defined as follows:

FORMULA 8.4

$$RDR = WACC = r_E \cdot \frac{E}{E+D} + d \cdot \frac{D}{E+D}$$

The first ratio (weight) represents the proportion of total capital funded by equity; the second represents the proportion funded by debt. Formula 8.4 deals with two sources of capital funding. If an additional source of funding were to be considered, the denominator would be expanded and an additional term would be added. For example, if preferred stock (P) is also to be considered, the denominator of each term would be E+D+P. In addition, a third term, the cost of preferred stock (p) multiplied by the weight P/(E+D+P), would be included. Additional sources of capital would be similarly treated. However, the convention has been to deal with two sources, common equity and conventional debt.

The cost of debt should be readily obtainable from financial institutions. Based on a company's credit rating and debt capacity, money can be borrowed at a specific spread over the risk-free rate. Since debt service is generally tax-deductible, the after-tax cost of debt (d) is the pre-tax cost multiplied by one minus the tax rate. The cost of equity capital is not as straightforward and merits separate discussion.

Cost of Equity Capital

One method to derive the cost of equity capital frequently encountered in finance theory is the capital asset pricing model (CAPM). CAPM provides a logical framework for deriving the cost of equity capital and ultimately the RDR. The cost of equity capital can be derived from the CAPM as follows:

Let:

r_f = the pre-tax risk-free rate of return

r_M = the expected market total rate of return on equities

$(r_M - r_f)$ = the market equity risk premium

β = a standard measure of risk (volatility) of a given company relative to that of the market (e.g., S&P 500)

Then,

FORMULA 8.5

$$r_E = r_f + (r_M - r_f) \cdot \beta$$

Some have used an expanded version of CAPM to include more than one beta, each measuring a specific risk (as with arbitrage pricing theory (APT) and the Fama-French three-factor model). Others have used CAPM with an adjustment for company size, implying that CAPM might not adequately capture the additional risks associated with small companies. In this regard, a size premium would be added to the cost of capital derived from CAPM. Despite any perceived limitations of CAPM, Formula 8.5, the traditional version of CAPM, is most often encountered in practice.

A brief discussion of the risk-free rate, the equity risk premium, and beta (β) is in order.

The Risk-Free Rate

Typically, in the United States, the risk-free rate is taken from the U.S. Treasury spot yield curve. For other countries, the equivalent government yield curve would be used, if one exists, or the closest corporate equivalent. Not all countries have a government-supported risk-free equivalent of the U.S. Treasury yield curve. Also, the question of which spot rate to use also arises. For example, choices might include the 30-day, one-year, five-year, or long-term spot rate. A government bond index might also be considered.

It might be helpful to consider that from an investor's point of view, the choice is to invest risk-free or buy stock in the company. In this regard, as a starting point, the duration of the risk-free rate might be chosen to match the duration of distributable earnings. For much embedded value work, which also works with the concept of distributable earnings, a fairly long-term risk-free rate is assumed for inforce business, typically 10 years.

The equity risk premium is inextricably connected to the risk-free rate and should not be set in isolation.

Equity Risk Premium

Equity risk premiums derived from historical data have been over 7% (based on Ibottson Associates historical data from 1926 through 2002). However, a number of studies have suggested that a lower equity risk premium would be more suitable for projection. For example, The Canadian Institute of Actuaries document, "Guidance Note for Calculation of Publicly Disclosed Embedded Value," suggests an equity risk premium of 3% to 4%.

It is important to note the characteristics of the risk-free rate used in any study and whether the rate is the continuous short-term rate of return, a long-term rate, or something in between. Choice of the equity risk premium should be consistent with the underlying risk-free rate and should reflect then-current market conditions and perceptions of the time.

Beta

Beta for a company is a measure of the volatility of its stock relative to the general market (e.g., S&P 500). With μ_X and μ_Y being the mean of x and y respectively, variance, covariance, and the correlation coefficient are defined in standard statistical notation respectively as:

$$\sigma_X^2 = \sum \frac{(x-\mu_X)^2}{n} \; ; \; \sigma_{XY} = \sum \frac{(x-\mu_X)\cdot(y-\mu_Y)}{n} \; ; \; \rho_{XY} = \frac{\sigma_{XY}}{\sigma_X \sigma_Y}$$

Using subscript S for the stock of the company and M for the market, with standard statistical notation for variance and covariance, beta is defined as follows:

FORMULA 8.6

$$B_{SM} = \frac{\sigma_{SM}}{\sigma_M^2}$$

By multiplying numerator and denominator by σ_S, beta can be expressed in terms of the correlation coefficient as follows:

$$B_{SM} = \frac{\sigma_{SM}}{\sigma_M^2} = \frac{\sigma_{SM}}{\sigma_M \sigma_M}\cdot\frac{\sigma_S}{\sigma_S} = \frac{\sigma_{SM}}{\sigma_M \sigma_S}\cdot\frac{\sigma_S}{\sigma_M} = \rho_{SM}\cdot\frac{\sigma_S}{\sigma_M} = \frac{\sigma_S}{\sigma_M}\cdot\rho_{SM}$$

Substituting the correlation coefficient form of beta in 8.5 gives:

FORMULA 8.7

$$r_E = r_f + \frac{(r_M - r_f)}{\sigma_M} \cdot \sigma_S \cdot \rho_{SM}$$

Formula 8.7 has an interesting intuitive interpretation. Given the market's expected total return in excess of the risk-free rate, as measured in terms of the market's standard deviation (volatility), the stock's total return is expected to exceed the risk-free rate by the same number of its standard deviations multiplied by the correlation coefficient.

For many insurance companies, a beta of less than one is deemed appropriate. However, even within a particular company, the beta for its lines of business (products) can vary substantially. For example, referring to embedded value reporting, some companies use the same beta and RDR for computing the embedded value of all inforce business. Others choose RDRs specific to the risks associated with a particular blocks of inforce contracts. Certainly, when purchasing a specific block of inforce business, the latter would be preferable. However, when purchasing an entire company, it would not be unusual to encounter the former in practice.

While further discussion of beta and equity risk premiums is beyond the scope of this chapter, they can be key components of RDR determination and should be given serious attention at the time of valuation. At the time of valuation, data on recent purchase transactions and embedded value disclosures may be available to help validate the RDR derived from CAPM.

8.2.7.5.2.4 Embedded Value Approach to VOBA: PVDE Less RC

Embedded value consists of insurance business value (IBV), which is the value of inforce business, and adjusted net worth (ANW), which is the realizable value of capital and surplus (i.e., the marked to market and tax-effected value).

As previously discussed, the geography of RC is unimportant. For simplicity, it was assumed that RC would be allocated to inforce business and PVDE would be derived. By subtracting RC from PVDE, the IBV encountered in embedded value analysis is obtained.

Because this may not be intuitively obvious, it may be worthwhile to develop the formula for IBV from Formula 8.1, which is restated below.

Restated, Formula 8.1: $DE_t = BP_t + i_A \cdot RC_{t-1} - (RC_t - RC_{t-1})$

Subtracting and adding $RDR \cdot RC_{t-1}$ in the right side of the equation gives:

FORMULA 8.8

$$\begin{aligned} DE_t = BP_t &- (RDR - i_A) \cdot RC_{t-1} \\ &+ (1 + RDR) \cdot RC_{t-1} - RC_t \end{aligned}$$

Formula 8.8 is intentionally shown on two lines. The second term in the first line represents a required capital use charge (RCUC). Investors expect to earn the risk rate of return on their entire investment. To the extent RC cannot be distributed, investors expect to be compensated at the RDR. However, while RC resides in invested assets, it would earn an after-tax rate of return.

The present value of the first line in Formula 8.8, projected from t to the end of the projection period, gives the standard definition of IBV_{t-1}: the present value of book profits (PVBP) less the present value of RCUCs, computed at the end of period t-1. The present value of required capital use charges (PVRCUC) is usually referred to as the net cost of capital (NCC). For convenience, IBV, computed at the end of year (or accounting period) t-1, is shown in Formula 8.9:

FORMULA 8.9

$$IBV_{t-1} = PVBP_{t-1} - NCC_{t-1}$$

The second line of Formula 8.8, $(1+RDR)\cdot RC_{t-1} - RC_t$, when projected and discounted at the RDR, degenerates to just RC_{t-1}. This may seem anomalous at first, but as t advances, a telescoping sum emerges, causing all terms to cancel except for the first and last. The last value of RC at the end of the projection period will be zero; the first value is RC_{t-1}. Eliminating subscripts for convenience, this means that PVDE can be expressed as follows:

FORMULA 8.10

$$PVDE = IBV + RC$$

Therefore,

FORMULA 8.11

$$IBV = PVDE - RC$$

Formula 8.11 is important because PVDE is often computed as part of the appraisal process. IBV certainly includes the cost of RC, but not the RC itself. Also, IBV is after-tax, because book profits and RCUCs are computed on an after-tax basis. This makes IBV a starting candidate for the unadjusted after-tax value of VOBA.

8.2.7.5.2.5 ***Fair Value***

As previously mentioned, SFAS 141 and SFAS 142 deal with fair value concepts. PVDE has been deemed to be the purchase price of inforce business, which would imply fair value. IBV is a derivative of PVDE and is the same value excluding RC. By association, IBV appears to represent fair value as well. Either can be used to derive fair value of liabilities. This is more clearly demonstrated by a simple example. Suppressing subscripts,

let:

Reserve = Account value = 1,000
Required Capital = 50
Invested Assets = 1,050
PVDE=150
PVBP = 120
Net Cost of Capital (NCC) or PVRCUC = 20

Then, using Formula 8.9,

IBV = PVBP-NCC=120-20 = 100

Alternatively, using Formula 8.11,

IBV = PVDE-RC = 150-50=100

Assume that inforce business described above is purchased for exactly 150, the PVDE. Assume further that this is deemed to be a fair price and that no other intangible assets, free surplus, or ability to write future business is purchased. This should make goodwill zero. However, because some have suggested that VOBA should be PVDE, it is worthwhile to go through the mechanics of goodwill to confirm that the value that must be assigned to VOBA to cause goodwill to be zero is indeed IBV, 100, and not 150 in this example.

Goodwill and Fair Value

The definition of goodwill is the purchase price less net assets acquired. The term net assets acquired is the fair value of assets, including intangible assets, less the FVL. In formula form:

FORMULA 8.12

$$GW = price - (FVA - FVL)$$

Now, the fair value of assets is composed of the fair value of tangible assets (mostly investments) and the fair value of intangible assets. Define MVA as the fair value (market value) of invested assets and assume the only intangible asset is VOBA. Formula 8.12 can then be expanded to:

FORMULA 8.13

$$GW = price - [(MVA + VOBA) - FVL]$$

Maintaining the simplifying assumptions that statutory reserves, GAAP reserves, and net tax reserves are equal and that book values, market values, and tax basis values of invested assets are equal, MVA would be 1,050. This is composed of 1,000 backing statutory liabilities and 50 backing RC. Substituting IBV of 100 for VOBA in Formula 8.13 gives:

$$GW = 150 - [(1{,}050 + 100) - 1{,}000] = \text{zero}$$

This derivation of goodwill unveils a number of important observations:

- The choice of VOBA of 100 is the IBV type. That is, it is the PVBP less the net cost of capital. If PVDE, 150, were chosen to represent VOBA, goodwill would not be zero. This is because the RC, 50, is already included in the market value of tangible assets, 1,050. Since PVDE is IBV increased by RC, its choice would have resulted in double counting of RC.
- VOBA does include the cost of capital. Had it only included the PV of book profits, 120, goodwill would not have been zero. This appears to make a case for including the cost of capital in VOBA.
- The reserve is the account value, 1,000, clearly a book value and not the FVL. However, its substitution in Formula 8.13 results in the correct goodwill, zero. This may seem anomalous at first and in need of further explanation. It is correct that if the account value were examined in isolation, clearly, it would be deemed a book value. However, when combined with VOBA, forming a net GAAP liability, it becomes a surrogate for FVL. Specifically, AV-VOBA equals 1,000-100, or 900. This 900 represents the market value of the net assets that would be transferred from the seller to the buyer.

Expanding on the last bullet above, for 900 of assets, the buyer would be willing to take on liabilities of 1,000 and put up RC of 50. If all assumptions worked out as modeled, the buyer would earn the RDR for its investors over time. The 900 can be derived from two different perspectives. Working with PVDE, the buyer would ask for 1,050 of assets (reserves plus RC) less a price of 150, PVDE. Alternatively, working with IBV, the buyer would ask for assets equal to 1,000 (reserves) less a price of 100 (IBV). In either case, net assets whose fair value is 900 would be transferred from the seller to the buyer. The buyer would then add 100 to be statutorily solvent and 50 for RC. So, in either case the buyer's investment would be 150.

In concluding, FVL can be derived by subtracting VOBA from the corresponding PGAAP reserve. Alternatively, subtracting PVDE from the fair value of assets supporting modeled liabilities and RC can also derive FVL. This is the indirect method of deriving FVL (Girard 2000).

CRYPT 8.1

Paying The Piper

This audit client was a serial acquirer. I was auditing the PGAAP on a new acquisition. I was happy that VOBA was no longer being accreted at 15%, but I was alarmed at the size of the goodwill. I thought I was missing something. I talked to the actuary, who was new and hadn't been involved in the acquisition.

He said they used to have a corporate actuary, Colleen, who did all the acquisitions. But apparently she gave management too much reality in her evaluations because the company hadn't been able to submit winning bids with her numbers. Perhaps that was why after Colleen left the company, the pace of acquisitions accelerated.

Back then, goodwill didn't have to be tested for recoverability, so this massive monument to excess remained on the balance sheet in accordance with GAAP. With some foreshadowing, the new actuary did admit that this recent acquisition would have never occurred had Colleen still been around.

Three acquisitions later, the company collapsed and went into Chapter 11.

You should listen to your actuary, and you should walk away if the bids are too high. Goodwill should not be a monument.

8.2.7.5.2.6 ***Alternative Computations of VOBA***

The VOBA derived thus far can be described as a statutory after-tax VOBA. Before discussing adjustments required to convert this VOBA to a pre-tax GAAP basis, some alternative computations of VOBA should be considered.

While SFAS 141 requires a fair value balance sheet at the date of acquisition, the market for insurance companies and/or blocks of inforce business is far from deep, complete, or efficient. Few transactions occur in the course of a typical year. In addition, such transactions might reflect the particular circumstances of the buyer or seller, resulting in unique opportunities for expense synergies, growth, tax advantages, and other advantages, without necessarily reflecting true market conditions.

In addition, accounting guidance for the computation of an initial VOBA is almost nonexistent. While the AAM discussed thus far can be demonstrated to be consistent with fair value principles and financial economics, it is not the only method that has been applied in practice. Several other methods have been in general use for some time.

Under certain conditions and with certain assumptions, these other methods can produce results not materially different from those delivered by AAM. However, at times, results can differ significantly. Nevertheless, because such methods have been accepted in practice, the more common alternative methods will be presented below. Where applicable, the support for the method and the advantages and disadvantages will be highlighted.

VOBA = PV of GAAP Book Profits

Support for this alternative computation of VOBA may be traced to EITF 92-9. In that document reference is made to PVP, the present value of profits. The EITF may give the impression that for SFAS 97 products, for example, VOBA would be the present value of GAAP book profits.

If VOBA were set equal to the present value of GAAP book profits without a reduction for cost of capital, investors would not be expected to make the RDR on the entire investment over time. Investors would expect to earn the RDR on present value of book profits (PVBP) but only the after-tax rate of interest on RC. The blended rate of return on the total investment would fall short of the RDR. Although not an accounting requirement, earning the RDR on the total investment is often sought because it is consistent with the derivation of the purchase price. The purchase price would indeed reflect the cost of capital, hence, some would argue, so should VOBA.

VOBA = PV of GAAP Book Profits Less PV Cost of Capital

This method should produce results identical to those derived by AAM. VOBA derived thus far has been on an after-tax statutory accounting basis. As will be subsequently discussed, adjustments will need to be made for GAAP and statutory reserve differences.

An alternative approach that deals with GAAP book profits can also be used. However, to express VOBA as the present value of GAAP book profits less the present value of cost of capital requires the level of RC to be adjusted to a GAAP basis. This will be further discussed in a subsequent section.

VOBA = PVDE

The advantage of this choice of VOBA is that PVDE can be extracted directly from the actuarial appraisal, if one exists, or from a model rerun. However, setting up a VOBA that includes RC creates a potential future income inconsistency.

More specifically, while releases of RC certainly contribute to distributable earnings, they do not contribute to GAAP income (i.e., releases of RC do not flow through GAAP income). Hence, by including RC in VOBA, the amortization of VOBA would also amortize RC, reducing income without the benefit of a GAAP income counterpart to absorb such amortization.

VOBA = BVL - FVL

VOBA can be determined as the book value of liabilities (BVL) less the FVL. However, it requires the FVL to be computed directly. Subtracting PVDE from the market value of supporting assets has been called the indirect method. Luke Girard has demonstrated their equivalence in his paper, "Market Value of Insurance Liabilities: Reconciling the Actuarial Appraisal and Option Pricing Methods" (Girard 2000). J. Peter Duran, in his discussion of a Girard paper (Duran 2002), has demonstrated the equivalence of the indirect method (AAM) and three different approaches to the direct method, valuing FVL using an asset earnings rate, a liability rate, and the hurdle rate (or RDR).

In addition, risk-neutral valuations, consistent with approaches to valuing securities and options, have also been used to fair value certain liabilities, such as SFAS 133 embedded derivatives. Hence, there has been an array of approaches offered to calculate insurance liabilities on a fair value basis.

This approach to VOBA is complex. There is some controversy surrounding the choice of market value margins (MVMs), margins to be added to best-estimate assumptions to value liabilities on a market-consistent basis. Likewise, some controversy surrounds the level of required profits that might be added to projected liability cash flows to achieve a market-consistent valuation. There are also issues with respect to assumptions, such as whether company-specific assumptions or market-based assumptions should be used and whether realistic or risk-neutral probabilities should be assumed with portfolio rates or risk-free rates of interest.

FVL valuation techniques are complex, evolving, and beyond the scope of this book. If FVL obtained by direct computation matches that obtained by the AAM in an acquisition, certainly it would be appropriate for VOBA to be defined as the difference between the BVL and the FVL so derived.

PGAAP Reserves = FVL, VOBA=Zero

Assuming methods and assumptions for computing FVL have become generally accepted, some would prefer setting PGAAP liabilities directly at FVL. This would satisfy the fair value requirement of SFAS 141 at the date of acquisition. This implies that VOBA would be zero because VOBA emerges solely because liabilities in PGAAP are not shown at their fair value.

VOBA is a type of correction to the PGAAP liability to allow FVL to emerge. Hence, the PGAAP liability (a book value) less VOBA becomes a surrogate for FVL. If the PGAAP liability were directly established at fair value, some would conclude that there would be no need to establish VOBA.

Except for certain liabilities that must be carried at fair value, US GAAP does not allow post-purchase reserves to be fair value. As a result, immediately after purchase, standard HGAAP reserves would generally be held. For example, post-purchase reserves on SFAS 97 UL-type products would generally be policyholder account value balances. Consequently, PGAAP liabilities are most often deliberately chosen to match the form of post-purchase HGAAP reserves. Hence, typically PGAAP reserves are account values, NLP reserves, DIRM HGAAP reserves, etc.

In addition, if PGAAP liabilities were established at fair value, the difference between post-purchase HGAAP reserves and such PGAAP reserves would still have to be recognized and amortized. Otherwise, there would be a discontinuity immediately after purchase, resulting in a gain or loss at the time that HGAAP reserves replace PGAAP reserves.

While there may be some support documentation for the method of amortization of an intangible asset over its useful life, the method of amortization of reserve differences originating at the date of acquisition is far less clear. One might make the leap to categorize reserve differences as the equivalent of VOBA and proceed to apply VOBA amortization rules, which will be discussed subsequently. However, other patterns of amortization, such as one based on a constant percentage of book reserves, might also be proposed.

The upshot is that the difference between post-purchase HGAAP reserves at the date of acquisition and PGAAP FVL would produce the equivalent of a VOBA. However, post-purchase amortization rules might not be quite as clear.

CRYPT 8.2

Super Sensitive Discount Rate

My client, Fairfield Life, was sold to an investor group. I was retained to do the post-purchase accounting.

After weeks of education and deliberations, Fairfield settled on PGAAP methodology. We started putting everything into place. All the assumption setting, both research and documentation, was going smoothly, with the exception of one item, the investor's expected return for taking this risk.

I had asked several times for this number. After several rebuffs, I got a reply I never expected. The new owners wouldn't disclose what their expected ROE would be. They intended to resell the company three years later and didn't want any prospective buyers to know what their profit expectations were.

I'm still wondering what to do. The editors of this book need this story now. I guess you'll have to wait for the second edition to see what we did.

8.2.7.5.2.7 **Adjustments to VOBA for GAAP Reserves, Assets, and Deferred Tax**

Up to this point it has been assumed that statutory reserves, GAAP reserves, and net tax reserves are equal, and that book, market, and tax values of assets are equal. This section will remove simplifying assumptions and address the complexities that were previously deferred.

Adjustments for GAAP/Statutory Reserve Differences

The AAM led to an IBV based on statutory book profits. To the extent GAAP reserves do not equal statutory reserves, VOBA must be adjusted. VOBA derived thus far can be considered to be an after-tax VOBA based on statutory reserves. GAAP reserves, net of any deferred tax asset (DTA), should be compared to the statutory reserves at the date of purchase. Any excess (deficit) would be an addition (reduction) to VOBA. Working with the previous example, the following additional assumptions are made:

Let:

Tax Reserve = 950 [For simplicity, assume proxy DAC is zero.]
Tax Rate = tr = 35%
GAAP Reserve = Account Value (AV) = 1,050 [This is a change from the previous example.]
Statutory Reserve = 1,000 [unchanged, but no longer assumed to equal AV]

Based on the above assumptions, a DTA of 35% of the difference between the GAAP reserve and the tax reserve would be established. This gives: 35%*(1,050-950) = 35. The pre-VOBA net GAAP liability (reserve of 1,050 less DTA of 35) is 1,015. However, a statutory reserve of 1,000 was used to generate book profits. Hence, VOBA should be increased by 15 (1,015-1,000).

Some have asked why a dollar-for-dollar adjustment is appropriate when the difference between GAAP and statutory reserves would run off over time. That is, the present value (at the RDR) of the releases of excess GAAP reserves into book profits and additional investment income on such excess reserves while held would not equal the initial excess.

This is true when examining the PVBP in isolation. However, the total required assets are equal to the statutory reserves plus RC. The total required assets less those required to compute GAAP book profits would constitute an adjusted base for computing cost of capital, a type of GAAP RC.

In this example, the initial RCUC should now be based on 35, not on the actual RC of 50. This smaller initial RC base emerges as the difference between total required assets of 1,050 (statutory reserve plus RC) and the net GAAP liability of 1,015 (GAAP reserve less DTA).

The upshot is that while the PVBP would not be expected to increase by the entire net GAAP/statutory reserve difference, an additional increase to VOBA coming from a reduced net cost of capital would account for the residual. When combined, the resulting increase to VOBA would exactly equal the net GAAP/statutory reserve difference at the date of purchase.

Adjustments for Market/Book Differences in Asset Values

Another simplifying assumption for invested assets was that the market value of assets (MVA) was exactly equal to the book value of assets (BVA) at the date of purchase. If statutory book profits were computed using book rates of return, then regardless of their market value, the supporting assets are already spoken for in the VOBA computation.

FVL can be thought of as the market value of the basket of assets transferred to the buyer, which have already been established as the reserve less the after-tax VOBA (representing the purchase price). Market/book differences do not create a problem directly in the VOBA computation. Rather, it is what purchase accounting requires that can create a potential error.

If the PGAAP balance sheet required that only free surplus be marked to market, no VOBA adjustment would be necessary. However, purchase accounting requires all tangible assets to be shown at their fair value, even those supporting reserves and RC in the VOBA computation. Without an offsetting adjustment to VOBA, goodwill would be out of balance.

This can be seen by revisiting the goodwill example and making an assumption that the fair value (market value) of invested assets is 50 higher than the statutory book value, resulting in a total market value of 1,100. All other assumptions are assumed to remain the same as was exhibited in Formula 8.13. For convenience, Formula 8.13 is restated:

Restated, Formula 8.13: $GW = price - [(MVA + VOBA) - FVL]$

Or, GW = 150 - [(1,050+100)-1,000] = zero

Then, substituting 1,100 for MVA in 8.13 gives

FORMULA 8.14

$$GW = 150 - [(1,100 + 100) - 1000] = -50$$

Without reducing VOBA, goodwill would become negative 50. This is because all invested assets must be marked to market. The simple solution is to reduce VOBA by exactly the same net unrealized gain of 50. Hence, VOBA would be reduced from 100 to 50. Recomputing goodwill,

FORMULA 8.15

$$GW = 150 - [(1,100 + 50) - 1,000] = 0$$

Rather than applying the above adjustment, some prefer a revaluation of VOBA based on then-current market rates of return on new money investments. In such a case, some of the value of VOBA computed above might migrate to goodwill or vice versa. However, because the simple adjustment is often encountered in practice, the rest of this section assumes the simple adjustment applies without VOBA revaluation. Finally, the above adjustment to VOBA, without an additional adjustment for deferred tax, applies in the United States when an IRC Section 338(h)(10) election is made for tax purposes.

Adjustments for Deferred Tax

With an IRC Section 338(h)(10) election, the tax basis of all invested assets becomes the market value. This is sometimes called a "stepped-up" basis. In addition, the PGAAP balance sheet marks all invested assets to market. Hence, at the date of purchase, both the book value and tax basis value of invested assets are adjusted to equal the fair value of invested assets. Therefore, there would be no deferred tax liability (DTL) or DTA associated with any net unrealized gains (since they would not exist at the date of acquisition).

When a stepped-up basis is elected, VOBA can be reduced dollar for dollar by any net unrealized gains on supporting (modeled) assets.

If a stepped-up basis is not elected for tax purposes and book value returns have been modeled for VOBA, then the reduction to VOBA should be net of DTL (DTA). In principle, VOBA is deemed to be correct prior to the creation of the PGAAP balance sheet. If supporting assets are marked to market, but an associated DTL (DTA) is set up on the PGAAP balance sheet, then VOBA should be decreased by the net impact (i.e., the unrealized gains (losses) less associated DTL (DTA)).

In short, whatever adjustments to supporting assets are necessary to create the PGAAP balance sheet, the objective is to unwind them by making offsetting adjustments to VOBA as the following example illustrates.

Assume a 35% tax rate in the previous example and no IRC Section 338(h)(10) election (i.e., no stepped-up basis). Assume also that the tax value of assets (TVA) equals the BVA. VOBA would then be reduced by 32.50 (i.e., net unrealized gains of 50 less DTL of 35% of 50). Goodwill can then be appropriately derived as follows:

$$GW = 150 - [(FVA{=}1,100)-(DTL{=}17.50)+(VOBA{=}100-32.50)-(AV{=}1,000)] = 0$$

FORMULA 8.16

IRC Section 848 requires a percentage of premiums (depending on the product type) to be added to taxable income. This amount can be taken as a deduction to taxable income ratably over the following 10 years (for most companies). At the valuation date, the remaining future deductions become a tax basis asset, to be gradually released against future taxable income.

In this regard, such asset appears to be gradually amortized into income as an expense, similar to DAC. Often this asset is called the proxy DAC. For convenience, the above examples assumed that proxy DAC was zero. To the extent proxy DAC exists, it can simply be treated as a reduction to the tax reserve; the net tax reserve can be considered to be the tax reserve less proxy DAC. All other mechanics would work the same, supplanting the tax reserve with the net tax reserve.

Another subtlety is the interaction between modeled statutory book profits and deferred tax. Modeling of book profits is often performed ignoring deferred tax. In essence, invested assets are assumed to equal book reserves without regard to the existence of DTLs or DTAs. Taxes in book profits would be computed by exact modeling of net tax reserves and the timing of their release. In this case, projected current taxes, as opposed to the sum of current and deferred taxes, are modeled. The resulting VOBA (PVBP less NCC) would be correct without adjustment if deferred tax did not enter the picture. However, on the balance sheet, if a deferred tax asset (liability) were set up for the difference between GAAP reserves and net tax reserves, VOBA would have to be reduced (increased) by such deferred tax asset (liability).

By analogy, the same holds true if exact modeling of taxable investment income is performed (which often is not the case). VOBA would again be correct without adjustment if deferred tax were not established. However, on the balance sheet, if a DTL (DTA) for net unrealized gains were established, VOBA would have to be increased (decreased) by such DTL (DTA).

Finally, since VOBA must be adjusted to offset a DTA arising from book tax differences, a similar adjustment would apply to the extent any tax basis goodwill or newly computed proxy DAC is allocated to inforce business.

Whether actuaries initially deliver an after-tax or a pre-tax VOBA, close communication should be maintained with tax accountants to ensure appropriate adjustments are made to deliver the final VOBA on a pre-tax basis, the required basis for PGAAP reporting.

8.2.7.5.2.8 ***Summary of VOBA Development***

The development of VOBA as outlined in this section is summarized below.

- $DE_t = BP_t + i_A \cdot RC_{t-1} - (RC_t - RC_{t-1})$
- $IBV_{t-1} = PVDE_{t-1}@RDR - RC_{t-1}$

Alternatively,

- Required Capital Use Charge: $RCUC_t = (RDR - i_A) * RC_{t-1}$
- $NCC_{t-1} = PVRCUC_{t-1}@RDR$
- $IBV_{t-1} = PVBP_{t-1} - NCC_{t-1}$

Typical after-tax adjustments:

- + [(GAAPRes-DTA)-StatRes], where, DTA= tr*[GAAPRes-(TaxRes-ProxyDAC)]
- - [(MVA-DTL)-BVA], where, DTL = tr*(MVA-TVA) or, with IRC 338(h)(10) election, DTL=0

Subtotal = $_{AT}$VOBA

Final gross-up to pre-tax value:

- VOBA = $_{PT}$VOBA = $_{AT}$VOBA/ (1-tr)

The PGAAP balance sheet would then show an additional DTL equal to the pre-tax VOBA times the tax rate. However, the net impact on equity would still be the after-tax VOBA. That is, the PGAAP VOBA will have already been grossed-up to offset the impending DTL that would ultimately be set against it on the PGAAP balance sheet.

VOBA Development Summarized in Formula Form

The development of VOBA illustrated above can be summarized in formula form by using two basic equations to derive a third. For brevity all subscripts are eliminated and the following short-form definitions replace the previous symbols.

GRes = GAAP reserve (previously GAAPRes)
SVL = Statutory value of liabilities (previously StatRes)
TVL = Tax value of liabilities (previously TaxRes-ProxyDAC)
TVA = Tax value of assets (if IRC Section 338(h)(10) is elected, will also equal MVA)

FORMULA 8.17

$$VOBA = IBV + (GRes - SVL) - (MVA - BVA) + DTL$$

Equation 8.17 is a basic equation that defines VOBA in terms of IBV, a type of after-tax statutory VOBA, plus adjustments for differences in GAAP and statutory liabilities and market value and book value of invested assets, plus a net deferred tax liability. The result is a pre-tax VOBA, the required balance sheet item.

FORMULA 8.18

$$DTL = tr \cdot [(MVA - TVA) - (GRes - TVL) + VOBA]$$

Substituting the right side of 8.18 for DTL in 8.17 and solving for VOBA gives:

FORMULA 8.19

$$VOBA = \frac{IBV + [GRes - tr \cdot (GRes - TVL) - SVL] - [MVA - tr \cdot (MVA - TVA) - BVA]}{1 - tr}$$

As can be observed, the procedure for developing VOBA, shown in bullet form at the beginning of this section, is summarized in formula form by 8.19. The numerator of 8.19 is the after-tax VOBA. By dividing by one minus the tax rate, the pre-tax VOBA emerges, which is the VOBA required for the PGAAP balance sheet.

Numerical Example

Relying on the actuarial appraisal example of Chapter 4, key PGAAP balance sheet items will be derived.

The basic appraisal supporting the purchase price is repeated as Table 8.1. For computational ease and illustration simplicity, it is assumed that VOBA is the only intangible asset acquired apart from goodwill.

UL SAMPLE PROJECTION
Summary of Actuarial Appraisal Values
As of December 31, 2004
(in millions after tax and cost of capital)

Component of Value	Discount Rate		
	10.0%	12.0%	14.0%
1) Adjusted Statutory Book Value	100.0	**100.0**	100.0
2) Value of Business In Force as of December 31, 2003			
UL	212.1	185.0	163.1
Subtotal Pre-Tax Existing Business	212.1	185.0	163.1
Federal Income Taxes	(64.5)	(56.3)	(49.6)
Cost of Capital Based on 200% RBC	(24.7)	(29.5)	(33.0)
Subtotal After-Tax Existing Business	122.9	**99.2**	80.4
3) Ten Years of New Business from December 31, 2003			
UL (Including Unallocated Expense)	219.0	166.6	128.2
Subtotal Pre-Tax Future Business	219.0	166.6	128.2
Federal Income Taxes	(105.7)	(85.8)	(70.6)
Cost of Capital Based on 200% RBC	(34.3)	(36.7)	(37.0)
Subtotal After-Tax Future Business	79.0	**44.1**	20.6
4) Total Value			
After-Tax: (1) plus (2) plus (3)	301.9	**243.3**	201.0

TABLE 8.1

Because an actuarial appraisal may serve as a starting point for negotiation, quite often valuations are performed at more than one RDR. However, a range of values for VOBA cannot be booked for PGAAP purposes. A single best estimate is required. The following example assumes the final choice for RDR was 12% and, based on the actuarial appraisal, the actual purchase price was 243.3 million.

Working with the 12% discount rate column of Table 8.1, it can be seen that the after-tax statutory based VOBA ("Subtotal After-Tax Existing Business" in the table) is 99.2 million. This is the appraisal value of inforce business. The appraisal value of future new business is shown as 44.1 million. When added to the adjusted statutory book value of 100.0 million, a purchase price of 243.3 million is derived.

Table 8.2 compares key statutory, tax, and PGAAP balance sheet items.

UL SAMPLE COMPANY
(in millions of dollars)

Item	Statutory	Tax	PGAAP
Invested Assets	903.4	903.4	903.4
DAC	0.0	54.2	0.0
VOBA	0.0	0.0	**308.7**
Goodwill	0.0	0.0	**44.1**
Total Assets	903.4	957.6	1,256.2
Policy Liabilities	803.4	782.4	1,000.0
Deferred Tax	0.0	0.0	**12.9**
Total Liabilities	803.4	782.4	1,012.9
Capital	100.0	175.2	243.3

TABLE 8.2

Given statutory and tax balance sheet items, PGAAP liabilities of 1,000.0 million, and a purchase price of 243.3 million, remaining key PGAAP balance sheet items in Table 8.2 will be derived with the formulas of this section.

The TVL is defined as the tax reserve of 782.4 less the proxy DAC of 54.2, giving 728.4. Using Formula 8.19, VOBA can be derived.

$$VOBA = \frac{IBV + [G\mathrm{Re}s - tr \cdot (G\mathrm{Re}s - TVL) - SVL] - [MVA - tr \cdot (MVA - TVA) - BVA]}{1 - tr}$$

$$VOBA = \frac{99.2 + [1000 - 0.35 \cdot (1000 - 728.2) - 803.4] - [903.4 - 0.35 \cdot (903.4 - 903.4) - 903.4]}{1 - 0.35}$$

The numerical result is a VOBA of 308.7 million, validating the VOBA shown in Table 8.2.

It can be seen that the adjustment for asset differences (second bracketed term in the numerator) is zero. This is because a Section 338(h)(10) election is implied, and actuarial modeling was performed with the fair value of invested assets and market (new money) rates of return.

Table 8.2 does not split capital (100) between RC and free surplus. However, since MVA, TVA, and BVA are equal, all assets are included in the bracketed term for convenience. If such values were not equal, only those assets supporting statutory reserves and RC would be included in the bracketed term to derive VOBA. For deriving DTL and goodwill, however, all assets should be included.

Using Formula 8.18, the net DTL can be derived.

$$DTL = tr \cdot [(MVA - TVA) - (G\mathrm{Re}s - TVL) + VOBA]$$

$$DTL = 0.35 \cdot [(903.4 - 903.4) - (1000.0 - 728.2) + 308.7] = 12.9$$

The numerical result of 12.9 million matches the DTL in Table 8.2.

Finally, goodwill can be derived by use of a pre-tax counterpart to Formula 8.13. Formula 8.13 deals with an after-tax VOBA, hence, the conspicuous absence of a DTL. For convenience, Formula 8.13 is restated with a subscript emphasizing the after-tax status of VOBA, followed by Formula 8.20, its pre-tax counterpart.

Restated Formula 8.13: $$GW = price - [(MVA + {}_{AT}VOBA) - FVL]$$

FORMULA 8.20

$$GW = price - [(MVA + VOBA) - (FVL + DTL)]$$

Again GW can be interpreted as price less net assets acquired. Using Formula 8.20,

$$GW = 243.3 - [(903.4 + 308.7) - (1000.0 + 12.9)] = 44.1$$

The numerical result of 44.1 million matches the goodwill in Table 8.2. Because no other intangible assets were assumed to be acquired and because the actuarial appraisal computed the value of future new business directly, goodwill could have been set equal to 44.1 million as shown in Table 8.1. However, generally there are many considerations beyond the appraisal value in establishing a final price. Hence, it is safer to solve for goodwill as a residual.

The actuarial appraisal projection, converted to a GAAP basis, is provided in Table 8.3. The projected emergence of GAAP earnings and the corresponding return on equity (ROE) would be of particular interest to the purchaser and its investors.

UL SAMPLE COMPANY
Line of Business GAAP Projection
(in millions of dollars)

Baseline Growth
Ten Years of New Business

Year Ending December 31,	2004	2005	2006	2007	2008	2009	2010	2011	2012	2013
Existing and Future Business										
Premium Income	0.0	0.0	0.0	0.0	0.0	0.0	0.0	0.0	0.0	0.0
Policy Charges	72.4	83.4	95.6	109.1	124.0	140.3	158.3	178.0	199.6	223.3
Investment Income	63.7	75.5	89.3	104.9	122.5	142.0	163.7	187.6	214.1	243.3
Total Income	136.2	158.9	184.9	214.0	246.4	282.3	322.0	365.7	413.8	466.7
Death / Health Claims	20.5	23.5	27.1	31.3	36.1	41.8	49.2	57.7	66.8	76.4
Interest Credited	58.6	69.3	81.5	95.1	110.4	127.3	146.0	166.7	189.4	214.5
Other Benefits	0.0	0.0	0.0	0.0	0.0	0.0	0.0	0.0	0.0	0.0
Benefit Reserve Incr (Incl FLR)	0.0	0.0	0.0	0.0	0.0	0.0	0.0	0.0	0.0	0.0
Expense (Incl Unalloc)	18.9	20.4	21.8	23.4	25.7	28.5	31.6	35.0	38.7	42.7
Commission	51.2	55.5	62.1	69.2	76.9	85.0	93.7	103.1	113.6	125.0
DAC Capitalization	(54.5)	(63.3)	(71.2)	(79.8)	(89.1)	(99.0)	(109.4)	(120.8)	(133.3)	(147.0)
VOBA / DAC Amortization	17.6	21.8	26.2	31.0	36.3	41.9	47.5	53.4	60.0	67.6
Total Benefits and Expenses	112.3	127.1	147.4	170.2	196.2	225.7	258.6	295.1	335.2	379.1
Goodwill Amortization	0.0	0.0	0.0	0.0	0.0	0.0	0.0	0.0	0.0	0.0
Total Pre-Tax Earnings	23.8	31.8	37.5	43.8	50.2	56.7	63.4	70.5	78.6	87.5
Federal Income Tax (35.0%)	(8.3)	(11.1)	(13.1)	(15.3)	(17.6)	(19.8)	(22.2)	(24.7)	(27.5)	(30.6)
After-Tax Earnings	15.5	20.7	24.4	28.5	32.6	36.8	41.2	45.8	51.1	56.9

GAAP Balance Sheet - EB + FB										
Assets	1,010.8	1,200.0	1,415.2	1,658.5	1,929.0	2,230.5	2,564.8	2,934.5	3,342.2	3,791.4
DAC + VOBA Balance	345.6	387.1	432.2	481.0	533.8	590.8	652.7	720.1	793.4	872.9
Goodwill	44.1	44.1	44.1	44.1	44.1	44.1	44.1	44.1	44.1	44.1
Total Assets	1,400.4	1,631.2	1,891.4	2,183.6	2,506.9	2,865.4	3,261.6	3,698.7	4,179.7	4,708.4
Benefit Reserve	1,187.8	1,401.1	1,641.3	1,910.3	2,209.8	2,542.1	2,909.2	3,313.9	3,759.4	4,249.4
Deferred Tax Liability	12.7	12.9	13.0	12.6	11.7	10.7	9.8	9.0	8.2	7.2
Total Liabilities	1,200.5	1,414.0	1,654.4	1,922.9	2,221.5	2,552.8	2,919.0	3,323.0	3,767.6	4,256.6
Equity	199.9	217.2	237.0	260.7	285.4	312.6	342.6	375.7	412.1	451.8
Return on Equity	7.0%	9.9%	10.7%	11.4%	12.0%	12.3%	12.6%	12.8%	13.0%	13.2%
Return on Equity Excluding Goodwill	8.7%	12.6%	13.3%	13.9%	14.3%	14.5%	14.5%	14.6%	14.6%	14.7%

TABLE 8.3

8.2.7.5.3 VOBA Amortization (EITF 92-9)

The Emerging Issues Task Force document, EITF 92-9, indicates that VOBA should be amortized in accordance with the method of DAC amortization for the underlying contracts. This implies that VOBA associated with SFAS 97 UL-type contracts would be amortized as a uniform percentage of estimated gross profits (EGPs). Likewise, for long-term traditional life insurance contracts valued in accordance with SFAS 60, VOBA would be amortized as a uniform percentage of gross premiums.

However, for traditional limited payment contracts, amortization of VOBA over the premium-paying period may not be appropriate because the remaining premium-paying period may be short or non-existent. For example, for single premium immediate annuities (payout annuities), no future premiums remain. As a result, an alternative amortization base, such as insurance in force or annuity benefit payments (as recommended by SFAS 97 for amortization of unearned revenue), can be considered. Although EITF 92-9 predates SFAS 120, by analogy VOBA associated with participating contracts valued in accordance with SOP 95-1 would be amortized as a uniform percentage of gross margins.

VOBA amortization, as specified by EITF 92-9, will not result in investors achieving a constant ROE equal to the RDR. This will be true even if actual experience exactly matches all underlying assumptions. EITF 92-9 does not allow VOBA to be amortized at the RDR. If it did, the ROE would equal the RDR (if actual experience matches assumed).

The required use of the GAAP rate in amortization generally speeds up amortization in the early years after purchase and, hence, reduces the ROE below the RDR (assuming the GAAP rate is less than the RDR). However, over the remaining life of the inforce business, investors can be expected to realize the RDR overall.

Because unlocking takes place for DAC amortization under SFAS 97 and SFAS 120, it must take place for VOBA arising from such contracts. For SFAS 60 contracts, unlocking does not take place unless a premium deficiency is recognized (loss recognition). Consequently, VOBA from SFAS 60 contracts should continue to be amortized at the same rate (percentage of gross premium), locked in, unless determined to be unrecoverable.

Finally, for SFAS 60 long-duration contracts, some companies have computed the initial VOBA as the present value of a uniform percentage of gross premiums. This method has been accepted for traditional products and is consistent with existing accounting guidance.

However, even for such traditional products, the initial VOBA (before adjustments) can be computed as the present value of statutory book profits less the net cost of capital. The resulting initial VOBA might more closely resemble a purchase price obtained by the actuarial appraisal method. Also, as previously discussed, there is a wide range of acceptable PGAAP reserves.

As has been demonstrated, any excess of PGAAP reserves over statutory reserves directly increases VOBA. This might give the impression that PGAAP reserves are irrelevant because required assets (statutory reserves plus RC) drive purchase price and VOBA. However, it is unlikely that the pattern of amortization of VOBA will exactly match the pattern of release of excess reserves. As a result, different PGAAP reserves, while having no immediate balance sheet impact at the date of acquisition, will have a different impact on the incidence of post-purchase GAAP income.

This same phenomenon will become apparent upon examination of the pattern of ROE exhibited in Table 8.3. Even though the purchase price was derived with an RDR of 12%, a constant 12% ROE is not achieved.

CRYPT 8.3

Look Before You Speak

VOBA and goodwill have always been lively topics.

One insurance conglomerate computed the present value of profits of current inforce using very high discount rates, such as 20% or even higher, an approach that was popular during the early 1990s. This approach tended to minimize the VOBA, which maximized the slow-amortizing goodwill.

The VOBA then accreted at the same discount rate of 20% or more, which caused negative amortization and deferred real amortization into the distant future.

I attended a financial accounting seminar where this corporation's CFO was the featured speaker. I couldn't believe that he expounded on, if not boasted about, using this method. Perhaps there was an attendee from the FASB there because shortly thereafter FASB issued EITF 92-9, banning this practice.

8.2.7.5.4 SFAS 115: Shadow VOBA

SFAS 115, "Accounting for Certain Investments in Debt and Equity Securities," requires that assets designated as available-for-sale (AFS) be carried on the balance sheet at fair value. However, net unrealized gains on AFS assets do not flow through income. Rather, they flow into other comprehensive income (OCI).

EITF D-41, "Adjustments in Assets and Liabilities for Holding Gains and Losses as Related to the Implementation of FASB Statement No. 115," treats this issue directly. It specifies that in addition to deferred tax, registrants should adjust other assets and liabilities that would have been adjusted if the unrealized holding gains or losses (net unrealized gains) from securities classified as AFS actually had been realized.

For example, for SFAS 97 UL-type products, generating net realized gains would impact gross profits, which in turn would impact the amortization of DAC (hence, the term, "shadow DAC"). However, DAC might not be the only item requiring adjustment. For SFAS 97 and SFAS 120 contracts, where certain assets and liabilities are amortized or accrued in proportion to gross profits/margins, a number of other shadow counterparts emerge. Examples of other assets and liabilities with shadow counterparts include unearned revenue liability (URL), accrued bonus liability, terminal dividend liability (TDL), policyholder dividend obligation (PDO), reinsurance asset/liability, and VOBA.

To the extent VOBA is amortized as a uniform percentage of gross profits or gross margins, the realization of net unrealized gains on AFS assets would result in an adjustment to VOBA. The adjustment would be the same in form as the shadow DAC adjustment. Some companies assume that the sale of AFS assets alters future projected investment income and, hence, future gross profits. VOBA is then recalculated based on a revised projection of EGPs. Other companies apply the percentage used to amortize VOBA to net unrealized gains to derive the shadow adjustment.

The difference between the VOBA supporting the income statement and the recalculated VOBA is the shadow adjustment. As with other shadow adjustments, the shadow VOBA adjustment flows through OCI.

8.2.7.5.5 Loss Recognition Testing

Just as unamortized DAC must be tested for its ultimate recoverability, having established that VOBA is a counterpart of DAC, exactly the same rules would seem to apply to testing the recoverability of unamortized VOBA. In essence, to test recoverability of unamortized DAC, a gross premium valuation is performed with best-estimate assumptions (i.e., no provisions for adverse deviation). If the gross premium reserve is greater than the net GAAP liability (e.g., book reserves less DAC), DAC must be reduced.

Some shortcuts are taken in practice. For example, for SFAS 97 UL-type contracts, if the present value of gross profits, computed with best-estimate assumptions, is less than the unamortized DAC, loss recognition takes place and DAC is reduced. The same rules and procedures applicable to loss recognition testing for DAC should be applied to VOBA.

It might be asked whether an intangible asset, such as VOBA, should be tested for recoverability by comparison to its fair value at the date of valuation. Fair value principles are applied to establish VOBA on the PGAAP balance sheet. However, after the date of acquisition, VOBA is amortized and carried at its unamortized value. Hence, VOBA is carried at book value and not at fair value. Loss recognition testing as prescribed by SFAS 60 is performed utilizing best-estimate book value assumptions—not fair value principles and assumptions, which might be applicable to shadow loss recognition under SFAS 115.

8.2.7.6 *Other Intangible Assets*

As discussed in section 8.2.7, generally, the largest identifiable intangible asset for a life insurance company is VOBA. However, an acquirer must go through the process to determine if any other identified intangible assets exist. SFAS 142, Appendix A, lists intangible assets that could be identified in a business combination. The major classes of intangible assets listed in SFAS 142 (not an all-inclusive list) are set out below. These intangible assets are not specifically related to the insurance industry:

- *Marketing-related*—trademarks, trade names, Internet domain names, non-compete agreements, etc.
- *Customer-related*—customer lists, customer contracts and related customer relationships, noncontractual customer relationships, etc.
- *Artistic-related*—copyrights, etc.
- *Contract-based*—favorable and unfavorable lease agreements, license and royalty agreements, employment contracts, etc.
- *Technology-based*—patented and unpatented technology and computer software.

Intangible assets (not all-inclusive) that are specific to the insurance industry include: (i) VOBA (discussed extensively above beginning at section 8.2.7.5), (ii) state licenses, (iii) distribution channels, (iv) reinsurance treaties (ceded and assumed), (v) health provider contracts, and (vi) product approvals and registration.

Most of the intangible assets mentioned above are minor compared to VOBA. A company may regard its acquired distribution channel as an intangible asset. Some believe that the value of distribution channel is inherent in VOBA.

Accordingly, an entity that completes a purchase price allocation under SFAS 141 that does not result in the recognition of intangible assets listed in Appendix A must be prepared to demonstrate that no such intangible asset exists, that it does not meet the criteria for recognition apart from goodwill, or that the value is not material. An assessment of materiality, especially in the absence of a complete fair value measurement, will require an analysis of the specific facts and circumstances by the acquirer.

8.2.8 ACQUISITION RESERVES

Acquisition reserves (also commonly referred to as "exit costs") can be established as part of the purchase price allocation if certain conditions are met. Per EITF 95-3, "Recognition of Liabilities in Connection with a Purchase Business Combination," these reserves could include the costs of a plan to: (1) exit an activity of an acquired company, (2) involuntarily terminate employees of an acquired company, or (3) relocate employees of an acquired company.

In other words, severance costs, employee relocation costs associated with closing duplicate facilities, and similar costs incurred by the seller may be recorded as part of the purchase price allocation. However, in order to record these reserves, the acquiring company must formalize a plan and complete it within one year. EITF 95-3 lists an abundance of conditions that need to be obtained to capitalize acquisition reserves. Costs related to activities or employees of the acquiring company are not considered in the purchase price allocation. Also, integration costs are expensed as incurred.

Examples of anticipated expenses that qualify as exit costs are costs of involuntarily terminating employees of a plant to be shut down, the remaining term of noncancellable operating leases after operations cease, and a lease cancellation penalty. Examples of anticipated expenses that do not qualify as exit costs are costs of new computers needed to upgrade an acquired company's systems and costs to retrain existing employees who will be part of ongoing activities.

If the actual exit costs are less than the amount recorded as a liability in the allocation of the initial purchase price, the excess should reduce the cost of the acquired company. Alternatively, if the actual cost exceeds the amount recorded as a liability in the allocation of the initial purchase price, the excess should result in a higher purchase price only if an adjustment to the original estimate is determined within one year of the acquisition date.

CRYPT 8.4

Gold Standard

We acquired ALC in 1994 and inherited a complex legal issue. ALC owned its home office building, but not the land on which it rested. The land was leased under a 99-year land lease contract, originating in 1917. The company had built the building but at the end of 99 years (2016) ownership of the building will revert back to the landowner.

Rent was $1,916.67 per month but, under the terms of the original lease, it could be demanded in gold coin valued at its 1917 value. This was commonly known as a "gold clause" and was designed to protect the lessor against inflation. I was told it was not unusual in the early days of the century. If the lessor demanded such payment in gold, the rent would be multiplied by a factor of 10 at then-current prices, which could represent an additional expense of roughly $5,000,000 to the company over the remainder of the lease.

In 1933 Congress, in response to monetary issues of the Great Depression, declared these clauses illegal. This effectively nullified the gold clause in ALC's lease agreement. However, in 1975 legislation provided that the 1933 statute would not be applicable to contracts initiated after October 17, 1977. This permitted new gold clause contracts to be entered into.

ALC's parent corporation had transferred ownership of the building and obligations under the lease to ALC from an affiliated company in 1990. The novation agreement that accomplished the transfer specifically embraced the terms of the 1917 lease agreement. The lessor contended that the novation had created a new contract, which could validly contain a gold clause in light of the 1975 statute, and in late 1993 notified ALC of its intent to demand payment in gold at a greatly inflated value in 90 days (this notice was required under the lease).

In an interesting twist of events, ALC believed that it could prepay the remaining rent (through 2016) in cash prior to the expiry of the 90-day notice period and promptly wrote a check for $515,583.33. The lessor refused to cash it, insisting on monthly payments in gold. The lawsuit followed shortly thereafter.

In the end the courts upheld the gold clause, and ALC paid the gold equivalent rent. However, the company sued the law firm that had done the novation agreement for legal malpractice. We won that suit, though our recovery did not match the loss on the gold clause.

In our PGAAP treatment of the merger, no provision for this loss had been made. We relied heavily on legal advisors concerning the gold clause. In retrospect it appears that making no provision for the gold-related costs was perhaps unwise, though litigation provisions are always difficult to assess.

8.2.9 GOODWILL

The excess of the cost of an acquired entity over the net of the fair value of net assets acquired (including the amount of identifiable intangible assets) and liabilities assumed is recognized as an asset referred to as goodwill. An acquired intangible asset that does not meet the criteria in SFAS 141, paragraph 39, should be included in the amount recognized as goodwill.

In rare instances, the fair value of net assets acquired exceeds the cost of the acquired entity. This was previously known as "negative goodwill." Negative goodwill is not allowed under SFAS 141. SFAS 141, paragraph 44, states that the "excess shall be allocated as a pro rata reduction of the amounts that otherwise would have been assigned to all of the acquired assets except (a) financial assets other than investments accounted for by the equity method, (b) assets to be disposed of by sale, (c) deferred tax assets, (d) prepaid assets relating to pension or other postretirement benefit plans, and (e) other current assets."

The purchase price allocated to the above assets is not reduced because they are viewed as having a more reliably determinable fair value. In the context of an insurance company, the majority of its assets are investments, thus the only other material assets that could potentially be pro rata reduced would be identifiable intangibles (i.e., VOBA).

If any excess remains after reducing to zero the amounts that otherwise would have been assigned to those assets, the remaining excess will be recognized as an extraordinary gain. The extraordinary gain will be recognized in the period in which the business combination is completed unless the combination involves contingent consideration that, if paid or issued, would be recognized as additional cost of the acquired entity. If an extraordinary gain is recognized before the end of the allocation period, any subsequent adjustments to that extraordinary gain that result from changes to the purchase price allocation are also recognized as an extraordinary gain.

8.2.9.1 Goodwill Amortization and Impairment Testing

Goodwill is not subject to amortization but is to be tested for impairment at a "reporting unit" level on a frequency at least annually. This requires that all purchased assets and liabilities, including goodwill, be allocated to a "reporting unit." An impairment exists if the carrying amount of goodwill exceeds its implied fair value.

8.2.9.1.1 Reporting Unit Identification

The first part of the analysis is to identify the reporting units of the combined entity. SFAS 142, paragraph 30, states "a reporting unit is an operating segment or one level below an operating segment (referred to as a component). A component of an operating segment is a reporting unit if the component constitutes a business for which discrete financial information is available and segment management regularly reviews the operating results of that component.

"However, two or more components of an operating segment shall be aggregated and deemed a single reporting unit if the components have similar economic characteristics. An operating segment shall be deemed to be a reporting unit if all its components are similar, if none of its components is a reporting unit, or if it comprises only a single component."

This paragraph suggests that the reporting unit should represent the level of internal reporting that reflects the way an enterprise manages and operates its business and to which goodwill would naturally be attributable.

The relevant provisions of SFAS 131, "Disclosures About Segments of an Enterprise and Related Information," and related interpretative literature shall be used to determine the reporting units of the entity.

Determining whether a component of an operating segment is a reporting unit is a matter of judgment based on an entity's specific facts and circumstances. Although SFAS 142, paragraph 30, includes a number of characteristics that must be present for a component of an operating segment to be a reporting unit, no single factor or characteristic is determinative.

Clearly SFAS 131 guidance applies for this purpose. As a result, the FASB staff believes that how an entity manages its operations and how an acquired entity is integrated with the acquiring entity are key to determining the reporting units of the newly formed entity.

An acquiring entity can redefine a reporting unit upon the acquisition of another company. The process can result in combining business segments of the acquired operation with that of the acquiring entity to maximize future operating efficiencies, allocating the cost of the acquired entity, and allocating goodwill associated with the purchase. If an acquiring entity redefines a reporting unit or establishes a new reporting unit for the acquisition, it should be determined shortly after the acquisition.

8.2.9.1.1.1 Assignment of Assets and Liabilities to Reporting Units

After the entity's reporting units have been identified, the next step is to maintain records of the assets and liabilities of each reporting unit. SFAS 142, paragraph 32, requires "for the purpose of testing goodwill impairment, acquired assets and liabilities shall be assigned to a reporting unit as of the acquisition date if both of the following criteria are met:

- The asset will be employed in or the liability relates to the operations of the reporting unit, and
- The asset or liability will be considered in determining the fair value of the reporting unit."

Corporate assets and liabilities that meet the above criteria are also required to be assigned to a reporting unit. Examples of items that could be allocated are pension assets and liabilities or corporate debt. As a general rule, if an asset or liability would not be included if the reporting unit were to be sold, no assignment should be made, and that fact should be considered when determining the fair value of the reporting unit.

8.2.9.1.1.2 Goodwill Assigned to a Reporting Unit

For the purposes of goodwill impairment testing, all goodwill must be assigned to one or more reporting units. Allocation of the goodwill should be to reporting units of the combined operation that are expected to benefit from the synergies of the combination even though other assets or liabilities of the acquired entity may not be assigned to that reporting unit.

The FASB staff indicated that goodwill is allocated to each reporting unit by determining the fair value of the acquired business (or portion thereof) to be included in a reporting unit—in essence a "purchase price" for that business. The entity would then allocate that purchase price to the individual assets acquired and liabilities assumed related to that business (or portion thereof). Any excess purchase price is the amount of goodwill assigned to that reporting unit (for carrying amount purposes). The overriding principle for assignment of goodwill to a reporting unit is that it should be done in a reasonable and supportable manner.

8.2.9.1.2 Two-Step Impairment Test

As mentioned, SFAS 142 requires at the date of acquisition that goodwill be allocated to reporting units of the combined entity. Subsequently, goodwill must be tested for impairment at least annually.

SFAS 142 prescribes a two-step impairment test. Step 1 compares the fair value of a reporting unit (RU) to its carrying value, which includes goodwill. If the fair value of the RU exceeds its carrying value, goodwill is deemed not to be impaired.

Once goodwill is allocated to an RU, the entire value of the RU is available to cover its carrying value. Sometimes business in the acquired company is allocated and combined with similar business in the acquiring company to form a combined reporting unit. As a result, the fair value of such a combined RU might include the fair value of inforce business that was written by the acquiring entity prior to the date of acquisition.

In addition, any new business written in the RU after the date of acquisition that is in force at the valuation (testing) date is also available to contribute to the fair value of the reporting unit. Sometimes such business is referred to as internally generated goodwill.

SFAS 142 acknowledges that after goodwill has been allocated to an RU of an acquiring company, distinguishing on an ongoing basis whether future new business would be attributable to the pre-existing distribution system and management of the acquirer or solely to the acquired entity will be difficult. As a result, SFAS 142 allows any value of future new business of the combined reporting unit to be included in the estimation of its fair value, which provides an opportunity for defining an acquisition strategy that maximizes the leverage inherent in scale (the increased size of an operation).

However, if the Step 1 test is failed (i.e., the fair value of the RU is less than its carrying value), the Step 2 test requires a more rigorous valuation of the implied fair value of goodwill (discussed below in section 8.2.9.1.3). In essence, the RU is valued as if it were being sold.

The amount of goodwill write-down (the impairment) is defined as the excess, if any, of the carrying amount (book value) of the RU goodwill over its implied fair value. An impairment in one RU cannot be offset by excess value in another RU. Goodwill must be recoverable at the reporting unit level. Hence, each RU is valued on a stand-alone basis and the goodwill allocated to it must be tested for impairment.

8.2.9.1.3 Implied Fair Value of Goodwill Derived from the Fair Value of a Reporting Unit

Fair Value of a Reporting Unit

There is no active, complete, and efficient market for the sale of insurance companies, blocks of business, and, hence, RUs. As a result, for the purpose of the Step 1 impairment test, a number of valuation methods have developed in practice. A multiple of earnings, the market capitalization (possibly adjusted to reflect a control premium), a comparison to a recent sale of a similar entity, discounted cash flow, published embedded values, and other methods and sources might be used for the Step 1 test to demonstrate that it is unlikely that goodwill would be impaired.

However, if the Step 1 test is failed, a more rigorous valuation technique should be considered for the Step 2 test to more accurately quantify any potential write-down. In this regard, one technique considered to be fairly rigorous is the actuarial appraisal method, introduced in Chapter 4 for valuing companies and further illustrated in this chapter for the computation of VOBA.

Because the objective is to value the RU as if it were being sold, all assumptions should be best estimates and reflect then-current market conditions. This is also the case for choosing the risk discount rate (RDR), which should be based on the then-current cost of equity capital and debt and reflect the market's standard blend.

Market expenses might be quite different from the company's best estimate. However, if the RU were put up for sale, the valuation would be based on expense assumptions encountered in the marketplace and would reflect any available expense synergies. This is consistent with FASB Concepts Statement 7, which indicates that fair value measurement should reflect estimates and expectations that marketplace participants would use in their estimates of fair value. To the extent possible, all assumptions should reflect then-current market conditions and perceptions.

In summation, the fair value of the RU would be the excess of the fair value of tangible assets over the fair value of liabilities, plus the value of intangible assets, including the value of inforce business, plus the value of future new business capacity

Implied Fair Value of Reporting Unit Goodwill

The fair value of the RU can be considered to be the deemed purchase price (i.e., the value of inforce business plus adjusted net worth of capital and surplus plus the value of future new business capacity and other intangible assets). Net assets of the RU include both the excess of the fair value of tangible assets over fair value of liabilities plus the fair value of intangible assets, such as the value of inforce business (similar to a recomputation of VOBA at the valuation date).

PGAAP computations of assets and liabilities in the RU are made to derive the equivalent of net assets acquired in a purchase. The excess of the deemed purchase price (fair value of the RU) over the net assets deemed to be acquired is the implied fair value of goodwill. If the actuarial appraisal method is used to derive the fair value of the RU, the implied fair value of goodwill can be derived directly as the value of projected future new business (see Chapter 4).

The carrying amount of RU goodwill cannot exceed the implied fair value of RU goodwill. Hence, the write-down (impairment) of RU goodwill can be defined as the excess, if any, of the carrying amount of the RU goodwill over its implied fair value.

8.2.9.1.4 Example of the Two-Step Impairment Test

The two-step impairment test can be illustrated with the data of Table 8.4. Again, for simplicity, it is assumed that VOBA is the only intangible asset apart from goodwill.

GOODWILL IMPAIRMENT TEST
Reporting Unit Balance Sheet
(in millions of dollars)

Item	Carrying Value GAAP BV	Fair Value Recomputed PGAAP	FV-BV
Invested Assets	1,250	1,250	-
DAC	50	-	(50)
VOBA	200	323	123
Goodwill	**100**	**80**	(20)
Total Assets	1,600	1,653	53
Policy Liabilities	1,350	1,350	-
Deferred Tax	50	93	43
Total Liabilities	1,400	1,443	43
Equity: RU Value	**200**	**210**	**10**

TABLE 8.4

An actuarial appraisal, such as the one in Table 8.4, would not normally be available to support the Step 1 test, although embedded value analysis might be available. Nevertheless, the components of value are exhibited in Table 8.4 to illustrate the concepts at play.

The carrying value of the reporting unit is the GAAP book value. In this case the carrying value of goodwill is 100. The fair value of the reporting unit for the Step 1 test can be derived by a variety of acceptable valuation methods. In Table 8.4, the fair value can be thought of as the equity on a recomputed PGAAP balance sheet. In the table, the fair value of the RU exceeds its carrying value by 10. Hence, the Step 1 test is passed and there would be no need to consider a goodwill write-down.

Goodwill is deemed to be unimpaired even though the recomputed goodwill of 80 is less than its carrying value of 100. The main contributor to the RU's increase in value is the inforce business, a recomputed VOBA. The carrying value of VOBA, 200, represents the unamortized value. The recomputed VOBA includes the value of any business written by the RU after the date of acquisition as well as any business written by the acquiring entity before the date of acquisition that still remains in force in the RU at the valuation date (testing date). Although DAC is eliminated, a significant net gain is achieved in this example.

Although the test was passed, there is not much cushion to absorb a further loss in the value of future new business capacity (implied goodwill). This is illustrated in Table 8.5.

GOODWILL IMPAIRMENT TEST
Reporting Unit Balance Sheet
(in millions of dollars)

Item	Carrying Value GAAP BV	Fair Value Recomputed PGAAP	FV-BV
Invested Assets	1,250	1,250	-
DAC	50	-	(50)
VOBA	200	323	123
Goodwill	**100**	**60**	(40)
Total Assets	1,600	1,633	33
Policy Liabilities	1,350	1,350	-
Deferred Tax	50	93	43
Total Liabilities	1,400	1,443	43
Equity: RU Value	**200**	**190**	**(10)**

TABLE 8.5

Examining the fair value column, goodwill has declined from 80 in Table 8.4 to 60 in Table 8.5, perhaps due to lower expected sales or reduced expected profitability of future new business. While the above actuarial appraisal directly quantifies the value of future new business, 60, it is the value of the reporting unit, 190, that is critical for the test.

For this example, it can be assumed that another valuation method, although possibly not delivering a separate value of future new business, would still show the reporting unit to be worth 190. This decline is sufficient to fail the Step 1 impairment test. The carrying value of the reporting unit, 200, is greater than its fair value, 190. Hence, the Step 2 test must be performed to determine any write-down of goodwill.

The Step 2 test can be performed with a variety of valuation techniques. If the fair value of the RU is determined by a valuation technique other than an actuarial appraisal, the implied fair value of goodwill is a residual. That is, implied goodwill is the fair value of the RU less net assets deemed to be acquired, which include tangible and intangible assets, liabilities, and deferred tax. Assume the valuation exhibited in Table 8.5 is of sufficient precision to qualify as a Step 2 impairment test. Then using Formula 8.20 and values from Table 8.5, implied goodwill could be derived.

$$GW = price - [(MVA + VOBA) - (FVL + DTL)]$$

$$\text{Implied GW} = 190 - [(1250+323) - (1350+93)] = 60$$

If the actuarial appraisal method were used, the implied value of goodwill can be derived directly. Often it would equal the actuarially computed value of future new business capacity.

Although the Step 2 test was failed by only 10, goodwill would not be written down by just 10 (i.e., from 100 to 90). Rather, the implied value of goodwill, 60, replaces the carrying value of goodwill, 100. Hence the goodwill write-down is 40.

CRYPT 8.5

Goodwill Skyscraper

I had been the auditing actuary for a smaller life and credit life holding company, working for a regional accounting firm. The company switched to a national audit firm; at the same time, the financial reporting actuary left. So I switched hats and became their consulting actuary. I dusted off my flight guide and maintained my eight-year relationship.

This company had a successful record of acquiring blocks of business or small companies. They had a track record of growing by acquisition every other year.

The chairman of the company, Tim, an attorney, had been doing the acquisitions for the past 20 years. Based on emerging experience, Tim had done a good job of locating pursuit-worthy targets, avoiding bad assets, identifying synergy, and settling at a reasonable price.

At the onset of my initial consulting year, they acquired a credit life company. This company was based in a large city and had a hold on nearly all the auto dealer business in its county of a million plus people.

Because it was short-term credit insurance, the company's accounting staff had prepared the reserves, the DAC, and the VOBA. I reviewed these calculations to my satisfaction. I was about to move on when I noticed a very disproportionate number next to the VOBA. There was a huge entry for goodwill associated with this company.

At that time, goodwill was not tested for recoverability. Nevertheless, I felt compelled to understand more about this transaction. So, I did a recoverability test on my own.

I found a Rand McNally road atlas. I looked in the index to see how many people lived in the county. I assumed a ratio of one car for every two people.

Knowing the profitability of these credit contracts, it was easy to back into how many people needed to be buying cars and taking out the insurance. In order to create earnings equal to the goodwill, every other person in the county would need to be buying a new car every three years ... for the next 25 years. Further, this assumed that all people would buy credit insurance through this company, implying the relationships remained intact and no competition entered.

I just couldn't believe the numbers I was looking at. I must have missed something. I went into the CFO's office and explained my bewilderment.

The CFO paused, then looked at his shoes, which wasn't a good sign. A few weeks earlier, he had come to the same conclusion and had searched for an answer.

It seems that Tim, the chairman with the successful track record, had been lured into a bidding war. Somehow, it had become personal; the chairman was determined not to lose this acquisition. So who checks the chairman's bid? In this instance, the board of directors had traditionally performed that responsibility. But the board had been lulled to complacency by the chairman's good track record. They didn't challenge the proposed price and approved the acquisition.

This cash drain mortally wounded the company. It never came close to recouping the purchase price. Bit by bit, the company sold off blocks until it was just a shell of itself.

A good track record is nice, but it doesn't guarantee success for the next venture. That much goodwill was a foreshadowing of the company's demise.

8.2.10 COMPARISON OF HGAAP TO PGAAP

GENERAL COMPARISON OF HGAAP AND PGAAP

	HGAAP	PGAAP
Accounting models	SFAS 60, 91, 97, and 120	SFAS 60, 91, 97, and 120
Basis for applying models	Product level	Product level
Asset valuation	Book values generally based on cost at the acquisition of the asset	Fair value at purchase date; becomes cost basis going forward
Basis of assumptions	Best estimate at date of issue (SFAS 60 and 97 LP); current best estimate for other models	Best-estimate at date of purchase for acquired business; same as HGAAP for new business
PAD in assumptions	SFAS 60 and SFAS 97 LP only	SFAS 60 and SFAS 97 LP only
DAC asset	Yes for all models, based on SFAS 60 criteria, amortized over period that revenues are recognized	Only for post-purchase business and future deferrable costs on acquired inforce; amortization as for HGAAP
Discount rate for DAC amortization	GAAP earned rate for SFAS 60, 97 LP, and 120; assumed credited rate for SFAS 97; break-even rate for SFAS 91	GAAP earned rate for SFAS 60, 97 LP, and 120; assumed credited rate for SFAS 97; break-even rate for SFAS 91
VOBA asset	None	Yes, replaces existing DAC at purchase
Discount rate for VOBA determination	Not applicable	Risk discount rate (RDR) based on cost of capital and market conditions
Discount rate for VOBA amortization	Not applicable	Same as for DAC on new business issued at time of purchase
Goodwill	None	Excess of purchase price over net assets acquired, including VOBA asset, at purchase
Policyholder liabilities	NLP basis, based on assumptions at issue (SFAS 60 and 97 LP); AV or discounted CFs at assumed credited rate (SFAS 91); AV (SFAS 97 UL and IC); NLP basis, based on dividend basis assumptions (SFAS 120)	Fair value at the time of purchase but reported going forward under the appropriate SFAS models
Deferred FIT	Yes, based on timing differences between HGAAP and tax basis	Yes, based on timing differences between PGAAP and tax basis

TABLE 8.6

8.2.11 EXAMPLE A—DETERMINE PURCHASE PRICE AND GOODWILL

Table 8.7 provides an example of purchase accounting from HGAAP to PGAAP for an acquired insurance company. This is assuming that 100% of the entity is acquired and that no IRS Section 338 election (stock acquisition treated as an asset acquisition with a step-up in basis for purchased assets) has been made for tax purposes.

PURCHASE ACCOUNTING EXAMPLE
As of the Purchase Date

Balance Sheet Item	HGAAP	Adjustments		PGAAP
Investments	$ 175,064	$3,640	(a)	$ 178,704
Other assets	20,931	0		20,931
DAC	102,836	(102,836)	(b)	0
VOBA	0	138,201	(b)	138,201
Other intangibles (brand name & distribution channel)	0	10,500	(c)	10,500
Goodwill	0	25,486		25,486
Total assets	298,832	74,991		373,823
Reserves	177,562	(668)	(a)	176,894
Other liabilities	6,003	0		6,003
Deferred income taxes	11,290	17,393	(d)	28,684
Shareholders' equity	103,977	58,266		162,243
Total liabilities and equity	$ 298,832	$74,991		$ 373,823

DEFERRED TAXES

	PGAAP	Tax Basis		GAAP/Tax Difference
Investments	$ 178,704	$174,604		$ 4,100
Other assets	20,931	19,386		1,545
VOBA	138,201	0		138,201
Other intangibles (brand name & distribution channel)	10,500	0		10,500
DAC tax	0	15,424		(15,424)
Reserves	(176,894)	(123,886)		(53,008)
Other liabilities	(6,003)	(2,042)		(8,044)
Identifiable net assets	$ 165,440	$83,487		$ 81,953

GOODWILL CALCULATION

Amount paid	161,658
Direct acquisition costs incurred by the buyer	584
Total purchase price	162,243
Tangible net assets acquired	199,636
VOBA	138,201
Other Intangibles (brand name & distribution channel)	10,500
Reserves and other liabilities	(182,897)
Deferred tax liability (e)	(28,684)
Total net assets acquired	136,757
Excess - Goodwill	$25,486

Notes:
(a) assets and liabilities are recorded at relative fair values.
(b) Elimination of DAC and creation of VOBA (based on value of existing business only).
(c) Recording of identifiable intangible assets in accordance with SFAS 141.
(d) Recalculate deferred taxes based on new bases.
(e) Calculated as 35% of the GAAP/Tax Difference of $81,953.

TABLE 8.7

8.2.12 EXAMPLE B—PURCHASE PRICE AND GOODWILL CALCULATION

On June 15, 2003, Company A (a public company) announced its intent to acquire 100% of Company B for 10,000,000 shares of Company A common stock. The transaction is as follows:

- Company A's common stock traded at $5 two days before the announcement (including the announcement date) and increased to $10 for the two days after the announcement (the deal was announced after the market closed).
- Company A incurred $2 million and Company B incurred $1 million of direct and incremental costs as a result of the transaction, respectively. Company A incurred $1 million in internal costs related to its mergers and acquisition department.
- The fair value of the tangible net assets of Company B equaled $50 million.
- Identifiable intangible assets were valued as follows:
  - Brand name—$1 million
  - Assembled workforce—$500,000
  - Distribution channel—$2 million.

Calculation of purchase price and goodwill recorded:
Determining purchase price:

1	Fair value of securities issued (a)	$75,000,000
2	Direct and incremental costs (buyer) (b)	$ 2,000,000
Total Purchase Price (1 + 2)		$77,000,000

(a) As discussed earlier, the SEC has viewed that the market price of securities issued be determined over a reasonable period of time before and after the terms of the acquisition are agreed to and announced. A "reasonable time" has generally been interpreted as two days before and ending after the date of the acquisition. In this case, the average of the stock price has been used in this example.

(b) In accordance with SFAS 141, paragraph 24, only the buyer's direct costs of the business combination can be included in the cost of the acquired entity. As a result buyer internal costs and all seller's expenses (whether direct or indirect) are expensed.

Calculation of Goodwill:		
1	Purchase price	$77,000,000
2	Fair value of tangible net assets	$50,000,000
Identified intangibles:		
3	Assembled workforce	$ 0
4	VOBA	$20,000,000
5	Brand name	$ 1,000,000
6	Independent agency force	$ 2,000,000
7	Fair value of net assets acquired (2, 4, 5, 6)	$73,000,000
Excess – Goodwill (1-7)		$ 4,000,000

As discussed earlier in the chapter, goodwill is the excess of the cost of an acquired entity over the fair value of its net assets (including identifiable intangible assets). An assembled workforce is specifically excluded in SFAS 141 as an identifiable intangible asset. An acquired intangible asset that does not meet the criteria in SFAS 141, paragraph 39, is inherently included in goodwill.

8.2.13 ASSUMPTION AND INDEMNITY REINSURANCE

A common form of insurance business acquisition is through indemnity or assumption reinsurance. Reinsurance is the transfer of invested assets and insurance liabilities to an acquirer. Indemnity reinsurance is the most common form because it does not require policyholder consent and contract novation (a legal action that extinguishes the ceding entity's liability to the policyholder).

Under assumption reinsurance, policyholder consent is required, which is generally a lengthy and costly process. These acquisition mechanisms would be available as long as the acquirer has the appropriate licenses to write the transferred insurance liabilities. As mentioned earlier, these transactions may constitute a "business" and if so would follow SFAS 141 accounting. It is likely there will be no goodwill on such a transaction. If the transaction does not represent a "business," the accounting would follow reinsurance accounting in accordance with SFAS 113. EITF Issue No. 98-3, "Determining Whether a Nonmonetary Transaction Involves Receipt of Productive Assets or of a Business," provides guidance on what constitutes a business.

For example, Company XYZ enters into an assumption reinsurance agreement with Company ABC in which Company XYZ assumes all existing insurance policy liabilities of Company ABC's workers' compensation line. In addition, Company XYZ also acquires all of Company ABC's employees and information technology. Company XYZ met all the requirements for a "business" in accordance with EITF Issue No. 98-3. As a result, Company XYZ would follow purchase accounting in accordance with SFAS 141.

8.3 STATUTORY ACCOUNTING PRINCIPLES

Financial statements that are submitted to insurance regulators are required to be filed using statutory accounting principles (SAP). The major purchase accounting provisions under SAP are outlined in the remaining sections of this chapter. It should be noted that there could be prescribed accounting practices by state that could differ from the NAIC accounting policies and procedures manual (manual) that describes the SAPs. Prescribed practices by state supersede those of the manual.

8.3.1 PURCHASER'S ACCOUNTING

SSAP 68, "Business Combinations and Goodwill," governs statutory accounting for the recording of acquisitions and goodwill. According to SSAP 68, a business combination can generally be accounted for as either a "statutory purchase" or a "statutory merger."

Statutory purchase is referred to as an acquisition in which a parent-subsidiary relationship exists. The acquiring entity records the acquisition as an investment at its purchase price (referred to as "cost"). No consolidation of subsidiaries is required under SAP.

The cost of the acquired entity could include: (a) any cash payments, (b) fair value of other assets distributed, (c) fair value of any liabilities assumed, and (d) any direct costs of the acquisition. The difference between the purchase price and the historical book value of the acquired entity is recorded as goodwill on the acquiring entity's books. Under SAP, no identifiable intangibles other than goodwill are recorded.

Statutory merger is referred to as an acquisition in which equity of one entity is issued in exchange for the equity of another entity and then subsequently canceled. Prospectively only one entity exists and is accounted for as a "statutory merger." Both entities' statutory balance sheets are simply combined. No goodwill is generated and no adjustment is required to mark assets and liabilities to fair value. Any goodwill that exists on either entity is eliminated by a charge or credit to surplus immediately.

8.3.2 ACQUIRED ENTITY ACCOUNTING

Under the statutory purchase method, the acquired entity continues to use its historical basis in valuing assets and liabilities on the statutory financial statements. As a result, no pushdown accounting is permitted (i.e., no recording of goodwill and adjusting assets and liabilities to fair values at the acquired entity level). As discussed above, the acquiring company records the goodwill generated by the acquisition.

8.3.3 GOODWILL ADMISSIBILITY

The admissibility of goodwill varies on a state-by-state basis. However, under SSAP 68, goodwill is admitted subject to limitation. Goodwill is limited to 10% of the acquiring entity's capital and surplus, excluding any goodwill, electronic data processing (EDP) equipment, operating systems software, and net deferred tax assets. Based on this limitation, any non-admitted goodwill is charged directly to surplus.

Goodwill (positive and negative) is amortized to unrealized gains and losses over a period not to exceed 10 years. Goodwill impairment analysis is required. If there is a decline in the fair value below cost and the decline is considered other than temporary, the investment should be written down to fair value.

Chapter Nine

Merger Integration

9.1 INTRODUCTION

Numerous books have been written on change management. Core topics encompass re-engineering, re-structuring, and turnaround strategy (titles of popular references are found at the end of this chapter). These themes have much in common with merger integration; many of the same "rules and tools" apply. Yet one could be an expert in all of them and still not understand the scope of the special challenges facing a full M&A integration process, much less how to increase the probabilities of success.

Merger integration is no more (and no less) than an intricate, high-stakes exercise in change management. Essentially, management is placing bets on a portfolio of operations that are regularly evaluated and fine-tuned in order to optimize return. Resources (time, money, and personnel) are finite and must be allocated to maximize return. Organizations that learn faster, act quicker, and shift gears more efficiently during the integration process are able to capture more value than their peers. This is done by collecting the information needed to make informed decisions, prioritizing it effectively, and linking resource allocation to sustainable value creation.

The goal of the integration is to capture the value drivers (the deal's financial and strategic objectives) used to justify the acquisition. It takes leadership, planning, and hard work. Ultimately, the successful outcome of the transaction for the acquirer depends on the effectiveness of its integration activities. Yet all too often the time, money, and energy spent to purchase a company far outweighs the investment in making it work. Integration becomes an afterthought when the kudos have been lavished on the deal execution team while the spade work is left to overworked task forces and teams.

Acquirers who consistently meet or exceed deal expectations have strong leaders, leverage a thorough due diligence to prepare the high-level integration plan so project teams can hit the ground running, pay a fair price that does not overstate synergies or expense saves, negotiate a sound contract that protects their interests, and communicate often and effectively with stakeholders.

Finally, integration must focus on people. Many assume that integration is about programs, processes, and systems. There is always plenty of this work, and it is relatively straightforward by comparison; the key, and usually the trickiest part, is getting the people issues right.

While each deal is different, the integrator will be successful if the lessons presented in this chapter are heeded.

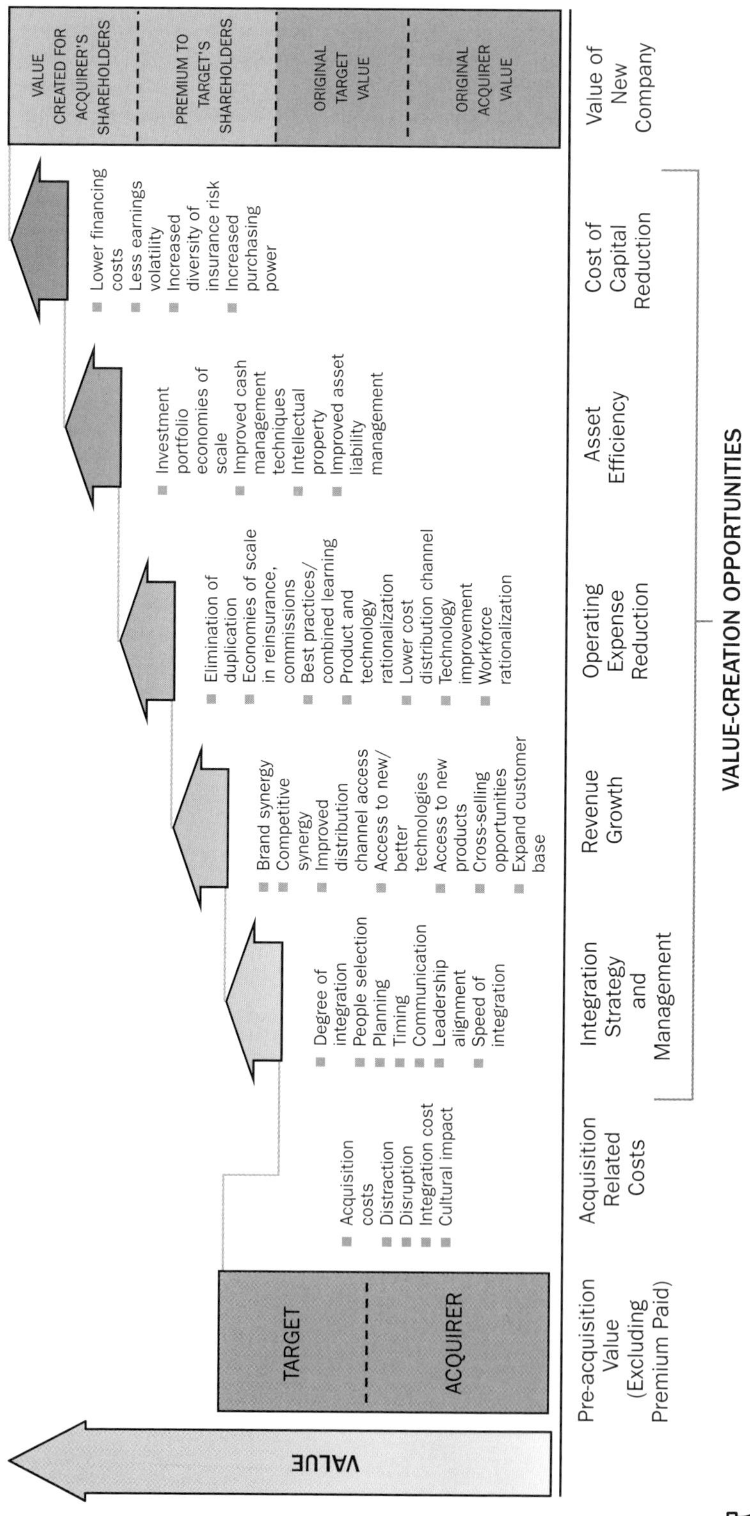

FIGURE 9.1 **Source:** Deloitte & Touche LLP

9.1.1 THE IMPORTANCE OF LEADERSHIP

Executives who have not been involved in M&A before may believe their role in the transaction is over once the purchase agreement has been inked. Yet even if the decision is to maintain relatively separate, stand-alone businesses, this attitude is like sending the entire coaching staff home at halftime and leaving the players to call the game. No matter what the degree of cohesion required, integration execution will determine the ultimate success or failure of the transaction.

First, the leadership of the new entity must be determined. Leadership roles should be clearly stated early on, optimally in the transaction announcement itself. Detailed integration planning in advance of establishing leadership may be a fool's errand if the new CEO decides to go off in a different direction. While presumably validating the acquisition strategy, leaders play a crucial role in setting the agenda and confirming the roles of those managing the transition.

Management from both organizations must work together to promote the benefits of the transaction to the various stakeholders. Management needs to begin communicating as early as possible a vision of what life in the merged enterprise will be like, with special attention paid to employees, distributors, and policyholders. Sometimes both CEOs remain for a defined period, with one staying on to help with the transition before moving on. Of course, these agreements do not always work out as planned, and one or the other may leave earlier.

Change starts at the top. Executives must lead by example; rank and file will take their cues from how leadership behaves and acts. The corporate jet should not be flown to meetings to discuss the latest cost-cutting measures and layoffs. Successes should be acknowledged widely; failures should not remain unpunished. Responsibility must be accepted and the team must move forward.

9.1.2 SPEED MATTERS

Maintaining business continuity and generating momentum during the integration stage is the single most important factor in the ultimate success of the transaction. Achieving these sometimes-conflicting goals requires a well planned, disciplined, and efficient implementation process.[1]

All things being equal, the faster a target is integrated, the higher the probability of success. Leisurely transitions are like a crash in slow motion accompanied by a painful soundtrack. The goal is not to optimize processes but to develop solutions that work well enough for everyone to focus on their work. If integration takes longer than planned, the effective cost of the acquisition goes up. Every time financial statements are published, the progress of the transaction will be scrutinized.

Employees do not relish change for its own sake; policyholders do not appreciate uncertainty. Long delays increase uncertainty and the perception that no one is at the helm, ultimately affecting customer retention as employee attrition, process uncertainties, and communication breakdowns degrade service. Employees will rise to the challenge more effectively if definitive milestones are set and the length of time people are affected is limited. Day one, week one, month one, month three, month six, and year one are typically important milestones.

To accelerate the process, integration planning needs to start early in the transaction—as soon as the target is being seriously evaluated. Members of the transition team need to be intimately involved in the due diligence process. As soon as the transaction is closed, the goal is to hit the ground running, leading off with a well-orchestrated day-one agenda. Early successes that are well communicated will translate into enthusiasm and greater levels of support in the trenches, generating all-important (but difficult to quantify) momentum. By the same token, it can be extremely difficult to recover from early failures.

[1] Schmidt, Jeffrey, Ed., "Making Mergers Work: The Strategic Importance of People," Towers Perrin/SHRM Foundation, 2002, p. 6.

CRYPT 9.1

Take Over The Business As Quickly As You Can

Years ago, when it was possible to do assumption reinsurance without policyholder consent, we agreed to buy a block of business from a company that urgently needed to raise capital. The structure of the transaction was to be coinsurance, with servicing by the ceding company for the first six months, followed by assumption reinsurance and full policy servicing by us after six months.

We knew that the selling company was short on capital. However, we assumed that the value of their inforce, along with our ceding allowance, would keep the selling company going for several years.

We were wrong. Four months after we closed the transaction, and while the business was still under the coinsurance arrangement, the selling company was put under regulatory supervision. All of a sudden, we wondered if we would ever recover our purchase price, and we wondered if the policyholders who we hoped to assume within two months would, instead, get letters from the state regulators telling them that they were policyholders of an insolvent insurer.

Thankfully, after several days of frenzied activity, we were able to work out the situation to our benefit. We moved the transition of administration up by one month and did a conversion in five months instead of six. The regulator who took over the company allowed us to assume the business as planned, and our policyholders never got a letter from the regulator telling them that their insurer was insolvent.

Today, in all instances, we move as rapidly as possible to bring in the administration.

9.1.3 COMMUNICATION

The importance of timely and frequent communication cannot be underestimated in making integration, and ultimately the transaction, work. A company that communicates its vision of the combined entity, the integration strategies, and ground level tactics improves the probability that the value contemplated by the transaction will be realized. Because of its importance, communication is often the sole responsibility of a separate team.

9.1.3.1 *Formulating a Strategy*

When the deal is announced, there always will be two pieces of information broadly disclosed: why the deal is being done and why it is good for stakeholders. The price may also be revealed, thus disclosing to the world the value of the integrated companies. Stakeholders will not lose sight of this. A significant challenge facing the organization is getting all these different groups, each with different agendas, pointed in the same direction, supporting the transaction.

Senior management, with the help of a public relations team, will formulate a communication strategy that sends clear and consistent messages to the company's stakeholders. The first communication announcing the transaction is usually a well-orchestrated media event using a meticulously crafted statement. But it cannot stop there; stakeholders need regular communications during the course of the transformation. Otherwise, ill-informed, less forgiving sources may take over in the vacuum.

Below are various considerations in creating an effective communications plan for an integration project:

- Communications should be timely and frequent.
- All messages should be grounded in the strategic rationale for the transaction.
- Spin should be avoided in order to maintain credibility.
- Tough messages should be delivered in the context of the broader economic environment or industry-specific realities.
- Messages should be repeated and reinforced by using multiple channels (webcasts, e-mails, memos, group meetings, and company publications).
- People should be given a mechanism for providing feedback.

Face-to-face discussion is the first choice for distributing important internal messages such as communicating vision, mobilizing support, and removing uncertainty. Just as importantly, it gives people the opportunity to engage in dialogue. Leaders need to be prepared to answer inquiries about the transaction; most questions can be anticipated. The leadership and communications team should identify the main concerns of each audience and prepare the executives to respond effectively. Shooting from the hip can indicate a lack of interest or concern in the executive branch, a sure de-motivator, rumor mill stoker or, worse, exit door.

9.1.3.2 Target the Audience

Stakeholders consist of groups with different interests and agendas. Audiences that will be receiving messages include employees, distributors, policyholders, investors, financial analysts, rating agencies, lenders, community organizations, regulatory bodies, competitors, and the media. While messages must be consistent, they should also be tailored to address the concerns and interests of each audience.

In a field as complex as insurance, it is advisable to anticipate and confirm the stakeholders' concerns. Regulators who hold approval authority for the transaction and ratings agencies are particularly important. This is also true with regard to policyholders and distributors; competitors may be anticipating their concerns. It is incumbent upon the communications team to make sure critical issues are identified and addressed.

9.1.3.3 The Rumor Mill

Rumors are a symptom of a lack of information and the ensuing sense of uncertainty. Given the seriousness of the repercussions of uncertainty, incomplete news or bad news is better than no news. It is advisable to have a regular process to communicate status. Some companies provide financial details to stakeholders to quantify progress. This may seem unnecessary, but because quarterly results are public, it may be better to interpret and distribute results internally than to leave the job to outsiders.

In order to minimize rumors, a description of integration plans, an explanation of how they were made, and details of execution tactics should be provided to employees as early as possible. This needs to be carefully communicated to line managers so there is no disconnect with those actually involved in the implementation. Line managers serve as the messengers of validation, reinforcement, and reiteration. Any disconnect will be duly discussed in the rumor mill and only serve to unsettle both the managers and employees.

CRYPT 9.2

Musical Chairs

Looking back at my seven-year accounting career in the life industry in the Midwest, I am already a refugee from not one but two acquisitions. The memories mostly involve the new owner breaking the news to the employees that our jobs were going away.

In the first acquisition, the accounting department was pulled together and we were informed reorganization was in the works. The new parent would merge three of its accounting departments to make one "shared service" that would provide financial reporting for all entities within the new organization. We were told that most likely all accounting functions would be moved to our location.

Six months later, management announced its reorganization plans. During the time spent waiting for the decision, the members of our department became convinced that the "shared service" was coming to our location since our department employed 35 accountants and we were already preparing the financial reporting and accounting functions for seven insurance companies, three holding companies, two non-insurance companies, and two separate accounts. The other two competing locations combined had 10 employees in their accounting departments and were providing financial reporting and accounting functions for just three companies.

The day the announcement was scheduled, our accounting department was called together. All of us had expectations of integrating the remaining three companies into our area.

As we entered the room, we noticed human resources (HR) representatives attending with a stack of manila envelopes. With pale faces, we realized these weren't new charts of accounts.

Obviously, we did not hear the announcement we expected. The CFO from the Atlanta regional office seemed scared to death, shaking and sweating profusely as he broke the news. We were devastated with the announcement that we were not the survivors.

Not only would we lose our jobs, but we would have to transfer our work to individuals who had no life insurance or annuity experience. We had to train the individuals replacing us, not only about our specific jobs, but also about life insurance and annuity concepts. The severance packages and stay bonuses were attractive enough to entice most of the accounting department to stay to the end of the transition period.

However, my time with this company did not end there. Three months before the ending date, the organization realized that it still needed three accountants in the Midwest location. I was asked to fill one of those positions. I accepted; the first assignment was to complete a conversion to a new general ledger system. So I was now an employee of the new parent.

Maybe we finished the general ledger conversion too quickly. At its completion, the remaining valuation actuaries and we accountants were called into a video conference. As we walked in the room we again noticed HR people with a stack of manila envelopes. Also, sitting in the corner was the individual who had done outplacement counseling with the first transition. Needless to say, we knew we weren't about to be congratulated on a job well done. On the video screen, a vice president delivered the news that our positions were moving to another location within six months. Also, we would not be moving with them. So the transition began again. Not only did the individuals we trained not have any life insurance or annuity accounting experience or knowledge, but we even questioned their knowledge of basic accounting concepts. Wouldn't you wonder if someone asks whether debits have to equal credits?

We failed to view the deal from new management's perspective. From our perspective we never could figure out why management made the decisions that they did. We thought that we were safe because we had a far more experienced staff, we were managing more entities, and we were more knowledgeable about both general and industry-specific accounting procedures and issues. Perhaps we did not have all the facts that the new management had; perhaps we tried to fit the facts into an optimistic interpretation of what would happen. Next time, I will remember these painful lessons when setting my expectations.

9.2 INTEGRATION PLANNING

Integration planning is a dynamic process. While forward looking, it must be responsive to the realities of the current environment. While each plan must be tailored to the transaction at hand, companies who are routinely active in M&A have developed checklists of integration considerations, not unlike their due diligence lists.

Integration implications should be contemplated throughout the due diligence process. Its cost and timing should be taken into consideration in the bid price. The better the job performed in due diligence, in particular transferring and incorporating key information to the transition team, the smoother the transition will be and the more likely it will be to capture the transaction drivers of value.

The purchase agreement may be structured in such a way that certain conditions or ground rules are set for the integration. The acquired company may insist on some degree of job security for its employees or a certain number of seats on the new board.

Activity during the period from transaction announcement to the closing date continues to the extent possible, but is hobbled by limits on the sharing of information due to anti-trust concerns. Formal integration begins in earnest on day one and only concludes when the synergies that management intends to capture, extract, or build are operational.

For the target, the role is obviously more reactive than proactive. However, targets can and do make an important contribution and shape the direction of integration in a meaningful way.

Buy A House, Get A Job (Maybe)

CRYPT 9.3

The board of our company had accepted a takeover offer from another financial services firm. That company began sending its key personnel to our offices to go over the procedures for the transition and the takeover. We in the actuarial department were told that about one-third of us would be offered positions at the new company. Those positions would require relocation from our current city.

About a month before Thanksgiving, the firm's actuarial officers invited me to travel to their home office for an interview. Wanting to keep all my options open, I readily agreed. The date was set for the second Friday before Thanksgiving. I was to fly with one of my subordinates, who was also to be interviewed, which seemed normal enough.

A day before the trip, each of us got an agenda. We were each going to meet with five people on their staff, with no overlap between us except for the chief actuary. That also seemed normal enough. However, the final agenda item of the day was to meet with a local real estate agent to visit houses in the area. That started to seem strange, since we were looking in quite different price ranges.

We went and talked to the various people. Although no offer was forthcoming, the chief actuary and his top assistant told me to stay close to the phone because I would be contacted before Thanksgiving. The implication was that I would be getting an offer, although I had no clue what it would be. My subordinate had a similar experience.

We then met with the real estate agent. She took us around for about two hours. Half the time we looked at houses in my price range, and half the time we looked at houses in my subordinate's price range. During the latter half, having time to mull things over, I thought, "Here I am looking at houses, when I don't yet have a job offer. Even if I get an offer I don't know if it will be any good, and even if it is good I don't know yet if I would accept it. Buying a house is the least of my concerns here." Nevertheless, I went back and stayed close to the phone.

The Friday before Thanksgiving, the takeover deal collapsed. The phone never rang.

9.2.1 STEERING COMMITTEE

The role of the steering committee is to plan the integration from a broad perspective, make big-picture decisions, and see that the plan moves ahead smoothly and efficiently. A critical part of the team's responsibility is to align corporate, operational, and integration strategies with the goals of the new organization. As in any high stakes process, it is critical to align incentives and outcomes; those responsible for structuring the deal should bear some responsibility for execution.

A core team of five to eight senior executives may be selected to lead the integration process for a large transaction. This steering committee should be composed of executives who are already deeply involved in due diligence and thus intimate with the issues as well as the transaction's value drivers. These individuals may include the chief financial officer, chief actuary, chief technology officer, general counsel, vice president of HR, heads of major lines of business, chief risk officer (CRO) and chief compliance officer (CCO). The inclusion of the CRO and CCO makes sense given Sarbanes-Oxley and the need to ensure that the combined company understands and manages its risk exposures from the start.

Another important criterion is that the selected executives should be overseeing and/or managing the new entity's day-to-day operations. This will help ensure that they own both the integration planning and the execution. Most of these individuals will have been involved with the transaction from the beginning, so they should have the best perspective as to what the combined companies should look like after a successful integration.

Many companies also hire outside consultants with extensive integration experience to assist in facilitating the process.[2] Outside facilitators should not vote on outcomes. While their experience, expertise, and objectivity can add significant value, the best choices come from those who have a vested interest in the outcome.

9.2.2 THE STRATEGIC PLAN

The first responsibility of the integration steering committee is to define how the newly formed company will operate. This task is jump-started by building on information obtained during due diligence. Existing knowledge of the target organization serves to inform how the new entity will function. These functions include strategic positioning, competitive advantages, operational performance, management capacity, technology infrastructure, staffing, and other resources.

First, the steering committee decides on an end-state for the process: a target (but not a blueprint) for what the end result of successful integration will look like. Once the end-state is articulated, the steering committee creates a plan for reaching the destination. The plan outlines when, how, and to what degree the resources, processes, and commitments of the two firms will be combined in the new structure. Senior managers and the board should refer to the plan in making their decisions. A feedback mechanism is needed should changes in the plan be required.

In this short timeframe, firms focus on the archetypical 20% of the actions with the highest probability of success that are likely to drive 80% of the economic value. A process for reaching agreement on these priorities in an orderly fashion is described in a book by Mark

[2] "A group facilitator is an independent 3rd party who helps the group identify problems, find solutions, and make decisions. Independent means that the person should be neutral with respect to the matters being decided and should have no decision making authority within the group. Obviously, to be effective, the facilitator should be someone who is acceptable to all members of the group. Facilitators can be helpful to many groups, particularly those that are susceptible to dominance by or deadlocking." Reed, Stanley Foster and Alexandra Reed Lajoux, *The Art of M&A*, 3rd ed., New York: McGraw-Hill, 1998, p. 655.

Feldman and Michael Spratt:[3] In order to maximize return, the steering committee needs to prioritize the value drivers on the basis of financial impact, time frame, and chances for success. Then, resources are allocated to those actions with the highest chances for success. Resources are thus leveraged by concentrating them on areas with the highest potential impact. This process ensures that the leaders of the firm reach consensus on priorities and lessen the likelihood of disruptive conflicts during integration.[4]

Like any battle where logistics are important drivers of success, the key is to concentrate resources at tipping points. Integration is not an exercise in precision but in relative values. Getting senior management to buy into the process and own the decisions is more important than getting all the precise input values correct. Information from due diligence, perhaps with some scrubbing, suffices for this purpose. During integration, the team should avoid spending time on multiple rounds of fact finding and reconciliation of sources.

9.2.3 DEGREE OF INTEGRATION

The degree of integration must be decided early. There is a full spectrum of possibilities from stand-alone to fully absorbed and everything in between.

Although there is certainly some discretion in the details, the extent of integration will largely depend on the strategic and financial objectives of the transaction. A transaction whose rationale is based on geographic expansion will require a different degree of integration, and have different challenges, than one justified by operational efficiencies. Companies with "roll up" strategies[5] will place a premium on flexibility, scalability, and speed.

CRYPT 9.4

Target Bucks Trend; Stays Self-Standing

We were for sale. We saw several bidders; one emerged as the preferred buyer. It had a track record of absorbing every acquisition it made. We could read the handwriting on the wall. As employees, we were doomed.

For me, I just kept on doing my job, irrespective of the impending change in ownership. I provided the information it needed, on a timely and accurate basis. I was responsive to follow-up questions.

During the due diligence phase, we were told that it would discontinue the operations. While very disappointed, I did not see any reason why I should not be cooperative.

It had lots of questions on pricing, financial reporting, and reinsurance. Since I was responsible for all three functions, I became the point person for it to get answers. Fortunately, being a person who wanted to know all the details helped me in providing timely responses. It had confidence in me.

There was a gleam of hope. The company decided to continue marketing operations. Our CEO was able to continue as head of marketing. He was often inside the parent and quickly realized that our shop was running more efficiently. He presented the case that integrating some of the functions would only increase our cost structure. Also, at this time, I was implementing PGAAP. Our reserving methods and financial reporting were much more transparent than what it was used to. We proceeded to implement PGAAP in a relatively short time and with a lower budget than it had anticipated.

This put us over the hump. We were able to persuade it to leave us self-standing. We have been delivering top and bottom line ever since. Thank goodness we remained professional throughout due diligence and demonstrated we could deliver the value it sought. We bucked the trend when our companies weren't physically integrated, for good reasons.

---

[3] Feldman, Mark and Michael Spratt, *Five Frogs on a Log*, New York: HarperCollins, 1999, Chapter 5.

[4] Gora, Jean, "Planning and Managing Insurer Merger Integration," LOMA, p. 120.

[5] Larger, stronger organizations buy smaller, weaker companies and fold them into their operations with the goal of leveraging the acquirer's better rating and operational skills to add value to the stock.

Typically the worst performing transactions are so-called "mergers of equals," where two of everything are kept, from the CEO on down. Combinations billed as a merger of equals usually evolve to become acquisitions. Ultimately, there is a shakeout and the real business of integration gets started, months or even years later. The rest of this chapter assumes a whole-hearted integration process.

9.2.4 REGULATORY APPROVALS

One of the unique challenges of an insurance transaction is dealing with state regulation in addition to normal federal regulations involving mergers of listed companies. In addition to federal anti-trust regulation (typically not an issue in the fragmented insurance industry), companies need to obtain approval from the appropriate state regulators. Regulators in the state of domicile of both companies, but particularly the target, will take a keen interest in the transaction. Other states may also become involved, especially in situations involving the rehabilitation of failed companies, due to the potential impact on their policyholders and state guarantee funds. As a result, there is typically a delay of three months or more from the announcement of the transaction to the actual closing.

This reality is in direct conflict with the injunction to proceed as rapidly as possible. This window gives competitors an opportunity to sow uncertainty and disruption among distributors, employees, and policyholders. For this reason, having a communications program in place to address the concerns of these constituencies during this key period is critical.

This makes it all the more important that plans are in place to hit the ground running on day one. Legal experts generally agree that some information sharing may occur before the official go-ahead is received, but prudent acquirers only proceed with information sharing to the degree that legal counsel approves. At a minimum, teams should complement publicly available information with as much data from due diligence as possible in order to help develop a preliminary integration plan.

Some organizations use independent third parties to collect information that cannot yet be shared between the two entities in the transaction. These "clean teams" can prove to be an accelerator of the integration planning process while allowing the companies to fully comply with legal restrictions. Because of the costs associated with this approach, it is typically utilized only when time is of the essence. This tactic may be particularly useful in situations where there is an emphasis on quickly capturing expense savings or dealing with over-capacity.[6]

9.2.5 BRAND MANAGEMENT

Much of the value ascribed to the new business valuation can be attributable to brand. Branding and brand valuation are beyond the scope of this text, but they should be considered in both large and small transactions.[7]

In large transactions, consultants specializing in brand management will be brought in to assist in the transition to ensure brand value is maximized. In general, 85% of merged entities are named after the acquirer, 1% are named for the target, and 14% receive a new name.[8] The decision depends on the relative strength of the respective brands and the degree of integration of the new entity.

[6] Gora, Jean, "Planning and Managing Insurer Merger Integration," LOMA.

[7] For a groundbreaking treatment of valuation, brands, and the financial services industry, refer to the paper, "Brands and Customer Values," by Andrew Leifer, Philip Simpson, and Mike Wilkinson, The Staple Inn Actuarial Society, 2002.

[8] Reed, Stanley Foster and Alexandra Reed Lajoux, *The Art of M&A*, 3rd ed., New York: McGraw-Hill, 1998. p 674.

In insurance, the value of the brand is based on trust and integrity; change puts that value at risk. Word of mouth is important, particularly with distributors who are gatekeepers with the power to place your product or choose another provider. This is especially true with annual renewable policies such as property and casualty and large group policies. Sensitive corporate buyers will be the first to depart if they have any concerns, financial or otherwise, about the transaction.

9.3 IMPLEMENTATION

At its core, a merger is no more than an oversized group of interrelated projects with an extremely sensitive public relations element. Some of the projects are relatively predictable and their coordination is routine. Other aspects are dynamic and need adroit leadership capable of responding rapidly to changing conditions. Incentives need to be put in place to underscore the notion that superior performance by team members is good for both the new organization and the future careers of its members. The structure and management of the implementation teams must facilitate both needs.

As discussed earlier, the steering committee creates a strategic plan. The work of reducing this broad plan to the level of concrete deliverables and specific timetables is left to implementation teams. On their own, implementation teams may find themselves at cross-purposes and need to resolve conflicting directives or, more likely, find that they are dependent on one another. The steering committee may or may not have time to address issues at the detail level. As a result, there is often an additional layer of coordination between the steering committee and the implementation teams. Companies that are regular acquirers may have designated "go-to" individuals or full-time staff devoted to the role in the form of a corporate integration unit.

9.3.1 CORPORATE INTEGRATION UNIT

A corporate integration unit (CIU) is no more than a special purpose project management team. Many experts recommend using the CIU as the center of a "hub and spokes" type approach, with the CIU coordinating the project on behalf of the steering committee and limited scope implementation teams addressing specific tasks.

The CIU is typically delegated the responsibility of choosing individuals to lead the implementation teams. The CIU maintains a master project plan and issues list using agreed-upon project management tools. They maintain contact with the implementation teams on an ongoing basis, charting progress and coordinating communications with and across the various teams.

The CIU is responsible for incorporating issues that inevitably arise into the plan and deciding when to involve the steering committee for direction. Working with one or more members of the steering committee, the CIU assists in preparing communications for stakeholders to ensure a consistent message is delivered. This approach leverages the competencies of line management while sparing them from some of the labors of project management.

The CIU is the logical place to manage clean room activities and to maintain a centralized information resource, starting with collecting and updating information from due diligence. The CIU is typically responsible for quantifying the costs and benefits of alternative integration approaches at the bequest of the steering committee or on their own initiative. This is also the logical area to manage the integration of corporate functions such as finance, accounting, and HR.

This arrangement has a number of advantages. Acquired merger competencies can be leveraged from the CIU as members learn and pass along their experience to individuals on other teams. Implementation team leaders report back scheduling and resource conflicts to the CIU, who, with perspectives across the entire scope of the project, can make informed decisions. Having full-time staff allotted allows for the opportunity to build internal expertise, using each transaction to build competence. A recommended practice is debriefings for participants after the merger to discuss lessons learned and to create references to guide future acquisitions.

9.3.2 IMPLEMENTATION TEAMS

Once the priorities are set, specific assignments can be handed off to implementation or project teams. Keeping teams small focuses accountability, facilitates scheduling, and aids communication. The charge for these teams is to develop solutions for achieving the end-state defined by the steering committee. These teams should involve line management to ensure their buy-in. Team members should be selected and be ready to start work officially on day one. To speed up progress, teams should have access to relevant pre-transaction due diligence analysis. Unless there is a reason not to, maintaining the due diligence data room is a useful frame of reference whose resources may already be familiar to many participants.

Implementation teams can be structured in a variety of ways. To produce quality results, companies must staff these teams with the most talented people available without consideration for the organization they represent. Two common approaches to organize teams are to:

- Establish teams that reflect the various functions of the organization. For example, there might be an underwriting team, an actuarial team, a claims team, an HR team, an information technology (IT) team, a finance team, and a marketing team.
- Create teams that support the different business lines of the combined companies. For example, a life insurer might include an individual life team, a health insurance team, a long-term care team, a disability income team, and a corporate team.

The team coordinator, often a line manager, is appointed by the CIU to lead the team. The key responsibility of the team coordinator is to define information requirements from other teams and other processes. The coordinator has to understand the bigger picture so he or she knows how the timing of the team's work affects other teams, which is critical to ensure that tasks are staged in the right order.[9] The team coordinator is also responsible for providing regular progress updates to the CIU.

The project teams must be provided a clear charter. People need to know what they are expected to do, what the timetable is, and what the goals are for capturing value, creating controls, and stabilizing processes. Implementation teams are accountable to the CIU for delivering timely results. The CIU, in turn, is responsible for monitoring progress of individual teams and reporting overall performance towards the objectives outlined by the steering committee in the strategic plan.

[9] Rosenblatt, Alice et al, "How to Avoid Common Pitfalls of Health Plan Mergers," *SOA Record*, Volume 26, #1, 2000, p. 17.

SIDE NOTE

BEWARE BEST PRACTICES

In approaching integration, teams need to find the middle ground between inertia and change for the sake of change. In deciding what and how to integrate, the participants must be aware that "no change" is a valid option for the right reasons. This is not the time to reference the re-engineering manual and look at each process to try to develop best practices. The idea is to get up and running as soon as possible.

A "best practices" strategy can quickly deteriorate into turf battles and bitter debate over aspects that do not matter and do not return value. Resources can be locked into protecting their turf rather than focusing on achieving the goals of the transition. Processes are part of larger systems. Grafting a process from one organization into the corporate host may be rejected, the victim of unintended consequences. Planners must carefully consider critical interdependencies. The purpose is not to optimize processes but to ensure that people are working on activities that add real value.

Even though implementation teams take ownership of specific assignments, in large projects with lots of moving parts, situations may be expected to arise between teams regarding prioritization, resource allocation, and timing, which will require resolution. Typically, inconsistencies can be resolved more effectively by filtering them to a higher level, such as the CIU or the steering committee, which can look at conflicts from a bigger-picture perspective. This helps ensure that a decision made in one area of the business does not make a commitment that is impossible for another part of the organization to carry out or, worse, that threatens the overall transaction value.

Implementation teams must set a high bar for the results desired. High expectations motivate people and keep them engaged. The assumption is that if people face aggressive requirements, they will not devote a lot of time to activities that do not add value. Expectations must be balanced with the reality that it is not possible to tackle every part of the plan at once. By recognizing and focusing on the most critical activities of merger integration, bigger payoffs, and more rapid progress are achievable.

As near-term goals are achieved, recognition of accomplishment is in order, which is beneficial to everyone involved because explicit communication and recognition increase confidence that the integration is moving according to plan. Recognition builds support for the plan across the organization.

Success is best achieved when companies set tangible and realistic milestones that can be clearly measured. It is important to be realistic about the time involved; missed deadlines have implications both internally and externally. Integration is an arduous process that can take months or years to accomplish. Instead of focusing on the single grand win, teams should attack smaller goals that can be executed successfully in a short time frame. In practice, impressive results can be delivered and people kept motivated when manageable, short-term deadlines are applied. Smaller goals foster an environment that enables people to exceed expectations, which is reinforced with rewards and incentives that encourage continued success.

Smart organizations use their best people on all aspects of an acquisition to increase the chances of success, particularly in due diligence and integration. However, since companies do not have excess staff, acquisitions require significant amounts of overtime because individuals must complete their regular jobs in addition to M&A-related responsibilities. Due to constant pressure with few resting places, projects may seem like they will never end. The organization must monitor the workload and employee well-being or risk increased error rates and loss of key people.

9.3.3 DAY-ONE ISSUES

There is a whole category of problems that needs to be addressed and fully implemented on day one (the day the transaction legally closes). The efficiency of day-one handling (or lack thereof) will reflect on the acquirer. The initial conduct creates memories and establishes a reputation that are long-lasting. It is wise to remember that one never gets a second chance to make a first impression.

Day-one readiness focuses on being able to operate the new business from the moment the acquisition is closed. Main areas of consideration include:

- reinforcement of vision and strategy for the new organization
- financial controls
  - assets
  - claims/benefit payments
  - areas writing checks and dealing with money
- employee communications
  - compensation and benefits
  - performance and incentive plans
  - scope and timing of likely layoffs
  - severance package and support services to be offered to laid-off workers
  - interim reporting relationships
  - opportunities and training programs
- technology
  - common payroll (which typically drives management information)
  - common communications (voicemail, e-mail, etc.)
  - security issues.

CRYPT 9.5

Curious Assets

In making acquisitions over the years, we've tried our best to get good quality assets to back the liabilities. Cash is always best—investment grade bonds are fine—and good quality mortgages are acceptable. But when you're buying a company, or taking over a block of business that's in receivership, sometimes you get assets that are not as desirable.

In the past, our company has received some peculiar assets in acquisitions. At one time, we were the proud owners of what must have been the ugliest 20-story office building in the state of Oklahoma. Along with the office building came an adjacent hotel, which the inspectors told us "had more asbestos than they had ever seen in one building." It took six months for the men in spacesuits to remove the asbestos from the building, during which time no guests were permitted to be in the hotel. We've also been the proud owners of a very high-quality health club and restaurant combination, which would have been a wonderful property in a major metropolitan area, but was entirely uneconomic since it was located in a rural town of 15,000 people.

Our most interesting asset came from an insolvent company many years ago. We took ownership and operating control of a cemetery in a small town in North Dakota. Not only did we have no experience in the cemetery business, but we soon learned that the ground froze so hard that the caskets of those who died during the winter were stockpiled until the spring thaw came. We got out of the cemetery business as fast as we could find someone to take it off our hands!

Of course, my company had correctly identified these assets as illiquid or inappropriate for a life company investment and had suitably discounted their value in the offer price. So there were no surprises during integration.

The HR staffs of both companies need to prepare, in advance of day one, answers to easily anticipated questions. Individuals who communicate with customers need to be ready to respond to questions. A helpful approach is to establish a clearinghouse of frequently asked questions to coordinate responses to questions from internal and external stakeholders. To the extent possible, these front line workers need to be able to explain how the transition works and what can be expected during the process.

9.3.4 TECHNOLOGY

Technology in the insurance industry is a world unto itself. Systems proliferate at insurance companies. Software and hardware are necessary for product development and pricing (actuarial modeling systems), marketing (illustrations, new business, and field management), underwriting, administration, asset management, claims, commissions, and accounting. Each area has its own software and often a separate technology platform with its own in-house gurus. The decision to combine or maintain separate systems each must be made individually.

Due to the degree of customization in the products, most policy administration packages require customization. In decades past, acquirers believed they could extract expense savings by combining platforms and IT projects. Current wisdom allows inforce to run on existing systems while implementing a single platform for new business.

The costs of systems development and conversion are significant. Companies considering embarking on a series of acquisitions need systems that accommodate expansion and control costs. Frequent acquirers and companies pursuing a roll up strategy need to develop capabilities to facilitate technology integration. The operation needs to be more predictable than tailored, typically assuming most processes are folded into the acquirer. As such, information systems for frequent acquirers need to be open and scalable.

9.3.5 PROCESS CONTROL

One of the first tasks for an acquirer is to stabilize processes. While not on anyone's list of value drivers, synergies, or cost saves, these are part of the table stakes that must be addressed. Left unattended, the potential downside is too great.

A company needs to deliver consistent processes so that distributors, customers, and employees know how to interact with it. The handling of applications and claims greatly impacts relationships with distributors. Some companies may have strict interpretations of published rules while others may provide a great deal of leeway. Misunderstandings and policy changes may cause a great deal of consternation to various constituencies. Merging companies need common policies and processes or confusion and distribution channel conflict may flare up. Companies that are not proactive in managing their processes may end up with the worst and most expensive of both worlds.

9.3.6 PROJECT MANAGEMENT TOOLS

Large integration projects involve dozens of teams and hundreds of concurrent projects. Large transactions are typically coordinated using a single set of project management tools. Smaller ones may or may not use these tools depending on the culture of the company or the requirements of particular managers.

In order to manage projects across departments, physical locations, and time zones, companies are increasingly turning to the use of intranet-based project management software. This places more responsibility and control in the teams, providing easier access to information while implicitly recognizing the interdependence of the sub-projects. This provides more flexibility in updating progress than centralized planning tools, enhancing the timeliness and accuracy of information flow.

In addition to tracking progress and resources, these tools provide assistance in developing schedules, building teams, and managing resources. Developing an in-house competency with project management software can pay significant dividends, particularly for companies using a corporate integration unit. As an added bonus, the project management skills learned in integration are directly applicable to other large corporate projects.

9.4 PEOPLE ISSUES

In any merger, the impact of the transaction on employees and others who work closely with the company is profound. Managing this impact is a crucial dimension in a successful transformation from two independent entities into a single enterprise with common, shared strategic vision.[10] As discussed in Chapter 6, HR and benefits experts must be introduced early in the process to get a sense of the challenges facing them. The information gleaned in due diligence must be leveraged to facilitate the integration process.

The chart below illustrates how employees go through several psychological stages during an M&A transaction.

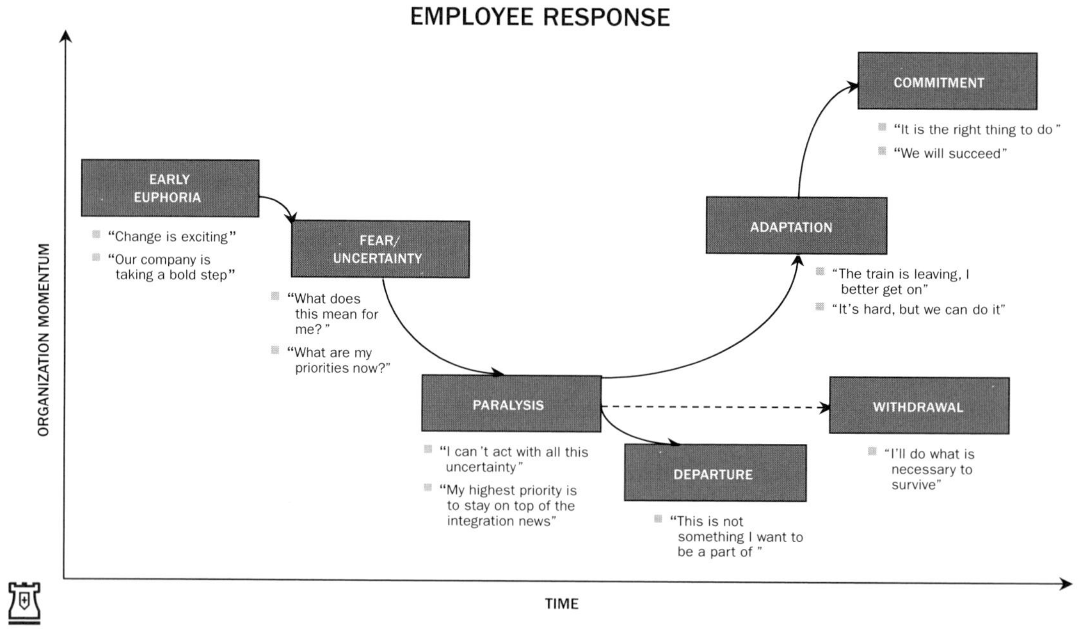

FIGURE 9.2 **Source:** Deloitte & Touche LLP

When the deal is first announced, a feeling of euphoria emerges. People are excited about what the transaction might mean for the business, their departments, and their careers. But this mood eventually shifts to one of uncertainty and sometimes fear. The uncertainty is often accompanied by a dip in performance as a sense of paralysis sets in. Anxieties distract employees from their work and more time is spent "around the water cooler" stoking the rumor mill. At this stage, one of three things is likely to happen:

[10] Schmidt, Jeffrey, Ed., "Making Mergers Work: The Strategic Importance of People," Towers Perrin/SHRM Foundation, 2002, p. 21.

- Employees leave the company because they don't want to be part of the new organization.
- Employees stay with the organization but with less commitment to the business, seeing their work as "just a job" that they will do to survive.
- Employees adapt to and champion the transaction.

The paralysis and performance dip can be short-circuited by giving employees a clear sense of direction about what they have to do to fit into the new organization. This will help boost the comfort level of people who are already committed to the new entity.

As employees move through these stages to acceptance, senior executives must be mindful of leadership's impact on the organization. The communications and actions of senior executives will set the tone for all employees. As role models, leaders must keep in mind that they cannot just "talk the talk." Their actions speak louder than words, and people are watching more closely than ever.

9.4.1 EMPLOYEE RETENTION

Insurance processes are complex. They rely heavily on technology and require skills that are not easily transferable or obtainable in the marketplace. Pricing, underwriting, investing, and claims handling are specialized functions that differ greatly by line of business and market segment. As such, many of the most valuable people in insurance companies have significant specialized training. Others have knowledge of the history and quirks of the company that is quite literally irreplaceable. They may view change as an indictment of their legacy. If these individuals leave, they take part of the value of the company with them.

The uncertainty surrounding a merger can significantly disrupt any business. Employees immediately assume that there will be fewer positions in the newly merged company. People realize they may have to compete directly with their counterparts in the acquiring organization in order to retain their current positions, a distinct disadvantage. Within hours of the announcement of a transaction, competitors will try to recruit the best employees. Since virtually every transaction considers at least certain employee groups to be a key component of value, the full potential of the merger may be immediately at risk. To address this situation, companies need to make retention a top priority.

Typically, three employee groups are identified in the transaction: 1) permanent preservations, 2) immediate layoffs, and 3) temporary retentions.

CRYPT 9.6

Keep Your Options Open

Our company had agreed to be sold to another company, which had a reputation for completing takeovers with little retention of the personnel. The takeover company's top executive in charge of the merger, Mr. Smith, came to our offices and announced at a company-wide meeting that they liked our operation and that they foresaw making no changes—in personnel, procedures, or location.

I had a few of our employees ask me individually what I thought of the announcement. I replied that I could not advise them what to believe or what to do, but that they should try to keep all their options open.

About two months later, Mr. Smith announced at a company-wide meeting that in fact they would only be retaining at most one-fourth of our people and that they would have to relocate out of state. You could hear the wailing and gnashing of teeth. Although I was not thrilled by the announcement, I was not surprised given the history of the acquiring company.

A few weeks later, on a cold and rainy night, a small commuter plane unfortunately went down near our office, killing all on board. The next day, more than once I heard the remark, "I hope Smith was on that flight." (He wasn't.)

Looking at it in a coldly rational way, Smith was merely doing his job and his second announcement could have been expected. Perhaps the biggest error he made was making the first announcement. Perhaps my fellow employees made a bigger error by not being prepared—assume the worst, hope for the best, and keep your options open.

9.4.1.1 Adverse Selection in Employee Retention

Those familiar with the science of risk selection are familiar with the concept of anti-selection, where individuals at greater risk are more likely to pursue the purchase of insurance to cover those risks. The same principle is applicable to employee retention. When a company is on the block, employees assess their prospects in the new organization. If they do not believe they have viable career opportunities in the new entity, they will attempt to depart as soon as possible. The best performers typically will not lack options, leaving behind colleagues whose career choices are not as robust. Simply put, the most valuable employees are the ones most likely to leave. This saddles the passive acquirer with a poorer performing group of employees, thus increasing the risk of the transaction failing to meet expectations.

This calls for implementing a selection process that identifies and proactively attempts to retain the most talented people in both the acquiring and target companies as soon as possible. If key members of the new entity's senior management have been identified and commitments obtained prior to the transaction announcement, shareholders and other constituencies gain confidence that substantial preplanning has already been conducted.

These executives will then begin to assemble their teams. It is vital to identify and keep employees with important stakeholder relationships. These employees may hold the key to retaining value. If necessary, retention bonuses and non-compete agreements can be used to retain key personnel (consideration must be offered for a non-compete agreement to be valid). Of course, the cost for these programs must be incorporated into the purchase price.

One of the challenges for the acquirer is to discover the target's talent and take advantage of it to upgrade its own talent pool. Smart companies use due diligence as an opportunity to get a head start on identifying the best people in the combined organization. Normally, the individuals involved in due diligence interview their counterparts in the target to obtain information about operations. This interview is also an opportunity to evaluate the background and qualifications of these peers.

These pre-transaction interviews take place in the real world. People participating in them understand that they might soon be competing head to head with the person sitting across the table. It would take an extraordinarily candid and objective individual to admit that the person across the table would be more valuable to the new organization than him or herself. As a result, in situations where personnel cuts are anticipated, companies may hire consulting firms to help to evaluate staff and make retention recommendations.

The acquirer's leadership usually has the upper hand in deciding which employees will be placed in management and other positions. However, if it is perceived that one group is getting all of the best jobs, the other's best employees in that area will depart. It is important for the process to treat all employees fairly both in appearance and fact.

Us Versus Them

CRYPT 9.7

A common initial reaction of a buyer in an acquisition situation is that the buyer has superior knowledge and skills on most things in comparison to the acquired company. The initial temptation is to impose the methods, systems, controls, philosophies, etc., of the buyer onto the acquired company. However, some companies go through an exercise of determining what the "best practices" are between the parent and acquired companies. Unfortunately these exercises are somewhat superficial some times. The end result is usually that the majority of best practices are being performed by the parent company, and the acquired company has few best practices.

We went through an acquisition in which one of these exercises was conducted. The result was that the best practices were virtually all determined to be those of the acquiring company. The senior management team reviewed the recommendations and sent them back for further analysis by the integration team. The senior management team did not believe that the acquired company did not have any best practices. Upon further "review" a more balanced analysis of best practices was achieved and the integration of the acquired company went very smoothly.

It is natural for an acquired company to feel some uneasiness and resentfulness toward the company that purchased it. The new parent company will typically send in teams of people to review how the acquired company does business. Most companies that have never been acquired are not accustomed to answering detailed questions about their business. Also, most companies have a few "skeletons in the closet" of things that have been done in the past that do not make sense unless the entire context of the situation is understood.

Once a company is purchased, it is best for the acquired company to lay all of its cards on the table so that the new parent can understand exactly what is going on in its new company. A problem for the acquired company may be that it has many business practices that "have always been done that way" but have not been reviewed recently. Though some of these practices may be embarrassing, hiding any facts from the parent can only lead to a bad relationship and distrust. In this same light, the acquired company should go out of its way to ask probing questions to understand the requirements of the new parent company.

9.4.1.2 Personnel Cuts

The other side of the retention issue is identifying the people who will not be needed by the new organization. This is not a subject to be treated lightly because the manner in which this group of employees is treated will say a lot to those staying for the long term. Just as importantly, it sends a clear message to those who will be asked to stay on to help complete short-term transition projects.

Members of this second group typically come from areas where the acquirer may already have the scale to accommodate the combined workload or the acquirer does not intend to use the outputs of these workers (e.g., discontinuing a line of business). It is advisable to identify the layoffs as quickly as possible to minimize the uncertainty for all involved. Once identified, it is advisable to release the affected individuals as soon as possible because people who will not be part of the organization going forward may poison the environment for those staying behind.

Putting equitable severance policies in place will help ease the pain of employees who cannot be retained. However, developing severance plans is a balancing act. On the one hand, management does not want to unnecessarily incur expenses for which it has no legal obligation. On the other hand, the company wants to signal to retained employees that even while making tough business decisions, the company can do so in a way that is respectful to employees and recognizes their prior contributions.

Severance packages tend to fluctuate with the strength of the economy and other external factors. Compensation and benefits specialists should be consulted to provide guidance in determining the components to be granted as well as to estimate the potential cost. Besides cash compensation, companies may offer severance benefits, such as outplacement services, job training, use of office facilities for job hunting, and extended medical coverage.

Cost cutting, particularly through employee severance, is no panacea for reaching transaction objectives and should be approached with trepidation. According to four separate PricewaterhouseCoopers surveys, the reduction of operating expense through the capture of scale economies is one of the least achieved objectives in a merger.[11]

Nothing can demoralize an integration team more than being given unrealistic targets or being required to make shortsighted cuts to cover for bidding errors. Savings only "count" if they are net savings, after payment of termination benefits and netting out of lost revenue. Up-front payments can lead to large one-time charges, depressing short-term financial performance. There is also evidence that downsizing results in the filing of more disability claims for longer periods of time.[12] Ultimately, the productivity of those who remain behind may suffer.

9.4.1.3 *Temporary Employees*

Often, a third group of employees who will not be retained in the long-term are needed for the short- to medium-term to maintain operating performance or to help complete some portion of the integration. This group is always the most difficult to manage. Experience has shown that these employees must have clear objectives with compensation linked to both retention and performance to maximize the value of the relationship. The short careers these employees will have with the new entity typically result in the need to pay them above-market rates and/or retention bonuses.

9.4.2 DISTRIBUTION

Acquirers face exceedingly complex decisions regarding agent retention and loyalty. Because of their close relationship to the home office, distributors will often learn about possible merger plans before the general public, which gives them ample time to evaluate their prospects and negotiate contracts with competitors. Due to the nature of the customer/agent relationship, when the distributor is lost, a significant portion of the business it has written may depart as well. Acquirers need to decide how far they will go to honor special deals the target may have made with individual producers. If these arrangements are cancelled, the buyer risks losing both current and future policyholders. It these arrangements are retained, the buyer's own distributors may become dissatisfied.

The acquiring company will need a well-planned strategy for securing the business of and relationships with distributors. Communication will be critical. Some successful practices include on-site visits by company senior executives, webcasts explaining benefits of the transaction, a hotline for agent questions and complaints, and bonus commissions for a limited period. In an effort to "influence the influencers," the highest producers may get special treatment.

---

[11] Feldman, Mark and Michael Spratt, *Five Frogs on a Log*, New York: HarperCollins, 1999, p. 124.

[12] Reed, Stanley Foster and Alexandra Reed Lajoux, *The Art of M&A*, 3rd ed., New York: McGraw-Hill, 1998, p 695.

Many insurance companies use independent agents to distribute their products. These independent contractors are the link between the insurance company and the policyholder. Typically, these agents, rather than the insurer, own the relationship with the policyholder, which is different from career agents who are more closely tied to the insurance company. Too many companies fail to understand this dynamic. Distribution is one of the key transaction drivers, yet it is also the area where acquirers can most quickly destroy value.

The acquirer must protect and grow this important asset. It must be understood that independent agents are just that: independent. They have multiple insurance company relationships where they can place their clients' business. Competitors will pursue these independent agents with a tremendous effort to try to induce them to move their business. Typical inducements include extra marketing allowances, override commissions, or preferred agent status. While tactics may differ, competitors will be relentless from the time the acquisition is announced.

Some question the difference between protecting and integrating employees and protecting relationships with independent agents. Acquirers are generally limited or even prohibited from talking directly to independent agents during the due diligence process. However, once the transaction is announced, there is nothing to prevent the acquirer from approaching or soliciting independent agents.

9.4.3 POLICYHOLDERS

One of the most important and easily quantifiable tasks for acquiring companies is to keep the inforce business on the books. But due to anti-competitive concerns, the acquirer cannot communicate directly with policyholders between the transaction announcement and the closing date, which can be months apart.

A common mistake of acquiring companies is to focus initially on employee and distribution contacts and delay contacting policyholders. It is critical for the acquirer to reach out as soon as possible to this group to protect its investment. Once the transaction is announced, competitors and their agents will be eyeing the target's customer base, offering compelling arguments to switch to them as the carrier. Without attention, a significant component of the transaction value may be eroded in as little as six months.

The initial contact with policyholders usually is in the form of written correspondence. This correspondence will inform the insured of the nature of the transaction, indicate any possible impact on the policyholder, and may describe benefits the acquirer believes will be available to the policyholder. Because of the nature of the relationship between the insured and insurer, and the extent of the contact between them, the impact of a transaction on policyholders varies between long- and short-term contracts (e.g., life vs P&C) and whether the contracts are commercial or individual.

Typically, policyholders are somewhat "sticky" due to a certain degree of inertia. A policyholder's biggest concerns are solvency and stability. This is manifested most clearly to the policyholder in two ways: independent ratings of claims paying ability and service. If a company's ratings are maintained but service deteriorates sufficiently, customers may be motivated to overcome the sense of inertia and transfer to a new insurer. For this reason alone, some degree of continuity in customer service personnel is desirable.

9.5 THE IMPORTANCE OF CULTURE

Integration is a change process. With all great change there is resistance whether the status quo is perceived as optimal or not. Much of the resistance or acceptance, and even the manner in which these feelings are expressed, is a direct result of corporate culture. Employees from a company with an entrepreneurial outlook may be frustrated with the pace of progress at a firm with multiple layers in the decision making process. Employees used to a hierarchical structure may or may not thrive at a company whose rewards emphasize speed over deliberation. Companies with similar organizational architecture may still stumble over any number of other cultural issues, including incentives, compensation structure, and controls.

9.5.1 WHAT IS CULTURE?

The dynamics of culture are so ingrained that they are nearly invisible to people inside the company. While people outside the company may readily perceive cultural characteristics, it can be difficult to analyze them objectively and be even more daunting to quantify them meaningfully. Most organizations have a difficult time understanding what their own culture is, much less how to add, subtract, or multiply the cultures of two independent organizations. Because of this, many acquirers ignore culture in the integration process and assume it will resolve itself. This can be a big mistake. Survey after survey consistently shows cultural issues to be one of the greatest challenges to successful integration. According to a Deloitte survey, 85% of transaction failures have cultural undertones.

CRYPT 9.8

New CEO Dismembers Old Culture

We had a situation in which the parent purchased a company that was not operating efficiently. The value of the acquisition to the parent company involved three primary items:

a. Significant cuts in expenses in the acquired company
b. Continued profitability from a solid block of inforce business
c. Utilization of independent field force with strong loyalties to the acquired company.

The acquiring company did not realize how interrelated these three items were. The plan was to fire most of the acquired company's senior management and replace them with several people from the parent company and several new hires. The person who was inserted as the new president had been in the insurance business for many years and appeared to have an understanding of field force dynamics and administrative issues.

However, the new president did not respect the culture of the acquired company and attempted to impose immediate harsh arbitrary guidelines on the home office and field in order to achieve the necessary expense cuts. Almost overnight, the field force became dissatisfied and many previously loyal agents left the company. When the agents left the company, they took with them a lot of the inforce business that they had written over the years. As a further expense cutting measure, the company offered an early retirement program that provided incentives for people over 55 to leave the company. The "take-rate" on this offer was almost 100%.

So, within a year, the new management had alienated the field force, lost a lot of the profitable inforce business, and lost a huge block of historical knowledge from the "early-retirees."

It would have been prudent for someone in the acquired company to make the problems known to the parent. However, there was nobody in the acquired company (outside of the new management team) who had developed a relationship with the parent company. Thus, nobody could let the parent company know that value was being destroyed by the new management team. When the parent company finally figured it out (and replaced part of the management team again), a lot of damage had been done.

The new management took a different approach and restored some of things that had been taken away by the first team of new management. Certain agent perks were restored, a field advisory council was established, and efforts were made in the home office to build the morale. Some of the "old culture" was re-established and a more incremental approach was decided upon to achieve the targeted expense savings.

In summary, the parent company initially failed to respect the culture of the acquired company. Understanding and respecting the culture of a company and the relationships within the home office and with the field force are essential before successful changes can be made. However, it is important the new culture begin to be inserted early. If a company is allowed to continue to operate without changes to the culture, then it is significantly more difficult to implement the cultural changes later.

The culture must be understood before it can be adapted. Business people usually make decisions based on quantifiable facts. Culture does not lend itself to quantification. Culture is not, as some believe, embodied in a mission statement, a statement of values, or an employee handbook. According to James Brickley, "Corporate culture encompasses the ways *work and authority are organized*, the ways *people are rewarded and controlled*, as well as organizational features such as *customs, taboos, company slogans, heroes, and social rituals*."[13] (emphasis added).

Culture consists of the principles and values, the beliefs and behaviors, and the expectations and etiquette that shape every company's personality. Culture is reflected by the nature of employee empowerment and incentive. A merger will impact all of these features.

9.5.2 CREATING A SHARED CULTURE

It is the rare acquirer that understands the importance and impact of cultural issues. A successful acquirer deals with cultural transition proactively. If an acquirer cannot articulate its own culture, it will be unable to identify the culture of its target, much less design the cultural integration process.

The easiest time to change corporate culture is during a merger. Stakeholders anticipate major changes during a transition, which provides ammunition against firmly entrenched interests and offers a window of opportunity for change. A major concern of investors, creditors, and analysts is the inability to act. Companies that move quickly, decisively, and effectively shield themselves from unwelcome scrutiny.

There are various ways companies can overcome cultural integration hurdles and take tangible steps towards creating a shared culture. Interactions between leaders of the two organizations are often a reliable way to gauge the potential for cultural compatibility. Tactics such as site visits, employee interviews, employee surveys, and third-party assessments can be used to learn about another organization's culture.

An insightful exercise in cultural exploration is to have each company's executives reply to a set of prepared questions about their own culture, about their merger partner's culture, and about their merger partner's perceptions about their own culture. By comparing the answers of the two companies, clear differences in perception can be observed. This exercise makes management of the two firms aware of cultural assumptions and provides a common vocabulary for dealing with them.[14]

As a result of the transaction, neither culture will remain the same as it was before, even if the institutions remain completely separate. Objectives and rewards will change, sending ripples through existing corporate culture as the organizational structure realigns to support

[13] Chew, Donald, Ed., *The New Corporate Finance*, 3rd ed., New York: McGraw-Hill, 2001, p 113.

[14] Gora, Jean, "Planning and Managing Insurer Merger Integration," LOMA, p. 112.

achieving these targets. For this reason, it is recommended that the steering committee conscientiously consider the end-state for the new organization's culture. The cultural target should be closely related to the transaction's value drivers. Companies would be well advised to connect cultural change to measurable business objectives because business outcomes can be used as a means to mold and reward desired cultural behavior.

A successful integration demands more than gaining insights into the potential compatibility between the two organizations and targeting an end state. The real engine of cultural change is the observable behavior of the senior management viewed as role models. If their conduct is inconsistent with the messages being disseminated, the inconsistency will be evident and a Pandora's box of potential problems will be opened.

By aligning incentives with outcomes, acknowledging publicly successful role models, and sending consistent messages to stakeholders, the company will be well on its way to inducing cultural change. Over time, by aligning policy with consistently reinforced desired behavior, a company can shape its culture in a proactive fashion.[15]

9.5.3 CULTURAL MODEL

At this point, the question becomes, "What is the right culture?" Of course, there is no single right answer to this question. Some highly effective companies foster a culture that is top-down and hierarchical. Others boast a free-form, entrepreneurial climate that is equally successful. While no single cultural model will fit every organization, this is not to suggest they are by any means interchangeable. The integration should focus on defining a culture that supports the business model. Everyone in the merged organization should understand what the elements of the new culture are with emphasis on how incentives are tied to outcomes.

Firms with different value propositions must critically evaluate their integration plan. A company whose business model embraces being a low-cost provider should think twice if it intends to merge with a company whose value proposition is full service. Difficulties during such a transition should be expected. Friction and conflict will arise as individuals confront behavior and expectations they don't understand.[16]

Planned well and communicated effectively, the process of developing the culture of the new firm can engage employees and help forge their relationship with the organization. Communication and culture can combine to create a sense of shared vision and purpose that helps employees embrace rather than resist change. As people increase their understanding of the new organization's culture, its success measures, and consequent rewards, they will gain confidence in their ability to participate in the changes. Ultimately, employees must feel their role is key to the success of the new enterprise.

[15] The new CEO for a troubled firm faces many of the same challenges as those in a merger, but without the excitement of the bidding. In the 1980s, David Kearns changed corporate culture at Xerox to focus on quality. In the 1990s, Lou Gerstner turned around IBM by changing their focus to service. Both of these are textbook examples of cultural change from the top, with plenty of relevant documentation for the interested reader.

[16] In nature, when two baboon troops are combined, troop dynamics are unstable and individuals are anxious until the alpha males and females are established and the new social hierarchy is settled.

9.6 KEY MEASURES OF SUCCESS AND REASONS FOR FAILURE

For a transaction to be considered a success on Wall Street, it must create shareholder value in both the short term and the long term. The combined company must also perform better than its peer group. The relative performance of the pre-merger entities is seldom reported because separate books tracking the financial performance of the pieces are not made public under normal operating conditions (holding companies being the primary exception). Ultimately, the judgment of success or failure of the transaction is reflected in the stock price. It can be difficult to isolate the causes of stock dips and flutters unless there are serious, visible problems. Deciding that a transaction is successful often comes down to Wall Street chatter—what analysts are saying about the transaction—three, six, and 12 months down the road.

M&A transactions fail for three main reasons. The first reason is poor strategic choice—"It seemed like a good idea but it wasn't." This type of failure typically occurs early in the transaction process, perhaps when a poor initial assumption set driven by an eager transaction team cascades through the decision making process, almost with a mind of its own.

The second reason is that a good property is identified but too much is paid. No matter how expert the due diligence and integration teams are, there is no way to get 20 from 10. This is known as the "winner's curse." Synergy estimates tend to rise in an auction as companies try to support a winning bid. But once a winner has been selected, managers with "buyer's remorse" may back off their synergy commitments. A best practice is to link management compensation to achieving the value drivers identified during the diligence phase, which helps the company bid a realistic price and avoid overpaying for the target. It also keeps participants focused on the economic reality that whatever they buy they have to take home and integrate (the reverse Pottery Barn rule).

The third main reason for M&A failures occurs due to poor integration, or execution risk. The main problems in any integration are:

- poor communication
- inadequate linkage between objectives and performance targets
- lack of accountability
- poorly defined objectives
- incorrect assumptions
- key commitments not in writing
- schedules not based on realistic time frames
- failure to learn from mistakes.[17]

But it is not simply bad strategy or paying too much that causes failures; people issues are frequently the underlying problem. Key managers or talent may leave unexpectedly. Valuable operating synergies may evaporate because cultural differences between companies are not understood or are simply ignored. Cuts or significant changes in pay structure and benefits may create ill will, reducing productivity. If management does not communicate its business rationale or goals for the new company, employees may flounder in the ensuing confusion.[18]

---

[17] Adapted from "*Project Management for Dummies*," Stanley Portnoy, Indianapolis: Wiley Publishing, Inc. 2001.

[18] Schmidt, Jeffrey, Ed., "Making Mergers Work: The Strategic Importance of People," Towers Perrin/SHRM Foundation, 2002.

CRYPT 9.9

Bait And Switch

An old-line manufacturer bought a life company. The insurer was run by a flamboyant dealmaker. The acquirer had been drawn to the table by the lure of the future of direct response. The insurer's CEO was touting the values of direct response insurance sales and was totally committed to make this happen.

However, once the sale was completed, mass marketing was relegated to the back burner. The CEO instead concentrated on completely unrelated endeavors, such as developing traditional lines of business (not even the new universal life) and negotiating to acquire other life companies (with the new parent's money).

The parent never pressed him to honor his pre-acquisition strategy. The parent never saw its anticipated return on investment (ROI) either.

9.6.1 SURVEYS

M&A is a fertile field for academic and business research for a significant reason: money. Huge amounts of it are made or lost as it sloshes in and out of shareholder buckets. Returns that prove modest may indicate the endeavor wasn't worth the effort. M&A is awash in qualitative surveys identifying reasons for success and explanations for failure. Quantitative studies of post-transaction financial performance attempt to define whether transactions do or do not add value to shareholders. A book by Stanley Foster Reed and Alexandra Reed Lajoux, *The Art of M&A,* compared the results of 17 major studies of long-term post merger performance conducted between 1965 and 1997 and found that the verdict was split 45%/55% between success and failure.

Survey results should not be viewed with 100% reliability. Survey questions are open to interpretation, data sets may not be complete, and publicly available information may not be error-free. Regulations change, tax regimes come and go, and accounting standards evolve. Even the definition of success and failure can be inconsistent between studies.

9.6.2 COST OF CHANGE

The decision to grow by acquisition is not to be taken lightly. In addition to the financial cost and increased risk exposures, mergers bring extraordinary opportunity costs by disrupting business, distracting employees, and diminishing current performance.[19] Employment cost is raised in terms of increased turnover, absenteeism, conflict, workers' compensation, and disability claims.[20]

Organizational change is not new. Change itself does not equate to progress. Frequent changes harm productivity and demoralize the workforce. In constantly changing environments, employees have limited incentive to learn new job assignments, devise more efficient production processes, or develop relations with co-workers. Frequent restructuring causes uncertainty about job assignments and promotes actions that focus on short-term payoffs rather than long-term investments.

Before undertaking major organizational changes, management should have a good understanding of how the target arrived at its existing organizational architecture and, more generally, why particular types of organizations work well in given competitive and regulatory environments. Such an understanding is important if only because the costs of organizational change can be so large.

---

[19] Feldman, Mark and Michael Spratt, *Five Frogs on a Log,* New York: HarperCollins, 1999, page 15.

[20] Olin, Meike, "Managing the Risks of Mergers and Acquisitions," Marsh Inc., 2004, p 17.

9.6.3 SO WHY DO IT?

Despite the spotty track record, many companies continue to pursue M&A over other growth alternatives. There are several reasons why buyers pursue acquisition targets. One obvious explanation is the management agency problem—incentives for executives are not aligned with the interests of stockholders. This can be seen in some high-profile instances where management benefits from rich severance packages despite the diminishment, if not evaporation, of earnings. M&A does create an exciting work environment, which may attract (or reflect) a type of executive staff different from the type of executives which are attracted to companies that pursue organic growth strategies.

Another aspect is more visceral than logical. For the same reason people buy lottery tickets knowing full well aggregate losses are 50%, the potential for a huge payoff to the winner exists. In the lottery, the one sure winner is the lottery sponsor; in M&A, sure winners are the investment bankers and consultants.

Of course, there are companies that do M&A for a living and do it well. Stockholders know these companies are valuable and pay a premium to join as investors. Unfortunately, developing M&A competency is a problem for first timers—there is no safe way to practice a first acquisition.

9.6.4 INCREASING THE ODDS

Some companies have a better track record at M&A than others. They know how to pick their properties, have smart due diligence teams, and negotiate good contracts. But it does not stop there. Companies that consistently deliver above-average results know how to integrate towards their objectives in a way that maximizes the value of the deal. These companies have managed to develop the integration competency.

Integration is a skill that can be learned as an organization. Unfortunately, there is no substitute for experience. Reading a textbook or planning in meetings cannot provide the entire roadmap to success. Like learning to ride a bicycle, the successful practitioner needs the experience. Companies typically need to go through several transactions before the milestones in the process become familiar. Every time is unique and there are inevitably surprises along the way. To quote one veteran participant, "Once you have seen one acquisition, you've seen one acquisition."

A company aspiring to become an M&A player can hire outside consulting talent to bootstrap inexperienced teams or to add strength in areas an experienced team lacks. Even companies with a solid M&A track record use transition specialists to assist in the process and to take the burden off of stretched internal resources. Used effectively, outside talent may accelerate the process or produce a superior end result.

9.7 CONCLUSION

Managing a merger integration is a complex, labor-intensive process. Large transactions typically entail a multitude of cross-functional activities across multiple sites involving numerous people. The challenge is to manage this process seamlessly while staying focused on core business operations, which has to be accomplished without hurting customer service for both new and existing customers and while maintaining financial performance for the new group. It's a tall order.

Merger integration experts underscore one critical point: to capture the financial and strategic objectives of the deal, companies need to take a comprehensive approach to the integration process with process ownership high in the organization. Companies can improve their probabilities of success by incorporating best practices discussed in this book:

To summarize lessons presented in this chapter, successful practitioners:

- identify value and bid appropriately
- protect their investment with careful due diligence
- negotiate terms to safeguard the deal
- get appropriate outside expertise to complement in-house experts
- have those responsible for structuring the deal bear responsibility for execution
- prepare for rapid deployment by doing comprehensive planning
- integrate efficiently
- focus on capturing the drivers of value
- align incentives and outcomes
- resolve employee retention alternatives early
- address cultural issues in a timely and forthright manner
- communicate, communicate, and communicate again.

The ideas introduced and discussed in this book can make the difference between success and failure in a merger or acquisition. Applying these practices effectively will result in the company's recognition as an elite firm that completes M&A transactions successfully.

APPENDIX

APPENDIX A1

Confidentiality Agreement

PERSONAL AND CONFIDENTIAL

[DATE]

[NAME]
[TITLE]
[RECIPIENT COMPANY'S NAME]
[ADDRESS]
[CITY, STATE ZIP CODE]

Re: CONFIDENTIALITY AGREEMENT

Dear _____________:

In connection with your consideration of a possible transaction ("Transaction") with XYZ, Inc. (the "Company"), you have requested certain confidential and other information concerning the Company. ABC Investment Bank Capital ("ABC") is the financial advisor to the Company.

You agree to treat any information concerning the Company, whether furnished to you before or after the date of this letter, together with any and all analyses or other documents prepared by you or any of your directors, employees, advisors, attorneys, accountants, consultants, representatives, or lending institutions (collectively, "Representatives") that contain or otherwise reflect such information (collectively, "Evaluation Material"), in accordance with this agreement. The term "Evaluation Material" does not include information that: (a) was already in your possession prior to the time of disclosure to you by the Company or ABC, (b) was or becomes generally available to the public other than as a result of a disclosure by you or your Representatives, or (c) becomes available to you on a non-confidential basis from a source other than the Company or ABC, provided that such source is not known by you to be bound by a confidentiality agreement with the Company or otherwise prohibited from disclosing the information to you.

The Evaluation Material will be used solely for the purpose of evaluating the Transaction between the Company and you and will be kept confidential by you and your Representatives, except to the extent that disclosure: (a) has been consented to in writing by the Company or ABC, (b) is required by law or other applicable judicial or governmental order, or (c) is made to your Representatives who need to know such information for the purpose of evaluating the Transaction (it being understood that such Representatives shall be informed by you of the confidential nature of the

Evaluation Material). In any event, you shall be responsible for any disclosure of Evaluation Material by your Representatives that would constitute a breach of this agreement.

In addition, without the prior written consent of the Company, you will not, and you will direct your Representatives not to, disclose to any person: (a) that the Evaluation Material has been made available to you or your Representatives, (b) that discussions are taking place concerning a Transaction, or (c) any terms or other facts with respect to the Transaction, including the status thereof.

In the event that you or any of your Representatives are requested or required by judicial, legislative, or regulatory process to disclose any Evaluation Material, you will provide the Company with prompt notice of any such request or requirement so that the Company may seek a protective order or other appropriate remedy and/or waive compliance with the terms of this agreement. In the event that such protective order or other remedy is not obtained, or that the Company waives compliance with the terms hereof, you may disclose only that portion of the Evaluation Material that is legally required.

It is understood and agreed that money damages may not be a sufficient remedy for any breach of this agreement and that the Company is entitled to seek specific performance and injunctive or other equitable relief. Such remedy shall not be deemed to be the exclusive remedy for breach of this agreement, but shall be in addition to all other remedies available at law or equity to the Company.

Neither the Company nor ABC shall be deemed to have made any representations or warranties as to the accuracy or completeness of the Evaluation Material. Only those representations or warranties that are made by the Company in a final definitive agreement regarding a Transaction, when, as, and if executed, and subject to such limitations and restrictions as may be specified therein, will have any legal effect.

Within 10 days after being so requested by the Company, except to the extent you are advised by legal counsel that complying with such request would be prohibited by law, you will return or destroy all Evaluation Material. You shall confirm any destruction of materials in writing. Any Evaluation Material that cannot be returned or destroyed (such as oral Evaluation Material) shall remain confidential, subject to the terms of this agreement.

This agreement binds the parties only with respect to the matters expressly set forth herein. As such, unless and until a subsequent definitive written agreement regarding a Transaction between the Company and you has been executed, (a) neither the Company nor you will be under any legal obligation of any kind whatsoever to negotiate or consummate a Transaction, and (b) you shall have no claim whatsoever against the Company or ABC or any of their respective directors, officers, owners, affiliates, or representatives arising out of or relating to any Transaction.

Additionally, you agree not to solicit for employment any Company employees to whom you may be introduced or otherwise had contact with as a result of your consideration of a Transaction for a period of one year after the date of this agreement, provided that you shall not be restricted in any general solicitation for employees (including through the use of employment agencies) not specifically directed at any such persons, and provided further that you shall not be restricted in hiring any such person who responds to any such general solicitation.

This agreement shall be governed by the internal laws of the State of   , without regard to conflict of laws principles. This agreement may be amended only in writing. No failure or delay by the Company or ABC in exercising any right hereunder or any partial exercise thereof shall operate as a waiver thereof or preclude any other or further exercise of any right hereunder.

Your obligations under this agreement shall remain in effect for a period of ______ years from the date hereof, unless and until this agreement is terminated by the Company or is superseded by another agreement with you that concerns your use of the Evaluation Material.

The Company is a third party beneficiary of this agreement.

Please confirm that the foregoing is in accordance with your understanding by signing and returning to us a copy of this letter.

Very truly yours,

ABC INVESTMENT BANK

By:
[NAME: ______________________]
[TITLE:]

Accepted and agreed to as of:

[RECIPIENT COMPANY]

By: ______________________
Name:
Title: ______________________

APPENDIX A2

Bid Process Letter

PERSONAL AND CONFIDENTIAL

[Date]

[Name of Contact]
[Title]
[Name of Company]
[Address]
[Address]

Dear [Contact]:

Thank you for your interest in a possible acquisition of [Name of Company]. The Company was previously code-named "[Name of Company]" in the Confidentiality Agreement that you executed. The enclosed Confidential Memorandum is being furnished to you to assist in your evaluation of a possible transaction with the Company. The information contained in the Confidential Memorandum is provided pursuant to the Confidentiality Agreement that you have executed and returned to ABC Investment Bank ("ABC"). The following letter outlines how we intend to proceed with the sale process, which has been designed to ensure the equitable treatment of all interested parties.

If you have an interest in [Name of Company], please advise ABC by [Date] 5:00 PM EST in writing, ([Fax:], Attention: [Name]), that subject to further due diligence you have a bona fide interest in acquiring the Company. Written indications of interest should include:

(i) a preliminary non-binding estimate of the purchase price;

(ii) a description of the proposed consideration to be received by the shareholders (stock, cash, etc.) with as much detail as possible regarding any possible restrictions, contingencies attached to the consideration;

(iii) your intentions with respect to management as it relates to their growth plans outlined in the Confidential Memorandum;

(iv) source of financing, if necessary, to consummate the transaction; and

(v) any material preconditions to the consummation of a transaction, including shareholder approval, regulatory approvals, etc.

ABC will be available to consult with prospective purchasers prior to the deadline in order to provide guidance in submitting Indications of Interest. [Name of Company], with the assistance of ABC, will decide based upon your Indication of Interest whether it is appropriate to proceed to the second phase of the sale process. The Company presently anticipates selecting only a limited group of qualified parties to undertake a more complete evaluation of the Company, which will include the opportunity to meet with management, tour the facility, visit a data room of additional information (legal, financial, corporate, etc.) and conduct other appropriate due diligence, as required.

The individuals at ABC listed within the Confidential Memorandum should be the sole points of contact for the transaction process. You may contact any member of the ABC team at our main phone number (312) 765-4321. Neither the management, directors, nor any employees of [Name of Company] should be contacted directly. We would appreciate your strictest confidentiality with respect to this sale.

Thank you for your interest in this opportunity.

Sincerely,

[Name]

[Title]

ABC Investment Bank

Enclosure

Appendix A3

Preliminary Bid Letter

PRELIMINARY BID LETTER KEY ECONOMIC AND STRUCTURAL TERMS	
Transaction Overview	BUYER ("BUYER") to purchase 100% of the equity of SELLER.
Consideration to be Paid at Closing	A total consideration; including the assumption of $20.0 million in debt; to be paid at closing based on 86.0x SELLER's LTM Net Income or $115 million, whichever is greater.
Form of Consideration	Restricted stock, no par value, and cash as follows: (i) Restricted stock of $10 million, paid to management and certain insider shareholders (based on an assumed ownership level by management of 10%); (ii) Cash of $5 million paid to management and certain insider shareholders; and (iii) Cash of $100 million, paid to all other shareholders.
Additional Contingent Consideration	Additional contingent consideration of up to $17.5 million will be paid, in the form of five-year restricted stock to current insider shareholders, if SELLER achieves a 15% Net Income margin on average for five years.
Retention / Employment Agreements	Additional contingent consideration payments will be paid irrespective of continued employment of the recipient. Additional contingent consideration will not be made available to non-shareholding employees at the time of the transaction. A separate retention pool, non-competition, and long-term employment agreements are to be negotiated separately with certain key employees and other individuals as designated.
Restricted Stock Issuance	Issue amount of restricted stock will be calculated based on the greater of: (i) The trailing 30-day average BUYER stock price for the relevant payment period (either the close of the transaction for the initial consideration paid or, for the additional contingent compensation amounts, the respective measurement period); or (ii) $10.00 per share.
Antidilution	Restricted stock grants will be subject to reasonable and customary antidilution provisions.
Vesting, Transfer Restrictions	Restricted stock will vest immediately, but will have transfer restrictions that lapse in increments of 10% for the first 4 years and 60% in year 5.
Dividend	All shares issued in the transaction are eligible for dividends, as applicable.

Net Working Capital at Closing	Current assets of the SELLER must be at least $2.0 million greater than the current liabilities at time of purchase. To the extent there is less than $2.0 million net working capital, purchase price will be reduced by such shortfall.
Indemnification	***Cap:*** to be determined. ***Term:*** Claims for indemnification may be made at any time during the two calendar years post-closing. ***Priority:*** Claims made for indemnification are to be pro rata first from the additional contingent compensation payments; the remainder, if any, from the escrow account funded on behalf of all shareholders.
Payment	Restricted stock will be issued in Treasury shares at the closing of the transaction.
Anticipated Closing	________, _____.
Other	Reasonable and customary representations, warranties, covenants, and closing conditions to be negotiated. Other terms and conditions as necessary for recipients of additional contingent consideration to receive capital gains treatment, as practicable.

APPENDIX A4

Form A

FORM A

STATEMENT REGARDING THE
ACQUISITION OF CONTROL OF OR MERGER WITH A DOMESTIC INSURER

____
Name of Domestic Insurer

BY

Name of Acquiring Person (Applicant)

Filed with the Insurance Department of

Dated: , 19

(State of domicile of insurer being acquired)

Name, Title, address and telephone number of Individual to Whom Notices and Correspondence Concerning this Statement Should be Addressed:

____

____

____

____

ITEM 1. METHOD OF ACQUISITION

State the name and address of the domestic insurer to which this application relates and a brief description of how control is to be acquired.

ITEM 2. IDENTITY AND BACKGROUND OF THE APPLICANT

(a) State the name and address of the applicant seeking to acquire control over the insurer.

(b) If the applicant is not an individual, state the nature of its business operations for the past 5 years or for such lesser period as such person and any predecessors thereof shall have been in existence.

Briefly describe the business intended to be done by the applicant and the applicant's subsidiaries.

(c) Furnish a chart or listing clearly presenting the identities of the interrelationships among the applicant and all affiliates of the applicant. No affiliate need be identified if its total assets are equal to less than 1/2 of 1% of the total assets of the ultimate controlling person affiliated with the applicant. Indicate in such chart or listing the percentage of voting securities of each such person which is owned or controlled by the applicant or by any other such person. If control of any person is maintained other than by the ownership or control of voting securities, indicate the basis of such control. As to each person specified in such chart or listing indicate the type of organization (e.g., corporation, trust, partnership) and the state or other jurisdiction of domicile. If court proceedings involving a reorganization or liquidation are pending with respect to any such person, indicate which person, and set forth the title of the court, nature of proceedings and the date when commenced.

ITEM 3. IDENTITY AND BACKGROUND OF INDIVIDUALS ASSOCIATED WITH THE APPLICANT

State the following with respect to (1) the applicant if (s)he is an individual or (2) all persons who are directors, executive officers or owners of 10% or more of the voting securities of the applicant if the applicant is not an individual.

(a) Name and business address;

(b) Present principal business activity, occupation or employment including position and office held and the name, principal business, and address of any corporation or other organization in which such employment is carried on;

(c) Material occupations, positions, offices or employment during the last 5 years, giving the starting and ending dates of each and the name, principal business, and address of any business corporation or other organization in which each such occupation, position, office, or employment was carried on; if any such occupation, position, office, or employment required licensing by or registration with any federal, state, or municipal governmental agency, indicate such fact, the current status of such licensing or registration, and an explanation of any surrender, revocation, suspension, or disciplinary proceedings in connection therewith.

(d) Whether or not such person has ever been convicted in a criminal proceeding (excluding minor traffic violations) during the last 10 years and, if so, give the date, nature of conviction, name and location of court, and penalty imposed or other disposition of the case.

ITEM 4. NATURE, SOURCE, AND AMOUNT OF CONSIDERATION

(a) Describe the nature, source, and amount of funds or other considerations used or to be used in effecting the merger or other acquisition of control. If any part of the same is represented or is to be represented by funds or other consideration borrowed or otherwise obtained for the purpose of acquiring, holding or trading securities, furnish a description of the transaction, the names of the parties thereto, the relationship, if any, between the borrower and the lender, the amounts borrowed or to be borrowed, and copies of all agreements, promissory notes, and security arrangements relating thereto.

(b) Explain the criteria used in determining the nature and amount of such consideration.

(c) If the source of the consideration is a loan made in the lender's ordinary course of business and if the applicant wishes the identity of the lender to remain confidential, he must specifically request that the identity be kept confidential.

ITEM 5. FUTURE PLANS OF INSURER

Describe any plans or proposals which the applicant may have to declare an extraordinary dividend, to liquidate the insurer, to sell its assets to or merge it with any person or persons or to make any other material change in its business operations or corporate structure or management.

ITEM 6. VOTING SECURITIES TO BE ACQUIRED

State the number of shares of the insurer's voting securities which the applicant, its affiliates, and any person listed in Item 3 plan to acquire, and the terms of the offer, request, invitation, agreement or acquisition, and a statement as to the method by which the fairness of the proposal was arrived at.

ITEM 7. OWNERSHIP OF VOTING SECURITIES

State the amount of each class of any voting security of the insurer which is beneficially owned or concerning which there is a right to acquire beneficial ownership by the applicant, its affiliates, or any person listed in Item 3.

ITEM 8. CONTRACTS, ARRANGEMENTS, OR UNDERSTANDINGS WITH RESPECT TO VOTING SECURITIES OF THE INSURER

Give a full description of any contracts, arrangements, or understandings with respect to any voting security of the insurer in which the applicant, its affiliates, or any person listed in Item 3 is involved, including but not limited to transfer of any of the securities, joint ventures, loan, or option arrangements, puts or calls, guarantees of loans, guarantees against loss or guarantees of profits, division of losses or profits, or the giving, or withholding of proxies. Such description shall identify the persons with whom the contracts, arrangements, or understandings have been entered into.

ITEM 9. RECENT PURCHASES OF VOTING SECURITIES

Describe any purchases of any voting securities of the insurer by the applicant, its affiliates or any person listed in Item 3 during the 12 calendar months preceding the filing of this statement. Include in the description the dates of purchase, the names of the purchasers, and the consideration paid or agreed to be paid therefor. State whether any shares so purchased are hypothecated.

ITEM 10. RECENT RECOMMENDATIONS TO PURCHASE

Describe any recommendations to purchase any voting security of the insurer made by the applicant, its affiliates, or any person listed in Item 3, or by anyone based upon interviews or at the suggestion of the applicant, its affiliates, or any person listed in Item 3 during the 12 calendar months preceding the filing of this statement.

ITEM 11. AGREEMENTS WITH BROKER-DEALERS

Describe the terms of any agreement, contract, or understanding made with any broker-dealer as to solicitation of voting securities of the insurer for tender and the amount of any fees, commissions, or other compensation to be paid to broker-dealers with regard thereto.

ITEM 12. FINANCIAL STATEMENTS AND EXHIBITS

(a) Financial statements and exhibits shall be attached to this statement as an appendix, but list under this item the financial statements and exhibits so attached.

(b) The financial statements shall include the annual financial statements of the persons identified in Item 2(c) for the preceding 5 fiscal years (or for such lesser period as such applicant and its affiliates and any predecessors thereof shall have been in existence), and similar information covering the period from the end of such person's last fiscal year, if the information is available. The statements may be prepared on either an individual basis, or, unless the Commissioner otherwise requires, on a consolidated basis if consolidated statements are prepared in the usual course of business.

The annual financial statements of the applicant shall be accompanied by the certificate of an independent public accountant to the effect that such statements present fairly the financial position of the applicant and the results of its operations for the year then ended, in conformity with generally accepted accounting principles or with requirements of insurance or other accounting principles prescribed or permitted under law. If the applicant is an insurer which is actively engaged in the business of insurance, the financial statements need not be certified, provided they are based on the Annual Statement of the person filed with the insurance department of the person's domiciliary state and are in accordance with the requirements of insurance or other accounting principles prescribed or permitted under the law and regulations of the state.

(c) File as exhibits copies of all tender offers for, requests or invitations for, tenders of, exchange offers for, and agreements to acquire or exchange any voting securities of the insurer and (if distributed) of additional soliciting material relating thereto, any proposed employment, consultation, advisory or management contracts concerning the insurer, annual reports to the stockholders of the insurer and the applicant for the last two fiscal years, and any additional documents or papers required by Form A or regulation Sections 4 and 6.

ITEM 13. SIGNATURE AND CERTIFICATION

Signature and certification required as follows:

SIGNATURE

Pursuant to the requirements of Section 3 of the Act has caused this application to be duly signed on its behalf in the City of and State of on the day of , 19 .

(SEAL)

Name of Applicant

BY

(Name) (Title)

Attest:

____

(Signature of Officer)

____

(Title)

CERTIFICATION

The undersigned deposes and says that (s)he has duly executed the attached application dated ____________________, 19________, for and on behalf of ____________________ (Name of Applicant); that (s)he is the ____________________(Title of Officer) of such company and that (s)he is authorized to execute and file such instrument. Deponent further says that (s)he is familiar with the instrument and the contents thereof, and that the facts therein set forth are true to the best of his/her knowledge, information and belief.

(Signature)

(Type or print name beneath)

Appendix A5

Form E

FORM E

PRE-ACQUISITION NOTIFICATION FORM
REGARDING THE POTENTIAL COMPETITIVE IMPACT
OF A PROPOSED MERGER OR ACQUISITION BY A
NON-DOMICILIARY INSURER DOING BUSINESS IN THIS
STATE OR BY A DOMESTIC INSURER

Name of Applicant

____

Name of Other Person
Involved in Merger or
Acquisition

Filed with the Insurance Department of

Dated: , 19

Name, title, address, and telephone number of person completing this statement:

____

____

____

____

ITEM 1. NAME AND ADDRESS

State the names and addresses of the persons who hereby provide notice of their involvement in a pending acquisition or change in corporate control.

ITEM 2. NAME AND ADDRESSES OF AFFILIATED COMPANIES

State the names and addresses of the persons affiliated with those listed in Item 1. Describe their affiliations.

ITEM 3. NATURE AND PURPOSE OF THE PROPOSED MERGER OR ACQUISITION

State the nature and purpose of the proposed merger or acquisition.

ITEM 4. NATURE OF BUSINESS

State the nature of the business performed by each of the persons identified in response to Item 1 and Item 2.

ITEM 5. MARKET AND MARKET SHARE

State specifically what market and market share in each relevant insurance market the persons identified in Item 1 and Item 2 currently enjoy in this state. Provide historical market and market share data for each person identified in Item 1 and Item 2 for the past five years and identify the source of such data.

For purposes of this question, market means direct written insurance premium in this state for a line of business as contained in the annual statement required to be filed by insurers licensed to do business in this state.

NOTE: State Insurance Departments may additionally choose to make these calculations using their own data or data provided by the National Association of Insurance Commissioners.

APPENDIX B

Actuarial Standard of Practice 19

The version of this ASOP reprinted in this book is for illustrative purposes only. This standard may have been amended or repealed subsequent to its inclusion in the book. Actuaries wishing to practice in this area should obtain a current copy of the standard and not rely on the version that appears in this textbook.

ACTUARIAL STANDARDS BOARD

Actuarial Standard
of Practice
No. 19

Actuarial Appraisals

Developed by the
Actuarial Appraisals Task Force of the
Actuarial Standards Board

Adopted by the
Actuarial Standards Board
October 1991

(Doc. No. 034)

TABLE OF CONTENTS

January 1992

TO: Members of Actuarial Organizations Governed by the Standards of the Actuarial Standards Board, and Other Persons Interested in Actuarial Appraisals

FROM: Actuarial Standards Board (ASB)

SUBJ: Actuarial Standard of Practice No. 19: *Actuarial Appraisals*

Enclosed is the final version of this standard, adopted by the ASB on October 10, 1991. The standard was twice exposed to the profession, and a total of sixty-two comment letters, many of them lengthy, were received. Both exposure drafts, and the final version, were developed by the ASB's Actuarial Appraisal Task Force, which was formed in May 1989 to prepare a standard in this area. The task force's mission was defined as follows:

> To develop a standard of practice for actuarial appraisals which provides consistency between life insurance and casualty insurance situations. The standard should provide guidance to developers and users of such actuarial reports, leaving room for variations in those items that differ between life and casualty work. Thus, this standard will deal with those issues that are universal to appraisals of insurers and other related organizations.

The task force recognized its responsibilities to provide consistent guidance to life and casualty actuaries working in the identified subject areas, as well as to maintain a high level of credibility for such actuaries when they work in the areas of actuarial appraisals and mergers/acquisitions (M&A).

The task force members include life and casualty actuarial practitioners in actuarial, accounting, intermediary and insurance firms, as well as two investment bankers with substantial insurance M&A experience.

In its initial meetings, the task force addressed a number of critical issues, including:

1. How should the standard deal with the evolving research, technology, and literature in many areas (e.g., stochastic processes)?
2. How should the standard reflect (appropriate) variations in perspectives on value?
3. What is the appropriate basis for earnings in an actuarial appraisal?
4. How should the actuary deal with the cost of capital, varying buyer perspectives, and different client needs?
5. Is there such a thing as one intrinsic value for an insurance company?
6. How should the actuary deal with oral (vs. written) communications?

Actuarial appraisal assignments are completed for a wide range of users with varying objectives and needs. The standard needs to reflect these realities in order to be of maximum value to our practitioners and the industries we serve. Users include management groups, buyers, sellers, advisors, intermediaries, investment bankers, investors, analysts, regulators, and the Internal Revenue Service.

The actuary developing an actuarial appraisal should be aware of and follow this standard. Since many users will not be aware of this standard, the actuary is responsible for making clear the nature and range of intended use of the actuarial appraisal to anyone who is exposed to the work. For example, an actuarial study which, from its form or conclusions, might be reasonably construed by a user as an actuarial appraisal, but is not, should contain an admonition clearly pointing out this fact. A more complex situation might be illustrated by a study completed by a pricing actuary or a valuation actuary which could, in certain cases, appear to be an actuarial appraisal although it was never intended to be considered as such.

Often, this work must be done under extreme time pressure and in the absence of complete data. In order to frame properly the project approach and documentation, the practicing actuary needs to address carefully the following questions:

1. What is the context of the assignment?

2. What are the needs, areas of expertise, and expectations of the user?

3. Are there users of the report beyond the client?

4. How much will the user rely on the work product of the actuary?

5. Will the actuary be functioning as an advocate?

6. How much time was provided to complete the assignment?

7. How much access to data was provided?

8. What assumptions are appropriate?

9. What methods are appropriate?

Comments on the First Exposure Draft

The first draft of the standard was exposed for review in a document dated April 1990, with a comment deadline of September 1, 1990. Thirty-eight letters of comment were received. After reviewing these, the task force identified five primary areas where suggestions were made:

1. Improving the applicability of the standard to the property and casualty (P/C) business. The responses identified a number of differences in perspective and approach between life and P/C appraisals. The task force's objective was to have the appraisal standard apply to both life and P/C insurance. Hence, a subgroup of the task force, headed by P/C actuaries, reviewed and revised significant portions of the text.

2. Clarifying the appropriate earnings bases to be used in actuarial appraisals. The task force tightened the language related to earnings basis, reconfirming that statutory accounting is the appropriate basis for developing an actuarial appraisal.

3. Tightening and clarifying recommended practices for valuations of existing business in tax liquidations. There was a difference in viewpoint as to how the requirements of tax accounting should be reflected in the determination of value. The subsection on Tax Liquidations (5.10) was modified to allow for this difference. However, it was stated that the valuation of existing business for tax purposes "is an actuarial appraisal and would embody the same methodologies and assumptions prescribed in this standard." Note that the actuarial appraisal is an important element in estimating fair market value in tax appraisal and other situations.

4. Clarifying the application of the standard to health insurance, reinsurance, and other specialty lines of business. Several modifications were made to the original draft as a result of suggestions received. An example was the development of the new subsection 5.6.3 (Premium Changes).

5. Improving the style and structure of the standard generally. Substantial editing was done to tighten the language and structure of the original exposure draft.

All suggestions were considered carefully and many were directly reflected in the second exposure draft. The task force believed the revised document was substantially improved as a result. At the same time, the changes made warranted a second exposure.

At the direction of the ASB, the second draft was exposed in January 1991 with a comment deadline of April 30. Twenty-four letters of comment were received.

Comments on the Second Exposure Draft, and Task Force Responses

The task force has summarized below what it considered significant issues and questions contained in the comment letters. The task force's responses appear in **boldface**.

Need for the Standard

Several respondents objected to the promulgation of the standard: there was no demonstrated need for it, there were no real situations where the standard would improve the importance, credibility, or correctness of actuarial appraisals. And one reader pointed out that failing to consider an element required by the standard could expose an actuary to criticism. **The evidence leading to the creation of an actuarial appraisal task force by the Actuarial Standards Board suggested that there is a need for a standard in this area. The members of the task force, and the exposure draft commentators, represent a broad cross section of those who perform and use actuarial appraisals; the great majority of these demonstrated a belief that there is a clear need for the standard. On the last point raised, the task force agrees that an actuary failing to consider an element required by the standard could be subject to criticism, or even discipline.**

Name of the Work Product

One respondent suggested substituting the term "actuarial valuation" for "actuarial appraisal." **Within the insurance and actuarial communities, the concept of actuarial appraisal connotes the development of the underlying economic value.**

Discounting Rate

It was suggested that actuaries should give clients more advice and information on the discounting rate, especially the reason for the choice of rate, how the rate relates to underlying investment and reinvestment assumptions, how it relates to risk, and so on. **The task force believes that subsections 2.7, 5.2.2, and 6.1.10 provide sufficient guidance for minimum standards on the choice and disclosure of discounting rates.**

Cash Flows or GAAP Earnings vs. Statutory Earnings

Several respondents repeated earlier suggestions for permitting or requiring earnings on bases other than statutory earnings, e.g., GAAP earnings, cash flows distributable to shareholders, or other alternatives. **The task force considered these alternatives in a number of its earlier discussions, and reviewed its thinking in the light of the latest comments. It again concluded that statutory earnings are the appropriate minimum standard. Subsection 5.2.1 of the standard details the reasoning behind this choice. The actuary is free to apply a more stringent standard as circumstances dictate.**

Market Dynamics

One respondent suggested that appraisals should use assumptions that reflect the dynamics of the markets served by the company. **The task force strengthened the wording in the standard on this issue (see subsection 5.6).**

Adjusted Net Worth

The adjusted net worth represents a stream of earnings just like the value of existing or future business. Hence it will have different values at different discounting rates, unlike what is often displayed in actuarial appraisal reports. **The task force's response is that the actuary should disclose the basis used to value adjusted net worth and any provision for cost of capital (see subsection 6.1.9). Depending on the circumstances surrounding the appraisal, the actuary *may* value adjusted net worth as a discounted stream of future earnings, using either the assumed rate of investment return or a risk-adjusted rate of return. The actuarial report should make clear the meaning of each number presented.**

"Laundry Lists"

The comment was made that "laundry lists" such as the lists in subsections 5.6.10 and 6.1.1 through 6.1.9 are unnecessary in standards. **Subsection 5.6.10 was deleted from the text in recognition of this comment, but the list is reproduced here with the understanding that the actuary should consider items such as the following in selecting assumptions:**

a. policyholder dividends
b. asset securitization programs
c. premium-collection patterns on short-term contracts
d. potential future premiums on retrospectively rated contracts
e. claim payment patterns
f. market value of nonadmitted assets or the emergence of nonadmitted assets into earnings
g. the cost of involuntary insurance programs such as those applicable to workers compensation and automobile insurance
h. the future emergence of environmental liability costs for casualty insurers, epidemic-related claims for life and health insurers, and other special claims situations
i. foreign-currency exchange issues
j. guarantee fund obligations
k. projected future earnings on riders
l. the implications of assessable policies or possible restrictions on the amount of profits arising from participating policies which can inure to the benefit of shareholders of mixed companies
m. the effect of policy loan utilization
n. other nonrequired liabilities of an actuarial nature, such as post-retirement health care benefits and unfunded pension obligations

With regard to subsections 6.1.1 through 6.1.9, the task force believed it desirable to specify within the standard certain key items that should be included in an actuarial appraisal report, since many users of such reports are not actuaries and it is important to communicate all the information called for in subsections 6.1.1–6.1.9 to these users. Also, many actuaries have limited experience in performing actuarial appraisals, and the same information would be useful to them. The task force believes that many reports produced do not contain all the information called for in these paragraphs.

Stochastic Analysis

Two respondents took exception to an apparent suggestion in subsection 5.6 that stochastic analysis is needed in many areas, pointing out that this is only one of a number of tools an actuary could use; also, little guidance was provided as to when to use it. **The task force believes that traditional deterministic processes are inadequate in some areas and that the practitioner should apply stochastic analysis when it is deemed material to the appraisal.**

Events after the Appraisal Date

A writer suggested that the actuary should comment on material events that have (or have not) happened after the appraisal date and before the issuance of the report. **Because of the detailed analysis inherent in actuarial appraisals, determining what is material might require extensive work. Much as in the appraisal of a house or a car, it is difficult to establish standards for what may have happened after one has "seen" the entity.**

Treatment of Assets

Several reviewers expressed concern that the proposed standard did not deal adequately with assets. In particular, issues raised were: should all marketable assets be revalued to market, should default costs be required to be addressed by the actuary, and should future increases in the mandatory securities valuation reserve (MSVR) be deducted from projected statutory earnings? **The task force revised subsection 5.6.1 to call for consideration of the financial effect of asset defaults in projecting investment rates of return. Adjustment of marketable assets to a market valuation basis was not deemed necessary in the standard, which contemplates a statutory projection—usually in a going-concern context. Once default costs have been considered, the adjustment of assets to market in conjunction with a concurrent selection of appropriate market rates of return should produce values consistent with statutory-basis projections. The task force believed that future increases in MSVR need not be deducted from projected statutory earnings, since MSVR is being treated as allocated surplus in the context of this standard.**

Made-to-Order Results?

One reader expressed the view that the third paragraph of subsection 5.2 perpetuates the concept that the actuary will supply any answer that the client or primary user desires. **The task force believed that it is crucial to recognize that circumstances, needs, and perspectives do vary. However, recognition of this does not constitute a license to supply "any answer." The**

actuary is required by several explicit provisions of the standard to comment on the reasonableness of the assumptions used.

Written Reports

One reader asked if there can be an actuarial appraisal without a written report. **The task force intended that a written report would be preferable for most actuarial appraisals. An actuarial appraisal might be concluded with an oral report, but if so, the task force intended that the oral report would include all the applicable elements of section 6 of the standard. Otherwise, disclosure of deviation from the standard must be made under the terms of subsection 6.4.**

Actuarial Appraisals of Other Financial Institutions

The suggestion was made that financial institutions other than insurance companies should not be precluded from the standard. **The task force meant the standard to apply only to insurance and insurance-like situations and not to the broader universe of financial institutions.**

"Cookbook Approach"

Several commentators said the standard calls for "a cookbook approach," which should always be avoided. **The standard has been revisited to eliminate some elements that some considered to be of this nature.**

"More Detailed Requirements Are Needed"

A commentator wanted the standard to contain more detailed requirements on model building and validation. **The task force believed it was necessary to strike a balance between the inclusion of sufficiently explicit descriptions of what should be considered in performing an actuarial appraisal, and the avoidance of discussions not sufficiently general to be applicable to all situations. Some commentators viewed the standard as overly explicit. Probably no one approach will be totally satisfactory to all. The task force believes that the standard in its final form strikes a reasonable balance.**

Opinion and Report

A commentator said that what distinguishes an actuarial opinion from an actuarial report should be addressed before the adoption of this standard. **The task force changed the wording in subsection 6.1 so that an *actuarial opinion* is no longer defined as different from an *actuarial report.***

Specific Stream of Earnings

A reviewer asked, should the reader infer that any valuation which does not project a specific stream of statutory distributable earnings and then produce a value by discounting that stream at a specific, risk-adjusted discounting rate, is not covered by the standard? **The task force responded that the standard is meant to apply to calculations involving either an explicit or implicit approach of projecting statutory earnings and then discounting. In addition, much of the standard may have relevance for other assignments that are not specifically covered by the standard.**

New-Business Capacity

A reader asked why should the appraisal of new-business production capacity be limited to business reasonably attributable to the company structure as it existed on the appraisal date. **The task force responded by changing the wording in subsection 5.6.9 to allow the flexibility to use varying assumptions regarding new-business production, as long as the relationship of the new-business assumptions to the company's structure as of the appraisal date is disclosed.**

Different Rate of Discounting

A commentator said the standard should provide for a different rate of discounting, depending on the nature of future obligations and cash flows. **The task force responded that the standard already accomplishes this.**

IRC Section 338 Appraisals

Some respondents expressed the view that the standard permitted the use of either statutory earnings or tax-basis earnings for purposes of appraisals done in connection with Section 338 of the Internal Revenue Code (IRC). One respondent said the standard was too vague in regard to the proper earnings basis; it did not offer sufficient guidance. One alternative suggested was that the standard exclude appraisals done in connection with IRC Section 338 from the definition of an actuarial appraisal. **The task force concluded that an appraisal done in connection with a Section 338 election was an actuarial appraisal which should be under the purview of the standard, because such an appraisal embodies many of the same methods and assumptions used in the valuation of an insurance company.**

The task force has purposely not mandated a specific methodology to compute the tax benefits attributable to an IRC Section 338 election. Rather, the language adopted indicates

that statutory and tax-basis items may differ, and leeway is allowed in the choice of methodologies to reflect that in the actuarial appraisal.

Appraised Value and Sale Price

A reviewer suggested adding a new paragraph saying that "an actuarial appraisal done for purposes of purchasing or selling a business should include a statement that the calculated value(s) should not be considered the sole determinant of sale price." **The task force believes that the standard already addresses this point in subsection 5.2, where it is said that the actuarial appraisal value "does not necessarily define an appropriate sale price."**

Client's Assumptions

A reviewer commented that when actuaries are requested to use a set of assumptions by a client, such assumptions should be disclosed and evaluated. **The task force recognized this point in modifying the wording of subsection 6.1.**

Confidentiality of Information

A reviewer suggested adding a statement cautioning the actuary to use utmost discretion and be guided by the highest standards of professional integrity in handling confidential or proprietary information gathered in the course of an appraisal. **The task force noted that Precept 10 of the AAA Code of Professional Conduct (effective January 1, 1992) covered this issue.**

The revised version from the second exposure was adopted by the ASB at its October 1991 meeting, effective for appraisal reports dated on or after January 10, 1992.

Actuarial Appraisal Task Force

Robert D. Shapiro, Chairperson

Robert Beisenherz	James A. Hall, III
Charles Carroll	Reuben Jeffery, III
Robert L. Collett	Allan M. Kaufman
Leandro S. Galban, Jr.	Stephen P. Lowe
Patricia L. Guinn	Gary N. See

Actuarial Standards Board

Walter N. Miller, Chairperson

Edward E. Burrows	Frederick W. Kilbourne
Gary Corbett	Harry L. Sutton, Jr.
Willard A. Hartman	Jack M. Turnquist
James C. Hickman	P. Adger Williams

ACTUARIAL STANDARD OF PRACTICE NO. 19

ACTUARIAL APPRAISALS

PREAMBLE

Section 1. Purpose, Scope, and Effective Date

1.1 Purpose—This actuarial standard of practice sets out the considerations that bear on the actuary's professional work in performing actuarial appraisals. The standard prescribes appropriate procedures for performing actuarial appraisals and for documenting assumptions and methodologies in an actuarial report.

1.2 Scope—Actuarial appraisals are developed for use in many areas, including (but not limited to) facilitating the financial management of an insurance company; estimating the value in the acquisition or sale of an insurance company, insurance marketing organization, or block of insurance contracts, and determining the value of insurance companies, insurance marketing organizations, or blocks of insurance contracts for tax purposes. This standard applies to appraisals that are performed on entire insurance companies, on segments of insurance companies (for example, the group insurance line of business), or on existing or potential future blocks of insurance contracts (or both).

Elements of the actuarial appraisal generally involve actuarial assumptions about the future growth and experience of the evaluated business; making financial projections of future cash flows, earnings, taxes, assets, and liabilities, and selecting risk-adjusted rates of return for computing the present value of these projected quantities. In the actuarial appraisal of an insurance company, the reported capital and surplus of the company will be evaluated as a part of this process. Each of these elements is discussed in this standard.

An actuarial study should indicate its nature and intended use. Where an actuarial study could reasonably be construed, on the basis of its form or conclusions, to be an actuarial appraisal but it is not, a clear statement and explanation of this fact should be provided.

1.3 Effective Date—This standard is effective January 10, 1992 for actuarial appraisal reports dated on or after that date.

Section 2. Definitions

2.1 Actuarial Appraisal—An assessment of value based on projections of expected future earnings, discounted to present value at appropriate risk-adjusted rates of return. For the purposes of this standard, an *actuarial appraisal* is further defined as an assessment of value of an insurance company, a segment of an insurance company, or a block of insurance contracts ("the evaluated business").

2.2 Actuarial Appraisal Calculations—Any derivation of value or range of values based on projections of anticipated future quantities associated with the evaluated business, discounted to present value at appropriate risk-adjusted rates of return.

2.3 Actuarial Appraisal Report—A document which sets forth the procedures, methods, data, and assumptions used in actuarial appraisal calculations, as well as the results of these actuarial appraisal calculations.

2.4 Actuarial Appraisal Value—A value or range of values derived from actuarial appraisal calculations.

2.5 Appraisal Date—The date as of which actuarial appraisal calculations are derived.

2.6 Existing Business—Policies in force on the appraisal date, including any remaining obligations and risks that relate to coverage provided previously (e.g., the runoff of claim liabilities).

2.7 Risk-Adjusted Rate of Return—An expected or target annual return to the investor that includes a risk-free return that compensates the investor for the use of the funds (recognizing anticipated inflation so as to maintain the real value of those funds), plus a risk premium above the risk-free rate that compensates the investor for the risk that actual returns will deviate from expected. The size of the risk premium varies with the degree of risk associated with the returns.

Section 3. Background and Historical Issues

Actuaries perform actuarial appraisal calculations for a number of purposes and for a variety of users, including sellers, buyers, management, or regulators. It is important that these users understand the work the actuary has done, the limitations of that work, and any reliance the actuary may have placed on others.

The key element in an actuarial appraisal is the projection of the future stream of earnings attributable to the evaluated business. This includes the runoff of claim liabilities. This stream of earnings is projected using actuarial assumptions relating to such items as claims, expenses, and investment return. The projections may be done for existing and new business separately, or in combination. The projected earnings are then discounted at appropriate risk-adjusted rate(s) of return to derive value.

Section 4. Current Practices and Alternatives

An actuarial appraisal has become recognized in the business community as a critical element in placing an overall value on an insurance-related business or in establishing separate values for components of a company for tax or other purposes. In part because of the expected continued high level of mergers and acquisitions, actuarial appraisals will continue to be important and visible.

As practice has evolved, some methodologies have become fairly well accepted, and some differences have emerged. There is less literature available and more variation in practice for property/casualty and other short-term insurance contracts than for whole life and other long-term insurance contracts. In addition to differences in methodology, practices have varied as to the data employed in the calculations and the choice of actuarial assumptions. A standard of practice is needed for reconciling these differences and defining the range of acceptable practice.

In performing an actuarial appraisal calculation, an actuary has a myriad of assumptions and data sources from which to choose in developing financial projections and ultimately deriving a value or range of values for the business. In actual practice, appraisal values are sometimes based on extensive analysis of confidential or proprietary information, from which thorough testing of key assumptions can be performed. In other instances, appraisals are based on more limited analysis or data because of materiality considerations or time limitations, or because internal company data are unavailable and only publicly available information can be used.

Differences in approach may have an impact on the proper interpretation of the actuary's opinion as to appraisal values. This suggests that formal requirements for disclosure are desirable.

STANDARD OF PRACTICE

Section 5. Analysis of Issues and Recommended Practices

5.1 Consideration of Code of Conduct and Qualification Standards—In performing actuarial appraisals, actuaries hold themselves out to be experts in the process of actuarial appraisal work as well as experts in the lines of business being appraised. The actuary should be familiar with or review the Code of Professional Conduct and the Qualification Standards of the American Academy of Actuaries as to these separate considerations.

5.2 Basic Concepts—Actuarial appraisal calculations may be performed, and appraisal values derived, for isolated segments of an insurance company's business or for the insurance company's entire book of business. Similarly, calculations may be performed on existing business only, or on new business only, or on both taken together.

The value of an insurance company or related organization is often estimated by an actuarial appraisal of its existing business and future business capacity, with consideration of the capital and surplus of the entity.

It should be recognized that such an actuarial appraisal value is a measure of the value of the business to a particular user (e.g., prospective buyer, prospective management, or regulator), under a specified set of assumptions. Since circumstances, needs, and perspectives vary from one user to another, the assumptions and the resulting values will also vary among the users. The assumptions used in the appraisal should be consistent with the circumstances of the user who makes decisions based on the appraisal, so that the measure of value will be relevant to that user. While this measure of value includes an examination of the earnings potential of the company, it does not necessarily define an appropriate sale price.

A characterization of the assumptions, both individually and collectively, as to their level of reasonableness in the particular context should be disclosed in the actuarial report.

5.2.1 Distributable Earnings—For insurance companies, statutory earnings form the basis for determining distributable earnings, since the availability of dividends to owners is constrained by the amount of accumulated earnings and minimum capital and surplus requirements, both of which must be determined on a statutory accounting basis. Distributable earnings consist of statutory earnings, adjusted as appropriate to allow for the retention of a portion thereof or the release of a portion of prior accumulated earnings therein, in recognition of minimum capital and surplus levels necessary to support existing business.

Economic value generally is determined as the present value of future cash flows. Statutory accounting determines the earnings available to the owner. Hence, while future earnings calculated according to generally accepted accounting principles (GAAP) will often be of interest to the user of an actuarial appraisal, as may other patterns of earnings, the discounted present-value calculations contemplated within the definition of actuarial appraisal in this standard should be developed in consideration of statutory earnings, rather than some other basis. Special considerations for tax appraisal purposes are discussed in subsection 5.10 of this standard. The actuary's report should include a discussion of factors, such as capital needs (whether perceived by the actuary or imposed by an external entity such as a regulator), that may cause the earnings available for shareholder or policyholder distribution to be different from statutory earnings.

5.2.2 Risk-Adjusted Rates of Return—The rates used for discounting future earnings should reasonably reflect risks inherent in the realization of such earnings, and should be representative of the returns desired by the buyer, seller, or owner of the enterprise. Since risks vary by product line and between inforce and new business, it is natural that risk-adjusted rates of return might vary similarly. Also, in the selection of risk-adjusted rates of return, the actuary should consider the actuarial methods and assumptions used.

5.3 Estimated Value of Insurance Company—Based on actuarial appraisal calculations, the value of an insurance company is often, but not necessarily, divided into the following three components as of the appraisal date:

a. Adjusted net worth

b. Appraisal value of existing business

c. Appraisal value of future business capacity

The items included in each of these categories may vary on the basis of the type of business being appraised, the needs of the user, and other circumstances. For example, the value of loss reserve deficiencies may be determined as a part of adjusted net worth or as a part of the value of existing business. The actuary should describe the items included in each component.

5.3.1 Adjusted Net Worth—This component normally includes the following:

a. Statutory capital and surplus

b. Any statutory liabilities that, in essence, represent allocations of surplus (e.g., mandatory securities valuation reserves, statutory portions of casualty Schedule P reserves)

c. Any statutory nonadmitted assets that have realizable value

d. Reduction for surplus items that represent obligations to others

e. Adjustment to reflect the difference between market value and book value of those assets which are in support of all or a portion of adjusted net worth

5.3.2 Value of Existing Business—This component equals the present value of future earnings attributable to business in force on the appraisal date, including any remaining effects of coverage previously provided.

5.3.3 Value of Future Business Capacity—This component equals the present value of future earnings attributable to business issued or acquired after the appraisal date and attributable to the existing new-business capacity of the enterprise. Future renewals of existing contracts may also be included in this component. In certain cases, this component could be measured on the basis of the market value of the company's charters and licenses and other components of goodwill.

5.4 Capital Needs—Part or perhaps even all of capital and surplus on the appraisal date, as well as some portion of future after-tax earnings on existing and new business, may need to be retained within the company, and future capital contributions may be needed to support the risks on existing and new business. The actuary should disclose the manner in which capital needs were considered, and may include an estimate of the cost of such capital.

5.5 Allocation of Assets—The assets of the company on the appraisal date should be allocated to existing business and to adjusted net worth. Consideration should be given to the allocation of assets by type, quality, and duration to the various segments of existing business and adjusted net worth. Appropriate recognition should be given to the difference between statutory accounting value and market value of the assets, either in terms of the assumed rate of investment return or changes to adjusted net worth. The use of a market-value adjustment for assets allocated to the adjusted net worth can serve as an alternative (in whole or in part) to discounting projected statutory earnings on adjusted net worth, and may appropriately differ from the treatment of assets allocated to existing business. In any event, the valuation of assets on the basis of market, statutory, or other basis should be consistent with the assumed earnings rate for those assets.

5.6 Assumptions—Assumptions regarding future experience should be reasonable, and, to the extent possible, should take into account the actual historical and current experience of the company, adjusted to reflect known changes in the environment and identifiable trends. Experience studies should be reviewed, and the results should be disclosed. If experience studies are not available, they should be developed where appropriate and practical. In some instances, data may not be available or may be insufficient to provide a credible basis on which to develop assumptions. Consequently, it may be necessary to rely more on judgment, taking into consideration the company's pricing and/or reserving assumptions and the experience of other companies with comparable products, markets, and operating procedures. Key assumptions and their sources should be disclosed.

Certain assumptions may require input or expertise which the actuary does not have. In setting assumptions, the actuary should obtain any necessary input from persons possessing the relevant knowledge or expertise, and should give due weight to their input. Such special knowledge areas may include asset default rates, investment new-money rates, marketing, expense control, property/casualty underwriting and claim operations, reinsurance availability, and tax laws.

It is important to recognize that the assumptions will be used to project future results, and should therefore be selected with due regard for the future context or expected future operating environment of the company. Thus, they may or may not be consistent with past experience.

Also, in many areas, such as evaluating interest-sensitive and variable life insurance and annuity products, deterministic approaches may be inadequate for properly evaluating and projecting financial results. The actuary needs to examine each assumption critically in this regard, and apply stochastic analysis where the tools exist and where stochastic analysis is deemed material to the appraisal.

The assumptions used in an actuarial appraisal need to be specific to the type of entity being appraised—e.g., property/casualty or life/health—as well as the kinds of products underwritten and markets being served by the entity. Therefore, the actuary needs to be familiar with all products that contribute materially to the value of the business subject to the actuarial appraisal. Furthermore, the actuary should recognize that issues common to all appraisals may require different treatment when applied to short-term contract business (property/casualty, group insurance, etc.) compared to long-term contract business (whole life insurance, annuities, etc.).

The remainder of this subsection covers certain key assumption areas. The list of assumptions discussed is not all-inclusive; the actuary should consider any item that could have a material effect on results.

5.6.1 Rates of Investment Return and Assets—The level of detail required for this item varies by product type.

For products in which the investment component is significant (e.g., whole life and annuities), the analysis should include consideration of the asset maturities and cash flows from current invested assets and insurance operations, new-money investment-yield assumptions, a variety of future rate-of-return scenarios, and risk level associated with changes in future rates of return.
For products in which the investment component is less significant (e.g., casualty, group health), the analysis may be limited to a review of current rates of return and a consideration of reasonable rates of return in the future.

The actuary may wish to perform projections under a number of future rate-of-investment-return scenarios and determine values based on an analysis of the results obtained. To the extent this approach is taken, the risk related to changes in future rates of investment return will have been taken into account in projecting earnings.

The actuary should also consider asset quality as it relates to the risk of delayed collectibility, default, or other financial nonperformance.

5.6.2 Lapsation or Nonrenewal of Insurance Contracts—These assumptions are most important on long-term contract business, such as whole life and annuity business, and on direct-response business where the insurer has a significant investment in developing the existing business.

When this item is significant, the effect of lapsation or nonrenewal activity, premium change, and premium suspension on flexible-premium products should be considered in the evaluation of historical experience and the development of the actuary's assumptions as to future anticipated experience. In addition, the actuary should consider the potential for unusually high rates of lapsation or non-renewal resulting from a proposed merger or acquisition transaction, and make appropriate provision for it.

5.6.3 Premium Changes—In dealing with business where premium is subject to change after the origination of the contract, consideration should be given to regulatory limitations, time of implementation of future changes, effects of antiselection on expected claims and persistency, and the effect that historical premium changes might have had on prior company experience.

5.6.4 Expected Claims—In developing expected future claim levels, the actuary should consider the experience of the appraised entity, the experience of other comparable entities, and the potential for future changes, favorable or adverse. Future changes to consider include underwriting cycles, mortality trends, tort reform, etc. The actuary should consider the ability of the entity to adjust rates in response to future conditions.

5.6.5 Expenses—These assumptions are generally analyzed in greater detail for long-term contract business than for short-term contract business. For all types of products, the selected expenses, including commissions and investment expenses, should be reasonable in light of the projected circumstances.

A detailed analysis of the type typically applied to some life insurance products should include consideration of whether the current levels of expenses may exceed those which would be developed by the application of unit expense factors deemed reasonable for long-term projection purposes. Such excess expenses might, for example, be attributable to nonrecurring expenses or production, administrative, or overhead capacity in excess of that required for the volume of insurance written and in force. Certain of these excess expenses might be diminished as a result of increases in existing business, economies of scale, and expense-reduction programs. The amount of such excess expenses and the actuary's treatment of them should be disclosed.

5.6.6 Inflation—Inflation should be considered. The inflation assumption that is explicit or implicit in the choice of claim and expense assumptions should be consistent with the new-money investment rate(s) of return selected by the actuary.

5.6.7 Reinsurance—Provision for the cost of reinsurance should be made if it is deemed material. Particular care should be taken in analyzing and reflecting the effect on value of financial reinsurance transactions entered into for surplus relief or other capital and earnings purposes. Some reinsurance transactions may be more appropriately reflected in adjusted net worth.

5.6.8 New Business Production—The assumptions regarding new business production should be selected with consideration of history and anticipated future conditions. The actuary should disclose the relationship of the new-business production assumptions to the company's structure as it existed at the appraisal date.

The actuary may wish to provide a range of new-business production scenarios.

5.7 Federal Income Tax—In any consideration of future income taxes, it should be recognized that the taxation of insurance companies is not only complex but also subject to change.

The most meaningful estimate of the effect of federal income taxes on appraisal values is made when the amount of federal income tax has been calculated on a year-by-year basis for the company as a whole.

The actuary should consider all of the major items affecting the calculation of taxable income. It is recognized, however, that the tax status of a potential purchaser may be unknown at the point of calculation.

5.8 Modeling and Model Validation—The detail of the model of future earnings should be appropriate for the situation. For short-term policies, the model might relate to the company as a whole or to particular lines of business. For long-term contract business, more detailed

models are often useful. In such cases, separate models might be developed for each line of business, separately for risks underwritten prior to the appraisal date and for new business.

As a general rule, separate models should be developed for each line of business, separately for risks underwritten prior to the appraisal date and for new business. Even within a line of business, it is frequently desirable to construct submodels by type of business or market, or by significant contract design differences—e.g., by state—to facilitate the validation of assumptions, to evaluate the reasonableness of the results developed, and to improve the work product.

Any model used in a projection should reproduce the premiums, volumes of insurance, and statutory statement reserves of the risks underwritten prior to the appraisal date within close tolerances in the aggregate. The "fit" comparison of premiums, volumes, and reserves normally would be examined on a line-by-line basis or even a plan-by-plan basis and, where necessary, adjustments made to the modeling parameters to produce the proper representation.

The validity of the model and the experience assumptions used in developing the projections should be tested against actual experience immediately prior to the appraisal date and against any available plan information for time periods immediately following the appraisal date.

5.9 Sensitivity Analysis—The actuarial assumptions chosen to value existing and new business normally are chosen to be reasonable for a particular scenario. The sensitivity of appraisal values to a particular risk is assessed by testing different assumptions regarding future experience. Testing of different assumptions regarding future experience is usually designed to cover circumstances that seem plausible, but it cannot cover every conceivable circumstance. Sensitivity testing is particularly recommended when assumptions have been based on very limited data, when deviations from expected values may be very large, or when an assumption is deemed particularly critical.

5.10 Tax Liquidations—Section 338(h)(10) of the Internal Revenue Code essentially allows an election to treat the acquisition of stock of an insurance company as the acquisition of the company's assets, including an asset attributable to the value of existing business. In many instances, the actuary is asked to determine a value of the existing business for this purpose. Such a determination is an actuarial appraisal and would embody the same methodologies and assumptions as prescribed in this standard, although recognizing that tax-basis assets, liabilities, and earnings may differ from statutory.

Section 6. Communications and Disclosures

6.1 Actuarial Appraisal Report—An actuarial appraisal report should be prepared which summarizes and places in context the actuary's conclusions from the appraisal calculations that have been performed. The report should include, at a minimum, the following items:

6.1.1 Scope of Assignment—Reference should be made to a letter of engagement, if used. The report should discuss the depth of the assignment, and any limitations imposed by the user, the time available, or the availability of data. The scope of the assignment should be consistent with the intended use of the report, as discussed in the following paragraph.

6.1.2 Intended Use—There should be a clear description of the intended purpose of the report, and if necessary, a statement of how or why it might be inappropriate for purposes other than the one for which it was intended. This description should be consistent with the scope of the work done. It should contain any limitations on distribution of, or reference to, the report.

6.1.3 Reliances—The report should identify the information, documents, and data used for which no independent verification was undertaken by the actuary.

6.1.4 Limitations—The report should identify limitations attaching to the values developed, and their applicability to specific situations, as the result of items or lines of business excluded, lack of reliable data, recent or pending changes in operations, time constraints, or other considerations.

6.1.5 Description of the Entity Being Valued—There should be a description of the corporate organizational structure, stating which of the companies are the subject of the actuarial appraisal and delineating any material intercompany financial relationships. There should be a discussion of each subject company, its marketing, lines of business, and products. The appraisal date should be clearly disclosed.

6.1.6 Actuarial Appraisal Value—The report should state the value or range of values obtained from the actuary's appraisal calculations. This may be a point estimate, a range, or a table of alternative values.

The report should also include a description of the extent and depth of testing that underlie the calculations, including a description of sensitivity tests that have been made.

6.1.7 Methodology—For each component of value, the report should contain a description of the techniques employed and the methodology used.

6.1.8 Validation—For each line of business that was valued, there should be a description of the validation techniques and results.

6.1.9 Cost of Capital—The actuary should disclose the basis used to value adjusted net worth, and what provision, if any, is made for the cost of capital.

6.1.10 Assumptions—If any assumption was selected by someone other than the actuary, the actuary should disclose that fact and the source of the assumption. The actuary should characterize the assumptions, both individually and collectively, as to their level of reasonableness in the particular context and whether they:

i. are consistent with past experience, or

ii. are not consistent with past experience, but are attainable under reasonable, specified conditions.

The risk-adjusted rates of return should similarly be characterized as to their level of reasonableness.

Assumptions used should be set forth in detail. Each material assumption should be described as to the basis for its determination. Discussions should include the following:

a. Where assumptions are based on company or other experience studies, the report should describe the studies in enough detail to allow the user to evaluate their appropriateness.

b. Where assumptions are based on judgment or industry experience, the actuary should discuss any relevant factors that led to the choice of assumptions.

c. Where assumptions differ from recent experience because of trends, known changes in the environment, or anticipated changes in the operations of the company, the actuary should discuss the trends or anticipated changes that led to the assumptions used.

d. Where assumptions were set using input or expertise from outside sources, the report should disclose the sources of such information and the reasons for reliance on it.

e. Where the actuary has knowledge of factors that may have a material bearing on one or more of the assumptions, the actuary should disclose such factors and the results of sensitivity tests that have been made.

6.1.11 Federal Income Taxes—The report should disclose the extent to which taxes have been considered, and on what basis. If federal income taxes are not directly provided for, the actuary should state the need for the user to consider them and include information to assist the user in estimating the effect of federal income taxes.

6.2 Disclosure If Not an Actuarial Appraisal—An actuarial study should clearly indicate its nature and intended use. Where an actuarial study could reasonably be construed, on the basis of its form or conclusions, to be an actuarial appraisal, but it is not, a clear statement and explanation of this fact should be provided.

6.3 Other Disclosures Prescribed in This Standard—The following subsections of section 5 of this standard prescribe additional disclosures concerning the subjects listed:

5.2 Basic Concepts: reasonableness of assumptions

5.2.1 Distributable Earnings: factors that could affect earnings

5.3 Estimated Value of Insurance Company: components of value

5.4 Capital Needs: how considered

5.6 Assumptions: assumptions and sources

5.6.5 Expenses: amount and treatment of excess expenses

5.6.8 New Business Production: relationship of assumptions to existing company structure

6.4 Deviation from Standard—An actuary who uses a procedure which differs from this standard must include, in any actuarial communication disclosing the result of the procedure, an appropriate and explicit statement with respect to the nature, rationale, and effect of the use of such a procedure.

Appendix C

Sample Due Diligence Life Insurance Company Information Request

Below is a sample due diligence information request for a hypothetical multi-line company. Not every item will be appropriate for each transaction. Each company's distinctive nature dictates that additional items will need to be addressed during review. Serial acquirers will develop their own standard lists and customize them for each transaction, updating them regularly for lessons learned.

The due diligence team should track when each item was requested and when it was received.

I. Corporate development, organization, and structure

A. Describe the Company's general development and its business performance.

B. Describe the Company's overall strategy.

C. Describe all new business initiatives.

D. Provide a copy of the strategic business plan for each line of business.

E. Describe the legal structure of the Company, indicating the purpose of each subsidiary and affiliate. Provide a copy of the organizational chart showing all the Company's subsidiaries and affiliates (including all joint ventures in which the Company holds an interest).

F. Describe the Company's functional and departmental structure. Provide a copy of the organizational chart showing the Company's functional and departmental structure.

G. Provide a schedule of all companies or partnerships in which the Company holds an interest, including the percentage of interest held in each such company or partnership.

H. Indicate the total number of shares issued by the Company, including a breakdown by type and class.

I. Provide a schedule of all of the Company's shareholders, including the total number of shares owned by each shareholder (including a breakdown by type and class) as well as contact information.

J. Provide access to the corporate books reflecting issuances, cancellations, and transfers of Company shares.

K. Indicate whether the Company has issued any convertible shares. If so, describe the quantity, holder, and convertibility conditions.

L. Indicate whether there exists any proceeding to increase the Company's capital. If so, describe the proposal, indicating the issuance value of the shares, the subscription conditions, and the status of the proceeding.

M. Provide a schedule of all liens, pledges, or encumbrances on the Company's shares that are either registered in the corporate books or known by the Company, including a brief description of each such lien, pledge, or encumbrance.

II. Management, employees, and outside consultants

A. Provide a copy of the management organizational chart showing the name and title of each member of management and the overall chain-of-command.

B. Provide summary biographical information for each member of management, including each member of the board of directors.

C. Employees

1. Indicate the total number of employees employed by the Company, including a breakdown by geographic location and function or expertise (e.g., sales, underwriting, actuarial, etc.).

2. Indicate the average number of years that the Company has employed the employees.

3. Provide a schedule of all employees employed by the Company (including all employees employed by the hour as well as all independent workers). Include the salary of each employee and indicate which employees are expatriates or foreigners.
4. Provide a copy of the current payroll.
5. Indicate whether there are any employment or consulting agreements with directors, officers, or employees of the Company that are currently in effect or intended to be in effect following the proposed transaction. If so, provide details.
6. Describe all benefits granted to employees (including post-employment benefits for retirees), either mandatory or at the Company's discretion, indicating the granting criteria as well as the costs for the Company and for the employees. The information requested in items (a) to (i) immediately below should be included in or supplement the description.
    a) Indicate whether any employees participate in profit sharing plans or any related incentive plans (e.g., premiums, bonuses, allowances, etc.). If so, describe the plans in detail (indicating regularity and goals to be met in order to qualify) and provide a copy of all documentation in connection therewith.
    b) Indicate whether there is any variable compensation for employees. If so, describe the variable compensation system and provide a copy of all documentation in connection therewith.
    c) Indicate whether there are any other benefits, which are, or have been, granted, such as housing plans, financing for acquisition of movable assets or real property, etc. If so, describe each of the other benefits and provide a copy of all documentation in connection therewith.
    d) Indicate whether there are any supplementary benefits (including vehicles, clubs, special medical assistance plans, housing, etc.) granted to the executive employees. If so, describe each supplementary benefit and provide a copy of all agreements, contracts, acts, internal memoranda, and regulations in connection therewith.
    e) Provide a copy of all additional social security plans, including pension funds, supplementary retirement plans, and medical assistance plans, along with all regulations, statutes, and documentation in connection therewith.
    f) Indicate the amounts paid by the Company to employees for each type of benefit (e.g., sick leave, vacation, etc.) during the prior 12 months.
    g) Provide a copy of the most recent valuation reports of the Company's (i) pension fund and (ii) profit sharing fund.
    h) Indicate whether the benefits granted to employees are competitive relative to the market; provide details, including current comparative data.
    i) Indicate whether the benefits are integrated in the employees' salaries for purposes of calculating social security contributions and income taxes. If so, provide a copy of all agreements or regulations in connection therewith.
7. Describe the Company's policy concerning salary increases for, and promotions of, employees, indicating how often salary increases are granted as well as the criteria for salary increases and promotion of employees.
8. Provide a schedule of all employees who have ceased to work for the Company during the current year and the prior three years.
9. Provide a copy of all outstanding severance agreements.
10. Provide a copy of all agreements concerning the retirement or early retirement of employees.
11. Indicate whether any employees are unionized. If so, provide details, along with a copy of all current labor or collective bargaining agreements as well as all consents, waivers, or amendments thereto.
12. Assess the quality of employee relations. Provide a schedule of all labor disturbances during the current year and the prior three years, other than routine grievances.

D. Outside consultants

1. Describe the Company's use of outside consultants and/or freelance workers.
2. Provide a schedule of outside consultants and/or freelance workers who are currently rendering services,

or have rendered services during the prior 12 months, on behalf of the Company, including a brief description of the services rendered, or being rendered, by each such outside consultant and freelance worker.

3. Provide a copy of all agreements or contracts between the Company and companies (or individuals) that are currently rendering legal, accounting, actuarial, marketing, medical, or dental services, or have rendered legal, accounting, actuarial, marketing, medical, or dental services during the prior 12 months, on behalf of the Company.

III. Products

A. Describe each of the Company's products, including the following information about each product:

1. Function(s), purpose(s), and use(s);
2. Special benefits and/or features (e.g., guaranteed issue, pure endowments, etc.);
3. Targeted market(s); and
4. Policy limits.

B. Provide a copy of all policy forms for both new and inforce business.

C. Provide a copy of all marketing material and brochures, including all product brochures.

D. Describe all historical and/or planned changes for each line of business or product.

E. Describe all new products under development.

IV. Marketing and distribution

A. Describe the Company's key customers (e.g., demographically, geographically, etc.).

B. Customer database

1. Describe the Company's customer database, indicating the following information:
   a) How the data are collected;
   b) The capabilities for data mining and other analyses;
   c) Whether the data are policy-based, customer-based, or a combination of the two; and
   d) Whether the data are collected for each line of business.
2. Describe how the Company uses the customer database to generate sales.

C. Internal marketing and sales organization

1. Indicate the Company's total number of in-house marketing and distribution management personnel.
2. Indicate the average number of years the in-house marketing and distribution management personnel have been employed by the Company.
3. Describe the organizational structure of the Company's marketing efforts. Provide a copy of the organizational chart showing the structure of the Company's marketing function.
4. Describe all special incentive arrangements made available to marketing and distribution management personnel.
5. Describe the Company's use of outside marketing expertise.

D. Distribution network

1. Describe the distribution channels used by the Company (e.g., bancassurance, agents, brokers, mass marketing, telemarketing, etc.) for both individual and group business, including the historical development of each channel. The information requested in items (a) to (k) immediately below should be included in or supplement the description.
   a) Describe the distribution network management and support structures (along with geographic distribution of sales offices and/or producers). Provide a copy of the organizational chart showing the Company's distribution network management and support structures.
   b) Indicate the total number of producers, including a breakdown by type of producer (i.e., captive agents, independent agents, brokers, etc.). For each type of producer, indicate the total number of active producers.

c) Provide net earned premiums, net losses, commissions, other issue costs, other maintenance costs, number of policies sold, total sum insured, and average policy size, along with a summary of reserves and first year and renewal premiums, for each distribution channel for the current year and each of the prior two years, including a breakdown by line of business and type of business (i.e., individual versus group business).

d) Agents and brokers

(1) Provide a schedule of all key broker relationships.

(2) Indicate whether any single agent or broker controls more than 10% of any line of business. If so, describe the volume of business and the terms of the contract for each such agent or broker.

(3) Provide net earned premiums and net loss ratios for the top five brokers and for the top five agents for the current year and each of the prior three years, including a breakdown by line of business and by type of business (i.e., individual versus group business).

(4) Agent and broker contracts

(a) Provide a copy of the standard agent and broker contracts.

(b) Provide a schedule of each agent and broker whose contract contains an exception or modification to the standard agent and broker contract, including a brief description of each such exception or modification.

(c) Indicate whether there are any plans to modify the standard agent and broker contracts. If so, provide details.

(5) Provide a copy of all material correspondence with brokers or agents for the current year and the prior three years.

(6) Provide a copy of all loan or credit agreements with agents or brokers.

(7) Indicate all benefits to agents or brokers not specified in the standard agent or broker contract.

e) Describe the Company's direct marketing and telemarketing activities, including organizations the Company has distribution agreements with, the types and amounts of business written, profitability, penetration, etc.

f) Describe all of the Company's cross-selling activities with its affiliates, indicating the types and amounts of business written, profitability, penetration, etc.

g) Indicate whether there are any exclusive third-party distributors. If so, describe the volume of business and the terms of contract for each distributor.

h) Describe all unique aspects of the Company's distribution network.

i) Provide a copy of all agreements with third parties for direct marketing, telemarketing, or use of databases or listings.

j) Describe distribution channel development plans.

2. Distribution network performance

a) Key performance indicators

(1) Provide key performance indicators (e.g., productivity, retention, persistency, etc.) for each distribution channel for the current year and each of the prior three years.

(2) Where appropriate, compare the key performance indicators to the key performance indicators as:

(a) Projected by the Company;

(b) Reported by the Company by class of agent;

(c) Reported by the industry; and

(d) Reported by the industry by class of agent.

b) Describe all unique performance measures for non-agency distribution systems.

c) Provide comparative cost information concerning each distribution channel.

d) Provide a copy of all studies concerning each distribution channel, such as expense or productivity studies.

3. Describe the compensation/incentive system for producers. The information requested in items (a) to (b) immediately below should be included in or supplement the description.
   a) Describe all changes to the compensation/incentive system implemented in the current year and the prior three years.
   b) Indicate whether there are any planned changes to the compensation/incentive system. If so, provide details.
4. Describe how funds to producers are paid (i.e., check, EFT, cash, etc.).
5. Describe the licensing and appointment process for each type of producer.
6. Describe cash disbursement procedures and associated controls.
7. Describe premium collection procedures and associated controls.
8. Provide a copy of all sales office audit results for the current year and the prior three years.
9. Describe sales office MIS and illustration systems.
10. Provide access to producer manuals and training materials.

E. Advertising and promotion
1. Describe all significant marketing programs currently being conducted or that have been conducted during the current year and the prior three years.
2. Describe all marketing programs recently discontinued, along with the reasons therefor.
3. Describe the effectiveness of each type or channel of advertising and promotion.
4. Describe the importance of each of the following to the Company's marketing efforts:
   a) Product differentiation (e.g., brand name, quality image, technological or other superiority, etc.);
   b) Favored customer relationships; and
   c) Servicing.

V. Risk management

A. Provide detailed information concerning the Company's risk management program, indicating the following information:
1. The Company's risk management philosophy, policies, procedures, and guidelines;
2. The types of risk (e.g., market risk, credit risk, liquidity risk, pricing risk, operational risk, legal/regulatory risk, reputation risk, etc.) monitored, measured, and managed;
3. How the risk management function is organized, including the roles and responsibilities of the Company's risk managers; and
4. How the risk managers currently monitor, measure, and manage each type of risk.

B. Provide a description of each property, general liability, automobile, workers' compensation, and umbrella insurance policy issued to the Company, along with a copy of each such policy. Include a schedule of all pending issues concerning each policy, the respective amount involved as well as the current stage of the negotiation. In addition to the foregoing, for each policy issued to the Company, specify the following information:
1. Name of carrier;
2. Premium;
3. Coverage;
4. Self-insured retention, co-payment, and/or deductible; and
5. Type of policy (i.e., claims-made versus occurrence).

C. Concentration of risk (by line of business)
1. Indicate whether any single risk (or group account in the case of group business) accounts for more than 10% of the Company's exposure. If so, provide details concerning the nature and the term of each such contract.
2. Indicate what percentage of the Company's business is derived from companies or business affiliated with the Company's parent company.

3. Describe all large accounts that are not characteristic of the general book of business of the Company, including a description of all limits offered and deductible or self-insured retention.
4. Assess the Company's exposure to mass tort claims (such as asbestos and pollution) and to possible future mass tort claims (such as tobacco).

VI. Product management

A. Universal Life Products
   1. Provide summary of products with bonus provisions and sales inducements.
   2. Provide summary of GAAP DAC amortization ratios.
   3. Provide recap of current COI and current interest determination policies.

B. Fixed Deferred Annuity Products
   1. Describe how assets are assigned to blocks of policies for interest crediting purposes.
   2. Provide summary of how current interest rates are determined, including the number of interest crediting cells.
   3. Provide summary of GAAP DAC amortization ratios.

C. Variable Annuity Products
   1. Provide itemization of all funds available.
   2. Provide summary of special features by policy form.
   3. Itemize counterparties for hedging and reinsurance providers.
   4. Provide summary of GAAP DAC amortization ratios.

D. Participating Products
   1. Policyholder dividends
      a) Describe the Company's dividend philosophy and how it relates to its competitive position and marketing goals.
      b) Describe the dividend formula utilized by the Company.
      c) Describe all restrictions on dividends (e.g., regulations, company charter, etc.).
      d) Provide a summary of the current dividend schedule.

E. Income Pay Guarantees
   1. Summarize all annuity policies by mortality table guarantee.
   2. Summarize all annuity policies by interest rate guarantee.

F. Term Products
   1. Provide summary of products by GAAP net/gross premium ratio.
   2. Describe management practices at policy anniversaries where significant premium increases occur.

G. Health Products
   1. Provide a copy of all provider contracts.
   2. Indicate all changes in provider costs during the current year and the prior three years.
   3. Indicate whether provider discounts are handled in the claims system or off-line.
   4. Describe frequency with which provider contracts are reviewed.
   5. Describe provider quality assurance program.
   6. Describe utilization controls in place and how effectiveness is measured.
   7. Describe hospital pre-admission approval procedures and appeals process.
   8. Indicate whether the Company administers self-funding plans for employers or other groups. If so, describe how the programs are structured and indicate whether the Company has any liability in any self-funded programs (if so, provide details).

H. Disability Products
   1. Indicate the frequency of review of disability claims.
   2. Describe all rehabilitation or return to work programs in place.
   3. Describe how disability benefits are coordinated with other benefits such as Social Security.
   4. Describe how disabilities are certified.

VII. Actuarial

A. Provide a copy of all internal financial models prepared during the current year and the prior three years, including validation reports and supporting documentation.

B. Provide a copy of all external actuarial evaluations or reports prepared during the current year and the prior three years.

C. Provide current inforce policy count, reserves, average premium, average face amount, and average issue age as well as inforce policy count, reserves, average premium, average face amount, and average issue age at the end of the prior year broken down by age, sex, duration, and policy form.

D. Provide historical and projected gross premiums written, net premiums written, and net premiums earned for each of the prior three years, the current year, and the next three years broken down by line of business, type of business (i.e., individual versus group business) and product.

E. Provide net premiums earned (annualized premium basis preferred) for the current year and each of the prior three years, indicating the split between new business and renewal business.

F. Provide the amount of new business written by month for the current year and each of the prior three years by line of business.

G. Provide a schedule reconciling gross premiums written to net premiums earned by line of business detailing discounts, lapses/cancellations, change in unearned premiums, reinsurance, etc.

H. Provide the earned exposures underlying net premiums earned for the current year and each of the prior three years, indicating the exposure basis used for each line of business (e.g., sales receipts, number of beds, etc.).

I. Provide distribution of net premiums earned and/or exposure for the current year and each of the prior three years by:
   1. Policy limits;
   2. Deductible/retention size;
   3. Type of policy (i.e., claims-made versus occurrence basis);
   4. State or region;
   5. Policy term; and
   6. Class or special program within line of business.

J. Provide historical and projected gross and net loss experience by line of business and product for each of the prior three years, the current year, and the next three years.

K. Provide historical and projected expense experience by line of business and product for each of the prior three years, the current year, and the next three years.

L. Provide historical and projected loss and expense ratios by line of business and product for each of the prior three years, the current year, and the next three years.

M. Provide historical and projected indirect administrative costs by line of business and product, including explanations for significant fluctuations between periods, for each of the prior three years, the current year, and the next three years.

N. Provide historical and projected unallocated loss adjustment expense estimates as well as issue and maintenance cost estimates by line of business and product for each of the prior years, the current year, and the next three years.

O. Provide details on all events considered by the Company to be considered unusual or non-recurring.

P. Provide a copy of the following experience studies by line of business (include actual versus expected) for the current year and the prior three years:

1. Mortality;
2. Morbidity;
3. Medical utilization reports;
4. Claim frequency;
5. Claim severity;
6. Claim inflation trends;
7. Lapse and renewal; and
8. Premium payment patterns.

Q. Provide actuarial loss data (gross and net of ceded reinsurance), including triangles data, where available, with annual valuations of each accident year (for occurrence coverages) or of each report year (for claims-made coverages), separately by line of business (for health and property and casualty only). Specify if data is to be provided either by (i) policy year or underwriting year or (ii) territory, market segment, or profit center. Loss triangles should be provided as follows:

1. Paid losses
    a) Closed claims
    b) Open claims
2. Paid allocated loss adjustment expenses
    a) Closed claims
    b) Open claims
3. Reported losses (i.e., paid losses plus case reserves)
4. Reported allocated loss adjustment expenses (i.e., paid allocated loss adjustment expenses plus case reserves)
5. Claim counts
    a) Reported
    b) Closed with loss payment
    c) Closed with allocated loss adjustment expenses payment only
    d) Open
    e) Data to reconcile to company financials:
        (1) Non-reviewed lines
        (2) Residual market/pools
        (3) Bulk reserves
            (a) Fast track
            (b) Transactions awaiting system input

R. Provide a schedule showing the number of outstanding claims by categories or size of claim by line of business.

S. Provide a schedule of all individual claims over a given amount (e.g., claims greater than 90% of retention). Include the following information for each claim:

1. Accident date;
2. Report date;
3. Coverage;
4. Policy limits;
5. Losses paid to date;
6. Loss reserve;
7. ALAE reserve;
8. Description of claim;

9. Current claim status; and
10. Development history.

T. Provide an analysis of liabilities or other similar risks in run-off.

U. Indicate how the Company guards against anti-selection and disintermediation.

V. Provide detailed reserve calculations for selected policies.

VIII. Underwriting (by line of business)

A. Philosophy

1. Describe the Company's underwriting philosophy and all changes that have occurred during the current year and the prior three years. Indicate whether there are any plans to change the underwriting philosophy. If so, provide details.

B. Processing

1. Describe the underwriting process and all changes that have occurred during the current year and the prior three years.

C. Audits

1. Describe the frequency and nature of internal checks.
2. Describe all problems that have been discovered through audits.
3. Describe all external audits that may be performed (such as by reinsurers).

D. Pricing

1. Describe the Company's pricing philosophy and how it relates to its competitive position and marketing goals.
2. Describe all major pricing changes that have occurred during the current year and the prior three years. Indicate whether there are any planned pricing changes. If so, provide details.
3. Describe pricing profitability goals.
4. Describe the importance of each of the following factors when pricing products:
   a) Competitor's prices;
   b) Regulatory standards; and
   c) Internal analysis.
5. Compare actual claims, lapses, surrenders, and investment yield results by product to pricing assumptions.
6. Describe the line of authority in establishing prices.
7. Describe pricing assumptions for products by line of business (e.g., mortality/loss ratios, lapse/renewal rates, expenses, commissions, etc.).
8. Provide the most recent pricing information and technical notes for each policy form.
9. Provide a copy of rate books and rate cards for each line of business for the current year and the prior three years.
10. Provide all information not included in the rate books and rate cards that would otherwise be expected to be included in the rate books and rate cards.
11. Provide a copy of all rate adequacy reviews and studies of variance from manual rates.

E. Miscellaneous

1. Provide a copy of the underwriting manual and procedures (including audit procedures concerning underwriting).
2. Indicate the amount of substandard business written during the current year and each of the prior three years.

IX. **Claims (by line of business)**

A. Philosophy

1. Describe the Company's claims settlement philosophy and all changes that have occurred during the current year and the prior three years. Indicate whether there are any plans to change the claims settlement philosophy. If so, provide details.

B. Claims processing

1. Describe how a claim is received and handled.

C. Reserve practices

1. Describe reserve-setting procedures for each line of business, including the statutory requirements and all deviations from those requirements. Provide a copy of all internal documents prescribing or describing the Company's reserving methodologies and procedures.

2. Provide a copy of all actuarial studies, reports, opinions, and certifications prepared by independent actuaries (including accounting firms) concerning the Company's reserve calculations and adequacy as well as particular risks or events (e.g., effects of legislation, changes in coverage offered).

3. Provide a copy of all actuarial studies, reports, and opinions prepared by the Company's internal actuaries concerning the Company's reserve calculations and adequacy as well as particular risks or events (e.g., effects of legislation, changes in coverage offered).

4. Provide copies of all material correspondence among the Company and its lawyers and accountants for the current year and the prior three years concerning the accuracy or appropriateness of the Company's reserves and reserving methodologies.

5. Provide access to actuarial work papers supporting the calculation of reserves.

6. Provide historical and projected loss and loss adjustment expense reserves by line of business on both a gross and net basis for each of the prior three years, the current year, and the next three years.

D. Audits

1. Describe the frequency and nature of internal reviews of:

   a) Claims procedures;

   b) Case reserves; and

   c) Paid claims.

2. Describe the external auditing process.

3. Describe all problems that have been detected through internal or external audits.

E. Personnel

1. Describe claims staffing by function.

F. Miscellaneous

1. Provide a copy of the claims manual and procedures (including audit procedures concerning claims).

X. **Reinsurance**

A. Describe the Company's reinsurance philosophy.

B. Describe the Company's reinsurance programs, indicating the following information (separately for ceded and assumed reinsurance by accident year or report year, where appropriate):

1. The lines of business and exposures covered;

2. The retention levels per claim or occurrence;

3. The aggregate retention levels;

4. The type of policy (i.e., claims-made versus occurrence basis);

5. The width of reinsured and coinsured layers;

6. The amounts of reinsurance and coinsurance by line of business;

7. The annual premium as a percentage of coverage (i.e., rate-on-line);

8. The reinstatement premiums;

9. The reinsurance and coinsurance recoveries by line of business;
10. The reinsurance and coinsurance ceding commissions;
11. The names of all reinsurers and coinsurers, along with a copy of all contracts or treaties entered into with each reinsurer or coinsurer; and
12. The current reserves.

C. Provide a copy of all actuarial reports on assumed reinsurance.

D. Provide a schedule of reinsurance recoverables.

E. Indicate whether any contracts are currently non-performing, in dispute, in arbitration, non-collectible, or slow paying. If so, provide details.

F. Indicate premiums ceded for the current year and each of the prior three years.

G. Indicate loss and loss adjustment expenses ceded for the current year and each of the prior three years.

H. Indicate premiums assumed for the current year and each of the prior three years.

I. Indicate loss and loss adjustment expenses assumed for the current year and each of the prior three years.

J. Provide a copy of statutory statements or management reports for the current year and the prior three years, broken down as follows:

1. Before reinsurance ceded and assumed;
2. Reinsurance ceded and assumed; and
3. After reinsurance ceded and assumed.

XI. Information systems

A. Describe the Company's data processing and operation systems with respect to:

1. Product development;
2. Underwriting processing;
3. Policy administration, including claims processing;
4. Compensation;
5. Sales and marketing;
6. Illustrations;
7. Commissions;
8. General ledger;
9. Investments; and
10. Human resources.

B. Provide a schedule of the Company's data processing and operation systems (i.e., personal computers (including desktops, servers, and laptops), mid-range computers, etc., as well as software).

1. Indicate the following information for each personal computer, mid-range computer, etc.:
   a) Whether it is leased (and, if so, from whom and on what terms; in addition, provide a copy of each such lease agreement) or owned;
   b) The type and age;
   c) The estimated capacity utilization;
   d) Whether any related licenses exist (if so, provide details, along with a copy of each such license);
   e) Whether any indemnification agreements exist (if so, provide details, along with a copy of each such agreement); and
   f) Whether any of the licenses are transferable (if so, provide details, along with a copy of all documentation in connection therewith).
2. Indicate the following information for each type of software:
   a) Whether any related licenses exist (if so, provide details, along with a copy of each such related license);

b) The source (i.e., package or internally developed);

c) Whether any indemnification agreements exist (if so, provide details, along with a copy of each such agreement); and

d) Whether any of the licenses are transferable (if so, provide details, along with a copy of all documentation in connection therewith).

C. Provide a schedule of each information systems contract, including all expenses related thereto. Provide a copy of each such contract and all other documentation in connection therewith.

D. Databases

1. Describe each type of database used by the Company, indicating which databases are leased (as well as from whom and on what terms) and which are owned.

2. Describe the associated gateways to transport the information among the offices.

E. Compare the Company's IT support to that of the industry.

F. Systems audits

1. Describe all recent information on system audits, indicating the associated issues found.

2. Provide a copy of each system audit.

G. Describe architecture, standards, and technology plans for the future.

H. Describe all outstanding IT projects.

I. Describe the Company's backup and disaster/recovery plans.

J. Management Information System budget material

1. Provide flow charts of business.

2. Provide individual unit costs (i.e., people versus machines).

3. Provide production and revenue data.

K. Describe the Company's communications and network protocols, including information about each of the following:

1. Network protocols that connect the branches;

2. Cabling within the administrative and sales offices

3. Hardware inventory to support the network (e.g., routers); and

4. Telephone systems.

L. Describe the Company's IT function. Include the following information: structure, skill assessment, training programs, and opinion surveys. In addition to the description of the structure of the Company's IT function, provide a copy of the organizational chart showing the structure of the Company's IT function.

M. Provide historical and projected capital expenditures for each of the prior three years, the current year, and the next three years.

XII. Legal and regulatory

A. General

1. Provide a copy of the Company's articles of incorporation.

2. Provide a copy of the Company's by-laws along with all amendments thereto.

3. Provide a copy of all of the Company's shareholders' agreements, along with evidence of knowledge of each such agreement by the Company.

4. Provide a copy of all other agreements or documents providing for registration rights, preemptive rights, or options to acquire, rights of first refusal, or securities convertible into or exchangeable for, shares of the Company, along with evidence of knowledge of each such agreement or document by the Company.

5. Provide a copy of all agreements, contracts, and arrangements, with shareholders, or related companies or persons of shareholders, including, but not limited to, those agreements, contracts, and arrangements concerning services, technology transfer, and licensing.

6. Provide a copy of all minutes of meetings and written consents of the board of directors for the current year and the prior three years.
7. Provide a copy of all resolutions of the board of directors for the current year and the prior three years.
8. Provide a copy of all minutes of the annual, ordinary, extraordinary, and special shareholders' meetings, along with all written consents of the shareholders, for the current year and the prior three years.
9. Provide a copy of all resolutions of the shareholders for the current year and the prior three years.
10. Provide a copy of all materials for the current year and the prior three years concerning the solicitation by the Company of shareholder proxies.
11. Provide a copy of all proxies granted by shareholders of the Company during the current year and the prior three years.
12. Provide a copy of all minutes of meetings and written consents of all other corporate body for the current year and the prior three years.
13. Provide a copy of all contracts in connection with each commitment of purchase and sale, option, and repurchase of shares.
14. Describe all controversies between shareholders and the Company concerning increases in capital, execution of corporate acts, structure of corporate bodies, shareholders' agreements, voting agreements, etc.
15. Provide a copy of all documents concerning the approval of issuance of other securities, along with all amendments thereto, as well as all printed advertisements distributed to the public in connection with such issuance (e.g., offering circulars or memoranda).
16. Provide a schedule of all mergers, acquisitions, joint ventures, and divestitures entered into or made by the Company in the past, along with a copy of all documentation in connection therewith.
17. Indicate whether the Company has discontinued any of its activities during the current year or any of the prior three years. If so, provide details.
18. Indicate whether any goodwill has been acquired or sold during the current year or any of the prior three years. If so, provide a schedule of each agreement creating or transferring the goodwill, along with a copy of each such agreement.
19. Indicate whether any of the Company's premises have been closed during the current year or any of the prior three years. If so, provide details.
20. Indicate whether the Company's head office has changed address during the current year or any of the prior three years. If so, provide details.
21. Indicate whether the Company aids, or has aided, the community in those locations where the Company has a physical presence, such as providing regular access to any of its facilities for community, religious or supportive purposes. If so, provide details, along with a copy of all documentation in connection therewith.
22. Provide a schedule of all licenses, permits, or other approvals required from each federal, state, or local regulatory body in order to carry out any aspect of the Company's business. Indicate the purpose as well as the issue and expiration date, of each such license, permit, or other approval.
23. Indicate whether the Company has adopted an ethics and compliance program. If so, provide details, along with a copy of all documentation in connection therewith, including a copy of all manuals.
24. Provide access to the customer complaint log and the customer complaint files, including all summaries of such logs or files, for the current year and the prior three years.
25. Provide a copy of all material correspondence with all policyholders for the current year and the prior three years.

B. Insurance regulatory

1. Provide a copy of the certificate of authorization issued by the insurance regulatory body, along with all amendments thereof.
2. Provide a copy of all insurance regulatory filings for the current year and the prior three years, along with all annual statutory statements as well as all interim statutory financial reports of the Company.
3. Provide a copy of all reports of examination of the Company done by or for each insurance regulatory body

during the current year and the prior three years.

4. Provide a copy of all market conduct examination of the Company done by or for each insurance regulatory body during the current year and the prior three years.
5. Provide a copy of all actuarial studies of the Company done by or for each insurance regulatory body during the current year and the prior three years.
6. Provide a copy of all information (e.g., correspondence, regulatory notices and actions, litigation files, etc.) concerning issues with each insurance regulatory body that (i) remain outstanding or (ii) arose during the current year and the prior three years but have since been settled, along with all documents evidencing settlement of each such issue.
7. Provide a copy of all material agreements, undertakings, or understandings between the Company and each insurance regulatory body in effect at any time during the current year and the prior three years (along with all correspondence in connection therewith).
8. Provide a schedule and description of impending regulatory investigations and/or inquiries concerning the Company's compliance with insurance laws and regulations, including, but not limited to, insurance sales and advertising practices (along with all correspondence in connection therewith).
9. Provide a copy of all other correspondence exchanged with each insurance regulatory body during the current year and the prior three years.
10. Describe all current or historical disputes with each insurance regulatory body not mentioned above.
11. Provide a copy of all rulings issued by the insurance regulatory body to the Company during the current year and the prior three years.

C. Other regulatory

1. Provide a copy of all information (e.g., correspondence, regulatory notices and actions, litigation files, etc.) concerning all significant issues with each non-insurance regulatory body that (i) remain outstanding or (ii) arose during the current year or any of the prior three years but have since been settled, along with all documents evidencing settlement of each such issue.
2. Provide a copy of all material agreements, undertakings, or understandings between the Company and each non-insurance regulatory body in effect at any time during the current year or any of the prior three years.

D. Contracts

1. Provide a schedule of all real estate lease agreements, whether the Company is lessor or lessee, along with a copy of each such lease agreement and the receipt of payment concerning the last month of each such lease agreement.
2. Provide a schedule of all other lease agreements, whether the Company is lessor or lessee, along with a copy of each such lease agreement and the receipt of payment concerning the last month of each such lease agreement.
3. Provide a schedule of all financing or loan agreements in which the Company is obligor (including sale/leasebacks, credit agreements, and letters of credit) and all financial or hedging instruments to which the Company is party (e.g., swaps, foreign exchange, etc.), along with a copy of all documentation in connection therewith. Where appropriate, indicate the following information for each item included in the schedule:
   a) The entity that is the obligor; co-obligor or guarantor, if any; and obligee;
   b) The current stage of compliance; and
   c) The current amount outstanding.
4. Provide a schedule of all commitments, guarantees, or warranties given by the Company in connection with each of the items included in the schedule requested immediately above or otherwise, along with a copy of all documentation in connection therewith. Indicate the current stage of compliance and the current amount outstanding for each such commitment, guarantee, or warranty.
5. Provide a copy of each agreement entered into with a bank or another insurance company.
6. Provide a schedule of all of the Company's indemnification agreements with third parties whether the

Company is indemnitor or indemnitee, along with a copy of each such indemnification agreement.

7. Indicate whether there are any other agreements between the Company and its affiliates, controlled companies, and companies in which the Company holds a considerable interest that do not fall into any of the categories mentioned above. If so, provide a copy of each such agreement.
8. Provide a schedule of all agreements entered into on an exclusive, reciprocal or non-competitive basis, along with a copy of each such agreement.
9. Provide a schedule of all other agreements with a nominal value of at least $10,000 wherein the Company stands as a party, along with a copy of each such agreement.
10. Indicate whether there are any approvals or consents required that relate to any contract in which the Company is a party that are necessary to consummate the proposed transaction. If so, provide details.
11. Indicate whether there exists any default or event of default in connection with any of the contracts referred to above, whether any party has given notice of or has otherwise asserted such default. If so, provide details.

E. Technology and intellectual property

1. Provide a schedule of all license agreements in which the Company is licensor or licensee concerning all of the technology or intellectual property utilized by the Company, along with a copy of each such license agreement.
2. Indicate whether there exists any default or event of default in connection with any of the licenses referred to above, whether any party has given notice of or has otherwise asserted such default. If so, provide details.
3. Provide a schedule of all trade secrets and know-how of the Company in any way concerning the technology or intellectual property (a) of the Company, (b) licensed by the Company, or (c) otherwise utilized by the Company, anywhere in the world, including a description of the efforts taken to protect each such trade secret or know-how.
4. Provide a schedule of all copyright registrations, pending applications, or copyrightable subject matter in any way concerning the technology or intellectual property (a) of the Company, (b) licensed by the Company, or (c) otherwise utilized by the Company, anywhere in the world, including software, flow charts, manuals, etc.
5. Describe the Company's copyright policy.
6. Provide a copy of all forms of agreement for the purchase, license, and sale of copyrighted material.
7. Provide a schedule of all trademarks, trade names, service marks, trade dress, slogans, or trade phrases ("Trademarks") of the Company in any way concerning the technology or intellectual property (a) of the Company, (b) licensed by the Company, or (c) otherwise utilized by the Company.
8. Provide a copy of all registration certificates and all renewals thereto, along with evidence of actual use by the Company of the Trademarks, during the current year and the prior two years.
9. If any Trademarks are not registered, indicate whether any applications are pending. If so, provide a copy of each such application.
10. Provide a schedule of abandoned applications or canceled registrations for the Trademarks.
11. Provide a schedule of all intellectual property not identified above that is used by the Company.
12. Provide a schedule of all franchise agreements entered into by the Company in any way concerning the technology or intellectual property (a) of the Company, (b) licensed by the Company, or (c) otherwise utilized by the Company, along with a copy of each such agreement.
13. Indicate whether there are any claims, asserted or unasserted, that the Company has against any third party in respect of the intellectual property identified above, including any claim that any of such third party's intellectual property infringes any intellectual property right or trade secret of the Company as well as any pending or threatened litigation by the Company (including infringement suits) concerning all intellectual property rights. If so, provide details.
14. Indicate whether there are any claims, asserted or unasserted, that third parties have against the Company in respect of intellectual property. If so, provide details.

15. Indicate whether there are any restrictions on expanding the use of any of the technology or intellectual property identified above which is known by the Company. If so, provide details.
16. Indicate whether there is any restriction on transfer of any of the technology or intellectual property rights identified above which is known by the Company. If so, provide details.
17. Indicate whether there are any encumbrances on the technology or intellectual property identified above. If so, provide details.
18. Indicate whether there are any title defects or chain of title problems with any technology or intellectual property identified above. If so, provide details.
19. Provide a schedule of contracts with all independent contractors that assisted in the development of the technology and intellectual property identified above.

F. Real estate and movable properties

1. Provide a schedule of all real estate owned by the Company, along with a copy of (a) the respective deeds, agreements, and instruments for each property included in the schedule and (b) all third-party appraisals. Include the property type (i.e., commercial, residential, industrial, etc.), geographic location, occupancy, book value (broken out by cost and accumulated depreciation), and market value of, as well as the corresponding rental income for, each property.
2. Provide a schedule of all movable properties (whether leased or owned by the Company) with a nominal value of at least $10,000, indicating which properties are leased (as well as from whom and on what terms) and which properties are owned.
3. Provide a schedule of all liens and encumbrances on the Company's assets, along with a copy of all documentation in connection therewith.
4. Provide detailed information concerning all notice letters, requests for information, claim or investigation by, or communication with all governmental authorities or other persons in connection with (a) potential liability for the clean up of contaminated properties, or the violation of environmental laws or regulations and (b) all violations of zoning laws or regulations, along with a copy of all documentation in connection therewith.

G. Litigation and other proceedings

1. Provide a schedule of all court or administrative proceedings, as well as all arbitration and mediation cases, of any kind in which the Company is a party, indicating which proceedings and cases are of utmost importance to the Company considering the subject matter or amounts involved. In addition, include the following information for each proceeding or case:
   a) The subject matter, amount involved, jurisdiction, and status;
   b) The person in charge (in case of an independent lawyer, include the law firm, address, telephone, and facsimile number as well); and
   c) Whether the Company has reserved for any potential liability that may arise and, if so, the amount of the reserve.
2. Provide a schedule of all pending issues with shareholders, financiers, suppliers, buyers, distributors, and other third parties, including governmental agencies and bodies, not scheduled above, including the amount involved and status for each such issue.
3. Indicate whether the Company (or any of its officers, directors, or affiliates) is under investigation for any reason whatsoever. If so, provide details.
4. Indicate whether there are any actions, suits, claims, proceedings, or investigations threatened against the Company or any of its officers, directors, or affiliates. If so, provide details.
5. Provide a schedule of all other contingent liabilities of the Company.
6. Provide a copy of all reports forwarded to independent auditors either by in-house or independent lawyers concerning administrative or judicial proceedings in their charge in the current year and the prior three years.
7. Provide a copy of all actualized reports on administrative and judicial proceedings under the responsibility of in-house and independent lawyers.

8. Provide a copy of all letters from independent counsel to the Company's independent auditors for the current year and the prior three years concerning contingencies as well as potential unasserted claims and assessments in connection with the preparation of financial statements or otherwise.

H. Employees

1. Provide a copy of all of the different types of employment agreements used by the Company.
2. Provide a copy of all agreements, contracts, or similar instruments concerning secrecy or intellectual property entered into by the Company and employees or third parties.
3. Provide a schedule of all employees' associations or similar associations, indicating each associations' activities (e.g., cultural, credit cooperation, etc.).
4. Indicate whether the Company financially contributes to any of the associations referred to immediately above. If so, provide details, along with a copy of all documentation in connection therewith.
5. Provide a copy of all agreements entered into between the Company and all employees' associations.
6. Indicate whether there are employees of any employees' associations rendering services, or that have rendered services during the prior 12 months, either inside or outside the Company's premises. If so, provide a schedule of the agreements in connection therewith, along with a copy of each such agreement.
7. Indicate whether the Company usually requires its employees to submit to medical examinations prior to hiring, periodically (indicate period in between), upon readmission and dismissal. If so, provide a copy of all forms used for each examination category.
8. Provide a schedule of employees performing activities under health hazardous conditions, including the position and salary of, as well as the activity or activities being performed by, each such employee.
9. Provide detailed information concerning projects aimed at reducing or avoiding labor accidents, including all information on investments already made and planned.
10. Provide a schedule of all indemnities paid in the current year and the prior three years or to be paid by the Company due to labor accidents.
11. Provide a schedule of all employee labor claims (including a brief description of each), along with a copy of all documentation in connection therewith. Include the following information for each such claim:
    a) The court or regulatory/administrative body;
    b) The amount involved;
    c) The current status; and
    d) The expected result.

XIII. Tax

A. General

1. Provide a copy of all federal income tax returns for the prior six years, along with the work papers supporting installment payments for the current year.
2. Provide a list of net operating loss carryforwards and foreign tax credit carryforwards by year of expiration. Indicate the extent to which these tax attributes are attributable to extraordinary transactions (i.e., not in the ordinary course of business), and include a detailed description of when and how such transactions occurred.
3. For each insurance company, provide a reconciliation of (a) GAAP income to (b) statutory income for the prior six years, along with the work papers supporting GAAP and statutory book accruals for taxes for the prior year.
4. Provide a detailed schedule and explanation of the GAAP and, for each insurance company, statutory reserves for contingent tax liabilities at the end of the prior year, along with the supporting work papers in connection therewith.
5. Provide recent (i.e., within the last six years) (a) reports of examining agents of the tax authorities; (b) tax payer protests, appeals, and settlements; (c) copies of document requests from the tax authorities; (d) copies of requests for private letter rulings, along with responses from the tax authorities; and (e) information concerning all threatened and/or proposed assessments for any current examination.

6. Indicate what tax years are open. Indicate what tax years are pending in an administrative or judicial appeal. During the prior six years, indicate what issues have been resolved in administrative or judicial appeals, and what issues are unresolved. Indicate whether any audit, administrative appeal settlement, or judicial appeal settlement will carry over to future tax years. If so, provide details.
7. Indicate what tax years are currently under audit, what issues have been proposed for adjustment, and what items are currently under audit review. For each item, list the potential effect on tax payable to the tax authorities.
8. Provide deferred tax work papers for the prior three years, including GAAP and, for each insurance company, statutory tax accrual work papers, along with a tax basis balance sheet.
9. To the extent not already provided, provide a copy of all documentation concerning acquisitions, reorganizations, redemptions, dividends, divestitures, share issuances, and shareholder loans for current year and the prior six years, including tax opinion letters and related administrative rulings received from the tax authorities.
10. Provide a schedule of tax elections made for the prior six years.
11. Provide a schedule of all changes in tax methods or procedures implemented during the current year and the prior six years.
12. Provide a schedule of inter-company transactions, including amounts of income or loss deferred, determined separately for each company. Provide a copy of all advance pricing agreements for related party transactions with the tax authorities.
13. Provide a copy of all tax opinion letters and administrative rulings from the tax authorities in connection with all significant reinsurance and coinsurance contracts.
14. Indicate what foreign activities are undertaken directly or through foreign subsidiaries, partnerships, or other types of entities.
15. For each partnership, limited liability company, or other legal entity in which the Company owns an interest (either directly or indirectly), provide details concerning the future tax effects.
16. Indicate how investments are identified as "held to maturity" or "available for sale."
17. Indicate how investments are hedged for tax purposes. Describe all derivatives transactions and their treatment for tax purposes.
18. Indicate whether there are any separate account assets where the tax basis does not equal market value. If so, provide details.
19. Indicate whether there is or was any seed money in separate accounts in any open year. Indicate how it is treated on tax returns. Describe all procedures used to allocate income/deduction items between the seed money and variable contracts.

B. Tax reserves, deferred acquisition costs, and certain miscellaneous items

1. Provide schedules for the prior three years showing all reserves furnished in the annual financial statement filed with each insurance regulatory body and the corresponding tax reserves. The schedule should set forth items separately for each company, line of business, product, and issue year or blocks of issue years using the same table, interest rate and reserve method. It should also indicate how the tax reserve was computed (i.e., table, interest rate, and reserve method).
2. Provide an explanation of the major differences between statutory reserves and tax reserves in B.1 above and, for blocks where the statutory reserve equals the tax reserve, the reason this is the case.
3. For each reinsurance and coinsurance contract, provide GAAP, statutory, and tax reserves ceded or assumed.
4. Indicate whether any reserves are attributable to foreign risks. If so, describe.
5. Indicate what method is used to determine the tax reserve offset for due and deferred premiums by line of business and, if relevant, by major product type.
6. Indicate whether there are any statutory premiums (which are deferred and uncollected) that are accrued as income for tax purposes. If so, provide details.
7. Indicate how policy acquisition expenses are treated for tax purposes. Provide worksheets of deferred

acquisition costs computations for the prior three years.

8. Indicate whether there are any policyholder dividend liabilities accrued on the tax return.

C. Recordkeeping, withholding, and reporting

1. Income tax withholding for products and personnel

a) Describe the procedures, including the methodology, used for all income taxes being withheld by the Company.

b) Provide a schedule of each state and locality for which taxes are being withheld, indicating the procedures and methodology used.

c) Provide a copy of all forms and notices to policyholders/accountholders concerning tax withholding.

d) Provide copies of all rulings received from federal or state tax authorities concerning taxation of payments made from products in question which would affect future tax withholding, depositing, and/or reporting obligations.

e) Identify and provide copies of all special agreements entered into with employers that would impact tax withholding, tax deposit, and/or reporting obligations.

2. Recordkeeping

a) Provide a list of all life insurance contracts with loans outstanding. For each contract, indicate the amount outstanding.

b) In connection with name/address files, indicate whether a special "tax address" is maintained. If so, indicate whether it is online.

c) Indicate how cash transactions are recorded and reported.

3. Sales and property tax audits

a) Provide a schedule of sales and property tax audit assessments during the current year and the prior six years.

b) Provide a schedule of all sales and property tax audits currently open, indicating the status and potential assessment.

c) Provide an analysis of all contingent reserves concerning sales and property taxes.

D. Tax structure

1. Provide detailed information concerning the tax structure of the Company, including all information on tax exemptions, special tax regimes, and incentives, along with a copy of all granting instruments and covenants. Also provide a schedule of entities included/excluded from the Company's consolidated federal, state, and local tax returns.

2. Provide a copy of all correspondence with auditing companies and law firms on the tax structure of the Company, along with the responses and opinions in connection therewith, concerning the current year and the prior six years.

3. Provide a schedule of all of the Company's joint ventures, indicating the party responsible for tax return preparation.

4. Provide a copy of all tax sharing agreements entered into by the Company.

E. Product qualification

1. Provide an analysis of tax issues concerning the insurance and annuity products issued by the Company and the marketing of such products. This analysis should review how products sold by the Company qualify/comply with all product definitions under the law and with the tax purposes for which they were sold.

2. Provide a copy of all tax opinions, private letter rulings, and tax memoranda concerning the insurance and annuity products issued by the Company.

XIV. Investments

A. Provide detailed information concerning the organizational structure of the Company's investment management function (both oversight and operational components), including all information on portfolio management as well as asset origination/administration activities.

B. Provide detailed information concerning the Company's investment management philosophy, policies, procedures, and guidelines, including information concerning identifying problem assets, establishing asset reserves, and matching assets and liabilities. Provide a copy of all asset/liability and spread management studies.

C. Provide a copy of the investment plan for the current year and the prior two years.

D. Describe regulations concerning investments, indicating all incidents of non-compliance for the current year and the prior three years.

E. Provide the estimated current market value of the Company's investment portfolio.

F. Provide historical and projected investment performance for each of the prior three years, the current year, and the next three years.

G. Describe the current investment portfolio, including the following information:

1. A breakdown by category (e.g., fixed income, equity, real estate, commercial mortgages, etc.);
2. A breakdown of fixed income investments by range of scheduled maturities, type of issuer, and rating. For ratings, indicate whether they are assigned by the Company or an independent agency (identifying it by name), and if by the Company, indicate briefly the basic methodology used;
3. A breakdown of commercial mortgages by range of scheduled maturities, property type, and quality;
4. A breakdown of low-quality investments by basic categories (if any) used by the Company (e.g., "watch list," non-performing, restructuring, foreclosure, etc.);
5. A breakdown of derivative instruments;
6. Any special investments, highlighting international/offshore investments;
7. Returns by category, including a comparison of returns by investment category to an appropriate index for the current year and each of the prior three years;
8. The concentration by maturity;
9. The concentration by issuer;
10. All recent turnover by asset class;
11. The liquidity of the portfolio; and
12. All problem investments.

H. Provide available comparative information. This may include assessments of results against any outside benchmarks as well as peer companies.

I. Provide a schedule of the Company's outside managers and advisors, including the following information for each outside manager or advisor:

1. The accounts or portfolios under management;
2. The applicable fees; and
3. A track record.

J. Provide a schedule of all significant commercial mortgage loans outstanding, indicating amount, property type (i.e., commercial, residential, industrial, etc.), quality, location, and basic terms. Also, specify non-performing or questionable loans.

K. Provide a schedule of equity investments in unconsolidated subsidiaries. Include the percentage of ownership and the accounting treatment for carrying value for each such equity investment.

L. Provide a copy of all financial or forward-looking analysis of problem asset exposures, in particular with respect to real property investments, commercial mortgages, and high-yield bonds.

M. Provide a schedule of all investment reserves and all write-offs or write-downs of, or all determinations to write-off or write-down any of, the Company's assets or properties during the current year and the prior three years.

N. Describe interest rate risks and steps taken by the Company to mitigate them.

O. Describe actions taken by the Company if interest rates shift substantially.

P. Describe the impact on the Company of lower investment yields.

Q. Provide detailed information concerning all investment systems and applications in use by the Company, including information on all near-term development plans.

XV. **Corporate treasury**

A. Describe the Company's corporate treasury organization, including the roles and responsibilities of the people within the corporate treasury organization. Provide a copy of the organizational chart showing the structure of the Company's corporate treasury function.

B. Describe corporate treasury (including cash management (e.g., collections, disbursements, etc.) policies, procedures, and guidelines.

C. Describe controls concerning corporate treasury and banking activity/transactions.

D. Describe liquidity management.

E. Provide a schedule of banking, custody, and borrowing relationships.

F. Provide a schedule of all bank accounts, along with the balance of each such account for each of the prior 12 months.

G. Provide a schedule of all lines of credit, indicating the portion that remains unfunded for each line of credit.

H. Indicate whether there are any other unfunded sources of liquidity of the Company currently in effect. If so, provide details.

I. Provide a schedule of all compensation paid to each third party for corporate treasury services for the prior 12 months.

XVI. **Financial**

A. Provide a copy of the Company's audited consolidated financial statements, along with a copy of the independent auditor's opinion, for the prior three years as well as unaudited consolidated financial statements for each quarter of the current year. In the event that the financial statements for any quarter of the current year have been audited, provide a copy of the audited consolidated financial statements, along with a copy of the independent auditor's opinion, for that quarter in lieu of the unaudited financial statements.

B. Provide a copy of audited financial statements for each subsidiary/affiliate, along with a copy of the independent auditor's opinion, for the prior three years as well as unaudited financial statements for each subsidiary/affiliate for each quarter of the current year. In the event that the financial statements for any subsidiary/affiliate for any quarter of the current year have been audited, provide a copy of the audited consolidated financial statements for each such subsidiary/affiliate, along with a copy of the independent auditor's opinion, for that quarter in lieu of the unaudited financial statements.

C. Provide a copy of each auditor's management letter or controls observation summary for the current year and the prior three years.

D. Provide a copy of all internal audit reports for the current year and the prior three years.

E. Provide access to detailed internal financial records by major account for the current year and the prior year.

F. Provide detailed internal financial records (i.e., general ledger summary by major account) for the current year and the prior year by line of business consolidating to the comprehensive group financial results/position.

G. Provide a schedule of adjustments to reconcile from the internal financial records to the audited financial statements for the current year (if available) and the prior year.

H. Provide access to independent external auditor work papers for the current year (if available) and the prior year.

I. Provide a copy of all internal financial or management reports by line of business, including related studies (e.g., business plans, budgets, reserve studies, experience studies (see below), commission studies, expense studies, premium rate studies and filings, etc.), for the current year and the prior three years.

J. Provide financial statement projections by line of business for the remainder of the current year and each of the next three years, including an explanation of each major underlying assumption.

K. Financial reporting systems, policies, and procedures

1. Describe internal control review, including a description of internal controls.
2. Describe reporting systems and arrangements.
3. Describe internal audit processes and procedures.

L. Provide copies of all required capital/target surplus reports for the current year and each of the prior three years.

M. Provide historical and projected solvency margin calculations for each of the prior three years, the current year, the next three years.

N. Describe the Company's dividend policy, indicating the following information:

1. The amount of dividends paid during the current year and each of the prior three years;
2. Whether there are there any dividends, either cumulative or not, pending payment (if so, specify the accounting period(s) related thereto); and
3. Whether the Company has determined in the current year and the prior three years to withhold or to not distribute profits.

O. Provide a schedule of all agreements or other arrangements between the Company and any of its subsidiaries and affiliates (including arrangements pursuant to which investment advisory or management, administrative, or other services are performed; risks are shared (including support agreements); inter-company funds transfers are effected; and balances (if any) are documented), along with a copy of all tax sharing or indemnification agreements.

P. Provide details of all earnout payment agreements in connection with any acquisitions.

Q. Provide a schedule of all off-balance sheet liabilities entered into or incurred by the Company during the current year and the prior year.

R. Describe possible cost reduction efforts and quantify each.

S. Identify all changes in accounting methods or procedures implemented during the current year and the prior three years.

T. Provide a premium receivable aging schedule for the current year and the prior year.

U. Provide an analysis of allowance for doubtful accounts/premium cancellations for the current year and the prior year.

V. Provide a schedule of all receivables (other than premiums and agent balances receivable) for the current year and the prior year.

W. Provide a schedule of deferred acquisition costs for the current year and the prior year. Include a description of the methodology for capitalization and amortization of deferred acquisition costs by line of business. Also include a sample calculation of the deferred acquisition cost asset, along with formulas.

X. Provide a schedule of all other deferred costs for the current year and the prior year, including amortization schedules.

Y. Provide a schedule of property, plant, and equipment, along with accumulated depreciation, for the current year and the prior year broken down into category totals (i.e., land, building, equipment, etc.).

Z. Provide a schedule indicating capital expenditures by category for the current year and the prior year.

AA. Provide a schedule of accounts payable (aged, if available) for the current year and the prior year, including a reconciliation to the general ledger.

BB. Provide a schedule of all other accruals and liabilities (e.g., commissions, bonus plans, utilities, marketing programs, deferred revenue). Include a description of the calculation methodology for each such accrual or liability.

CC. Provide a schedule of the unearned premium reserve by line of business for the current year and the prior year. If the unearned premium reserve has been subject to a system audit by independent auditors, provide access to external auditor work papers for such audit procedures and conclusions. If no such audit has been performed, provide access to the unearned premium reserve master file in order to be able to perform a system recalculation.

DD. Provide a copy of all significant internal financial and forward-looking analysis of significant business issues or problems.

XVII. Other

A. Describe all non-insurance-related businesses of the Company.

B. Facilities/branches

1. Provide the number of facilities/branches.
2. Describe the location, purpose, and monthly expenses of each facility/branch.
3. Indicate which facilities/branches are leased and which are owned. If leased, provide the square footage, the monthly rent, and the material terms of the lease.

C. Provide a copy of all presentations or reports prepared by the Company for rating agencies for the current year and the prior three years.

D. To the extent not covered elsewhere, provide a copy of all recent analyses of the Company prepared by investment bankers, management consultants, accountants or others, including marketing studies, credit reports, and other types of reports.

E. Provide copies of all news releases concerning the Company during the current year and the prior three years.

F. Provide sample statements sent to producers and policyholders.

G. Provide any other significant proprietary information that would be helpful to understanding the Company and its business(es), including all significant analysis or report (not otherwise covered by this list) prepared by the Company, its consultants, or advisors concerning material financial, operational, or other business issues.

Appendix D

Sample Due Diligence Employee Benefits Information Request

EMPLOYEE BENEFITS
DUE DILIGENCE INFORMATION REQUEST

PLANS TO REVIEW

The review of employee benefits should include a review of qualified plans, non-qualified plans, and group benefit plans.

Qualified plans include pension plans, savings plans, profit sharing plans, and employee stock ownership plan. Non-qualified plans include supplemental executive retirement plans, benefits in excess of qualified plan limits, and deferred compensation. These plans are broken into defined benefit and defined contribution.

DEFINED BENEFIT (QUALIFIED AND NONQUALIFIED) PLAN DATA REQUIREMENTS

- Plan document(s) and amendments thereto
- Administrative forms and notices (e.g., joint and survivor notice and direct rollover notice)
- Current summary plan descriptions and all summary of material modification statements
- Most recent determination letter and IRS filing submission
- Insurance contracts used to fund the Plan
- Three most recent Summary Annual Reports
- Trust agreement(s)
- For nonqualified plans, a list of participants and the accrued benefit of each (include date determined)
- Written administrative procedures (e.g., qualified domestic relations order procedures)
- Any plan administrative or investment committee minutes for the three most recent plan years
- Any correspondence from the IRS, the DOL, or the PBGC for the past 12 months, including any pending determination letter requests filed with the IRS
- Complete PBGC Form 1 for the last three years
- List of personnel responsible for administering the Plan, their locations, and the duties performed by each (include professional service providers and contact names and duties)
- Three most recent actuarial valuations
- Three most recent Form 5500s, including audited financial statements
- Most recent trustee's report, including listing of plan assets, investment activity, and contributions
- List of any plans which merged into the Plan in the prior three years
- DOL top hat filing for nonqualified plans

The following items are useful, if available:

- Copies of completed distribution packages and benefit calculations (including work sheets, if any) for the last five retirees
- Copies of completed distribution packages and benefit calculations (including work sheets, if any) for the last five terminated vested participants receiving voluntary distributions
- Copies of the completed distribution packages and calculations for the last five participants receiving voluntary lump sum distributions
- Copies of all paperwork (including benefit calculations) for the last five participants receiving involuntary lump sum distributions
- Copies of benefit calculations for the 10 most highly compensated employees

DEFINED CONTRIBUTION (QUALIFIED AND NONQUALIFIED) PLAN DATA REQUIREMENTS

- Plan document(s), including all executed amendments thereto and trust agreement(s)
- SPD and SMMs
- Written administrative procedures (e.g., loan and hardship procedures)
- Process for reconciliation for recordkeeper to trustee balance
- For nonqualified plans, list of participants and account balance of each
- All administrative forms and notices (e.g., joint and survivor notice, in-service withdrawal (including hardship), loan request, direct rollover notice, distribution, and enrollment forms)
- Three most recent Form 5500s, including audited financial statements
- Most recent trustee's report, including listing of plan assets, investment activity, and distribution activity
- Listing of investment choices and informational materials that are provided to participants
- Most recent IRS determination letter and IRS filing submission
- Participant investment election forms and procedures, including procedures for transfers of existing funds
- Most recent ADP/ACP final test (including data used in running the tests) and any preliminary testing done for the current plan year
- Most recent Code Section 415 test results (including dual plan limit results)
- For nonqualified plans, DOL top hat filing

The following items are useful, if available:

- List of all Plan participants receiving distributions, loans, and in-service withdrawals during the most recent year (including name, Social Security number, hire date, termination date (if applicable), and date and type of the "event" (e.g., date of loan, withdrawal, or distribution));
- List of all Plan participants who have reached age 70_, who are on a leave of absence, who have been disabled, who have died, or who had one or more breaks in service during the most recent plan year
- Sample recordkeeping reports (monthly/quarterly) including sample participant statements

GROUP BENEFIT PLANS

Group Benefit plans cover a wide array of items including vacation policy, medical, prescription drugs, dental, disability, vision, life, and miscellaneous benefit programs ranging from employee assistance programs to family leave to education and legal benefits. Severance policies and flexible benefits (including spending accounts) also fall under the aegis of group benefits.

The review of group benefit plans is split between active and retired employees and should encompass:

ACTIVE EMPLOYEES

- VEBA trust funds
  - Financial statements
  - Actuarial reports
  - VEBA document
- Flexible benefits program
  - Plan document (with applicable amendments)
  - Pending amendments
  - Union or other variations by employee group
- Insured benefits
  - Insurance contracts
  - Experience reports
  - Statement of reserves
  - Recent rate changes
- Self-insured benefits
  - Administrative agreements
  - Financial statements
- Claim experience for each benefit area (last three years) and any claim data analysis available
- Outstanding liabilities and reserves associated with projected liabilities—FAS 112 valuation or analysis, if available
- Vendor contracts (HMOs, utilization review, carriers, brokers, consultants, accountants, attorneys, etc.)
- Health care continuation plan rates required by the Consolidated Omnibus Budget Reconciliation Act (COBRA)
  - Basis for COBRA rates
  - COBRA liabilities
  - COBRA violations
- Section 125/129 nondiscrimination testing for flexible benefits and dependent children account plans
- Employee communications other than SPDs
  - Enrollment materials
  - Newsletters
- Description of any broad-based severance plan (even if not treated as a "formal" plan).

RETIRED EMPLOYEES

- Statements/communications regarding retiree benefits (especially medical)
- Postretirement medical data
  - Analysis of Seller's current liabilities
  - Historical cost analysis
  - Detailed plan features
- Employee contributions and any historical changes
- Most recent FAS 106 valuations (last three years if available)

APPENDIX E

Sample Due Diligence Corporate Insurance Programs Information Request

CORPORATE INSURANCE PROGRAMS
DUE DILIGENCE INFORMATION REQUEST

Information required for due diligence of corporate property casualty risk and insurance programs.

Initial data request for preliminary review - Short list

1. Summary or schedule of the current property-casualty insurance program including but not limited to: workers' compensation, general liability, product liability, automobile, property, crime, D&O, E&O, employment practices, surety bonds, etc. Summaries should include: name of insurer, exposure covered, claims-made coverage (where applicable), policy limits, deductibles, annual premium, rating structure (fixed premium or adjustable premium), and endorsed exclusions. Please include both domestic and international coverages. Note any significant changes in the program during the past five years.
2. Name and contact number for the corporate risk manager and/or officer responsible for placing the property and liability insurance program. Please include a copy of the most recent renewal presentation prepared by the insurance broker if one is available.
3. Summary sheet showing balance sheet accruals during the past three years for property and liability risk and insurance. These include accrued liabilities for self-insured losses, prepaid insurance, loss fund deposits, and reinsurance recoverable.
4. Summary sheet showing charges to earnings for property and liability risk and insurance, which include premiums, paid losses, claim administration costs, defense costs, and changes in the balance sheet accruals for self-insured losses.
5. Summary sheet listing all security requirements including letters of credit and surety bonds.
6. Please provide copies of all actuarial reports, audit work papers, and other management reports used to develop the estimates of ultimate settlement costs and estimates of accrued liabilities for all self-insured exposure for the past three years. This report should include the retention limits and associated reserve estimates for each type of exposure. If no reports are available, detailed loss reports will be requested.

ADDITIONAL INFORMATION REQUIRED WHEN SELF-INSURED EXPOSURE REPRESENTS MATERIAL ACCOUNT BALANCES.

1. The most recent valuation of the Company's loss experience showing total paid losses, outstanding losses, incurred losses, number of reported Claims, and number of open claims for all policy years that were self-insured or where the Company purchased a large deductible policy or retrospective rated policy. The experience report should be provided by type of coverage (i.e., workers' comp, general liability, product liability, auto liability, etc.). If available, please provide company-specific loss development data.

2. A summary sheet describing changes in self-insured retention levels for the past 10 years.
3. For policies with retrospective rating provisions, please provide copies of the endorsement or summary of key plan parameters, including loss conversion factor, basic premium factor, loss limit, and minimum and maximum premium.
4. Large loss report showing detailed information for any claims that may exceed the company's retention.
5. Provide the following for the past five years and an estimate for the next 12 months:
   a) Payroll (by class code if available)
   b) Employee head count
   c) Sales
   d) Vehicle count (show separate counts for private passenger vehicles and trucks)
   e) Insured value of real property, personal property, and business interruption. List any new or discontinued products. For discontinued products please list termination year and associated sales total.

6. Copy of all contracts with third party administrators (TPA) providing claim-handling services. Alternatively, please provide a description of TPA fee structure (life of claim or life of contract) for all open policy years and a description of cash flow for loss and expense payments (i.e., the TPA is reimbursed on a monthly basis for losses paid or a pre-funded loss account is funded quarterly).

Additional information when the Company uses a captive insurer

1) Provide financial statements and any actuarial reports for the captive insurance subsidiary for the past three years.
2) Please describe how the insurance subsidiary's results are reflected in the target company's earnings.
3) Please describe how captive premiums are determined.
4) Describe how premiums and losses are charged to subsidiaries or divisions for each type of coverage.
5) Copies of captive insuring agreements.
6) Copies of captive reinsurance policies.

Other unique exposure and risk management data requested

1) Have any past insurance carriers become insolvent?
2) Provide list of acquisitions/divestitures during the past five years including any indemnification obligations and assumption of self-insured exposure.
3) Does company have exposure to claims from asbestos, silica, or pollution liability?
4) Have there been any recently reported losses or settled legal cases that could impact the company's future business? This would include large losses, product recalls, exposure claims, multiple claimant, or class action claims.
5) Please provide copies of product brochures.
6) Does the company offer warrantees on any of its products or completed operations?
7) Are any operations subject to one-of-a-kind machinery, plans, or facilities that would be extremely difficult to replace?

8) Please provide a copy of the Safety and Loss Prevention Program, Risk Management Manual, and any loss control reports issued by insurance companies.

9) Is there any international exposure? Does the company maintain currency exchange coverage?

10) Describe inland or ocean marine shipments.

11) Do you own, lease, or charter aircraft or watercraft?

Appendix F
Insurance M&A and GAAP Evolution

A veteran actuary shares his recollections and perspectives as a crew member on the HMS PGAAP Beagle *as it sailed from the early 1970s through the mid 1990s.*

Statutory accounting principles have been with us since the beginning of the 1900s. Practitioners were intimately familiar and comfortable with statutory presentations. Some people thought there could be no other way of viewing the financial condition of a life company.

Generally Accepted Accounting Principles were introduced in the early 1970s. By the mid-'70s, the industry realized that one key to understanding GAAP versus statutory had been the deferred acquisition cost (DAC) asset. This intangible GAAP item usually meant that total GAAP assets and yearly earnings would exceed statutory.

Once upon a time, a large, old-line manufacturing company was looking for diversification and studied life companies. It commissioned a valuation on another old, established insurer. The consulting actuary used a straight 20% discount for future production, and, probably, 15% discount for current inforce profits. Unfortunately, the 20% discount gave quite a bit of weight to early duration statutory losses and too little to positive renewal statutory profits. As a result, the present value of future production came out negative, although, on a lifetime level margin basis, results were profitable.

The total value of the company came out less than the GAAP book value. In discussions, the directors were bitterly divided over whether to accept this valuation, thus selling the company at what some thought was an excessive bargain price. The prominence of the consulting firm involved carried considerable weight. Shoving matches even broke out between a few directors. Nonetheless, the divided board approved the sale at this price, which corresponded to the actuarial appraisal report numbers.

Publicity over this acquisition encouraged other manufacturing companies and conglomerates to establish their own insurance acquisitions. As almost always happens, competition drove prices up.

Consultants then developed an analytical theme for would-be acquirers. An insurer's surplus was valued at itself. In other words, the present value of interest on capital and surplus was discounted at the same earned rate, resulting in the surplus account itself. The present value of current inforce profits was discounted at a risk rate, a rate higher than current earned rate, to reflect risks inherent in long-term contracts. The agency force was valued by the present value of its expected future production; its profits were discounted at a still higher rate. Instead of using a straight 20%, some firms used 20% up to the point of production, then 15% or the same discount rate as for current inforce thereafter.

One consideration that arose related to these present values. If the acquired company employed GAAP accounting, should these present value projections be based on GAAP profits instead of the traditional statutory basis? For current inforce, this change wouldn't necessarily matter much. However, for future business, values could be increased dramatically. Flows of profits under GAAP would normally be positive from day one, rather than the statutory pattern of initial loss then renewal profit.

It was pointed out that projections of future production were speculative and subject to the vagaries of agent relationships. One renowned Big Eight audit partner was vehemently opposed to any use of GAAP in projecting future production, and he embarked on a crusade against this approach. Even the consultant who made the original statutory projections that showed negative value on future business joined in the denunciation. In any event, calculations of discounted future production, as opposed to actual yearly projections, remained almost universally on a statutory basis.

Even if the present value of future production, using statutory earnings flow, turned out positive, it still wasn't used in financial statements. The incidence of earnings inherent in future production would go up each year, as more layers of production years were added. Amortization of the initial asset would understandably be negative (thus, an increasing asset) for a number of years before turning into positive charges. In fact, the degree of negative amortization would depend on the number of production years included in calculations.

Not without good reason, many accountants balked at the idea of negative amortization of an intangible (wasting) asset. Hence, the present value of future production never made its way into balance sheet respectability.

At higher prices, some acquirers grew discouraged at what seemed to be low returns on equity from the transaction. The entire purchase price represented beginning equity of the acquired company if the transaction was accounted for as an official "purchase." Some transactions, if they were all stock/no cash, and fulfilled several other requirements, qualified as "poolings." Poolings had the advantage of retaining the acquired company's historical GAAP (HGAAP) equity.

Since most transactions were classed as "purchases," questions about transaction or purchase accounting were critical. To a considerable extent, everyone was feeling his or her way, which was especially true since the entire insurance industry had only adopted GAAP several years earlier.

Purchase accounting at the time was governed by Accounting Principles Board (APB) opinions ##16 and 17. They were not specific to insurance. In general, assets and liabilities should be adjusted to "current values," so that purchase GAAP (PGAAP) balance sheets and earnings would replace historical versions.

Rules were plain enough for invested assets. They were interpreted to mean write-off of existing DAC and any goodwill from previous acquisitions. Policy reserves would be adjusted to "current assumptions." However, there remained much vagueness as to what assumptions should be used for reserve net premiums. Should they use current assumptions from original issue date, from current durations after acquisition, etc.? One approach that gained some acceptance was to divide the present value of gross premiums into components: the present values of benefit premiums, renewal expenses, and commissions. The balancing item would become the present value of profit margins. The first present value would offset the present value of benefits to provide PGAAP policy reserves. The present value of renewal expenses and commissions would be offset by the second component, often resulting in a small asset or liability. The remainder would represent the present value of profits.

In earlier acquisitions in the '70s, some controllers of acquiring companies claimed that no new intangible asset was appropriate to replace DAC other than goodwill. However, the argument that prevailed was that the acquirer had purchased the inherent value of long-term contracts. This identifiable value was the proper, new intangible asset under PGAAP.

Thus, the following steps emerged to adjust opening balance sheets from HGAAP to PGAAP:

a. Substitute a present value of profits of current inforce for DAC.

b. Substitute reserves using an approach with current assumptions for HGAAP reserves.

c. Adjust invested assets to market value, replacing mostly historical cost values under HGAAP. When interest rates were high, in the late '70s and early '80s, the write down to invested assets was often very significant. Some companies were chagrined to discover that, if these market values had been used under statutory accounting, they would be insolvent.

d. Write-off HGAAP deferred federal tax liabilities and replace it by the "tax effects" (deferred taxes) (both liabilities or assets), either added to or subtracted from the above.

e. The balancing asset, so that equity would equal the purchase price, would be goodwill.

f. For subsequent earnings, for new production, HGAAP would be re-introduced. The present value of profits would be amortized. Total PGAAP reserves would generally increase for a few years, just like HGAAP reserves, and then be released. The market value write down to invested assets would gradually be written up (into earnings) as assets such as bonds approached maturity.

As commercial companies and other insurers became interested in insurance acquisitions, purchase prices started to climb. One prominent acquisition of a large insurer was at two times HGAAP book value, while another smaller insurer was sold for three times HGAAP book. It was almost inevitable that large amounts of the balancing item, goodwill, would be generated, since it was very difficult to qualify as a pooling transaction.

Controllers became interested in the effect of PGAAP adjustments on subsequent earnings. Often, future earnings would be less than HGAAP earnings would have been, for several reasons:

a. The present value of profits was often larger than DAC; hence, there was more to write-off.

b. If PGAAP reserves on current assumptions were less than HGAAP reserves, there was less available for later release; hence, earnings were lower.

c. Goodwill had to be written off, no slower than 2.5% per year.

d. Only the release of market value write-down of invested assets into earnings was a source of higher profit.

Concerned acquirers often looked to consultants or other advisors to mitigate this future strain on earnings. One controller stated, "Just take care of us for five years, and we will let inflation cover things after that." Achieving this objective was easier said than done.

Acquiring companies took widely varying views toward goodwill. Some viewed goodwill as almost the devil's work because goodwill signified an excessive purchase price, a bad deal. One actuary always started transactions by saying, "My board will fire me if I approve any purchase with goodwill."

On the other hand, some companies wanted to maximize goodwill. Since this type of asset was written off at 2.5 % annually, they believed that its amortization scale was more favorable than, say, present value of profits or large reserve differences. They considered themselves clever—the more they could balance the new PGAAP equity with goodwill, the cleverer they were.

A few purchase transactions developed what was known as negative goodwill. When identified purchased assets were matched with the sum of purchased liabilities plus equity (purchase price), the assets were too high. The resulting balancing item to assets was considered "negative goodwill."

When this oddity was generated, people had different reactions. The ones preparing calculations thought, "What error did I make?" Sellers who were made aware of this outcome often thought, "We just sold at a fire sale price and will be castigated by our board of directors." Buyers were sometimes happy at a result that indicated a favorable purchase price. In other cases, however, buyers were suspicious of the calculations and the assumptions and demanded that they be redone.

Another approach to acquisitions, taxable transactions under Internal Revenue Code Section 334(b)(2), entered the picture. Many earlier transactions, as described above, whether purchase or pooling for accounting purposes, were still classed as tax-free exchanges for federal income tax (FIT) purposes. However, if the seller was, for various reasons, to enter a taxable (to the seller) transaction, the buyer received a significant benefit. The present value of profits of current inforce would be tax deductible.

The present value of profits, in this case, was of tax return profits. Often, in those days, FIT reserves exceeded statutory amounts, which often meant that release of FIT reserves was greater, causing the present value of FIT profits on current inforce to exceed the PGAAP present value. A related benefit was in computing PGAAP deferred taxes or tax effects. Now this effect would be generated from the difference between two assets. Often, a deferred FIT equivalent asset was the result, which resulted in reduced goodwill.

The history of the next 25 years should be just as interesting.

BIBLIOGRAPHY

Actuarial Standards Board. Actuarial Appraisal Task Force. *Actuarial Standard of Practice No. 19, Actuarial Appraisals*. Washington, D.C.: Actuarial Standards Board, 1991.

Anderson, J. C. H. "Gross Premium Calculations and Profit Measurement for Nonparticipating Insurance," *Transactions of the Society of Actuaries*. Vol. XI (1959): 11-61.

Association of British Insurers. *Supplementary Reporting For Long Term Insurance Business (The Achieved Profits Method)*. London: Association of British Insurers, 2001.

Black, Kenneth Jr., and Harold D. Skipper Jr. *Life & Health Insurance*, 13th ed. Upper Saddle River, NJ: Prentice Hall, 2000.

Bluhm, William F., ed. *Group Insurance*, 4th ed. Winsted, CT: ACTEX Publications, 2003.

Bowers, Newton L., Hans U. Gerber, James C. Hickman, Donald A. Jones, and Cecil J. Nesbitt. *Actuarial Mathematics*. Itasca, IL: Society of Actuaries, 1986.

Brealey, Richard, and Stewart Meyers. *Principles of Corporate Finance*, 7th ed. New York: McGraw-Hill, 2003.

Bridges, William. *Managing Transitions: Making the Most of Change*. Cambridge, MA: Da Capo Press, 2003.

Burling, Irving, and David Whitsett. "Achieving Successful Organizational Integration." *SOA Record*, Volume 22 (1996), No 3. *http://library.soa.org/library/record/1990-99/rsa96v22n380cs.pdf*.

Canadian Institute of Actuaries. *Committee Role of the Appointed Actuary—Guidance Note for Calculation of Publicly Disclosed Embedded Value*. Ottawa, Ontario: Canadian Institute of Actuaries, 2000.

Carroll, Charles, Scott Littlejohn, and Deborah Whitmore. "Making Acquisitions for Stock: How Sweet it Is." 1999 Valuation Actuary Symposium Proceedings, Session 26PD. *http://library.soa.org/library/valact/1985-99/VA99_26PD.PDF*.

Casualty Actuarial Society. *Foundations of Casualty Actuarial Science*, 4th ed. Ch. 4, pp. 149-195. Arlington, VA: Casualty Actuarial Society, 2001.

Casualty Actuarial Society. Task Force on Fair Value Liabilities. "White Paper on Fair Valuing Property/Casualty Insurance Liabilities." Arlington, VA: Casualty Actuarial Society, 2000.

Chernow, Ron. *The House of Morgan: An American Banking Dynasty and the Rise of Modern Finance.* New York: Touchstone, 1990.

Chew, Donald, ed. *The New Corporate Finance.* 3rd ed., New York: McGraw-Hill, 2001.

Cummins, J. David, Sharon Tennyson, and Mary A. Weiss. "Consolidation and Efficiency in the U.S. Life Insurance Industry." A paper for The Wharton Financial Institutions Center. Philadelphia: The Wharton Financial Institutions Center, 1998.

Davis, Mark, Kevin Mackay, and Joseph Rafson. "Mergers and Acquisitions." 2000 Valuation Actuary Symposium Proceedings, Session 18PD. *http://library.soa.org/library/valact/2000-09/VA00_18PD.PDF.*

Deloitte Touche Tohmatsu. "Business Combinations." In the *Deloitte Accounting Manual.* Wilton, CT: Deloitte Touche Tohmatsu, 2002.

Deloitte Touche Tohmatsu. "Goodwill and Other Intangibles," In the *Deloitte Accounting Manual.* Wilton, CT: Deloitte Touche Tohmatsu, 2002.

Duran, J. Peter. Discussion of Girard's "An Approach to Fair Valuation of Insurance Liabilities," *North American Actuarial Journal.* Vol. 6 (2002), No. 2: 41-46.

Evans, G. Heberton. "The Early History of Preferred Stock in the United States." *American Economic Review.* Vol. 19 (1929), No. 1, pp. 43-58.

Fama, Eugene F. "Random Walks in Stock Market Prices." *Financial Analysts Journal*, September-October, 1965.

Fama, Eugene F., and Kenneth R. French. "Common Risk Factors in the Returns on Stocks and Bonds." *Journal of Financial Economics.* Vol. 33 (1993), No. 1: 3-53.

Feldman, Mark, and Michael Spratt. *Five Frogs on a Log.* New York: HarperCollins, 1999.

Ferenczy, Ilene. *Employee Benefits In Mergers & Acquisitions*, 2003 ed. New York: Aspen Publishers.

Financial Accounting Standards Board. "Business Combinations Purchase Method Procedures and Certain Issues Related to the Accounting for and Reporting of Noncontrolling (minority) Interests." *Summary of Tentative Decisions—FASB Board.* Norwalk, CT: Financial Accounting Standards Board, 2003.

Financial Accounting Standards Board. "Combinations Between Mutual Enterprises." *Summary of Tentative Decisions—FASB Board. Norwalk*, CT: Financial Accounting Standards Board, 2004.

Financial Accounting Standards Board. "Determination of the Measurement Date for the Market Price of Acquirer Securities Issued in a Purchase Business Combination." In *Emerging Issues Task Force Topic No.99-12.* Norwalk, CT: Financial Accounting Standards Board, 1999.

Financial Accounting Standards Board. "Recognition of Liabilities in Connection with a Purchase Business Combination." In *Emerging Issues Task Force Topic No. 95-3*. Norwalk, CT: Financial Accounting Standards Board, 1995.

Gaugan, Patrick. *Mergers, Acquisitions and Corporate Restructuring*, 3rd ed. New York: John Wiley & Sons, 2002.

Gerstner, Louis. *Who Says Elephants Can't Dance?* New York: HarperCollins, 2002.

Girard, Luc N. "Market Value of Insurance Liabilities: Reconciling the Actuarial Appraisal and Option Pricing Methods." *North American Actuarial Journal*. Vol. 4 (2000), No. 1: 31-49.

Goodheart, Lawrence B. *Abolitionist, Actuary, Atheist: Elizur Wright and the Reform Impulse*. Kent, OH: Kent State University Press, 1990.

Gora, Jean. "Planning and Managing Insurer Merger Integration." A study by LOMA. Atlanta: LOMA, 2002.

Harris, Timothy, et al. "Valuation of Health Business for Mergers and Acquisitions." *The Record*, Volume 23 (1997), No 1. *http://library.soa.org/library/record/1990-99/rsa97v23n115of.pdf*.

Hawawini, Gabriel, and Claude Viallet. *Finance for Executives: Managing for Value Creation*. Cincinnati: South-Western College Publishing, 1999.

Horbatt, William, Charles Carroll, and Herbert Goodfriend. "Let's Make a Deal: Life and Health Mergers and Acquisitions." *The Record*, Volume 24 (1998), Nos. 1 & 2. *http://library.soa.org/library/record/1990-99/rsa98v24n151cs.pdf*.

Hull, John C. *Options, Futures, & Other Derivatives*, 5th ed. Upper Saddle River, NJ: Prentice Hall, 2002.

Ibbotson Associates. *Stocks, Bonds, Bills, and Inflation—Valuation Edition 2003 Yearbook*. Chicago: Ibbotson Associates, 2003.

Jordan, C. Wallace. *Life Contingencies*, 2nd ed. Chicago, IL: Society of Actuaries, 1967.

Lam, James. *Enterprise Risk Management: from Incentives to Controls*. Hoboken, NJ: John Wiley & Sons, 2003.

LaSorella, Kenneth A., and Edward L. Robbins. "Internal Rate of Return as an Evaluator of Tax-Planning Strategies." *Transactions of the Society of Actuaries*. Vol. XLIV (1992): 175-191.

Leifer, Andrew, Philip Simpson, and Mike Wilkinson. "Brands and Customer Values." A paper for The Staple Inn Actuarial Society. London: Staple Inn Actuarial Society, 2002. http://www.sias.org.uk/papers/brands.pdf.

Littmann, Mark, Dan Thomas, Marcus Tarrant, and Sam Gutterman. *An Investigation of Practical Matters Relating to Implementing Fair Value Accounting for Property/Casualty Loss Reserves*. New York: PricewaterhouseCoopers, 2004.

McGill, Dan M. *Fundamentals of Private Pensions*, 7th ed. For the Pension Research Council. Oxford, England: Oxford University Press, 1996.

Malecki, Donald S., and Arthur L. Flitner. *Commercial Liability Insurance and Risk Management*. 4th ed. Vol. 1. Malvern, PA: American Institute for Chartered Property Casualty Underwriters, 1998.

Modigliani, Franco, and Merton H. Miller. "The Cost of Capital, Corporation Finance and the Theory of Investment." *American Economic Review*, June 1958.

Moorhead, Ernest J. *Our Yesterdays: the History of the Actuarial Profession in North America*. Itasca, IL: Society of Actuaries, 1989.

Morrell, Margot, and Stephanie Capparell. *Shackleton's Way: Leadership Lessons from the Great Antarctic Explorer*. New York: Viking Press, 2001.

National Association of Insurance Commissioners. "Life, Deposit-Type and Accident and Health Reinsurance." *Statement of Statutory Accounting Principles* No. 61. From the Accounting Practice and Procedures Manual as of March 2003. Kansas City, MO: National Association of Insurance Commissioners, 2001.

Olin, Meike. "Managing the Risks of Mergers and Acquisitions," *Risk Alert*, Marsh Inc., 2004.

Patterson, Edwin W. *The Insurance Commissioner in the United States: A Study in Administrative Law and Practice*. Cambridge, MA: Harvard University Press, 1927.

Portnoy, Stanley. *Project Management for Dummies*. Indianapolis: Wiley Publishing, Inc., 2001.

Ratajczak, Meredith, Michael Hughes, and Bradley Smith. "Mergers and Acquisitions/Appraisals." 1998 Valuation Actuary Symposium Proceedings, Session 19PD. *http://library.soa.org/library/valact/1985-99/VASP9816.PDF.*

Reed, Stanley Foster, and Alexandra Reed Lajoux. *The Art of M&A*, 3rd ed. New York: McGraw-Hill, 1998.

Rosenblatt, Alice, et al. "How to Avoid Common Pitfalls of Health Plan Mergers." *SOA Record*, Volume 26 (2000), #1. http://library.soa.org/library/record/2000-09/rsa00V26n178if.pdf.

Schmidt, Jeffrey, ed. *Making Mergers Work: The Strategic Importance of People*. Alexandria, VA: Towers Perrin/SHRM Foundation, 2002.

Schreiner, J. "Actuarial Considerations in Evaluating a Life Insurance Company." An internal paper for Milliman & Robertson, Inc., 1989.

Schroder Salomon Smith Barney. *Life Insurance—The American Way of Life*. London: Schroder Salomon Smith Barney, 2002.

Skipper, H. *International Risk and Insurance.* New York: McGraw-Hill, 1998.

Society of Actuaries. *Part 7 Study Notes: Valuation of Liabilities*. Chicago, IL: Society of Actuaries, 1979.

Starr, Jeremy, James Dallas, and Timothy Gaule. "Use of Reinsurance in Mergers and Acquisitions." *The Record*, Volume 25 (1999), No 1. *http://library.soa.org/library/record/1990-99/rsa99v25n171pd.pdf.*

Stowe, John D., Thomas R. Robinson, Jerald E. Pinto, and Dennis W. McLeavey. *Analysis of Equity Investments: Valuation*. For the Association for Investment Management and Research. Baltimore: United Book Press Inc., 2002.

Tiller, Denise F., and John E. Tiller. *Life Health & Annuity Reinsurance*, 2nd ed. Winsted, CT: ACTEX Publications, 1995.

Tilley, James A. "The Pricing of Nonparticipating Single Premium Immediate Annuities." *Transactions of the Society of Actuaries*. Vol. XXI (1979): 11-61.

Toole, Jim. *Actuarial Considerations in Insurance Mergers and Acquisitions: An International Perspective.* Schaumburg, IL: Society of Actuaries, 2003.

Turner, Samuel H. "Actuarial Appraisal Valuations of Life Insurance Companies." *Transactions of the Society of Actuaries*. Vol. XXX (1978): 139.

Van Mieghem, Dennis P., and other partners at KPMG Peat Marwick, eds. *Federal Taxation of Insurance Companies*. New York: Research Institute of America, Inc., 1991.

Welch, Jack. *Jack Welch and the GE Way*. New York: McGraw-Hill, 1999.

Wiening, Eric A., George E. Rejda, Constance M. Luthardt, and Cheryl L. Ferguson. *Personal Insurance*. 1st ed. Malvern, PA: American Institute for Chartered Property Casualty Underwriters, 2002.

Winterhof, Bruce. *Actuarial Appraisals for Life Insurers*. New York: Practising Law Institute, 1999.

Zollo, Maurizio, and Dima Leshchinkskii. "Can Firms Learn to Acquire? Do Markets Notice?" A paper for The Wharton Financial Institutions Center. Philadelphia: The Wharton Financial Institutions Center, 2001.

Index

D

E

H

I

T

U